0056775

W9-BKK-536

CULTURAL EXCURSIONS

NEIL HARRIS

CULTURAL EXCURSIONS

MARKETING APPETITES AND CULTURAL TASTES IN MODERN AMERICA

....

The University of Chicago Press · Chicago and London

NEIL HARRIS, professor of history at the University of
Chicago, is the author of *The Artist in American Society: The
Formative Years, 1790–1860* and *Humbug: The Art of P. T.
Barnum*, both published by the University of Chicago Press.

The University of Chicago Press, Chicago 60637
The University of Chicago Press, Ltd., London
© 1990 by The University of Chicago
All rights reserved. Published 1990
Printed in the United States of America

99 98 97 96 95 94 93 92 91 90   54321

Library of Congress Cataloging-in-Publication Data
Harris, Neil, 1938–
      Cultural excursions : marketing appetites and cultural
tastes in modern America / Neil Harris.
          p.   cm.
      Selected essays written over a period of fifteen years.
      ISBN 0-226-31757-9 (cloth)
      1. United States—Popular culture—History—20th
century.
      2. Arts—United States—Marketing.   I. Title.
      NX180.S6H325   1990
      306.4'0973'0904—dc20   89-28045
                                                              CIP

To the memory of Robert Rosenthal

CONTENTS

● ● ●

INTRODUCTION

The essays that follow were written over a period of fifteen years, in response to a variety of occasions, requests, and assignments. A number of them have not been easily accessible because of the circumstances of their publication. They were selected from a larger assembly because of this, and in the interest of thematic connections.

It is tempting, in an anthology of this kind, to try to find consistencies and continuities. And certainly there are some repetitions. But almost any reader can uncover opinions that have changed and viewpoints that have shifted. As I have gone over many of the essays I found myself qualifying arguments and amending conclusions. I wish that I had available, at the time of my writing, the stimulating, highly original, and erudite studies of American culture that have subsequently appeared. This rich field is in a state of continual revision and reexamination.

But the book's tripartite organization does represent with some fairness several major interests that continue to shape my research and teaching. Rather than provide new levels of interpretation or offer apologies for specific inconsistencies, I will use this brief introduction to explain how each group of essays came into being, and to suggest some of the links that I find among them. They are presented in their approximate order of writing and/or publication, the two activities never quite as neatly aligned as authors would wish. And, with some minor changes to correct typographical errors, they are printed as they originally appeared.

The first section is built around the history of cultural institutions, most particularly, the evolution of American art museums. My absorption with museums goes back many years, reflecting experiences I share with others of my generation. Taken by teachers or parents to the large, imposing, metropolitan institutions that encase our icons of art and science, most of us have responded with mixtures of delight, boredom, veneration, and resentment to what have been variously described as treasurehouses, amusement palaces, or educational laboratories. In my case the mixture was enriched by spending several years in Europe after graduating from college, seeing regularly and repeatedly the foreign analogues of the institutions I had visited in New York. At that point, in the 1950s, I had begun to take some notice of museums as settings and meeting places, watching visitors, I suspected, even more intently than I looked at art.

But it was only when I began to read about museum history, upon entering graduate school in the early 1960s, that I became fully engaged with the subject. The founding years for many of the great American private libraries, museums, and universities coincided with a period that had earned the patronizing contempt of many cultural historians, contempt for its political corruptions, stylistic eclecticism, and intense materialism. The Gilded Age still provoked, at that point, angry indignation or comic irony, depending whether one read Matthew Josephson and Charles A. Beard or Thorstein Veblen and Thomas Beer. The wealthy, pretentious, intimidating, and formidably endowed symbol of rapacious wealth that was the art museum seemed an apt symbol for the period's self-absorption, a far cry from the popular, educationally sophisticated, open-minded institution it seemed to have become generations later, at least according to the whiggish views then prevailing.

My own research suggested something else. Looking through trustee minute books, official publications, professional meeting agendas, and newspaper editorials convinced me that museums had always incorporated many kinds of motives and cultural responses, and they did not easily fit within the cultural straitjacket some historians had prescribed. The first essay I ever published concerned the establishment of one such institution, the Museum of Fine Arts in Boston. I tried to document the serious interests the first trustees took in industrial, educational, and mass taste, and their commitment to accessibility as opposed to masterpieces.

I may have overreacted a bit, for some of these early reflections now seem to me oversimplified. The richly diverse studies on American merchandising, consumption patterns, therapeutic strategies, and psychology that have been published in the last two decades did not yet exist when I began to work. Nor had urban cultural institutions been examined with the care they would receive in the 1970s and 1980s. But I was concerned, at the start, with issues of periodization and typology. I thought it important to acknowledge that institutions of culture had their own histories, could develop in unexpected directions and with unanticipated consequences, and could reveal traces of local experience as well as cosmopolitan ambitions. As I proceeded further I was able, as my citations reveal, to rely on a growing literature of commentary and analysis, oriented around a series of analogous issues.

Although I was drawn backward in time from the Gilded Age by my dissertation and other scholarly projects, I remained absorbed by the multiple personalities of these cultural institutions, and the challenge of locating them within a rapidly changing urban society. Writing a biography of P. T. Barnum furthered my interest in urban exhibitions and a move to Chicago in 1969, indeed my living alongside the site of America's greatest exposition, the World's Columbian Exposition of 1893 in Jackson Park, sharpened my awareness of the extraordinary role of world's fairs in the late nineteenth and early twentieth centuries and forced me to consider more closely the physical shape as well as the timing of these massive social interventions. My first extended essay on the subject was written for a conference on Japanese-American relations, and more particularly the images of the other each society entertained. As I began to explore the rich materials, I realized that these expositions were sources that influenced (or at least occasions to express) a broad range of opinions about the world in general. In the United States fairs were also moments of great importance to museums, libraries, universities, among other instruments of high culture. They helped focus energies and attention upon municipal identities, and left behind structures, artifacts, and shared experiences. For another conference, this one focused upon material culture and American life, I was able to compare museums and exhibitions and draw as well on the history of commercial presentation, most notably the urban department store.

As I was extending my work on museum history, I found it enriched unexpectedly by administrative and consulting service. In the 1970s I was appointed to the board of a new federal agency concerned with financial support of museum operations. This was complemented by service on the board of trustees of a museum of American decorative art, and membership on the Smithsonian Council. These practicalities led to further reflections upon the history of museums as functioning entities and made it clear that traditional characterizations and categorizations did not easily capture the problems confronting managers of such institutions. Contemporaneous attacks on museum management and practices, debates about hegemonic values, analyses of philanthropic support patterns and social ambitions, all led me to suspect that it was necessary to study these institutions in a more holistic fashion than was traditional, to see the connections among fund-raising, architecture, museum publicity, educational programs, exhibition strategies, gift shops, patron interests, and ethnic politics.

The rise of the museum to public consciousness, increasing evidences of an international tourist culture, problems of conservation, blockbuster exhibitions, and concern about the museum's role in shaping public values have, in the last decade particularly, led curators, administrators, and foundations to subsidize ever more ambitious studies. Conferences, seminars, newly organized institutional archives, all testify to the renewed attention paid to exhibitions and their influence in shaping social values. The opportunity to talk to museum professionals shaped several of these essays, notably the piece on museum advocacy and "Museums: The Hidden Agenda." The same practicum influenced my essay "Great American Fairs," for it was stimulated by the aborted plan to hold an international exposition in Chicago in 1992, to honor the Columbian Quincentenary. My involvement with various local boards and committees emphasized, even more clearly than my research, the tangled complexities and mixed motives attending the planning of such events.

There are some who believe the new electronic culture, the growing ease of international travel, and the permanent Disney installations doom future expositions. But there were, several decades ago, analogous fears voiced about our museums. Today American museums are flourishing and experiencing enormous growth in numbers, scale, budget, and attendance. The meaning of this growth continues to be debated, however, along with the museum's status within the hierarchy of metropolitan institutions. What was once securely positioned within the world of high culture has apparently been moved into the realm of popular culture, an aggressively merchandised, often trendy, lavishly supported meeting place. And it is, in a sense, the boundaries and intersections of cultures and media that form the occasion for the second group of essays. Although divisions among technologies, senses, and constituencies have formed the very basis of critical analysis and historical genre, it is the confusion of these genres that provides some of the excitement for modern cultural historians—a confusion that owes much to the novelties of new sources of power and instruments of mechanical reproduction.

My interest in one of the subjects I treat, utopian fiction, arose from developing a course in culture and technology. The novels that streamed from American publishers in the wake of Edward Bellamy's *Looking Backward* had generally been examined by social historians, intent upon explicating their reform logic and ideological origins. Certainly, on the face of it the lengthy discussions of property divisions, classlessness or class structure, state-owned enterprises, and changing standards of living suggested that the novelists were indeed economic reformers. But as I read dozens of these texts it seemed they were talking about other things as well, grievances connected with the physical shape of their society, its novel conveniences, its rituals and ceremonies, its transport, communications, and sanitation systems. Generic boundaries were not helpful in defining some messages of these books. They had been placed within too confined a category.

But not all writers found the commercial expansion of American life a source of criticism or complaint. Indeed, as I looked for other interactions between the worlds of merchandising and literary culture, I found a growing delight in specification and a series of insights which intimated absorption and appreciation as well as irony and contempt. "The Drama of Consumer Desire" was written for a conference on the American System of Manufactures that was held at the Smithsonian in the mid 1970s, and was meant to suggest that the glories of mass production had a counterpart in the glories of mass consumption; both were, quite properly, the subjects of artistic reflection, and in the past few years these interests have received more systematic attention than I had time and space to give them.

It was in the area of public performance, however, that one saw even more emphatically the mixture of genres that could be found in democratic taste. And it was in John Philip Sousa that I found an impressive blend of the missionary, the artistic, and entrepreneurial, well suited to the marketing of both popular and high culture. I had, as an amateur musician, found myself playing in the percussion section of bands while in high school and college, and the figure of Sousa was a formidable one in the band literature. His marches remained the staples of our repertory, and it was as a prolific and imaginative composer that I had come to know him.

The Sousa of pre–World War I America turned out to be a still more impressive figure, a giant of the concert hall and of the Sunday supplements, with opinions and accomplishments in many areas besides music. Sousa helped popularize live versions of classical music; his transcriptions (and his own band concerts) provided many Americans, in the years before the phonograph's dominance, with their first experience of Beethoven, Verdi, Mendelssohn, and Wagner. Sousa sought to be a mediator, to spread knowledge of and affection for serious music even while he entertained groups seeking simple diversion. Like many other merchandisers his strategies were self-conscious and elaborate. The clipping books he assembled and left behind after his death, revealed the patterns he employed in his performances. Again, it was not always clear where Sousa should be stationed within the hierarchy of cultural leadership. Looked up to as well as looked down at, Sousa was interested in more than profits and popularity, though both were important to him. He valued and respected serious musical traditions and condemned both modernism and mass media, but he was comfortable within the setting of the resort hotel and the band shell. His mission to the middle class involved a redefinition of boundaries.

There were more obvious signs of strain between the demands of a mass audience and traditional art forms in another essay I have included here; it examined the property value of Superman. Written for a conference on modern mythology, the paper grew out of some legal research I had been doing. My knowledge of copyright law remains superficial, but judicial decisions determining the ownership of popular heroes raised important problems of definition for me. Most of the commentaries I encountered were concerned largely with the economic and legal implications of case law and new legislation. The concepts involved, however, went to the heart of contemporary American culture. The voracious appetites of radio, television, film, and newspapers, and the huge stakes in devising successful formulas combined to suggest new strategies for purveyors of public amusements. The fact that ideas were more easily borrowed when they were satirized could not have been overlooked by producers and publishers. And the consequences of systematic mythic degradation were bound to be significant. Again, traditional boundaries separating popular culture and high art seemed irrelevant to the issues at stake.

The final essay in this section was written for an art catalogue, and might seem better placed among the earlier group on museums and cultural institutions. But it seems to me appropriate to set it here because J. Pierpont Morgan's fabulous collecting career reflected some of the confusion of cultural realms I have been discussing. Morgan's own institutional loyalties, his strong support of the Metropolitan Museum of Art over which he presided, his involvement with the American Academy in Rome, his creation of university chairs and of the great library that bears his name, all suggested a concern with traditions of high culture, cosmopolitanism, and aesthetic sophistication. Unlike many other American collectors of his generation Morgan was formally educated in Europe and had pretensions to erudition and critical judgment. Opinions varied about his taste and acuteness, but he was not simply the dupe of dealers or bent upon a trail of conspicuous consumption. His collecting was more programmatic than that, with serious intentions.

Nonetheless, the scale of his purchases, when combined with his own fame (or notoriety), made Morgan's activities into quintessential newspaper fodder. The extraordinary prices he was willing to pay for artworks, the eclecticism of the objects he sought, the romance involved with their movement from continent to continent, the rumors of smuggling and secret deals, the antiquity and fame of particular pieces, the foreign anger and indignation, all combined to produce a long-running story of considerable popular appeal. Inevitably enough the pursuit of high art became translated into the adventure story it has become today, and long before the artworks entered the precincts of museum and library they had been translated into commodities whose values were debated down to the last penny. It was impossible, in this era of publicity, instant communications, nationalistic competition, and bourgeois display, to avoid mingling the politics and psychology of collecting with its artistic objects. Morgan's princely ambitions and ample purse set the rules for a new game, one which contemporary observers like Henry James were quick to translate and interpret. The game is with us still.

The final group of essays confronts themes I have worked on since my doctoral dissertation: the social history of art and architecture. While writing *The Artist in American Society*, I sought to understand how ante-bellum Americans valued visual media, and how they organized symbolically the new landscape they were creating for themselves. Although my primary concern was the legitimation of the visual arts and the creation of the professional artist's career, I found it useful to examine as well the settings and vocabularies developed by architects and sculptors, and to analyze the linkages among foreign travel, patronage, and social description. It seemed natural to pursue some of these subjects in later periods, although I could not anticipate their directions. The conjunction of preparing a new course in the history of the American landscape, and some visits around the Chicago area to stores and shopping districts, led me to the first of a series of short pieces for the *New Republic* on designed spaces and public facilities.

At this point, in the mid seventies, things were happening which would soon suggest that news of the death of the American city had been much exaggerated. Since Minerva's owl continues to fly only in the gathering dusk, historians had only just begun to pay attention to the evolution of suburban structures and life-styles. New and rather exciting commentaries were decoding the landscape of the highway and the roadside stand, treating automobiles as design sources, analyzing the creation of developer suburbs and tract housing. But there was little of significance on the history of an extraordinary new building type, the enclosed shopping mall. These complexes were only a couple of decades old at that time. The opportunity to explore some of their evolution was stimulated by the creation just then, in Chicago, of what appeared to be a hybrid form, the vertical urban mall. This had almost everything its suburban cousin possessed except for parking. The structure that opened on Michigan Avenue in 1976 proved a forerunner of similar things to come, in this city and elsewhere. Smaller versions of the urban mall began to serve as spearheads of the commercial gentrification which has transformed real estate values in central cities even while it has raised complex and sometimes unpleasant political and social questions. The shopping center seemed an excellent place in which to examine the transfer of urban and suburban values and architectural expectations. With the construction of tall buildings and urbane office parks many miles from the central city, this transfer has become even more marked in the last decade. Highly polished and elegant shopping malls serve suburbanites, while city officials and developers have attempted to trade on nostalgia for the gaudy urban past, anxiously shoving old movie palaces, department store buildings, arcades, and trolley barns out of the path of the wrecking ball and the magic siren song of urban renewal. The history of merchandising and commercial architecture seemed an opening into a larger story of urban sentimentalism and a search for acceptable contemporary monumentality.

The story broadened when the renaissance of the great hotels was brought into consideration, the hollowed-out towers with their plant-bedecked atriums that spread from Atlanta to cities throughout the country. Their public spaces not only revealed that taste for enclosure, control, and ease of access that the shopping centers demonstrated; their glitter and scale also recalled an earlier era of the urban downtown when lobbies in many kinds of buildings functioned as extravagant heralds of fantasy. The language of postmodernism was as yet unavailable to me when writing these architectural pieces, but it seemed probable that a new era of decorative exuberance was making an appearance. And, in a number of cities, its boundaries have been extended to include even that most mundane of urban structures, the parking garage, whose facades now resemble automobile grilles and public monuments and which differentiate one floor from another with flags and national anthems and playing card symbols.

The popular absorption with landscape changes, the growth of amateur preservation movements and architectural nostalgia, the trendy concern with building styles and spatial values, all have resulted in part from a vastly enhanced system of visual reproduction. Glossy magazines with enticing color inserts, films, television news stories and documentary features can and do focus on certain aspects of design. Armed with well-illustrated guidebooks and local histories tourists and urban homesteaders alike can involve themselves in issues of landscape management. But this is a fairly recent moment in human history, the availability of so inexpensive, diverse, and evocative a set of visual images. The rest of the essays in this group concern themselves with various aspects of this revolutionary set of changes whose origins go far back in time but which were quickened, first, by the development of photography in the early 1830s, and, fifty years later, by the acceptance of halftone techniques for process printing. Image-making itself has a limited impact until the pictures can be easily distributed and popularly viewed, and this began to come true in the late nineteenth century.

It was not only the halftone, of course, which supported the vast expansion of pictorial information. Lithography, lantern slides, pocket cameras, movies, three-color printing, rotary presses, billboard and poster art, postcards, postage stamps, paper currency, catalogues, advertising brochures, all contributed well before World War I to the flood of images. It is not easy to understand the difference made by these innovations, just as it has taken some time to understand the changes brought by the printing revolution several hundred years earlier. But many of the same issues—political and cultural authority, authenticity and originality, class differentiation, mobility, educational methods and opportunities, the status of traditional learning, the functions of art—were implicated in each event.

The relationships between cultural values and technological changes are examined not only in "Iconography and Intellectual History," but in the two essays that follow it. One of the most powerful and dramatic changes in visual rendition permitted during the past hundred years has been the inclusion of color. Before the mid-nineteenth century color printing was generally either very expensive or very crude. A series of innovations allowed for increasing use of color in book illustration, magazines, photographs, and newspapers. A conference on the history of mass communications organized by the late Catherine Covert at Syracuse University, allowed me to look more closely at issues raised by color translation in media other than printing. Like many other "improvements" we have come to take for granted, the coming of color was seen as a threat as well as a benefit. But its penetration became more pervasive (and less problematic) in film and television than it did in printing. Some of these differences had a technical basis, but not all of them. Innovations are made and exploited within specific cultural settings. Traditions of interpretation and craftsmanship which in printing, photography, and even film dignified black and white (or tinted) practices, were simply not present when it came to television. The coming of color, like the coming of many other innovations, involved issues of authority and authorship, and the recent debate over colorization of formerly black and white motion pictures demonstrates just how deeply such commitments can run.

Authority was also an issue when it came to illustrations for fiction and magazine articles. The tensions between an author's conception and an artist's vision troubled a number of critics. A divided command might confuse the readership, or worse still force them to depend upon visual translation rather than their own imaginative faculties. The senses were ranked in a hierarchy long after a rich and sophisticated menu of imagic possibilities had been developed. The printed word was privileged by many commentators, who suspected the ease of understanding associated with pictures. Addressing a conference on the history of American illustration, it seemed appropriate to emphasize that the virtuoso achievements of a distinguished set of American artists, to say nothing of a succeeding generation of photographers, had aroused consternation as well as admiration. The debate revealed the continuously shifting boundaries organizing the world of culture, as well as the realm of the senses.

The book's final essay examines, among other things, the image-making capacities of American mass media, but it also links up with an earlier theme, the confusion of realms occasioned by revolutions in merchandising and distribution. The character of American commercial design has benefitted enormously, since the 1890s, from the expansion of American advertising. Newspaper and magazine advertisements, posters, leaflets, calendars, all have required the services of artists. Some of these designers were extremely talented and imaginative, but for much of the twentieth century they coexisted with complaints about the crudity and vulgarity of commercial publicity. After all, it was frequently supervised by businessmen and ad men who knew little and cared less about the demands of art. As the control of advertisement shifted increasingly into the hands of advertising agencies in the interwar years, more ambitious strategies were plotted. Serious artists of unquestioned reputation, modernists as well as traditionalists, were brought into the service of corporate salesmanship. The precise contrast between commercial art and high art grew cloudy, as printers, typographers, painters, and advertising agents alike joined forces to award prizes and hold exhibitions for the commercial graphic art they admired.

My own essay was touched off by presentation of the art commissioned by the Container Corporation of America for its advertising campaigns to the Smithsonian Institution. But it was also an opportunity to consider just how conflated art, business, patronage, promotion, collecting, and museums could become in twentieth-century America. The involvement of business corporations in museum exhibitions, art commissions, and systematic collecting is of recent origin. But the mixture has proven to be both a powerful source of support for some artists, dealers, curators, and museums, and a spring of controversy. The issues raised focus, once more, on boundaries, categories, changing standards of legitimacy, and appropriateness for both private action and for state action. Concern for the political and cultural implications of visual art goes back to the earliest days of the American republic and the austere visions of revolutionary virtue projected by some of the founding fathers. Then the anxiety built around the dangers of state and church. Today it reflects concerns with corporate capital. But much of the debate involves familiar points of opposition.

This continuity is but one of many explored in these essays. In work that is ongoing I am dealing with these themes in the hope of better understanding and keener resolution. But since I believe that a good question can be more valuable than a good answer, I will be happy if I have complicated rather than simplified our sense of cultural history.

●

ONE

Four Stages

of Cultural Growth:

The American City

Since the era of the American Revolution, it has been a national sport to ridicule or despise the city. From Jefferson through Frank Lloyd Wright prominent Americans have argued that great cities were to a national community like sores to a healthy body. Corruption, crime, poverty, and congestion were nourished by the anonymous urban masses; better by far a nation of yeomen than a people of city-dwellers.[1]

But despite the national mythology, the religious suspicions, and the patriotic warnings, our cities grew at an unprecedented pace. Up through the Great Depression of the twentieth century, millions of people flocked to urban centers, and their pressure of numbers helped produce the complex networks of goods and services that characterize the modern city. Why did they come? Some, obviously, had no alternative; boats and trains deposited them in cities and they could never find the money or energy to leave. Others came principally for economic reasons, to find better jobs or to abandon demeaning ones. But for many the city was a magnet because it offered experiences and opportunities

From *History and the Role of the City in American Life* (Indianapolis: Indiana Historical Society, 1972), 25–49. © 1972 by Neil Harris. All rights reserved.

impossible anywhere else, a cure for loneliness and isolation, a source of variety, amusement, education, and information.

We now live at a time when cities are undergoing unprecedented crises. Pollution, social tension, and congestion have driven millions into the suburbs. Instead of being a place of hope, the city for many has become a symbol of despair and a demonstration of failure. It is hard to recall the bright promises once held out; we remember the warnings instead.

Crises, however, if they do little else, usually stimulate historians to action. When going arrangements are challenged or break down, the commonplace acquires a new relevance, and scholars reexamine old assumptions. Thus the last ten years have produced a series of important urban studies concerned with issues long neglected by historians. For the first time we have studies of police force development, the birth and maintenance of urban ghettos, the nature of commercial and professional elites, and the patterns of urban land use.[2]

But despite our new knowledge of neighborhood development, economic specialization, and geographical determinism, we are not much closer to learning more about the noneconomic appeals cities made to earlier generations of Americans. We have not begun to categorize the motives and effects of urban institutions concerned primarily with a people's habits, values, and diversions. In other words, we have still to sketch the outlines of our urban culture.

This, it seems to me, is an important issue. Our great urban institutions, which no longer seem to enjoy their older attractions and compulsions, possess histories; over time their purposes and clienteles have changed. If we are interested in urban communities whose members believed in the city as a way of life, we must try to understand the role cultural institutions played, and the threats they operate under today. The cycles of urban culture remind us that present arrangements have evolved, and need not be accepted as permanent solutions if they are inadequate.

I should like to make a start toward explaining the changing appeal of the city by constructing an overview of urban culture as its institutions developed in America during four separate periods. First, and most briefly, the colonial background; second, the period from the early republic to about the 1870s; third, the years from the seventies to some time before World War II; and finally, most indistinctly and tentatively of all, our own times.

These periods do not break neatly or evenly; there are interstices between them, and they do not apply equally to every large city. Depending on location, demography, and era of settlement, some of our cities skipped one or more of these periods entirely, and telescoped others. Moreover, I must operate at a highly abstract level, and run the risk of oversimplifying and overgeneralizing. But before there is more research and interest it may be necessary to provoke debate by offering models, however flawed, and to pose questions which can guide the individual investigator. Establishing a sequence may help the larger enterprise.

Before beginning, though, I must say something about the word culture. It has had a complex history and is the subject of continuing debate. Until the nineteenth century changed its meaning, culture was more an activity than a state of being; it represented growth or nourishment and could be applied to almost anything. Some years ago Raymond Williams showed how Victorians made culture into a noun signifying the highest and most valued human activities, connected particularly with the high arts.[3] People were defined as cultured according to their interest or proficiency in certain traditional areas: music, painting, architecture, belles lettres. In the twentieth century the word culture has been transformed again, made more comprehensive and catholic. We assume that every people, every civilization, and even every subgroup possesses a culture of some kind, that is, a pattern of value structures, mores, and institutions. It may be a nonliterate, or a violent, or a preindustrial culture, but a culture it is, nonetheless.

These changing definitions of culture must inevitably color any study of urban institutions. When I describe culture in the colonial period and the early nineteenth century, I refer to its original meaning, as growth; when I discuss the period from the mid-nineteenth century to the interwar years, I refer to its second, normative definition, as the highest and best mankind has produced in the arts; and when I analyze the changes occurring in our own days, I employ the third, most comprehensive meaning. It is obviously necessary to avoid imposing a definition which transcends historical experience, and there are great temptations to do this with culture.

Let me turn, then, to the character of urban institutions in the colonial period. What cities existed, in this era, were of course confined to the eastern seaboard; in retrospect they seem overgrown towns. A population of 10,000 or 15,000 was enough to qualify a community for urban status, and only a few places, like Boston, New York, Philadelphia, and Charleston, attained this level before the Revolution. They remained islands in an agricultural sea, and few worried about their drawing power. Dominated by the needs and interests of the propertied, urban institutions fulfilled their special requirements at work and at play. Schools and churches were located not only in towns but in villages as well, and therefore do not fall into our consideration; but mercantile exchanges, where information was transmitted and commercial transactions concluded, coffee houses, dancing assemblies, debating societies, library companies, racing associations, fishing and hunting clubs, these could not be duplicated without the patronage of concentrated wealth and gentility.[4]

The function of our urban culture, in the eighteenth century, was to transcend the limitations of time and place which the uncultivated wilderness of the New World had established. The ambitions of urban aristocracies, both North and South, centered about the re-creation of an environment recalling the Old World at its most sophisticated. Gentry in Boston, New York, or Charleston would have been flattered if visitors told them they were becoming as fashionable as Bristol, Edinburgh, or London itself. Their style of life was meant to be cosmopolitan and international, not tied to geography or nationality.

The chief economic interest of these towns, trade, itself worked toward international contact and beyond local concerns. The function of urban institutions was to promote knowledge of European news, entertainment, art, and scholarship. They were meant to collect, display, and record the work of others across the water. There were, of course, variations from city to city. Bostonians still restricted some of the more daring aspects of urban culture, such as the playhouse, while Philadelphia, under Franklin's leadership, developed a set of self-supporting institutions; its hospital, fire companies, and insurance firms went beyond Old World models. But despite these qualifications we can still argue that urban culture in the pre-Revolutionary era was not distinctive nationally or sectionally. Cities were physical entities not obviously different in character from the rest of society; they were agglomerations of population offering certain conveniences and elegancies. A town house was occupied by many for only a portion of the year.

It was presumed, then, that the transit from country to city could be made naturally, for business or pleasure, by those whose needs took them that way. Urban laborers and mechanics, of course, did not enjoy the luxury of several residences, but the presumption ran that many urban artisans would end up owning their own land and go into farming as soon as they could afford it. The city was not yet a drain on the countryside, an engrosser of its talents and resources. For ordinary men its institutions were not open or characteristically special. Country pubs could take the place of coffee houses; library companies and theaters were still for educated folk; and it was unnecessary, in the country, to form fishing and hunting associations for healthy exercise. Urban culture in this period, then, acted neither as a lure to ruralites, nor existed as a distinctive entity. It represented simply an extension of certain European expectations, a translation of older traditions. When we speak about the degree of imitation in early American colonization we are apt to dwell on rural life, but the level of imitation may well have been greatest in the establishment of urban areas and the social life that their excess wealth permitted.

In urban culture, as in so many other aspects of American life, the Revolution marks a great divide. Not all its implications were immediately apparent, and some would not become obvious for several decades, but the shift is undeniable. Self-consciousness about the role of the city in a young republic develops, and alongside it appears criticism of traditional urban amenities and amusements. Some of this is owing to the revivals of evangelical religion at the turn of the century, some to lingering Puritan suspicions, but even more is caused by the new political ideology which rejects many English and Continental social traditions. The city becomes suspicious from two different points of view—as a stronghold of the idle rich who pose a threat to republican security and as a haven for the mob, who endanger the future from an opposite direction. The disturbances of the eighties and nineties in London and Paris acted to create permanent associations in the American mind between radical violence and the city. There had always been connections between royal pomp and city life. These two elements were supplemented by other things such as the devastating epidemics of yellow fever and later cholera that decimated our urban areas. As a threat to health, sanity, simplicity, and honest government, the city becomes the subject of such fiction writers as Charles Brockden Brown, Poe, and Hawthorne, as well as of the more sober writings of ministers and political leaders.

Self-consciousness also developed as the economic needs of the city and countryside began to diverge in the older states. As cities grew their services— water, sanitation, policing, fire fighting, street repair—grew also, and within state legislatures expensive choices had to be made. The city also attracted notice because of the increasing number of immigrants who began to crowd it— Irish and German—whose religions, languages, or living standards differed significantly from native citizens. Warnings increased in the early nineteenth century about the snares and corruptions of an urban proletariat, and so did fears of public disorder.

But, despite changes and challenges, the city was not abandoned in this early time of troubles. More research is necessary, but it seems clear that social, mercantile, and political elites did not desert their communities, throw up their hands in horror, and move away. In many cases they remained committed to the cause of cosmopolitanism which eighteenth-century urban life had symbolized, and they now had powerful patriotic considerations as well. For it seemed clear that whatever inspiration romantic writers and artists might find in the countryside, the creation of a national art, the fulfillment of the genius of democracy, required communities of writers and artists, living in cities, nourishing one another's ambitions, supported by generous civic patrons. The great centers of foreign art lay in capitals such as Paris and London. A sense of competition with Europe, for the greater glory of republicanism and American nationalism, seemed to argue for the establishment of institutions aimed at producing great artists, and educating the public sufficiently to appreciate them.[5]

One sees, therefore, in the first half of the nineteenth century, an extraordinary range of institutions created, having as their goal some form of art popularization or patronage. Libraries, historical societies, art unions, art academies, lyceums, theaters, and opera companies appear, not only in eastern cities but in the newer western towns such as Lexington, Cincinnati, Pittsburgh, Buffalo, and Indianapolis. Obviously levels of attainment varied according to the wealth or age of the community; New York and Boston afforded more variety and sophistication in their amusements and recreations than did Pittsburgh and St. Louis. But the factor bringing all these institutions under one heading in this period was the zeal of residents in publicizing their home cities as places deserving outside respect (and patronage) because of their cultural amenities. Literary societies and academies were advantages alongside convenient railroad lines and fine harbors. Guidebooks and newspapers, both in New York and in smaller towns, presented their panoply of institutions as proof of urbanity and wealth. "Need we name our two museums, both respectable," wrote one Cincinnati newspaper, listing the city's advantages, "our schools and academies, both numerous and respectable; the academy of fine arts, yet in its incipient stage but establishing on a firm basis; the circulating library," and so on.[6]

In the West as in the East cities vied for the title "Athens of America" and sought institutions truly popular in their clientage and effects. Where once, in the colonial period, American cities sought to ape foreign examples in the attention paid the genteel arts, now imitation was no longer enough. The genius of democracy and local pride required institutions that were patronized by the whole community, that succeeded in integrating the population, bringing together representatives from all social grades in the pursuit of intellectual, aesthetic, and moral improvement.[7]

To a remarkable extent these institutions were indeed integrating. One source of evidence comes from the long list of foreign travelers repelled by the public habits of Americans. The revulsion of visitors such as Harriet Martineau and Frances Trollope was based on the strange American juxtaposition of institutions normally associated with elite patronage in Europe, with ordinary, coarsely dressed, less polite Americans. Behavior in theaters, for example, was a continual source of irritation to the genteel—the nursing of babies which went on in boxes, the catcalls and yelling, the eating and drinking, the general rowdiness of audiences watching anything from the latest melodrama to Shakespeare. This naturally aroused the ire of strangers who expected better behavior. But what such unruly public conduct demonstrated was the lack of compartmentalization among American urban audiences in the Jacksonian period, the fact that all types and conditions were jammed together within theaters, museums, and concert halls, sometimes lowering the artistic atmosphere, but making up for it in enthusiasm and size.

Moreover, the great tours which European artists such as Fanny Ellssler, Ole Bull, Jenny Lind, and Teresa Parodi undertook in the pre–Civil War era, are further pieces of evidence.[8] They were made under the aegis of impresarios such as P. T. Barnum, men who employed all the arts of publicity and exaggeration that they could to entice urbanites to part with some cash. The crowds in the new urban theaters and concert halls were enormous, sometimes more than 5,000 a night, returning rich profits to the artists and their managers, but representing a surge of truly popular interest. The fact that American audiences were cleverly manipulated by these early Sol Huroks is less significant than that they were truly mass audiences, heterogeneous groups of men willing to take off their hats and open their pocketbooks for art, but demanding entertainment at the same time. High culture was not yet separated from popular culture. Museums, such as Barnum's in New York, Kimball's in Boston, Peale's in Philadelphia, or the Western Museum in Cincinnati, mingled together all sorts of oddities—Indian arrows, dinosaur bones, two-headed pigs, along with casts of Greek sculpture, and paintings by Gilbert Stuart and Thomas Sully.[9] The arts and sciences would be gathered hospitably together under one roof, open to anyone with curiosity and the price of admission. And that they were run for profit, with commercial possibilities, was not considered shameful.

For the visual arts, more specifically, there were great art unions, enrolling tens of thousands of members in the 1840s, acting as distributors for native painters.[10] Five or ten dollars entitled a member to a ticket in the lotteries distributing the artworks, as well as to engraved copies of the most-prized objects, copies which themselves were works of art. The trustees of these art unions were frequently self-made, newly rich merchants, operating, to be sure, with some class bias, but brushing shoulders easily with the artists they supported and the ordinary citizens who used their institutions. Their emphasis lay on participation; the presence of profits only reemphasized the civic and patriotic imperatives of wide support. This cultural leadership had few pretensions to exclusivity; involvement was meant to testify to civic pride rather than class membership.

And there was a real competition among communities to attract larger numbers of artists and writers to their midst, and in following the efforts of local boys trying to make good in the great world of the metropolis, either in New York or Europe. Many a starving young American painter or poet was rescued in France or Italy by the friendly interest of a merchant in his home town, eager to see one of his fellow townsmen succeed. The comparative poverty of American cities in original art works seemed to argue a collective approach which would permit citizens to pool their resources and talents. Few studies have examined the range of these urban institutions in the first half of the nineteenth century, nor have their managers and promoters been subjected to the kind of scrutiny which would permit supported generalizations about their background and motives. But this era of urban culture is characterized by an emphasis on popular distribution, an openness of management, and a willingness to accept commercial profit as a legitimate goal.

Indeed it is in this period that we find, in large cities, an institution run entirely for profit, which is not usually included with other cultural forces—the American hotel. With their hundreds of sleeping rooms, libraries, great dining areas, and immense marble lobbies, hotels were one of the institutions not easily duplicated in small towns, which forced urbanites together and gave a focus to municipal pride. In hotels, wrote Sarmiento, the Argentine visitor to America in 1847, "the marvels of art are lavished on the glorification of the masses." In New Orleans the dome of the St. Charles Hotel brought to his mind the image of St. Peter's in Rome, and Sarmiento argued that in America, while the power of the church diminished in proportion to the multiplicity of sects, "the hotel inherits the dome of the ancient tabernacle and takes on the aspect of the baths of emperors."[11]

His reminiscences of the American hotel prompted Sarmiento, in fact, to provide evidence for a point I made earlier: that Captain Marryat, Mrs. Trollope, and other travelers would have changed their minds about uncouth American manners if, "in England and France the coal miners, woodcutters, and tavernkeepers were to sit down at the same table with artists, congressmen, bankers, and landowners, as is the case in the United States."[12] The hotel was one of the urban institutions which brought such human varieties together and encouraged acceptance of a common mode of behavior. Any town with pretensions required a great hotel, as much as it did a theater, opera house, and mercantile exchange. Along with the museums, academies, and libraries, the hotel must take its place as one of the integrating instruments of urban culture in the antebellum era.

How long this popularizing phase lasted varied from city to city. Even before the Civil War there were signs that the character and motivation of urban patrons were beginning to change in the older eastern cities, while in western towns such as Chicago, Denver, and San Francisco this earlier period lasted somewhat longer. But at some point in the nineteenth century emphasis shifts away from participation and more to what I would call certification, certification of either the experiences or objects the institution protected, or of the good taste and social standing of its supporters. From being devices which brought the population of cities together, self-conscious cultural institutions now started to segment portions of the citizenry, and their managements became preoccupied with different problems, and defensive about their own social status. On the face of it, this was the most creative period in the history of our cultural institutions, the years between the 1870s and the First World War.[13] One thinks, for example, of the Museum of Fine Arts in Boston and the Metropolitan Museum of Art in New York, both founded in 1870, of the Boston Symphony of 1881, the Chicago Symphony of 1891, the Philadelphia Orchestra of 1900, the Art Institute of Chicago, and the Metropolitan Opera, to name just a few. These were the years when great temples and palaces were built to house the new orchestras, libraries, and museums; they often were grouped together in great plazas or squares near the city's center. These enterprises were noncommercial in their objectives, but they continued to be popular in objective: their goal was public enlightenment, the same goal proclaimed by earlier founders of cultural institutions.

But the circumstances had changed. Efficiency combined with class bias to dictate that the new cultural institutions be organized more with an eye to protecting the standard of the arts than with the theatricality and mingling of tastes which might have drawn mass audiences. The new interest in achievement and cosmopolitan excellence was not solely a product of snobbishness, as many critics of the Gilded Age have charged. The fact that many sponsors of the institutions were business tycoons meant that masterful and rather decisive temperaments directed the cultural reorganization going on. Their products would bear some of the same marks the newly organized businesses wore. Professionalization began to overtake the ranks of museum directors and opera managers, as it was coming to dominate the worlds of higher education and business management.

In the course of creating this new institutional world, many of the old informalities disappeared. Monopolization of talent and markets was not confined to commerce or manufacturing. One could take as an example the creation of our great symphony orchestras. Before 1850 many of our orchestras and opera companies were organized on a joint-stock basis. The musicians and singers themselves shared the profits, if there were any, or attempted to meet the losses, a more normal situation. They were often managed by impresarios whose goal was also private profit. The New York Philharmonic Society, organized in 1842 as one of our first orchestras, was just such an institution.[14] Its conductor was elected by vote, and its income was distributed among orchestra members. Musicians were not tied down to the one organization; they floated in and out, performing when they got engagements, rehearsing when they found time, quitting occasionally at short notice when enticed by more favorable prospects. The levels of musical performances, as a result, were uneven, and American critics complained of shoddy playing and indifferent interpretations. To set up a different kind of symphonic institution required an authoritarian management; profits had to be taken away from the musicians who would then, like small businessmen and independent entrepreneurs during the same era, sacrifice independence for security, and become employees of the management.

The New York Philharmonic tried to hold on to its cooperative machinery, and did so much longer than other musical groups, but by the beginning of the twentieth century its coherence broke down and it capitulated. Men such as Rockefeller, Carnegie, and J. P. Morgan contributed large sums to create an endowment, but they insisted on certain conditions. Among them was the creation of an outside board of control which would make policy decisions, hire the conductor, and fix the salaries. These practices are so common today that when musicians, as they did in Cleveland recently, express a voting preference for individual conductors, opponents label this a heresy, opposed to tradition and common sense. Actually, this practice is older than the custom of turning power over to boards of trustees.

In Boston, Henry Lee Higginson, a successful businessman and an active philanthropist, was determined in the early eighties to raise the level of musical performances there. He acted partly from a sense of civic obligation and partly from his own passion for music. Higginson began to hire musicians for an orchestra, but he insisted, after the first year of operation, that these musicians agree to perform only for the Boston Symphony. He insisted also that they put aside several days each week for rehearsal. The orchestra was run like a business organization with time schedules, enforced discipline, and threats of dismissal presented to recalcitrant musicians.[15]

This new policy met great opposition. Some Bostonians charged Higginson with cornering the musical market and centralizing symphonic activity, in much the same way they attacked the oil, steel, and coal tycoons. And in a sense this was what Higginson was doing. One Boston newspaper argued that Higginson was threatening the entire city; either it took his gift or faced musical starvation. "It is as if a man should make a poor friend a present of several baskets of champagne, and, at the same time, cut off his whole water supply." Totally unimpressed, Higginson threatened to hire musicians outside the United States if his demands were not met. Like the New York Philharmonic orchestra, the musicians capitulated and Boston got its permanent symphony.

But it was not only the new institutional rigor which contrasted with the antebellum scene; there was also the character of the audiences attracted. In place of the heterogeneous mingling which visitors found so annoying in the earlier period, crowds attending symphony concerts were decorous, well-bred, and middling to wealthy. New practices of dressing and ticket prices combined to squeeze out many of the poor. A letter writer in Boston complained in the early 1880s that among symphony audiences he saw "but few whom I should believe to be poor or even of moderate means . . . 'Full dress' was to be seen on every hand. I should be very glad to take my family to hear these educating and refining concerts," the correspondent went on, "but I have not the means to go in full dress; neither can I afford to pay a spectacular double the price for tickets that is asked by the manager."[16]

One can find similar comments on the part of other observers, but sometimes they were coupled with approval rather than criticism. When the Boston Symphony made its appearance in New York in 1887, a writer reported to the *Boston Traveller* that it was a lovely evening. "In place of the face of foreign types which accompanies one everywhere in cosmopolitan New York, here right alongside was one of the loveliest old New England grand mammas, with a bevy of nephews and nieces; in the next row a group of fine fellows, New Yorkers, it may be, but Harvard men undoubtedly, while it was such a pleasure to see all about the faces with which one felt a kinship." He did not mean to disparage foreigners, the correspondent went on, but he had been really homesick "for the sight of a *family* face when for any cause brought into a promiscuous company in New York."[17]

This rather revealing comment testifies to one of the things the new institutions were doing in this period: separating audiences out, by class, wealth, or ethnic background, dividing up what had become for many participants an impossibly heterogeneous gathering. No longer meant to gather profits, the institution's function was one of accreditation, and its major interest the perpetuation of a world of older objects and experiences. Museums, libraries, and orchestras were meant to be asylums—the word is used frequently—refuges for the best that world culture had produced. Unlike the antebellum institutions, the new temples were not expected to fit into the pattern of national life; they were consciously erected to move across these patterns, to improve, oppose, protect, and conserve. Although museum promoters argued that their enterprises relaxed and softened the rigors or urban life, they did not constitute a means for adapting to it. Rather, for the happy few who made use of them, they challenged such conditions. This notion of culture as being not the art and spirit of the society enveloping it, but rather a set of alien standards to which men could repair in times of flux, was not solely American; it recurs in the writings of many European critics, most notably Matthew Arnold and John Ruskin. But the distance between actual society and cultural ideal was more obvious in America because most European industrial states possessed at least the physical heritage of their own art; their turn was to an organic and therefore comprehensible past.

Certainly, there was some continuity between these institutions and their predecessors. Among art museum founders, particularly, one finds evidence that the new patrons were interested in reaching the mass of the population, and also in affecting the level of American art and industrial design.[18] The influence of the South Kensington Museum in London, later the Victoria and Albert, was critical. American museums pioneered in a variety of programs to get the public into their buildings. Classes, lectures, improved labeling techniques, free or very low admission charges, physical accessibility, these were among the methods attempted. Patriotism also played its part, as it did in the antebellum years, the notion that by bringing together masterpieces and arranging them attractively and intelligibly an uplifting effect would be had, not only on the crowds of spectators but on the ranks of American artists as well.

Moreover, there was considerable variation from city to city. In places like Pittsburgh, Cincinnati, St. Louis, and Chicago, with large numbers of German immigrants, the city's great musical organizations were formed with the support and under the leadership of German-Americans. Thus at least one immigrant group was able to impress its stamp on the character of formal municipal culture, although many of the other newcomers were as distant from the symphonics and operas as they were in cities like Boston and Philadelphia.

But even the museums, which were far more oriented to public service than the other cultural institutions, represented a freezing of older notions of patronage. Instead of money going to living artists, it went to dealers and other collectors. Inevitably these diversions of income sources hurt American designers. Membership on museum boards, despite the rhetoric, remained largely confined for many years to representatives of old and established families. One museum trustee announced on his election in the 1890s that he felt as he "were entering a church."[19] Improvement was to come not by stimulating the living art of the day but by "knowledge of the masterpieces of the past."[20] Inevitably then, despite the high attendance figures and the active lecture programs, museums cut themselves off from much of the life of their cities. Visits to museums were for many like visits to sacred services, and in place of comprehension there was frequently simple awe.

This is not, I repeat, to impugn the motives of the founders. Though some were attracted to institutions by the exclusive character of the management, and others hoped to improve their social status, many early trustees were sincerely committed to raising the levels of public taste. But as the collections grew in size and value, as the cost of opera houses and symphony orchestras and theater maintenance increased, so did conservatism about use and concern about protection. The investment in these large physical collections and the buildings which housed them was expensive enough to require expert control, and institutional life acquired a logic of its own which effectively locked out portions of the community.

But if the wealthy urban classes encouraged the construction of these great institutions, the city supported contemporaneously other institutions which nourished other cultures—cultures with class, ethnic, or generational ties. What one sees in the late nineteenth century is the creation of many spheres within city populations, rarely touching except in moments of crisis, each supplies with its own forms of expression and means of recreation.[21] Each duplicated the other's institutions—newspapers, clubs, fraternal societies— but none of these institutions was inclusive enough to comprehend more than one group. Cultural institutions became badges of membership, not in the larger municipal or national community, as they had been in the early nineteenth century, but in a group or class which provided the necessary support. So these institutions merely mirrored the increasingly sharp divisions which made up the metropolis of some eighty years ago.

As I say, I am presuming a lot on rather slender evidence. We do not know a great deal about the audiences or backers of these various enterprises. But there is some evidence, at least, that this segmenting trend was especially striking among theater audiences. Even the vaudeville theater was specialized. In the words of one of its students, it "was most appealing to the rising class of white-collar workers."[22] This group, whom Albert McLean has labeled the "New Folk," was no longer the heterogeneous mixture that had filled theaters in the early nineteenth century. It was genteel, well-behaved, and appreciative of the great palaces that entrepreneurs such as B. F. Keith were building for it. Ethnic groups, particularly the Italians and Jews, had their own theaters.

Even among the totally commercial institutions, which in their quest for profits tried not to separate out their clienteles, greater variety and concentration made it possible to pick and choose. Thus expensive hotels and exclusive department stores no longer had to cater to the masses, as their predecessors did in the earlier part of the century. The carriage trade could support them, as it supported increasingly exclusive private schools, clubs, genealogical societies, and summer colonies. And in spectator sports, long presumed (without sufficient evidence) to be among the most integrating areas of urban culture, onlookers began to divide themselves according to class, with polo, cricket, and college football at one end, boxing on the other end, and baseball somewhere in between. Private athletic clubs made it possible, of course, for exercise and spectatorship to be pursued in still more sanitized surroundings.

The one exception in this mass of competing and differentiating institutions, the one enterprise which did manage to bring the people of cities together, and mingle them with strangers and visitors, was the series of great expositions which many American cities sponsored at some point between the 1870s and World War I.[23] The greatest of these events were held in Philadelphia, Chicago, St. Louis, and San Francisco, but major fairs were also sponsored by Buffalo, Atlanta, Nashville, Portland, New Orleans, San Diego, and Omaha. These festivals celebrated historical events, commercial trade routes, and investment opportunities, but what many were striving for was some visible unity to the social, economic, and artistic lives of their divided communities. It is not surprising, then, that such epochal observations on the state of national unity and purpose as Frederick Jackson Turner's frontier thesis and Booker T. Washington's racial cooperation speech occurred within the confines of these expositions. Attracting huge and heterogeneous crowds, the fair managers sought to legitimize, by sheer numbers, the principles of historical continuity and moral gentility which official urban culture enshrined. The many foreign exhibits, each housed in its own pavilion, symbolized for some the variety of America's own population. The acres of painted allegory and the sculptured figures of Patriotism and Fame stood in miniature though not minute fair cities, demonstrating that it was possible to objectify the spiritual values which a community might hold in common.

The fairs, however, although they influenced a generation of urban planners, were evanescent glimpses of an imaginary world, a realm of concord guided by the ideals of art, as the middle classes conceived them. Behind and beyond the White City was the Black City, and temporary festivals were inadequate solutions to the problems of division. The civic squares, the courthouses with their Latin mottoes and patriotic statuary, the war memorials, and great public libraries were tributes to an ideal, not an actuality.

Divisions in urban culture between its most esteemed formal institutions on the one hand and the recreational and commercial enterprises serving separate classes on the other continued well on into the twentieth century. Boards of trustees and patrons remained dominated by special if expert interests, emphasizing certification and refinement. But several things, in the period between the wars, began to weaken the notion that these formal institutions constituted urban culture. The almost automatic respect for the pronouncements of curators and managers started to diminish.

We approach our own times, when historical judgments must become still more tentative, but two important trends have helped undermine the meaning of urban culture in its traditional forms. The first was the growth of the mass media—motion pictures, radio, picture magazines, and television. Obviously it is impossible to say much that is new about the enormous effects of media growth, particularly in a few minutes, but it might be noted here that they constituted, from one angle, a challenge to the carefully gathered treasures of the older cultural institutions. The ability to popularize on a huge scale objects of art, images, and living styles helped thrust urban culture into a new stage. For one thing, the media pioneers, the early directors, producers, and editors were successful because they knew how to exploit public taste and manipulate the new possibilities. But unlike the curators, conductors, and librarians, these men lacked formal accreditation and advanced education, for they were operating in a field where innovativeness, flexibility, and sensitivity to client demands were paramount. They were not responsible to conservative boards of trustees, but to bankers or stockholders who demanded profit, not aesthetic accomplishment. In some way their motives resembled those of the urban impresarios of the middle nineteenth century; movie makers integrated enormous audiences and sought inclusiveness and comprehensibility. Their films were frequently as oddly assorted as the curiosities that filled Barnum's Museum, and as uneven in quality. But there were differences.

From one point of view, radio and film might seem to signal the urban takeover of American culture, and they have often been represented as such: urban mobility and moral relativism replacing the older fixed standards, agrarian and small town, which had dominated the public mind. The glitter and glamour of city life beckoned from the urban settings that the radio and films projected.

But from another point of view, the mass media challenged and erased the city's older cultural advantages and replaced urban culture with a new amalgam of its own. For the media now permitted Americans everywhere to duplicate the possibilities which only physical concentration had previously permitted. Once variety and professionalism in recreation and art had belonged exclusively to communities which could physically afford to house theaters, libraries, museums, and opera houses. Now these accumulated treasures could be expended over the microphone or through the camera and sent anywhere electricity and receivers existed. Smaller groups of people could replicate the advantages of cities. Radio, film, and later television replaced older urban entertainments; motels and shopping centers competed with central hotels and department stores. One might speculate whether or not the middle classes would have fled in such numbers to suburbia without the protection of the media, the knowledge that physical removal did not mean empty leisure hours or abandonment of traditional amusements. The media, in this sense, represented not the triumph of urban values but a menace to urban existence, a destruction of once exclusive privileges. The cities hospitably took in the radio stations and the movie theaters and the publishing empires, but they may have turned out to be another Trojan Horse.

The homogenizing world of the mass media, moreover, contradicted the values of separated heterogeneity that had constituted urban culture in the previous period. That most powerful influence of all, motion pictures, was produced not in the atmosphere of an urban setting like New York or Chicago (except for a brief period in its early years), but in the hothouse environment of a Los Angeles suburb where weather and terrain, rather than traditional cultural strengths, proved to be the most important determinants. Early students of film, such as the poet Vachel Lindsay, hoped that "Los Angeles may become the Boston of the photoplay," America's new cultural capital, and argued that it was "thrillingly possible" for California and cinema "to acquire spiritual tradition and depth together," but whether they did remains an open question.[24] The Hollywood achievement is too complex to summarize in a few sentences. But the fact that this great cultural expression was created far from the nation's centers of publishing, writing, and artistic activity, may make suspect the generalization that mass media reflected urban values and expectations.

The media indirectly undercut both levels of urban culture—the upper middle-class facade of formal institutions and the competing heterogeneity of various classes and ethnic groups. In the last two decades a more frontal assault on the character of municipal institutions has destroyed further the acquiescence that guardians of culture had grown accustomed to receiving. Various groups within the community are no longer willing to permit their own identities and achievements to be ignored by public spokesmen. The incongruity of boards of trustees who are unrepresentative of municipal populations yet speak in their names has become more evident. And the art, music, and literature which urban libraries, museums, and concert halls celebrate has also been challenged. Cultural fortresses such as the Metropolitan Museum can no longer consign minority cultures to their own enclaves. Insulated and separated institutions, such as existed in the late nineteenth century, are not enough; official recognition and support are demanded.

The value of spending so much money and space on a relatively small segment of human achievement has also been criticized. Art workers have grown more vocal in criticizing the protective cordon thrown about art objects and the rituals associated with certain forms of spectatorship. In Europe as well as in America boards of trustees have been faced with protests sometimes taking bizarre forms. The trustees of the Metropolitan Museum of Art were invaded by cockroaches at a dinner meeting recently, a gift from members of the Art Workers Coalition who were protesting the spirit of acquisition that seemed to characterize the Museum.[25] For the first time since the early republic, urban cultural institutions are being asked to reflect as well as nourish the actual life of the communities which house them. Commitment to an ideal which exists apart in time and space, accreditation, preservation, protection, these no longer seem worth the effort to many urbanites.

Temples of course continue to rise, such as the Kennedy Center in Washington, and attendance is enormous at our great galleries. But along with the criticisms, the entertainments and exhibitions have grown more various. Ethnic culture can be presented inside the buildings once reserved for traditional masterpieces, and jazz and rock can share the orchestra halls with Mozart and Beethoven. Perhaps we are witnessing the transformation of these institutions, at last, to integrating forums, where all the arts and crafts mingle. Or perhaps we are witnessing their reduction to entertainment palaces where useful distinctions are being blurred into shapelessness.

It is difficult to foretell what will be the fate and new shape of our urban institutions. Orchestras, operas, museums, and theaters will continue to exist in some form, although both municipal budgets and private contributors seem unequal to the tasks of support. More and more, in fact, these institutions are coming to be seen as national rather than local possessions, owned not by particular cities but by society as a whole. This may be a symbol of the fact that city and hinterland are not the separate entities they were when such institutions were founded, and that indeed federal subsidies to urban orchestras and museums follow logically upon the nationalization of culture. In one sense then, our museums and orchestras may be acting as spearheads in the reintegration of national life. Their recognition as national institutions may prefigure the day when boundaries no longer cut off artificially our urban from our suburban areas, and when the city itself is transcended by more logical and livable administrative arrangements.

2

All the World

a Melting Pot?

Japan at American Fairs,

1876–1904

The great fairs of the nineteenth and twentieth centuries offer unusual opportunities for the study of international communications. In these controlled settings nation-states set out their artistic and industrial achievements before enormous audiences. Reactions varied, of course. But for certain cultures there was special meaning in these international displays.

The Japanese exhibits at American fairs attracted particularly strong attention. Some of the American interest was aroused by the inherent excellence of the Japanese displays, their novelty and ingenuity. Some was stimulated by the contrast between oriental design and the preponderantly European art and architecture at the fairs. But another reason for American interest had to do with a special feature of Japanese culture—its tension between the pull of modernization and the antiquity of native traditions. For reasons that are fundamental to the character of American civilization, this bifurcation of energy, between ancient arts and modern industry, echoed a different kind of bifurcation in American life. Examining American reactions to the Japanese exhibits

From Akira Iriye, ed., *Mutual Images: Essays in American-Japanese Relations* (Cambridge, Mass.: Harvard University Press, 1975), 24–54. Reprinted with permission.

we can find clues to the special place of Japan in the American mind of the nineteenth century.

Most Americans made their first contact with Japanese culture at one of the international expositions.[1] American contacts with China go back to the late eighteenth century and involved a variety of commercial, cultural, and missionary expressions. But Japanese exclusion meant that, except for a few sailors and shipwrecked civilians, there was absolutely no interaction between Japan and the United States before the mid nineteenth century, and very little information about Japan diffused in this country before the Centennial Exhibition of 1876. In the post-Perry era of Japanese-American relations there had been one outstanding incident: the 1860 visit of the Japanese envoys. Their nationwide tour caused a brief sensation and a flurry of writing about Japanese customs. But the Civil War years quickly eclipsed this one experience. As a result, the various fairs made up the only concentrated encounter Americans had with Japanese life and whetted a taste for more information. This was serviced, in the late nineteenth century, by periodical articles and books of description written by travelers or Americans resident in Japan. The fairs not only acquired great importance for Japanese-American relations, they also gave the Japanese government an unparalleled opportunity (not shared by most foreign powers) to define the kind of impression they wished Americans to possess. Visitors to the fairs would have little with which to correct or supplement the official displays, for almost everything they saw or learned at the fairs was new. There is an element of control about these experiences that is quite novel and unusual in the study of mutual images.

International expositions must be considered one of the hallmarks of nineteenth-century civilization. To many contemporaries they symbolized the world of peaceful progress that religion and technology seemed combining to establish. Although national expositions had developed in the eighteenth century, the first modern world's fair is generally accepted as the Crystal Palace Exposition held in London in 1851.[2]

Having made its point (and returned a profit), the international exposition was soon imitated in many countries. Americans erected a Crystal Palace in New York City in 1853, but their exhibition had much less impact than its British model. The French, however, took the institution and carried it to new heights of size and artistic elegance. The Paris world's fairs of 1855, 1867, 1878, 1889, and 1900 cost impressive sums of money and attracted millions of visitors. The 1900 fair, the largest of all, was viewed by almost 50 million people.[3] Instead of being placed within a single large building, the fairs of the late nineteenth century spread out over sites of many acres. The landscaped grounds were dotted with national pavilions and enormous palaces of agriculture, transportation, manufacturing, horticulture, and liberal arts. Here the latest achievements of industrial civilization could be viewed.

Although the Paris fairs were the most spectacular, major exhibitions were held in many other places. Vienna hosted one in 1873, on an area of parkland along the Danube. Brussels in 1883 and 1897, Antwerp in 1893, London in 1862, Dublin in 1853, Florence in 1861, Amsterdam in 1864, even far off Sydney in 1879 and Melbourne in 1880 sponsored important exhibitions. And, more to our point, in 1876 the United States got involved and began its own series of spectacular exhibitions.

Most of the major American fairs had as their justification some great national anniversary. However much the fairs turned into booster events for the host cities, the original themes were never forgotten. It was appropriate, therefore, that our first major exhibition celebrated national independence itself. It ran for six months in Philadelphia in the summer of 1876.[4] Planning for the festival began early. In March 1871 Congress passed an act to provide for celebrating the centennial, but it did not provide any funds. It did, however, establish the United States Centennial Commission to encourage foreign participation. One year later Congress established a Centennial Board of Finance to manage the budget of the exhibition, construct buildings, pay debts, and supervise the sale of stock to the public. After various delays, the officers of the fair were appointed in 1874, contracts were let out, and construction was begun on a site in Fairmount Park along the Schuylkill River. The exhibition was to cover some 236 acres, and the managers began with totally uncultivated grounds. All the details of drainage, sewerage, water supply, and plantings had to be undertaken upon this swamp, in addition to the construction. Some 249 buildings would be erected, many of them quite small but others among the largest in the world. The main building would cover twenty acres and Machinery Hall would cover fourteen. The centennial eventually cost several million dollars and recorded more than 10 million admissions. All in all an enormous undertaking, and the first of its scale to take place in the United States.

Because of the importance of the anniversary and the scale of the projected exposition, Americans were eager to learn the response of foreign states. The fair was designed to demonstrate that the United States now possessed the fruits of Western civilization and could rival in splendor and elegance, as well as practicality, the great fairs that Europe had hosted. But without generous international participation, without the national pavilions, art collections, and examples of industry gathered from all over the world, the Centennial Exposition would be unable to make major claims.

As expected, the larger European powers responded. Great Britain appropriated $250,000 for its display (an amount supplemented and even surpassed by its private exhibitors); Germany followed close behind; France, Sweden, Austria-Hungary, Russia, and Italy also responded. Latin America made a good representation. All of this was very gratifying to Americans. "A unanimous, graceful and cordial bow of acceptance" swept "round the globe in response to the invitation of the youngest member of the family," wrote one contemporary historian, self-conscious about America's entry into the world of expositions. Many foreigners, he suggested, still had the impression that their host "was not yet fully out of the woods, that the chestnut-burs were still sticking in his hair, and that the wolf, the buffalo and the Indian were among his intimate daily chums."[5] But they would find something different. The "country cousin" would surprise his guests with "city hospitalities." It was not the American's habit "to aim too low."

Anxious to redeem themselves from the charge of boorishness and materialism, Americans were grateful for the scale of foreign participation. But there were other foreign powers, also new to the crowded stage of expositions, and as eager as the Americans to make a good impression. Foremost among these was Japan. The country had first been represented at the Paris fair of 1867, where the Shogunate and two provinces (Satsuma and Hizen han) had mounted small-scale displays. But the fair coincided with the turmoil of the Meiji Restoration, and it was not again until the Vienna fair of 1873 that the national government took charge of the Japanese effort. Preparations for the Vienna show were hurried. An official commission was not appointed until June 1872, barely one year before the fair opened. This did not allow enough time for the elaborate planning that was necessary. The American fair was another story. The Japanese learned about the centennial celebration as early as June 1873 and decided to participate in June 1874. They officially responded to the invitation six months later.[6]

Soon afterwards, Japanese carpenters traveled to Philadelphia to erect the national pavilion. Two structures were put up near the west gate of the grounds, one, a small bazaar and tea house, the other, a large, two-story building that contained, among other things, residential quarters for the Japanese commission. Besides this there were Japanese sections in Agricultural Hall and in the main exhibition building. The placing of the Japanese display in the main building revealed how literally Americans interpreted the power of national character and the peaceful competition of the fairs. Japan was placed in the western section of the building, next to China. This corresponded to its geographical location relative to the United States. "France and Colonies, rep-

Japanese builders at work, Philadelphia Centennial Exposition, 1876

resenting the Latin races," reported the director general, "was given space adjacent to the northeast central tower. England and Colonies, representing the Anglo-Saxon races, were given spaces adjacent to the northwest central tower. The German Empire, and Austria and Hungary, representing the Teutonic races, were granted space adjacent to the southwest tower."[7] To make racial installation and identification complete, the commissioners tried to place around France those peoples of Latin extraction, and around Germany those of Teutonic extraction. Despite the optimistic environmentalism that dominated American thought, the careful racial classifications indicated that Americans were prepared for the hereditarianism that would become increasingly popular in the late nineteenth century.

More than thirty nations participated in the centennial. Japan's exhibit, however, stood out sharply. It had accepted early and the preparations were extensive. Japan shipped more than 7,000 packages to Philadelphia, exceeded only by Great Britain.[8] With 17,831 square feet in the main building and some 284 separate exhibitors, the Japanese were surpassed by only a few, countries much larger or much closer to the United States. And Japan had one of the nine foreign government buildings.

But the size and costliness of the display was not its chief characteristic. Rather, Americans reacted to its total novelty. The Japanese art wares were different from anything seen here before. The sense of newness spread even before the centennial opened. In February 1876 the *New York Times* described the Japanese workers building the official pavilion.[9] Crowds gathered daily to scrutinize the strange, "almond-eyed" carpenters and their bizarre methods. The tea house, constructed in Japan and put together in Philadelphia, resembled "an ingenious puzzle which was being connected." No nails were employed and the framework rested on posts, rather than the usual masonry foundations. The Japanese exuded an impression of neatness and precision. Their craftsmanship contrasted with that of the Chinese, the only Asians Americans knew. "Contrary to what has been observed of the Chinese in California and the mining regions," the *Times* continued, "the children of the Flowery Land do not burst into song when plying the implements of carpentry, but work away in absolute silence." Ignorance of Japan made any details welcome. The workers "wear a thick blue garment . . . and dark-blue pants, with some stout shoes apparently soled with paper. Their doublets are embroidered on the back with white, and have large loose sleeves." The *Times* declared that the people of Philadelphia were delighted and wished only for a bit more animation, distrusting "the cold reserve" of the Japanese workmen. "Some of the lookers-on certainly believe all Japs to be acrobats, and I overheard a young lady ask her mother if the Jap who was hammering one of the lengths of the upright post with the other would not climb up and balance himself on the top." Because he did not, the girl said she wouldn't have come "through all that mud and clay if she hadn't thought that they were real Japs, but now she saw that they were only imitation ones."

What articles like this revealed was the local thirst for exotica. Americans longed for the quaint and the different and were invariably disappointed at half-measures. In one of his pieces on the centennial, published in the *Atlantic Monthly*, William Dean Howells recorded his disappointment on seeing only one Japanese man in national costume. The others wore Western dress "which they had evidently but half subdued to their use." "It is a great pity not to see them in their own outlandish gear, for picturesqueness' sake," Howells went on; "the show loses vastly by it; and if it is true that the annoyances they suffered from the street crowds forced them to abandon it, we are all disgraced by the fact."[10] The Japanese example was imitated by many. "There is a lamentable lack of foreignness in the dress at the Centennial. The costumed peoples have all put on European wear." Americans expected foreigners to behave like foreigners; imitation seemed a form of cultural dilution, all the more objectionable in a land without much picturesque diversity. "In the cities of Europe," according to the *Atlantic,* "the spectacle of people from far-off countries in strange, picturesque garb is an every-day matter, and fails to raise the emotions it does with us."[11]

But if Americans could not encounter Japanese costume, there remained much that was strange and interesting in an exhibit "whose beauty has nothing to do with newness or utility." Americans seemed to take a special pleasure in the fact that Europe's boasted antiquity was dwarfed by this visitor from the East. The Orient could be used to strike back at the pretensions of the Old World, which for so long had reminded Americans of their youth and lack of cultivation. Compare Japanese antiques with the treasures of famous Christian shrines, one critic suggested. "What barbarous lumps of gold and silver stuck full of jewels of the rudest shape are the crowns." The very preciousness of the materials and the size of the diamonds and rubies only aggravated "the clumsiness of design and execution." But in Japanese handicrafts, 800 years old or more, one found "a grace and elegance of design and fabulous perfection of workmanship which rival or excel the marvels of Italian or ornamental art at its zenith." Moreover, there was "no decline nor degeneracy, no period of corruptness and coarseness, such as the Renaissance shows in its decay."[12]

The Japanese section in the main building featured porcelains, bronzes, silks, embroideries, and lacquered ware. With a frontage of some 100 feet, Japanese exhibitors arranged two large rectangular platforms, placed diagonally to the main avenue. In the middle of the triangle formed by the platforms stood a large bronze fountain, and flying above all was the flag of Japan.[13] According to James McCabe the display was "one of the great surprises of the fair." Visitors to the exhibition would have to amend their ideas about Japan, McCabe continued. "We have been accustomed to regard that country as uncivilized, or half-civilized at the best, but we found here abundant evidences that it outshines the most cultivated nations of Europe in arts which are their pride and glory, and which are regarded as among the proudest tokens of their high civilization."[14] Once again the theme of orientals beating Europeans at their own game appealed to Americans. "After the Japanese collection everything looks in a measure commonplace, almost vulgar," ran one comment.[15] The Japanese "have all the willing courtesy and readiness to show attention so often ascribed to the French people," went another observation, "but they have super-added thereto the same simplicity and artlessness in their manners which one cannot but recognize in the aesthetic work of the nation, and which crowns the knowledge and skill so conspicuous in it with a higher grade."[16] The fact that the most striking vase in the Japanese exhibit went to an English purchaser caused Edward Bruce to pause. "Think of such a concession from the conceit of Western civilization!" exulted Bruce. "It is content, at the first summons, to accept instruction in one of the highest walks of industrial art from what it has been wont to style the effete and mouldy civilizations of the extreme East."[17] American schools and museums were also heavy purchasers and in Bruce's account further testified to the new obeisance being paid the Orient.

A number of things can be generalized from reactions to the Japanese exhibit. First of all, despite occasional recognition of Japanese efforts at modernization, most attention was lavished on Japanese art and craftwork. Indeed, there was some criticism of the fact that the government decided to emphasize so heavily the aesthetic aspects of its culture. One Philadelphia newspaper, noting that "this veritable wonderland" was "constantly thronged by sightseers," took the Japanese commissioners to task. They should have remembered that the world wished to know more of Japan. Instead of turning their exhibit into a salesroom for bronzes and porcelains, it would have been better if "the commissioners had done more towards making us understand their country and the life of the people." The Japanese bazaar could have concentrated on selling and exhibiting. The public would have enjoyed learning more about Japanese schools, industries, and customs.[18]

But most observers did not criticize the concentration on art; they simply enjoyed it. Presuppositions that Eastern aesthetic principles were grotesque eroded as Americans reconsidered their faith in realism. The year following the centennial, the *New York Times* insisted that "a correctly-drawn, much less a noble, human figure never came from the brain of a Japanese draughtsman," but it allowed the Japanese "delicacy of fancy, a thorough sympathy with a few aspects of nature, a fine sense of humor, and an intimate acquaintance with the use of the primitive colors."[19] Most other commentators were still more enthusiastic. One newspaper was impressed with "the subdued elegance, the subtle and delicate taste, the symbolism of art" that lay everywhere. There was nothing suggesting Greek or European plastic art, and no exaltation of the human body. But this could bear interesting interpretation. "The Japanese artist seems to sink the human personality in deference to the vast personality of nature, and oftener humbles the former by putting men and women into pantomime, comedy, grotesque, and ridiculous situations, than ministers to human pride by anything grandiose or dignified."[20] This may produce, the writer concluded, the "utter absence of conceit" that marked the Japanese character. The grotesque was rarely employed in depicting natural objects, such as trees or mountain ranges, which indicated that "the instinct of sublimity" remained part of the Japanese artist's sensibility.

A second and related aspect of the American reaction was not simply an interest in art but particular delight in certain aspects of it. Instead of praising Japanese restraint, harmony, and reticence (although occasional comments appeared), Americans enjoyed Japanese profusion, costliness, and adornment. Japan had escaped the domination of machine-made objects, "mouldings . . . run out for us by the mile, like iron from the rolling-mill or tunes from a musical box."[21] In place of hackneyed forms Japanese art used original and intricate designs. It was "gorgeous" and "delicate." "There is no repetition of parts on different sides or faces" of the objects being exhibited, marveled one reporter. "The variety, the patient originality, has no limit."[22] The fountain that dominated the entry to the Japanese section was "inlaid with silver, covered with raised figures, and more crowded with embellishment than a Gothic shrine. Beyond this is literally a forest of bronze, with interlacing stems, leafage and feathered, scaled and furry inhabitants. Penetrate it, and you find that like other forests it separates into individual members, vases of various hue and shape representing the trees." Even the gardens, as Americans described them, were profuse and lavish, rather than economical and restrained.[23]

Everything, in fact, gave an impression of patient work. In an America where labor was dear, this meant extreme costliness. Visitors and guidebooks alike emphasized how long it had taken to manufacture various items and how expensive it would be to purchase them. One vase on exhibition, reported J. S. Ingram, represented the equivalent of 2,250 days of steady labor for one man, and the $2,000 price did not seem excessive.[24] Marietta Holley, author of a series of books narrated by an American Mrs. Malaprop, Samantha, developed this theme. "Such nicety of work, such patience and long sufferin' as must have gone into their manufactorys," observed Samantha. "Why there was a buro, black and gold, with shelves and draws, and doors hung with gold and silver hinges, and every part of that buro clear to the backside of the bottom draw was nicer, and fixed off handsomer than any handkerchief pin. They asked four thousand five hundred dollars for it, and it was worth it." The vases stood higher than Samantha's husband, and the handles were "clear dragons . . . and a row of wimmen a dancin' round it, each one carryin' a rose in her hand bigger than her head, and up the side of it was foxes in men's clothes. And the handles of another vase was a flock of birds settlin' down on a rock, with a dragon on it, and on top of it a eagle aswoopin' down onto a snake."[25]

Creators of such delicate objects had to be sensitive themselves. The Japanese men at the exhibition ("though dark complexioned," complained Samantha) were so patient and polite answering questions, "not losin' their gentle ways and courtesy, not gettin' fractious or worrysome a mite." [26] Their art work seconded the impression of Japanese character that Americans had held since the Perry expedition. The 1860 visit, according to American commentators, showed how polite, disciplined, and imperturbable were the Japanese. "They are the sweetest-voice, gentlest-manner folk," said one visitor to the fair, "and it is impossible to look from their small forms to their exquisite productions without an uncomfortable misgiving that they may feel like so many Gullivers in Brobdingnag." [27] The *Atlantic* made the connection between art and national character most explicit, when it described the "doll-work" of the park and bazaar and noted that the railings around the lily garden were "about as stout as a sandalwood fan." If this served as protection in Japan, not only the men but the beasts themselves "must be as gentle as the lilies of the field." [26]

Thus Japanese screens, porcelain, silks, and bronzes were welcomed. American parlors and drawing rooms of the 1870s featured profusion and redundancy, cabinets filled with curios, carpets with complicated patterns and rugs over them, antimacassars, flowers, carvings, paintings hung from ceiling to floor. Although Japanese art was exotic it suited American tastes and fitted American expectations. [29] This combination accounted for the craze that succeeded the exposition, a popularity that permitted Tiffany's to make profits from Japanese imports and that prompted the Japanese government itself to open an agency in New York to distribute its native products. In the years that followed tens of thousands of fans, vases, and bronzes flooded middle-class households.

Although this exotica was popular because it fitted American taste, Americans had a third and paradoxical reaction to the Japanese exhibits: one of anxiety and concern. They feared that Western patronage might destroy the distinctive Japanese characteristics they claimed to admire, and substitute subservience to European and American taste and shoddiness of manufacture and design. Japanese art is excellent and honest, Charles Wyllys Elliott conceded in the *Atlantic*, but it would "certainly go down before the arrogant demands of trade. Already there is sufficient evidence that they are perceiving the desirableness of shoddy and the importance of cheapness; already they are making us pay 'through the nose.'" [30] The *New York Times*, in its critical report on Japanese art, suggested that the only changes it had undergone were "for the worse," from a foolish desire to please the West. [31] Oriental designs based on French or Dutch models were hideous. "Some travelers complain that the people of Eastern Europe and Asia are losing their old-time picturesqueness," noted the *Philadelphia Bulletin* in an article on Japanese preparations for the fair. "Many of these natives are fast adopting the manners and customs, as well as the costumes, of Western civilization. By and by they will cease to make the curious things with which we have always identified them." China and Japan will continue to export silk, tea, and carvings, but "we shall have no more cloisonné, jade-work, wonderful lacquer-ware, and eggshell porcelain, if the Asiatics do not get over their rabid eagerness for sewing-machines, planes, and self-raking reapers." It was fine, as Carlyle put it, to watch an oriental nation "getting tragically out of bed," but "sentimental and poetical people say that the world is losing an element of pictorial beauty which it cannot afford to spare." [32]

The *Bulletin* refused to despair. It admitted that the mikado in high hat and pantaloons might lose dignity, "but we are bound to believe that his subjects are to be better, by the moral and material changes which come in with that awkward garb." Despite its brave front, and Edward Bruce's denial of the charge that the Japanese were no longer independent of European artistic influences, [33] one finds in these comments a curious mixture of deference and unquiet. Almost without exception guidebooks, newspaper comments, and visitors' reactions were favorable. It was not simply novelty, for the Chinese exhibits were either ignored or downgraded. "China and Japan are both queer," Samantha reported, "but Japan's queerness has a imaginative artistic quirl to it that China's queerness don't have." [34] If Japan was China's student, wrote Edward Bruce, "the pupil has surpassed the teacher." [35] "We relegate the Chinese to the half-civilized class without hesitation," offered one Philadelphia paper, "or without feeling that any indignity has been offered, and this fact shows what an important difference there is between Japanese and Chinese civilization." [36] For various reasons Chinese art had deteriorated, while Japanese art had still maintained its purity. The Japanese artists and craftsmen exemplified discipline, patience, and quaintness.

But what at first glance seems love for the exotic was basically assimilatory. The Japanese did not present fundamental challenges in their first appearance. The sense that Japanese civilization was an alternative (and superior) mode of life to Western models would come later. Yet the Japanese were admired, paradoxically, both because they respected the West and because they resisted it. The fear that communication would bring homogeneity was a real one. Just as Japanese nationals at the fair had lost picturesqueness by donning Western dress, so cabinetmakers and potters might abandon native gifts in favor of client orientation. The *Bulletin*'s conviction that loss of picturesqueness would mean physical improvement was equivocal. The dilemma of how to accept the prospect of westernization crystallized American attitudes toward national difference generally: on the one hand, a tendency to see Americanization as a sign of progress; on the other, a desire to freeze national customs into a picturesque whole. One of the two effects produced on fair visitors was a feeling "that they are glad that they are Americans," wrote a visitor to another exposition. "And the other one is that they know, as they never knew before, that not by any means all of the world is in America, nor even all the best things."[37] The Japanese raised the problem graphically. "In view of the education, intelligence, and refinement of the Japanese," one newspaper argued during the centennial, "it seems hardly consistent to class them with the 'half-civilized' races, and yet the gulf between them and the highest civilization is hardly less than on the other hand is that between the American Indians and themselves." It might be allowed, the newspaper continued, "from a partial view that Japanese culture is the highest of its kind, and that the kind is one peculiar to the East," but we must have standards, "and Europe is that standard."[38] Confronting real difference, Americans drew back; confronting the uniformity that would come from westernization, they had their doubts as well. The paradox that would come to dominate mid twentieth-century reactions to industrial and technological change was thus demonstrated in this first experience with Japanese culture.

In the wake of the Philadelphia show knowledge about Japan increased among Americans. William Griffis's *Mikado's Empire* became a major source of information, supplemented by travel reminiscences and periodical articles about Japanese art, religion, and modernization. These pieces were designed for highly literate audiences and frequently took on an academic and scholarly tone. Ernest Fenollosa, Percival Lowell, Edward Morse, Lafcadio Hearn, and Sturgis Bigelow, collectors, architects, philosophers, and artists flocked to the East in greater numbers. They grew convinced that Japanese attitudes toward family life, rituals, and personal relationships were complex and worthy of study, if not emulation. More Americans than not, however, received information about Japan from occasional newspaper articles or pieces run in semipopular magazines like *Harper's Weekly*. But there were more fairs to come.

After the centennial the Japanese went on exhibiting in European expositions, but the government also paid attention to smaller American shows. In 1885, for example, New Orleans hosted a fair in which the Japanese participated. Lafcadio Hearn, later an influential commentator on Japanese life, was working as a newspaperman in New Orleans at the time. He gave extensive coverage to "The East at New Orleans" for *Harper's Weekly*.[39] Japanese emphasis had changed somewhat. Japan now featured its educational advances, universities, scientific apparatus, and publishing industry. Hearn argued that the scientific volumes he examined at New Orleans compared favorably with the best French work. Moreover, the Japanese showed great ingenuity in the design of scientific instruments for teaching, particularly when they were unable to purchase what they needed. Hearn paid his respects to the bronzes, the ivories, the fans, and the animal paintings, but unlike the commentators at Philadelphia he spent more time describing Japan's response to the modern world and its rapid strides in science and education.

The New Orleans exhibit, however, was just a taste of what would come at Chicago in 1893. The World's Columbian Exposition, held in Chicago to celebrate the four hundredth anniversary of Columbus's landing, was probably the single most successful exposition held in America. No other fair ever matched its reputation for beauty and harmony, a brilliant technical display of what Victorian administrative genius and building ability could accomplish at their best.[40]

Everything about the Chicago fair was bigger than its predecessor. The Jackson Park site was 686 acres, and the official expenditures on the exposition came to more than $28 million. The number of foreign buildings was doubled from Philadelphia to Chicago and the number of exhibition palaces more than tripled. Around the palaces and pavilions clustered hundreds of concessions that brought the fair authorities thousands of dollars from various restaurants, foreign villages, and amusements. All in all some 25 million people visited the fair, and its greatest single day, Chicago day, saw a crowd of more than 600,000 struggle into the park grounds.

Like many other governments Japan sought to participate in this great festival, which had so many more assurances of success than the affair in Philadelphia two decades earlier. Indeed, Japanese participation revealed a special intensity of interest, because of the circumstances under which it was demonstrated. In March 1890 the Imperial Diet was holding its first session, in Japan's initial attempt at parliamentary government. Although an official invitation from the Columbian Exposition had not yet been received and despite the strain between the Diet and the executive concerning the national budget, the Diet voluntarily proposed that provision be made for Japanese participation in the Chicago fair and agreed to appropriate the funds when necessary. In November, six months later, a supplementary appropriation of 630,000 yen for participation was submitted to the Diet by the government and passed unanimously. Six months later the emperor appointed a commission to supervise preparations. It was placed directly under the government's control, the minister of agriculture and commerce becoming the ex officio president of the commission. To widen support and improve communication, an advisory council was appointed that included manufacturers and merchants.[41]

The care and self-consciousness that marked the creation of the commission also characterized its later works. The commission declared that the selection of Japanese artifacts and manufactured goods was to be representative of the country's actual production, not specially chosen for high quality nor given misleadingly false prices to attract international attention. The same items employed in domestic use were to be shown in Chicago. The one exception concerned art; here, stung by previous criticisms about the westernization of Japanese artists and already caught up in the revival of interest in Japanese traditions that succeeded the westernizing craze of the 1870s, the commission announced it would be carefully selective. In each Japanese prefecture local commissions were appointed to examine and advise potential exhibitors. As before, the government promised to pay the freight on exhibits, in addition to insurance and storage charges which the long trip inevitably would require.

This concerted national effort resulted in an enormous quantity of goods. Originally, Minister Tateno noted, the government had expected that 1,000 tons of material would be shipped to Chicago, three times the weight shipped to Philadelphia and triple even that sent to Paris for the great 1889 fair. When local commissions forwarded their proposals, however, the total amounted to 7,000 tons, and it was only after considerable effort that a final figure of 1,750 tons, more than five times the Philadelphia total, was arrived at.

With all these preparations it was of course vital that adequate space be obtained at Chicago. Here the authorities were under great pressure from exhibiting countries, each wishing better locations and larger sites than could be made available. The Chicago managers, after some early arguments, agreed to make available for the official Japanese display a 40,000 square foot site on the Wooded Island, a small piece of land located near the Illinois Building and a superb spot for visual relief from the overpowering classicism of the exposition. Originally Frederick Olmsted, who supervised the fair's landscaping, wanted to keep the island a refuge from all formal fair activities. But the Japanese, who promised to present their buildings as a gift to the people of Chicago, managed to change the commission's mind. In addition to this central display the Japanese were to have sections in the Palace of Manufactures and Liberal Arts (40,000 square feet), in the Fine Arts Palace (2,850 square feet), in Agriculture, Horticulture, Forestry, Mines, and Fisheries, and a large spot on the Midway Plaisance, where the amusement and refreshment concessions were located, for a tea house and bazaar. Although the Japanese building on the Wooded Island took up only a small part of the site, the rest being devoted to landscaped gardens, the Japanese building was still the seventh largest at the fair, exceeded only by the great powers and various Latin American countries.

As in Philadelphia, the preparations made by the Japanese attracted great attention. Everything about the national effort seemed praiseworthy. *Harper's Weekly* ran a little note in the spring of 1893 about Japanese skill at unpacking the delicate artworks. Packers could learn much from "the patient and careful Japanese, who do this thing to perfection. Not only is each article put away so that there is no chance for breakage, but after the case is fastened tightly provision is made against mishaps from rough handling."[42] The Japanese indicated by marks the side to be placed uppermost, apparently an innovation, and placed handles on their cases so that stevedores could move them conveniently.

But the unpacking was trivial compared to the construction efforts. Even while the snow from Chicago's winter still covered the Wooded Island, Japanese joiners began to construct their pavilion, surrounded by curious crowds. "And what bright and nimble fellows these workmen were," reported *Harper's*. "It may be that they were picked men, selected for their skill and intelligence. . . . It seems almost a pity that these carpenters could not be kept at work all during the fair."[43] The numbers gathering to watch the workmen were so great that ropes had to be put up to keep them from the construction site, and they plied the workmen with questions about the novel techniques they were employing. The carpenters, according to observers, retained their good humor and answered the inquiries.

What they were building represented an ambitious attempt to sum up important periods in the history of Japanese art and architecture. The pavilion actually consisted of three separate parts, designed to resemble the plan of the Hō-ōden or Phoenix Hall, built at Uji near Kyoto in the twelfth century. This now version of the Phoenix Hall was designed by a government architect, Kuru Masamichi. The north wing was set up to display the art of the Fujiwara era, with ornamental doors, paintings, and objects appropriate to the period. The south wing was done in the style of the Ashikaga period and contained several rooms including a library and a tea room. A central hall, which connected the two wings, was done in the elaborate style of the Tokugawa period and included an interior that duplicated one in Edo castle. The total supposedly cost the Japanese government more than $100,000, but if the delighted response of visitors was any test, the sum was a good investment. Moreover, portions of the building remained standing well into the twentieth century, and some years later, the Japan Society built a tea house on the Wooded Island which remained in use until the 1940s.

The Chicago building, argues Clay Lancaster, the best student of Japanese architectural influence in America, was both more significant and more elegant than the centennial effort. Its structural honesty and craftsmanship contrasted with the huge plaster palaces that stood nearby, a building that was "human in scale and appealing," showing that "architecture—real architecture—need make no apologies for its use of simple, everyday materials."[44]

Besides the building on the Wooded Island, the Japanese made extensive exhibits in the other buildings already mentioned. Their fine arts display was particularly impressive (270 of the 291 items of decorative art in the Palace of

Fine Arts were Japanese, although they contributed only 24 of the 1,013 sculpture works and 55 of the 7,357 paintings), and unlike at Philadelphia the manufacturing and educational aspects of Japanese life were well treated also. There were 72 exhibits of rice, 215 exhibits of tea and tobacco, specimens of vermicelli, hemp, mineral waters, umbrella handles, artificial fruits, photographs of railroad lines and telegraph systems, surgical instruments, textbooks, statistics of life insurance and crime, razors, safes, buttons, silverware, toys, perfumes—in short, everything that any Western nation was producing could be found in the Japanese display.[45]

The response to the Japanese exhibits took note of both the objects of art and the objects of industry, but the art continued to attract the most attention. Again the carvings in wood, ivory, and bronze, the vases decorated with dragons, the incense boxes, metal screens, embroideries, cut velvets, portières, all attracted admiration because of their marvelous colors and elaborate detail. That it was different from Western art did not seem to matter to the visitors. "Having no lumps of Parian marble with all but speaking tongues, and no canvases that the royal palaces might covet," wrote H. D. Northrop, "Japan welcomes the nations to see gems in pounded brass and chiseled ivory and carved wood and inlaid gold." Their art presented "life as the people of the rising sun know it, muscles and bones and sinews as their athletes possess them, flowers and rivers and mountains such as their country affords. No foreign school of any age or any clime has warped the native taste."[46] Once again, as in Philadelphia, it was costliness and elaborateness that attracted Americans, things like the $30,000 tapestry displaying a festival procession with more than 1,000 separate pieces. That the strange animals and vegetable forms might be termed grotesque some admitted, but "there is no gainsaying the extreme delicacy of execution and design."[47]

Americans now felt it easier to generalize about the Japanese character and to couple their praise for art with admiration for Japanese modernization. The enormous Japanese school system, with its eight "higher schools" and tens of thousands of primary schools, was displayed in photographs and pamphlets. The Japanese ability to gain discipline without punishment was longingly described by Americans, who did not know how to accomplish it in their own land. One visitor reported on the reaction in Japan when the emperor published an address inculcating moral duties that was hung in all the schools. In America such a statement, issued by the president, "would have invited every mischievous boy in school to aim paper wads and bits of crayon. But in Japan the effect was tremendous. Children looked up to the address as a thing to remember and ponder. Both they and the teachers made obeisance to the photograph before they began the school work of the day."[48]

Japanese courtesy provided an object lesson for *Harper's Weekly* while the fair was still on. Angry because the United States Senate refused to pass needed legislation during the financial panic of 1893 (senators insisted that the opposition be permitted to oppose aid to the unemployed for as long as they wished to talk), *Harper's* labeled this a false politeness. "What might have been the effect on American manners if the gentle Japanese had been held up to our childish eyes as our models of propriety," the magazine wondered. "For what the Japanese call politeness springs from the heart, and is the simple expression of kindly feelings. Think of cities where the potter places the still moist products of his wheel out in the middle of the street to dry in the sun, and where the children in their play step carefully around among the fragile wares lest they work injury to the trustful artisan." [49]

Politeness remained the overwhelming characteristic Americans associated with Japan. The ubiquitous Samantha also visited the Columbian Exposition, as she had the centennial, and reported that the Japanese temple was gorgeous but queer. "But then," Samantha theorized, "I spoze them Japans would call the Jonesville meetin'-house queer; for what is strange in one country is second nater in another." [50] "The Japans," she went on, "are the politest nation on the earth; they say cheatin' and lyin' haint polite, and so they don't want to foller 'em; they hitch principle and politeness right up in one team and ride after it." [51] Politeness was coupled with a childlike nature; the Japanese were invariably termed "little," and Samantha philosophized that "The Japanese are a child-like people easily pleased, easily pleased, easily grieved— laughin' and cryin' jest like chidren." [52] For Americans in the late nineteenth century docility and childlike behavior were often associated with laziness and backwardness. A favorite theme of southerners was the "childlike" character of the Negro. The Japanese, however, belied this image because they added to politeness and docility tremendous industry and discipline. Denton J. Snider, an American philosopher, found its unified excellence the most impressive feature of the Japanese displays. It was not only their art that pleased: their exhibit in the Liberal Arts Building was "large, very attractive, and well-ordered." "We meet them everywhere, and they are doing their best." [53]

So clear was Japanese energy and advancement that comparisons with China now flooded to the surface. "The Japanese," wrote H. G. Cutler, a visitor to the fair, "have not the staid, placid dispositions of the Chinese. They are more light-hearted, and even at table often enliven the simple courses with music upon the guitar." [54] For Mrs. D. C. Taylor, China was a "strange, cold, homeless, heartless, heathen land!" It was filled with "down-trodden women, priests, and tyrant-ridden men." A "strange depression of mind and sickness of heart" came over her when she thought of the Celestial Kingdom. Japan, however, was quite different, the "suave, smiling" Japanese just the opposite of the "pigtailed, avaricious Chinese."[55] Julian Hawthorne, son of the famous novelist, found Japanese art humorous and lively, but Chinese humor reminded him of a "weird grimace," and he assumed the Chinese were "without souls" in their worship of antiquity and their earthly everlastingness.[56]

The unexpected combination of industry and docility puzzled some commentators, who found other paradoxes to ponder. It is a wonder "how so mild and good-humored a people as they evidently are," commented H. G. Cutler, "can live under so sanguinary a code of laws. Death is the general penalty."[57] The combination of chrysanthemum and sword was noted early by American visitors.

The popularity of the Japanese displays was attested to by more than the comments on the official pavilion and the manufacturers' show. The Midway Plaisance featured a myriad of amusements. They grossed more than $4 million during the exposition, ten times what the concessions at the Philadelphia fair had taken in. There were such popular features as "Cairo Street" where "Little Egypt" danced, "Old Vienna," "Hagenbeck's Zoological Show," "Donegal Castle," and many others. Almost four hundred concessions competed for public favor. One of the most popular shows on the Midway, certainly within the top ten of the foreign exhibits, was the Japanese bazaar, operated by Y. Maurai. It was "dretful ornamental," said Samantha, who wandered about looking at Japanese spinners, weavers, dyers, and musicians, visiting houses made of bamboo without nails, and, of course, the tea house. The Japanese bazaar did a business of more than $200,000 in the six months of the fair, and the Nippon tea house took in an additional $23,000.[58]

For the second time, then, Japan had succeeded in making an enormous impact on the visitors. Everything Japanese excited interest. Wherever "the flag of Japan was displayed," wrote Tudor Jenks in a children's book about the fair, "the boys never grudged time for examination. That artistic little nation can always teach a lesson to natives of the young occident."[59] Even the grocery displays in the Manufactures Building revealed a special touch and elegance. The Japanese government seconded its exhibitions by large amounts of printed material, books, and pamphlets listing Japan's recent statistical triumphs, timetables, travel literature, and comprehensive catalogues. "I just made up my mind that if they were heathens," said the hero of Carl Western's novel about the exposition, "there were lots of things we could learn from them."[60] "I don't see," observed another visitor in similar terms, "the use of sending missionaries to Japan. I suppose they do worship all them things, but even if they do, I think that if they had as much pretty china to home as they've got here, I'd be inclined to worship it myself. . . . I should think the Japanese would almost feel like sending missionaries over here."[61]

There remained, of course, some sense of the dangers of modernization. Hubert Bancroft complained that as a result of the great demand for Japanese articles "the simple characteristics of earlier Japanese work have become somewhat vulgarized, for the restless commercial spirit has seized upon Japanese and American alike, and lowered the former standard."[62] Nevertheless, the anxiety level seemed lower than at Philadelphia. "They have grown quite accustomed to our ways," proclaimed the official directory to the fair, "and do not surrender their methods in favor of ours unless the superiority of the new over the old is apparent."[63] Few commentators bothered to say much about the dangers of Japanese assimilation.

So impressive was the Japanese effort that some felt it needed to be explained. The energy put by Japan into the fair argued that it was demanding more respect than the world had paid it previously. The carvings, the ivory, the porcelain and lacquer work, "all arranged faultlessly and displayed with the peculiar smiling self-confidence which marks the race," wrote Joseph and Caroline Kirkland, "seemed to say 'We belong among you; we have something to teach as well as something to learn.'"[64] Denton Snider thought the Japanese exhibit so conspicuous that it demanded commentary. "The Japanese are plainly the vanguard in the Occidental movement toward the Orient," he argued. Historically, the movement of civilization had been east to west, coming from western Asia, through Europe, America, and now Japan. The Japanese were the bearers of the new order and stood confronting the Chinese, representing the old. "We are, therefore, inclined to read in this attempt of Japan the effort to put itself into line with the world-historical movement of the Occident. It allies itself with the nations of the West, especially does it appeal to the United States," Snider noted approvingly. "One cannot help noticing here the care with which the Japanese man explains that he is not a Chinaman."[65] Snider felt that Japan was preparing for an approaching struggle by winning the sympathy of the West. This was the reason for the many books and pamphlets reporting on Japanese progress that the government was distributing in Chicago. Snider agreed with the Kirklands. The Japanese message was "I am one of you."[66] Japan will remain Japan, he concluded, and would not lose its individuality, but it had nonetheless joined the march of Western civilization.

The Chicago exposition, then, had meaning both for the Americans and the Japanese. American visitors, still clinging to their image of the Japanese as a childlike, humorous, artistic people, now began to acknowledge that this oriental civilization had somehow managed to achieve a parity of sorts with the industrial West. The Japanese welcomed the tributes paid their arts and manufactures. Travelling in Japan in the 1890s William Elroy Curtis noted how the White City had advertised Chicago in Japan. "Everybody knows about it," he wrote. "Three or four years ago the ordinary Japanese tradesman and mechanic knew of the existence of London, Paris, and New York, and many of them were familiar with the name of San Francisco." Now, however, "every school-boy and girl, even the little tots in the kindergarten, are familiar with the name and the location of Chicago and with the appearance of the buildings of the exposition, and when an ordinary merchant or mechanic heard I was from that city he looked up with a gleam of gratified recognition—as if he had met an old friend." The Japanese, reported Curtis, called the exposition "Dai Bankoku Hakuran Kwai," or "the great place for seeing objects from all countries." [67]

Some years later an English visitor to Japan, A. Herbage Edwards, made a similar discovery. On a pilgrimage to Izumo in western Japan, he visited a temple at Kizuki. The priests greeting him took him to a plaster statue of the sun goddess, who bore proudly on her wrist "a much-worn ticket, stating in printed Roman capitals, that 'This exhibit has won a Prize at the World's Fair at Chicago.'" Edwards recalled the "white sunlight filtering through the yellow matting" falling on "white-robed priests who serve a temple worshipped through two thousand years" and "on the faded ticket on the arm of the Sun-Goddess." [68]

The Japanese had specific hopes for Chicago. Describing the exhibition in the *North American Review,* Tateno Gōzō closed by hoping that Japanese efforts would entitle them to "full fellowship in the family of nations, no longer deserving to labor under the incubus which circumstances forced upon her." Tateno was referring to the treaties Japan had signed granting foreign powers certain extraterritorial rights. The restrictions may have been necessary originally, he admitted. But the Japanese felt the restrictions constituted an "unnecessary, incumbering vestige of the past" and hoped for their removal. They welcomed the Columbian Exposition "as one means of proving that they have attained a position worthy of the respect and confidence of other nations." [69] In fact, the centennial display had stimulated some Americans to demand the return of the Shimonoseki indemnity, some $750,000 paid to the United States as a result of an 1863 incident in which Samurai of Chōshū attacked foreign ships. [70] Obviously, the Japanese now hoped for similar rewards from Chicago.

At Philadelphia, the Japanese made their first entry into the popular consciousness as an exotic but artistic people whose ornamentation and aesthetic fantasies fit well the eclectic taste of Victorian America. At Chicago they broadened their claim on public attention by demonstrating their feats of modernization and their architectural skill. Japan was emerging as an alternative rather than a supplementary culture, worthy of understanding on its own terms. But something more was necessary to raise respect to veneration, and this came about in 1904, with the combined triumphs of the Japanese in the Russo-Japanese War and at the Louisiana Purchase Exposition in St. Louis.

St. Louis had been disappointed in its effort to host the Columbian Exposition. But it was the natural site for the fair held nine years later to celebrate the centennial of Thomas Jefferson's Louisiana Purchase. The area that Jefferson had purchased from France was now a thriving and well-populated region of twenty-three states, and St. Louis was its chief city. As with other American expositions, planning began several years in advance. Originally, it was supposed to take place in 1903. When Japan was invited, local attention was concentrated on a great exhibition in Osaka. The government thereupon declined. When the Louisiana Purchase Exposition was postponed until May 1904, the Japanese accepted the invitation, after sending several representatives to visit St. Louis, early in 1903.[71]

The Louisiana Purchase Exposition was constructed on a scale exceeding even that of the Columbian Exposition.[72] Located in Forest Park, the grounds of the fair totaled some 1,272 acres. As one historian has pointed out, this was nearly equal to the combined area of all previous expositions.[73] More than 1,500 separate buildings were put up, 15 of which were exhibition palaces. As in Chicago, classical themes predominated, but the total effect was more exuberant and more fanciful. The palaces themselves were constructed on a monumental scale; some were more than 1,500 feet long. Despite the attractions which the exposition authorities provided, including automobile and balloon races, the international Olympics, and visits by heads of state, the total attendance of about 19 million was considerably below that of Chicago. Nevertheless, foreign states were eager to participate. Twenty-one of them, more than at Chicago, had national buildings, and some put up more than one.

The Japanese had now participated in more than two dozen exhibitions and, as usual, their careful preparations stood out. The Japanese exhibit was the only foreign display ready when the fair opened, despite the fact that the government was fully involved in the war with Russia. It had appropriated $800,000, and Baron Matsudaira Masanao, the vice president of the imperial commission, supervised the actual preparations.[74] Japan received more than 150,000 square feet, making large displays in the palaces of Industry (27,000 square feet), Manufactures (54,000 square feet), Education (6,300 square feet), Transportation (14,000 square feet), Fine Arts (6,800 feet), Mines (6,900 square feet), and Agriculture (8,600 square feet). Private exhibitors were better organized now than ever before. Every Japanese exhibitor was a member of the Japan Exhibit Association. One week after the government decided to participate in St. Louis, a meeting was held in Tokyo of the representatives of the various commercial associations throughout the country. A business organization was formed to consolidate the exhibits, and government appropriations helped them. A year before the fair opened representatives were sent to St. Louis to examine the site. Not only did individual firms such as the Japanese Mail and Steamship Company prepare displays, but associations of companies—the Kyoto Chamber of Commerce was one—also demonstrated the skills and resources of areas within the country. Ōtani Kahei, president of the Japanese Exhibitors Association, and other representatives of the association were in charge of installing all the exhibits, distributing information, handling sales, and shipping back what was left to Japan. The display was twice as large as the immense display at Chicago and three times as big as the important Paris exhibition of 1900. The fine arts collection was particularly noteworthy. So important did the Japanese government conceive it that before the artworks left Japan 3,000 artists visited the collection in Tokyo, by government invitation.

Besides the industrial and artistic objects scattered through the exhibition palaces, there were two other displays of the Japanese effort at St. Louis. One was the official government exhibit, the Imperial Japanese Garden. In a setting of landscaped gardens, water, and bridges, a group of buildings was put up. The major building was a replica of the Kinkaku, the Golden Pavilion built for the Shogun near Kyoto at the end of the fourteenth century. Uncannily, as Clay Lancaster has pointed out, the Kinkaku shared some features with indigenous design in the lower Mississippi Valley: the hipped roof, the open galleries resting on slender supports—both characteristic of Creole architecture in the eighteenth century. That the Japanese buildings made such an impact in St. Louis, Lancaster concludes, was due in part "to their own aesthetic and structural merits, in part to their affinities to pre-existing building forms. . . . The design of the Kinkaku mirrored a local type in the deep South, and in turn itself was reflected in the New Orleans suburbs in combination with belated Mississippi steamboat and contemporary bungalow elements."[75] Along with the Kinkaku there was a bamboo tea house, representing newly acquired Formosa, a commissioners' residence, a reproduction of a reception hall from an imperial palace at Kyoto, and, of course, the gardens. "A visit to the Japanese pavilion on the hill is one of the pleasantest experiences of the whole fair," a writer reported in *The World's Work*.[76]

Aside from the displays scattered through the palace and the official pavilion, an unofficial group of buildings called the Japanese Village took up a spot on the Pike, the fair's amusement area and its counterpart to Chicago's Midway. These included several gateways, a tea house, a bazaar, and a Japanese theater. One of the gateways, a replica of a gateway to the tomb of Ieyasu at Nikko, rose 100 feet above the Pike. The Japanese Village attested to the public's interest in Japanese curiosities. There were 540 separate concessions in St. Louis, including 60 restaurants, 53 amusements, 11 transportation com-

*The Japanese
Pavilion, St. Louis,
1904*

panies, and 153 souvenir and novelty centers. The village, which took in
$205,000 proved to be the tenth most popular concession, exceeded only by
the largest and most elaborate displays such as the Tyrolean Alps and the Trans-
vaal Military Spectacle. The Japanese bazaar produced an additional income of
$85,937.[77]

The separate areas permitted Japanese exhibitors to satisfy a wide variety
of tastes. Connoisseurs of art could linger in the Fine Arts Building; businessmen and educators could examine displays in the Manufactures and Education
buildings; casual sightseers could stop in the Japanese Village; and lovers of
Japanese gardening and architecture could wander through the official pavilion
and its landscaped grounds. The latter were opened with a reception, on June
1, with more than 200 guests served tea by geisha girls. Baron Takahira Kogorō,
the minister at Washington, along with Matsudaira Masanao, stood at the head
of the receiving line. The guest of honor was the president's daughter, Alice
Roosevelt. During the six months the fair ran, other celebrations—the Mikado's
birthday, for example—were held as well.

The comments made about the various Japanese displays continued the
trend of earlier observations. That is, they were extremely favorable. Perhaps
the most overwhelming effort at the fair was made by Germany, enticed by the
large number of German-Americans in the St. Louis area, but after Germany

there was no question that Japan created the most excitement. The ever-present Samantha, also a visitor to St. Louis, felt the Japanese had outdone everyone. On the one hand, Samantha was still impressed by the ornateness of the Japanese objects and their expense. In the Temple of Nikko, in the official pavilion, she saw one pair of vases "worth ten thousand dollars. . . . There is one spring room in it that holds the very atmosphere of spring. The tapestry and crape hangings are embroidered with cheery blossoms. . . . And there wuz an autumn room, autumn leaves of rich colors wuz woven in the matting and embroidered in the hangings, the screens and walls white with yellow chrysanthemums."[78] Still another room, with walls of carved wood and rich silk hangings, cost $45,000 and was therefore even more impressive. Thus the tradition of delight in Japanese profusion, established at Philadelphia, continued.

On the other hand, even Samantha was impressed now by other things, including efficiency, modernization, and cleanliness. "In cleanin' house time, now I have fairly begreched the ease and comfort of them Japanese housewives who jest take up their mat and sweep out, move their paper walls and little mebby and there it is done. No heavy, dirt-laden carpets to clean, no papered walls and ceilings to break their back over. . . . Kind hearted, reverent to equals and superiors, trained to kindness and courtesy and reverence in childhood when American mothers are ruled and badgered by short skirted and roundabout clad tyrants." Japan was becoming more of a total civilization, to be studied not merely on antiquarian grounds but because it had accomplished things westerners seemed unable to do. "I set store by the Japans and am glad to hear how fast they're pressin' forwards in every path civilization has opened," Samantha concluded. "They could give Uncle Sam a good many lessons if he wuz willin' to take 'em."[79]

Particularly interesting, from the American view, was the display of the Red Cross in the official pavilion. "This is the only hint this courteous country gives of the great war going on at home that would stop the exhibit of most any other country."[80] The Red Cross seemed to symbolize not only Japan's new military power but also its commitment to obey the rules governing international relations, its assumption of a "civilized" role, even when fighting a "Western" country, Russia.

Reactions to the fair exhibit could not be separated from the loud American admiration for Japanese military prowess. While the exposition was in progress, American magazines were dominated by detailed news of the conflict in the Far East and by overwhelmingly favorable reports on the morale, abilities, and restraint of the Japanese armed forces. Military success, more than any fair exhibits, demonstrated what the Japanese government had been trying to show: that Japan had managed the adjustment to modern industrial conditions with great skill. The St. Louis fair concentrated American attention on achievements such as the Japanese telegraph system, only thirty years old but with 60,000 miles of wire; the railroad network, more than 4,000 miles, constructed in twenty years; the elaborate postal system, which in 1903 handled 902 million pieces of mail; the Japanese textile industry, which was employing more than 700,000 persons; and so on. More than 80,000 exhibits in the name of some 2,000 firms and individuals represented Japan at St. Louis, and the displays skillfully used photographs, topographical maps made of rice paper, mechanical models, and carefully prepared handbooks. In the electricity palace a map thirty feet high and twenty-five feet wide showed the Lake Biwa Canal connecting Lake Biwa with Kyoto; a mine was reproduced in its entirety, along with a first-class salon on a ship of the Japanese Mail Steamship Company. "In arrangement and detail," wrote Isaac Marcosson, "the national pavilion shows that, to the achievement of commerce and industry, the Japanese have brought the perfection of landscape beauty, another expression of the genius of a people who, in the art of war and the pursuits of peace, are steadily making their way to a large place in world power. For this is the real significance of the Japanese exhibit at St. Louis."[81]

But beneath this praise, and more explicitly in articles dealing with Japanese power generally, Americans revealed concern about what was happening to Japan's distinctiveness in its mad zeal to imitate the West. The anxiety penetrated comments on Japanese art. The *Nation* reported that although the Japanese exhibit in the Varied Arts Building was large, "table after table is crowded with common ceramic ware (it is a shame to apply such a term to it) and poor modern bronzes." "A few dealers gain by selling the trash, but the public estimate of Japanese technical skill suffers."[82] Mabel Loomis Todd described the Japanese paintings by artists trained in foreign lands. "It is good painting, the technique cannot be criticized, the scenes depicted recall vividly the flowery country; yet it is wholly unsatisfying. Even the faint odor of Japan which always hovers about any considerable collection from its shores, and which touches all these rooms with a reminiscent charm, fails to idealize these good Japanese paintings by Japanese artists done in 'foreign' style."[83] The president of the fair himself, David R. Francis, in his official history recalled that the Japanese were urged to exclude from their art galleries works painted under Western influences, and the government did in fact segregate such work in a separate room. But although the major part of the collection demonstrated purely native qualities, Francis regretted the strong tendency, "shared by so many of the younger Japanese, to forsake the purity and fine qualities of their native art for characteristics, the outgrowth of a civilization and educational training opposite to their own."[84]

Popular American appreciation of Japan as a total civilization, then, was growing even while Americans were wondering how long such a civilization could survive the experience of gaining world influence. Articles appeared bearing titles like "Is Japanese Progress Changing Japanese Character?" in which the writer concluded that the Japanese were not changing as rapidly as Westerners thought and argued that it was not "morally reprehensible" for them to remain distinctive and separate.[85] The *Nation*, however, satirically suggested that the Japanese, so successfully imperialistic, be admitted into the Anglo-Saxon club and their military leaders become honorary Roughriders. "In such company even the courteous and inoffensive Japanese might in time learn to bluster, swagger, talk volubly of war and preparedness for it, and become an international nuisance." How can we take up the white man's burden, asked The *Nation* with heavy irony, if our yellow and brown brothers are to act like this? "How are you going to civilize people who have a pure joy in being killed in battle?"[86]

Many lessons were taken from the Japanese victories. Among them was the argument that the military successes validated the whole Japanese way of life, its system of art, education, and philosophy. "Whatever be the final result of the war," wrote one journal, Japan "will henceforth command a degree of respect that she could have won in no other way so quickly. We had a similar experience after our little war with Spain."[87] In an extraordinary essay published in The *Nation*, the author rested Japanese success on classical education and abstract training. The spectacular practical results were produced by impractical interests. "What has really made the Japanese mind the superb instrument it is daily proving itself to be is the habit of abstract meditation—of separating the operations of the intellect from those of the emotions. For some 2,000 years the best minds of Japan have had the habit of hard and consecutive thinking along metaphysical lines. . . . From the China Seas comes the startling message that your best engineer comes from generations of mystics, that, by a strange perversion, the soul of Siddartha is controlling with a precision before unknown the weapons forged by Thornycroft and Krupp." The lesson for this American was obvious: the rigors of modern life demanded classical education. Japanese success "is a warning to them not too readily to give up the educational standard under which they are conquering, and a reminder to us not to substitute workshops and sham practicalities for the old liberal training that makes the mind hardy enough to answer all challenges, and steady enough to meet the most exigent practical demands."[88]

Thus, even at the moment of Japanese victory American commentators could not escape the issue of traditionalism as a strength or a weakness. The great interest taken in Japanese culture was more than a fascination with the exotic. Japan telescoped a major American problem. In the late nineteenth century anxiety was growing about the menacing character of modernization and the effects of industrialization and massive immigration. Americanism itself had never been easily defined, for membership in our national community was theoretically not racial but ideological. This, at least, was the lesson of the revolution. But as millions of immigrants with distinctive physical, linguistic, and cultural traits entered the country, the question of assimilation grew more insistent. Were old-stock Americans to train these millions to already extant models of culture, deportment, and value orientation, or would immigrants retain their cultural peculiarities, enriching with heterogeneity a society that had not yet assumed any fixed form? In 1878 the *Atlantic Monthly* reported a decline of American confidence in their ability "to receive from all other countries the most incongruous and unfavorable materials, and assimilate and transmute them all into the texture and substance of a noble national life."[89] This led, in time, to a growing interest in immigration restriction and an increasing set of pressures on public schools to "Americanize" newcomers and melt them down into an approved mold. But other Americans favored individuality and variety; traditions of diversity would fulfill rather than subvert the national genius.[90]

Japan presented an analogous problem. Americans were fascinated by the rapidity and completeness of Japanese modernization; they approved of the new school systems, railroads, telegraphs, and military skill. At the same time, the only reason the Japanese were special lay in their distinctive preindustrial arts, habits, and mores. If the Japanese modernized, would they lose their special contribution to world civilization? If they did not modernize, could they survive as an independent state and resist the blandishments and intimidations of Western powers? Different Americans arrived at different conclusions concerning both the actual and the normative aspects of Japanese development. But the comments on expositions may suggest that this problem underlay the fascination Japan held for Americans. The gradual appreciation of the fact that pottery, bronzes, and silks were products not of unconnected and incidental craft skills but of a civilization with special emphases and loyalties can be found in the decennial revivals of concern with foreign cultures that expositions sponsored. At just the same time in American cities, settlement workers like Jane Addams were finding in immigrant craft skills and family organization a rich social texture capable of resisting the oppressive features of urban life and preserving human dignity and diversity. The trend toward larger generalization and increased concern with Japan that reached its apogee in St. Louis in 1904 reflected more than American efforts to understand the Japanese. It was also an attempt to examine the future shape of their own civilization, one in which modernization itself would soon form the only tradition.

3

Museums, Merchandising,

and Popular Taste:

The Struggle for Influence

T he relationship between the museum and that elu-
sive phenomenon labeled public taste has always
been problematic. By that is meant two things: first,
that the relationship has more often been assumed
than defined and, therefore, exists in an unspecified
limbo, making any judgments difficult to defend;
and second, that partly because of this obscurity,
results have always been outstripped by expecta-
tions. Vagueness and imprecision have led invariably to disappointment and
suspicion about what in fact museums can do to influence public taste.

Like so much else in the world of American art, justifications for museum
support have been instrumental. They were never more so than in moments of
institutional formation. Whatever their psychological, social, and economic
motives, museum founders, trustees, and donors emphasized, publicly and privately, the potential influence of museums on every aspect of national life.[1]
Founders assumed that they were competing for money and attention with other
worthy enterprises—hospitals, colleges, libraries, and settlement houses—
and, therefore, would have to demonstrate the importance of museum support.

From Ian M. B. Quimby, ed., *Material Culture and the Study of American Life* (New
York: W. W. Norton, Winterthur Book, 1978), 140–74. Reprinted by permission of the
H. F. DuPont Winterthur Museum.

Thus, high hopes were married to a sense of crisis in the late nineteenth century, that period when so many of our great art museums were established. The crisis—symbolized to some by the quality of American achievements in the Centennial Exposition—was an impoverished national taste, a struggling and depressed class of artists, and a debased and vulgar stock of consumer goods. Americans had supposedly been suborned by the machine or deluded by national conceit into an affection for meretricious ornament and sentimental, crudely wrought art. In the arena of international competition, which once again the Centennial Exposition highlighted, Americans looked crudely mercenary and badly educated. Museums were meant to redeem the fortunes spent creating them by raising the level of public taste.

Now what was public taste? Although rarely specified, it seems probable that the notion meant then, and means now, the aesthetic knowledgeability, experience, and preferences of the entire population. But because taste involves some kind of expression, the population can be divided, by transaction, into three separate groups: producers, sellers, and consumers. Together they make up the national marketplace. Influencing public taste, therefore, means increasing knowledge, expanding experience, and shaping preference for all or some of these groups. These were the objectives that lay behind the grand rhetoric of educators, millionaires, and curators when they laid cornerstones, cut ribbons, opened exhibitions, and generally performed the rites of passage for the new museums. There existed then, however, and there remains now, a large problem. Museums were intended to have a broad impact and appeal. But producers, sellers, and consumers of art represented only a tiny fraction of the American public. How, then, could museums of art create the results that they promised?

Several strategies were available and museum officials debated their relative value. One was to concentrate upon artists and designers in museum schools, hoping that the accumulation of objects would help improve the future producers of textiles and furniture, as well as the coming painters and sculptors. Another was to assume that comprehensive, well-planned exhibitions would increase public knowledge of design principles by exposure to the history of the world's art. And, finally, some argued for intensive aesthetic experiences, avoiding comprehensiveness for specific effect; by accompanying the art with carefully chosen accouterments, the lessons of harmony and joy that aesthetic mastery could teach would inspire visitors with a sense of new standards. The arguments were often confused and imprecise. But clearly museums' success, as their founders defined it, depended upon their effectiveness in reaching a large lay audience, capturing its attention, increasing its knowledge, and shaping its sense of possibility.

But by the early twentieth century, even more clearly by the 1920s, art museums had apparently abandoned their lay clients; according to critics they had turned into storehouses, paradise for the curator or researcher, but hell for the serious amateur and the ordinary visitor. The art museum, it appeared, had become a depository, a subtreasury of art and valuable artifacts, with only a peripheral influence on knowledgeability and public preference. How this view developed, and why, is the subject of this paper. The argument can be stated briefly. In the period of their founding, museums opted for a consumer orientation to justify their existence. They faced competition but a competition that merchandised in a similar or an analogous fashion. During the interwar years, however, the museum, as a setting, fell behind in its techniques of display, and thus built up a fund of resentments. Making up for lost time, starting in the late 1930s but increasing dramatically in the postwar period, the museum did indeed become a more self-conscious and successful merchandiser of taste, or at least of knowledge and experience, but there have been costs involved which deserve further mention. The late nineteenth century makes a good starting point for discussion.

Besides the museum, there were two other settings, both enjoying their vigorous youth in the Gilded Age, where objects were exhibited in great number and variety, and which had strong connections with public knowledgeability. The first was the ritual of the World's Fair. Beginning, in a systematic way, in 1876 (previewed in 1853), great expositions appeared regularly in the United States.[2] Between the early 1880s and World War I they loomed every four or five years. Major exhibitions were held during this era in New Orleans, Atlanta, Chicago, St. Louis, Buffalo, Nashville, San Francisco, San Diego, Seattle, Omaha, and Portland. They were supplemented by great industrial fairs, the series held in Cincinnati and St. Louis, for example, and by state and county fairs. Contemporaries perceived both the aesthetic and the educational values that expositions projected. Many Americans had their first contact at fairs with serious art, and with a series of major innovations: autos, typewriters, airships, telephones, new furniture and construction methods, electricity, synthetic materials. In booths and pavilions thousands of objects were available for handling and close comparison.

The fair's educational work was universally recognized. The very word *exposition,* which was first applied to fairs in London in the 1750s, referred to the great change that overtook the modern fair. No longer primarily a merchants' encounter, an exposition's primary appeal was now to consumers. It became a giant advertisement organ rather than a protected site used to seal commercial transactions. Thus the spectacle of the fairs became steadily more extensive and more elaborate. The "Short Sermon for Sightseers," in the *Art Handbook* of the Pan-American Exposition of 1901, advised its readers, "Please remember when you get inside the gates you are part of the show."[3]

Because of their size and complexity, the fairs quickly developed their own groups of experts trained to supervise everything from architecture and lighting to sanitation and landscaping and who moved from one exposition to another, increasing their skills in handling large crowds and exploiting sites. Charles Howard Walker is one example; a Boston-born architect who became a vice-president of the American Institute of Architects, he was a member of the planning board for the Louisiana Purchase Exposition and designed the Massachusetts Building and the Electricity Building for the same fair; his firm prepared the general plan and designed the Administration Building for Omaha's Trans-Mississippi Exposition. William J. Hammer is another; a consulting engineer for the Edison Company, both in England and America, he installed the lighting for London's 1882 exposition and built for it the first electrical sign ever made; took charge of the eight Edison exhibits at the International Electrical Exposition the Franklin Institute held in Philadelphia in 1884; was appointed in 1888 as consulting engineer to the Cincinnati Centennial Exposition, and designed its lighting; in 1889 represented Edison at the Paris Exposition; and helped organize the International Electrical Congress and served on a jury at the St. Louis Fair. Bradford L. Gilbert, architect and inventor, designer of railroad stations for Octave Chanute, completed a special station for Chicago's 1893 fair; supervised and designed the construction of the Atlanta Cotton States Exposition in 1895; and was architect for the South Carolina Interstate and West Indian Exposition of 1901. Charles Kurtz, director of the art department for Louisville's annual Southern Exposition; became assistant chief of the art department for the Columbian Exposition; was given the art directorship of the annual St. Louis Exposition in 1894; aided the art department of the Trans-Mississippi Exposition; became assistant director of fine arts for the United States Commission to the 1900 Paris Exposition; and in 1901 was appointed assistant chief of the Louisiana Purchase Exposition.[4] The sole point is that planners and department chiefs moved from fair to fair, building up a capital of experience to make the sophisticated, innovative, and effective displays which comprised the expositions.

Attendance was vast; the Chicago fair of 1893, the best attended, recorded more than 25 million visits (in a population of 70 million). Philadelphia, St. Louis, and Buffalo were also particularly well-attended expositions. Fairgoing was a typical experience for the American at the turn of the century.

If fairs are defined as competitors to museums in their ability to present large selections of the world's art and artifacts, arranged according to specific principles of classification and designed both for aesthetic pleasure and edifi-

*Opening
ceremonies at
Memorial Hall,
Philadelphia
Centennial*

cation, their presence must be taken seriously. However, although the fairs were run generally by different people and contained more inclusive exhibits, they did not really challenge the basic thrust of the new museums. For one thing, expositions preserved the hierarchical approach to classification, a hierarchy basic to the museum's principles of organization. Exhibits were segregated. Almost all the artwork, for example, was housed in a separate building (or palace). The highest encomia were usually reserved for these canvases and statues gathered from all over the world and presented in close juxtaposition under one roof. Art, then, was granted a special, reserved, and lofty status among the interests of the world, set off from more mundane pursuits, and glamorized by pompously ornate settings.

Indeed, fair buildings generally resembled museum structures in their turn-of-the-century expression; they were heavily reliant upon classical forms—the Chicago buildings were the single most influential ensemble—but even Philadelphia, as John Maass has shown, set a precedent for future museums in Schwarzmann's Memorial Hall. Those fair buildings that were designed for permanence usually became museums; this happened in St. Louis, Chicago, Philadelphia, San Francisco, and Buffalo, among others. And fair collections, at Chicago, for instance, and at Cincinnati, became the basis for future museum foundings.

Not only did the expositions present hierarchies of function, they protected hierarchies of quality as well. Juries and panels of experts awarded gold, silver, and bronze medals to distinguished entries, in somewhat the same manner that art exhibitors had traditionally been rewarded. Fair organizers insisted that while the exposition must be inclusive, it also had to represent a culling of the best of the world's goods. To be sure, a subversive principle was at work here, subversive, at least, of the premise of the major art museums: the best beer, the best roller skate, the best sewing machine could get as much serious attention from a panel of judges (and as elaborate a medal) as a painting or bas-relief. And this should not be underestimated in evaluating the total effect of the fairs. Nevertheless, in format, influence, and organization, the expositions, like the turn-of-the-century museums, functioned as educational pleasure grounds, designed or at least intended to have a pervasive if vaguely defined improving effect upon the practice of the arts and the sciences. And they treated the traditional organization of human ideas and activities, particularly intellectual activities, with reverence. Fairs of ideas coincided with the expositions of material objects at both Chicago, which hosted the Parliament of Religions in 1893, and St. Louis, which hosted the Congress of Arts and Sciences in 1904.

Animal pleasures and pastimes, trivial delights, Little Egypt, and the ice cream parlors were also present, but given allotted spots outside the fairgrounds, on the midways or pikes. But even in the official areas of the fairs, great efforts were made at differentiation. Most visitors to the Columbian Exposition, according to the *Chicago Record*, which chronicled the history of the fair, "must have been impressed by the great contrast between their southern section and their northern one. In the first, the effect aimed at is that of the formal, the academic, the ceremonial. In the second, art makes some concession to nature and the balance and symmetry required by the classic style give way to an adjustment that permits a free expression of the informal and the picturesque."[5]

Some displays were sophisticated and technically impressive. Expositions were electrical innovators; Luther Stieringer pioneered with lighting by glow, reflecting rays from a dull white surface at Chicago, Portland, and Omaha. At Omaha, Stieringer did light paintings by hiding and juxtaposing lights with different voltages, highlighted the building's architectural ornaments with multicolored lights, and experimented with indoor lighting as well.[6] Frederick W. Putnam's anthropological displays brought great praise at Chicago as did the general use of relief maps.

But many interiors were still crowded with oddly assorted piles of objects that leaned toward the ingenious rather than the impressive. Like museums, fairs seemed intent on showing everything they had all at once. And the displays reflected the still heavily agricultural character of the country. As the *Chicago Record* pointed out, if Philadelphia had its Sleeping Beauty sculpted in butter "the present exhibition has its prune horses and orange lighthouses from California and its cows and horses and spread-eagles done in Iowa corn."[7]

*Mines and Mining,
Columbian
Exposition,
Chicago, 1893*

The *Nation* charged that Columbian interiors contrasted poorly with their magnificent façades; the installation of machinery exhibits seemed only to heighten the planning defects.[8]

But despite unequal achievements, the fairs had decisive effects upon the respectful crowds, not least upon their manners (another echo of older museum ideals). "You may be crowded with a thousand American mechanics and their wives in the blocked avenues of the Exposition, and you shall not hear an oath or an ill-humoured word," reported the *New York Tribune*. One happy symptom of the American temper, reported the same newspaper, "is the promptness with which the Exposition is recognized and received by the masses of our own people, not as a show place but as a school. There is very little idle sauntering. . . . In the groups surrounding an exhibit the faces of Americans, keen, alive, quick-eyed, are distinguishable from all others, and the questions asked by them are unusually shrewd and intelligent." How different from the French, who came to their expositions, according to the *Tribune*, "as to a fete."[9] And Paul Bourget found the multitudes at the Columbian Exposition striking "by the total absence of both joy and repose. . . . They went about examining the interior and the exterior of the Exposition with a sort of blank avidity, as if they were walking in the midst of a colossal lesson in things."[10] Bourget insisted that the visitors were more interested in instruction than in entertainment. The

Scientific American made the same observations of the crowds at the St. Louis Fair of 1904.[11]

These expositions, then, were mass encounters with the art and objects of the modern world, dramatic, persuasive, self-consciously designed to produce a maximum effect, and having at least as much influence upon the knowledge and the taste of the American public as all the art museums put together. If fairs did not before World War I challenge the logic of museum presentation, they nonetheless represented an alternative experience.

The second major competitor to the museum as a display area for artifacts was less clearly idealistic and educational than the exposition but also served a consciousness-expanding end. And that was the department store.[12] Many commentators, both friendly and hostile to the metropolitan museum, have noted the relationship between the store and the great museum, and have pointed to the centralizing principles and merchandising techniques endemic to both. American department stores were approximately the same age as the modern museum. There had been major dry goods stores in the pre–Civil War era, most notably A. T. Stewart's New York establishment, but it was not until the 1860s and 1870s that the set of conditions which define the department store came together in Marshall Field's and The Fair in Chicago, Macy's in New York, and John Wanamaker's in Philadelphia. By the 1890s every large American city had several immense emporia with armies of employees. In New York, Bloomingdale's, Lord & Taylor, B. Altman, Ohrbach's, Bergdorf Goodman were all founded before 1900, to say nothing of firms like McCreary's, Siegel-Cooper, Stern's, Arnold Constable, and Best and Company, which are no longer operating. Outside New York, Strawbridge and Clothier in Philadelphia, Filene's in Boston, Carson Pirie Scott in Chicago, Hudson's in Detroit, Rich's in Atlanta, Bullock's and Robinson's of Los Angeles, and Magnin's in San Francisco were all products of the last decades of the century. The large department stores were determinants of the urban real estate market, its office districts, its newspaper industry, and its transportation networks as well.

Like museums, department stores were selective concentrations of merchandise, merchandise grouped by functional categories rather than by age and nationality. Novelists, journalists, and ordinary consumers testified, even more than advertisements did, to the overpowering effects of the commodities and settings of the large metropolitan department store. In a sophisticated retail manner, merchandising was really born in the post–Civil War era; John D. Wanamaker declared in 1912 that the art was really less than forty years old. A. T. Stewart's great store in New York, the largest and most imposing commercial building in America, was not particularly impressive in its interior; floors were uncarpeted, furnishings and fixtures were plain, goods generally were piled casually upon shelves with little attempt made to create special displays. But in the 1870s, 1880s, and 1890s, precisely in those decades that the art museums began operations, shopping manners changed. Innovative merchants realized the advantages that lay in courting women customers by settings that played upon fantasies of luxury. American retailers traveled abroad, studied the *grands magasins* of Paris—the Louvre, the Bon Marché—and returned home to lavish on their own buildings handsome restrooms, writing rooms, art galleries, restaurants, and elegant draperies and fixtures. The drama of shopping probably reached its high point in Chicago and its most sensitive cultivation in the great stores of Marshall Field. Field, seconded by Gordon Selfridge, his most aggressive and innovative manager, put on a show in State Street that enthralled the city.

The new store rested on basic changes. Until the late nineteenth century big money was made in the wholesale rather than the retail trade. That was true of Stewart's and it was true of Field's. From 1871 to 1877 Field's retail profits were $300,000 compared with wholesale profits of more than $5 million.[13] But then the retail explosion began. In the words of sociologist Hugh Dalziel Duncan, "Chicago merchants made their stores great stages for the enactment of their roles as 'servants of the public.' Far from being too proud to clerk in their stores, they gloried in the art of presenting themselves to customers as friendly yet elegant hosts and appeared before their clerks as grand masters in all the arts of management. Chicagoans thought of their stores as social centers."[14] The department store experience, like the museum, was treated respectfully by all participants; clerks and shoppers dressed up for the encounter. Selfridge, for example, who toured Field's several times a day, changed his clothes just as often. As early as the 1868 store, the fittings were designed to bring out the most sensuous materials: displays of furs and silks to tempt the shopper, frescoed walls, brilliant gas lighting. The great new show windows in the department stores presented their own tableaux. "The Loop became a vast promenade of huge glass windows in which mannequins stood as mistresses of taste to teach people how to embody their secret longings for status in things of great price."[15]

In Macy's, with somewhat greater austerity in the windows and the store fixtures, new standards of luxury were created in the 1890s. The ladies' waiting room, placed in the 1891 addition to the Fourteenth Street store, was, according to advertisements "the most luxurious and beautiful department devoted to the comfort of ladies to be found in a mercantile establishment in the city. The style of decoration is Louis XV, and no expense has been spared in the adornment and furnishing of this room." On their way to it, customers would pass through an art room, containing "a carefully selected line of onyx" and bronzes.[16] In the first decade of the twentieth century, Macy's, Wanamaker's, and Field's all erected giant new stores, with ranks of elevators and escalators, with huge restaurants and elegant tearooms, special departments for costly rugs, jewels, antique furniture, and art. Wanamaker, who was an enthusiastic purchaser of modern academic artists like Munkacsy, Alma Tadema, Troyon, Schreyer, and Bouguereau, filled his stores with pictures, careful to select and hang them to maximum effect. He objected to the crowding of pictures in museums, which he likened to a three-ring circus. "In museums," Wanamaker declared, "most everything looks like junk even when it isn't, because there is no care or thought in the display. If women would wear their fine clothes like galleries wear their pictures, they'd be laughed at."[17] Wanamaker installed in his Philadelphia store the first electrical system placed in any building used by the public. His New York store, which opened in 1907, had built into it a twenty-two-room private home, "The House Palatial," with hall, staircases, and auditorium, and a series of period furniture displays. Field's new store, built by D. H. Burnham and Company, opened sections in various years from 1902 on. It had an enormous glass dome by Tiffany, rare Circassian walnut paneling and blue Wilton carpets for the tearooms, a Louis Quatorze salon for gowns, an Elizabethan Room for fine linens, an Oak Room for antiques, a French Room for lingerie, and an American Colonial Room. The Belgian sculptor Gustav Van Debergen, who would subsequently work on the St. Louis exposition, developed a series of sculptured motifs on the history of merchandising for the building. The stores proudly seized on expositions held in their cities to publicize their own merchandise, and in advertisements in 1893, Selfridge declared Field's to be "an exposition in itself."[18]

The department store, then, like the exposition, challenged the monopoly of the new museums in the collection and display of art and of costly manufactured objects. Nevertheless, there were parallels and complementary effects in the store displays. The atmosphere of a great department store was not totally disparate from that of a museum. Academic tastes and traditional formalities dominated both. The deference of the properly dressed and quiet clerks, the doormen at the carriage entrances, the frock-coated managers, formally dressed floorwalkers, and elegantly dressed women shoppers gave, to the more fashionable stores, a certain panache. Moreover, the dark wood cases, the cluttered interiors, the sense of compression all paralleled the display techniques of fairs and museums.

Second, the architecture and general design of the stores was traditional and palatial. Although museums typically had colonnaded porticos and pediments, which the stores lacked, the stores with their greater height, resembled great chateaux looming impressively on city streets. Often built around courtyards to increase their light and air, the huge floors acted like little galleries in

Left, the Tiffany dome in Marshall Field & Co., Chicago Right, entrance hall of the City Art Museum, St. Louis

themselves. If the atmosphere was less sacred and hushed than in the museum, it was still special and self-contained, and buyers respected the same standards of costliness, elegance, and tradition—in higher-priced items—that exposition managers and museum curators had appropriated.

Before World War I, then, if one examines institutional influences on what Americans knew about art and style in objects, one has a giant triptych: museums in the center flanked by fairs on one side and great retail establishments on the other. All were different, but all worked in the interests of an art ideal that stressed continuity with the past and respect for the old masters. All gave to art in its high sense—painting and sculpture—a special place and believed in surrounding it with the marble and fine woods that went into every great house. During the interwar years, however, the great art museum, in its capacity to display, moved out of phase with its two partners. Its ability to influence public knowledge and preferences was called into question. Always vulnerable, the museum became even more so as it was outdistanced by commerce. Changes in the architecture and display methods of expositions and retailers lessened the effectiveness of museum displays, raised public expectations, and so rendered the museum less powerful as a force shaping that abstraction called public taste. Consider briefly the history of expositions during the interwar years.

The Great Court in
Wanamaker's,
Philadelphia

On the face of it, the power of expositions as an experience had lessened, if the number of major international shows held in the United States is any index. There were really only three of any true consequence, all held in the 1930s, in New York, San Francisco, and Chicago, although a number of important events like Philadelphia's Sesquicentennial in 1926 cannot be overlooked. But the three great fairs of the 1930s, taking place as they did during the Depression, were noteworthy events and in their own way became physical symbols for their decade as compelling as the Columbian Exposition or the St. Louis fair had been for their own days. It does not take long, however, to detect a major difference between the two fair-going generations. Before World War I the fairs were great academic festivals, glorifications of conventional wisdom in the arts and in architecture. They were manned by the orthodox, and their exhibition settings and art, like their exhibition materials themselves, were highly traditional in orientation, even if they were innovative in method. By the 1930s this had changed; to a certain extent the avant-garde, or at least a self-proclaimed avant-garde, took charge of fair-planning. Stimulated, perhaps, by the influence of the Paris fair of 1925 on merchandising and style in the decorative arts, the fairs became streamlined and frankly embraced the machine and its culture. The shapes of the buildings, the symbols used for the fairs—abstract pylons or bridges in place of art palaces or giant statues—and, most of all, the lavish and startling exhibition halls put up by huge companies like Ford, General Motors, and General Electric, reflected a world in which the new was worshiped and the emphasis was on sensation and novel perceptions rather than the absorption of data. Prepared for novel experiences by motion pictures and national advertising, the public moved through these fairs in a less reverent and more aggressive fashion than had their nineteenth-century ancestors. Young designers like Walter Dorwin Teague and Norman Bel Geddes were able to experiment with new ways of entertaining large audiences. The world of the 1930s was much less certain of its relationship to intellectual generalization than was the world of forty years before; the emphasis now lay on titillation and sensation rather than on synthesis. It was knowing how things worked, rather than knowing what things were, that was important. This concern with process, and its greater relativism, naturally produced a less formal atmosphere. Malls, flags, processions, concerts, uniforms—all these, it is true, still appeared at fairs, but the asymmetrical, stark, glass and metal buildings created an atmosphere that was unsettling to traditional ceremonies and experiences. This was the world of the Future seeking objectification; the nineteenth-century fair was the Present, a backward look at many conquests already achieved.

It was hard to know just what the fairs of the 1930s signified to students of the science of display, but that they were different and somewhat innovative seemed clear. With this in mind the Rockefeller Foundation determined to support a tour of the two fairs of 1939, in New York and San Francisco, by museum specialists who could determine the implications of the fairs for museum management. Chairing this group and writing up his general impressions, was Carlos E. Cummings, director of the Buffalo Museum of Science. His book was published under the title *East is East and West is West*.[19] The implication of the title—that fairs were fairs and museums were museums and never the twain shall meet—was not quite the argument of this lengthy, discursive, and not always persuasive commentary on exhibition management. Cummings isolated various unsuccessful exhibits and pointed out the many problems and the many opportunities that fairs possessed which museums did not. Although Cummings gleaned a number of important principles from the art of fair display, particularly the tremendous effect of some company pavilions, he did not, however, hit upon the central fact. Visitors touring the fairs of the 1930s had an experience very different from that generally available in museums. They entered interiors that were planned and decorated around a few central ideas. Huge photomontages, movies, and abstract illustrations enhanced the power of the objects under display. Crowd movements became, according to one observer, part of the exhibition. Overhead mirrors and fluid structures, sophisticated neon lighting, and ambulatory stages and auditoria were exploited imaginatively.[20]

In a real sense, selectivity was the key to this success, selectivity and association with enticing ideas. A designer of the Indian artifact display in the Federal Building on San Francisco's Treasure Island, summed it up, according to Cummings. He declared that in each exhibit hall "some single dominating item, displayed in a conspicuous manner, should be so placed as to arrest the attention of everyone entering the room before his eyes fall on anything else; this should instantly create a mental symbol, a main theme if you choose, under the aegis of which all the items in the room should be gradually gathered."[21] Cummings called this a "theory of mind-control or subjective guidance." He was not certain that the planners were always aware of the psychology involved in their management, but he was impressed. Not impressed enough, to be sure, to single it out as the chief lesson of the fairs, but then he never did draw up a set of detailed conclusions.

The viewers going through the fairs, however, were grateful for the care taken to attract and hold their attention. The fairs of the 1930s pioneered in client-centered displays which relied upon surprise, arresting juxtapositions, and a high degree of selectivity to make their points. They no longer needed to present the comprehensive products of world civilization. Instead, it was argument and dramatic impact that counted, a channeling of attention to a specific quality or effect. The lessons of advertising, an industry that had grown enormously in size and self-consciousness in the interwar years, were applied to fair merchandising, and the unclear results still put museums and their directors on the defensive.

Just as merchandising and architectural motifs had changed considerably in the fairs, they had changed in the great stores of the interwar years. The modern department store of the 1930s was a considerable modification of the environments planned by Levi Leiter, Gordon Selfridge, and John D. Wanamaker. Store modernization, in fact, had become a lucrative specialty among architects, and dozens of articles were published in professional journals during the 1920s and 1930s, indicating the kinds of changes that could be wrought in store interiors without necessarily tearing down the whole structure. Although conditions worsened during the Depression, hard times had come to many retailers even during the boom years of the 1920s. In 1923 the average net profits of stores doing an annual business of over $1 million were only 3.6 percent of net sales; in 1924 they dropped to 2 percent; in 1927 to 1.7 percent; and by the 1930s they were almost zero.[22] In this competition for increasing sales, American retail establishments could not move much further in the direction of increased efficiency; instead, they turned to the architecture of merchandising, hiring well-known architects and designers to dress up their stores; change their show windows; modify their internal shopping arrangements; add new technologies of lighting, cooling, and heating to increase client comfort; improve parking facilities; and generally stimulate customer imagination. Dramatically different new stores appeared in major cities, like Bullock's on Wilshire Boulevard in Los Angeles; Saks Fifth Avenue in Chicago and New York; Jay-Thorpe and Bonwit Teller in New York. By 1937 retail merchants were spending almost $70 million annually for modernization of existing facilities; Franklin Simon, Lord & Taylor, Macy's, Field's in Chicago, and Burdine's in Miami were among the big spenders, as were chains like Woolworth, Montgomery Ward, and Sears. Small stores shared the spirit, streamlining their exteriors, putting in neon lighting, removing excess counters. Architectural firms like Ross-Frankel specialized in commercial modernizations, prefabricating and assembling complete stores in New York and then disassembling them and shipping the parts to small towns throughout the United States. High-priced specialty stores, like Peck and Peck, went even further, hiring well-known interior designers to manufacture interiors that gave a maximum of encouragement to the eager customer.[23] Antique dealers and specialists in valuable curios of all sorts did the same thing when they could afford it. Israel Sack of Boston, one of the country's major dealers, produced the King Hopper Store on Chestnut Street, a handsome Palladian shop front with more than 1,500 feet of display, including a seventeenth-century room. John Russell Pope, the architect who

The Helicline, New York World's Fair, 1939

worked on Yale's college system and the Lincoln Memorial, designed a small rug shop, Whittall's, using paneling and antiques to show off a large assortment of rare old carpets.[24] Both furniture stores and department stores began to arrange their merchandise in model rooms; some had as many as several dozen complete rooms; Macy's at one time had sixty-five. Although museums had pioneered with period rooms at the start of the century, by the 1920s and the 1930s the stores had far outdistanced them.

The department stores, moreover, now went in for more overt cultural activities. At one store in the late 1930s, as many as 3,000 people attended a single lecture and lamp display, an exhibition of the history of lighting "from 600 B.C. to the present." Other store exhibits demonstrated how customers could save space by rearranging or buying double-duty furniture.[25] Cooking classes, art classes, child-development classes, and classes in glass and new materials like plastics supplemented store exhibits. As educators in the quality of American design, these great displays were probably more popular and even

more influential than any but a few museums. The thrust of the merchandising revolution within the stores was to lighten the interiors, to be more selective in displaying objects, to lessen clutter and dramatize blank spaces and lighting, to surround the shopper with a sense of adventure, and to underline this by the continual display of new objects. If the dark mahogany and traditional styling of the department stores complemented museums at the turn of the century, by the 1930s stores had moved to different settings altogether and were challenging rather than supporting the museum atmosphere. The shared monopoly of the early years was no longer effective, and, as arbiters of American taste, despite their lecture series and occasional exhibitions of industrial design, the museums were slipping. One president of the Metropolitan Museum of Art, Robert W. de Forest, actually told a group of department store executives to remember that their influence was far greater than that of all the museums combined. "You are the most fruitful source of art in America," de Forest exclaimed, urging them to become missionaries for beauty.[26] In some cases department stores themselves retailed original paintings, etchings, and antiques. Douglas and Elizabeth Rigby have amusingly described the use of store outlets to dispose of part of the enormous Hearst collection. At Gimbel's, Field's, and Saks Fifth Avenue, valuables were sold by the thousands. Gimbel's took over the Clarence H. Mackay sale and the collection of Warner S. McCall. "Have you always wanted one piece of genuine old Wedgwood, but thought it was forever beyond

*Left, the hat
department, Meier
& Frank Store,
Portland, Oregon,
before 1933
Right, the hat
department, Meier
& Frank Store,
Portland, Oregon,
after 1933*

you?" the department store asked. "Come find one here—browse around to
your heart's content." Implicit in many of the advertisements was hostility to the
museum, now associated with snobbish seclusion. "Artists never made them
[artworks] for museums and galleries. They made them to be worn, to be used,
to be looked at, to be appreciated, to be loved"[27] Apparently, the department
store could encourage appreciation more than the art palace.

Although critics of museums during the interwar years frequently berated
them for their gargantuan size and holdings, they nonetheless liked big department stores; their criticisms clearly reflected the new standards of customer
service that the stores had developed. In the *Century Magazine* Forest H. Cooke
entitled his attack, "Culture and Fatigue," rebuking poor ventilation, superflu-
ity of exhibits, and the absence of resting places; museums, he insisted, by
their very size and stolidity were projecting a civilization based on quantitative
rather than qualitative criteria. However well they preserved the past, they gave
little inspiration for future work, according to Cooke. "The rooms open to the
public should be of great beauty as rooms, well ventilated, restful, and inviting
leisure. They should contain very few objects of exhibition, and these should
be so placed as not to detract from each other. There should be comfortable,
movable chairs."[28]

Although Cooke did not speak specifically of modern stores in this article, they exemplified what he had in mind: merchandising that maximized

physical comfort and exploited the dramatic possibilities of empty space and
selectivity. Some museum directors, like the iconoclastic John Cotton Dana of
the Newark Museum, insisted that the buying public learned more about fine
art from shop windows and travel than from museums. Heaping scorn on the
museum's claim to hold a monopoly on influencing public taste and legitimizing
objects, Dana argued that the average citizen exercised his taste when he selected "a cravat or a table cover or a rug or a chair." He should transfer to the
"designer of good umbrella handles" the same respect he felt for the artist
dignified by museum exhibition.[29] The *Saturday Evening Post*, complimenting
the Metropolitan on the installation of its American wing and the Philadelphia
Museum on its period rooms, urged other museums to move away from being
"bleak storage warehouses for the protection of art objects" into popular displays which better exploited modern technology. The department store entered
the *Post*'s editorial inadvertently. The magazine spoke warmly of the recent
transformation of the public library into a community center, a change forced
upon readers "by arts just as skillful as those employed by department store
proprietors to crowd their aisles with eager customers."[30] Writing in the *Commonweal Magazine*, Frederic Thompson called American art museums tombs

*Window display by
Arthur Fraser,
Marshall Field &
Co.*

and safe deposit vaults. He insisted that there was "scarcely any attempt to make museums, inwardly or outwardly original in design, or beautiful in themselves."[31] He urged philanthropists to help living artists, rather than museums.

Specific reforms surfaced. Set designer Lee Simonson was not complimentary in comparing the museum with the department store, for he thought museums had overexpanded and produced a new malady named "museum fatigue." Museums themselves were overstocked and stuffed full because their directors had never properly conceived of "the problem of organizing countless 'art objects' in a way that will make their aesthetic value clear and their social importance effective." Curators had assumed that it was enough simply to show sufficient numbers of bronzes, marbles, and paintings, in order to "endow the uneducated with an abiding sense of the good, the beautiful and the true." In actual fact, the business of a museum "is not to chronicle art as a fact but to enact it as an event and to dramatize its function. Its role is not that of a custodian but that of a showman." And the way to make this possible was through the simplest application of a few principles of stage setting and architectural arrangement."[32] Instead of organizing "in a procession of showcases" five thousand examples of Japanese art, swords, lacquer, vases, and paintings, museums should build a Japanese room, arrange within it the one painting it was meant to frame and select the other appropriate details. Although the objects might amount to one five hundredth of those now displayed in any important Oriental collection, the most casual visitor would receive a better impression of the true meaning of Japanese art. What was true of Japanese art was true also of Swiss or American or Hungarian.

The skyscraper tower of twenty or thirty stories that Simonson proposed permitted concentration by avoiding the inevitable distractions visitors faced when they walked from collection through collection in order to see specific objects. Irrelevant objects inevitably distracted the student or art critic. Traditional museum arrangements depleted "the kind of attention that opens into criticism as effectively and methodically as it fails to focus on the visitor who comes in without any specific purpose whatever."[33] A skyscraper needed no skylights and so would avoid the repetitive use of parallel walls and their parade of pictures, arranged in "regimental perspective," permitting new and critically more appropriate hanging methods. If museums are to become alive, Simonson concluded, they had to do more than hold occasional exhibitions of silverware or furniture. "Unless they are structurally reconceived, the really formative moments in the development of American taste will be the moments when increasing hordes of Winter and Summer travelers stand for the first time under the columns of the Parthenon, or see the roseate temple, Der el Bahari, across the Nile at Luxor."[34]

Simonson is quoted at this length, not because his skyscraper museum possessed peculiar virtues or because his indictment made so much sense. But his call for a structural reconception typified the phenomenon that I have been describing. In the 1920s and 1930s a series of experiences—on stage and screen as well as in fairs and retailing—called attention to new and dramatic possibilities of museum rearrangement. Merchandising techniques had become so numerous and impressive, that museums were now being asked to exploit possibilities that they had in fact originated—such as period rooms—but which they had nonetheless failed to develop fully. The planning, reconstruction, and building of museums during the interwar years, recognized some of the necessary changes. But it was a slow conversion given the heavy capital investment museums had in their existing physical settings. In his 1950 survey of museum buildings, Laurence Vail Coleman dated a massive shift of design to 1933. He argued that by 1942, when the war interrupted further construction, more than fifty modern museum buildings had been constructed, including Goodwin and Stone's Museum of Modern Art, and art museum buildings in Hartford, Colorado Springs, Dallas, West Palm Beach, and Des Moines.[35] But if Coleman had numbers on his side, the exceptions he named were obviously of much greater importance in terms of their collections and their audiences. The later classical buildings included Philadelphia's Franklin Institute, the National Gallery in Washington, and the art museums of Kansas City and San Francisco. Building additions, while modern in some aspects, continued to echo the more traditional monumentality, and some of the new buildings themselves were simply a transcribed form of the older verities without much change in display methods.

It is, nonetheless, impossible to deny that museum planners were becoming sensitive to new possibilities and aware of the advances that stores and fairs had made in influencing public taste. The arrival of émigrés like Alexander Dorner also had some influence.[36] Lighting, more effective use of space, new materials, improved visitor facilities, novel display cases and cabinets, more varied room sizes and greater tolerance for ordinary and novel objects reflected the many studies undertaken by the American Association of Museums in these years. Nevertheless, the fruition of these efforts would await the postwar period, and the museum's position as a monopolizer of art and objects was further challenged by completely new developments in the mass media, most notably in film, which fall outside the realm of this paper.

To sum up the interwar years, then, the merchandising revolution which overtook fairs and department stores, and which spread to smaller stores as well, placed museums in a laggard position, which helped feed the resentments expressed in the press. As an influence on public taste, the American museum faced powerful challenges. Knowledgeability, experience, and preference patterns, the three elements of public taste, were all more dramatically shaped by other institutions. That museums recognized the new source of energy can be seen in one of their chief responses: displays of industrial art and consumer design which the Museum of Modern Art and the Metropolitan Museum hosted.[37] As popular and interesting as they were, these exhibitions nevertheless consisted of selected reactions to the power, prestige, and inventiveness of another world of merchandising. A certain legitimation was, of course, conferred by museum approval, but the true source of influence was merely acknowledged, rather than transferred, through these exhibitions.

The postwar decades, however, took a different direction. Among many other changes six factors have helped somewhat to shift the balance of influence away from certain competitors and back to the museum. The first change is the decline in strength of the central city, particularly of its retailing. The litany of downtown woes is long and depressing and unnecessary to repeat here. Among the major casualties, in terms of relative influence, have been the great downtown department stores. In the last three decades, dozens of apparently permanent establishments have gone out of business or shifted their primary emphasis to the suburban shopping center.[38] Shopping-center settings are often highly dramatic spatial ensembles, and they have continued and expanded upon the advances in lighting and merchandising developed during the interwar years. However, if the techniques of display are more impressive, the collection of objects in the center cannot compete with the older department stores and central cities; for various reasons—the size of the stores, the financial needs of the centers which rest upon franchised operations, the character of the suburban market—there is an extraordinary degree of replication in goods and services offered within the shopping center and from one shopping center to another. It contains few surprises, a factor which perhaps has led to its innovativeness in designing an overall setting. As merchandising competitors, retail establishments have suffered from this decentralization.

The other great competitor of the museum, the fair, has itself ceased to be an important factor in introducing people to new goods and services, partly because new media, like television, and increasingly easy travel have made the fairs superfluous except as purely promotional or symbolic devices. Among the three great central institutions that once shared control over object display, the museum has retained its essential power better than the others, simply because it has not decentralized, and its exhibits are less easily replicable.

Second, the museum itself, while retaining its collection of objects, has modernized its settings to an extent just dimly forecast in the late 1930s and 1940s. An extraordinary variety of museum environments have been created in this country since 1950; the plans, scale, materials, and the logic of museum display have all excited considerable debate and controversy. But this controversy reflects the fact that museum design, instead of reflecting the most traditional wing of architectural practice, has attracted innovative practitioners who have seized public attention, if not public approval.[39] The Guggenheim was an early example of the modern controversial museum; since then, California, New York, and Texas have hosted dozens of new settings—suspended, underground, undulating, rectangular, monumental, domestic—which incorporate almost every possibility for manipulating objects, and bring to bear upon the museumgoer the whole force of a broad repertory of designer methods. These great settings, according to some critics, detract from the primacy of the object on display. Nevertheless, they have added to the dramatic appeal of museum-going and to the sense of luxury associated with the institution, an association which attracted bitter commentary and hostility in the late 1960s, but which increased the theatrical impact of the museum experience in much the same way that movies were aided by their fantasy palaces and department stores by their rich appointments. In their variety and ingenuity, modern museum display techniques rival, and often outdistance, the most advanced retail methods.

A third factor that has increased the museum's influence on public knowledgeability is a spectrum of publicity gestures, the most notable example of which is the great purchase. Once again, we encounter a practice that has borne the brunt of considerable criticism, but whose impact upon museum consumers has been undeniable. Perhaps the most famous, although no longer the most expensive of these gestures, was the Metropolitan's purchase of Rembrandt's *Aristotle Contemplating the Bust of Homer*. In a sense, the great purchase simply is an extension of commercial advertising methods that were well established before the postwar years. Merchant princes like Wanamaker and Field well understood the customer appeal of such dramatic gestures, and benefited from the resultant publicity. The art museum becomes, therefore, in the public mind at any rate, the kind of dramatic arena where gestures like this can be expected, and a pecuniary symbol of considerable importance. The ultimate value of these gestures may well be open to question, but they do enhance its ability to influence a heterogeneous clientele that has few aesthetic assumptions or pretensions. While the glamor of the shopping and exposition rituals has dimmed, the glamor of the art museum experience has become either a target for criticism or an experience to cherish. If the ability to influence requires the association of honorific and attention-getting devices, the museum would seem to have recaptured, albeit in Veblenesque terms, a degree of public attention it had previously lost.

Fourth, museum directors, curators, and exhibition organizers have demonstrated an ability to create exhibitions that have an immediate impact upon observable public taste. Rather than merely reflect this taste, as did the industrial art exhibitions of the interwar years, with proper planning and publicity these exhibitions have shaped it. One case in point is the revival of interest in Art Moderne, sometimes, if too loosely, called Art Deco. It is interesting that the many varieties of modernistic interwar design, which were stimulated in the first instance by a world's fair, were restimulated to a large degree by museum exhibitions, in particular the exhibitions organized at Finch College in 1970, and the Minneapolis Institute of Arts in the summer of 1971, which had the benefit of a catalog text by Bevis Hillier.[40] Many factors stimulated the revival of interest in the furniture, pottery, glass, textile, and skyscraper designs of the 1920s and 1930s, and there were clearly presentiments and publications of importance which occurred before the exhibitions of the early 1970s. But in retrospect (and judging from the attentions of the mass media), the exhibitions seem to have been critical to the dispersion of public knowledge and commercial imitation. By joining the power of media to the dramatic gesture, the mu-

A Rembrandt on display at Parke-Bernet Galleries

seum has shown an ability to use a single exhibition with remarkable effectiveness. Although there apparently are no comparative studies that analyze the
effects of museum exhibitions in different periods, the present moment does not
seem to indicate a low ebb. If anything it suggests the opposite.

Fifth, the museum as an institution in the postwar years applied direct
merchandising methods through the institutionalization of its own retail outlets—stores—which, particularly in the last decade, have become ever larger,
more profitable, and more important elements in the museum's total operation.
The museum store sells not only postcards and slides but reproductions of
pottery, fabrics, statuary, and jewelry. It handles books, uses greeting cards to
popularize knowledge of the museum's holdings, and generally functions as a
commercial publicist. The immediate gratification felt by the department store
customer in the act of purchase, and the experience of handling objects and
learning more about them, which was the joy of the fair-goer, are united in the
museum store, and seal the museum-going experience for many visitors. Appropriately enough in our culture, it is a commercial setting which legitimizes
an aesthetic setting. However late the discovery was in coming to museums, no
one can now accuse them of backwardness in exploiting it. The importance of
the store lies not simply in its financial returns but in the means it offers for
the museums to influence directly consumer taste. In a sense, they can create
their own instant customers. The museum store comes closer than one might
expect to the vision of galleries of casts and reproductions which colored the
motives of early American museum founders, depressed about the cost of importing masterpieces from abroad.

The sixth and final element in the museum enterprise is a public mood
which is difficult to define but pervasive in its effects, and which demands a
total immersion in nostalgic evocation.[41] The roots and directions of contemporary nostalgia are still unclear, but they include an affection for physical
objects and details that is quite astonishing in its inclusiveness and perhaps in
its lack of discrimination. Public absorption with mementos of a past that is
continually recorded and yet recedes into memory as styles change can be
satisfied ultimately only by total environments. The museum alone has the
stock of objects to permit total immersion. There is, for example, an increasing
tendency to place building façades, interiors, and details under the shelter of
the art museum; for example, in New York the park façade of the original Metropolitan and in Chicago the trading floor of the old Stock Exchange now placed
in the Art Institute's new wing. Exhibitions of costumes, quilts, comic books,
and other artifacts have become standard operating procedures at major museums, while the displays of period rooms have become more elaborate and
more numerous. In a sense, the museum's stock of nostalgia has increased

relative to the difficulties of maintaining period buildings and objects in the world outside it. Modernization and mobility, twin themes of American social and environmental life, have probably increased the appeal of nostalgia, while they have reduced the ordinary capacity to service it. The museum's age, size, and vast holdings, in the interwar years a handicap in merchandising, have in response to the new public mood become advantages to exploit. A revival of interest in Victorian and Beaux Arts architecture has also helped.[42] The relationship between these new advantages and public taste is not easy to determine except to note, among other things, that museum exhibitions have stimulated manufacturers to produce replicas. Certainly knowledgeability about the history of design has been increased as a result, and the nostalgia boom has helped nourish bands of culturists with commitments to particular kinds of objects and styles.

To summarize then, a series of weaknesses in competing institutions and environments, a set of merchandising advantages and innovations, and a public temper have combined to make the museum stand out today as the single most dramatic setting for the display of art and objects. The costs of consumer orientation do exist, of course, and were present right from the start in the never-ending debates about the function of museums. If attractiveness and public appeal become the museum's objectives, how in effect does it differ from any commercial institution which exists chiefly for the purpose of selling? Are public knowledgeability and experience increased at the cost of stating any preferences, a practice which might appear unseemly or arbitrary to an audience which simply desires entertainment? Has the museum, as a new entertainment palace, become merely another asylum, an asylum not for objects and art but for special kinds of memory baths and gallery-going rituals, a quantified, certified, collective encounter that may shape purchase patterns but hardly improve them? At one time museums were charged with paying too little attention to the wants and needs of millions of laymen. Now, in another era, they are taxed with pandering to delight in relevance, drama, and popularity. Evaluation of the consequences of this shift must be left to another time, but the changing fortunes of the museum as a public influence suggest capacities that are great, growing, and endowed with almost infinite variation. Having survived a series of competitive challenges, the art museum must now demonstrate that the victory was worth it and that its repertory of merchandising techniques can be put in the service of clearly defined, significant, and worthwhile goals.

A Historical Perspective

on Museum Advocacy

As a historian, I find it strange that the issue of advocacy has taken so long to develop in museums. Speaking or acting in support of something has always been inseparable from the basic nature of any institution. From hospitals, prisons, and libraries, to conscript armies, professional societies, and museums, institutions are created to meet needs. Their very existence represents specific assumptions about contemporary problems. One is not surprised to find members of the bar debating legislation licensing lawyers or hospital staffs absorbed by laws fixing medical liability. Institutions have a stake in evaluating policies that affect their constituencies.

The problem of museum advocacy, then, concerns its limits and constituencies, not its legitimacy. Most American institutions have been embroiled in debates about the limits of their responsibility for public action, the neutrality proper for issues of popular importance, the self-restraint and objectivity appropriate to their power and status. One thinks, for example, of the evolving role of American clergymen and American churches in political debates; of universities, school systems, and textbooks; of the political expression deemed

From *Museum News* 59, no. 3 (November–December 1980): 60–86. Reprinted with permission of the American Association of Museums.

appropriate for civil servants, military officers, and enlistees; of the constraints imposed upon public airwaves and commercial advertisers. Barrels of ink and years of discussion have been spilled in the interests of these questions. Yet, until recently, museums have been largely immune to such involvement. Why? Has the question emerged because of changing museum policies and operations? Because of new public attitudes and values? Or both?

Historically, musuems have not, as a group, been totally free from controversy. In the last century and a half, American museums, their trustees, and administrators have been embroiled in a series of issues that some would consider solely contemporary. Should the museum emphasize the generation or the diffusion of knowledge? Should it aim at a broad, diverse public or reserve its efforts for a smaller group of experts and connoiseurs? How aggressive should it become in attracting attention to itself or even decentralizing its collections? Should the museum charge admission? Should it aim for broadly educational exhibits or for the selective display of masterpieces? These questions and many others concerning the museum's audience and display methods have been around for more than a century. George Goode, Joseph Henry, Benjamin Ives Gilman, and John Cotton Dana are among the major figures in museum history who have taken positions on them. Museum historians encounter continual debates about the dangers of pandering to, rather than sharpening, public taste and of using admissions figures to establish significance rather than internal standards of excellence.

But whether the museum should take positions is, I believe, a rather new question and has much to do with the relationship between museums and society. The museum has, in fact, become more sensitive to issues of public importance, and its ongoing activities are subjected to more critical review. Advocacy itself is but a part of this change. I believe that three major shifts in perception have contributed to the awareness of museums as potentially controversial institutions, shifts larger than the museum and over which it has very little control. But these changes have substantially modified the perspective of both the museum-goer and the museum-manager and have produced occasional confrontations where earlier there had been agreement or indifference. These new controversies testify to the museum's social importance. They should be welcomed rather than deplored, for they indicate an awareness that museums are powerful institutions whose policies produce an impact.

The first large change is the erosion of broad-based, consensual agreements about basic social arrangements in America and the substitution of values that emphasize personal fulfillment and individual value judgments as the basis of life styles. That such a shift has apparently occurred is no well-kept secret. For the past three decades, historians, sociologists, political scientists, and journalists have been busy writing books about the transformation of American life. The titles of some of their texts have a faintly antique and embarrassed air, reflecting the aroma of forecasts gone sour. Others retain a primitive vigor. But they suggest the character of the change. In the fifties and early sixties, texts like *The Lonely Crowd; The Organization Man; The Hidden Persuaders;* and *The Power Elite* suggested fears of conformity and social sleep-walking which had overtaken a population caught in the grasp of powerful opinion-makers and concentrations of power. But in the later sixties and seventies the trajectory shifted. *Growing Up Absurd; The Greening of America; The Making of a Counter Culture; The Politics of Ecstasy; The Feminine Mystique; The Electric Kool-Aid Acid Test;* and *The Culture of Narcissism* emphasized different themes, a fear or glorification of a culture of personal liberation at the expense of established institutional patterns and commitments. Satiric, admiring, loathing, or detached, these social commentaries produced a powerful reaction, for they were related to fundamental social movements at work at the time.

The hierarchies that divided the power and opportunities of American life according to sexual, racial, or cultural status were challenged more fundamentally, and often more successfully, than ever before in our history. This struggle was accompanied by questioning values and institutions that many Americans still clung to—the fundamental roles of monogamous marriage and the family; the virtues of free enterprise and private property; the special status of professional training and expertise; the centrality of religion, as a set of institutions, if not as an ideology; the value of high culture as a pursuit and group of ideals; and the virtues of self-denial, discipline, and thrift. Basic convictions concerning the beneficent course of American material progress have been, and are, under attack by spokesmen for the natural environment. Ethnocentric notions of cultural supremacy, centered on the arts and civilization of Western Europe and America, have been eagerly assaulted. These categories are simply culled from a longer list; every commentator has his favorite combinations. But whatever the specific terms employed, the result has been to make conventional wisdom seem neither wise nor conventional.

These shifts in values and behavior have inevitably affected the character of cultural institutions as well. They have done this by removing them from a "neutral" region and relocating them in a sphere of special interests and social manipulation. One can see this in a number of ways; one is through the self-proclaimed aims of the museum. The rhetoric of museum literature has recently been invested with greater significance, because its apparently commonplace truths and assumptions no longer stand unchallenged. In the late nineteenth and early twentieth centuries, when thousands of cornerstones were laid throughout this country for libraries, art museums, historical societies, zoos, and museums of science, the messages at dedications were self-confident and impassioned restatements of a semiofficial vision of culture. And this was a dream of the redeeming power of art, science, and education as a way to transcend the gross inequities of daily life. The goals sought were idealistic and unembarrased in their emotional intensity. Opening the Museum of Fine Arts in Boston in July 1876, Mayor Cobb spoke for the managers. Here, he predicted, "will be a favorite resort of the cultured few who find a supreme delight in the finer creations of art; and, what is more important, all classes of people will derive benefit and pleasure from barely looking upon objects that appeal to the sense of the beautiful. Even the least favored and least cultivated persons cannot fail to derive some refining and elevating influences from the sight of beautiful things." The museum, like the public library, would be "the crown of our educational system." Here, declared Dr. Samuel Eliot on the same occasion, "are forms which have proved their power for hundreds, some of them for thousands of years; here are truths expressed . . . which have proved capable of moulding the minds and purposes of generation after generation." The exhibitions, the lectures and educational programs, all reflected social policy. Officials could assert publicly their wish to instill awe, reverence, respect, affection, commitment, and decorum, and it was understood that these were necessary and useful attributes that could be harnessed to the larger goals of the entire community.

But when social goals and social structure themselves become charged with controversy, no institution has the luxury of making its didactic intentions known without facing possible challenge. Museums, like libraries and universities, have had to adapt to changing circumstance. The rhetoric of uplift has been shifted to language more suitable to the new hedonism. The museum-goer is now given the right to find personal fulfillment through the diverse set of objects on display. And he or she can find a group heritage documented in them. In ministering to a new search for social identity, the museum can manipulate its justifying rhetoric.

Moreover, special interests can create their own museums to represent their point of view. Ethnic, religious, geographical, minority, and occupational groups have, in fact, treated museum-founding as a means of asserting their special claims.

But the larger, publicly subsidized museums, meant to serve the whole community, have special dilemmas. When fundamental collective values fragment, and truisms are challenged, then these museums can be seen as serving special interest groups. The earlier neutrality is presented as a subterfuge, and exhibitions are subjected to searching examinations for social, cultural, political, or sexual commitments. Museum purchases or accessions can now be charged with controversy. Reflecting the self-consciousness of groups within the community, museum boards and governing bodies must be balanced to mirror the diversity of this larger constituency. This has happened to most other social institutions; the museum is now included because its pose of neutrality has been challenged. The assumption behind these challenges is that museums emit particular and even peculiar visions of history, art, and science; their catalogues, shows, and great purchases are praised or objected to as instruments of cultural advocacy. Museums then have become victims of more searching questions about the relationship between power and culture. With hierarchies discredited and values disputed, any institution that bestows status upon whole classes of artifacts can be controversial.

Museum founders of an earlier era tended to see the museum's educational functions in a prfoundly conservative way; the shapes of the buildings, the arrangement of permanent exhibitions, the messages, murals, or mottoes adorning the walls were all ways of transmitting attitudes about the achievements of Western civilization. That anyone could object to these achievements would have seemed astonishing seventy-five or a hundred years ago. And so would the counterargument that museums should attempt to challenge or even subvert existing truths and support—through visions of art, history, or science—radical conceptions of human nature or social organization.

There was a reason for the failure to acknowledge these aspects of the museum's role, for they presented special problems. The museum had goals in common with a broad range of other educational institutions—schools, libraries, and universities, among them—but those were, in a sense, far less authoritarian. In a library users could select which books to read and check out. Even where prudery or conservatism controlled acquisition policies, the ultimate choice was the reader's. In colleges and universities discussion and debate were increasingly part of the teaching method. Individual instructors could well be classroom tyrants, but there were many opportunities to challenge the lecturer's logic or the accuracy of his evidence.

But how, in fact, did one argue with an exhibition? The curator's selection was final; so was the choice of exhibition themes. It was difficult to talk back to the objects on display or to argue about items not included. Critics and reviewers could suggest alternatives, but the ordinary museum-goer was hostage, in a sense, to the taste, standards, and goals of the specialists organizing the display. This appearance of finality was fine as long as the museum's authority was unquestioned and its values identified with a larger community interest. But when exclusions began to be noted, values challenged, and authority questioned, the apparent neutrality of the museum became less convincing. In the postwar years of the fifties and sixties, as women and minorities scrutinized their disabilities, as colloquial and popular art forms grew in popularity, and postatomic views of science and technology became modified, dissent could be heard more loudly. Older policies of inclusion and exclusion suggested that museums had already been taking an advocate's position and that official ideologies represented only a partial interest. It did not seem inappropriate to demand that museums pay closer attention to arguments, categories, artists, and cultural types previously neglected. This demand simultaneously swamped universities, asked to provide new curricular approaches, but those institutions at least had some tradition of pedagogic controversy. Along with all this came a more radical institutional historiography. Historians, in the sixties and seventies, began to reexamine the motives and policies of cultural institutionalists and to reevaluate cultural events like world fairs. Chicago's Columbian Exposition of 1893 and the St. Louis Fair of 1904, famous for their elaborate assemblies of beaux arts buildings, their anthropological collections, and scholarly congresses, were now presented as ethnocentric exercises in cultural propaganda, underwriting a special kind of racism. There was an earlier tradition of attack upon fairs as conservative bastions—one need only recall Louis Sullivan's famous comments on the 1893 Exposition—but what was new was the larger political and cultural bias being suggested by the critics.

This revisionist movement, bent on exposing the museum as the socializing instrument of special interests, was accompanied by public awareness that the form of any presentation, the logic of its display and image selection, could reiterate its message. The sources for this new awareness were multiple and recent. Newspaper reading, attendance at debates, and the study of literary texts had accustomed the public to verbal technique as an instrument of persuasion, but the history of visual and dramatic art were more eccentric parts of the school curriculum before the 1950s. The new mass culture spawned by the communications revolution remained a relatively unexplored area for teaching and investigation. But all that soon changed. In the fifties and sixties, a series of exposés of American advertising techniques, ranging from Vance Packard's *Hidden Persuaders* to Marshall McLuhan's *Mechanical Bride*, began to explore the strategies used to excite the imagination and stimulate the purchasing power of American consumers. The phrase "Madison Avenue" became synonymous with this continuing war for sales power. Suspicion of rhetorical technique and the inflated claims of manufacturers and distributors was not new to American life. Consumer protests and hostility to governmental or industrial propaganda had a long history and were particularly active in the 1920s, partly as a reaction to the excesses of World War I messages. What was new was the precision evident in the analysis of visual techniques and their psychological overtones. This muckraking literature appealed in part because it dissected the advertiser's use of images so skillfully; the colors, models, situations, and story lines were all decoded with unexpected and sometimes rather amusing results. Reexamining ads for hidden Freudian twists, attempting to examine their "subliminal messages" became a popular parlor game.

The growth of movies had contributed to the interest in visual decoding, but in the fifties and sixties the explosion of television-viewing was an even more emphatic influence. Television combined the frequent commercial messages of radio with the visual appeal of film, and by 1952 its invasion of the political process was becoming a major theme in journalistic commentary. How presidents smiled, dressed, gestured, and moved, first in black and white and then in color, became a subject of political analysis. From Nixon's Checkers speech to the Army-McCarthy hearings, Americans became aware of the visual methods by which politicians could manipulate the sentiments of the electorate. By the sixties it was commonplace to acknowledge, in McLuhan's phrase, that "the medium was the message"; sustained cultural criticism of the electronic mass media helped create an environment receptive to a new kind of exhibition criticism. Even if museums had done nothing after the war to change their exhibition policies, even if there had been no major new museums built or additional wings constructed, some public response would have occurred.

But as things stood, the responses multiplied. Curators and museum planners were as much influenced as anyone by the new opportunities media offered, and they responded to public interest in contemporary modes like photography, videotapes, and multimedia performances. Moreover, within the space of twenty-five years, hundreds of millions of dollars were spent on splendid new museum buildings. No longer conservative affirmations of traditional architectural values, museum buildings were hotly debated as bold or ugly or incomprehensible or dazzling in their modernness.

The most famous—or notorious—instance of controversial design was, of course, Frank Lloyd Wright's Guggenheim Museum. There the external design was so untraditional and the internal organization so unusual that critics quickly began to speculate on how the environment and the art would interact. But the Guggenheim was simply an early version of a new museum modernism that spread quickly throughout the country. While American museums had once sought to project images of stability and respectability through their architecture, during the postwar years many museums allied themselves with dynamic, contemporary trends, and even with gestures of revolt. It was inevitable that this realignment could be read by some as advocacy of a whole series of positions.

The feeling that exhibition planning was advocacy and the choice of objects a form of indoctrination was aided by other phenomena of the 1950s. One was the cultural cold war, which made creative art a weapon in the struggle to justify the Western political system. American artists, novelists, poets, athletes, and architects were pressed into service to demonstrate the cultural advantages of capitalism. In the nineteenth century Americans had been content to let their material products speak for themselves. But they were no longer sufficient, and the museum stocked with American-owned or American-made objects became an instrument with international political overtones. One moment of cultural confrontation came at the Brussels World's Fair of 1958, when the two superpower pavilions—the American designed by Edward Stone—contended with one another. Here, critics argued, the form of presentation was part of the message. The lighter, more ironic touch of the American displays, the selective and relaxed salesmanship, the lack of emphasis on capital goods in favor of celebrities, services, and mass entertainments all contrasted with the crammed overkill of the Soviet exhibition, bursting with tractors and industrial hardware. Exhibition management was put not only in the hire of culture, but in the hire of patriotism itself.

The museum's increasingly vulnerable stance had still another source beyond the attenuation of consensual values and the new awareness of display as argument. This third source is both more difficult to describe and more fundamental than the other two. It has to do with the increasing popular interest in artifacts and objects, art or otherwise, as historical talismans and a corresponding concern with their preservation and conservation. What this meant in the end was a shift of museum constituencies, a broadening of interests and responsibilities.

During the nineteenth and early twentieth centuries, most of our museums saw their principal concern as the education and refinement of their visitors. It is difficult to overemphasize the stress they placed upon their pedagogical functions some hundred years ago and the benefits they promised for industrial production, scientific curiosity, and historical consciousness. In their earliest days museum planners envisaged close relationships with school systems, universities, libraries, and publication programs. This emphasis went back to the first American efforts to establish collections of rare and curious objects, some of which had commercial ends as well. Charles Willson Peale, the prolific painter, inventor, and man of letters, sought a steady source of income for himself and his large family in the series of museums he established, but profit was overshadowed by his wish to promote useful knowledge through the gathering of specimens, models, and objects. Groups like the American Philosophical Society, the American Antiquarian Society, and the Philadelphia Academy of Natural Sciences, along with local colleges, historical societies, and clubs of scientific or artistic amateurs busied themselves with creating cabinets of curiosities to further the advance of knowledge and enlighten the public.

In their early years, these American collections, the stock of our first museums, were heterogeneous in subject and quality, miscellaneous jumbles of the valuable and the valueless, the genuine and the sham. Biblical relics, historical documents, vaguely but ambitiously attributed oil paintings, strange weapons, and fossils mingled with stuffed animals, Indian portraits, anatomical rarities, and sculpture casts. Captain Marryat, a visitor to Jacksonian America whose caustic comments have enlivened the pages of many subsequent histories, argued that American museums had collections "as would be made by schoolboys. . . . Side by side with the most interesting and valuable specimens, such as the fossil mammoth . . . you have the greatest puerilities and absurdities in the world."

Such jumbles may indeed have resisted quality control and made the visitor's task more complicated. But they did have the great advantage of encouraging American museums to emphasize pedagogy rather than masterpieces. Claims were made for objects of rarity and reputation, but they were so often exaggerated that they were easily dismissed. The museum existed through the 1870s or 1880s as a set of experiences designed to instruct or amuse, casual, haphazard, and often arbitrary. During the great era of institution-founding, from 1870 to World War I, new standards of rigor and comprehensiveness were applied to collecting, and more dignified, consistently serious postures toward culture were adopted, but the educational legacy remained attractive in an era of increasing immigration and industrial conflict.

This was, moreover, a culture dominated by words and print. During the American museum's formative years the primary method of transmitting information was verbal; although oral instruction remained important, the printed word was central. The museum's objects were read about before or after the visit. As in foreign travel, the preparations for the encounter, the standards to validate and organize the experience, were frequently literary. Historical knowledge, principles of aesthetic criticism, and scientific investigation were transmitted through the pages of books, supported by reproduced illustrations and lantern slides. Characteristically, early museums amassed collections of slides, as well as graphs, charts, and other visual aids.

These aspects of museum operation were transformed in the twentieth century. While the educational emphasis continued, it was changed as the museum's exhibits became more and more expensive, particularly in art museums, and the process of authentication became more important as a certificate of entry into the collections. Professional skills grew specialized and expert in most curatorial areas, and collections were pruned of their more doubtful elements. Educational programs, which had once relied upon models or replicas to introduce visitors to themes and larger movements, were now reconstructed on the basis of originals. And, ironically, it was this transfer of interest to original artworks and authenticated historical relics that would make the museum a truly popular institution.

The metamorphosis of the museum from a group of educational warehouses into a set of artistic, historical, and scientific treasure chests coincided with a public obsession with collecting as the key to enriched experience and entry into a world of specialized knowledge. Most of us are familiar with the enormous growth of private collecting that has taken place in the last twenty years or so, encompassing everything from the high and decorative arts to bourbon bottles, beer cans, posters, and barbed wire. Journalists have turned out scores of articles on what has been labelled a nostalgia boom, although I think the interest is broader than that. Some of the more recent interest, no doubt, is economic, a function of severe inflation. Objects, limited on the basis of authenticity, appreciate faster than money, which can be reproduced by governments in apparently unlimited amounts. The enormous sums paid for artworks, autographs, books, and historic relics have added to their glamour in a society where monetary value plays so great a role in fixing comparative status.

The economics of collecting, however, are only part of the story. One must also take into account several generations of sophisticated consumers who, having been exposed to a vast array of mass-produced objects, are trained to differentiate among brands, models, and product lines and to gauge cost, age, and utility. With the largest stock of personal possessions a people has ever gathered—clothing, utensils, automobiles, furniture, books, appliances—Americans have become accustomed to using physical objects as devices to project historical time. Hollywood costume dramas played their part here; so did the world of advertising and industrial production. But it is the museum where objects and material culture have become most effective in establishing a sense of the past. Today, encounters with material culture have become primary rather than supplementary; the museum functions like the library, as the broker between the information seeker and the data.

The museum, moreover, as a repository of extraordinary collections, is culture-resistant in a special and appealing way. The electronic media can simulate and project almost total illusions of time and space, but this multiplication of experience only makes more valuable the nonduplicatable qualities that authentic remnants possess. It has been noted that in a world of duplicatable experience the museum possesses a monopoly of the inimitable. Commercialism may taint but not destroy this power. Replicas sold in museum shops no more detract from the drawing power of the original than do postcards from the special powers of great paintings or great buildings. Publicity can make objects clichéd and tiresome, but they more normally graft onto the inherent appeal new levels of fascination.

Thus, the absorption of our civilization with objects gives the museum, with its tested claims to authentic possessions, special power. But it also raises questions that relate to the larger issue of advocacy. The wide public interest seeks to shape or at least to influence museum policy and to define museum responsibilities. Because the modern museum has increasingly become an asylum for cultural remnants, it has been thrust into the hard problems of cultural conservation. Who owns the objects on display in museums or, more precisely, to whom do they belong? Should the museum return artifacts to the cultural groups whose inheritance they form? Should it concern itself with the continuing sale, destruction, or disappearance of objects? Should curators become involved in preservation and conservation programs, which may frequently involve complex community decisions in anything from pollution control and dam construction to downtown redevelopment and diplomatic immunity? And should the museum be willing to host exhibitions that take stands on any of these subjects? These questions rest on the growth of object consciousness and an increasing sense of responsibility for the survival of the physical world. The museum has become embroiled precisely because of its newfound persuasiveness. Its broad range of clients make it the focus for a series of struggles. Some of its objects are inherently valuable; others rare as the work of unique masters or as part of historic events; and still others, newly important because they represent whole classes of things that have disappeared, important because typical. Who speaks for these endangered cultures and their disappearing symbols? Increasingly, voluntary associations organized around the goals of preservation and conservation do so, and they turn to museums as an appropriate shelter and home. Nineteenth-century museums were frequently indifferent to problems of conservation; it is rare to find them tied to campaigns or programs aiming to preserve man's cultural heritage for future generations. Cornerstone-laying rhetoric, so quick to seize upon the apparently neutral terrain of national enlightenment, left such matters alone. This is not because people didn't think objects would be safer inside the museum than outside—although nineteenth-century museum fires may have discouraged this notion also. It was rather, I suspect, because they were less concerned about disappearance as such. In the late nineteenth century some of this may have been a function of vulgar Darwinism, an assumption that survival resulted from natural processes best left undisturbed. Evolution was painful, and even the most obvious victims of civilized progress—the animal kingdom—were slow to awaken sympathy. Humane societies, animal welfare leagues, and conservation groups were largely an invention of the late part of the century, but by its end public opinion was more convinced that it made for good policy and wise morality to be concerned about animal welfare and species survival. In this, zoos played a role, an early example of the close connections between larger public policy and museums as institutions.

The interest in objects and the built environment emerged more slowly. Nineteenth-century Americans were still largely absorbed by their sudden productive expansion. So many new categories of objects had been created that it was difficult to be concerned about the survival of individual examples, particularly if they were relatively recent. And during the era of museum-founding, policies of Americanizing immigrants were pursued at the expense of savoring and nurturing cultural distinctiveness. Only rare exceptions, like Jane Addams, developed museum ideals that stood out against this trend. Only after several generations had experienced the multiplication of commodities did they discover how vulnerable they were to destruction or disappearance, and how easy it was for whole classes of things to vanish completely. It was the common, ordinary, mundane objects of daily use that ran the greatest risk; they could literally be used up, having never been granted the privileged status that belonged to objects of greater expense. The modern, produced with such profusion, was also strangely delicate, its life span limited not only by consumership but by cheaper materials and modes of production. Our libraries have certainly come to learn this irony full well; seventeenth- and eighteenth-century printed materials remain in good states of preservation while the paper products of the nineteenth century begin a process of irretrievable decay.

Along with this growing realization of the vulnerability of the modern came a new interest in cultural multiplicity and a sense that it was biologically dangerous and culturally irresponsible to permit the extinction of any elements of our physical and social world. We have, paradoxically, become obsessed during the past few decades with saving as much as we possibly can of our animal and artifactual world, at just the moment when our productive power suggests the capacity to manufacture almost anything we want. This passion for material conservation is related to our interest in objects as representing moments in time. In this sense the museum has become a vital humanistic instrument, a device for reasserting human-oriented values and respect for natural processes even while we simultaneously pursue, through technologically sophisticated support systems, ways of constructing surrogates for human judgment and natural forces. Because museums affect us so deeply, because the display of objects triggers memories and satisfies tastes in ways achieved by no competing forum, it is inevitable that those caring deeply about policy toward history, culture, and environment should look to the museum for leadership and support. The museum is, after all, an institution that is centrally concerned with preserving, cataloging and exhibiting persuasive physical records. How can it avoid taking positions on anything that is related to the survival of this record? And, fortunately or unfortunately, almost everything is connected with such survival. To protect its sources, to indicate concern for the creative process, to nurture the capacity to preserve, the museum is potentially involved with a broad range of policy decisions finding expression in legislative, judicial, and administrative decisions.

The wonder is not that the contemporary museum faces controversial problems, but that the debates are not more frequent, and more bitter. One reason, perhaps, is that many realize the delicacy of the museum's position, given our variation of life-styles, our awareness of display bias, and the importance of the exhibition experience. We realize, as generations earlier did about universities, that it is dangerous to react too forcefully when decisions have been made or arguments voiced that we dislike, so long as equitable procedures have been followed. Nothing would cripple the operations of museums more devastatingly than a constantly nagging public or legislative opinion, predisposed, as in politics, to suspect and criticize the motives, the character, the skills, and the judgments of museum officials and museum boards.

Nonetheless, restraint will not operate universally or permanently. Museums must debate their relationship to controversial public issues which they may affect. And, in spite of the problems institutional analogies invariably possess, I would urge greater consideration of the evolution of universities, public and private, and their reasonably successful resolution of this problem. Museums, if they are to continue as major educational institutions, will have real impact on ways of viewing reality and therefore will have to intrude upon many levels of personal policy judgments. Like the university, the museum can and should advocate to protect its institutional self-interests. Like the university also, however, the museum must avoid confusing its privileged status with specific political judgments best made by individuals. How to separate professional from political issues, then, becomes the crucial and the maddening problem, and no formula will ever quite solve it.

Argument—about science, art, technology, and history—must remain a museum function. I do not believe it is always possible to separate fact and value judgment in presenting displays, or that it is appropriate to insist upon total neutrality. Exhibition is an authoritarian form; when conclusions can be separated from display materials, they should be. But to insist that a museum bar advocacy from its exhibitions would be like insisting that a university bar argument from its classrooms: unthinkable not simply because such a ban interferes with a statement of opinion, but because it inhibits thought and constrains experience. If the museum's educational functions are serious, its displays must be created seriously. And that means, among other things, permitting an interpretative frame and encouraging visitors to understand more clearly the character of display as argument.

I am, as I indicated at the start, a historian and am uneasy about offering policy advice to those so much more experienced. I conclude then simply by reiterating that current controversies indicate no degeneracy or devolution. They are signs, instead, that museums have become central forces in the shaping of opinion and are responsible to broader constituencies than ever before in American history. And that achievement deserves celebration as well as scrutiny.

5

Cultural Institutions

and American Modernization

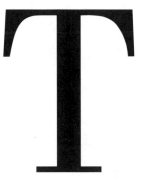hose familiar with recent American library history will recognize at once the names of John Colson, Phyllis Dain, Elaine Fain, Dee Garrison, and Michael Harris. Their books and essays have pushed forward a set of vigorous scholarly disagreements, particularly over the public library movement. Running through most of their contributions has been a call, voiced again and again, for American library historians to join (or rejoin) the main body of American historians, to apply their critical methods and share their major discussions. The urgency of this demand has grown so self-conscious as occasionally to seem self-defeating. But it has helped produce a new level of reintegration.

This change in emphasis, however, has not been accomplished without cost. And that cost involves an understanding of the complex relationship between the founding of our cultural institutions and the ongoing efforts to modernize national society. By bridging the historiographical gap with an ideological connection, the controversy gains strength but the subject is occasionally obscured. I am, I must admit, uncomfortable with the term *modernization*, par-

From the *Journal of Library History* 16, no. 1 (Winter 1981): 28–47. Reprinted with permission of the University of Texas Press.

ticularly when it is applied to modern American history. It has become something of a buzzword among social scientists, and when coupled with detailed historical models it inevitably begs some questions. But I know of no surrogate for this notion of a society developing rituals, values, skills, legal relationships, structures, expectations, life experiences, functional to fundamental economic and technological changes.[1] In America the modernized world would be dominated by the principles of industrial capitalism and mass democracy; accompanying the shift were inevitable rearrangements in work and leisure, family and class structures, savings and consumption patterns.

I believe that historical understanding of our cultural institutions involves making sense of their position within this broad movement. The status, rhetoric, and strategies of the founders and early administrators suggest their concern, from one standpoint or another, with this relationship. But before we can examine the connections, we must contend with a significant historiographical shift that has taken place among cultural historians within the last two decades, a more combative and critical stance toward our institutions, which has served as a bridge for the public library debate to enter the larger arena. This shift has sharpened our vision but also, in some cases, distorted our aim. Having abandoned one set of presentist dead ends, we may be constructing another. Let me specify my observations by moving through three different but related subjects. First, identifying and accounting for the massive historiographical change I have just referred to. Second, raising some questions about its conclusions and their relationship to modernization. And third, most briefly, reflecting upon the connection between history and contemporary policy debates.

Twenty-five years ago most histories of cultural institutions were self-confident and optimistic. Almost any institution that had managed to survive—zoo, hospital, library, museum, college, professional society—was admired, a tribute to sacrificing founders bent on combining the democratic genius with obvious needs for enlightenment, recreation, standardization, or reform. It was a credit, also, to patient clients and supporters who nurtured these institutions when they were young and vulnerable and saw them mature into strong and influential entities, capable of commissioning, or at least sustaining, a historical narrative.

These were, in the large, company histories. Their authors were not unaware of larger currents of argument or the multiplication of scholarly monographs. Indeed, they supplemented their observations with references to major figures like Beard, Turner, Parrington, Schlesinger, Fish, and others. Charles Beard's notion, for example, that social and cultural institutions were not automatic responses to challenge but rested on intent, analysis, and deliberation, all deserving scrutiny, helped stimulate historical investigation of subjects like the museum and the library, neglected because taken for granted.[2] Any number of institutional historians were sustained by the status of a new scientific history introduced from Europe through the seminar system, which had led to rigorous analysis of the evolution of American political instruments like the town meeting, universal suffrage, federalism, and party competition. Fond in their early days of employing "germ" metaphors to indicate their concern with institutional roots, these historians happily drew on the prestige and comprehensiveness of the Spencerian persuasion, that grafting of Darwinian theory to social analysis. These institutional narratives were as much influenced by the genial determinism of evolutionary history as was the better-known new political and economic history. Primary energy frequently went into cataloguing the predisposing factors encouraging the creation of an institution. Judgment was exercised by evaluating their comparative strength.

This is not to say that these historians presented no conflicts or tensions. Some cultural institutions were begun too late and perished because they were unequal to the occasion or to the problem. Others were born too early and had to await refunding or reformulation. There was occasional venality, mismanagement, and fanaticism. Useful changes could arouse bitter resistance, and there was always the presence of conservatives moving too slowly or radicals moving too fast. But in general there were few guiding questions to help shape what inevitably became a homogeneous, affirmative, and noncritical literature, concerned with demonstrating an almost teleological necessity for the emergence of particular institutions and supplying a wealth of detail that permitted some kind of chronological organization to emerge.

This, I repeat, was the condition of a broad range of institutional history in the fields of education and culture. If intellectual whiggism was inevitable, immense amounts of labor reconstructed long-buried traditions and helped preserve and organize invaluable records. While burdened with the tasks of simply creating coherent narratives, these historians often managed quite evocatively to summarize the eloquent calls to arms that initially activated so many of the organizations they described. And their texts still form the substantive basis of our current knowledge. What they did not do was supply any set of tests, questions, or arguments that could be extracted and applied to other areas or other institutions. Despite their sensitivity to ongoing historical generalizations, the books were institution-specific in all but the blandest ways. And, to some extent, they were out of touch with popular opinion and revisionist historiography at large, both of which raised questions about the motives, conduct, and impact of many of these same institutions.

Thus Thorstein Veblen, for example, had been able to turn upside down this benevolent and affirmative evolutionism into an ironic and uproarious set of juxtapositions; these colored popular consciousness, and even sophisticated historians who concentrated on other areas accepted Veblenian notions of conspicuous consumption and pecuniary emulation. But institutional historians tended to ignore such critiques when they examined single subjects or communities. They were sealed off from this critical tradition. Indeed, the Veblenian polemic did not really service serious intellectual investigation; if it supported anything, it nourished a vague, often unspecified set of grievances about the character of our high culture, making it out to be forbidding, irrelevant, vulgar, or self-interested. There seemed little connection between popular attitudes to libraries, universities, museums, and schools and the histories written about them, partly, perhaps, because the density of detail and repetition of argument gave institutional histories little to interest the lay public.

But then something happened. Beginning, perhaps, in the late 1950s, quickening in the 1960s, and multiplying still further in the 1970s, a set of speculations, investigations, and monographs transformed what I take to have been a somewhat sluggish field into one of the liveliest arenas of historical debate, so comprehensive and sharply etched that it affected both public conceptions and the work of scholars in other disciplines. Dozens of books and many times that number of articles spelled out, in these years, a set of critical and sometimes hostile questions about the beneficence, disinterestedness, and effectiveness of some of our most revered cultural institutions, applying in their examinations a range of new techniques and an international context. Listing these books and articles in their entirety or even in numbers suggesting their influence would be tedious; let me recount a few titles, however, to indicate their variety of subject matter: Daniel Calhoun, *Professional Lives in America* (1965); Roger Lane, *Policing the City* (1967); Michael Katz, *The Irony of Early School Reform* (1968); David Rothman, *The Discovery of the Asylum* (1971); Anthony Platt, *The Child-Savers* (1969); David F. Noble, *America by Design* (1977); Marvin Lazerson, *Origins of the Urban School* (1971); Stanley Schultz, *The Culture Factory*; Helen L. Horowitz, *Culture and the City* (1976); Jerold Auerbach, *Unequal Justice* (1976); Laurence R. Veysey, *The Emergence of the American University* (1965).[3] There are forthcoming monographs on the history of American hospitals, baseball and sports management, prisons, and other subjects, which promise to continue this critical tradition and to provoke renewed controversy and debate. And this, of course, is in addition to the heated discussions among library historians, and the biographical research that in some instances has contributed to the revisionist thrust. What happened to produce a historiographical movement with so broad a sweep, so many common concerns, and such powerful effects? There are a number of reasons that deserve exploration. Many of these fall within the profession itself, growing rapidly in number during these same years, fed on one end by expanding Ph.D. programs producing larger numbers of dissertations, and nourished on the other by growing college and university systems meant to provide ultimate employment for the new scholars.

But growth was merely one of the general conditions. There were others more specific. First of all came the appearance of classic texts, books that became exemplary and influential as a result of their cogency, persuasiveness, and obvious applications. One of these books appeared in 1960, during the early years of the larger historiographical movement; its contribution to revisionism is interesting given the attacks mounted by radical historians some years later. That was Bernard Bailyn's *Education in the Forming of American Society*, which helped make American educational history one of the shock fronts for radical speculation about institutional history, a model-bringer to many other areas of historical research. Bailyn's impact came about not only through his specific arguments about early American educational history or his exploration of the social functions of formal institutions. These were important. But it was his commentary upon the historiographical tradition he confronted that gave his book such special status, his concern with the depressing effects of historical plenitude.

Bailyn was, after all, evaluating a field rich with monographs and syntheses. But despite the scale of historical research, we had "almost no historical leverage on the problems of American education. The facts, or at least a great quantity of them, are there, but they lie inert; they form no significant pattern."[4] The reason for this, Bailyn argued, again in terms that had great meaning for institutional historians generally, was that the history of education had been written and taught by educationists, by missionaries whose scholarly activity constituted a demonstration of the theoretical and procedural centrality of their own institutions. Thus the schools were "self-contained entities whose development had followed an inner logic and an innate propulsion." The restriction of educational history to formal instruction, argued Bailyn, resulted from a conviction that "the past was simply the present writ small. It differed from the present in the magnitudes and arrangement of its elements, not in their character. The ingredients of past and present were the same. . . . They had no capacity for surprise." These creators of institutional history "lacked the belief, the historian's instinct, that the elements of their world might not have existed at all for others, might in fact have been inconceivable to them, and that the real task is to describe the dawning of ideas and the creation of forms—surprising, strange, and awkward then, however familiar they may have become since—in response to the changing demands of circumstance." Institutions represented solutions to problems, then, rather than predetermined or preordained symbols of progress. Their origins were not understood because scholars approached them with condescension. Seeking familiarity "in an unfamiliar past," these historians "had no choice but to accept crude facsimiles, deceptive cognates." This foreshortening produced a past differentiated from the present "mainly by its primitivism," the rudimentary character of the institutions and ideas whose ultimate development the writers were privileged to know so well."[5] Such condescension exaggerated the quaintness of the institutional ancestry, and sacrificed indispensable historical leverage.

I think Bailyn's remarks offer an exceptionally perceptive glimpse into the structure of the earlier historiography, into the relationship between the authors' assumptions and their modes of investigation. In the opening pages to his book Bailyn did far more than open up the question of public education or insist upon the need to integrate questions of family structure, denominationalism, economic activity, and land ownership with educational theory. He also provided a charter of liberation for historians who wished to escape the constraints professional loyalties had imposed upon institutional history. The peculiar combination of presentism and condescension that Bailyn diagnosed would survive in newer, more disguised forms; Bailyn's call for approaching earlier social history with respect for difference, complexity, and surprise was not invariably obeyed. But his suggestion that institutions be examined, not necessarily as revelations of cultural strength but also as demonstrations of social weakness, building upon the disintegration of traditional structures, would help color the working world of institutional historians for the next twenty years.

There were other classic texts besides Bailyn's, some of them produced in Europe by a group of French and British historians, who had broadened the subject matter of historical investigation to include activities and values that had never quite attained legitimacy in the United States, ranging from what would later be known as material culture to the study of alchemy, magic, witchcraft, and mental disease. In the pages of some of their journals, particularly *Annales* and *Past and Present*, the work of Braudel, Bloch, E. P. Thompson, and Brian Harrison, a set of traditions was being created that would feed later institutional work.[6]

Their texts, in fact, bring up a second source for this historiographical revolution, and that was the steadily easier communication, during these twenty years, between historians and their colleagues in the humanities and social sciences. Interdisciplinary fashions now pervaded university curricula and foundation grants and inevitably affected the character of historical research. Taste for other fields was catholic, and many of the trends had little to do with institutional history. But many of them did, particularly in anthropology, political science, and sociology. I need mention only the names of Simmel, Parsons, Lévi-Strauss, Lazarsfeld, Adorno, Mannheim, Foucault, Goffman, Durkheim, and Gramsci to give some sense of their scope and variety. Increasingly, historians were arming themselves with theoretical insights before constructing research projects and using them to help form a narrative strategy. While such influences produced many different outcomes, the heavy concern with mass society and collective behavior and the role of Marxist social science, so rich a source for European thinking, both proved eminently useful to historians of culture. With the assumption of a more critical view of the development of society and a conviction that institutions reflected, in some measure, both the level of economic organization and the division of power, a range of new questions was opened up. Individual institutions could be placed within a landscape acknowledging their particularity but assigning them specific functions. Ideal types provided a set of standards, a scale system by which to weigh the impact of everything from professional associations and learned societies to newspapers and museums. Although the social sciences were used more heavily for certain classic areas of economic and social history, it was inevitable that the integrated social view they encouraged should stimulate new thinking about the evolution of culture itself.

All this was aided by still another historiographical stimulus, the creation of sophisticated generalizations that reworked the periodization of American history and that drew upon the social sciences. Instead of relying upon once sacrosanct political subdivisions, historians like Richard Hofstadter and Robert Wiebe, George Mowry and Henry May, Gabriel Kolko and Samuel Hays provided new benchmarks to separate generations of people and generations of institutions.[7] The functions of status revolutions, efficiency ideals, bureaucratic management, and technological imperatives invaded histories of politics, judicial decision-making, industrial growth, and urban government, inviting once again new statements about the symbolic function and intended role of the cultural institutions.

To all of these historiographical influences—supplemented by the growing popularity of methods like prosopography—must be added new social and professional attitudes held by many American scholars coming to intellectual maturity during the 1960s and 1970s. Replacing an older set of satisfactions with the development of major cultural institutions, a sense of victories won and successes gained, were a long list of discontents, suspicions, and criticisms. These focused on the unequal distribution of power within American life, the continued exploitation of minorities, the power of sexual discrimination, the military adventurism of American governments, the enormous power of advertising and corporate influence, and the cooptation, by those with economic and political power, of cultural institutions that had once appeared to be independent or at least neutral. Indeed many protesting intellectuals in the sixties and seventies took it as their mission to demystify relationships between power and culture so as to indicate the overwhelming strength of the establishment and its capacity to shape any set of values or institutions. Classic figures in American political or social reform from Horace Mann and John Dewey to Jane Addams and Walter Lippmann were redefined and reclassified as futile or paradoxical gestures in the face of a larger movement of economic rationalization. Modernity was seen as a set of repressions, exerted through the same instruments of culture that had once been portrayed as liberating or enlightening. Social control was the goal of the powerful, fear of disorder or revolution their anxiety, and civilization but another name for their obsession with order. The free market, mobility, individualism, and equality were basically rhetorical strategies, for they contained contradictory tendencies that could never be simultaneously achieved.[8]

This bundle of dissatisfactions, which built upon undeniable frustrations and realistic fears, was as influential upon historians as earlier consensual satisfactions had been. Obviously it did not affect all who wrote institutional history, nor all professionals who traced the evolution of their specialties. But it posed a set of dynamic questions for institutional historians. Instead of a success story, one could now develop tragic failure, institutions exploiting and even worsening the plight of those whom they claimed to serve and benefit. Created by privilege, cultural institutions serviced the needs of privilege. There did not need to be villains or evildoers in this process, cardboard caricatures who had for so long dominated late nineteenth-century political history. That was the beauty of the new arguments. For there was self-delusion as well as purposiveness involved, not only on the part of founders and donors but also of professionals and administrators. Teachers, principals, doctors, lawyers, hospital administrators, university professors, settlement house workers, guidance counselors, librarians may indeed have believed in the social utility of their labor, the neutrality or beneficence of their professional standards, or the value of their social prejudices. But in fact such individual commitments were not the crucial aspects of the larger institutional effects. Whether or not their planners and governors realized it, such institutions expressed, through their rituals of use, their appearance, their patterns of consumption, their presentation of values and information, the driving needs of an economic system that required the maintenance of unequal power distributions, passively satisfied labor forces, punctual, obedient, industrious workers and ambitious, hungry, manipulable consumers.[9] The logic of cultural institutions—those concerned with instruction, certification, indoctrination, and entertainment—was conservative and designed to strengthen the system as it was already structured.

The monographs and syntheses concerned with a revisionist interpretation of these institutions ranged far back in American history, some of them confronting the colonial period, others examining the Age of Jackson and the purported radical democracy of free school and asylum reformers like Dorothea Dix and Horace Mann. But the period enjoying most attention was the late nineteenth and early twentieth centuries, when wealth, need, urban growth, and immigration combined to create the system of cultural institutions that still survives in the form of public school systems, universities, libraries, museums, and professional and learned associations. It was a period of special ingenuity and creativity so far as the shaping and direction of cultural institutions are concerned, but also one of extraordinary instability and social unrest. Thus the very institutional creativity could be explained in terms of the special challenges conservatives faced, the intensity of their anxieties being related to the increasing pace of foreign immigration, violent strikes, the spectre of international socialism, and a new political radicalism. Many of these institutions had to invent the very diseases they were meant to treat, because without a sense of social defects they could hardly be justified. So juvenile delinquency became popular as a device for justifying the institutionalization of potentially dangerous youngsters from unstable or broken families. And mental disease was specified and redefined in an effort to remove other sources of social instability.

Institutions with overtly compulsory aims—schools, hospitals, prisons, asylums—do not exhaust the larger category. What of those in which attendance was more voluntary, or whose certification was a response to individual ambition or mobility? Zoos, libraries, museums, universities, professional societies, all multiplied rapidly during the Progressive Era.[10] Here some of the new history has been particularly valuable in categorizing the variant forms that emerged and tying them to specific social needs: coping with the vast increase of information and of records, with the requirements of expert training, particularly in the sciences, with the development of professionally specialized subcultures, and providing avenues of instruction, amusement, diversion, or inspiration for an increasingly urbanized industrial population.[11]

It is here that we come to the question that interests me most, and for which, I add, I have no easy answer. How instrumental were these new cultural institutions in meeting the social needs of a modernizing society, in lubricating the economic and political engines of progress? The assumption, unspoken in many cases, of some contemporary cultural historians is that, in fact, these institutions were supported by monied or politically powerful elites because they would contribute to the security and efficiency of the community as a whole. One historian of the library movement concludes that public library support was "one of the movements of urban reform designed to cope with the problems of industrialized society. Seeking orderly cohesion, library leadership was essentially conservative in purpose and sought to impose the cultural and social norms of the upper class." But were the cultural and social norms of this class appropriate to American modernization or not? For Dee Garrison goes on to say that the result of this movement was an estrangement between the public library and the working-class community, a divorce between library ideology and reality, an emphasis upon critical functions and irrelevant if traditional values. "Like other custodians of culture in this era," she concludes, "the librarian tended to resist, rather than to facilitate, the coming of modern values." [12] With this last statement I agree. Many of the custodians of culture, although not all, did resist modern values. But what, in fact, are such values? The only indication given in this context is that modern values have something to do with democratic reality.

But if we include modernization in the category of the modern, we must also examine, among other things, first, the increasing specialization of social and economic functions, the new professionalism with its lengthened training periods and modes of certification; second, the greater emphasis, in production, advertising, and marketing, upon mass consumption and the creation of hungry and manipulable consumers; third, a secularizing insistence upon rationality and bureaucratic efficiency rather than sentiment or religion as the source for social reform and the basis for human relationships; fourth, a bias toward national integration, economic, social, and cultural, and an increasing reliance upon planning; and finally, an ever larger role for government as arbiter, standard-setter, rate-fixer, regulator, and taxer. Occupational specialization, consumer orientation, efficiency-based values, national integration, and governmental supervision: these were all aspects of the modernizing process, well under way by the early twentieth century.

And this, I believe, introduces a new complexity. For these objectives were not necessarily inherently democratic, nor, on the other hand, were they associated with the upper-class elites, resistant to majoritarian democracy. If libraries, museums, or universities questioned or resisted some of these trends, they were not necessarily seeking to redress the distribution of power. They or their organizers were rather engaged in a struggle to govern the course of this modernization and the organizational logic of the modern world. We are less aware of this fact than we should be, because many of the new institutional studies do not clearly reconstruct the old alternatives, or suggest the kinds of choices institutions represented. Goals and motives were highly mixed, and subservience to political establishment was not the invariable result.

One of the cultural revisionists has, rather eloquently, reminded us how easily misinterpretation can develop. Anthony Platt, introducing a second edition of his book, *The Child Savers: The Invention of Delinquency*, eight years after its initial publication, confessed that he had failed to relate the movement to other institutions of the new welfare state or to explain the timing of its appearance, its sources of support, or the nature of the opposition. "Criticism," Platt concluded, in self-reproach, "no matter how well documented and substantiated, is an insufficient basis for action unless it is grounded in an overall conceptual framework and a thorough understanding of history."[13] By criticizing reformers who created the juvenile court system, his book seemed to imply that they alone were responsible for its unpleasant consequences and that more enlightened people could have constructed a better system. Drawing such an inference, Platt insisted, was improper, for it ignored the actual alternatives of the day.

It is this recovery of alternatives, of both the symbolic and practical implications of institution-founding, that will constitute its real integration with the larger field. The evocation of complexity and surprise, ambition and anxiety, which Bailyn described, seems called for. From my own work I believe that many cultural institutions were formed to reshape aspects of modernization, in the name of traditional values. But these values often sat uncomfortably with the new lords of business and commerce, the political power brokers, and the new professionals and efficiency experts. Just as we have rediscovered the power of the domestic sphere as an alternative as well as a helpmeet to worldliness, so the nature of culture as a value system in itself must help shape the new institutional history. Here the names of Carlyle, Ruskin, Morris, and Arnold are vitally important as spokesmen for an ideology that was, in part, antiindustrial and antimodernist.[14] This ideology contained, to be sure, particularly in its English manifestation, elements of what is now labeled elitism, and greeted democracy skeptically.

But in important ways this antidemocratic sentiment was diverted, in America, toward a concern with personal fulfillment and individualistic moral and aesthetic standards. We are just beginning to understand, for example, the powerful dimensions of that large and multifaceted artistic movement that paralleled the official American Renaissance of McKim, Mead, and White and Daniel Burnham and has been labeled the Arts and Crafts Movement. Here, for several decades, a search for personal expression and a revulsion against aspects of the new industrialization combined to produce widespread activity in the creation and consumption of furniture, glass, pottery, printing, weaving, and bookbinding, activities representing a defection from the mass-production trends of the new factories, department stores, and mail-order houses.[15] In various cities like Chicago, Detroit, and Boston, members of the movement were involved in the policy-making of the new libraries and museums. We know, moreover, that some businesspeople were openly hostile to the goals of collegiate liberal education. The insistence upon common instruction in art, history, philosophy, literature, and science as sources of personal integration, critical thought, and social harmony was opposed by advocates of vocational-ism. It is true that many apologists for liberal culture held conservative social goals. But they also argued that colleges and universities could strengthen val-ues resistant to efficiency-oriented modern trends. The paradox that lay at the heart of progressive educational methods—socialization to a competitive socio-economic order through immersion within a cooperative, comprehensive school society—affected many other cultural institutions as well.

And so did the knowledge that this might produce critical discontent with the arrangements of modern life. Both adaptation and resistance were mingled. Thus American museums were born, in part, from anxiety about the poverty of American design, the apparent inability to compete effectively with European makers of jewelry, silver, furniture, and textiles. Businesspeople were inter-ested in developing the taste of both artisan and customer, and comprehensive historical exhibitions of the applied arts could help. The museum was an aid to early industrial design training, and the museum movement can be seen as part of a modernizing impulse toward improving American productive efficiency.[16] But museums were also places to display masterpieces whose transcendent aes-thetic standards suggested something else, a world where economic competition did not set values, and where the experience of the art encounter substituted, in its own fashion, for an earlier generation's religious passion. The culture of the museum, like the culture of the church, contained both sources of accom-modation and sources of resistance to dominant social modes and values (see chap. 3, above). Thus Josiah Royce (a central figure in R. Jackson Wilson's *In Quest of Community*), an opponent, like J. Mark Baldwin and G. Stanley Hall, of regimentation, standardization, and modern rootlessness, sought in provin-cial museums, regional folklore, and the city beautiful a revival of local loyal-ties to limit the ongoing social disintegration.[17] Along with the museum, the university, the learned society, and the library combined in volatile quantities the modern era's capacity to gather, organize, and manipulate experience in the interest of modernity, and the same era's infatuation with the simpler verities of an earlier day.

Such division of loyalties may account for the arresting combinations of internal efficiency and external archaicism characteristic of the richer institutions. The newborn universities' dedicated researchers worked in laboratories modeled on medieval chapter houses, or in quadrangles that sought the instant appeal of antiquity. The libraries' efficient stack and delivery systems stood alongside muraled reading rooms or cloister courts, whose paint and marble instilled a sense of ages past to the visitor. The templelike museums developed new labeling and display methodologies. It was not always clear whether such institutions were to be engines of culture, as one historian described the museum, or temples of culture, generators or asylums.[18]

Henry James, describing his return visit to America in 1904, caught this sense of institutional strain as he toured the Boston Public Library in Copley Square. Noting the hostility of social democrats to the survival of penetralia, so necessary, in James's view, for study and meditation, he was caught by the splendor of the library building, the main staircase with its "amplitude of wing and its splendour of tawny marble, a high and luxurious beauty," bribing the visitor to enter a courtyard and inner arcade that, "when the afternoon light sadly slants," seemed like "one of the myriad gold-coloured courts of the Vatican."

This was all fine, but James was also caught by the Boston concern with amusing children on rainy afternoons in this great palace, "so many little heads bent over their story-books that the edifice took on at moments the appearance . . . of a lively distributing-house of the new fiction for the young." James found the notes of cloistered reserve and busy service to be bewildering. Could one, he asked theoretically, "snatching the bread-and molasses from their lips, cruelly deprive the young of rights in which they have been installed with a majesty nowhere else approaching that of their American installation?" Labeling such a question abysmal, he fled from the library straight to the Museum of Fine Arts, where he found only temporary consolation.[19]

What we can see then, in the foundation of our cultural institutions, are divided loyalties concerning the character of national modernization. Were our libraries, museums, and universities, or our theater companies, motion pictures, and paintings, to stand for anything in particular, to provide standards of reference to measure the character of progress or to raise questions about the values of punctuality, hard work, and consumer salvation? Or were they primarily instrumental in character, designed to respond to socioeconomic needs rather than to question them, to speed the socialization of the dispossessed, to aid the efficiency of production and consumption sought by major interests? This choice of strategy, which I have reduced, I fear, almost to the level of caricature, affected almost every level of institutional operation, from physical location and architectural style to ease of access, budgetary emphasis, and relationship to public authority. The choices cut in many directions. Service orientation might aid the mobility and self-education of ambitious immigrants, eager to participate in the larger culture; or it might simply satisfy the light reading needs of overworked clerks. Physical grandeur might inspire; or then again it might intimidate. Those institutions seeking simultaneously to be everything to everybody might find their resources dangerously overstrained. Institutions rarely contained representatives of only one point of view and rarely maintained any single policy with total consistency over long periods of time. As we learn more from minute books, trustee meetings, newspaper accounts, dedicatory rhetoric, and abandoned plans, we will find more discrepancy, confusion, and uncertainty than some historians might have us believe. Coexisting within these institutions were unstable mixtures of preservation and popularization, dogmatism and tolerance, opposition to and acquiescence in mass taste. From an early date there is a surprising blending of high and popular culture in unlikely places such as Carnegie Hall, the Chicago Art Institute, and the Library of Congress. Whether the popular was acknowledged out of respect for its integrity or from a desire to reshape it is not always clear. But these institutions adopted a stance toward modernity that was both more skeptical and more probing than easy wisdom would suggest.

Before we can be sure of any conclusions we must know more about the history of libraries, museums, and universities as cultural institutions. I offer this summary as only one organizing device. But I offer it also because as a user of these institutions, particularly the library, I am not always encouraged by new statements of purpose. Increasingly, the road of total accommodation seems to be the preferred strategy, accommodation, that is, to directly utilitarian ends. Since our cultural institutions depend upon public subsidy, popular opinion must be a significant force in shaping policy. But not the only force. American popular opinion is itself affected by many factors, including the impact of political, institutional, and corporate advertising; it is not always either consistent or continuous. Private resources, endowments, self-perpetuating boards were once hedges against sudden shifts of opinion. They were often, admittedly, used to support unenlightened, narrow, and patronizing policies. But not always. The increasing insistence that institutions be cost-effective shifts the balance.

The older dream of bibliophilic grandeur is now passing from the scene. It was both a dream and a nightmare, as Jorge Luis Borges reminds us in his ironic, chilling, and mysterious tale "The Library of Babel." "Man, the imperfect librarian, may be the work of chance or of malevolent demiurges; the universe [which others call the library], with its elegant endowment of shelves, of enigmatic volumes, of indefatigable ladders for the voyager, and of privies for the seated librarian, can only be the work of a god."[20] The image of the eternal stacks ebbs, replaced by intercommunicating data banks, whose network maintenance now dominates professional planning. Increasingly, inquires must be packaged in content-specific terms; scholarly browsing, without apparent purpose, will be more difficult.

The approach to knowledge was once meant to possess, in itself, existential meaning. The encounter with the book, like the encounter with art, was supposedly distinguishable from commercial or industrial transactions. The cultural center, the art complex, was presented as an alternative world. This separation of spheres, I repeat, can be defined as acknowledgment that modern existence requires fragmented, atomized life sectors, specially shaped by distinctive purposes. Or it can be seen as a statement of resistance to the logic of modern commercial and work values. In any event, I believe that our earlier institutions were poised between a commitment to and a suspicion of the coming of modernity. The tension was accepted, by some, as a source of strength. Our present posture, perhaps through technological or fiscal imperatives, is more accommodating.

I confess that the more thought I have given this problem, the less certain I have become of any conclusions. Contemporary libraries and museums are classification systems that reflect our modern capacity to dominate experience by indexing and subdividing it. We can command the art and the knowledge of civilizations distant in time and space, but our very appetite for information and our rage for order can reduce and even trivialize their character, by deracinating belief systems and responses to experience.

On one level, then, the library and the museum are supreme tributes to the modernizing spirit, the same spirit that has produced a human-dominated nature and specialized industrial societies governed by bureaucracies absorbed with the tasks of regulating and rationalizing the conduct of life.

But on another level, despite the fact that they are conceits, contrived assumptions of power, these institutions can be asylums of experience as well. They were once given semireligious powers of legitimation. In their expressive gestures, libraries, museums, and universities, archaic as they sometimes may have been, represented possible challenges to the new way of life. To understand more fully the nature of this symbolism we must, I believe, cast off formulas that make some ends seem more or less democratic or enfranchising. We must see the creation of these institutions as responses to a world grown surprising, bewildering, and disintegrating. In so doing, we can avoid a new Manicheanism, which threatens an exciting moment of historical research.

6

Great American Fairs and American Cities: The Role of Chicago's Columbian Exposition

This presentation is a description of the cultural meaning of world's fairs in the last hundred years, more particularly, the meaning they had ninety years ago, and the role of Chicago's Columbian Exposition. As a teacher and writer, I have found expositions an almost inexhaustible source of information and example. They are such not only by reason of their detail, but also because they raise so many central questions. I would like to raise some of these now, to present not so much a chronology of American fairs, but an argument about their changing urban importance.

For various reasons this is a moment when world's fairs are being reexamined. For so many years ignored or relegated to library corners, fairs have recently spawned two schools of interpretation. One is a function of several trends, including what might be called urban sentimentalism. It began in the 1960s and 1970s as nostalgia and decorative exuberance began to permit new pleasure in traditional architecture; as historic preservationists began to defend environmental landmarks; as collectors enthused about previously despised

From *The 1992 World's Fair Forum Papers*, vol. 1 (Evanston: Center for Urban Affairs and Policy Research, Northwestern University, 1984). Reprinted with permission of the Center for Urban Affairs and Policy Research.

mementos; and as historians worked to treat material culture more seriously. Fairs assumed new importance. A society of world's fair collectors was organized; older histories and photographs were reprinted; new histories, the first in seventy years, began to appear. The general tone of this school was affectionate, elegiac, sentimental, evocative.

The fairs of the late nineteenth and early twentieth centuries represented a culture that seemed hopeful, energetic, optimistic. They were useful for a cause in distress. And that cause was a powerful and inspirational vision of city life. At bottom, as I hope to demonstrate, the great fairs of the late nineteenth century were testaments to the power of an urban dream, the first such dream to emerge in our country, for we still celebrated, rhetorically, the virtues of the countryside. The fairs suggested attachment to city living as an emblem of human progress and national greatness. In the 1960s and 1970s there was little to support this dream, given the gloom of so many predictions about the urban future.

Louisiana Purchase Exposition, St. Louis, 1904

The second school, more recent, more quiet, is really just emerging, but deserves attention all the same. It is primarily the work of professional historians but historians hostile to the pieties and power establishments of our past. And it is part of the fruit of a more aggressive historical revisionism bred in the 1960s, when dissenting and minority voices began to demand a share in reexamining our past. This group has treated the fairs as revelations not of the idealism of American society, but of its unequal distribution of economic power, its class organization, its subordination of women, its racism, and its materialism. The fairs' purposes were, in general, according to these analysts, mercenary and ideological, imposing on society a special image of the world. Expositions were not merely sideshows, the argument continues, they were weapons for the minds and hearts of Americans, and their ethnographic views, their sense of national superiority and racial genius, would have a powerful impact on the America of the twentieth century.

Since their very start, fairs have been mixtures of many things: They have simultaneously been a repository for high idealism, money-making, critical evaluation of the world, and message-sending. Their legacy has been just as ambiguous. They strengthened prejudices and liberated minds; they enriched individuals and benefited whole regions; they were moments of high culture and of crass advertising. As we discuss our own hopes for the Age of Discovery Exposition, and as we look at the complex and often magnificent settings the fairs created, we should not forget that we are dealing with an institution that has always been a medley of many interests, many motives, some noble and some not. If we are apt to be self-accusatory in these times and to feel humbled by the achievements of earlier days, it is useful to remember that these wonderful fairs also contained much that we would not be willing to tolerate today and, in my view, much that should not be tolerated today.

I will try first to introduce the history of the nineteenth-century fair, periodize it, and establish its fundamentally urban context. Next, I will specify some of the features that represented the late nineteenth-century urban ideal. And, finally, I will touch on some ambiguities of the legacy and what happened to American fairs in the middle of the twentieth century. Almost one hundred years ago the Columbian Exposition helped inaugurate a special phase of fair-making in this country which lasted for twenty-five years. It was succeeded by a different kind of institution in the 1920s and 1930s and we now face the possibility of returning the fair to its true urban roots. But more of all this shortly.

Fairs, as instruments of ecnomic exchange, as recreational or even religious festivals, as methods of disseminating information and values, go back far into human time. They were vital elements in the history of medieval Europe, but the modern international exposition, an elaborate, six-month display of art and industry in specially prepared buildings and grounds, attracting enormous crowds, was born in London's Crystal Palace Exposition of 1851, hosted in Joseph Paxton's famous greenhouse in Hyde Park. Nourished partly by the interest of Prince Albert, this fair mingled economic and ideological goals. It sought to demonstrate the superiority of European culture by emphasizing commercial competition as a replacement for military warfare and to stimulate, as well, the character of British industrial design.

The idea spread with incredible rapidity; two years later we held our first major fair in New York City. In 1853 an American Crystal Palace was erected on the site of what is now the New York Public Library on 42 Street. It was too far uptown to be truly successful, but in the next forty years cities all over the world began to construct giant buildings to display their wares; Paris, in 1867, 1878, and 1889; Vienna, in 1873; Dublin, in 1853 and 1865; Santiago, Chile, in 1875; Cape Town, Glasgow, Antwerp, Barcelona, Calcutta, Sydney, Melbourne, Brussels, and, of course, Philadelphia, in 1876.

These fairs, attracting millions of people, tended to be dominated by one or two immense buildings, filled with the manufactured and agricultural products of the world. Often, separate structures were devoted to art, horticulture, and the liberal arts, but through the 1880s, although the acreage was growing, particularly in Philadelphia, the one or two major structures and their contents counted most. This first phase was the Fair as Emporium, as Warehouse, as Market of the world's goods.

But it was not to last very long. A second phase, which Chicago helped usher in, was something more elaborate, tied to dreams of metropolitan expansion, and emphasizing not a single building but an ensemble, a grouping, a spectacular series of landscapes and structures. This was the Exposition as Heavenly City, a purified reflection of the actual character of the late nineteenth-century metropolis. The Columbian Exposition began a twenty-five-year history of such American extravaganzas. But it did not come to Chicago easily. In the 1880s, as American cities began to consider the four hundredth anniversary of the Columbian voyage, four in particular—New York, St. Louis, Washington, and Chicago—joined in a bitter competition. The prize was something more than financial profits, although increased tourism benefited realtors, hotel owners, retailers, and railroad managers. Rather, the prize was acknowledgment by the country at large—and the world—of the host city's importance. The closest analogy in our century may lie in the effort to host the Olympic Games. This dignity has involved a legitimizing function, for Tokyo, Mexico City, and Munich, in particular.

The competition among American cities for federal approval (and congressional appropriation) revealed how important they thought the Fair was to their several destinies. A lengthy and expensive lobbying war ensued. Cities reflected—unkindly for the most part—on one another's climates, transportation networks, hotel facilities, and patriotism. Chicago's comments on St. Louis and New York's reflections on Chicago were especially slanderous. But Chicago won out in large part because it managed to gain the support of Midwestern delegations in Congress, responsive to the issue of regional loyalty, resentful of the arrogance of New York, amused by the fragile pretensions of Washington, and suspicious about the capabilities of St. Louis. The Middle West was, in fact, eager to put its provincial capital on display for the world to see and admire—a Middle West which had begun to feed the world and was undergoing, simultaneously, a major industrial expansion.

In a country that still valued rural virtues, Chicago insisted on being an acceptable urban symbol of nationalism. "Chicago," wrote one of her novelists, "is the first of the great cities of the world to rise under purely modern conditions; what we see here is the product of democracy working in a new field . . . untrammeled by any precedent and frankly open to every new influence that

Chicago Day at the Columbian Exposition

stirs." In hosting the exposition, Chicago was making a claim for its greatness. And it was also, in a sense, speaking for the greatness of the city itself.

The relationship between fairs and cities was more than the simple urban quest for legitimacy, however. If we examine the appearance of this second phase of the world's fair, we find these heavenly cities exemplified the special character of their sponsoring communities. They did so on many levels. The first thing to be noted about the great new cities of the nineteenth century— from Berlin and Birmingham to Lyons and Chicago—was their immense concentration, the density of populations, services, and commodities they contained. This was just as true of the older cities that had experienced more recent growth—London, Paris, and New York.

Concentration had always been the essence of urban status, but its scale was now unprecedented. Western cities were, above all else, crowded. And the great fairs of this era, however expansively created, had this at their heart. They lived on crowds; they were busy, energetic, crammed with people, merchandise, and exotic experiences. Profusion was their hallmark. The photographs of the expositions in the books memorializing them emphasize the huge masses in attendance, particularly at dedications and on special days. Buildings and grounds were black with people. Chicago became the best attended of

A BUSY DAY ON
DEARBORN
AND RANDOLPH
STREETS
CHICAGO

the American expositions, indeed one of the largest the world had seen. Only Paris exceeded it. More than 20 million people visited Jackson Park in a six-month period. On certain days, half a million overflowed the park boundaries. The biggest day of all, Chicago Day, saw some 700,000 move through the gates, this at a time when the city itself contained little more than a million people.

Crowding was only one of the claims these cities made on contemporary attention. For these were not only the largest agglomerations in world history, they were newly dependent upon a broad range of systems: water supply, sewage treatment, electricity, steam, railroads, telephones, telegraphs, policing, fire-fighting, traffic control. To meet the extraordinary congestion, American and European cities had, by the 1890s, decades of ingenious invention and experiment behind them, and they were about to develop more. Rapid transit systems, bridges, and tunnels moved the populace through the logjam. Subways and elevated roads represented triumphs of engineering, and cities of the world competed in trying to lower death rates, improve their public health, and increase their physical attractiveness.

As miniature cities, the fairs of this period mirrored the larger concern: indeed, they attempted to perfect the ongoing experiments. The Columbian Exposition and others like it demonstrated that it was possible to take hundreds

Early twentieth-century traffic congestion at Dearborn and Randolph, Chicago

of acres and buildings and place them under effective control. Specially organized police and fire forces, new water and electrical systems, novel transport devices, all supported the visitor surges. There was an obsession with demonstrating the orderly management the expositions enforced on the perils of social congestion. These fairs were designed to be safe, clean, peaceful, and easy to move through.

With maps, uniformed guards, and ingenuity, the fairs did what cities were trying to do albeit more chaotically. Turnstiles were first used for world's fairs; so were new types of railroad stations and railroad cars, moving sidewalks, and a host of other innovations. The handling of these millions was a triumph of Victorian planning; like the cities, the fairs boasted of their achievement in their publicity literature. The amenities we now take for granted—comfort stations, drinking fountains, benches, varied refreshment stands, and restaurants—were, in their profusion and ease of access, a product of the new cities and their fairs.

The second aspect of the turn-of-century city translated by fairs was an unprecedented sense of contrast. Some of these contrasts the fairs sought to transcend rather than repeat. Urban growth, for example, stimulated enormous varieties of living style. Opportunities to display wealth multiplied. Great mansions, some on a European scale, now appeared. Wealthy urbanites developed spectacular methods of spending their fortunes, such as horse shows, costume balls, carnivals, and cotillions. Cities now contained boulevards for carriage drives and coach processions; house interiors were cluttered with the ornaments decorators provided.

But along with this elegance, there swelled simultaneously an underclass, living in crowded slums that seemed to deny all that republican virtue and democratic promise once symbolized. By century's end this complex of poverty, congestion, and disorder had invaded the national consciousness. It alternately repelled and excited well-to-do residents and urban visitors. Sharing the Victorian passion for exploration, they occasionally took guided tours of slum quarters, under the watchful eye of police. Much of the city was kept alien to respectable types in the late nineteenth century. It seemed too dirty, dangerous, or unprotected.

But the fair was different. These contrasts it avoided. All of it appeared open and accessible. Artists delighted in showing the fair with well-dressed, refined, obviously cultivated ladies and gentlemen strolling through its avenues, sitting in its gardens, admiring its monuments. Americans could wander with a permissiveness national police made possible in Old World cities, but not in the New. The exposition grounds were a giant promenade, and visitors could indulge the boulevardier habit. Here was the freedom of the city that properly belonged to cosmopolitanism, the artists suggested; here was the way the American city should look, at least to the middle classes.

But these were not the only urban contrasts of the 1890s. Fairs did better recalling the characteristic spatial contrasts; in contemporary cities, crowded downtown streets with newly tall buildings were juxtaposed against young park systems and squares with open spaces and greenery. These contrasted with the sprawling industrial and transportation areas, which included activities like slaughtering and printing. Such heavy land consumers challenged, in turn, neat, tree-lined sections of middle-class residences, well maintained and policed, which in turn contrasted with nearby commercial buildings, plastered with advertising signs or located by giant billboards selling corsets, liquor, hams, or free advice.

Henry Blake Fuller, the Chicago novelist, writing in the *Outlook* just a few years after the Fair, saw the city as a "jumble of incongruities and contradictions. It is at once smart and shabby, trim and slovenly. The permanent and the temporary stand face to face; the massive and the flimsy exist side by side; the grandiloquent future elbows the discredited past; the high and the low are met together in a union aggressively, vociferously, repellently picturesque."

As Fuller suggests, these sectors had an unhappy history of impinging upon one another's boundaries. Commerce and industry invaded previously quiet haunts. Their residents pocketed the high selling prices offered by retailers or wholesalers, abandoned their homes, and went off—farther north in both New York and Chicago—to found new, elite neighborhoods. With business invasion came new slums, taking over once fashionable housing and, by pressure of numbers and severe income constraints, reducing it to levels of dilapidation. The contrasts of the nineteenth-century city were not only dramatic in themselves; they were fluid, volatile, perpetually in motion, unpredictable.

Not so the Fair. The Fair was a city that worked. While it retained the appeal of urban contrasts, it attempted to freeze them into peaceful coexistence, seeking to control their energies as well as their picturesqueness. This was, if you will, both the great problem of the American city, and the Chicago Fair's accomplishment. It, and other fairs that followed, achieved this by three major devices.

First of all, they permitted and even emphasized a contrast between building exteriors and interiors. On the outside, the exposition palaces in Chicago, St. Louis, Buffalo, and elsewhere exemplified the harmonies of Renaissance and neoclassical architecture. Unlike the earlier buildings in Philadelphia and New York or London's Crystal Palace, they did not call attention to their structural materials. Rather they were decorous, serene, majestic, reposeful, untroubled, suggesting a secure order of things, tranquil, harmonious, permanent. But inside, the exposition palaces were all energy, profusion, and variety. The exteriors emphasized tradition, order and control; the inside, physical progress, activity, newness.

In another place I have argued that these fairs, in this dualism, did not differ so much from two other contemporary institutions—the museum and the department store. If one examines the palaces being built for urban consumption and urban culture, one finds the same ordered monumentality on the exterior and crowded, object-filled displays inside. There was so much to sell and so much to see, that crowding testified to Victorian ambition. Shopping arcades, another feature of the nineteenth-century city, presented the same contrasts. With all their sumptuous exteriors, the fair buildings were little more than huge sheds, filled with bazaars, pavilions, tents, booths, heaping on their shelves and cabinets the latest products of art, science, and industry. Some of the pavilions were organized by nations or states; others, by corporations which were like small empires themselves.

The contrast between the monumental exteriors and the more naked, cowded, structural interiors once seemed to some architects and architectural historians as evidence of dishonesty, or at least loss of confidence in the technical processes of production and engineering—a mask, a disguise, a false veneer reflecting on the false culture of the day. In fact, the fairs mirrored a set of existing conventions about appropriate urban appearance. In many areas— commerce, transportation, home design—formality and monumentality was shown to the outer world, while, within, a set of divergent and sometimes antagonistic activities took place.

The great commercial blocks, the stores, the hotels, the new palatial apartment houses, all of them containing hundreds of different and competing companies, or departments, or families, were built as single, unified structures, which to the casual observer might have seemed to be housing within one single family or one single firm. Palaces, after all, traditionally belong to a single family, and the Palazzo style reinforced an often misleading sense of unified control. This kind of contrast between outer and inner was not novel then. The fairs, in their exposition palaces, simply magnified, justified, legitimated it, dignifying the commercial pursuits that went on inside them.

Another version of urban contrast and variety was emphasized by a different aspect of the fair: its separation into specialized spaces. In their official presentation of self, these fairs—and Omaha, St. Louis, Buffalo, Atlanta, Nashville, Portland, Seattle, and Jamestown were no different from Chicago in this—employed formal vistas, grand axial boulevards, giant fountains with terraced approaches, statuary, colonnades, water terraces. These were the Sunday clothes of the exposition where monumental planning received its consumma-

Machinery Hall,
Columbian
Exposition

tion. This blending into overall ensembles suggested other ages and other places. In these grand spaces the most rapturous prose of visitors and journalists was poured out: another Greece, another Rome, another Paris. This is what we think of when the phrase Dream City or Ivory City or White City is brought up: squares, plazas, canals, often with gondolas floating upon them, bordered by the façades of giant neoclassical or neobaroque or neo-Renaissance palaces. Here was the visible center, the ordered heart, the source of control, and frequently the physical symbols of the fair.

But juxtaposed with this were other areas, in the case of the Columbian Exposition, at least two. One was Frederick Law Olmsted's Wooded Island, a carefully landscaped imitation of the natural environment—irregular, informal, secluded, picturesque, emphasizing privacy and quiet communion, intimacy, meditation, rather than the publicity of the formal vistas of the Exposition proper. Much to Olmsted's regret, the Wooded Island did house some Fair activities, most important the Ho-o-den, or Phoenix Villa put up by the government of Japan, and a teahouse. But if this represented some degree of control,

Manufactures Palace and the Ho-o-den, Columbian Exposition

at least it was different from the traditional formality of the exposition halls and the national and state buildings. This was a park, as many park-makers of Olmsted's generation perceived it, a relief, a contrast, an escape valve for urbanites to walk through meadows or thickets, to picnic, forgetful of the bustle that lay around them. One crucial aspect of large city parks, according to their most creative supporters, lay in this element of contrast, and they fought vigorously a series of monumental intrusions, like museums, memorials, and tombs, armories, and lecture halls, which threatened them. In the previous three decades American cities, all over the country, had been planning and developing park systems. This contrast evidenced the urban capacity for carefully staged variety to handle the needs and pleasures of a vast and concentrated population.

But there was a third need beyond the formal need for ordered beauty and the personal need for natural scenery. That was for amusement, participation in the trivial pleasures of mass entertainment. Every fair had its Pike or Pan or Trail or Midway, filled with fun palaces, rides, exotic villages, refreshment stands, dance halls, animal acts, strongmen, and beauty queens. Chicago's was the first to develop on such a scale, and the Midway gave the Fair something of its popularity and appeal. Little Egypt, Sandow, Borneo villagers, the Streets of Cairo, American Indians mingled together amidst the throngs that were themselves a part of the attraction. This was a way, as well, of handling exoticism and racial difference, of emphasizing the believed-in superiority of Western culture by showing so-called primitive peoples in an entertainment setting. The Grand Court was the formal public face of the city; the Wooded Island, the informal private face; and the Midway synthesized the two into the informal public face.

Gregariousness was at the heart of such areas. But it was not a gregariousness in search of learning or enlightenment; rather it took pleasure in pleasure itself, unashamedly pursuing the relaxed nonimproving attractions that eager entrepreneurs could gather. By this time every city of size had an amusement quarter, viewed either with tolerance or suspicion by city authorities. Such sectors existed on a spectrum, ranging from the semirespectable pleasures of theaters and new vaudeville houses downtown, through larger, more peripheral amusement parks, many of them outfitted with new electrical rides, down to the illicit red-light districts, with bars, brothels, and gambling dens. Indeed many of the attractions at the Midway in Chicago would reappear in Atlantic City or Coney Island. They would also find their way to St. Louis, Buffalo, Omaha, and other expositions.

In the actual city, the various areas that I have described were dynamic. They often intruded on each other, or on other quarters designed for housing or commerce; there was anxiety about the growth of pleasure quarters, or the threat to parks and neighborhoods, or the presence of advertising. But the fairs kept these areas separated and defined. As things of a moment, fairs could control the size and character of their various elements. They had opening and closing dates to insulate their existence. They were frozen environments, zoned, if you will, long before the concept had developed legal standing here. Their commitment to clear boundaries, their ability to maintain variety and coherence, was one feature serving to astonish visitors. They were cities that worked precisely because of this.

Finally, the fairs obeyed the urban laws of contrast through their presentation of culture, the vast range of art, music, scholarship, and performance that represented the acme of civilization in the Victorian world. In the late nineteenth century we see emerging, primarily in cities, the outlines of what has since been termed mass culture—spectator sports, pulp publishing, vaudeville, motion pictures, popular music. The fairs constructed a setting to reinforce prevailing notions of cultural hierarchy, but to include as much as possible of this variety. On one end of the spectrum were serious expressions of high culture—great libraries, museums, repertory companies, orchestras, opera houses. These were just beginning to attach themselves to the American city in the 1890s. Americans had no lengthy experience with them. So the fairs worked closely with these infant institutions, cooperating with them. The new Art Institute building in Chicago's downtown was built, in part, because the Columbian Exposition had a series of congresses there during the Fair. Historians, philosophers, critics, physical scientists, and educators met in a series of conclaves, the most spectacular of which was the World Parliament of Religions. St. Louis hosted an International Congress of Arts and Sciences in 1904. In the Chicago Fine Arts Palace (today the Museum of Science and Industry), paintings and statuary from throughout the world were put on display, as they were in Buffalo and Atlanta and St. Louis. This was before cheap travel had been opened to large numbers; for many, the displays were their first encounter with large assemblies of the fine arts.

The fairs also had festival halls for musical performances. In Chicago, one was designed to seat 4,000 spectators with room for 2,000 singers and 200 instrumentalists, capable of producing elaborate oratorio festivals performed by symphony orchestras and choral societies. There were recital halls for chamber music as well. Cities also had begun to feature permanent opera houses and musical academies. Older cities like New York and Philadelphia tended to stretch these facilities back to pre–Civil War days, but even they got new structures in the 1880s and 1890s, like the Metropolitan Opera House and Carnegie Hall, while the younger cities were just on the eve of establishing their own.

At the other end of the spectrum, the fairs were great centers for popular culture. Daily concerts of band music, performed by the leading bands of the world, played to crowds of ten thousand or more, not only marches and patriotic tunes but popular songs and theater music. The Columbian Exposition was the launching pad for the career of John Philip Sousa, who had just left the U.S. Marine Band. It also helped the early ambitions of Florenz Ziegfeld, who was sponsoring the great Sandow, the strongman; I have already mentioned the new amusement park entrepreneurs and their new rides and displays. Like the zones, popular culture and high culture were part of the controlled contrasts in the expositions; each was located in its own place, and neither threatened the other.

This brings up the final point about the fair environments: their commitment to comprehensiveness. By the 1890s the American city was a city of immigrants, its population spread across a variety of European, Asian, and African peoples. Ethnic food and native theaters were part of the new landscape; German beer gardens, Chinese restaurants, Yiddish and Italian theaters, artist bohemias modeled on the Parisian scenes described by DuMaurier, pushcart markets. The fairs exploited these new urban features, emphasizing

exotic variety on the midways. In Chicago, Frank Millet, a popular mural artist, organized a series of processions as part of his division of special events: Bedouins on horseback, Chinese with a dragon, Hindu jugglers, American Indians, Turks, Javanese, all met and performed in dances and tugs of war. This was also, as I've said, a way of coping with an exoticism that didn't seem to fit into the Anglo-American tradition, and many of the displays had a patronizing, even contemptuous air to them. But they were planned to catch this sense of urban variety.

There were also special days for states and cities when thousands of visitors, led by bands and distinguished citizens, would hold ceremonies and receptions in their state building. And then the new professional variety of the day was recognized as well. There was a Stenographers' Day, a Commercial Travelers' Day, and a Mechanical Engineers' Day. And there was pageantry involving the military detachments guarding exhibits; French marines, Italian, Spanish, and Russian sailors held their exercises as did West Point cadets and

French Colonies,
Columbian
Exposition

national guard detachments. The Fair was a continual parade of the sort that American cities had been experiencing for half a century—parades celebrating patriotic holidays, canal completions, foreign revolutions, local festivals, state visits, and presidential campaigns—but the Fair formalized these festivals, hinting at a new kind of pageantry which would develop in twentieth-century cities to aid Americanization and the schools.

Comprehensiveness had one last element that might deserve a speech all its own, and that was the subject of illusion. Traditionally, one of the city's features had been its capacity to disguise, to permit people to assume new identities, to exploit the anonymity of numbers by permitting men and women to shed unwanted appearances and seek the professional help of expert illusionists—showmen, actors and actresses, con men, advertisers. This was one reason why the city was feared by moralists and condemned by clergymen.

The fairs took the growing urban skill at illusion and extended it. All visitors knew they were walking on stage sets. The fairs were unreal, but then they were also part of the shifting panoramas making up the large city. They built upon interest in changing behavior and dress according to the environment. Cities had downtowns, parks, Coney Island, and home neighborhoods. The fairs brought these together and constructed imaginary landscapes recalling eras and cities long vanished. They were giant costume parties with large guest lists. As artists presented them—by moonlight, at sunset, illuminated by innumerable electric lights—the fairs projected this sense of time remembered.

Like the city, fairs were designed for a new sensibility, a product of this new era of transportation, communication, and mass production. And that sensibility was the tourist's. They were overwhelmingly sightseeing events and helped spawn or initiate souvenir industries which, once more, could barely be matched by anything that went before. Their hordes of products have since created a collector's paradise, and set the pattern for much that came afterward. Indeed the American picture postcard was essentially born at Chicago's Columbian Exposition, as were a host of other advertising novelties.

As comprehensive and responsive as they were, fairs in the era of the Heavenly City had serious limitations. I have barely touched upon their problems. They organized their territories according to strict middle-class categories. They largely excluded minorities from decision-making, and if they participated, it was frequently in highly selected or segregated areas. Serious exoticism was frequently relegated to the midways, food for amusement rather than edification. Problems of poverty, inequality, and urban housing were largely ignored.

But the dream cities did perform some major services and leave some major legacies. Let me review some of them as I conclude. First of all, these fairs helped create or improve the status of several municipal institutions, particularly museums of art and natural history and universities. Remaining buildings from the fairgrounds frequently became museums or administration buildings. The task of continuing education which the fairs broached was, thus, permanently assumed.

Second, by their encouragement of new park and transport systems, fairs contributed to the physical landscape. Jackson Park and the Midway were restored after the Fair closing; the sandy swamps existing before 1893 were transformed into a handsome, much-used public facility; the Illinois Central tracks, raised and expanded, served a growing population. In Forest Park, St. Louis, in Atlanta, Nashville, Seattle, and Omaha, similar facilities were improved.

Third, the fairs permitted cities to experiment; their innovations demonstrated how to handle large numbers of people safely and comfortably. They reflected back on existing methods of sanitation, policing, fire-fighting, electrical supply and other essential municipal services. Because of their remarkable safety record, they gave confidence to the great Victorian pioneers in public health whose work is just beginning to receive the recognition it deserves.

Finally, the fairs undoubtedly returned profits to certain entrepreneurs, aided local economies, and even encouraged further investment by individuals and corporations. Fairs served notice that their host communities were active and dynamic.

There are undoubtedly other specific legacies as well, but to these four I would like to add three others, more abstract, but perhaps more relevant to our present thinking. First of all, the fairs bequeathed a newly identified local leadership, committed to the growth of the community. The many needs—lobbying efforts, transport, new housing and hotels, sanitation, publicity, special festivals, money-raising—forced an orgy of civic activity in every fair city. Many participants—businessmen, professionals, academics, religious figures, artists, architects, union leaders—knew one another earlier. But not all of them. And not so well. Provision of a common task, a common goal, served as a municipal equivalent of war. It prompted in competing cities an esprit which is as difficult to recapture as it is to revive.

Second, fairs, beyond the leadership level, stimulated an onrush of local, even regional pride. As display arenas, they intended to reflect their surrounding communities, calling forth efforts from kindergartens and grammar schools to public stock subscriptions. Fairs were causes, opportunities to promote higher civic involvement, to develop loyalties. At times this civic boosterism could become shrill, arrogant, narrowly self-serving. But at other times boosterism generated support for public works improvements, tax assessments, administrative reorganizations, and voluntary aid societies, these functioning before the time when the federal government had acknowledged many of its social obligations. Most of our continuing urban systems—water, gas, electricity, streets, sidewalks, bridges, and viaducts—date from this remarkable era and their maintenance, expansion, and supervision were stimulated by the public awareness of their new role and interest in their operation. Fairs exemplified a risk-taking which permitted many ambitions to flourish.

Finally, this era of expositions testified to something I mentioned at the start: the power of the urban idea. At a time when so many American cities still seemed raw, unfinished, physically chaotic, fairs suggested an urbanity, a civility, an approach to human experience ideally associated with great cities.

It is no historical accident that the great city plans we associate with Daniel Burnham, Edward Bennett, and Arnold Brunner, with civic reform committees in Minneapolis, Cleveland, Philadelphia, San Francisco, Washington, Denver, and Seattle postdate the fairs; or that they relied so heavily on the classical order which the various expositions exemplified. Although these city plans were far more than façade shifts, involving as well basic changes in transport management, environmental protection, recreational facilities, and even governance, most of them incorporated grand formal elements as emblems of a more perfect city. Their axial avenues, plazas, vistas and uniform cornice lines, their monumental civic buildings reflected a dream nourished by the fairs. The planners saw this as a city purified. Some critics today see it as a city superfluously sanitized, made authoritarian, a tribute to power and hierarchy, not democracy and free movement. But however evaluated, fairs represented a significant sense of ideal city form, in both its spatial meaning and its carefully focused variety.

In my opinion, both this image and this commitment were weakened by two succeeding waves of fairs. One came in the 1920s and 1930s when Philadelphia, Chicago, Dallas, San Francisco, Cleveland, and several other cities hosted expositions. These fairs increasingly celebrated modernism, the untrammeled forms of a new machine age. The motto of Chicago's own Century of Progress was, after all: "Science Finds. Industry Applies. Man Conforms." New York's fair called itself The World of Tomorrow.

These fairs were major influences on industrial design and streamlining, powerful statements of a belief in progress in a decade threatened with fundamental loss of faith. They attracted millions of people; they entertained and instructed. But despite their immense influence they did not bear the same organic relationship to their host cities as the earlier fairs did. They were extravaganzas, featuring models for people to tour—like Norman Bel Geddes's famous Futurama for General Motors at the New York Fair, its most popular exhibit.

Once fair layout and organization symbolized a combination of the real and ideal city. Now visitors got a combination of science and fiction by corporate sponsors like Ford or General Electric. Or it could be argued that the jumbled array of buildings represented cities that had let their plans get away from them. These fairs took place in a world whose mass communications and entertainments had caught up with earlier promises. Radio, talking pictures, and television had begun to change the experience of average fair-goers; the automobile and airplane were transforming travel patterns as well. Visitors no longer depended on expositions for firsthand experiences with art and exotic culture. They had grown more cosmopolitan. And because they were more cosmopolitan, the fair idea was less dominated by specific location. Tourist benefits remained important; cities used fairs to celebrate recent achievements—in San Francisco's case, the two great bridges closing the Golden Gate and connecting to Oakland.

But, by the 1930s, the power to make illusions had begun to shift to suburbs. City centers, once monumental symbols of power, with their fountains, museums, and plazas, were becoming embarrassing reminders of changes of fashion. These 1930s fairs traded on a magic future rather than a purified present. In so doing, I believe, they posed a subtle danger to city images. For fair-builders of the earlier period understood the additive character of the city, its layering by different styles and different kinds of people. It was compressed and dense. Compactness, detail, ritual remained its principles. Ahistorical modernism, the new fair style, threatened the city's eclectic appeals; the fair's surfaces were now unencumbered by the burden of historic references or association. These were Buck Rogers cities, all new, featuring plastics and stream-lining. Their most powerful influences came from individual corporate structures, expressionistic in their pre–Las Vegas appeal. They outshone both national pavilions and most official buildings.

However powerful the fair idea remained in scientific or industrial terms, it had become fragmented, split among interest groups. Its overall visual character no longer reflected a single vision of what a Heavenly or Redeemed City should look like. This phase could be termed the Futurist Fair, as opposed to the Emporium and the Heavenly City. This phase was popular, memorable, even quite profitable, and recalled with fond nostalgia today. But I think it had much less influence upon its host cities than previous expositions and failed as accurately to mirror their changing character.

The Futurist Fair was succeeded in turn by still another round of fairs in the 1960s and 1970s. These are harder to classify, and I offer only an observation rather than a settled conclusion. They appear to me even less vitally

New York World's
Fair, 1939

related to the fate of their host cities. To borrow an ambiguous, perhaps misleading phrase, these might be labeled Post-Modern Fairs. Lacking any totally
confident vision of the future, they also could not project a sympathetic view of
the past. If anything, they were committed to the triumph of mass marketing,
popular entertainment, and electronic gadgetry. There was no longer any effort
to present a single version of modernist styles, as in the 1930s. Instead the fair
environments were bizarre landscapes whose structures fit no easy expectations, strange shapes that were triumphs of engineering without always suggesting why they needed to be. These were magic worlds, although several were
oriented to serious problems like energy and conservation. Cosmic, rather than
global in orientation, some of these fairs left specific services in their wake,

like monorails and housing complexes, but their attachment to a single host environment, compared with the fairs of an earlier day, seemed fragile.

The idea of the world's fair continues but its meaning seems confused. With Disneylands and Epcots, shopping centers and video cassettes, experiences that fairs once monopolized can be duplicated outside their boundaries. Why have a world's fair at all? Beyond the immediate returns of tourism and construction jobs, what purposes can it serve? There may be simpler, less expensive ways of throwing a party or enhancing the lakefront. What ideas and visions can be objectified uniquely and appropriately in a world's fair today? We cannot repeat the aspirations of another age. Too much has changed. In the 1890s, cities were just receiving the museums, libraries, universities, and historical societies fairs helped to stimulate. Parks and city beaches were new and needed development. Pollution, ecology, and environmental impact statements posed no obstacles. Decisions could be made quickly and efficiently by small groups of white male business leaders.

Today cities like Chicago possess far more complex institutional structures; they are no longer growing at an apparently infinite rate; maintenance rather than creation of new services seems a major problem; and more vigorously assertive popular constituencies are demanding their own right to participate. The fairs of the 1930s provide no necessary models either. Their often naïve faith in science and technology seems inappropriate today; a streamlined world of tomorrow no longer seems the solution to current problems.

How can the 1992 Fair, then, reflect its announced theme and yet address the problems of American cities? Without some animating objectives at its heart, the Fair would be a lost opportunity. The 1893 Fair and its era are gone; they cannot be recreated. That fair projected a specialized, a privileged view of the world, shaped around dominant class and civic values. However, even while it reflected power, it demonstrated insight into certain urban virtues and helped nurture a spirit of ambition which supported a wide range of other institutions. The fair of the 1990s must be different in spirit, but it must also in the end serve the needs of its urban host.

What are these needs? And how can a fair best meet them? These questions will have to be addressed in the coming months all over this city. I hope we have the energy, tolerance, and imagination that properly belong to this planning effort. And demonstrate the continuing capacity of our cities to sponsor and benefit from such giant enterprises.

7

Museums:

The Hidden Agenda

I have been invited by the planners of this conference to consider how shifts in values and social experience might affect the world of the museum in the years ahead. I am an historian, to be sure, and I will now speculate about the future and evaluate the present. These changes of tense may be liberating or they may be constraining. Readers will have to judge. But I have accepted the charge. Necessarily I will begin by talking about the museums of the past, whose plans, organizations, and intellectual assumptions have influenced us enormously. And then I will attempt to identify some broad social trends and note some of their implications for the museum world.

I do this with special humility because it was only two years ago, in 1984, that the Commission on Museums for a New Century issued its report. I will say more about that report shortly, but I do hope to complement rather than simply repeat its concerns.

My plan today is simple. I will focus on some contrasts between the energies supporting museum creation in the past, and the bursts of interest, the new commitments, the crises of knowledge and authority that are shaping today's museums and may well influence them in future. Speculation about things

From *Midwest Museum News*, no. 46 (Spring 1987): 17–21. Reprinted with permission.

to come is a form of gambling. But such speculation forces us, at a minimum, to identify existing patterns and may permit us to discover historic shifts. Even if the trends I suggest here are misplaced, or overgeneralized, I hope my analysis at least possesses some heuristic value. It is meant to raise questions as much as to answer them.

My basic assumption is that creating, building, and endowing a museum, gathering its exhibits, hiring guards, curators, and administrators, planning tours, publishing catalogues, all are acts requiring explanation. Museum creation is not a natural species response like hunting for food, building shelter, nurturing the young. It is an add-on made possible by the presence of social and economic surplus. As a powerful didactic presence the museum is not much more than 150 years old. Despite important precursors, analogues, and early models, publicly sponsored display settings for art, science, history, and technology do not go back much further than the early nineteenth century. Their multiplication takes place still later, and in any continuous way, in the United States at least, they don't get fully operational for another fifty years.

The process of separation from raree shows, cabinets of curiosities, and collections of dubious ancestry occurred slowly. We are contending with little more than a century of uninterrupted life. Where did the impulse for these enterprises come from? What provoked the considerable expenditures of time, energy, and capital they required? Answers are easily available but let me provide still another brief summary based mainly on the United States and by implication on Western Europe during this period. The museum explosion can be viewed in the light of several fundamental trends, themselves products of historical development. These, in their turn, stimulated the creation of museum policy as a whole. Although related and often porous, the trends are divisible. I will try to describe four of them and then suggest how museums fulfilled their logic.

First of all, by the mid-nineteenth century, the West was in the midst of an unprecedented extension of knowledge about the material universe, the result of extended research, experimentation, exploration, theorizing, and systematic institutionalization. A broadening consensus among the educated was revising previous estimates of the age of the earth, the size of the universe, the origins of species, the workings of the body, and the mysteries of creation. So extended, so comprehensive a revolution of consciousness demanded new instruments of expression and display. Schools, universities, research institutes, hospitals, and museums multiplied.

Accompanying and supporting this extension of knowledge was a second revolution, that of wealth. In the capitalist economies of Europe and America individual businessmen found themselves in possession of enormous fortunes.

Their levels of income exceeded the wealth of crowned heads. Many of them had surpassed the richest monarchs in the history of the world, particularly in liquidity of resources. These fortunes, like the new knowledge, called for expression. Consumption patterns were soon established, including philanthropic bequests and collecting obsessions. Libraries, colleges, park systems, orphanages, galleries, and observatories were built by the masters of transport, real estate, textiles, coal, iron, oil, and steel: Astor, Lenox, Vanderbilt, Girard, Lowell, Peabody, Johns Hopkins, and later Rockefeller, Carnegie, Morgan, Havemeyer, Stanford, Field. These names, and dozens of others like them, are indelibly associated with cultural institutions of great power and influence.

Third, accompanying the growth of knowledge and underwriting the expansion of wealth came an increase of domination over the physical world and the creation of centers of empire in Europe and North America. These centers exploited not only the resources of the earth its minerals, its foodstuffs, its timber, its animal life—but the cultures and peoples of every continent. This domination, fed by military, economic, political, and technological skills, produced unprecedented ease in assembling the art, artifacts, flora, and fauna of the earth. Journeys of exploration and tourism, military expeditions, trading and diplomatic contacts, all succeeded in returning to the centers of political influence a vast array of objects. Their possession testified to power and to the strength of human fascination with the so-called bizarre or exotic. Categories placed Western and non-Western arts and sciences within separate hierarchies. Along with wealth and knowledge, domination added an important element to the brew being cooked.

There was one final experience which was crucial to museum foundation. And this was a state of mind, a consciousness rather than a set of conquests or achievements. Throughout the nineteenth century, in Europe and America, there grew up an increasing sense of historical discontinuity, a feeling of interruption, of separation from thousands of years of human existence. The sources for this sensibility were several: industrialization, particularly the exploitation of steam and electricity; the growth of extended cities, cutting people off from contact with nature; increasing secularism and scientific challenges to the authority of religion, both of which eroded ancient distinctions between the sacred and profane; democratic revolutions which subverted the nature of political form and the concept of personal property. Also, there were massive migrations of peoples from one country to another and one continent to another, making common the experience of growing up within alien cultures or encountering newcomers who challenged social expectations with their new languages, rituals, religions, and traditions; and finally, toward the end of the century, a sense that human expression, in all the arts and crafts—plastic, graphic, musical, theatrical, literary—was being transformed radically. Machinery, mass taste, and scientific theory had led to manipulations of color, sound, space, line, and material in ways which slashed across ancient traditions. This break of continuity, felt intensely by many intellectuals, artists, political leaders, and social critics, led to a prevailing sense of anxiety about the cultural fabric and stimulated a turn to new institutions as a means of conserving, consolidating, and connecting. Among them stood public libraries, historical societies, patriotic lodges.

Now the four elements I have just described were enabling rather than directly causal. They set the conditions for the creation of museums, but they also set the conditions for many other institutional outlets. Power, domination, wealth, and anxiety led also to universities, to hospitals, to settlement houses. But museums were indeed specially suitable. And for several reasons. First of all, as responses to newly expanded knowledge they permitted large-scale restatements of the new learning. Science museums, technology museums, zoos, arboreta, botanical gardens, museums of natural history, all could display the post-Darwinian categories of the scientific credo.

Their effectiveness was aided by the fact that their principal rival in reaching the popular mind, up through 1910 or so, lay in printing, through words or illustration. Museums were impressive contrasts to the book, the newspaper, and the magazine. They had a scale and elaborateness that transcended the page. They could exploit various senses simultaneously. For believers in racial hierarchy, advocates of ethnocentric standards for intelligence and physical beauty, believers in eugenic planning and selective breeding, the museum and zoo, for example, were far more impressive than periodical articles or school textbooks.

The increasing mastery of taxidermy, the diorama and panorama presentations, the growing sophistication of exhibition science in general, all allowed important museums to popularize new ways of seeing the world. And the museums became laboratories for the new scientists themselves. Universities found them to be fundamental in research and teaching strategies; by the early twentieth century Pennsylvania, Chicago, Harvard, Yale, Berkeley, Stanford, all possessed their archaeological, geological, and anthropological museums, and a few had begun to develop historical and art museums as well.

As solutions to the second process I identified, the increase of personal wealth, museums were as convenient as they had been for the knowledge revolution. Not only did they justify large, costly buildings which required dramatic donations, but the continuing need to add to collections or erect additional galleries provided further opportunities to display personal cultivation and worth. Museums mingled the civic wealth of urban and university communities with the private fortunes of individuals in a collective display of prosperity. Communities frequently provided the land, often within municipal parks. Occasionally they built buildings or wings, and then private citizens provided the contents, the furnishings, and the adornments.

Indeed there existed a strong American presumption that private art purchases would, on the whole, eventually end up in public museums. When our millionaires began, by century's end, to ransom great European masterpieces, the newspapers all assumed that the community itself was the residuary legatee. Thus museums legitimated the pursuit of private pleasure, suggesting that collecting goals and object accumulation were public benefactions. And museums were increasingly presented as intelligent local investments, aiding citizens in their quest for tourism or corporate capital. The notion that young cities could increase employment and improve their economies by enhancing their cultural life is well over a century old in the United States. Finally, by presenting museum displays portraying the evolution of artistic form, including its expression in textiles, furniture, glass, silver, and china, museums apparently justified the heavy expenditures of the rich on antiques and personal possessions. With their presence the tycoons were not simply parading their wealth in a crude grab for attention but apparently participating in a long-standing, valued activity, working variations on the collecting patterns established by connoisseurs and royalty centuries earlier.

The third great feature of Victorian life that I isolated—growing domination over the physical world—also seemed made to order for museum foundations. It wasn't only sheer wealth which permitted the unprecedented transfer of objects from one hemisphere to another. It was also the continual movement of people from the centers to the peripheries, not necessarily the very rich but sightseers, administrators, explorers, and soldiers eager to share their experiences with those back home and objectify them by samples of the objects available. Often inexpensive, seemingly inexhaustible, these artifacts and art objects could be produced almost on demand.

The resulting displays of the civilizations of the world served educational and aesthetic functions: they reassured the dominators about their goodwill and cultural superiority. A stream of ethnic patrimonies was moved within the all-embracing arms of museums of history and anthropology, and, when they involved Europe and the United States, into museums of art as well. The careful divisions among art, history, and anthropology reminded casual visitors that some exotic cultures, however interesting, informative, or varied they may have been, perched more precariously than others on the ladder of human achievement. The uplifting, inspirational, cleansing, and refining arts of Greece, Rome, and Europe took their own reserved places. Domination produced a desire to record—in museums of technology and history, for example—the inevitable progress associated with the developing West. In museum foundation there existed the same passion to exploit and control the natural world which animated so many inventors and entrepreneurs. The museum was an obvious theater in which to sing praises to this dominion.

These three features of the Victorian and Edwardian world found easy expression in museums. But the fourth, the sense of discontinuity and alienation, had a more complex effect. Rather than serve simply as a receptive vessel in which could be poured the accumulated knowledge, wealth, and loot of a newly managed world, in response to these anxieties the museum also became a corrective, an asylum, a source of transcendent values meant to restore some older rhythms of nature and history to a fast-paced, urbanizing, mechanized society. Museums could be organized as settings to promote integration and solidarity, between social and economic classes, between humanity and nature, between mankind and time, or between human beings and the act of creation. Behind the energies of many museum foundations, particularly in this country, stood a sense of deficit about contemporary life, a fear that machines had replaced skilled craftsmanship in goods production, that vulgarized and distorted taste had shaped a market for cheap and monstrously designed objects of daily use, that rapid movement across national and regional frontiers had produced ignorance of both the landscape and its history, that city life had come to conceal the most basic facts of nature which were available to the simplest farm child, and that all human relationships had become victims of rapid change.

For the various lobbies which operated from a sense of deficit the museum offered a set of glittering promises. Here handcrafted objects could be put on display and admired. In evolutionary exhibits as well as study collections the taste of customers and workers alike could be instructed and refined. Patriotic relics and historic icons could mirror, more effectively than written texts, the sublimity of national history. Awe and respect for the natural world could be transmitted by the displays of animal and plant life. Above all by its architecture, its elaborate instructional programs, its air of gravity and propriety, and its wealth, the museum could testify to the serious character of culture as a larger activity, to the fact that there were agreed upon values and standards which could be applied to judgment, to history, to civilization itself. Such codification found expression and was worshipped in the palaces and temples so popular as museum structures. Museums were popularly expected to project cultural authority and therefore to represent the highest, most objective scholarship available.

True, problems did exist. Exhibits could be flawed by the presence of fakes. They could be criticized for being too crowded or not comprehensive enough, for being poorly labeled or badly lit. But their inner logic, their organization, and their contents rarely faced fundamental challenge. The assumptions that standards of taste and scholarship had objective reality and that museums could express them in three-dimensional form were universally accepted. Management lay in the hands of a cultural, artistic, scientific, and academic establishment. They faced many problems, fund-raising and audience attention among them, but self-confidence about their mission and their authority did not constitute one of their dilemmas.

It is against these fundamental experiences and objectives that I think we must examine the present state and future fate of the museum world. For we now live under very different social conditions, intellectual assumptions, and economic imperatives. It is certainly true that American museums, taken as a group, appear to be thriving. Their numbers, their wealth, the size of their collections, their increasing attendance, the recent spate of new buildings and enlargements, the growing sophistication of exhibition management and instructional technique, all suggest a high degree of progressive continuity with the world left behind, the world I have been attempting to describe. And they are accompanied by a high degree of optimism.

The sixteen recommendations proposed by the Commission on Museums for a New Century appear to acknowledge this. As suggestions for meeting the challenges of the future, they fall into four major categories: first, encouraging collaboration, both among museums and with other cultural institutions; second, increasing self-study to learn more efficiently about both the exhibition and the museum experience; third, increasing the sharing of information about everything from professional salaries to educational programs; and fourth, more aggressively publicizing museum operations in the interests of better public support. On the whole these are management rather than conceptual or programmatic issues. Little suggests that the museum of the near as well as the distant future confronts dilemmas attached to broad secular trends and needs.

What are these trends? What can be said of our world today which corresponds to the same broad level of generalization that I invoked when describing the late nineteenth and early twentieth centuries? These museums, I repeat, seem responses to a knowledge revolution, increased personal wealth, specific patterns of national domination, and anxieties about cultural continuity.

All of these elements remain present and continue to support the larger enterprise. But they have been supplemented by different sources of energy and complicated by different social challenges. These have, I believe, major implications for museum workers. They do not correspond precisely to the predecessor conditions I have just summarized, but they suggest some shifting in the social functions of museums, and perhaps some reorientation of practical imperatives. My five categories are: first, the growth of objects; second, the explosion of the canon; third, the spiral of selective costs; fourth, the increase of performance competition; and fifth, the eclipse of the word. Collectively they suggest a new world because they constitute circumstances which museums are already responding to, and will need, even more in the future, policy directions. Let me explain what I mean in somewhat greater detail.

First of all, I allude to the growth of objects. Now this is not really new. The Victorian World, the world of our predecessor museums, was itself caught up by the romance of proliferation, multiplication, and enhanced production, but it was a fascination with their contemporary rather than historical form and found truest expression in the international exposition rather than the museum itself.

Anyone who has examined reproductions of world's fair pavilions, with their extraordinary assemblies of tools, toys, clocks, soaps, surgical instruments, steam engines, furniture sets, glassware, tractors, knows how overwhelming was the urge to present the wonders of modern art and technology. Few of the exhibitors or visitors, however, reflected on what would happen when it came time to think of making these shows permanent, incorporating the nineteenth and early twentieth centuries into the world of history represented by the museum.

Their present has become our past. And by reason of the intense shifts of mood and attention which the present world contains, our own present very quickly becomes our own past. How are we to salvage, organize, house, and interpret the cornucopia of things which human genius has recently created, to say nothing of the natural objects and specimens which science continues to accumulate? Man is a collecting animal.

Cabinets of curiosities are no longer confined to the very wealthy or the privileged. Such multiplication adds to the challenge. Museums will have to cope with an enormous output of historically valued, sentimentally recalled, and technically significant objects. Sanctified by photography and mass media, heroicized by the legends of science and invention, purified in the heat of battle, everything from television props to campaign badges seems about to enter one or another museum. What standards can be invoked to determine inclusion? Who should formulate them? And how much investment, in a society with many pressing needs, can go into endless conservation and curatorial organization?

There is an interesting analogy here, I think, with extant interests in architectural preservation. For long a subject of controversies, a crisis has been caused by two recent developments.

First, growing attachment to industrial, commercial, and vernacular architecture. And second, increasing affection for Victorian, Beaux Arts, and

Moderne styles. Both elements have added to the universe of valued structures. This has further intensified debate between those loyal to historic buildings and planned landscapes and those seeking economic expansion through razing and rebuilding. The angry arguments have, in many areas, produced important legislative, judicial, and administrative solutions.

But they have also raised questions about entitlement, questions which museum administrators and curators would do well to study. What determines the importance of a structure? What justifies the higher costs involved in protecting its physical appearance? Who benefits from these protections? When should they be imposed? A veritable industry of consultation and mediation has been mandated by governmental impact statements, landmark registers, municipal ordinances. They deserve attention.

This problem has not yet hit the museum with full intensity. Occasional questions have been asked, but many more will come as a system of object triage is considered. And the thrust is different from that bedeviling early administrators, criticized for not throwing out enough, for not weeding their collections more ruthlessly, for not separating the meretricious and sentimental from the exemplary and significant. This trend does remain present, of course. Donors, critics argue, should not expect to have institutions display their mistakes alongside their happier choices. Taste requires pruning. Today, however, many museum boards and curators are under less pressure to divest than they are to be more inclusive, to represent within the museum's walls the clash of standards, interests, skills, and cultures that constitutes the larger world.

There is less expert confidence that particular subjects, art forms, and techniques should be excluded. And there may be even less confidence in the future, for inclusion in a museum legitimates not only the object's maker and its giver, but the category of objects itself and the group of producers as a whole. To be part of a collection, an exhibit, a museum holding is to gain importance. And it is natural for groups within American society seeking recognition to discover—if religious and cultural prohibitions are absent—that the museum is a reasonable source for such legitimation.

The proliferation of objects, however, is only one aspect of what might be called a larger crisis of choice. It is related to a second major shift which transcends the history of the museum itself and has far reaching implications. I call this the Explosion of the Canon. As my remarks have already suggested, it is not only that more and more objects have been created, accumulated, and discovered. It is that larger and larger classes of objects are now deemed worthy of public display. And this is a function of the fact that classification has come to be seen as an act of domination as well as of analysis.

Sociologists, historians, philosophers no longer consider it value-free, neutral, or objective, even when developed by trained professionals. Discriminations—of race, gender, class, ethnicity—were inevitable in the past. Their patterns have been revealed by a growing chorus of scholars studying the social construction of knowledge. Many now demand broader, more representative exhibition policies and greater self-consciousness about the political and social implications of apparently neutral arrangements.

Again, museums are not alone in being singled out for attention. In literature, music, drama, ethics, criticism, architecture, painting, and sculpture, the concept of the masterpieces, the tradition of the classic, the notion of approved criteria have been challenged again and again by scholars. Our college civilization courses are no longer exclusively western; our art history courses have grown more comprehensive; our science is no longer assumed to be value-free. Women's studies, black studies, gay and lesbian studies, popular culture studies, media studies, all have invaded the curriculum and reflect broader, nonuniversity interests as well. The trend has inevitably been felt in museum operation, exhibition planning, and curatorial training; it will continue to be felt in the future.

There have been several proposed solutions. One response has been balkanization of the museum universe, the creation of many institutions each representing some special interest: museums of women's history or women's art, museums of black history, museums of labor, peace museums, photography museums, Freemasonry museums. It is a long list.

Another response has been an attempt, within larger, older, more inclusive institutions, to present counter arguments to the themes of progress and achievement that have been intertwined so closely with many subjects. This has meant introducing, for example, issues of pollution, radioactivity, or public safety within displays on industry and technology; or suggesting the costs of economic development along with their gains; or focusing attention, within museums of history, on the anomalies and contradictions that hover around even our most celebrated national accomplishments.

Still a third response has been creation of special traveling shows to address important social or political themes or to represent constituencies poorly served by permanent installations. SITES has done this: so have individual organizations and institutions. In effect then, within the last ten or fifteen years the argumentative, polemical, ideological potential of the museum display has been more openly acknowledged. There is increasing self-consciousness of the political implications of exhibitions.

Again, such acknowledgments are still broader. Within the academic world a series of intellectual surges has widened the definition of texts and made the science of sign-reading more fashionable. Even conservatives accept the burdens of interpretation which semiotics, structuralism, and post-structuralism have placed on their shoulders. The museum's position is no longer seen as transcendent. Rather it is implicated in the distributions of wealth, power, knowledge, and taste shaped by the larger social order. This critical view will, I think, grow sharper in decades to come. The explosion of the canon still reverberates and the implications for museums as repositories of authority deserve further exploration.

The third shift meriting attention involves long-term changes in the comparative pricing of labor and energy resources—the Spiral of Selective Costs. Here I can only be suggestive. But it seems clear that many things—unionization, increased mass education, widely dispersed expectations of personal welfare, increased expenditures on health, greater consciousness of job discrimination—have combined with long-term energy scarcity to produce paradoxes for our institutions of culture. Sets of subsidies which once shielded true costs of operation are less obvious today and in some places are practically invisible.

It is difficult to find—and illegal to hire—qualified employees who accept salaries below minimum wage levels. Certainly museums, universities, libraries, and schools still benefit from the presence of thousands of volunteers who subsidize, in time and salary, their nonprofit employers. But certain inequities are no longer tolerated, nor is independent wealth an effective source of employee support. Voluntarism continues to be important, but it operates within an increasingly professionalized and guilded world.

A set of facts, disparate in nature, suggests something of the crisis. The costs of college education in private institutions have increased twentyfold in twenty-five years, far beyond the cost of living. Building maintenance and security costs have similarly skyrocketed. Museums now admit routinely into their budgets once neglected items like conservation and preservation. The result is that we sometimes starve in the midst of plenty.

I have yet to see a comprehensive audit of institutional time budgets but consider the following. Forty years ago the New York Public Library was open every day of the year but Christmas, and with extended services for much of the time. In 1930 the Cleveland Museum of Art was open 62 hours each week, and every day, with Sunday, Wednesday, and Saturday free; in 1980 it was open 40 hours each week. In 1921 the Art Institute of Chicago was open weekly for 60 hours; in 1980, it offered 40 hours. In 1910 the St. Louis Museum of Art was open 49 hours and 7 days; in 1982, 42 hours and 6 days. In 1914 the Museum of Fine Arts in Boston was open for 54 hours weekly; in 1979, 46 hours, and this marked a recovery from a lower ebb. With collections of unprecedented value and magnificence, with increased attendance figures and sometimes uncomfortable crowding, museums have been forced to limit hours of availability, reduce free days, raise prices of admission and, most of all, engage in complex and elaborate campaigns of publicity and promotion to attract a larger measure of financial support.

Obviously, not all institutions have suffered equally. And obviously as well, some of the effort to gain government grants and to tap private sources through membership drives, gift shops, innovative entertainments, and popular exhibitions has had beneficial results. But in the eyes of some critics these financial pressures have also introduced a vulgarized and distorting set of institutional goals, diverted attention and energy away from ongoing curatorial and administrative responsibilities, introduced a commercialized ethic and vending vocabulary, and generally exaggerated museums expectations and anticipated benefits to a point where they have been inevitably disappointed.

One symbol of this has been the debate, which continues unabated to judge from recent issues of *Art News*, over the blockbuster exhibition. One motive behind the rise of the blockbuster—and there have been several—is the need for large museums to increase memberships and attendance, obtain favorable media publicity, and identify new groups of patrons and supporters. Smaller institutions, presumably, have their own version of such activities.

Some of the effort to publicize the museum and popularize its functions is obviously the result of an ongoing desire to extend influence and outreach. But the insatiable economic demands of a labor-intensive, high energy-cost environment add to the urgency. There is no reason to believe these costs will decline in the next few decades. And every expectation that admission fees, reduced hours of opening, selective closures of specific galleries, will continue to be responses. The effects of crowding, hyperbolic publicity, high admission prices, and aggressive marketing will continue to worry those concerned about the quality of museum-going as a social experience and its significance as an instrument of communication.

A fourth large trend, which is related to the marketing of the museum, has been the rise of aggressive, attractive, competitive forms of mass entertainment—the Increase of Performance Competition. When museums were first established in some numbers during the late nineteenth century, a range of urban amusements already existed. Vaudeville, spectator sports, theatrical performances, lectures, concerts, amusement parks, circuses, all were in full operation by century's end; several had been popular diversions for millennia.

But in the twentieth century a succession of new, powerful, nationalizing media—film, radio, television—grew up to constitute an unprecedented and pervasive source of popular experience. Eighty years ago the museum exhibition, even under old-fashioned and crowded conditions, constituted an imposing event. Museum spaces in large cities were huge and impressive; their objects seemed overwhelming in number; and good reproductions of the art and artifacts were hard to find.

Mass media changed standards of receptivity. They provide images and information on a daily basis, fresh and immediate, easily available. They offer commentators of unimpeachable distinction. The color, the scale, the effectiveness of their presentations, oriented either to the comfort of a theater or a living room, has meant that for the last sixty years museums have been trying to catch up with the power of these new competitors. Once-imposing museum spaces soon appeared stodgy and fatiguing.

Exhibition planners, two generations ago, began to enlist the skill and attention of industrial designers, lighting specialists, and theatrical directors. By our own day performance media—movies, television, closed-loop slide shows, computer graphics—are increasingly incorporated within exhibitions. Films are frequent preludes or conclusions for displays. Visitors find recorded tours available, through wands and earphones. Some museums employ live performers, turning exhibits into stage sets for actors, musicians, dancers, clowns, and storytellers. Performance culture is acknowledged to be a powerful shaper of the exhibition.

The particular performance form dominating our culture, of course, is television. It includes a packaging model that shapes expectations for the receipt of information. And with the wider availability of video cassette recorders the television experience itself is undergoing change, increasing personal options. Exploiting performance techniques for exhibition purposes can, depending on one's point of view, enhance, amplify, gut, or distort museum-going. What does seem unquestioned is that the blurring of boundaries between performance and exhibition raises important issues. How much, in fact, does museum-going differ from television-viewing? How self-consciously should museums try to contrast or disentangle these experiences? What impact on concentration or patience in examining objects does a staple diet of screen-viewing produce? Have certain kinds of exhibition modes—in zoos or planetaria or science museums, for example—benefited more than others by the electronic revolution?

There are other issues as well. The filmstrips, videotapes, and motion pictures so often associated with exhibitions serve more than informational ends. These electronic representations help legitimate the objects on display, providing an aura that enhances the authority of the authentic objects. The instant replay enters the museum exhibition as well as the sports contest. Cross referencing between live experience and televised reproduction reflects the pervasiveness of these media as instruments of acculturation, standard setters, definers of experience. They distribute values. This dominance shows no sign of diminution. And its implications deserve extended discussion by museum specialists, not merely pragmatic adaptation by exhibition planners.

The power of electronic performance raises my fifth and final element: the Eclipse of the Word. This problem is very complex. One reason for the popular appeal of many museum exhibitions is the apparent relief they offer to those uncomfortable or unfamiliar with reading as a source of intellectual and aesthetic pleasure. Learning from objects is now presumed to have significant meaning for adults as well as juveniles. Museum displays promise to increase such accessibility. The democratization of audience goals, so long a part of the museum movement, has supported the institution's image as a cultural mixing place.

But there are paradoxes and associated ironies. Reliance upon object displays may well be an instrument to gather together portions of a varied and educationally heterogeneous public. But the effort to translate exotic or specialized experiences, objects, and skills can turn exhibitions into highly verbal settings. Large printouts sometimes accompany and even dominate the displays. Label writing has, of course, for long been a source of debate among museum staff members. The development of concise, coherent, authoritative object descriptions reflected a democratizing trend within the American museum world. It was evident even in the late nineteenth century and contrasted with developments in other places where connoisseurs and scholars did not require the mediation of labels to know that they were seeing. The label expanded the audience.

More recently, however, the written explanation has attracted extensive criticism, for its length and complexity can overshadow the objects it was meant to serve. We have all been struck by the sight of museum visitors patiently reading long paragraphs and practically ignoring the artifacts the paragraphs are meant to introduce.

Now if the label is more appealing than the exhibited piece why do I call this trend the eclipse of the word? Because, in my view, the inability to look at objects as themselves, without reliance upon written explanation, ironically enough reflects the fact that pictures have replaced words for many, as the basis for sharing experience. And pictures cannot always be used to explain pictures. Stationary objects suffer from an impoverishment of descriptive and analytic vocabularies.

The labels are drunk thirstily by audiences who find the words as exotic as the objects they are meant to explain. I am speaking here not simply about the effects of electronic media, but about the growth of photographs, illustrations, posters, cartoons, visual symbols of all kinds, logos, about picture postcards and home movies and snapshots. Museum shops sell books and catalogues but they sell even more cards, slides, photos, souvenirs, stationery, and posters.

How long can people stand in front of objects and enjoy them without some verbal frame of reference? And how can that frame be supplied when it is viewed as intrusive? Quite frequently, in art museums at least, the context of viewer comment is simple recognition. Because of visual reproductions the art object has become well known, a celebrity, and the chance to view the original is exciting. Once accomplished, however, there is little reason to stand in front of it for too long.

The paradox I am suggesting, then, is that when words are eclipsed, diluted, abandoned, transcended, or denigrated as instruments of communication and description, in favor of direct visual representation or reporting, then many museum visitors are literally abandoned to the objects. And, ironically enough, in their abandonment they can rely only upon label-reading or picture-taking as structuring devices. Words continue to structure visual and object experiences. Without them museum-going can be aimless, incoherent, and without measurable impact. Docents, guides, producers of tape-recorded tours recognize this, although all too often they simply provide organizing narrative rather than actual entry into the visual and tactile categories themselves.

What happens to the tens of millions of American museum goers? Which sensations have been altered? What have they learned that is unavailable in a book, if they could read it? What can they get if they cannot get a book? Despite many individual studies we still know little about what goes on among viewers and about the effect of museums as environments.

Oddly enough, in some ways less is written about the museum experience now than during an earlier day. The most memorable museum evocations of our time come through visual rather than verbal representation. In an earlier day travellers, novelists, journalists, and critics offered powerful portraits of museums as social settings. Samuel Butler and Henry James, Willa Cather and John Galsworthy, Balzac and Zola annotated the viewing environment. Today their descriptions have been replaced by Alfred Hitchcock and Brian di Palma, by Fred Wiseman and television documentaries and BBC Masterpiece Theater. Museum visitors are accustomed to receiving information and sensation as part of a seated audience observing action on a stage or screen, not moving through space in a self-propelled fashion, in charge of their own time and movements, making decisions about what to look at and for how long. Exhibit illiteracy is in its own way as much a problem as verbal illiteracy; and it is closely related to it.

Social conditions and social structures change slowly. The last few decades have introduced conditions that are likely to be around for a long time. The challenges to traditional museum organization and museum-going will probably not be fundamentally altered in the next fifteen or twenty years. Newly aggressive constituencies seeking legitimation in exhibition display, controversies over museums as transcendent authorities, a continuing spiral of selective labor and energy costs, the appeal of performance models of information and entertainment, and the relative decline of verbal literacy should be here to stay for quite some time. As museums reflect norms, tastes, and experiences rather than dispense standards and values, as they flirt with the familiar and domesticate the exotic they run risks other institutions have run before them. They have entered an entertainment marketplace. And they toy with the boundaries that once comfortably separated them from competitive forms.

The contrasts between exhibition and performance cultures may well be eroding in our society, and the larger undifferentiated world of raree shows, cabinets of curiosities, wildly mixed personal collections—the world of Barnum and Peale and Tradescant—may be returning. Could museums compete if they passed on their true costs in the same way in which a Disney World or a theater troupe or an opera company attempts? How can museums cope with the task of employing descriptive vocabularies and confront general ignorance of science and history? Is it appropriate to think about testing the museum's success in reaching its visitors? Do many of the objects displayed justify the increasingly high overhead required to exhibit, catalogue, conserve, and interpret them? Apart from visiting schoolchildren how heterogeneous is the museum audience, and which constituencies in this country are really being served?

I raised these questions in a sympathetic voice. The mission of museums is powerful and continuing. But there are discrepancies between generations of museum thought, the assumptions that underlay the creation of powerful institutions of the past, and the practices of the present. The questions are hard ones. Fortunately, for me, they are not mine to answer. It is museum directors, planners, designers, curators, education programmers who must contend both with the severe problems of daily survival and the longer-term issuing of policy statements and reexaminations.

The unexamined museum, like the unexamined life, resists fulfillment. It may be inappropriate or even unfair to pose questions so broad, general, and abstract. But the resilience, imaginativeness, and institutional flexibility of the American museum have already been demonstrated on many occasions. And the challenges of the hidden agenda can be met by these sources of energy.

••

TWO

8

Utopian Fiction

and Its Discontents

O ver one hundred utopian novels were published in America during the quarter century before World War I. In addition, there appeared a large number of science fiction epics, as well as romances set in exotic places. All these genres shared a concern with other worlds, realms of life that contrasted with nineteenth-century experience. Whether they fit precisely within a utopian category or not, these experiments in time and place played with social conventions and frequently suspended the laws of history and nature.

Judged by contemporary reputation or literary survival, most of the books are minor documents. But their subterranean anxieties, largely ignored by later historians, are absorbingly up to date.

Many of these novelists were not professional authors. They had sound reasons for avoiding such a career. Their urge to describe other worlds was rarely based on any need for artistic fulfillment. More often they wrote from a passion to communicate some special idea. Their books, in fact, demonstrate the impact of modernization upon American life, presenting worlds ruled by strange machines, crowded with masses of people, and reverent toward scien-

From Richard L. Bushman et al., eds., *Uprooted Americans* (Boston: Little, Brown, 1979), 211–44. Reprinted with permission of the publisher.

tific truth. The novels' solutions to political and economic problems built on the classic anxieties we associate with this period. But their fictional details answered more intimate and perhaps more fundamental personal fears. These crudely written books offer surprising insights into long-vanished sensibilities. Perhaps the best way to begin is to consider a few examples of this literature, and their rather unusual authors.

In 1895, in Cincinnati, a book was published which occasionally is described as a utopian novel and is invariably a part of science fiction bibliographies. It bore the unlikely title of *Etidorhpa; or, The End of Earth, the Strange History of a Mysterious Being and the Account of a Remarkable Journey.* The author was as distinctive as his title. John Uri Lloyd had been born in 1849 in upstate New York, the son of a surveyor and mathematician.[1] After an apprenticeship to several Cincinnatti druggists, John Lloyd (along with a brother) came to own a drug firm. Lloyd also involved himself in research. During a long life he published eight scientific books, patented fifteen inventions, originated three hundred seventy-nine elixirs, and produced several thousand papers. Lloyd's collections of pharmaceutical formulas became standard texts in American colleges of pharmacy, and he assembled a distinguished library on botany and pharmacy, a library which published its own quarterly journal on the biological sciences. Heading various scientific and medical societies, he found the time to publish eight novels, all but one centered in northern Kentucky. By the time of his death in 1936 Lloyd had accumulated many honorary degrees and a comfortable fortune. In short, he was one of those extraordinary figures of nineteenth-century science: scholar, businessman, and bellettrist.

But this respectable scientist also published *Etidorhpa*, a novel that went through eighteen editions (of undetermined size) and was translated into seven languages. Some of the reviews, which the author reprinted in later editions, were enthusiastic. Benjamin O. Flower, social reformer, sometime mystic, and editor of the *Arena*, suggested that Lloyd had surpassed Alexander Dumas, Jules Verne, and Victor Hugo. Another critic termed *Etidorhpa* the "most unique, original, and suggestive new book" of the decade.[2] There was nothing else like it in print.

The novel describes a strange journey, begun when the member of a secret fraternity is kidnapped by his brothers for threatening to divulge the order's secrets. The sequence suggests the supposed abduction of William Morgan in the 1820s, an event touching off a decade of anti-Masonic agitation. Both abductors and victim are involved with alchemy and esoteric knowledge. Sentenced to annihilation of identity, the potential apostate is suddenly transformed into an aged, unrecognizable man. Led by semihuman guides, he then enters worlds where space, heat, time, and energy assume bizarre properties.

In its scope, the journey resembles other famous quests in Western literature. But unlike most of them, the aim of this allegory is principally to reveal the laws of nature. These laws are more complex, and permit more variety, than scientists ever dreamed. Strange forms of animal and vegetable life appear, including forests of gigantic mushrooms. Gravity loss, light without shadow, water without currents, mysterious energy sources, giant hands, temptations from fiends, communion with angels—all are part of the book. Lloyd's fictive strategy is clever. He introduces a narrator who interviews the apostate and challenges his experiences. He is met by experiments, descriptions, and diagrams that prove their possibility (however much they interrupt the narrative flow). Man, insists Lloyd, is limited and puny. No one could have forecast the wonderful inventions of the late nineteenth century. The marvels of *Etidorhpa* are real possibilities. Wonder is only an exemplification of ignorance.

But although its author was a scientist, and the book employs empirical demonstration, *Etidorhpa* is frequently antimaterlialist. Experimental science is dangerous because it threatens the idea of immortality. Beware of the beginning of biological inquiry is Lloyd's warning. Beware of your own brain. Reality is more than materialism; in *Etidorhpa* thought force is used to transmit ideas. The guide promises it will eventually replace the inadequacy of vocal language. But before this can happen, men will have to study strange spiritual phenomena and science abandon its materialist concentration. Spiritualistic investigations "unfortunately are considered by scientific men too often as reaching backward only," when in fact they lead directly to a wondrous future.[3] For many such pages the book proceeds, interweaving bizarre experiences with practical experiments and ending with a mystical vision: the abducted victim stands on the brink of another world, the distant country, prefiguring the progress of humanity when, like him, it will have comprehended the laws of creation and the meaning of life. He has reached the end of the earth.

This then was *Etidorhpa*. Questions must remain on every level of the book's meaning, but larger than the intricacies of its allegories is the basic fact of its appearance. What was a distinguished scientist doing with such a book? Why his suspicion of science? Why the turn to alchemy and mysticism?

If *Etidorhpa* stood alone, one might continue to examine Lloyd. But it shared a life with dozens of bizarre works depicting the existence of other worlds. As did *Etidorhpa*, they frequently combined careful descriptions of physical marvels with a passion for religious discussion, social improvement, and spiritualist investigation. One example is Amos K. Fiske's *Beyond the Bourn: Reports of a Traveller Returned from "The Undiscovered Country."*[4] In his own way, Fiske was as remarkable as Lloyd. He had been born in New Hampshire in 1842 and orphaned at an early age. Although forced as a child to work

Etidorhpa

in a cotton mill, Fiske managed to attend Harvard College and graduate with honors in 1866. He married a sister of Francis J. Child, the Harvard philologist and ballad scholar, and became an editor for various newspapers including the *Boston Globe* and the *New York Times*. Fiske published only half a dozen books but demonstrated a comprehensive mind. His works include studies of the Philippines and the West Indies, an analysis of banking, several volumes on Hebrew mythology and history, a proposed reorganization of labor and management, and, in 1891, his one utopia, *Beyond the Bourn*.

Fiske's novel is simpler than *Etidorhpa*, lacking its complex allegorical organization. But there is an added attraction. Alongside an account of a utopian planet, further evolved than earth, Fiske added a description of heaven. His narrator, apparently killed in a train wreck, makes an ascent to heaven, where he meets a number of old friends and is taken by angels to view a more advanced planet; after returning to heaven he awakens to find that he has in fact survived the wreck.

In its basic argument, Fiske's novel is a self-conscious effort to combine traditional religion with Darwinian evolution. His utopian world is cooperative, brotherly, and technologically sophisticated. Air travel, submarines, selective breeding, and the security of immortality make life easy. But Fiske's description of paradise forms his most interesting contribution. The orthodox meet with some surprises. The spirits of the dead, stripped of selfish animal appetites, can observe without reliance upon physical sensation. They require no material substance to perceive form and color. Contrary to popular belief, they do not stand around idly singing hymns but are in constant activity. With millions of globes to learn about, each with its own inhabitants, there are continuing marvels to discover. Heaven is far from dull.

Despite this enthusiastic description, however, Fiske warned against efforts to communicate directly with heavenly spirits. "The craving for such revelations," he argued, "becomes morbid and absorbing; it blinds the judgment . . . and leads to deception."[5] Nonetheless, spiritualists and mediums must have read *Beyond the Bourne* with satisfaction, for here, along with the social analysis of a utopian society, appeared a noncorporeal spiritual world, defying known natural laws, and demonstrating the existence of life after death.

Fiske and Lloyd were joined in their fictional enterprises by many others of lesser fame and accomplishment. Cyrus Cole, for example, who published *The Auroraphone* in Boston in 1890, published nothing else.[6] But this novel also is a heady mixture of utopianism, romance, religious debate, and soul transmutation. A group of Americans, traveling out west, stumble on communication with Saturn, through an instrument which combines features of the telephone and the telegraph. They find a planet torn by religious dissension. Saturnians had once worshiped the sun, whose power was revealed by the appearance of his son, Creeto. Creeto taught a religion of future rewards and punishments. In a thinly veiled satire on Christianity, Cole describes the arguments erupting about the religious doctrines. The followers of Creeto, Creetans, accept as a principle the permutation of personality. In a universe of homogeneous atoms, some of which form the soul, every individual during the course of time will inevitably acquire the personality of every other living organism, experiencing every pain and joy the universe embraces. Existence is unitary; if one individual or generation bears greater burdens than others, they will eventually reap their rewards.

While this doctrine unites Saturnians for a time, they face other problems. Marvelous machines enable them to master their environment. One, labeled the Electro-Camera-Lucida-Motophone, reproduces past events; the American visitors witness the destruction of Pompeii, the Battle of Gettysburg, and the Chicago Fire. Saturnians have also managed to create duplicate human beings from matal, a strange element combining strength with lightness. The duplicates perform every function human beings do, except for reproduction; they are accountants, soldiers, and clerks. With the word *robot* still unborn, Cole happily had the Saturnians call their machines "dummies." But the dummies gain power, as Saturnian laziness leads to torpor. Learning to charge their own electrometers, the dummies revolt against their masters, killing thousands of citizens and capturing many cities. The Saturnians ruefully admit their mistake in moving forward so rapidly. "A certain amount of useful labor with the hands, daily performed," appears to be the price required by progress.[7]

The American visitors are impressed with Saturn's wonders, but even more excited by the Creetan theory of permutation. Without sacrificing belief in a benevolent deity, the creed explains all the evil in the universe. Knowing that one day even the fortunate and wealthy will experience the pains of the lower orders would surely produce greater social sympathy. This doctrine might permit brotherhood on earth. And Saturn's experiences, properly modified, would allow earthlings to avoid the dangers of machine insurrection.

Cole, Lloyd, and Fiske published their books within a period of five years. If talked about at all by literary historians, they are mentioned as part of the flowering of utopian fantasy which occurred in the two decades following publication of Edward Bellamy's *Looking Backward* in 1888. Their strange plots, metaphysical speculation, suspicion of science, and new mechanical marvels have usually been dismissed as irrelevant. Most commentators have concentrated upon the political and economic features of their utopian societies. The physical settings, the tastes of the interplanetary beings, and their religious convictions apparently required no explication.

Such selective analysis was partly accidental. Historians discovered our utopian literature in the 1930s and 1940s. This discovery became part of a larger effort to demonstrate a tradition of social and economic consciousness that American artists and writers could draw upon. Sensitive to charges of irrelevance and often committed to activist notions of the artist's political role, critics were delighted to demonstrate a pedigree for social involvement.

And the pedigree was comprehensive. More than one hundred ideal societies were depicted by novelists between the late 1880s and 1910; hundreds of other novels took as their themes labor strife and the class struggle. One early study of this literature, Claude Flory's *Economic Criticism in American*

Fiction, placed the utopias in the context of economic commentary. Flory insisted that the ablest American realists, from 1860 to 1900, were also the most vigorous economic critics. "The relationship," he explained, "is that both economic criticism—in the regular novel—and realism demand truth to life." Flory had located only sixty utopian novels; they did not fit his criteria for realism, to be sure. But he avoided the problem by declaring them a special genre, one which maintained an older, antebellum romanticism but was, "of course, almost exclusively economic" in its import.[8]

Other scholars—Alleyn B. Forbes, Lisle Rose, Walter Taylor, Robert Shurter—expanded the study of economic fiction; in 1947 Vernon Louis Parrington, Jr., published his study of utopian fiction, *American Dreams.* Several dissertations and more books supplemented these efforts and increased our knowledge of published utopias. But with some exceptions the thrust of this scholarship, and its invaluable bibliographies, has been largely to describe, annotate, and collate utopian fiction by economic and political themes.[9] The novels have been divided into collectivist, populist, nationalist, and single-tax categories, with descriptions of their solutions to agrarian discontent, monetary inequities, labor unions, and political representation. The physical details, the family structure, the social rituals, and the religious concerns have remained offstage, subordinated, and oddly separate. It is undeniable, of course, that most utopian novelists were vitally concerned with the pressing problems of industrialization—its economic hardships and inequalities. But they were dealing also with the cultural hardships of modernization; and on these their testimony is most eloquent.

All this, of course, in terms of larger effects and literary importance, was a peripheral literature; and one may gain more from scrutinizing what appear to be peripheral features than central objectives. Economic categorizing has isolated the utopian genre in America from other contemporaneous enterprises. A social link between the utopian peninsula and the literary mainland is achieved through the reputation of some of the novelists—William Dean Howells and Jack London, for example. But there are other ties with American intellectual history, and these ties are provided by the novels' physical settings, and more particularly, their fascination with technology.

The three novels by Lloyd, Fiske, and Cole share a delight in outlining various scientific marvels that men might yet experience. Utopian writers, more generally, depict various forms of radar and television, air travel, temperature control, new metals, exploitation of solar energy, and automated machinery. While utopians catalogue advances, however, they spend little time explaining their operation. The few who do are highly derivative, taking their information, without much change, from the pages of periodicals like *Popular Science.* Most critics, therefore, finding technological interests so clearly overshadowed by economic goals, have tended to ignore them or classify the inventions as further evidence of the authors' visionary character.

But if these technologies are examined, not in terms of originality or thematic centrality, but to determine the problems they were meant to solve and their role in establishing credibility, other conclusions develop. Many utopias are a part of the literature of American science fiction, as much as they belong to the literature of economic criticism. Some students—Robert Philmus, Thomas Clareson, David Ketterer—have developed interesting definitions of science fiction which deserve further exploration.[10] But in this essay I am less concerned with definitions of form than with common details. Joint consideration permits the isolaton of otherwise hidden themes, and these themes touch heavily on science and technology.

In the first place, technology was an enabling condition for the description of other worlds. In the early nineteenth century, American utopianism tended to be more practical than literary, household- or village-oriented, stressing primary relationships and work satisfactions. The famous experiments in group living scattered through New England and the Middle West sought to influence the rest of society by example. In Arthur Bestor's classic analysis, institutions seemed plastic; the country was young; and pure forms appeared attainable through isolation. Controlled experiments were social possibilities. The structure of national life, if illogical, was at least divisible; communication and involvement were voluntary acts.[11]

By the 1880s and 1890s it had become more evident that piecemeal reform was an unlikely introduction to utopian dreams. Urban and manufacturing technologies had created permanent interdependencies. The price of effective change was social comprehensiveness, on a national or worldwide scale. The continual attention utopian novelists gave to transport and communications reflected this commitment to interdependence. The very forms of their fictional societies would have been impossible without a new ecological consciousness, an awareness of the snowballing effects of physical innovation, and the need for their careful control. Henry Olerich, who published *A Cityless and Countryless World* in 1891, confronted these relationships directly. Physical change, he wrote, necessarily created social change. New locomotives produced new roadbeds, more rapid commerce, a transformed trade. "A system in order to be natural and harmonious must be connected whole." "The very act" of discussing "a single topic unconnected with others is a sign of mental incompleteness," he concluded.[12]

The social order, then, had to be transformed totally or not at all. No part of the community could remain outside, as either exemplary or cautionary. Hostility to private interests and selfish individualism was nourished by experiences with the machine as system builder. Many of the novelists were moderately successful technicians and inventors: Chauncey Thomas, author of *The Crystal Button*, was a New England carriage manufacturer; Frederick U. Adams, who published *President John Smith* in 1899, designed machinery, including electric light towers; John Bachelder, the author of *A.D. 2050: Electrical Development of Atlantis*, made important improvements on the sewing machine; Byron Brooks, still another utopian novelist, patented crucial improvements for the typewriter.[13] Some of these novelists, then, had been successful in adjusting to the occupational demands of the new industrial society; a few, like King Gillette, of safety-razor glory, even became wealthy. It was natural that they paraded gadgetry as proof of their own ingenuity and to demonstrate an appreciation of social complexity.

Technology served another major utopian need: it rescued far-reaching schemes from improbability. Henry Olerich introduced in his novel a man who claimed to have been born on Mars. Americans might find this hard to believe, Olerich admitted generously; but after all, many incredible things had happened in the nineteenth century. "Telegraphy seemed impossible to Washington and his contemporaries," Olerich argued; "so did a 60-mile-an-hour train. We have divested them of all mystery."[14] H. E. Swan, a Kansan whose utopian novel *It Might Be* appeared in 1896, introduced a time machine that permitted visitors to witness the Crucifixion and a wall paint that eliminated the need for artificial illumination by absorbing light during the day and emitting it at night. Some might scoff, but "had the picture of 1893 been drawn for our Puritan fathers, they would have called the artist crazy."[15] New machines were hostages, proofs that the limits of human intelligence could not be easily fixed.

A third value of technology to the utopians was its clear contrast with the wretched state of contemporary society. Machine efficiency might shame men into social improvement. "We have photographed stars too remote to be seen even with the most powerful telescopes," wrote Henry Olerich. "We have explored the bottom of the sea."[16] But women and children still spent long days in factories, farmers were abandoned to rural solitude, tramps terrorized the countryside. These disparities could not be tolerated. Machines raised expectations for physical comfort and social rationality. Their very presence invited dramatic institutional reform. Technology formed more than a footnote to utopian prescriptions; it lay at their heart.

But centrality was one thing, confidence another. Enthusiastic descriptions were coupled with doubts, strange speculations about heaven, mysticism, and timidities. Indeed, despite their technical daring and apparent self-confidence, many of these utopian novels were the products of worried minds and represented a flight from experience, adventure, and confrontation. The technological wonders were surrounded with restrictions and qualifications. Their purpose was to shield utopians from too much direct contact with either the organic world outside or their fellow human beings. The energies calling forth this literature of marvelous speculation were nourished by dreams of escape—escape from danger, from pressure, from threats both vague and specified. The keynote through all these novels was control, protection, security. Utopian societies were giant envelopes. Their combination of mystical religion and technological ingenuity is understandable when they are seen as anxious responses to a set of revolutionary changes undergone by this generation of Americans. These changes are associated with urbanization and industrialization, but they are the kinds of direct, physical experiences we often neglect in favor of larger abstractions. The changes that concerned them most, I believe, can be grouped within three large categories.

The first of these great revolutions was the harnessing of electricity. Up through the Civil War era the greatest symbol of scientific advance for the contemporary world was the steam engine, a gigantic emblem of natural power controlled by human ingenuity. But if steam power was ingenious, it was neither mysterious nor indecipherable. Its principles of operation were easily explainable; the energy that ran looms, boats, locomotives, and factories had obvious sources of fuel and comprehensible moving parts. Size and power stood in a direct relationship; great engines had the scale they seemed to deserve. Dirty, noisy, even threatening, the giant machines may have been, but they never disguised their nature or purpose.

Electrical energy, however, was less susceptible to ordinary logic; its systems were barely visible. The tiny wires and even the larger cables which transmitted the awesome power to move, to illuminate, to operate machinery seemed out of proportion to their task, minute conduits for a giant force. Experiments with electricity and writings about its properties had, of course, a long history by this time. In Europe, William Gilbert, Robert Boyle, and Otto von Guericke had experimented in the seventeenth century, and their efforts were expanded by Benjamin Franklin and Alessandro Volta. But despite Volta's famous 1800 paper on electrical generation and the work of nineteenth-century scientists like Faraday, Davy, and Joseph Henry, it was not until the 1870s that a larger public familiarity with the uses of electricity developed.[17] The single exception was the electric telegraph.

Beginning in the 1870s, however, a series of major innovations exposed laymen to the still-novel force; illumination, communications, transport, and machinery were all transformed. Arc lights and then incandescent lighting, electric traction for railways and streetcars, the telephone, sewing machines

(1889), automobiles (1892), vacuum cleaners (1899), all appeared in breathless succession. Electrical application appeared limitless, which is one reason why it figured so prominently in many utopian novels. Clean and portable, it seemed an ideal solution to problems of noise and pollution caused by steam.

But along with the sense of dominion which electricity stimulated there were forebodings and anxieties. The harnessing of natural forces, often far from the scene of application, seemed to some an arrogation of semidivine powers. The most dramatic symbol of this was the capture of that greatest token of the American sublime, Niagara Falls, to supply electricity for Buffalo in 1896. When this was accomplished, after years of effort and debate, the triumph of man over nature seemed assured.[18]

But so extraordinary a victory caused concern by its very scale. The new force was alternately dreaded and worshiped. Nowhere was this better evidenced than in the displays of late nineteenth-century world fairs. By the 1890s enormous palaces at these expositions devoted themselves to electricity, while evening illuminations formed one of the chief glories of the fairs. Awe and fear mingled with one another. Many descriptions have been penned, but one of the most interesting was written by Joseph and Caroline Kirkland, at the Columbian Exposition of 1893. The Kirklands had come to the Electricity Palace from the Mining Building. In the latter, they wrote, "we could touch, measure, weigh, describe, depict what we were talking about"; but electricity was different.

[We] can not perceive the matter itself by any of our senses. It is without weight, length, breadth, or thickness. We can only see, hear, feel what it does, not grasp it or even conceive it in our minds. Certain treatments of matter produce certain forces, which are surely not matter; and those forces proceed to act in certain invariable ways with fearful speed and strength—that is all we know. The why and wherefore is as inexplicable to us as why or wherefore a liberated stone falls to the ground, or a planted seed germinates. . . . We speak without being spoken to, and bow without being introduced. We hover around the beautiful, terrible stranger, but we do not—willingly—shake hands, His glance is blinding, his voice is deafening, his touch is death. He is a law unto himself, and his enactments are immutable.[19]

The semireligious tone dominates; electricity is a god whose laws must be obeyed without question, but whose aid knows no limits. Omnipotent, omnipresent, perhaps electricity is the source for all life. The Kirklands, in fact, end their description of electricity by quoting Emerson's "Brahma" entire. The harnessing of electrical energy fit an old strain in the American consciousness which found all reality an expression of the Over-Soul; here was evidence for the mystical power animating the universe. Another visitor to the same fair described her entry into the Electricity Palace as a penetration of "the Great Enchanter, the King of Wonders of the 19th century," and lapsed into silent awe.[20]

But awe was matched by practical awareness of electricity's dangers, and the popular press played up these concerns. Fears about electrocution were legion. "It is an uncomfortable fact that chain lightning is being recklessly dispensed all over town," the *Philadelphia Inquirer* complained in the 1880s about the installation of electricity.[21] The *Boston Evening Transcript,* commenting on the electrocution of a horse by a live wire in New York, noted that authorities insisted that "there is no danger in the wires; but nobody believes them any longer."[22] The employment of electric lights was "fraught with great perils," insisted the *New York Tribune,* before going on to name electricity as the source for all kinds of mysterious accidents.[23] Business competitors exploited these fears as well. In 1879 Dan Rice, the clown and showman, warned against the electric light being featured by Cooper and Bailey's Great London Circus: "Persons predisposed to pulmonary complaints" should avoid the light since "it will shorten their days and in many cases it affects the tender brain of children."[24] The National Safety Congress was created from the concern of electrical engineers intent on reassuring the public. Thomas Edison did not help much when he stressed the perils of electrocution in his ill-fated campaign against alternating current. Neither did the development of the electric chair, adopted by New York in 1888 and first used two years later, partly on Edison's advice.[25]

The rhetoric of those favoring the electric chair as a death penalty revealed some of these early concerns. Writing in the *Forum,* Park Benjamin insisted that "no other mode of inflicting death could inspire stronger fear" in the lawless classes. "Even those accustomed to deal with electricity every day of their lives cannot divest themselves of an undefined impression of mystery which seems to surround the form of energy," he continued. "People still attribute to electricity almost every out-of-the-way natural phenomenon which they cannot understand. . . . No death is more dreaded than that which is mysterious."[26] Benjamin added that fears of electricity were hundreds of years old, but now much more evidence justified these fears and allowed defenders of law and society to exploit public alarm.

With these sinister implications in mind, one can understand why so many of the novelists enthroned electricity as a divinity, capable of remarkable achievements but requiring careful worship. Clean, powerful, and quiet electricity may have been, but it needed continual monitoring. In John Bachelder's *A.D. 2050* electricity, applied to every form of power, is a state secret, entrusted to a government commission of six men.[27] In Jack London's "Goliah," the world

Rubber suits for protection against electrocution

is reformed by an inventor who has developed a new form of energy, resembling electricity, which can destroy at will.[28] The inhabitants of William Taylor's *Intermere*, a utopian novel of 1901, know how to take the dangers out of electrical current, but refuse to pass the knowledge on to earthlings. "Neither your people nor any other people could be trusted with this secret in their present moral condition," warns a leader of Intermere. "A few learned men dependent upon the rulers in one nation, knowing it, could and would plot the destruction and exploitation of others. The sacrifice of human life . . . would be appalling."[29] Not only its own power, then, but the unprecedented power it brought those who controlled it made electricity fearsome.

The electrical revolution, however, released other meanings. It permitted existing fears to be translated into demands for a risk-free environment. Electricity itself could be perilous. But its extraordinary capacities apparently justified dreams of total comfort and unmeasured independence, independence of nature, of other animals, of any reminders of vulnerability. Electrical energy stimulated a recital of these anxieties, and the novelists paraded their concerns about indiscriminate contact, exposure to the elements, bodily invasion. They sought a level of safety that was breathtakingly total. Many utopias were set underground or placed within vast domes. Temperature control meant transcendence of natural caprice. "In truth," confessed a character in Albert Howard's *Milltillionaire*, "we have absolute control of the weather, and may evolve any special weather from the elements that are at any moment to embellish the occasion."[30] No fog, mist, steam, smoke, or noxious gasses survived this atmosphere; even the crops were grown by electricity, a calorifico-electeric ether which had replaced sunlight.

Electricity protected against more personal threats which had grown under the pressure of urbanization. In *A.D. 2050* bedside keyboards were useful against burglars. "The building is guarded by an electric mechanism that notifies the occupants of the approach of anyone after the family retires. From the watch tower at Police Headquarters the whole or any part of the city can be instantly illuminated."[31]

No longer would man have to tolerate the presence of animals, or be distressed by claw and fang. The disappearance of horses, a prolific source of dirt and disease, was universally acclaimed. Utopian cities banished domestic animals. "Whatever the horse can do," promised one novelist, "the automobile can do a hundred times better."[32] Whole species were to be extirpated. "Humanity cannot but rejoice," cried a scientist in Chauncey Thomas's *Crystal Button*, "that the great carnivorous beasts of the feline, canine, and ursine families no longer exist." Their extinction resulted from "direct and systematic warfare in the interests of humanity." The hippopotamus, rhinoceros, crocodile, and tiger, Thomas continued happily, "have long since ceased to devastate and make afraid." And repaying a biblical debt, he also announced the total destruction of the entire serpent family, "a long-wished for riddance that has but recently been effected."[33]

Thus most utopians had little reverence for wilderness or unspoiled nature. The wild was dangerous because it was unpredictable. Utopian pleasures were taken in parks, and nature organized by electricity. Solitary confrontations with natural challenges—of weather, terrain, or animal rivalry—were defined out of utopias, along with other risks.

The need for animals was reduced, moreover, because of changes in eating habits. A large number of these fictional communities were vegetarian, both for health and for moral reasons. Dietary reform had long been associated with more comprehensive social schemes in the United States; its appearance in this literature is not surprising.[34] But the frequency and emphasis are still impressive, and the justifications are revealing. In *Equality*, Edward Bellamy's sequel to *Looking Backward*, improved health results from a vegetarian diet. But the impulses to this reform were ethical. According to Bellamy the abandonment of eating flesh "was chiefly an effect of the great wave of human feeling, the passion of pity and compunction for all suffering—in a word, the impulse of tender-heartedness—which was really the great moral power behind the revolution. . . . The sentiment of brotherhood, the feeling of solidarity, asserted itself not merely toward men and women, but likewise toward the humbler companions of our life on earth and sharers of its fortunes, the animals."[35] Men had come to conceive of themselves as elder brothers in a great natural family; eating animals seemed a kind of cannibalism.

While some utopians tried to forget man's debt to nature, others wanted simply to improve the master design by destroying all aggressive impulses. On the Mars of James Cowan's *Daybreak* horses had not disappeared, but people were too tenderhearted to enjoy riding them; the horses might become fatigued. Even animals ceased to eat flesh. They were trained not to do so, or bred until the carnivorous instinct had disappeared.[36] On another Mars, this one the creation of Gustavus W. Pope, Martians became vegetarians in order to transcend their baser appetites. "Animal food," declared a Martian doctor, "has the inherent tendency to depress the development of the higher and nobler attributes of man, the moral sentiments and feelings, and it has the worse effect, also, of stimulating and fostering the instincts and passions of our lower nature." Earth people, he warned, despite any advances in civilization they might make, would always have discord so long as they devoured meat. Meat, according to Herman Brinsmade, contained "all of the poisonous, unexcreted waste matter," of dead animals, overstimulating the "eliminative organs" and producing an enormous number of fatal diseases. In Brinsmade's *Utopia Achieved*, a single-tax community, one of the heroes was Horace Fletcher, the food reformer who gave up a life of ease to teach the poor how to chew. Broth, graham puffs, zwieback, and malt honey were healthful as well as ethical imperatives.[37]

The substitution of electricity for animal power and the complementary habit of vegetarianism were valued by the utopians as evidence of refined human feelings; stimulants which might lead to aggression or aggrandizement—alcohol, dirt, noise, animal food—were barred. Fears of aggressive energies, competitiveness, and self-enhancement dominate many of the novels. Activities which produced conflict or personal tension were discouraged. The reason for this obsession with order and regularity may lie in a second recent revolution which had affected the lives of millions of Americans, and that was the consciousness of crowding which invaded the late nineteenth-century mind. Recent scholarship has paid greater attention to the ecological aspects of rapid urban growth, but in this period of increasing urbanization all its victims knew that higher population densities were influencing every aspect of urban life. Transport, recreation, housing, commerce, and family life all bore marks of the strain placed by numbers on facilities. This social pressure had many effects; one, no doubt, was to increase interest in avenues of escape, the wilderness appeal that historians have lately described.[38] Another effect was to intensify demands for privacy, and strengthen the argument that population density was in itself a cause of poverty, crime, and social alienation. The novelists, however, were committed to community and not to isolation; somehow they had to evoke physical settings suitable for large groups, without any sense of pressure or tension. Continual contiguity led to aggression, loss of control, and social decline. "Contact breeds contagion and decay," wrote Captain Nathan Davis in *Beulah*. Dense "populations which are in constant contact breed moral contagion and deadly corruption."[39] The solution was to plan an environment that used space efficiently and avoided situations of crowding.

This, after all, was the first generation with so many indiscriminate crowd encounters; rural Americans, living on farms or in small towns, experienced large casual assemblages only occasionally, when they journeyed away from home or participated in political rallies and religious revivals. Even so, one finds among Poe, Hawthorne, and Melville an awareness of the nature of the pre–Civil War crowd. But the urbanites of the late nineteenth century, as the first generation of urban sociologists reiterated, were being bombarded with secondary contacts continuously, producing novel collective experiences. What arrangements could maintain order in so intense (and potentially anarchic) a social setting? This question was addressed by almost every utopian writer, whatever his economic orientation. The fictional strategy usually fell into three parts. First, avoidance of situations that involved social pressure, and a portrayal of the panic that would inevitably take place if control were to be lost. Second, construction of facilities which ordered public life and protected personal space simultaneously. And finally, encouragement of qualities of character and temper which preferred these controlled environments, and knew how to enjoy them.

On the first level, that of the object lesson, utopian novelists frequently referred to the horrors of social compression in contemporary America, contrasting them with the calm of utopian life. William Dean Howells's Altrurian traveler reacted with disgust to the noise and congestion of New York's elevated railroads. "Every seat in them is taken, and every foot of space in the aisle between the seats is held by people standing, and swaying miserably to and fro by the leather straps dangling from the roofs. Men and women are indecently crushed together, without regard for that personal dignity which we prize, but which the Americans seem to know nothing of and care nothing for. The multitude overflows from the car . . . and the passengers are as tightly wedged on the platforms without as they are within. . . . Those who wish to mount fight their way into the car or onto the platform, where the guard slams an iron gate."[40] Howells blamed such horrors on plutocracy; with ten men doing the work of one, the movement of people to and from business was enormous. Referring implicitly to the work of George M. Beard, an early psychiatrist whose book *American Nervousness* made direct connections between urban life and mental disease, Howells connected the noise of trains to the growing prevalence of "neurotic disorders."[41]

Public ceremonies were like public transport—disorderly, crowded, and threatening. According to utopians, decorum was maintained only by force. "I was once summoned as a witness in one of our courts," recalled an American visitor to Altruria, "and I have never forgotten the horror of it: the hot, dirty room, with its foul air, the brutal spectators, the policemen stationed among them to keep them in order."[42] Cosimo Noto, a physician and novelist, symbolized disorder by concentrating on accidents in crowded streets and on railroad trains.[43] Henry Olerich blamed many social evils on the indiscriminate concentration of people in apartments. "The old, the middle-aged, and the young are all crowded in one little apartment. Their natural inclination . . . is very unlike. Yet they are compelled to be together. . . . How many matured children," he asked his readers, "when living in the same . . . apartment, make your home a dungeon—a battle-field on which the better sentiments of both parents and children are slain?"[44] For Bradford Peck, whose very title, *The World a Department Store,* summarized his commitment to order, a major drawback of nineteenth-century life was the shopping scene, "when crowds of women, becoming as they did frantic and almost wild, pushed and crowded one another to gain an opportunity of purchasing something, because some other woman wanted it."[45]

Several of the utopian and many of the science fiction novels portrayed terrifying scenes of mass panic, when the normal controls failed. In Stewart Edward White's *The Sign at Six*, an old man holds New York in terror by cutting off electricity during the rush hour. "Where ordinarily is a crush," wrote White, "now was a panic—a panic the more terrible in that it was solid, sullen, inert, motionless. Women fainted and stood unconscious, erect. Men sank slowly from

*Utopian supply
store*

sight, agonized, their faces contorted, but unheard in the full roar of the crowd, and were seen no more. Around the edges people fought frantically to get out; and others, with the blind, unreasoning, home instinct, fought as hard to get in."[46] Several of the interplanetary stories feature cosmic catastrophe, meteor bombardments which reduce the delicate shell of civilization to rubble and send millions scrambling to escape destruction. In Louis P. Gratacap's novel of Mars, "strangely bewildered and uncontrolled" crowds fight to escape the meteor showers, the reverse of the buoyant throngs that the visitor had encountered just a short time before.[47] Panic scenes permitted writers to work out their fears, and sometimes to resolve them.

They did resolve them by devising miracles of ingenuity which carefully channeled the new crowds. Safety, dignity, and breathing space were stressed over and over again. Some novelists drew diagrams and maps of their ideal communities, scaled to the last foot of road width and building height. Mass transport, governed by elaborate mechanical safeguards, aided circulation. Garden cities and small towns replaced the dense concentration of urban life, while apartment hotels, with centralized cooking, eating, and washing facilities, were surrounded by parks and gardens. Neither concentration nor isolation was permissible, for each involved struggle and struggle meant anxiety. No device to ease worry was too small for discussion. In Albert Chavannes' Socioland, an ideal community set in Africa, streetcars were large, comfortable, and designed to reassure. At each end "is hung a large dial, and printed upon it are the names of the cross streets and important places passed on the trip. A needle on the dial, automatically moved by the running gear, travels in unison with the car, and always points to the exact spot reached, thus keeping the passengers informed of their present location. By this simple method much anxiety is avoided."[48] The great value of the telephone lay in its ability to bypass public encounters and crowd pressures. Broadcast sermons and music reached dispersed audiences. "Telephones have so far spoiled us," explained one utopian to a visitor, "that being in a crowd, which was the matter-of-course penalty you had to pay for seeing or hearing anything interesting, would seem too dear a price to pay for almost any enjoyment."[49] The population of Gustavus Pope's Mars was eight billion but there was no crowding; by a unique arrangement of great linear cities, some of them two thousand miles long, each family owned its own house, garden, and grounds.[50]

These technical contrivances, and the list could be extended indefinitely, all had a common objective: avoidance of confrontation and its resulting disorder. Utopians had an obsession with clarity. Everyone's place was demarcated. Some novelists prescribed uniforms (for men and women) as an effective means for social recognition.[51] Occasionally, in ominous prophecy, numbers were tattooed on the arm; elsewhere ceremonial parades demonstrated the coherence of the social order.[52]

But all these inventions, the novelists recognized, were doomed unless people adapted to crowd life by developing new, more regular habits. If social compression demanded mechanical resolution, it also required inner discipline and self-control. This was the purpose of education, explained one of Henry Olerich's Martians. We attach "a great deal of importance to order, promptness and regular habits," declared Mr. Midith. "We teach them to our children by practicing them ourselves. We are regular with our set meals, our work, our leisure, our exercises, our studies, our bathing, our dressing, our games, our rising, and our retiring. . . . We, no doubt, would be called cowards by you for not daring to infringe on our health by a night's carousal, the same as you would be called cowards by your savages for not daring to do what a cannibal delights in doing."[53] In Chauncey Thomas's city of Tone, citizens lived in giant apartment houses, resembling pyramids. While the earthly visitor is impressed by their cleanliness, he adds that if tenement dwellers at home were given such great buildings "they would soon reduce [them] to their own level of disorder, filth, and degradation. Of what account would be tiled floors, and porcelain walls . . . running water, ventilators, hot-air currents, and electric lights" to people who would not maintain them?[54] His utopian host, however, argued that the preliminaries of educating the workers in homemaking had been going on in Tone for centuries. Public instruction enabled workers' families to keep up their apartments.

The great state education systems promoted the transmission of these values, and public behavior, invariably restrained and peaceful, reflected their success. In Frank Rosewater's city of Red Cross, the earthly visitor winced a bit at the extremity of order. Underground subways led to electric car stations; no one ever faced bad weather; parkways were lined with temples for social relaxation. "This parked environment seems too dainty for an out-world barbarian," joked the earthling. "It reminds me of the restraint I felt as a boy, every time I had to don my Sunday clothes." "I suppose you'd rather wade in mud and filth, with the dust flying into your face and soot and cinders falling all over you," his hostess remonstrated.[55] The exchange illuminates the psychological restraints produced by sanitary compulsions. It seemed like a flight backward to childhood, stern parents warning their children against dirty faces and torn clothing. But according to the novelists, it worked; the "feverish haste and flurry" of American crowds was gone; drunkenness and rowdiness had disappeared, at least in public.[56]

With their physical innovations and new social values, the utopians had apparently conquered all the anxieties which tortured civilized society. There was one area, however, which gave even the utopians difficulty, and it was connected with the third great consciousness revolution which took place in the late nineteenth century: acceptance of the germ theory of disease. Like electricity, here was another set of discoveries which promised security but also intensified older anxieties. From the 1870s onward popular understanding of the work of Pasteur, Lister, and Koch broadened in America. New conceptions of the etiology of disease gained influence. Interestingly (and sadly) enough, newspapers and popular science journals picked up the new theories faster than did physicians and medical schools.[57] But within a generation ancient traditions of miasmatic sources and spontaneous generation were discarded in favor of the dangerous microbes—insidious, omnipotent, invisible enemies of humanity, able to attack anyone and anywhere. Older contagion theory had posited a variety of atmospheric hypotheses; with a few exceptions scientists did not hold organic entities or animate contagion responsible for the spread of disease. But by the 1880s science had located and identified these tiny animal beings; nature herself, rather than poisonous gases or waste, produced pain and illness. Old fears now gained precision and legitimacy.

Along with the expectations of progress grew new torments. "We are surrounded by invisible legions of enemies," complained the *Arena*, enemies which inspire "a certain uncanny terror unknown by war."[58] Postage stamps, doorknobs, theater audiences, even money became suspect as spreaders of saliva, dust, and morbid germs.[59] The *New York Times* charged that in founding public libraries Andrew Carnegie was "establishing breeding grounds for every kind and degree of microbe known to science" and warned that those coming to libraries to "quench their thirst for knowledge" would incur "the same risk as those who should drink of polluted waters." Books in public use fairly "swarm with spores, germs, cells, and ferments," and among the colonies they foster "may be found the representatives of every variety of evil thing in which reside the power and potency of death." Could it be, asked the *Times* disingenuously, that the lengthening of human life achieved in the recent past was largely the result of increased use of newspapers—less apt to be breeding grounds for microbes—and decreasing use of books?[60] Sharing the general hysteria, the Missouri Valley Homeopathic Association adopted a resolution declaring kissing to be unsanitary.[61] The health commissioner of New York proposed that every piece of money in circulation be disinfected; English medical authorities warned against the use of doorknobs, and advised designing foot levers to prevent "fouling of the hand."[62] And *Harper's Weekly* declared it "the age of the microbe." "He disports himself with equal satisfaction in the air, the earth, and the waters. He invades our beverages and our foods. He finds our mouths desirable lurking places, our hair and fingernails habitual outposts; on occasion he swims in our blood. Everywhere he is seeking his own selfish ends. He is the agent of decay and the messenger of disease. . . . The whole world, though it long denied him recognition, now bows to him as the mightiest of conquerors."[63]

It was natural, then, that the novelists, with their already developed concerns about pressure, danger, and bodily integrity, should display the cruelest anxieties about germs. "Little is known of the micro-organic world," Jack London wrote in an essay, "The Human Drift," "but that little is appalling; and no census of it will ever be taken, for there is the true, literal, 'abysmal fecundity.' Multitudinous as man is, all his totality of individuals is as nothing in comparison with the inconceivable vastness of numbers of the micro-organisms. In your body, or in mine, right now, are swarming more individual entities than there are human beings in the world to-day."[64] To London these facts had extraordinary meaning. They seemed nature's reassertion of Malthusian laws. When man increased too rapidly and invaded the sources of his food and space, nature would reply with a wave of "death-dealing microbes" to decimate his ranks and so restore the balance. *The Scarlet Plague*, which Jack London published in 1912, described a world population of several hundred, the few survivors of seven billion after a mysterious plague had struck.[65] The electrical age was succeeded by cavemen.

Many utopians shared London's phobia, but devised plans to overcome it. Communities could organize to fight the menace of the microbe; public health regulations and selective breeding would increase longevity and personal vigor. In Chauncey Thomas's Tone, citizens dealt "with disease as a deadly enemy that deserves no quarter." Marriage rules were strict. Invalids were treated within a domed hothouse, the Palace of the Sun, while monitoring stations searched for the presence of dangerous gases. The earthling applauded such innovations. "We used to be surrounded by invisible enemies that meant illness, if not death," he told his hosts, "and they found access not only to our factories and places of amusement, but also to our homes. Yet we had at our command no monitor to warn us of their presence. . . . The meters we most needed to cry 'Beware!' when the seeds of death hovered about us and our loved ones—those we lacked."[66] For the physician Cosimo Noto, disease was an obsession, justifying the most drastic methods of combat. Citizens of New Orleans, living under socialism and sanitation fifty years in the future, could not understand how nineteenth-century Americans could bear even to eat; there was "such a great number of microbes" in ordinary food that "everyone must have been constantly ill."[67] Science ran the spotless kitchens of utopian New Orleans. Dishes were sterilized after use, in specially designed machinery; the body was treated like "an electric battery," and rigorous legislation ensured that the air, water, and streets were spotless.

So strongly were utopians identified with sanitary regimentation that when a satire appeared, like W. N. Harben's *Land of the Changing Sun* (an attack upon socialism), it exaggerated for effect this worship of the body. Harben's dystopia exterminated all those found physically wanting. "Every heartbeat is heard by our medical men," reported the king, "and every vein is transparent."[68] Only the healthy lived in Alpha, under an electric sun, spied on continually by government agents.

Actually, Harben didn't have to travel far to exaggerate. In John Jacob Astor's *Journey in Other Worlds,* a utopian exploration which vaguely resembled *Etidorhpa,* earth people visited Saturn and Jupiter and observed with the eyes of a spirit what life really was like on earth. One visitor, demonstrating Astor's own anxieties, "saw not only the air as it entered and left his friends' lungs, but also the substance of their brains, and the seeds of disease and death whose presence they did not even suspect. . . . In some he saw the germs of consumption; in others, affections of the heart. In all he saw the malignant, omnipresent bacilli that the cells were trying to overcome."[69]

Of all these consciousness revolutions, microbe theory permitted the gravest of anxieties to surface, and this was the anxiety about death. In these worlds so controlled, so well planned, so secure, the ghostly stranger continued to appear. Death seemed anomalous to progressive thinkers in the late nineteenth century; it did not belong in a world so triumphantly organized. As Donald Meyer pointed out some years ago, for people "no longer disciplined to life and death by orthodox stoicism, no longer hedged narrowly by close economic and social circumstances," life was meant to join wish and reality. But no matter what marvels of machinery were achieved or what ingenious institutions were developed, "the body remained vulnerable. Death could strike. . . . Disease, sickness, death, bearing no relation to right moral order, manifesting alien, material, outside forces, defeated wishes unfairly."[70]

As the ultimate source of disorder and confrontation, the reality of death, its customs and ceremonies, formed an obvious subject for the utopian novelists.[71] The generation reading their books was fascinated with grief and mourning. In both Britain and America spiritualist societies enjoyed a resurgence. Hundreds of mediums held séances to stimulate direct communication with spirits. They published books dictated by the distinguished dead, offering advice on everything from politics to religion. Novelists of the period—Howells, James, Harold Frederic, Richard Harding Davis—treated the phenomonon as a major social issue.[72] University commissions held hearings to determine fraudulence; distinguished scholars like William James in America and Henry Sidgwick in England, celebrities like Houdini and Sir Arthur Conan Doyle, paid their respects to this quest for certainty. The growth of mind-cure religions, like Christian Science and New Thought, reflected this desire for victory over the bonds of mortality. The same energies which had wrought revolutions in science and technology, which had tamed nature and identified man's microbe enemies, could now be turned to the conquest of the nonmaterial world.

Along with others of their day, then, the utopian novelists took on this last anxiety which the race could be spared: death, preceded by debilitating old age. Selective breeding and elaborate public health programs, staples of the utopian genre, were tied to the prevention of physical decay. They studied "how best to nurture and care for those bodies," explained one of James Cowan's Martians, "and when that lesson was thoroughly learned, we found that sickness and pain were gone, and with them, also, all fear of death. For now we die when our days are fully ended. The span of our life has been doubled since we began to know and care for ourselves, and, at the close, death is anticipated and recognized as a friend."[73] Gustavus Pope's Martians were "free from those dreadful constitutional taints and inherited diseases, which have for ages past, and still afflict so many millions of our Terrestrial races. . . . Martians thoroughly understood the avoidable causes of disease and acted accordingly," their physicians exploring "the secret recesses of the human frame . . . with a skill unknown in our medical world," discovering and destroying the germs of disease.[74]

And when death eventually came, in utopia, it arrived gently, for mortals died in the full knowledge of their own immortality. They would simply move on to inhabit a heaven as advanced as their model societies, destined either for peace everlasting or passage to a new life. For Louis P. Gratacap heaven could be found on Mars; for Dr. Mortimore it was inside the sun; for Arthur Willink it lay in the fourth dimension. But that heaven existed, and could be described, was devoutly believed by most of the utopian novelists. [75]

Thus the religiosity, the antimaterialism, and the technological absorption of Lloyd, Fiske, and Cole, the strange combinations of interests which mark utopian literature, seem more understandable. Machines and mysticism had a common objective: the allaying of human anxieties, and most of all, anxieties about aggression, accident, old age, and death. These were ancient fears, as old as the race. They were not eclipsed by the more immediate confrontations of labor and capital, or the specter of class warfare. Instead they were revitalized by a series of modern discoveries which, tantalizingly, promised greater security even while they threatened imminent destruction. And running alongside the physical dangers was the spiritual catastrophe: that no future life awaited the soul to compensate for the pain of the earthly life. Scientific progress had not only abetted physical danger; by stimulating (and supporting) secularized ideals, it was annihilating the last, best promise of religion: future life.

There were, in the 1890s, masterly, vigorous spirits in America who, like Theodore Roosevelt, opted for the Strenuous Life; who preached football and risk-taking, and the expansion of experience as their response to an urbanizing world. The utopians, however, sought reconciliation and not challenge, and preferred comfort to confrontation. Despite its technology, advanced economics, and often rather aggressive secularism, this utopian vision was essentially religious, and aligned with a specifically American heritage. Like religious reformers of some three centuries earlier, faced with disorder the utopians sought to structure and even confine life, rather than expand it. The revolutions we have marked, until recently, as milestones of scientific progress, sobered them. Their optimism about the future rested on the achievement of an environmental stasis. Unlimited growth seemed as dangerous as decay.

That is why we can speak, with some justice, of the birth of the modernized sensibility in the utopian novel; for with all their strange trappings, their bizarre inventions, their scholasticism and occasional smugness, these utopians were awakening to the logic of the modern world. And many of them were afraid.

9

The Drama of

Consumer Desire

D escriptions of nineteenth-century industrial growth have considered a broad range of issues, including labor scarcity, patterns of imitation, primacy of innovation, and economies of scale. Studies of production and distribution abound. But the role and character of the retail buyer remain mysterious. Works are now in progress, or have been recently completed, which promise correction. As part of this enterprise I would like to examine a significant accompaniment to the expansion of the American system of manufactures—the creation of an American system of consumption, the establishment of relationships between Americans and a range of objects that were unprecedented in number and variety. These relationships were supported by a set of shopping rituals, and by habits of appropriation, which have become the commonplaces of modern capitalist society. They developed throughout the world. The pattern I present may or may not be applicable to Britain, France, or Germany during the same period. It is too early to engage in comparative speculation, and I wish to make no special national claims. But the process of identifying, describing, and evaluating the consumer, as a social type, proceeded steadily in the United States from the late nineteenth century on.

From Otto Mayr and Robert C. Post, eds., *Yankee Enterprise*, pp. 189–216. ©Smithsonian Institution, 1981.

I am concerned less with the objective history of the consumer and more
with consciousness of the consumer's role. For that reason my principal sources
will be works of fiction which placed the buying process within the social experience. My procedure has four steps. First of all, a brief summary of the
special national problems, primarily ideological in character. Second, some
reference to the initial age of consumer consciousness in fiction, coming at the
end of the last century. Third, a description of trends in the early twentieth
century, in particular during the 1920s, which intensified American object consciousness. And finally, some examples of the way in which mass distribution
affected the novelistic sensibility of the period. My argument, tout court, is that
mass-produced objects and object relationships came increasingly to enter the
American novel, both as symbols and as experiences. But the very standardization which produced such triumphs for the manufacturing and distributing systems is here defined as a major problem for the creative imagination. Thus a
national style of purchasing began to be adumbrated by our literary figures, and
fixed upon as a cultural metaphor.

If the American experience was not unique, it did offer, so far as historians of consumption are concerned, special circumstances. Public rhetoric, as
early as the seventeenth century, revealed such awareness. Moralists—political
leaders and religious advisers both—found that material prosperity posed grave
problems for the American colonists. Traditions of suspicion toward the effects
of comfort and security were especially powerful in New England and Pennsylvania. The fine edge of religious suspense was, after all, honed on a collective
sense of insecurity. Puritanism, and radical Protestantism generally, rested
upon an introspective obsession with determining the relationship between sign
and essence, sanctification and justification; any form of relaxation could be
dangerous. Wealth bred relaxation; it induced in sinners false confidence and
lessened their sense of dependence upon divine government. Economic success
might spell spiritual failure, and the Puritan ministry relentlessly explored this
paradox.[1]

It was also a problem for political leaders of the late eighteenth century,
sensitive to charges of mercenary ambition. Republicanism seemed to demand
austerity and restraint in personal life; the new task was to inspire the economic
energies that aided national advancement and independence without encouraging self-enhancement to assume a motive power all its own. That delicate
jewel, virtue, without which the constitutional mechanism was doomed, could
be marred by excessive appeals to personal advancement, yet qualities of discipline, industry, ingenuity, and audaciousness had economic gain and a higher
standard of consumption as their almost inevitable epilogue.[2]

The problem did not end in the American Enlightenment. If anything it assumed grander proportions during the Jacksonian era. Jeremiads multiplied warnings of the dangers inherent in personal wealth and the traps to virtue and piety that lay concealed beneath fancy clothes, large houses, silver plate, and fine furniture. One American historian analyzing the literature perceptively labelled the psychic drama of the Jacksonian period "Prosperity the Riddle."[3] There were, of course, always watchmen on the walls quick to spot any outbreaks of the materialistic virus which could bring on fatal attacks of self-indulgence. Busybodies, who have excited the scorn of native satirists and foreign critics alike,with their burrowing curiosity about the personal tastes and life-styles of private citizens, were nurtured in this hothouse of anxiety. What people drank, ate, wore, and consumed seemed to have direct relationships to their laws, their rulers, and their morals.[4]

But while there are continuities between pre- and postmodern fears of personal consumption, there are also contrasts. In general the buying habits that attracted criticism through the middle of the nineteenth century involved the purchase of luxuries and the search for sensual pleasure. The upholsterer, the parfumier, the milliner, the jeweler, all had benefitted for centuries from the patronage of the wealthy and the aspiring. And the national concern that a new aristocracy, eager to demonstrate its aesthetic tastes and well-bred gentility, would be a public danger by reason of its frivolity and social competition, this concern had already been voiced.

Yet there were also some special fears voiced. It was not only that the American experiment involved self-restraint; Americans seemed particularly vulnerable to a new kind of self-indulgence. One need turn only to that vade mecum of cultural insights, Alexis de Tocqueville's *Democracy in America*, to get a sense of the urgency. Tocqueville discovered, defined, and discoursed on American materialism. He found its blessings mixed. A concern with physical improvement encouraged a series of constructive pieties and useful disciplines, Toqueville acknowledged, but in this country it also constrained the role of idealism and the possibility for heroic acts. And the reason lay in the principle of equality. "The reproach I address to the principle of equality," Tocqueville wrote, "is not that it leads men away in the pursuit of forbidden enjoyments, but that it absorbs them wholly in quest of those which are allowed." The problem of American materialism—or its opportunity for American manufacturers and retailers—was not that it would corrupt a small number of community leaders, but that it would enervate, distract, and dominate the great masses. "The enjoyment of others is sanctioned by religion and morality; to these the heart, the imagination, and life itself are unreservedly given up, till, in snatching at these lesser gifts, men lose sight of those more precious possessions which constitute the glory and greatness of mankind."[5]

Tocqueville's generation was concerned with what has since come to be defined as the rise of mass society, and the conservative predilections of so many early sociologists helped shape much of their research and their writings. Later generations of critics would pick up and expand their message. American materialism was dangerous precisely because it did not confine itself to the exotic tastes of the wealthy and powerful. Objects more homely and more domestic than gold and silver or ivory and alabaster would, from the most pessimistic point of view, provide the bonds that would tie up the national imagination. "We are not prepared to allow that wealth is more valued in America than elsewhere," wrote the editor of *The American Whig Review,* "but in other countries the successful pursuit of it is necessarily confined to a few, while here it is open to all." No American was contented to be poor, he continued, and without any established limits there could be "no condition of hopes realized," or, in other words, "of contentment." This desire for physical possessions was "good and hopeful to the interests of the race, but destructive to the happiness and dangerous to the virtue of the generation exposed to it."[6] It was precisely that paradox, then, involving personal ambition and national advancement, which worried the Revolutionary generation.

The search for material happiness and comfort was not confined, during the first half of the nineteenth century, to the mere purchase of objects. It could be demonstrated, among other places, in the how-to-do-it literature which poured from American printers—the advice and directions given for home-building and house improvements, for furniture- and clothes-making, for cooking and machine-building.[7] Materialism, in the mid-nineteenth century, was tied both to production *and* consumption. If a man desired what he could not yet afford to buy, he could either enlarge his fortune or apply his own talents to imitation. Instead of going to expensive monopolists of skills and products, costly artisans and urban merchants, the individual consumer still had the capacity to create some of his own luxuries.

It is, I believe, the declining ability to manufacture one's own material environment that precipitates a growth of interest in the purchasing act. It first develops slowly in the last half of the nineteenth century and then flowers in the first few decades of the twentieth century. We are all familiar with the decline of household production, one of the results of the continuing process of industrialization, technological change, and urbanization. We are also familiar with the growing incapacity of consumers to match, in precision, variety, attractiveness, and especially cost, the profusion of objects produced by American manufacturers, from clothing and furniture to food and drink. To enhance consumer appeal, dramatic improvements in advertising and distribution capacities were made in the late nineteenth century. Newspaper and magazine advertisements grew in number and improved in quality, thanks to printing innovations and the new halftone engraving processes. Mail-order catalogues and a revolution in poster art enhanced display methods and increased public sensitivity to the attractions and variety of purchasable objects. And the enlargement and improvement of retailing operations—in large part through the construction of huge department stores, which achieved their modern physical forms in the twenty-five years preceding World War I—added to retailing temptations, as did the refinements of window dressing.[8]

Even before the Civil War, American magazines were peppered with stories about and comments upon the new retailing. *Harper's Weekly* in 1857 ran one picture of a shopping crowd entitled "The Dry-Goods Epidemic" and spoke of women "with faces like hawks and fingers like claws" surrounding the shopping counters. "The shopping mania," wrote *Harper's*, "ought to have received more attention than it has from the faculty. It is a species of absorbing insanity."[9] In the next several decades it would get more attention. Writing in *The Century* in 1901, Lillie Hamilton French sought to capture the spirit of New York's shopping district below Madison Square:

> There is no one part of the day from eight in the morning until six at night when the stores themselves are not full, and when out of doors you do not have to elbow your way . . . through throngs of people, men, women, and children, old and young, rich and poor. . . . The shop-windows, with their elaborate displays, their free exhibitions of the fashionable and the beautiful, are never without their crowds about them.[10]

The problems of consumption, shopping, and materialism were, by the late nineteenth century, increasingly identified with the classes and masses of the great cities, and it was probably inevitable that American novelists of this era, particularly those identified with a concern for realism, should analyze the relationship between consumer desire and personal wealth. They began to chart the rituals of American consumption, the new iconographies of possession and the competition for domestic luxury which lay behind the marketing success of so many American companies. William Dean Howells, the most perceptive of the social realists, observed the crowds of women thronging Washington Street in Boston, "intent upon spending the money of their natural protectors." Unconsciously echoing the imagery of *Harper's* a generation before, he evoked the fierce intensity of the female shoppers, clasping parcels to their hearts and coordinating the immense task of moving from store to store in search of bargains which they could tote back to their suburban homes.[11]

Howells's consumers, his admirers of fine things, were caught by tradi-

"The Dry-Goods Epidemic," 1857

tional problems. An ever broader slice of the population, they were still dazzled by visions of furniture, carpets, chandeliers, and bric-a-brac. And they fell prey to the moral dilemmas and unsatisfied desires that inevitably ensued.

Howells's greatest novel of social climbing and material desire, *The Rise of Silas Lapham*, focused upon this traditional dilemma by examining an ancient theme—the problems of the newly rich. The great symbolic act which informs the novel—Lapham's commissioning of a new house in Boston's Back Bay—is a translation of an immemorial gesture, indulged in by the new noblemen of Elizabethan England, the tidewater planters of the eighteenth-century Chesapeake, and the industrial millionaires of New York's Fifth Avenue. Lapham's own confrontation with social pretension and commercial dishonesty, the contact between parvenu money and genteel poverty, the personal tensions of urban living, all were explored by Howells with particular brilliance.[12] But the experience of consumption, the lure of material objects, did not absorb him as much as the comedy of manners provoked by the new scale of income.

There is, to be sure, a new level of specificity in Howells's description of the urban landscape and the interiors of middle-class housing and urban flats. The relationships drawn between personality and setting, between temperament and physical object, reached their apogee in Howells's famous descriptions. But the objects are generically classified and form the staple clutter, with some exotic twists, with which the middle classes had surrounded themselves from the mid century on. In *A Hazard of New Fortunes* the Basil Marches, searching for a furnished flat, encounter the bewildering forest of objects that make up the middle-class interior, and Howells enjoys recounting the details. Mrs. Grosvenor Green's rooms, for example, fairly swarmed with "gimcracks":

> The front of the upright piano had what March called a short-skirted portière on it, and the top was covered with vases, with dragon candlesticks, and with Jap fans, which also expanded themselves bat-wise on the walls between the etchings and the water-colors. The floors were covered with filling, and then rugs, and then skins; the easy-chairs all had tidies, Armenian and Turkish and Persian; the lounges and sofas had embroidered cushions hidden under tidies. The radiator was concealed by a Jap screen, and over the top of this some Arab scarfs were flung. There was a superabundance of clocks. China pugs guarded the hearth; a brass sunflower smiled from the top of either andiron, and a brass peacock spread its tail before them inside a high filigree fender; on one side was a coal hod in repoussé brass, and on the other a wrought-iron wood basket. Some red Japanese bird-kites were tucked about in the necks of spelter vases, a crimson Jap umbrella hung opened beneath the chandelier, and each globe had a shade of yellow silk.[13]

A furniture warehouse, in short, the loot from the bazaars of the world, its chief defect its clutter and eclecticism, its willful insistence upon disguise, upon torturing the material or the function or the appliance into something it was not meant to be. It was easy to project from these leavings the persona of their owner. The foibles of fashion formed a vulnerable and venerated target. Howells was cataloguing objects with brilliance and effecting a new social translation from an old mode of expression, but he was not transforming his characters fundamentally. Beyond the detail, this was a category of consumer which epitomized bourgeois acquisitiveness and, as such, had been around for quite a few decades.

There were some similarities of focus to be found in a contemporary of Howells's whose works are also filled with the physical details of America's Victorian age; but there is also now a new concern with the effects of consumership and mass appetite upon the life and ambitions of the working class. Theodore Dreiser's picture of the city, his evocative theatrical sets, fit a very old image of glitter and corruption, an image that moralizers of the seventeenth and eighteenth centuries would have recognized. But Dreiser's characterization added, through its drama and absorption with the effects of the material environment upon character, the manipulation of desire and appetite and portrayed a new setting for the terrible implications of American materialism. The corpus of Dreiser criticism and commentary forms a literature much larger than Dreiser's own output, and I am touching only lightly upon one of many directions in Dreiser's thinking. But many critics have noted his absorption with settings designed to enhance the urbanite's role as consumer—the theater, the hotel, the restaurant, and, above all, the department store. *Sister Carrie*, the novel which presented the drama of urban desire most evocatively, employs all these scenes and expresses Dreiser's fascination with the signalling devices, particularly the clothing, by which nineteenth-century Americans assumed their specified roles in the social drama. Within days of her hegira to Chicago, Carrie Meeber, as part of her search for work, finds herself in one of Chicago's new department stores, The Fair, which touches off Dreiser's brief disquisition on the history of this commercial enterprise. Carrie's encounter with the retail goods stands in miniature, for her encounter with the great promise of prosperity.

> Each separate counter was a show-place of dazzling interest and attraction. She could not help feeling the claim of each trinket and valuable upon her personally, and yet she did not stop. There was nothing there which she could not have used—nothing which she did not long to own. The dainty slippers and stockings, the delicately frilled skirts and petticoats, the laces, ribbons, hair-combs, purses, all touched her with individual desire, and she felt keenly the fact that not any of these things were in the range of her purchase.

Carrie's appetite and her sense of diminution are increased by the sight of other shoppers, "the fine ladies who elbowed and ignored her, brushing past in utter disregard of her presence, themselves eagerly enlisted in the materials which the store contained." The very shopgirls, pretty and well dressed, make her feel uncomfortable.[14]

The effort to make herself a respectable consumer, a shopper who not only looks but buys, forms one of Carrie's buried motives for leaving the dreary flat inhabited by her sister and brother-in-law. And, within a few chapters, beginning to respond to the wiles of Drouet, a drummer, Carrie is able to return to The Fair, to look at jackets. Dreiser entitled this chapter "The Lure of the Material: Beauty Speaks for Itself," and it is filled with images of Carrie's desire for finery, for shoes, stockings, a skirt and jacket. In The Fair, with Drouet's money, she indulges in one of the new consumer passions. "There is nothing in this world more delightful than that middle state in which we mentally balance at times, possessed of the means, lured by desire, and yet deterred by conscience or want of decision." Here, in this exploration of consumer sensibility, Dreiser has Carrie wander around the store, examining pieces of finery. "Her woman's heart was warm with desire for them. How would she look in this, how charming that would make her!" She moves from the corset department to jewelry, and Dreiser alludes to the earrings, bracelets, chains, and pins that she lovingly encounters. "What would she not have given if she could have had them all!"[15] Accompanying her in the store, advising her on purchases, Drouet employs the rich mercantile atmosphere as part of his courtship. The department store becomes the garden of desire, as suitable for American lovers at the turn of the century as a formal bower might have served couples centuries before. In describing the shopping rituals, the uncharted course of Carrie's wants, and the use of merchandise as a lure to win over her hesitations and suspicions, Dreiser has seized upon a central emblem for the new urban society. And throughout the book he uses the presence of consumer desire as a fever chart to indicate the health of his protagonists.

Thus Hurstwood's dissolution in New York, after the saloon owner abandons his family and flees with the stolen money, is defined in part by his demeaned consumer status, his dependence upon the sufferance of tradesmen, and his need to bargain and learn comparative shopping. He now grows aware of the price of meat, butter, and coal, searching the neighborhood for bargains or trying to do without the little luxuries. Carrie, having learned the pleasures of shopping without fear, reacts with bitterness. Such "miserable details ate the heart out of Carrie. They blackened her days and grieved her soul." Dreiser catalogues the minutiae. "Hurstwood bought the flour—which all grocers sold in 3½ pound packages—for thirteen cents and paid fifteen cents for a half pound of liver and bacon." Carrie, meanwhile, quarreling about debts with the milkman and the coal seller, goes for a drive, her eye "once more taken by the show of wealth—the elaborate costumes, elegant harnesses, spirited horses, and above all, the beauty. Once more the plague of poverty galled her, but now she forgot in a measure her own troubles so far as to forget Hurstwood."[16]

In detail, in drama, in its extraordinary setting of commercial and domestic scenes, Dreiser's novel broke new paths. But its ultimate meaning was, in many ways, highly traditional. At the end Carrie's search for material happiness contains a ring of doom. Surrounded by "her gowns and carriage, her furniture and bank account," by friends and the applause of her audiences, she remains unsatisfied. "Amid the tinsel and shine of her state walked Carrie, unhappy."[17] The objects surrounding her were reduced to false witness in the moralizing last vignette. Dreiser's challenge to conventional morality was his failure to punish Carrie for her fall from grace, leaving her with a successful stage career stretching ahead while Hurstwood commits suicide. But the challenge was not fundamental. In denying Carrie happiness, Dreiser simply extended an older, pietistic notion of the limitations of material success when divorced from spiritual progress. And his portrayal of the seductions of metropolitan life, along with his homilies on the happy family, could have fit comfortably within a whole series of more conventional sermons on the dangers of unchecked appetite.

Traditionalism also pervades human-object relationships in Dreiser's great trilogy on Frank Cowperwood. Cowperwood employs his wealth, in the second and most brilliant volume, *The Titan*, to establish himself as an economic and social force in his adopted city of Chicago. He pursues the usual millionaire's course of building a great house, collecting art, covering his wife with jewels, and generally maintaining the entourage of a grandee. Cowperwood, however, is neither dazzled nor seduced by his wealth. His object remains power, and for him power is a headier experience than mere financial expenditure. The corruptions he dispenses only emphasize his own transcendence of ordinary constraints and appetites, the superman-tycoon who shrugs off wounds which would fell ordinary mortals. Cowperwood in a sense is one of Tocqueville's aristocrats, self-made, but tolerating material losses with equanimity, made more determined than ever by setbacks and opposition. His conquest of society, incomplete and unsuccessful, nonetheless rests on a masterful self-discipline which stands impervious to the tinsel and glitter that seduce weaker spirits. The luxury surrounding the great businessman forms a series of props to his public presence, and, with the exception of his art collection, arouses none of the passion which it did in the heart of an arriviste like Carrie.[18]

The work of Howells and Dreiser, as the output of individual novelists, can hardly be termed representative, nor can it be fastened securely within the terms of an argument about consumer desire. But it testifies to the fact that well before World War I the buying drama had begun to serve as a symbol for modernity, and the buying experience had become a ritual worthy of examination, a metaphor for national mobility, social climbing, economic competition, and moral deterioration. On the whole the buying drama was still confined to women; its objects were generically described; its corruptions came principally through luxurious specialty items or through the transplanted and temporarily dispossessed, who would endure any privation to obtain a larger stock of the world's goods. But a change in sentiment was coming, a change which had its origins in the pre–World War I years but which intensified in the 1920s. American novelists in the twenties would also pay attention to the great American consumer, but there would be a shift of focus, a transformed manner of handling the relationship between people and mass-produced objects, a broader sector of the population to describe, an increased specificity, and a widening of critical attention to the buying act. The sensuality which Howells and to a much larger extent Dreiser located in the act of material possession now becomes a mass experience not confined to the stores or expensive merchandise. We enter, through the novels, a new world of merchandising, one closer to our own day. But before moving to consider these novels it would be useful, I believe, to review some aspects of the merchandising revolution in progress on the eve of the war, and intensifying during the following two decades. Each aspect I describe is merely a summary of a process which has received, or is capable of receiving, far more extensive and detailed treatment. But together they form what must be seen as a historic moment in the history of American selling: a moment which penetrates the world of American fiction, as novelists sense the struggle of the merchandisers to serve a new social type, and the needs people place upon objects as part of their social orientation.

One element of the merchandising revolution lay in the physical reconstruction of American department and specialty stores. Shopping architecture in the major cities was transformed as American retailers tried to incorporate some of the possibilities of modernism, as they had been evidenced at the great 1925 Exposition des Arts Decoratifs in Paris. Store owners, confronting narrow profit margins, increasing downtown congestion, the beginnings of the suburban exodus, and the challenge of chain stores and mail-order houses, began to mount a new and more aggressive campaign to capture consumer loyalties. "It is only in comparatively recent years," R. W. Sexton wrote in 1928, "that merchants have been brought to realize that art has a selling value. The keen competition amongst stores and shops in the congested shopping districts of the larger cities has already been responsible for the maturing of this appreciation of the commercial value of beautiful things." In his chapter "Stores and Shops," Sexton, a student of contemporary American commercial and residential building, argued that well-designed shops could differentiate themselves from one another through their displays, luring the "prospective customer in the expectation of finding there the unusual, the unique, things which they may not find in other places."[19] It was once believed, Sexton argued, that customers did not wish to be distracted from serious buying missions when entering a store. But driven by keener competition, shop owners now realized how crucial was eye appeal to retailing success. The new art of commercial display, John Taylor Boyd asserted in the *Architectural Record*, "aims less at making an exhibition of individual wares than it does at portraying those ideas of luxury, fashion, or style now so important in retail trade, as well as at impressing the public with the mastery on the part of the shop of fashion and style."[20] In place of merely showing goods, stores were displaying tableaux and pictures suggesting locale, mood, or historic incident. Captivated by such pictures, customers stopped, to purchase their ideals of fantasy as well as the specific commodity. Contemporary stores could not wait until customers were in absolute need of merchandise, Frederick J. Kiesler warned. "You must create demand."[21]

The redesign of store facades and interiors focused attention on the pervasive field of action available to the intelligent seller, on the lure of well-displayed objects and their aesthetic properties. Buying was now more than merely a survey of luxurious objects; it was a total experience in which the retailer became a subtle adviser on personal taste, a joiner who fit individual temperament with proper merchandise. The elegant store was less a bazaar and more of a fitting-room. The shop itself, rather than the array of items it displayed, became a muscular advocate for the buying drama.

Simultaneously there were other developments which demonstrated increasing sensitivity to the power of objects in exciting emotional loyalty and which increased awareness of their physical properties. One was a series of improvements in color printing and engraving, improvements which permitted large, full-page, full-color magazine advertisements to be far more faithful to the colors and textures of objects—particularly foods, textile, and automobiles—than ever before. Effective halftone advertising techniques were now more than a generation old, but problems of color reproduction had only recently been solved. This new control over visual advertisement gave manufacturers and retailers a further weapon in their struggle for popular interest.[22]

A third factor in expanding the issue of consumer consciousness could be found in the rationalization of advertising methods developed during the 1920s, stimulated in part by the experiences of World War I and by the more systematic application of experimental psychology to problems of motivating and channeling desire. This rationalization also owed much to the increasing self-confidence and articulateness of the advertising industry itself. Again the roots were prewar, but the science of selling was given, during the 1920s, special deference and attention. "Perhaps the most widely discussed subject in business today is the art of selling," Floyd Parsons announced in the *Saturday Evening Post* in 1920. "Efforts are now being made to develop definite methods for use in the selection of salesmen," he went on. The seller of goods must now be a psychologist, a statistician, a personality analyst, and a performer, in addition to possessing the skills of a merchant.[23] Book after book was written to describe the talents appropriate to salesmanship and to celebrate its social value. Bruce Barton's *The Man Nobody Knows* was merely the most famous example of a huge literature which justified the costs and energies consumed by selling and its advertising components. The rise of the public-relations counsel and the selling of character and personality were simple extensions of the method, once the parameters had been fixed.

Enough work has been done on the modern history of American advertising for this subject to be introduced without much further detail. The same is not true, however, of a fourth element enhancing the social role of consumer goods: the expansion of the American film industry. Profiting from the collapse of European competitors in the wake of World War I, American films dominated not only in this country but throughout the world market, establishing an international reputation for their stars, directors, and producers. Film's influence on consumer products, however subtle and complex, was probably almost as important as its provision of a new set of celebrities, for the image on the movie screen inevitably focused attention on the objects which formed part of its décor. The lingering close-ups, the use of music to emphasize mood, the employment of objects and sets as significant aspects of plot and character development, all emphasized the sensuous properties of what might have been seen, more casually, as mundane artifacts, hardly deserving of sustained attention. Because of the variety in film subject matter, the objects redeemed by the camera ran the gamut from expensive playthings, traditional objects of luxury, to the ordinary appliances of daily life. The presence of a certain style of clothing, a set of furniture, an interior décor, in a major film, could touch off considerable public demand. Films provided an underpinning for American faddishness, running all the way from hairdos and voice inflections to the design of offices and domestic interiors.[24]

Some of the object focus in film resulted from the association with stars, whose own consumption patterns received respectful and detailed attention from the news magazines, newspapers, and fan journals. The Hollywood style, a new blend of luxury and informality, projecting some of the qualities of southern California, set a consumption pattern that exerted considerable mass appeal.[25] Although the houses, the swimming pools, the extravagant art and furniture were clearly beyond the reach of most consumers, the cinema aristocracy inspired a good deal of less expensive imitation. In some ways this was a modern version of a traditional mode of style-setting, except that the pacesetters were now the creatures of a mass culture rather than socialites, military figures, wealthy businessmen, or any of the previous groups of fashion leaders. But the capacity of the camera to exaggerate material luxury, the exoticism of Hollywood's location, the size of the mass audience attending films, and the continual publicity given the stars, all created an unprecedented intensity and sharpness of focus. It is possible, occasionally, to document film's influence on fads or fashions. More difficult—and probably more important—are the undocumentable aspects of film's influence: the custom it inspired of examining the surfaces, shapes, and dimensions of objects with new interest as a result of their appearance on the screen; the stimulation of consumer consciousness because of the screen's capacity for memorable exaggeration. And all this was enhanced, of course, by the gorgeousness of the movie palaces: their opulence underlined the luxurious dreams played on the screen.

The new stores, the improvements in photography, the self-consciousness of the advertising industry, and the role of motion pictures were supplemented by other trends emphasizing the capacity of mass-produced objects to shape daily life. One was the advent of the industrial-design profession, a group that included Norman Bel Geddes, Raymond Loewy, Henry Dreyfuss, Gilbert

Rohde, Lee Simonson, and Walter Dorwin Teague. These men often had backgrounds in theater and set design and worked on products that would not only function effectively but create more compelling, saleable images.[26] They were client-oriented; several had already been employed to redecorate department stores and create retail liveries for store uniforms, delivery vans, wrapping papers, and so on. Their purpose was to demonstrate, to manufacturers and retailers, that attention to physical appearance produced larger profits. Loewy scored an early success by redesigning the Lucky Strike package and convincing hard-bitten George Washington Hill that he was worth his designer fee.

The industrial designers also claimed more disinterested objectives, seeking to develop art forms within machine-made objects that did not challenge the logic of their origins. Dispensing, as they did, with traditional decorative devices, sympathetic with contemporary European design, aware of the progress of the International school, the industrial designers confronted a characteristic dilemma: how to increase the allure of their products without relying upon the sentimental details and frills that had gained them customers at an earlier date. A certain amount of public education was necessary for potential audiences to appreciate the new uncluttered surfaces, the smooth curves, the dramatic lettering, the carefully planned knobs and controls in the redesigned refrigerators, stoves, alarm clocks, lighters, vacuum cleaners, hot-water heaters, and radios that flew off their drawing boards. But aided by the new photography, by the crusading of art publicists eager to legitimize modern design, by movies, by the railroad companies that popularized streamlined design in their search for more customers and were major patrons of Loewy and Dreyfuss, the industrial designers made considerable progress.

They were helped, also, by the great international expositions of the 1930s, in New York, San Francisco, and Chicago, where their work was displayed quite effectively.[27] Norman Bel Geddes, designer of the G.M. Futurama, and Walter Dorwin Teague, employed by Eastman Kodak, U.S. Steel, Du Pont, and Con Edison, were among the most visible designers of their generation. Surrounded with drama, greeted with excited enthusiasm by the press, their newly shaped objects achieved special immediacy and identity and seemed more intrinsically interesting than their predecessors. The movement by institutions like the Museum of Modern Art to collect well-designed objects of daily use added force to the designers' insistence that they were seeking artistic glory as well as increased sales. And the possibility of purchasing a mass-produced masterpiece added a certain piquancy to the consumer's activities. In sum, the contribution of industrial design provided, at a minimum, reinforcement to those seeking to increase the emotional energy invested in the adoration of mass-produced objects. And the designers managed this without associating

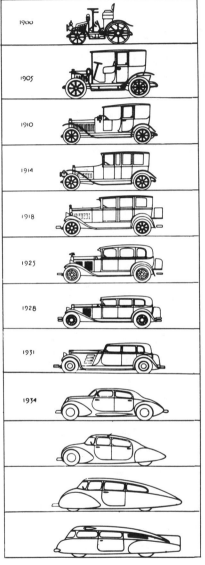

Raymond Loewy

such self-consciousness with dandyism or affectation, its standard earlier associations.

The achievement of the designers was complemented by another feature of the interwar years which has received extensive commentary in another context, and that was the popularity of the model change, particularly for automobiles.[28] It fitted easily into the heightened consciousness of object form that I have been trying to outline. Now it was not only the particular model that was important, but its vintage as well; the consumer was moving through time as well as space. How extensively and frequently manufacturers of consumer staples put model changes into effect varied, of course, according to the object, the state of technology, and the intervention of industrial designers. But there begins to be, in the 1920s, far less permanence in the appearance of many consumer products. This was one of the features that stimulated retailers to get involved with store renovation and to reconsider the appearance of the buying environment. A concern with up-to-the-minute fashion had once been reserved almost entirely to women's clothing; now it was extended to many other things. The consumer's notice was caught by continual demands that he move up to a new product, for the old model was deprived, through advertisement, of those magical intangibles which the copywriters fixed only on the newer model. It was also possible—in the case of automobiles, radios, phonographs, and refrigerators—to talk about technical changes which promised improved performance. The model change thus joins a lengthy list of influences stimulating sensitivity to the aesthetics of consumer goods.

One final element must, at least, be considered. It was not novel to the postwar period but rather was the final phase of a competitive era about to end. Combined with the other factors it was important. And this element was the number of brands available within any single object category. The coexistence of national advertising and a tremendous set of brand choices made the advertising pages of magazines take on almost encyclopedic detail. Looking back at the 1920s from the present, the merchandising world looks bewildering. In the mid-twenties, May Hoffman, director of research for a major advertising agency, examined the buying habits of small-town women, and in particular examined their brand preferences. The tabulated results are, in some ways, less interesting than the raw data. Some 210 women, for example, reported having purchased pianos in a town located near Kansas City, Missouri. But among the 210 the most popular brand, Gulbransen, had only ten buyers, Chickering, Kimball, Vose, and Steinway followed with six each. All the rest sold three or less. Among the 210 buyers, 101 separate brands were represented, most of which are no longer with us. For phonographs, although Victor was heavily dominant, there were twenty-six different brands represented, in addition to thirty manufacturers of radios, fifty different kinds of washing machines, and twenty-five different automobile makes, including the Essex, Oakland, Hupmobile, Franklin, Hudson, Maxwell, Packard, and Elcar.[29] Consumers confronted an extraordinary range of choices, and the competing manufacturers were forced into marketing strategies as ingenious and aggressive as the hard-pressed department stores. Like the model changes, this variety of brands stimulated interest in the object's symbolic properties. In the end it seemed to make the act of consumption a more significant statement of choice and preference and to increase the curiosity of friends and neighbors about the logic and meaning of specific buying patterns.

The range of trends, experiences, and innovations that I have just summarized, accompanied, I believe, a newer and sharper fictional exploration of the role and character of American consumption and helped stimulate a consideration of the function consumer goods performed in the imaginative lives and daily activities of many Americans. The shift had begun even before the war. But in the 1920s a larger discussion developed, accompanied by different emphases upon the consumer audience, its dependence upon material artifacts for identity as well as for identification, and the iconographic significance of brands and products. The wave of cultural criticism that succeeded the war, involving figures like Van Wyck Brooks, Harold Stearns, H. L. Mencken, George Jean Nathan, and Lewis Mumford, set the scene. In their *American Credo* of 1920, Mencken and Nathan redeemed Americans from charges of avariciousness and miserliness, only to substitute in their place a childlike insistence upon acquisition. Where an older generation put its money into banks or real property, "the young folks put their inheritance into phonographs, Fords, boiled shirts, yellow shoes, cuckoo clocks, lithographs of the current mountebanks, oil stock, automatic pianos," and in general into anything that could glitter and distract them. "Whatever is shiny gets their dollars. . . . They are, so to speak, constantly on a bust, their eyes alert for chances to get rid of their small change."[30] Lewis Mumford found the tension between the desire for acquisition and collection and the limited income of most workers, to provide the source for urban amusements; a temporary resolution came through the invention of the five-and-dime store. "People who do not know how to spend their time must take what satisfaction they can in spending their money. That is why, although the five and ten cent store is perhaps mainly an institution for the proletariat, the habits and dispositions it encourages are universal." The chief amusement of Atlantic City, Mumford went on, consisted not of its beach, or ocean bathing, but visiting the shops that lined the boardwalk. Consumption, in the eyes of these critics, had become a bribe; the "coercive repression of an impersonal, mechanical technique," Mumford went on, with his eyes on the larger industrial system, "was compensated by the pervasive will-to-power—or at least will-to-comfort—of commercialism."[31]

The corruptions that the eighteenth-century political scientists had feared, now flowered. The use of objects as distraction; their standardized plenitude (another example of the passion for conformity that seemed to have become a permanent presence in American civilization), and the substitution of goods and mechanical exercises for direct experience and spiritual values made the act of consumption take on larger overtones than it had for the prewar generation. To describe it became an act of criticism, criticism not of individual protagonists but of a larger system. Heavy reliance upon objects for satisfaction of psychological, sexual, or social needs became a characteristic theme for several novelists, and the relationship between Americans and their objects—their methods of buying, their systems of classification, their patterns of use—took on broader significance. Through further specification of product, dissection of the buying process, exploration of the psychology of the consumer, and, above all, direct connections between consumption and identity, several novelists of the decade created a portrait of the American buyer, and a revelation of changes in national character that remain evocative.

Thus one can turn to a writer who is not normally associated with the economic novel, F. Scott Fitzgerald. Fitzgerald's work is revealing, for purposes of this discussion, not because of the centrality of his interests in consumption, but because of certain changes of emphasis. Focusing upon the wealthy, upon consumers of luxury goods, Fitzgerald no longer presented generic categories, like Howells and Dreiser. He enjoyed the specific details, the brand names, the qualities of the object. It was part of the persuasive power that the Fitzgerald settings achieved. It may not seem much in 1945, John O'Hara wrote in his introduction to a Fitzgerald anthology, "but twenty-five years ago it was delightful to find a writer who would come right out and say Locomobile instead of high-powered motor car." Fitzgerald, insisted O'Hara, always knew his situations; unlike other writers he wasn't dependent upon the local branch library. "The reader usually knew, without stopping to think much about it, that if a family owned a Franklin it was because they didn't feel they could afford a Pierce-Arrow." O'Hara himself, in *Appointment in Samarra,* was to make much of the subtle distinctions among automobile makes, and he valued Fitzgerald's specificity as part of a pattern of description crucial for determining questions of taste, temperament, and class. [33]

Fitzgerald was concerned, moreover, with the consumption patterns of men as well as women, another new development for writers of the decade. The merchandising revolution of the postwar years involved both sexes; Fitzgerald's greatest consumer was, of course, Jay Gatsby. The pleasure domes constructed by the seekers for power included, among their brilliant attractions, a profusion of more ordinary items. Gatsby's shirts, for example, imported in shimmering colors and fabrics from England, achieve, through number and splendor, the status of a treasure house. Filling the "two hulking patent cabinets," "piled like bricks in stacks a dozen high," the shirts are displayed for Daisy, thrown on a table. The "soft rich heap mounted higher—shirts with stripes and scrolls and plaids in coral and apple-green and lavender and faint orange, with monograms of Indian blue," so beautiful that Daisy sobs in wonder. [34] The sadness and awe at Gatsby's innocent profusion catches, in miniature, the tragedy of denied fulfillment that Fitzgerald lifts to mythic proportion. And in another vision of the soured promise of America, the 1922 short story "May Day," Fitzgerald uses the image of piled-up shirts to project a contrast between two Yale classmates, Gordon Sterrett, who will commit suicide by the story's end, and Philip Dean, selfish, wealthy, and self-confident. [35] "May Day" is filled with references to commercial New York, discussions of haberdashery, reconstructions of shopping drama. "Fifth Avenue and Forty-fourth Street swarmed with the noon crowd. The wealthy, happy sun glittered in transient gold through the thick windows of the smart shops, lighting upon mesh bags and purses and strings of pearls in gray velvet cases; upon gaudy feather fans of many colors; upon the laces and silks of expensive dresses." The theme of unrequited love for earthly treasure is reconstructed by Fitzgerald to suit the urban crowd, working girls who, while they inspect wedding rings and platinum wrist watches, digest "the sandwiches and sundaes they had eaten for lunch.[36]

The sensual appeal of stores and the central modern experience of shopping are themes carried out in several Fitzgerald works, *Tender is the Night* particularly; according to some critics, they help give this novel much of its bite and irony. In one memorable and frequently quoted passage, Fitzgerald placed Nicole, daughter of a wealthy North Shore Chicago family, at the apex of a system that ran around the world:

> For her sake trains began their run in Chicago and traversed the round belly of the continent to California; chicle factories fumed and link belts grew link by link . . . men mixed toothpaste in vats and drew mouthwash out of copper hogsheads; girls canned tomatoes . . . half-breed Indians toiled on Brazilian coffee plantations and dreamers were muscled out of patent rights in new tractors—these were some of the people who gave a tithe to Nicole, and as the whole system swayed and thundered onward it lent a feverish bloom to such processes of hers as wholesale buying like the flush of a fireman's face holding his post before a spreading blaze. She illustrated very simple principles, containing in herself her own doom.[37]

Shopping is no longer, as it had been for Dreiser and his generation, the symbol of individual temptation or even personal exploitation. It has become an image for a planetary economic system, judged and found guilty of brutality, inequity, and even, in Fitzgerald's terms, of madness, doomed, in the long run, but meanwhile inspired to frantic activity. Consuming is one of the few art forms left to individuals; their expression of purpose and self must be in terms of what they can buy, for there is no other standard of value. When added to Fitzgerald's concern with enumeration and specification and placed within the richly populated world of his stories and novels, the social indictment exerts enormous power. The objects are no longer adjuncts; they dominate, dangling below them the personality of the protagonist. The American system of consumption has become a drama in which an old, sacred dream about the redemptive power of a landscape has been translated into a secular conviction about the saving power of merchandise.

But Fitzgerald's protagonists still represent a special section of the consumer world, the very rich. This was the setting he knew best, and in the 1920s the drama of buying shifted to a much larger public and to a far wider range of products, as my earlier survey attempted to indicate. And here, the most detailed, comprehensive, and emphatic portraits were drawn by the novelist of the American middle class, whose books from the twenties represent a commentary on national buying habits: Sinclair Lewis. Lewis was early attracted to the setting of the middle-class commercial world; one of his first novels, *The Job*, published in 1917, concerned itself with the new career woman and the state of manners and morals of metropolitan business. But it was in the twenties that his most popular books were published. In three of them, *Main Street*, *Babbitt*, and *Dodsworth*, all in print by 1929, Lewis examined buying, selling, and advertising in greatest detail.

In his brief preface to *Main Street*, Lewis stated explicitly the ironic relationship between the town culture he was examining and the course of human history. "Main Street is the climax of civilization. That this Ford car might stand in front of the Bon Ton Store, Hannibal invaded Rome and Erasmus wrote in Oxford cloisters."[38] The theme that Fitzgerald would imply in *Tender is the Night* was here stated more baldly. Carol Kennicott, absorbed by the task of bringing Gopher Prairie into the mainstream of civilization, is appalled not simply by the library, the schools, the theater, and other traditional hallmarks of the higher life, but by commerce, by buying opportunity, by merchandising displays. Her first tour of the town focuses upon the dull, sometimes dirty, invariably repellent atmosphere of the stores and shops, relieved only by the modern plate-glass windows of Harry Haydock's Bon Ton Store. Lewis's target in this architectural tour is apparently the rampant individualism of American architecture and town planning, the failure of buildings to harmonize with one another, the clutter of light poles and telegraph lines, gasoline pumps, and litter. "Each man had built with the most valiant disregard of all the others."[39] But this variety did not increase choice. Only in the metropolis—Minneapolis or Chicago—could the intelligent and venturesome consumer find goods to satisfy her heart. Small-town America, the target of so much cultural criticism in the early twenties for its creative repressiveness, its tyranny of opinion, its smugness, its xenophobia, its intolerance, provided too limited a field for Lewis to exercise his full descriptive skills, and, several years later, in *Babbitt*, he was able to give play to his concerns about consumer culture.

Babbitt remains perhaps the most detailed portrait of American consumption in our fiction. As Mark Schorer has pointed out, it is hardly a novel at all. As "the major documentation in literature of American business culture," the book consists of a series of "set pieces, each with its own topic, and all together giving us a punctilious analysis of the sociology of American commercial culture."[40] Individual chapters address domestic manners, marriage, Pullman Car culture, leisure time, conventions, and other features of bourgeois life. *Babbitt* consists of an endless set of inventories—inventories of clothing, of furniture, of automobile fixtures, of bathrooms and barbershops and haberdashers. Lewis is at pains to outline the symbolic system which surrounds the objects. Eyeglasses, shoes, and suits present the outer man, and automobiles fix his rank in the social world. In the city of Zenith, wrote Lewis,

> a family's motor indicated its social rank as precisely as the grades of the peerage determined the rank of an English family—indeed, more precisely. . . . There was no court to decide whether the second son of a Pierce Arrow limousine should go in to dinner before the first son of a Buick roadster, but of their respective social importance there was no doubt; and where Babbitt as a boy had aspired to the presidency, his son Ted aspired to a Packard twin-six and an established position in the motored gentry.[41]

The system of correspondences fixed by Lewis attracted his scorn precisely because it had become a system—regulated and fixed by external authority. "These standard advertised wares—toothpastes, socks, tires, cameras, instantaneous hot-water heaters—were his [Babbitt's] symbols and proofs of excellence; at first the signs, then the substitutes, for joy and passion and wisdom."[42] Tocqueville's prophecy could not have been more precisely summarized. The ownership of objects has become the chief goal of living, and self-understanding is possible only through contemplation of material possessions.

The standardized consumer goods that American industry labored to produce aroused in Lewis warring tendencies. On the one hand they symbolized reduced decision-making power, the buyer becoming simply the passive object of manipulators who were presenting him with objects which so closely resembled one another that there was little exercise of personality in the act of purchase. And since so much was now invested in the kinds of objects adorning the person, this loss of power threatened individuality. On the other hand, Lewis admired the predictability, the comfort, the convenience, and economy that standardization brought. In a debate taking place early in the book, Seneca Doane, Zenith's radical lawyer, admits to an affection for standardization even while he opposes conformity. The Ingersoll watch and the Ford car were, after all, reliable. "I know precisely what I'm getting, and that leaves me more time and energy to be individual in. . . . There's no other country in the world that has such pleasant houses. And I don't care if they *are* standardized.[43]

The relationship between the proliferation of comforts and the declining standards of excellence absorbed Lewis throughout the decade. There were many streams feeding this interest, going back to earlier generations of American artists, among them a wilderness urge which abhorred the soft life of the cities and found redemption only in the solitary confrontation with nature. But more often than not it was the metropolis rather than the wilderness which Lewis employed as his counterweight, a center of sophistication and cosmopolitanism in which broader and more sophisticated displays of consumer goods testified to a toleration for heterodox opinions. Merchandising, then, occupied a curiously ambiguous place in Lewis's scheme of things: on the one hand, testimony to the commercialization of American culture, the triumph of mass-produced objects over personality; and on the other, evidence of taste, culture, artistic accomplishment, and sophistication. Buying could be either an act of subservience to manufacturers and advertisers or a demonstration of individuality.

This bifurcation becomes most apparent in the third volume of what could be labelled a trilogy of consumer drama, *Dodsworth*, published in 1929. In this study of an American automobile manufacturer who travels to Europe in an effort to keep his wife and come to terms with the world of culture, Sinclair Lewis confronts most directly the problem of maintaining identity in a world of objects, only this time the objects include both the mass-produced goods of the New World and the luxury items of the Old. The precipitating event in Dodsworth's travels—the sale of his Revelation Motor Company to the giant Unit Automotive Company, with its millions of dollars of capital—was a symbol of the submergence of individual creations within much larger systems. Selling his company, Dodsworth tries to hide from himself the notion that the U.A.C., "with their mass production would cheapen and ruin the Revelation and turn his thunderbolt into a standardized cigar-lighter."[44]

The problem of standardization of goods recurs again and again. In England, Dodsworth is astonished to discover that older societies, spurning American methods, are still capable of producing impressive objects. Strolling down St. James's, he finds a window full of modern weapons. "He had not believed, somehow, that the English would have such beautiful shiny shotguns."[45] European selling he also finds superior to American in subtlety and manner. Commercial images abound in the book, and buying becomes itself a testing experience, a means of measuring the mettle of character. Boasting of bargains has become part of the common parlance of Americans, particularly of Fran Dodsworth, but the bargaining of Europeans takes on style, becomes a ritual which throws into the shadows the crude hustle of the American stores.[46] In the end Dodsworth sees his mission as achieving a union between American mass production and the attention to detail and comfort characterizing European design. Architecture, rather than motorcars, attracts him. "It came to him that now there was but little pioneering in manufacturing motors; that he hadn't much desire to fling out more cars on the packed highways. To create houses, perhaps less Coney Island–like than these—noble houses that would last three hundred years"—that would be interesting.[47] Suburban housing, which could unite the color and irregularity of the Old World with the built-in garages and American incinerators that symbolized modern technology—here was what he was looking for.

So the redemption of the manufacturer lies in reapplying the instinct for workmanship, and the redemption of the buyer lies in selecting goods which permit some kind of personal taste to shape the purchase. Carol Kennicott, the somewhat ineffectual aesthete, and George Babbitt, the mindless purchaser of the advertisers' fantasies, are brought together and reshaped in Samuel Dodsworth, who somehow dreams of supplying this mass market with objects that are not compromised in quality by number or economy. Dodsworth's tours of real estate developments and foreign automobile factories are in their own way reminiscent of the popularity of the do-it-yourself guides of a century before; the dream of prosperity can be attained, in his case, by active intervention, by a reentry into the manufacturing world, reasserting levels of craftsmanship that are gradually being abandoned. And in so doing the passive, tourist values which Fran Dodsworth exemplifies are repudiated. Submission is the feared luxury, the corrupter, not the provision of better objects for the American consumer.

So brief a summary cannot do justice to Lewis, but it may suggest some problems that novelists of the early twentieth century were beginning to examine in more depth, in particular the relationship between the objects of consumer desire and the creation of personality. It is not simply status that manufactured objects provide for members of the national community, but identity itself. The world of objects is no longer accessory, adjunct, scene-setting, as in Howells, or even Dreiser. And the quest for the object is no longer merely indulgence in sensual luxury and appetite. Objects have so multiplied that the ability to control them, to choose among them, to refuse to be overwhelmed by them, becomes a test of personal strength. The buying ritual is simultaneously an act of initiation, a competitive encounter, an exercise of judgment, and an assertion of individuality. In the 1920s, the flood of goods seemed impossible to dam; corruption could be avoided not by a refusal to participate in the great consumer drama, but by the exercise of choice and the determination of particular relationships between objects and individuals. Just as a system of interchangeable parts was becoming, according to its critics, a system of interchangeable workers who were metaphorically likened to cogs in machines, an image captured at this time by Chaplin, so the American consumer was threatened now with the same kind of interchangeability. Only by an act of will could this consumer avoid the anonymity which mass production encouraged, the infinite replicability of mass-produced furniture, and clothing, and appliances. The efforts of advertising men, photographers, film producers, architects and interior designers, and retailers to link their products with adventure, mystery, and romance, to graft narrative onto inanimate forms, and to develop aesthetic principles by which they could be evaluated, was a major aspect of American marketing. One can detect in our fiction a discovery of this process in operation, a concern with explicating and evaluating the modern situation so deeply colored by the consumer sensibility. Novelists witnessed and described the movement of objects from expressions of status to guarantors of identity. In so doing they helped map the ideology of a new American system, a search to individualize rather than standardize, by grafting onto mass production the alluring, psychological qualities that answered private dreams.

10

John Philip Sousa

and the Culture of

Reassurance

J ohn Philip Sousa and his America seemed made for each other. Their love affair, particularly during the Indian summer years preceding World War I, was neither coy nor covert, but entered into demonstratively and exuberantly by both sides. To later generations, caught up in waves of nostalgia and curious about a national mixture of assertion and self-confidence that seems impossible to recapture, Sousa continues to epitomize a whole way of life. His image evokes strutting drum majors, band concerts on soft summer nights, strolling couples, playing children, tranquil and reassuring evocations of a time of well-ordered pleasures. The marches remain a major national treasure, disciplined statements of national exuberance as unmistakably American as the Strauss waltz is Viennese.[1] Sousa has become, in short, a perfect textbook tag, a cigar-box label guaranteed to produce the proper associations. He is as useful an historical resource as, in his own day, he was a national possession whose presence immediately produced attention, respect, and patronage.

The creation of this spectacular success story, undarkened by all but the smallest cloud, poses problems for subsequent biographers. There seem to be no hidden corners in Sousa's life, no buried secrets, no squalid episodes to

From Jon Newsom, ed., *Perspectives on John Philip Sousa* (Washington, D.C.: Library of Congress, Music Division, 1983), 11–40. Reprinted with permission.

shock admirers or provoke defenders. In countless interviews, in articles and columns, in autobiography and public statements he acknowledged his ambition and his success openly; he refused to be intimidated by either. His political opinions resembled those held by most of his countrymen, nor was he swayed by particular emotion for any special cause or social reform. He was what he appeared to be: a hard-working, prolific, and energetic musical genius who marketed his special talents effectively (and profitably) for more than forty years. His compositions stir us, as they moved his contemporaries, for understandable reasons. His conducting technique, while not uncontroversial, employed established conventions. Examining the Sousa image then, seems doomed to footnoting the obvious generalizations: the story is too clear and uncomplicated to repay lengthy investigation.

But there may be some reasons for exploring Sousa more carefully; they lie in the very intensity and longevity of his success. The Sousa career was a managed one, created to stimulate and satisfy consumer interest and oriented to marketplace approval. Skillful publicists fashioned the Sousa image, appealing to the mass market created by modern journalism. Musical history contains many instances of masters writing on demand for fame or income. The impresario-performer, brought to prosperity by clever promotional techniques, was well established long before Sousa's birth. But rarely before had a composer-conductor so clearly identified himself with the cultural needs and public taste of his day. Seldom had an artist more easily made his peace with the commercial ethos surrounding him, or become so unambiguous a symbol of community ambition. And, in America at least, never had anyone achieved this for so long a period of time, basically unshaken in prestige by otherwise comprehensive changes.

American monarchs, royalty in a republican society, tend to reign in performing arenas—acting, sports, and music. The March King was, in his own way, as popular a figure as the Sultan of Swat. The fact that Sousa determined to document this role, in the eighty-five volumes of newspaper extracts which inform this essay, indicates a concern with reputation and a willingness to keep his clipping service busy recording it.[2] Sousa sensed, along with his audiences, that he had assumed a set of crucial cultural roles—pedagogic, patriotic, and paternal. His band and his music were unrivalled because they captured in sound the values official spokesmen celebrated verbally. Sousa's success built upon formula. The repeated conventions of a Sousa march, or a Sousa band performance, along with their timely adjustments to meet important events, were not entirely original. But the close fit they achieved, and never lost, owed much to Sousa's public personality.

In a country where artistic talent had generally been segregated from the active, practical skills of business and the professions, Sousa brought them together. During his lifetime the world of the performer became a highly specialized one, demanding the talents of managers, press agents, programmers, tour managers, theatre owners, and advance men. Sousa was a careful student of managerial skills; by his later years he had become a master strategist. The sense he had of American musical culture and his functions within it, the response of critics and audiences to his marches, both say something about the way this culture functioned. Sousa was an authentic cultural hero. His work reassured his countrymen about the essential benevolence of their national task, their political beliefs, and the vitality of their creative life. Courting the great middle classes who were his sponsors, Sousa realized that his strength lay in the close connections forged between performance and social confidence in Victorian America. Both the image and the image-making deserve some further attention.

Just as Edison did not invent electricity, Sousa did not invent the band. Two generations of Americans had been enjoying band music by the 1860s, the decade during which young John Philip grew up in Washington. As historians of American music have shown, there were several traditions to choose among.[3] During the 1840s and 1850s small groups of brass and reed instrumentalists performed assorted airs, waltzes, schottisches, two steps, ballads, and polkas for enthusiastic if informal audiences. This repertoire, popular and unselfconscious, was obviously not competing with the more complex compositions published in contemporary Europe which were rapidly assuming classic status. There were, in any event, few American ensembles capable of performing major symphonic works before the Civil War, although several orchestras had been organized.

But the popular bands shared attention with another variant, the military band, normally created by militia groups to provide music for social festivities and training exercises. The relationship between the wind band and the military band was centuries old by this time in Europe, and in one or another form it had existed in America since the eighteenth century. However, the absence of a standing army (or indeed of almost any type of uniformed service) and the unwillingness of public authorities to pay for such luxuries meant that support of military band music depended on the ambitions and self-respect of individual regiments, or occasionally on townships with a tradition of sustaining a musical organization. On the eve of the Civil War there were several reasonably accomplished such bands, the best of them being the group led by a young Irish-born musician who had emigrated after serving in the British Army in Canada, Patrick Sarsfield Gilmore.[4]

The bands, military and civil, were numerous and popular, but hardly dominated American musical life in the antebellum period. The paying public divided into two parts: first, a select group of subscribers to opera or symphony concerts, confined to the large cities and ritualistically maintaining a tradition of middle-class patronage modelled on Europe's.[5] The other sector, more heterogeneous and spasmodic, flocked to great discoveries and performing celebrities, also often European imports like Jenny Lind, Alboni, and the bandmaster Jullien.[6] These performers were the sensations of their age, centerpieces of elaborate and faddish worship, but their vogue usually ebbed in a short time and they returned home. So loose and ill defined was national musical life that immigrant groups, Germans in particular, found it necessary to establish their own musical organizations, singing clubs, tournaments, festivals, and music halls. German orchestras, choral societies, Saengerfest, Harmonieverein, Saengerbund, developed in cities like Cleveland, Cincinnati, Pittsburgh, Chicago, and St. Louis, but this active approach to performing was more an ethnic possession than an American characteristic.[7] With a small elite supporting the opera and symphony, a larger group dogging the footsteps of imported celebrities, and a set of people who simply enjoyed informal ensembles playing tunes of the day, the American public was served on the whole by small, badly equipped, and poorly trained bands, the largest of which had no more than fifteen or twenty members. And, according to touring artists and native critics, it was an audience prepared to accept poor musicianship and naïve programming in return for a little showmanship and diversion.[8]

Before the Civil War no great conductor had emerged in America, at least no one whose name alone could attract crowds. It was not very different in Europe. Historians argue that it was only in the 1840s and 1850s, with Musard in Paris, Jullien in England, and Strauss in Vienna, that the first celebrity conductors appeared, "able to draw audiences to the concerts . . . quite independently of any other attractions that were offered or of any other influences that were in operation."[9] And these three conductors featured dance music. Soloists and composers remained the dominant draw.

But the American band received a boost in popularity from the Civil War. Especially active in the early days of recruiting rallies and mass enlistment, military bands to accompany the troops were created in such numbers that Congress passed bills limiting their growth and forcing some reduction. Bands had traditional roles in warfare: the drum and bugle corps met important signalling needs, organizing the training camps and punctuating daily activities with their distinctive calls. In battle they relayed commands and, on occasion, bolstered morale; on the march they provided indispensable accompaniment and relief from the prevailing monotony. Above all the war evoked a spirit of

The first tours, certainly, were not easy ones. Sousa had already achieved some reputation as a composer of marches and he had transformed the Marine Band from a lackluster and little-known ensemble to a popular and well-supported group, at least in Washington, presiding over a broad range of official ceremonies. Indeed, Sousa's increasing dissatisfaction with the restrictions of governmental employment, and the publicity given his move to private management, mirrored the growing presence of a federal bureaucracy in the 1880s and 1890s. Sousa had to press to get permission for his Marine Band to tour under Blakely's management; general competition between military and civilian bands was a source of bitterness, not only in America but in Germany and Great Britain as well.[15] Military musicians, underpaid but also underworked, grabbed concert jobs at rates lower than those demanded by civilian bandsmen. In St. Louis, in the 1880s, five private bands were driven out of business when the cavalry department's recruiting band transferred there from Carlisle, Pennsylvania.[16] Although Sousa got the pay for Marine bandsmen raised in 1891, there was no question that military musicians suffered from official niggardliness. Sousa's departure from government symbolized the attractions of private capital, "Chicago gold," according to the New York *Evening Journal,* the same gold that allowed William Rainey Harper to raid the faculties of Europe and America for his new University of Chicago. "The East is becoming more and more disgusted every day with Chicago's way of doing things."[17]

Dreams of wealth appealed to Sousa; Blakely increased his income severalfold, and sales of his marches swelled agreeably. But Sousa was also attracted by the idea of creating a new kind of musical organization, one that would compete artistically with the greatest European bands, like the Garde Républicaine, but would also, with a newly arranged instrumentation, present a novel repertoire to popular audiences. In later years Sousa was asked why (as a former violinist) he did not become an orchestra conductor. His response was that the orchestra represented too confining a tradition. With no wish to perform "ponderous symphonies" or "massive preludes," and believing that "entertainment is of more real value to the world than technical education in musical appreciation," Sousa sought an alternative. The cabaret orchestra, one possibility, was too limited and the military band "too vague in its instrumentation." But "a new combination, unhampered by tradition, which could get at the hearts of the people was my desideratum." If his autobiographical reflections are to be believed, Sousa sought an original, innovative approach to performance and programming, and a special place for himself and his musical organization in the public heart. "I wanted to avoid those musical combinations governed by certain laws as enduring as those of the Medes and the Persians, and institute one which I felt would cater to the many rather than the few."[18]

Innovation and popularity, these two goals would dominate his activities.

Sousa's talents obviously impressed Blakely, despite the problems that his advance men were having publicizing the Marine Band's two early tours. J. H. Laine, one of them, wrote to Blakely from Indianapolis in 1891 that "the Marine Band did not take with the public so well in *advance work* as Gilmore or Strauss," and found it "dam [sic] hard work to boom or work up" the group.[19] The second tour, with better routing, tripled the profits, and Blakely's five-year contract practically guaranteed him a financial windfall. With his pick of potential attractions, the business manager determined that it was Sousa who had the brightest future.

Some of this appeal was highly personal. In the late nineteenth century the musical world contained more than its share of temperamental personalities, alternating bouts of romantic self-celebration with periods of guilt and depression. Many performers, moreover, had few attractions or accomplishments beyond their musical skills. Sousa, with only a limited formal education, somehow managed to acquire a certain polish and a set of broader interests, which he tied to a clearly stable and rather optimistic temperament. In mid 1892, when Blakely was still trying to put together a syndicate by selling shares, he wrote to a prospective purchaser. Hobart Weed of Buffalo, that Sousa would soon be appearing there. Invite Sousa to your club, he urged Weed; here was a "thoroughly polished gentleman, a magnificent musician, a remarkable composer, and a devilish good fellow generally," who would cause his host no blushes.[20] Sousa's carriage and self-discipline, combined with his gift for self-command, would make him a good gamble for the ambitious businessman.

There remained, to be sure, the unknown quality of his public charm. When Sousa began, the band field was dominated by the vigorous presence of Patrick Gilmore, now in his sixties and possibly on the eve of retirement, but certainly the most popular conductor ever to perform in America. Sousa would have to communicate some special excitement to be fully successful. J. H. Johnston, manager of the Pittsburgh Exposition, a lucrative engagement for a touring band, protested Blakely's demand for a $3,100-a-week contract. This was higher than he had paid Gilmore, and "it was Gilmore's strong personality that carried the day" rather than "*his Band.*" Pittsburgh, with broad exposure to a number of musical organizations, might be difficult. "Of Sousa's *personal characteristics* I know absolutely nothing," Johnson wrote, but "everything depends upon the *personal magnetism* of the leader. . . . *he has to prove his worth in this respect.*"[21]

The test would be met by Sousa's assembling a band to rival the best competition, and by Blakely's arranging for maximum possible exposure and publicity. About the first, the *Musical Courier* was not optimistic. Reacting, in

basically "a military orchestra, that is, a body of the usual instruments included in the makeup of a military band but capable of producing the effects commonly confined to the players of a concert orchestra."[35] The brass sections, noted another newspaper, were subordinated but not put out of hearing. Just as the beer in a shandy-gaff cut the acerbity of the ginger ale and the ale sweetened the bitterness of the beer, "so here the reeds temper the blare of the brass, and the brass spices the reeds."[36] In an era when the New York *Times* could argue that American brass bands were Bedlam and Pandemonium combined and suggest arranging bandstands on a pivot at seaside hotels "so that when the terrible creature within begins to lash himself into fury" the stage be turned to the sea "and the horrid voice of the monster poured out upon the illimitable ocean," this was high praise.[37] Here was a new sound developed by a "man of brains," and audiences were impressed.

During the first year or two of touring, observers raised themes which would continue to surface as responses to Sousa during the next three decades. One of them concerned his physical skill as a leader. Orchestral tone depended not only on practice, but on Sousa's capacity to direct it during performance. The "simple lash of his eye, the motion of his little finger," wrote an awed critic in the Worcester *Telegram,* "were sufficient to control the melodious noise of the hushed harmony of one of the finest bodies of instruments in the world."[38] Sousa "woos the harmony out of the men with the air of a master," a Midwestern newspaper agreed.[39] He had "such perfect control over his magnificent organization," the Williamsport *News* reported, "that every effect was brought out without any apparent effort."[40] "No conductor ever seen in Corning had his men under better or more complete control," ran another conclusion, a compliment whose sincerity compensated for its rather limited sphere of comparison.[41]

The conductor's magical control excited considerable comment during the late nineteenth-century performances.[42] Sousa's concert band was not huge by orchestral standards—containing nearly sixty men during a normal concert—but Americans were accustomed to the sloppy, ragged playing of much smaller amateur groups. And they were caught up by the subservience of this musical mammoth to the baton's movements. The posture and bearing of the conductor were important parts of any effective concert and the carefully groomed Sousa, clad in tight-fitting uniform and spotless white gloves, acted out the maestro for his audiences. Compared to the great and furious movements favored by some older leaders, his conducting style, at first, seemed modest and restrained. Sousa offered an intriguing but well-controlled set of motions, meticulously analyzed by music critics and journalists at a level of detail that reveals the importance of the concert's visual features.

The Saginaw *Globe*, for one, was impressed by the economy of his gestures. Holding his men "as under a spell," every baton motion brought a response. "Unlike the great Gilmore, Sousa does not make himself conspicuous
by his vigorous work, but is very quiet and unassuming. Yet the result is the
same."[43] The Brooklyn *Daily Eagle*, writing in the summer of 1893, shortly
after David Blakely had invited several hundred connoisseurs to watch Sousa
perform, apparently agreed. Gilmore, of blessed memory, the *Eagle* wrote, was
a passionate, spectacular conductor who employed energy and "snap" to intensify effects. "Gilmore wore the awful front of angry Mars when he worked up a
crescendo. He rode the harmonious storm as furiously as the wild huntsman
rides his phantom steed, dominating it and spurring it on to the climax." Organizing a diminuendo Gilmore was a different person, "smiling above his men
like the white winged cherub of peace."[44] The terrible warrior could suddenly
become an angel of light.

Sousa was something else. Apparently not a creature of moods he was "a
small man with a natty figure and a black beard. He is the quietest conductor
ever seen in these parts. He is not at all spectacular."[45] But if the fire did not
get into the conductor, it got into the music. And audience responses grew
stronger. The Duluth *Herald* labelled Sousa "an ideal leader. He is not overly
demonstrative and no violence characterizes his movements, but every motion
is graceful and expresses exactly what the music conveys. A deaf person might
almost watch Sousa and understand the music."[46] The Syracuse *Standard* described him as "the very personification of masculine grace," the Lewiston *Journal* applauded this "masterly yet modest way" of conducting, a baton with
"magic in it," vigorous yet with a "refined musicianly manner," and to the Duluth *Herald* Sousa's directions were so graceful that he seemed to be "waltzing
with the music."[47] A Syracuse critic applauded Sousa's avoidance of whole arm
movements, and his apparent reluctance even to use half arm gestures. He
possessed, instead, "a wrist made flexible by long practice with the violin bow
and it is with graceful wrist movements that he does most of his directing. He
adds force to any passage by movements of the body and the waist. His feet are
seldom moved."[48]

The combination of discipline and languor—in the same paragraph the
Buffalo *Enquirer* invoked gestures from a "lady-like shrug" to "the vigorous
action of a baseball pitcher"—was new and exciting.[49] It was an arresting synthesis of military precision and balletic grace. While one critic could liken
Sousa's conducting to "the sheer delight of a little girl playing mother with her
dolls," another described him as "a consummate general . . . alert, active,
watches every man."[50] Sousa's vigor, his energy, his masculine appeal rescued

managers to reach out and educate a broader mass, encouraging them to support the orchestras, opera companies, chamber music groups, and composers that a great civilization should possess. According to theorists of genteel improvement, serious-minded musicians had an obligation to raise the level of their audiences' musical desires, to instruct as well as to entertain. Certainly Theodore Thomas, in his tireless crusades to popularize European symphonic music, accepted such a role. Indeed he pursued it with such energy and singlemindedness that there were occasional complaints about his didacticism. Critics and musical educators argued furiously, of course, about the means of improvement. Some insisted that people who listened to music, any music, however common or popular, would gradually seek a higher standard. Others urged, from the outset, that trivial and trashy tunes be barred from performance in favor of higher standards. Pedagogues and promoters divided.

It was into this climate of anxiety about public taste, hope for improvement and concern with contemporary programming, that Sousa introduced his touring band. Bands had, traditionally, belonged to a lower part of the musical hierarchy than serious soloists, orchestras, chamber groups, and choral societies. They were identified with a more limited repertoire and with a performance style that exaggerated the vulgar, favoring flashy overtures, blaring marches, sentimental ballads, and incongruous pastiches. Even Patrick Gilmore disdained portions of the band repertoire. He upbraided David Blakely for trying to get him to perform a "false" and "inartistic . . . circus of war songs" in 1891. "I have fired the public beast through *cannon* and *anvil*," Gilmore admitted, "but I gave them great music *withal*. I would not touch the *War Song Panorama* for any amount of gold."[59]

Nonetheless, despite this protest Gilmore was widely identified with a relaxed and tolerant approach to programming. Gilmore's fame, the New York *World* explained, "was not based upon the satisfaction he gave our intellect; it rested upon the gratification he furnished to our senses. He played the simple melodies of our homes, and the tears filled our eyes." Gilmore knew public sentiment; he combined it with his own magnetism to fill men with "good nature" and make them "more contented, more cheerful and happier."[60] Gilmore, wrote the Kansas City *Journal*, "was more a caterer than a teacher," although he may well have been justified by the primitive level of national taste that existed when he began his conducting career.[61]

Sousa was harder to analyze. Articulate and aggressive about marketing his musical philosophy, certainly much more vocal and self-conscious than Gilmore had been, he gave concerts which appeared to be too heterogeneous and even volatile in quality for critics to take any clear line upon them. From the start he seemed more serious than previous band conductors, in part because of his heavier reliance upon winds and his concern with arranging more accurate and evocative transcriptions of orchestral compositions. Where Gilmore had sown, ran the refrain, Sousa would reap, appealing to and sustaining a more serious level of musical knowledge. This band leader "is not catering to popular taste," insisted the Elmira *Star* in early 1893. "He prefers a better quality of music than brass bands usually play or brass band audiences care to hear." [62] The playing of Grieg's Peer Gynt Suite, of Wagner's *Lohengrin*, of Schubert, Rossini, and Tschaikowsky revealed sophistication and skill. Even in lighter portions of the program, the Kansas City *Journal* wrote, there was a "dignity of treatment" which removed it from vulgarity. [63]

But most early comments about Sousa focused on his programming breadth and his playing of popular music. They did so, approvingly or disapprovingly, pondering the point of organizing a band so skillful and disciplined in order to play this more common range of tunes. Those who accepted Sousa's tributes to mass taste as a basis for programming agreed with him that there was nothing wrong with popularity. And a band was no fit interpreter of serious music anyway, some of them continued. "Mr. Sousa's excellent sense is shown in bowing to the popular will and giving the people what they want and what they pay for," a New York newspaper commented. Sousa had been advised to depart from the Gilmore tradition and emphasize classical music more, the paper admitted, but he realized his audiences did not come to be educated but to be entertained. [64]

The Chicago *Herald* agreed. Applauding Sousa's enormously popular performances at the Columbian Exposition, it attacked the Fair's musical directorate (including Theodore Thomas), who sought a means of "educating" the public. Many people, the *Herald* argued, found it "almost a punishment to hear classical music, while all their senses rejoice at listening to a simple and familiar melody." [65] Sousa's open air concerts, on the Grand Plaza of the fairgrounds, were an unexpected 1893 sensation and helped establish his early reputation.

But some reviewers were appalled by the heavy proportion of popular tunes and dismayed by the missed opportunities. The Duluth *Daily Commonwealth* detected a disproportion of "coconut dance and clog dance and Salvation Army parody" in Sousa's program, even while admitting that the audience seemed to love it. The "thousand people who heard with delight the overture to the Flying Dutchman and the Hungarian Rhapsodie" departed feeling "partly degraded" by this cheaper music. "A conductor should try to give his audience as much music as they can hold, and a Duluth audience has a better capacity than Mr. Sousa supposed." [66]

Other newspapers, reflecting the ambitions of the musically literate,

manly celebrity; a dramatic yet restrained platform manner; an articulate philosophy of musical composition and performance which supported the varied programming plans; and a set of devices, most notably the encore, for encouraging audience enthusiasm and allowing an immediate response to public preferences.

In addition to all this there was one final aspect to Sousa's career which brought him the personal power required by a great conductor. And that was his own massive contribution to musical composition, most particularly the Sousa marches that had begun to appear with regularity in the 1880s and continued to augment the American band repertoire for the next four decades. The marches were liquid bliss to expectant Americans, who were hoping for a native composer with an international reputation. Critics made extensive and repeated attempts to analyze the basis of their appeal, their capture of something incarnate in the national life. Almost from the first Sousa's marches were seized upon as quintessentially American in their bounce, their liveliness, their jaunty discipline. But the structure of the Sousa march and the mystery embedded in its evocation of national character are less relevant here than the authority they transferred to the conductor. Sousa's fame came through creation rather than performance. Even without the thousands who watched and listened to him, he had become a celebrity by the mid nineties. Composition brought the Sousa on the podium an additional source of magnetic appeal, a hint of personal genius which demanded audience attention. It was rare to see a genius in action, and a genius who so actively eschewed the affectations of the artist. Wearing "long hair, goggles, an air of mystery and . . . always smelling of Dutch cheese," Sousa told an interviewer for the New York *Advertiser* in August 1893, did not necessarily mean talent.[76] He contentedly obeyed the obvious conventions. Exuding a common-sense patriotism, Sousa differed from most of his audience only by his grander style of life, the material emblem of growing wealth. In place of his meager governmental salary, the rewards of private industry brought the musician the luster of financial success. By 1894 or 1895 he stood alone, setting the standard at which others aimed.

Many aspects of the Sousa legend, then, were firmly in place by the end of one or two years of independent touring. The search for Gilmore's successor was a short one; the gamble of establishing the new band seemed in hindsight nothing short of a sure thing. The nineties would be rich in band performance: Victor Herbert, Frederick Innes, Giuseppe Creatore, Thomas Brooke, Alessandro Liberati, Patrick Conway, and others provided stern competition. Some of Sousa's own instrumentalists would soon leave to found their own bands. Several of these leaders were brilliant musicians, a few were capable composers, and their tours often earned heady tributes from newspaper reviewers.[77] But it proved impossible to pass Sousa once he had hit his stride with the public. By the late nineties his energies overflowed into many aspects of creation and production, from musical comedy and light opera companies to writing fiction. "If there is any limit to Sousa's success as leader and composer," the *Musical Courier* wrote in 1896, it was not yet apparent. For four years he had continually been touring and giving concerts; "his face is probably more familiar to the people of the United States than that of any other public man in the country."[78] "Sousa earns over $100,000 a year!" exclaimed H. M. Bosworth in the San Francisco *Examiner.* "What fact can instance more emphatically the elevation of musical art in the popular estimation?"[79] He received more money than the president of the United States. That same year, in 1899, the Wilkes-Barre *Daily News* argued that "we can now look upon a tradition of Sousa compositions and Sousa concerts. . . . There's hardly a way now of comparing Sousa's Band, except with itself."[80] Sousa "is omnipresent," the Dayton *News* enthused. "In the military camp, in the crowded streets of the city . . . in the ball room, in the concert hall, at the seaside and on the mountains, go where you may, you hear Sousa, always Sousa. . . . It is Sousa in the band, Sousa in the orchestra, Sousa in the phonograph, Sousa in the hand organ, Sousa in the music box, Sousa everywhere," the man "not of the day, or of the hour, but of the time."[81]

Sousa furthered his reputation by extending the techniques he developed during his first tours. He was continually posing for newspaper photographers, interviewed on his love for horses, his bicycle riding, or his trap shooting, invited to judge contests and to offer opinions on the major controversies of the day. New York newspapers showed photographs of the conductor taking boxing lessons at Manhattan Beach. "Here, then, you see bared before the camera the muscular right arm that has wielded the baton to the delight of millions, the sturdy fist that wrote 'El Capitan.'" "Within a few years of hard training," his teacher, Jock Cooper, manager of the Manhattan Beach Race Track insisted, "Mr. Sousa could easily develop into a world beater."[82] His reading habits provoked observation; so did his views on cultural patronage, foreign music, national character, and international relations. Those who knew Sousa only from his conducting podium, one critic wrote in 1901, "know only half the man. The Sousa of keen insight, the Sousa of discriminating fancy, the student of musical tradition and of musical development; the man of affairs able to take up any of the questions of the day and dissect them; able to take his side of an argument and hold his own; the man of refinement and toleration, the patriotic American, the husband and father," here was the Sousa who was always "an inspiration to meet. . . . His intellectuality glimmers from as many sides as the facets of a diamond."[83]

ing to us. . . . . Get the American home life into your music and into the life of the musicians, and we will have the greatest musical community, in God's good time, that the world has ever known."[90]

In later years, also, Sousa identified more fully with the American businessman. His organizational gifts were evident from the start but some obstacles stunted his claims for commercial genius. In 1897, during the legal disputes that followed upon David Blakely's death, newspapermen stared at the earlier contracts in disbelief. "It looks as if Sousa had practically given the Blakely people something like an independent fortune," the Wilkes-Barre *Evening Leader* commented, "and as if his leg has been pulled to the stretching point." Why had Sousa made such a contract, giving away 80 percent of the profits and 50 percent of the march royalties? "There is hardly a record of such a gigantic swindle." The only easy answer was that "Sousa, like many another genius, hasn't got the band business head that looks out for his own interest," and so had permitted himself to be robbed by his ingenious manager.[91]

Of course this image of a bumbling businessman may have been spread by Sousa and his agents, to appear more favorably amidst the suits and countersuits that developed when Mrs. Blakely sought to impose the contract's terms and Sousa refused. But after the flurry had died down, Sousa devoted himself more emphatically to a business philosophy. "The organizing and maintaining of a superior band I regard in the light of a calm, calculative, business proposition," he wrote in the *Criterion* during 1900; the task was as practical as the selection of a bank teller. "As the head of a counting-house exercises powers of selection in gathering about him a staff as nearly perfect as possible, so is the bandmaster untiring in his search for the best available talent. . . . the principle of the survival of the fittest is strong."[92] Sousa's use of commercial similes, his friendship with entrepreneurs, his insistence upon established business practices, testified to his confidence in the marketplace.

His autobiographical reflections also emphasized a firm and practical approach to problem-solving, particularly when dealing with dishonest, incompetent, or unrealistic promoters. During a 1911 tour of South Africa he was startled by the naïveté of the arrangements. The Sousa Band was to give its concert in a public park "with no way of controlling the ingress or egress of the audience. That honest-hearted South African representative believed that the dear public would hunt up the ticketseller, buy tickets and wait in line to pass the proper entrance," even though no fence surrounded the park. Sousa immediately engaged the only hall in town, and filled it with an audience of 1,100. Thousands who had come to hear the band were disappointed. "But, since our expenses were $2,500 a day on the tour and we were certainly not touring for our health, we felt no compunction."[93]

Indeed, Sousa confessed that no less an authority than the great Theodore

Thomas had warned him to be careful about business matters. "Managers will stick close when you are making money," Thomas supposedly told him, "but they'll desert you without a qualm when the first squall blows up." Sousa distinguished himself from his great hero by his more diplomatic and prudent response to the opinions of others. While he admitted many parallels between Thomas and himself, Sousa felt less "given to irrevocable dicta. I would listen to advice, and if I knew it was no good, would quietly say, 'I'll think that over,' leaving the other fellow with no ammunition to discuss the matter further." Despite some unparalleled gifts, Thomas was "primarily an educator."[94] Tenacious of purpose, he lost his sense of proportion and came into occasional but sharp conflict with the public, who resented being told what they were meant to admire. Sousa's style better suited a country coming to value the power of salesmanship and the stern but self-restrained consistency of a successful business leader.

Sousa's assurances that American politics, values, and social habits were fundamentally healthy and not at all antagonistic to the arts gained in persuasiveness when he extended his foreign tours after 1900, and achieved, in effect, a conquest of European audiences. The *Musical Courier*, the premier professional periodical of the day, excitedly reprinted newspaper reports from the ancient cities of the Old World, attesting to his extraordinary popularity. Fannie Edgar Thomas sent back a description of the Paris Fair concerts in 1900 which was a veritable paean to Sousa's Americanism and his spirit of system. Even the very preparations stood out. When the trunks full of chairs and stands and platforms arrived on the scene in a cart, "instead of a regiment of useless and snarly old people surrounding" it, screaming themselves "hoarse and wearing themselves out in gesticulation, one very quiet young man in uniform was there . . . and without seeming to speak a word had the trunks unloaded and placed beside the place in a few seconds." French observers, according to Fannie Thomas, were amazed at the speed and silence with which a few Americans arranged the chairs and stands. The flag bearers "bore the pride of youth and health, and fearlessness of carrying the big flag of a big nation," and then came the bandsmen well groomed, well dressed, "straight, healthy, happy, clean and polished looking. . . . Without being rigidly disciplined, they have the impression of uniformity of movement. Without special grace, they were also without awkwardness." Most of the men, Fannie Thomas admitted, were in fact foreigners, German-born, but apparently that did not dampen their American appearance of sensible, well-organized, good humor. And finally there appeared the "quick, neat, fresh" and "radiant" Sousa himself, handsome and even exotic looking, his uniform "the perfection of fit and finish," who proceeded, on schedule, to dazzle his vast audience.[95]

The European triumphs underscored what many Americans already be-

ers royalties on their music. This seemed like simple theft, and he was an active force in the creation of ASCAP to protect and define the rights of creators.[102]

But Sousa's dislike of the phonograph was greater than simply economic. He realized that it threatened the monopoly of the performance as a musical medium. His own concerts were visual displays as well as musical renditions; the uniforms, the movements, the bearing of conductor and musicians added decisively to the impressiveness of the music. Sousa's is a pantomimic art, a Philadelphia paper commented. "At one of his concerts it is not alone the ear that is pleased and charmed, it is the eye also that is captivated and satisfied."[103] The New Haven *Leader* in 1899 used the phrase "see the original" in urging audiences to attend the concerts. "One does see Sousa's music; you see it grow under the magic of his baton, every note brought to life at its command as a picture grows under the artist's brush."[104] Sousa, wrote H. M. Bosworth in the San Francisco *Examiner,* was not so much a metronome as an expression. "What the physical illustration by face, attitude and gesture is to the spoken words of an orator the graceful attitude and gestures of Sousa are to the combined musical utterances of his executants."[105] They helped the audience enjoy the music. "Is there not possibly some occult power, some hypnotic spell, existent in that peerless back?" asked the Chicago *Tribune.* "And that matchless left hand, immaculate in purest white—what mystic magic lies concealed within it that it thus should set a-sway humanity's inmost being?"[106] If Sousa were placed behind a screen or made in some way invisible, the newspaper mused, the music could not possibly be as impressive. Sousa knew, then, that recorded he would lose much of his power, and it was as a performer that he received his fullest satisfactions.

Nonetheless, newspapers and magazines repudiated his assault on the phonograph. It was bound to improve public taste in the long run. "John Philip Sousa overindulges in mince pie, his dreams are filled with contorted talking machines and 'canned music' assumes the aspect of an ogre." "Sousa should be the last one to complain of mechanical music, however applied," another critic objected.[107] For once the bandmaster had miscalculated.

But with this exception, Sousa managed to affirm the taste and judgment of his audiences. "All the way through a Sousa program you can see the old flag waving, hear the clothes flapping on the line in the back yard, and smell the pork and beans cooking in the kitchen;" these homely metaphors were offered by the Topeka *Daily Capital* in 1902. "The principal soloist was born in St. Joseph, Mo., and the average man can pronounce the names of the members of the organization as they appear on the hotel register." There was admittedly, here and there a suggestion of "Die Wacht am Rhein" and a whiff of macaroni. "But Sousa's band is for Tom Jones and John Smith and their families."[108] The

Springfield *Republican,* in 1897, acclaimed Sousa's sway. "It seems as if he always gives just the thing that the audience is in the mood for . . . the delight he gives people is rather more unrestrained and unaffected than one ordinarily notes in audiences. Sousa and his hearers are thoroughly *en rapport.*"[109]

So powerful was the conductor's presence by the late nineties that sermons were preached and poems written as testaments to his power of inspiration. In May 1898, a Baptist minister used a Sousa concert as his text in a sermon that newspapers happily reprinted, "Spiritual Suggestions from Sousa." The conductor was transformed into a symbol of purity and leadership, a bringer of order from chaos. And his musicians represented the discipline of a well-run church, obedient and responsive. "The performers were content to play the score as it was given to them. They did not rewrite, compose a new one, or strike out in a few new lines. . . . If only the church and its preachers could be content with the faith once delivered to the saints." Each man played his own part, without worrying whether another's was better. There was variety to the music Sousa scheduled, a reminder that "in salvation's song something can be found fitted for every feeling, taste, aptitude." And the leader, controlling his men with "no contortion, no violent motion, no mighty sweep of his arm" recalled Christ's presence, quiet and continuing, even without obvious miracles or transfigurations.[110]

The conservative implications of a Sousa performance were complemented by its patriotism. The Sousa Band received many of its most tumultuous ovations during the war fever of the 1890s. "If the present Administration ever takes action against persons who arouse public patriotism," one newspaperman wrote, "John Philip Sousa should be selected as the first victim to be punished."[111] Sousa insisted upon playing the "Star-Spangled Banner" at his concerts, producing frenzied reactions among normally staid listeners. Some of the excitement was caused by the stirring themes of Sousa's new march, perhaps his most enduring one, "The Stars and Stripes Forever." If war came Sousa deserved government employment, argued one reporter. "One blast upon his bugle-horn would be worth 10,000 men."[112] Adapting himself to the bombastic rhetoric, Sousa created a new piece, "The Trooping of the Colors," grouping the flags of friendly foreign powers to the tunes of their anthems, and swaddling it all in patriotic melodies. The Chicago *Times-Herald,* a frequent critic of Sousa, was repelled by the promotional rhetoric of his management and worried about its injudicious advertisement of patriotism. It was a wonder that "the stars on the flag have not been transformed into boxes of soap, bicycles, and the photographs of political candidates," while the employment of patriotism as "a marketable ware is certainly not commendable, especially at the present time when cool-headed judgment is the better part of valor."[113]

the concert stage as American athletes were winning medals at the newly organized Olympic Games. He was conqueror, athlete, businessman, and sportsman, as well as genius.

The Sousa Phenomenon inevitably also became an anniversary event. Just as the programs tended to repeat their formulas from year to year—the mixture of operatic medleys, popular tunes, classical excerpts and Sousa marches serving his band as it would most of his competition—so the Sousa visits became devices to measure the passing years and the changing seasons. The annual stays at the Manhattan Beach, or the Willow Grove concerts near Philadelphia, were symbols of continuity in a civilization where so much else was changing. There was a certain irony in this, for Sousa's Band and its style were labelled, at various times in the nineties, a fad, a passing fancy which could be outgrown like so many other crazes. And Sousa did try to capture contemporary songs and events. Yet his band performances became a symbol of stability, of constancy, of predictability. As his conducting career became longer, observers loved to chart subtle differences in his appearance and technique—the figure growing stockier, the hair grayer, the gestures more languid and restrained—reluctant tributes to approaching age, or, in the case of the conducting techniques, signs of a new maturity and ever increasing mastery. The nostalgic aspects of the Sousa cult developed, in fact, within only a decade or so of the Band's actual premiere, so strong was the need for recurrence and so few the major entertainers with such staying power. Sousa continued to pour out marches and musical compositions right up through the year of his death, although his most popular compositions had been published, for the most part, by 1910. However, his gift for catching the public temper during moments of crisis remained, and the Sousa Band acted almost like an official representative for national spirit.

Into the teens and twenties Sousa remained an imposing figure. After American entry into World War I he assumed the task of training a band for the Great Lakes Naval Station, and his Jackies, as they were called, appeared at the band rallies which were a crucial part of the ongoing propaganda effort, along with movie stars, opera singers, and political personalities. Sousa no longer stood unrivalled as a stimulant to crowd emotion. Tin Pan Alley, through Irving Berlin and George M. Cohan, produced a series of songs that came to symbolize the American military commitment. But Sousa's "U.S. Field Artillery March," based on a song written by an army lieutenant, sold hundreds of thousands of records, and became as indelibly associated with the Army as "Semper Fidelis," written almost thirty years earlier, came to symbolize the Marines.

Some of Sousa's patriotic gestures were, of course, less successful. Sharing the fierce revulsion to things German, Sousa announced a substitute for the

German wedding marches that traditionally had accompanied American couples on their stroll down the aisle. After enormous publicity the "American Wedding March" appeared in 1918, but it failed to create a place for itself and, like Sousa's fierce rejection of German music, proved a transitory event.[124] The Oklahoma City *Oklahoman* pointed out that assigning Sousa to rewrite Mendelssohn and Wagner was "about as apposite as would be that of Bud Fischer to do a Mona Lisa."[125] Sousa's patriotism had become shrill, in keeping with the national mood.[126] And given his earlier popularization of German music, and the large number of German musicians in his organization, his exaggerated rhetoric about the war may have expressed a desire for expiation.

While he remained a figure of influence then, Sousa's most important years were probably the first two decades with his Band, before live performance was challenged so successfully by the new electronic media and before he was challenged, as well, by the steady growth of the two cultures he had attempted to straddle. Motion pictures, jazz, radio, comics, dance bands, automobiles, all represented forces paying little heed to many older cultural verities that Sousa, despite his quest for popularity, believed in. And on the other end of the creative spectrum, American poets, painters, museums, orchestras were now engaged in an international dialogue, achieving levels of performance, exhibition, and execution of serious art that were available in the America of the 1890s to only a few.

Sousa was in fact unhappy with the trends of modern music. Like the other arts, by 1910 it had borne aggressive rebellion against formal conventions. To Sousa music meant melody, rhythm, good humor, and sentiment. Like the older academic painters, angered and bewildered by the apparent defiance of craftsmanlike canons, he refused to accept the new trends. "The real development of music," he told a Spokane reporter in 1915, "will come no more through the efforts of the modern French school or strivings of Schoenberg and his class, than the real development of painting has come through futurists, cubists and all the other 'ists' of art." All of them, composers and painters alike, were "seeking a short and easy road to Mount Olympus, and it does not exist." The *Musical Courier*, reprinting the interview, vigorously agreed. "Tunes—real tunes, good honest tunes—that is what the public demands, and with absolute right."[127] Honest labor, evident in the score, without flimflam or cute tricks, not the lazy deceptions of the new Bohemians.[128]

Ironically, in view of the earlier fears of vulgarization, Sousa became an ideal to some conservative critics. Sousa's marches, wrote D. C. Parker in the *Musical Courier*, several years later, were a corrective "to all the vague syncopisings and sophisticated hesitations of the extreme anemic aesthetes. They said 'Yes' to life with unmistakable emphasis." Some had labelled Sousa's music

them frequently in the interest of reform. They held contemporary life up to other standards, contrasting the doubts of their day with the expansive force of another.

Sousa's was not a critical philosophy. He projected a supportive vision of national destiny that mingled folksiness, martial arts, gallantry, and commerce. To extract simply the marching tunes from his rich contemporary reputation is to lessen his impact and to dilute his goals. He took himself seriously (and so others took him) as a bridge between cultural communities. And as an instrument to lessen the forbidding awe felt for creative genius. The Sousa performance did more than merely display his marches to advantage. It was an occasion on which to reassure and conciliate an ambitious if unsophisticated public. We no longer have the performances; we do have the marches. If the legacy is reduced, it is no less real.

11

Who Owns Our Myths?

Heroism and Copyright

in an Age of Mass Culture

When we encounter a hero of extra-terrestrial origins, gifted with miraculous powers, overcoming enormous dangers, defeating stereotyped villains, enjoying universal recognition, and mouthing phrases that embody basic social, religious, and political values, we are probably meeting up with a mythic hero. In this essay I will treat one such figure, nurtured by broad cultural convictions and accepted almost everywhere with immense enthusiasm.

But I also ask what happens to this mythic figure as he fights for survival in our society. He exists in a world built around the twin notions of private property and liberty of expression. Ancient myths belonged to everyone, to be invoked and represented whenever the occasion suggested. Today's mythic heroes are more constrained. They can be copyrighted. Or, if they take special mechanical form, they can be patented. Or, finally, if they acquire specific associations, they can be registered. Plot, character, dialogue, appearance, all are protectable. At the same time, various forms of unlimited evocation seem

From *Social Research* 52, no. 2 (Summer 1985): 241–67. Reprinted with permission of the publisher.

indispensable in the interests of public welfare, free discussion, and artistic expression.

Dilemmas of fair use are endemic to disputes about artistic property. But they seem particularly intense when involving formula stories and heroes; these represent a fundamental collective consciousness. In this country during the last hundred years manufacturing energies, advertising ingenuity, and media appetites have combined to create a powerful postindustrial folklore. In their search for profits, merchandisers have hunted for persuasive versions of time-tested formulas, repeatable patterns that work. And having found them, they have managed to resell them. In effect, modern mythic heroes are franchised on a for-profit basis, rented out to sell products, experiences, or values. They are not available for indiscriminate appropriation. But paradoxically, it is earlier (and cheaper) to demean these heroes than to glorify them.

How has this happened? Answers can be found in a specialized and somewhat sequestered literature. For more than a century American courts and legislators have been attempting to formulate copyright standards appropriate to changing technologies and social uses. Casebooks incorporate these decisions; law review articles monitor their evolution. But it is a literature not well known outside courtrooms and law schools. I will draw on its rich variety, but it is impossible in so brief a space to synthesize its complex traditions. Thus I will focus on the vicissitudes of one modern hero who exemplifies the status of commoditized myths in daily life and raises questions about the logic of mass culture. I will describe first his antecedents, turn next to legal precedents and strategies adopted to protect his property function, and consider, finally, some problems arising out of his history.

If a modern myth has a point of origin it can obtain protection. For one particular myth a clear and undisputed chronology goes back now some fifty years to a Cleveland, Ohio, teenager. His name was Jerry Siegel. In 1932 he and a high school friend, an illustrator, produced a short story entitled "Reign of the Superman."[1] It featured a character possessing telescopic vision and great mental powers. After publishing in a magazine in 1933 the two young men thought of turning their story into a comic strip. In 1934 the author received a vision one summer night which he would later describe in some detail. The vision was of a dual-identity human avenger, simultaneously a mild-mannered newspaper reporter and a cape-powered, tights-wearing, extraterrestrial being to be known simply as Superman. The idea was clear and vivid. But it took four years for the author-illustrator team of Siegel and Schuster to persuade some publisher that it was worth purchasing. In 1938 they encountered a new figure in the comic book field. His name was Harry Donenfield and he offered the boys a deal. Although newspapers had been publishing comics for

more than forty years, until the 1930s most comic books had simply anthologized the newspaper strips. Rarely did they contain specially created plots and
characters. Donenfield had a new publication, *Action Comics,* and was searching for a lead feature. For $150 and some modest fees to draw and write the
episodes, the team of Schuster and Siegel assigned all rights over their creation
to Donenfield In June 1938 *Action Comics* number 1 appeared, bearing on its
cover the now familiar figure of Superman. Almost at once a powerful public
demand surfaced and an astonishing series of successes ensued. Within one
year Superman had his own comic book; within two years he was being syndi-
cated to dozens of major newspapers while the comic book ran into more than
a million copies an issue. Then followed radio, animated cartoons, special
Superman days and appearances, motion picture serials and features, and
eventually television and the stage. Apparently there was no medium in which
Superman could not flourish.

The scale of the response staggered even the most optimistic sponsors.
By 1941 "Superman" was appearing in well over a hundred newspapers with
combined circulations of almost 25 million. Ten weeks after "Superman" first
appeared on the radio it had become the most popular children's show ever to
be run on the airwaves. The serials remained among the most profitable filmed
serials ever made. Actors playing Superman or simply presenting his voice
became famous on that account alone. And "Superman" led a broader invasion
of comic books as a major publishing force. By 1943 the sales of comic books
had reached 18 million copies a month, more than the combined sales of *Life,*
Reader's Digest, and the *Saturday Evening Post.*[2]

But "Superman" did more than merely establish itself as gargantuan in
appeal, or expand the audience for each mass medium it penetrated. Its cast of
characters, its setting, its stock phrases, all entered common speech as reference points. So rapid and complete was this penetration that it provoked wonder, awe, and sometimes even anxiety among social commentators. There
seemed something fundamental to its appeal.

The author, Jerry Siegel, was as much a product as a creator of mass
culture. One magazine writer in 1941 described Siegel as a perfect clinical
illustration of psychological compensation: a myopic, overweight daydreamer
nourished on dime novels, comic strips, and science fiction. Recalling his great
moment of creative agony, tossing and turning in his bed one hot July night,
Siegel declared: "I conceive a character like Samson, Hercules and all the
strong men I have ever heard tell of rolled into one. Only more so. I hop right
out of bed and write this down, and then I go back and think some more for
about two hours and get up again and write that down."[3] By the next day he
and his partner had fashioned the first twelve "Superman" strips, creating a

Kryptonian scientist named Jor-1 who, just before cataclysms destroy his planet, sends his child into a rocket ship that lands in Smallville, U.S.A., 3 billion lightyears away.

Siegel's casual references to Greek mythology were not the last. In 1940, seeking to explain the phenomenal success of the cartoon hero in the *New Republic*, Slater Brown posited a combination of myth and modern demagogy. Superman was, he wrote, "handsome as Apollo, strong as Hercules, chivalrous as Launcelot, swift as Hermes . . . A Hero God . . . a protective deity" fulfilling popular desires for a more primitive religion.[4] Writing in *Commentary* nine years later, Heinz Politzer argued that Superman had about him "something of Goethe's Sorcerer's Apprentice, or Dr. Faust, of Hercules, and of Atlas. To be sure," Politzer continued, "Jules Verne and H. G. Wells also make their contribution to his costume and trappings, but essentially he owes his effect to the vanishing remnants of ancient mythology, that collective memory of mankind which has here been combined with utopian anticipation."[5]

More specifically, Hercules seemed the popular choice for Superman's true progenitor. The boy wonder who strangled snakes in his cradle, Hercules or Herakles was contemptuously labeled clumsy and muscle-bound by fifth-century Greeks, but he earned the titles of Defender against Evil, Tamer of Beasts and Criminals. These labels could surely be applied to Superman as well. One version of the myth gave Hercules a twin brother, Iphicles. In 1975 Kenneth Cavander argued that Clark Kent might be the mortal Iphicles to Superman. And it was easy to liken Metropolis, filled with corrupt politicians, to the Augean Stables.[6]

The owners of "Superman" in the 1980s take every occasion to present him as a mythic figure with ancient lineage. "Superman," writes his publisher, is "a masterwork of dream fulfillment, the indelible fusion of myth and desire. . . . Like Moses, like Odysseus, like every abandoned baby of heroic myth, he was cast afloat by his parents only to survive and become a savior himself." Superman was "the sun-god, flooding us with the warmth of his being," he was "this first god of a new mythology: definitely American, not borrowed, wholly our own."[7] It may be inconsistent to invoke an ancestry including Moses and Odysseus and simultaneously to insist upon radical novelty, but the publisher has a stake in protecting his property and too heavy an emphasis on ancient precedent might reduce unnecessarily the boundaries between private and public ownership.

Both at the time of his debut and today, other interpretations competed with mythic parallels to explain "Superman's" success. Some critics presented the economic despair and frustration produced by the Great Depression as fertile soil for the growth of superheroes charged with protecting the weak, raising the fallen, and persecuting evildoers. Among the figures emitted by radio and comics during the 1930s were Prince Valiant, Flash Gordon, the Lone Ranger, Dick Tracy, and Batman and Robin, all battling for justice. Some analysts compared them to Robin Hood, Tristan, and Amadis de Gaul as objects of "admiration, devotion and envy."[8]

Other critics connected Superman and his horde of imitators with the growing totalitarianism of their day and the gospel of action through violence. In the mid 1950s both Marshall McLuhan and Walter Ong argued that Superman bore the ideology of the superstate upon him as well as the mystique of fascism.[9] Politicians in Metropolis were invariably corrupt; scientists and intellectuals were bumbling fools. The Superman hero purveyed a philosophy of muscular anti-intellectualism and metapolitics; despite his slogans Superman expressed a fundamental contempt for law and order. The Superman formula, wrote Gershon Legman, amounted to little more than lynching. "'Superman' takes the crime for granted, and then spends thirty pages violently avenging it," Legman insisted in his vitriolic assault on American comics published in 1949. "No trial is necessary, no stupid policemen hog all the fun. Fists flashing into faces become the court of highest appeal."[10] Far from being an epic hero or chivalric knight, wrote one Chicago newspaperman, Superman peddled a version of hooded justice that resembled nothing more than the outlook of the Ku Klux Klan.[11]

Other explanations for Superman's popularity invoked neither economic circumstances nor a philosophy of violence but cited instead fundamental problems of national and sexual identity. Superman's divided self could be termed an emblem for a divided society. "The schizoid split within Superman symbolizes a basic split within the American psyche," argued one analyst. Like Superman, Americans were caught between dream and achievement, "between the theory that they are in control of their own lives and the reality of their powerlessness and weakness." Like Superman also, Americans were obsessed with self-identity. "It is because we have no sense of the past," Arthur Asa Berger explained, "that we have no sense of who we are."[12] Other critics paraded oedipal interpretations to justify the broad following this comic strip provoked, or concluded that heroes like Superman simply reinforced traditional beliefs, confirming widely held values and invoking frontierlike images of rugged individualism and heroic struggle against the environment.[13]

But the luxuriant train of interpretative possibilities, many of which focused on the meaning of popular culture writ large, rarely denied the mythic implications of the Superman formula. The ties seemed so obvious. That it was a formula promising success could be seen in the dozens of superheroes who fought for public attention in the 1940s and 1950s: Aquaman, Batman, Black

Knight, Captain America, Captain Marvel, Captain Midnight, Captain Triumph, Golden Arrow, Golden Law, Marvel Man, Professor Supermind, Skyman, Superboy, Supersnipe, Wonderman, Wonder Woman, an almost endless list.[14] The explosion testified to a broad public appetite that apparently justifies political, economic, *and* psychological explanations.

The imitation might have been flattering. But it was also threatening. The creators and owners of "Superman" responded quickly, if nervously, to competitive challenges. "Superman" had become an economic bonanza. And its story is significant not only because it was popular and transferable, but because its litigious spirit typified the high financial prizes rewarding successful fictional formulas.

From its earliest days the Superman property became involved with lawsuits, several of which earned classic status within the legal literature. In comics, as in some other areas of mass culture, it is the leading characters rather than the story lines which have been the crucial centers of argument. That is because characters are more easily conveyed to the vast range of advertised commodities so hungry for product identification. There exist in law several possible actions against those accused of appropriating an artistic property, including unfair competition and trademark invasion. But over the years the principal method of protection has been through copyright. One major concern of copyright law has been to shield legal owners "against those who appropriate another's work and present it as their own." The history of copyright, as idea and legislation, reveals an increasingly complex conception of artistic ownership.

Under English common law the right of an author to control his literary efforts included both printed and unpublished work; it was seen as something of a monopoly.[15] Not until the reign of Queen Anne, in 1710, did Parliament pass its first copyright act. This gave authors protection for a specified time after publication. The logic or equity of this arrangement disguised a shift in thinking. At one time literary property had been an ancient, broadly defined, individual right. Now it had become a statute-dependent privilege. For while an author still retained the right to determine if, when, where, and by whom his written work should be published, publication made it public property protected only by the copyright act from indiscriminate copying. Under Article I, Section 8 of the Federal Constitution, the purpose of copyright law is "To promote the Progress of Science and the useful Arts." This, rather than specific benefits to individual authors, is the basis of our copyright legislation, and it has been reasserted as a justification time and again as Congress debated successive statutes.

Our first copyright law was passed in 1790, only months after the inauguration of George Washington. Like the English law this statute granted authors and proprietors of literary texts the right of multiplication, but insisted on publication as a requirement for copyright and transferred the literary property to the public after a specified time. For our purposes the most significant piece of copyright legislation was the Act of 1909, which lasted in basic form for more than fifty years. While the 1909 act was passed after photographs, phonograph records, and motion pictures clouded previously clear definitions, it could not envisage the issues raised by xeroxing, television, video cassette recording, computers, and data banks. Thus copyright law continues to be an active and controversial area of legislative action and judicial intervention.

Concern about misappropriation of literary plots and characters intensified in the early twentieth century as comic strip and motion picture production grew and advertising methods became more varied. Litigation raised a number of issues, including the legal status of privacy, and several cases addressed the exploitation of popular figures—real and fictional—as product endorsements and trademarks. This was a new problem. During previous centuries fads and manias had often swept large masses of people, caught up in enthusiasm for a cause, a hero, or a work of art. Actors, generals, opera singers, politicians, artists, ballerinas, novels, all had demonstrated a capacity to influence daily fashions, social customs, or habits of consumption. From Jenny Lind to Georges du Maurier's Trilbymania, from Louis Kossuth to Lillian Russell, celebrities stood at the center of temporary epidemics. Hats, dolls, canes, bicycles, theaters, toys, dinnerware, furniture, cigars, liquors bore the likenesses, names, or special symbols of various personalities. Events, like fairs and anniversary celebrations, or places, like tourist centers and resorts, stimulated souvenir production. Fictional characters had mugs and spoons designed in their honor. Yet all this stimulated little litigation. Some unspoken assumption made famous people and literary characters a species of common property whose commodity exploitation required little control. Literature as such was protected by copyright (incompletely until the United States signed an international agreement in the 1890s), while hallmarks, patents, and eventually trademark registrations protected other brands and symbols.[16]

But pressure to extend concepts of ownership so as to cover plots and characters increased in the late nineteenth and early twentieth centuries, a product of a broader consumer market, the needs of filmmakers for best-selling ideas, and expanded mass distribution. One early case, *Empire City Amusement Co. v. Wilton,* revealed the new complexities of cartoons. As part of his aggressive program for the *New York Journal* William Randolph Hearst secured the services of several pioneering comic strip artists, among them Frederick Opper. With a colleague named Block, Opper had originated a cartoon strip called "Alphonse and Gaston," and transferred some literary rights to a company which promptly purchased a three-act comedy of the same name. But they were not alone. Another group, who would become defendants in this case, put on a play entitled *Loopin the Loop*, which featured two characters named Alphonse and Gaston, and advertised the play by posters. A federal court held this to be piracy and infringement. Copyrighted cartoons had dramatic rights as well.[17]

But complexities soon appeared. In 1914 litigation involved a play entitled *In Cartoonland*, which contained two characters named Nutt and Giff. Their names and their dress suspiciously resembled two popular cartoon figures, Mutt and Jeff. The defendant, however, insisted that his presentation was meant to be a burlesque. And the American stage had, for almost a century, been filled with parodies of current sensations. The federal judge, however, granted the plaintiffs relief. The owners of "Mutt and Jeff" were entitled to ask if the new play, parody or not, would "materially reduce the demand for the original." If it did, their copyright had been invaded. The only exception to this was a burlesque which lessened the original work's monetary value only by showing that it was not worth seeing in the first place.

Judge Rose concluded that there could be economic damage. "Those who saw 'Nutt and Giff' would have less keen a desire to see 'Mutt and Jeff,'" he determined. "Having seen the former they would be more likely to spend the next dime or quarter they had available for the purpose on a show other than the authorized dramatization." The impact of the original would be diluted. To indicate just how valuable cartoon characters had become, it was noted that the artist and author of "Mutt and Jeff" had earned more than $60,000 from the characters in only three years.[18]

But not everyone was prepared to accept the artistic integrity of all commercial designs. The Courier Lithographic Company, for example, sued a competitor, complaining that three chromolithographs advertising a performing family of bicyclists had been copied. Judge Lurton, a federal appeals court judge, found for the defendants. A print that was used solely for advertisement, he wrote, was not entitled to copyright for it possessed no value in itself. It did not promote "the useful arts, within the meaning of the constitutional provision." Mere labels, designating objects to which they were attached, could not be copyrighted. Thus "it must follow that a pictorial illustration designed and useful only as an advertisement, must be equally without the obvious meaning of the Constitution. It must have some connection with the fine arts to give it intrinsic value," Lurton insisted. Unable to discover "anything useful or meritorious" in the design, he refused to extend protection.[19]

For commercial artists this was ominous. Based on existing precedents Lurton may well have been correct. But his view was not to prevail. On appeal the case, now known as *Bleistein v. Donaldson Lithographing*, was sent to the U.S. Supreme Court. And there it encountered the elegant prose and subtle reasoning of Oliver Wendell Holmes. Holmes not only created a landmark copyright decision, he also raised a set of important questions about the dangers an emerging popular culture faced from conservatives unhappy about its direction or unaware of its logic. Overruling the lower court, he argued that artists were entitled to copyright anything they made, including copies of real persons or depictions of real events. "The copy is the personal reaction of an individual upon nature," Holmes explained, perhaps reflecting an increased consciousness of the aesthetic claims of photographers. Personality was always unique, expressing its singularity "even in handwriting," and the most modest grade of art contained "something irreducible." That something could be copyrighted. Despite Judge Lurton's suspicions, advertising chromolithographs were copyrightable illustrations. Works became no less artistic, Holmes continued, because they were attractive, increased trade, and made money.

For Holmes, then, self-conscious, aggressive commercial intentions did not taint an art form, at least not legally. And he added a final caution for jurists who found decision making an irresistible occasion for displaying personal taste. It would be dangerous, Holmes warned, for "persons trained only to the law to constitute themselves final judges of the worth of pictorial illustrations." The "taste of any public is not to be treated with contempt."[20]

So rich and powerful a decision had a major impact. It was frequently cited with admiration. Fifteen years later a circuit judge used it to agree with Dashiel Hammett's contention that he never abandoned to Warner Brothers exclusive use of *The Maltese Falcon* in future motion pictures, radio and television shows, or books. An owner had the right to use a character in sequels. "The characteristics of an author's imagination and the art of his descriptive talent," wrote Judge Stephens, "like a painter's or like a person with his penmanship, are always limited and always fall into limited patterns." Whatever those characteristics were, once copyrighted they deserved protection.[21]

During the next couple of decades, the 1920s and 1930s, judges steadily expanded the concept of artistic property. And they allowed its translation to commodities. In 1924 Judge Manton determined that a toy manufacturer had violated the rights of the owners of a comic strip featuring the exploits of Barney Google and Spark Plug. Copying, said this judge, cannot be confined to literary repetition but included many forms of adaptation. The Copyright Act was intended to protect the very conception of humor developed by a cartoonist.[22] Ten years later owners of another comic book character, Betty Boop, were protected

from dollmakers who insisted that the specific copyright notice placed on li-
censed toys was inadequate. "We do not think it avoids the infringement of the
copyright to take the substance or idea and produce it through a different medium," wrote Judge Manton. "Doing this is omitting the work of the artisan, but
appropriating the genius of the artist."[23] In the 1930s Walt Disney and Edgar
Rice Burroughs were beginning to realize large sums of money by franchising
out Tarzan, Mickey Mouse, and Donald Duck to watchmakers, clothing manufacturers, and food producers.[24] Long gone were the simpler days when famous
names, features, or props could be captured by any entrepreneur who wanted
to sell a product.

The thrust of literary protection enjoyed its rhetorical climax in a famous
1936 decision rendered by Learned Hand, enjoining a film entitled *Letty Lyn-
ton* from infringing a play, *Dishonored Lady.* Hand painstakingly compared plot
lines and characterization; in an argument which "Superman's" owners undoubtedly treasured, he insisted that it was irrelevant how much of a play or
fictional work had been anticipated by older literary forms falling within the
public domain. Some courts, Hand admitted, appeared to believe that "if a plot
were old, it could not be copyrighted." A myth, then, would be available for
anybody's use. But all this principle meant, Hand explained, was that plots
were public only in their broadest outlines. For "it is plain beyond peradventure
that anticipation as such cannot invalidate a copyright." And then Hand presented his oft-quoted example of last resort by noting that "if by some magic a
man who had never known it were to compose a new Keats's 'Ode on a Grecian
Urn,' he would be an 'author'" and if he copyrighted his poem, others could not
copy it with impunity (although they could still copy Keats's). It was no defense,
Hand added, to add new material to that which was stolen. "No plagiarist can
excuse the wrong by showing how much of his work he did not pirate."[25]

This summary of copyright decisions, however truncated, might seem a
detour in a discussion of mythic heroes. But in fact, legal precedents in place
by the time of "Superman's" 1938 arrival suggest a fully mature judicial awareness of the financial benefits of such a property. The apparently capricious
details of a fictional character's clothing and appearance translated into money.
Creators, even of humorous, superficial, critically scorned or stereotyped products, had proprietary rights to their exploitation. And even those claiming the
shelter of burlesque or criticism had to respect these rights. In the 1930s merchandisers of mythic formulas could find safety in the courts. The system made
judges and lawyers into literary critics, forcing them to evaluate even the sub-
tlest variations in story outline and character definition. But there was no reluctance to engage in the task. Equally refined judgments were required in
many other legal areas. And, one might add, equally arbitrary decisions were
rendered.

It was probably inevitable that so popular a hero as Superman would quickly be engaged in litigation. Within two years of the comic book's appearance a major suit developed. *Detective Comics v. Bruns Publications* found its way to the famed second circuit of the Court of Appeals, and a decision written by Learned Hand's brother, Augustus. In the wake of "Superman's" success the defendants, Bruns Publications, had brought out a cartoon figure named Wonderman. Like Superman, Wonderman concealed extraordinary strength beneath ordinary clothing. His skintight uniform was red while Superman's was blue. But this was apparently the major distinction. Each claimed to be a champion of the oppressed; each crushed guns with his bare hands; each leaped from tall building to tall building; each was described as the strongest man in the world. The defendants tried to avoid judgment by arguing that "Superman" did not deserve copyrighting. It was simply one more variation on an ancient theme, drawing on traditions developed in antiquity. Myths were common property; no one owned the gods and goddesses.

This argument did not impress Augustus Hand. If the author of "Superman" had indeed portrayed a "comic Hercules," Hand wrote, "yet if his production involves more than the presentation of a general type he may copyright it and say of it: 'A poor thing but mine own.'" The literary quality of *Detective Comics* might, Hand admitted, be "foolish" rather than "comic," but that was irrelevant. Here were original conceptions, and the defendants had appropriated not only "Superman's" general idea but specific details. Referring to his brother's opinions approvingly, Hand argued that even when an author drew on earlier materials "his own production cannot be copied." Hand did modify the sweeping language of a lower bench decision by Judge Woolsey (of *Ulysses* fame), but "Superman's" copyright was emphatically upheld.[26]

The legal tribulations began, then, on a bright note for "Superman's" owners. The first major challenge had been set aside. But the testing did not end then, nor did it end for similar creations. Several judges argued that characters were not protectable apart from the stories they appeared in. Some characters, after all, might be said to represent ideas, and ideas in themselves were not copyrightable. But this approach never constituted a majority view. Judges began to encounter stories whose characters constituted the only plot line. So the principle of a copyrighted hero gained persuasiveness.[27]

Some of "Superman's" legal troubles raised other issues. Schuster and Siegel, sadly aware they had signed away a fortune, contested their original contract. They decided to turn the tables by asking $5 million in damages, charging Donenfield and his syndicate with diluting their profits by introducing Batman, Superboy, The Flash, and Lois Lane as separate comic book heroes of their own. But the courts decided against them. After years of litigation the two originators signed a quitclaim in 1948 in exchange for $100,000.[28] Then they tried to market a new character, Funnyman. No Greek mythology here, only a comic seeking to capture criminals by wit and slapstick. And also, no major success. Siegel and Schuster confronted the bitter knowledge that they would never be able to duplicate their single astonishing breakthrough, achieved so effortlessly in their youth. Their later years were spent in discontented circumstances made slightly easier by small pensions the ownerships supplied.[29]

There were still other court tests for "Superman," however. The enterprising owner of a myth had to take all sorts of steps to protect it even from peripheral exploitation. "Superman's" owners covered as many bases as they could. Rea Irwin, a well-known cartoonist, discovered their ingenuity in 1943 when he started a new strip for the *New York Herald Tribune* entitled "Superwoman." It was intended as a satire. But Superwoman had already been registered as a trademark by *Action Comics* along with a set of drawings, to protect against just such an eventuality. Irwin canceled his plans.[30]

More complicated was another challenge, this by Fawcett Publications, which in 1940 began to feature the exploits of an unusual young man. Billy Batson was his name, a radio performer who, on the pronouncement of a magic word—"Shazam"—turned into an athletic hero complete with boots, skintight uniform, and flying cape. Captain Marvel (like Wonderman) dressed in red, Superman in blue, but both used similar dialogue rebuking villains who also suspiciously resembled one another.

Connections of Captain Marvel with ancient mythology were even more overt than the links with "Superman." The word "Shazam" was formed from the initials of six legendary heroes: Solomon, Hercules, Atlas, Zeus, Achilles, and Mercury. Republic Pictures produced a popular serial based on "The World's Mightiest Mortal," but Captain Marvel was probably the most simplistic of all the superheroes. A few suspected that he might simply be a spoof, a put-on. It was not easy to tell.

But "Superman" met here with its first check. Although action was instituted by *Detective Comics* in late 1941, the complaint was amended and a series of delays pushed the trial date ahead seven years, to 1948. The appeal was not completed until two years after that. The federal court believed that actual copying had taken place but decided against the owners of "Superman" on technical grounds.[31] The decision was so complicated that a petition for clarification was filed. Some of the "Superman" strips had omitted copyright notice, suggesting an unintentional surrender, but it was not clear which ones. Learned Hand did, however, insist that copyright was the comic strip's only protection. There was no misappropriation or unfair competition "for in the case of these silly pictures," he wrote, "nobody cares who is the producer—least of all, children who are the chief readers—; the 'strips' sell because they amuse and please," not because of their ownership.[32]

Eventually "Captain Marvel" was withdrawn, a "Superman" rip-off that temporarily escaped destruction because of technical obstacles. But the delay suggested some signs of softening. More to the point, "Captain Marvel" was just the sort of imitation spelling problems by reason of its very outrageousness and apparent irony. Could it really have been a parody? The comic book world was itself a caricature of the larger world outside. Colors, phrases, drawings, situations, all suggested distortion. Could one distort a distortion, pervert a perversion, falsify a travesty? If mythic narratives employed exaggeration to lampoon the hero as well as glorify him, if myths tamed dangerous emotions through this sort of deflation, couldn't parodists claim the same freedom of action? Imitation here could be seen as a form of criticism. As noted earlier, this argument had occasionally been trotted out by literary pirates, invoking freedom of speech to justify their thefts. It had been frequently rejected but as a strategy of defense it would prove increasingly popular.

For Superman, Batman, Captain America, Wonderwoman, and the other mythic figures of America's mass culture, as they aged and evolved, seemed both to incorporate and to invite increasing ridicule, from commentators and from rivals. By the 1960s and 1970s many of these characters had a generation or two of history behind them. They were no longer sudden intrusions into daily life and fashion. They were part of the record. Changes in appearance and characterization were inevitable as artists and authors retired or died and were replaced by others. Characters acquired new features. Superman gained relatives and a dog. The need to give his radio actor a vacation led to the invention of Kryptonite, the element which kept Superman helpless and, more to the point, speechless, until such a time as the producers could reengage the voice of the actor. Comic book specialists and expert fans examined new variations carefully, penning commentaries in the new learned journals that codified their increasingly abstruse lore. Critics took their own revenge. In "Superman Revisited," Roderick Nordell saw the Man of Steel following the route of Hercules and evolving into a figure of fun. In one comic, "The Three Generations of Superman," he had become a grandfather. Perhaps his next adventure would be to meet Donald Duck.[33]

In the 1970s it was a combination of this new, more ironic look, coupled with improvements in special effects, which gave "Superman" renewed life. Although there had been surges of interest occasioned by the renewed popularity of television serials like "Batman," although *Superman Comics* retained the loyalty of its readers through all these years, the decision to release two feature films on Superman in the late 1970s set new records of activity. By this time the marketing potential of fictional characters had eclipsed even the film profits. *Star Wars* toys brought more than $60 million on royalties alone, including items like bedsheets and bubblegum cards. The Pink Panther sold millions of bars of soap bearing his likeness. Walt Disney's creations had been garnering immense sums for decades. So it was natural for Warner to tie the new Superman films to a list of more than a thousand licensed items, mounting a publicity campaign that eclipsed everything since *Gone With the Wind*. Anyone wishing to use the name "Superman," of course, or details of the story, or the logo, would pay owners' fees.[34] Even the town of Metropolis, Illinois, founded with that name in 1839, had to purchase licensing rights to "Superman" from Warner Communications, in an ill-advised effort to promote the town by constructing a museum, theme park, and other tourist attractions.[35]

As the publicity surrounding the premiere of *Superman* rose to special heights, a new legal contest developed. The American Broadcasting Company began to publicize a fresh television series entitled "The Greatest American Hero." It featured a young high school teacher who, with the aid of a unique costume, discovered powers of flight, resistance to bullets, and superhuman strength. Unlike Superman, he performed these actions clumsily and sometimes ineffectively. The proper flight and landing instructions were never received; the flying teacher had to crash into obstacles in order to come to a halt.

Some of the details seemed to parody the original "Superman." But not all of them. Warner Communications sought, first, a temporary injunction to prevent the show from coming onto the air. Failing that, it sued for damages. The courts refused to award any. Warner could not claim "a protected interest in the theme of a man dressed in cape and tights who has the power to fly, resist bullets, walk through walls and break handcuffs with his bare hands."[36] Apparently these qualities were not specific enough. To warrant damages, evidence was needed that "the concrete expression of the Superman idea" had been appropriated. Quoting from various precedents, Judge Constance Baker Motley insisted that only a "substantial similarity" could support a determination of infringement. There were so many differences between the two stories that such similarity seemed insupportable. Admittedly, the court acknowledged, this was gutting Learned Hand's much-cited dictum that "no plagiarist can excuse the wrong by showing how much of his work he did not pirate," but that didn't seem important. More significant was the judge's observation that "Superman had become a 'folk hero' to the American public."[37] While this did not allow any and every liberty to be taken with the character, it suggested that his parody was a protected form of fair use.

Parody as protection was becoming an increasingly resonant judicial theme. Judge Motley could draw on several recent decisions protecting the burlesquing of copyrighted materials. In 1964 Judge Irving Kaufman upheld the right of *Mad Magazine* to print parodies of Irving Berlin songs. They included "The First Time I Saw Paris," a version of "The Last Time I Saw Paris."

This was allowable because, among other reasons, parody and burlesque were "independent forms of creative effort possessing distinctive literary qualities worthy of judicial protection in the public interest."[38] In another case "Saturday Night Live" was allowed to use the words "I Love Sodom" to the tune of "I Love New York," on the grounds that "in today's world of often unrelieved solemnity, copyright law should be hospitable to the humor of parody."[39] Lyrics, plot, characterization, symbols, and mythic heroes could all be exploited by strangers when their intention was parody. Some jurists argued that restriction on this kind of use might well constitute an infringement of the First Amendment.

It had not always been so. We have seen how parody was not an unassailable defense in the early twentieth century. As late as the 1950s Loew's won a controversial judgment against Jack Benny for a half-hour television burlesque of *Gaslight*.[40] Just a few months later, however, the same judge permitted a Sid Caesar spoof, "From Here to Obscurity."[41] Although Judge Carter, presiding in both these cases, denied that a doctrine of fair use existed specific to burlesque, Judge Kaufman's belief that "parody and satire *are* deserving of substantial freedom—both as entertainment and as a form of social and literary criticism," would dominate courts and legal commentators.[42]

We have arrived, then, at an interesting crossroads. Producers of mass culture obtained their legal protections after painful evolution. The artistry involved in caricature, jingle writing, commercial photography, zany name giving, all became recognized as property. No manufacturer, film director, or storyteller could plunder with impunity the stock of mythic variations which remained in copyright. Indeed, this sense of property has continued to broaden. In their zeal to protect the large financial interests at stake, some celebrities now seek to copyright their features and mannerisms for a period ending fifty years after death, so that their estates can enjoy the same benefits as the estates of authors. Lives have become texts, organized for public consumption.

At the same time alternate pressures mount. The appetite for diversion supports an elaborate network of parodists. At work on television, in radio, in theaters and nightclubs, in advertising, films, and comic books, these satirists burlesque the most untouchable icons, texts, and values. Such lampoons are defended as testaments to personal freedom, outlets for anger and frustration, opportunities for artistry, and social corrections for arrogance and egotism. Under such circumstances many jurists have happily offered burlesques refuge from charges of copyright invasion.

With modern mythic heroes as private property, contemporary authors, artists, and performers cannot easily employ them unless they are caricatured. The social function of myth becomes increasingly corrosive: a set of pranks and put-ons. This tendency is furthered by the fact that older, classic myths and heroes have long been freely available for any kind of exploitation. Automobiles, cement, cosmetics, athletic goods, confections, armaments, professional associations, all invoke the names and symbols of the ancient gods and goddesses. And they do this without paying any royalties at all. But these figures are already trademark symbols, to all intents. Their stories and associations are familiar on only the most general of levels. Contemporary heroes, whose formulaic exploits engage the fantasy lives of modern audiences on a daily basis, seem to be more potent. And they carry this potency from one story to another, and from one medium to another.

In essence, jurists have become the most authoritative new students of literary motif and potent definers of genre. Modern myths, in the end, seem most easily adaptable to rituals of degradation. The superhero confronts a series of diminutions. Superman's aging, and his modernization, made perfect targets. When George Reeves, one of Superman's portrayers, killed himself, headlines trumpeted that Superman had committed suicide.

There are some parallels with the fate of various religious creeds. Indeed, in the 1970s one Presbyterian clergyman published *The Gospel According to Superman,* arguing that Superman exemplified the human desire for a god, while his story encouraged an exploration of divine revelation.[43] Owners of modern myths can develop them in sustained and sometimes even poetic terms, to be sure. The Superman films of the recent past attracted critical attention partly because they were able to evoke a surprising sense of lyricism as they reenacted the creation of the foundation myth, or explored the more compelling powers associated with it, like the dream of personal flight. There was a shock in detecting touches of dignity and grandeur about so familiar and commercialized a story.

But these opportunities are available only to the owners. They alone have the power to develop, adapt, extend, and license their myths. Other serious artistic use must await the expiration of the copyright. Except, that is, for the intervention of parodists.

This paradox runs through a large sector of contemporary mass culture. Its formula entertainments are planned warily so as to capture large audiences and simultaneously avoid the legal challenges associated with copyright invasion. General formulas pose no problem. But details do, and they are what separate failures from successes. Discussing one modern formula some years ago, the gangster film, Robert Warshow wrote that the genre welcomed originality "only in the degree that it intensifies the expected experience without fundamentally altering it." Unlike other art forms its power did not rest on the life experiences of its audiences. It built, rather, on the audience's knowledge of the formula itself. "It creates its own field of reference."[44]

So do the commercialized myths. A transformed connection between myth and experience stands at their center. The new myths appeal by cross-referencing. They are stories everyone knows. But because ownership limits their boundaries, the mythic universe is subdivided. Mount Olympus has been parceled up. A self-referencing system of myths which relies upon parodied imitation as one of its central instruments of integration is a product of something beyond creative intention or legal history. And its social implications must be faced both by the courts and by its consumers.

Collective Possession:

J. Pierpont Morgan and

the American Imagination

The career of John Pierpont Morgan continues to fascinate the curious. In just two decades, during the 1870s and 1880s, his feats of financial management and consolidation brought him mythic status throughout the Western world. The Morgan touch—single-minded, far-seeing, concentrated—seemed never to fail. The Morgan style—terse, fierce, and audacious—made for lively journalistic copy. And the Morgan face and physique, crowned in later years by that diseased and disfigured nose, captivated photographers and caricaturists.[1]

The image of the all-powerful financial wizard whose decisions swayed empires and whose authority rivaled princes grew during the next twenty years. But it was supplemented in the two decades preceding World War I by another, newer reputation: the equally ruthless art acquisitor, the predatory treasure-hunter, the compulsive buyer whose wealth and ambition were transforming the

> *"It is preposterous to suppose that because a man is lucky in the stock market he is incapable of appreciating the very best things in art. He is not incapable; only he keeps his interests separate."*
>
> Simeon Strunsky, "Morgan" from *Post-Impressions*

From Linda H. Roth, ed., *J. Pierpont Morgan, Collector* (Hartford: Wadsworth Atheneum, 1987), 43–57. Reprinted with permission of the publisher.

world's art markets. Morgan's expenditure of tens of millions on a bewildering range of objects—books, paintings, miniatures, manuscripts, tapestries, porcelains, bronzes, textiles, furniture—shared the romance of the secret banking cabals and international agreements he was continually accused of masterminding. The annual trips to Europe, the forays to Egypt and the Middle East, the sudden raids on priceless hoards, all reaped their share of newspaper headlines.

The Morgan legend was aided, curiously enough, by the career of his banker son who bore the same name. In the minds of many Americans only the vaguest distinction separates John Pierpont, the railroad organizer of the 1870s, from J.P., the financier who appeared before the Pecora Committee in the 1930s, a midget seated on his knee. The name confusion has only added to the mystique.

But Pierpont Morgan himself was part of a larger story. His life and career suggest that the easy psychologizing of some Gilded Age analysts is insufficient to explain the collecting mania that overtook America in the late nineteenth and early twentieth centuries.[2] The well-educated, socially secure, personally fastidious son of a millionaire banker cannot be described by the phrases used to evoke self-made industrialists who found art either a road to respectability or a happy release from overstimulation. And these dismissals are equally inadequate when applied to many of the industrialists as well. Morgan did not invent the collecting type as a subject for inquiry; he was merely its most energetic and puzzling representative. Morgan was, wrote one museum director, "the greatest figure in the art world that America has yet produced....Never in the course of the history of collecting either in the United States or abroad has any private man . . . made so important or so generous a gift of art to the public."[3] He stood above the fray, but his collecting years, just a little more than twenty, witnessed a transformation of more general practices and attitudes. How this transformation occurred must be addressed before Morgan's own part is understood. He led the dance, but he did not dance alone.

When Pierpont Morgan began to collect seriously after the death of his father in 1890, several generations of American collectors had come and gone. And the institutional devices for receiving these accumulations had been revolutionized.

During much of the first half of the nineteenth century, American art collectors tended also to be art patrons; their interest assumed a patriotic air.[4] They not only imported artworks from Europe (benefiting from local auctions and foreign tours), they grew friendly with contemporary painters and sculptors and helped support the American art enterprise during its most fragile era.

Portraitists, landscapists, genre and history painters benefited from the interest of figures like the Baltimorean Robert Gilmor, the New York grocer Luman Reed, and from merchants like Charles M. Leupp, Robert M. Olyphant, and Jonathan Sturges. Dutch, Spanish, French, and Italian canvases, some of them spurious old masters, mingled in their collections with works by Thomas Cole, Asher B. Durand, William Sidney Mount, and Samuel F. B. Morse. Interest in art as such was suffused by a concern for national advancement. And this suggested support of the living. Only a few collectors took a systematic interest in representing the evolution of art, or attempted to assemble a body of chosen masterpieces. Exceptions like Thomas Jefferson Bryan and James Jackson Jarves, however celebrated and mourned by later generations of critics and historians, remain exemplary only from the standpoint of an interrupted tradition.[5] Their collecting ambitions, like their finances, suffered heavy blows.

Between the Civil War and the early 1890s many things changed. Trends were set which would mature during Morgan's collecting years. For one thing the links between collecting and interest in contemporary American work attenuated. Patron and collector split off. Americans attracted to nineteenth-century painting found French, German, and English art more agreeable than their own. A Gallic tone pervaded private galleries. Continentals like Corot, Meissonier, Troyon, Cabanel, and Ziem represented the acme of sophistication. Some American purchasers took personal interest in foreign artists, visiting them during their travels and writing letters of appreciation.[6] But although they occasionally picked up some American art and came to know a few native artists, there was little true enthusiasm unless the Americans were working abroad or had achieved European reputations.

Collecting ranks, moreover, were now invaded by the very rich. Antebellum collectors tended to be wealthy, but they were not dominated by vast fortunes. In the 1870s and 1880s, however, names like Vanderbilt, Belmont, Widener, and A. T. Stewart swelled the lists of art buyers. Expensive houses being built on Fifth Avenue, in North Philadelphia, on Chicago's Prairie Avenue, and in Boston's Back Bay often sported their own galleries. Dealers and auction houses, sometimes American-owned but often agents of European firms, appeared to serve these needs. By the 1860s Samuel T. Avery was buying and selling art at his rooms on Broadway and Fourth Street, aided by two Baltimoreans resident in Europe, George A. Lucas and William T. Walters.[7] In the 1870s Thomas E. Kirby came north to New York from Philadelphia, and began his lengthy auctioneering career with the American Art Association. The French dealer Durand-Ruel invaded New York in 1886 with several hundred paintings, exhibiting them at the American Art Association. Sales of the John

Taylor Johnston, George I. Seney, A. T. Stewart, and Mary Morgan collections brought in hundreds of thousands of dollars, although the most popular items tended to be by contemporary Europeans.[8]

The switch to European art and *objets,* the entry of the new millionaires, the dispersion of collecting focus, the higher prices, and the multiplication of dealers were seconded by a significant institutional development: the growth of the American art museum. By the 1880s the Museum of Fine Arts in Boston, the Metropolitan in New York, and the Art Institute of Chicago had begun to receive the collections (and bequests) of interested friends. Still housed in what would prove to be temporary homes, crowded with objects, experimenting with modes of self-government and staff appointments, happily welcoming casts, photographs, and personal gatherings of doubtful quality, the American museum had become a source for municipal pride and held out the promise of a better day.[9] Merchants, bankers, realtors, industrialists, and socialites mingled on its boards.

While Morgan was acquiring his financial fame, then—securing the basis of his fortune and strengthening the role of his House—the components of the art acquisition system were falling into place. But however the system was prepared for and anticipated before 1890, it was the next twenty-five years that would bring the basic changes.

The real impact of the art invasion rested on several things: first of all, fuller acknowledgment of the cultural power of the art object; second, greater understanding of the collector's role and the operations governing the art market; and third, an improved science of validation. As all this happened, America became not simply the refuge of human liberty, an asylum for millions of European immigrants, but also a storehouse of European art, the magnet for the privileged as well as the dispossessed. This was accomplished in the full light of publicity, as newspapers, magazines, and fiction of the day revealed. Journalists, novelists, and critics found the international competition for art, like the race for empire, a spectacle of considerable significance. They singled out for attention its various ingredients: the collectors, the expensive objects, the dealers, and the great museums. The paradoxes as well as the triumphs of this great transfer of ritual images and cult objects from one hemisphere to another formed a subject of consuming interest.

As a literary issue art was not new to Americans of this era. For decades American writers had depicted the desperate and sometimes farcical efforts of painters, craftsmen, sculptors, and architects to create objects of beauty for an indifferent and sometimes hostile audience. American artists confronted various constraints: the small range of older examples available in their own country, the inadequacies of specialized training, an apparent poverty of local subject matter, and the corruptions of emigration and transplantation. These themes had gradually entered the mainstream of national fiction.

But as the century closed and a new one dawned, it became increasingly fashionable to examine art collectors themselves, to consider the people who enjoyed the chase for objects, and to raise problems posed by such absorption. Theodore Dreiser, Edith Wharton, Robert Herrick, Henry B. Fuller, and above all, Henry James examined the nature of collecting. Europeans had explored the subject earlier, but more recent American experiences gave the theme a new intensity here.[10]

The collecting motif surfaced, appropriately enough, in an early Henry James novel, *Roderick Hudson*, published in New York in 1876. Though James here concentrated on a subject he would explore again and again, the plight of the working artist, he also considered the collector's needs. He did this by describing Rowland Mallet, the wealthy New Englander who supported young Hudson's tragic journey to Italy. Mallet reflected an older, antebellum tradition; he was both patron and collector. While he conceived his duty to involve supporting living artists, he also believed in the civic obligation to "go abroad and with all expedition and secrecy purchase certain valuable specimens of the Dutch and Italian schools." This done he could then "present his treasures" to an American city willing to create an art museum.[11]

Collecting exerted some romantic appeals. Mallet imagined himself standing "in some mouldy old saloon of a Florentine palace, turning toward the deep embrasure of the window some scarcely faded Ghirlandaio or Botticelli, while a host in reduced circumstances pointed out the lovely drawing of a hand." Here he would rescue for his countrymen some priceless legacy locked away from public view. But this fantasy hardly undercut the more utilitarian ideal that animated Mallet. As an art collector he tended to be rational rather than impassioned. Eager to be useful, he lacked "the simple, sensuous, confident relish of pleasure." Aware of this handicap Mallet longed for a painter's or sculptor's sensibility in place of his own "awkward mixture of moral and aesthetic curiosity." As it was "he could only buy pictures and not paint them; and in the way of acquisition he had to content himself with making a rule to render scrupulous justice to fine strokes of behaviour in others."[12] James centered his drama upon the artist's struggle rather than the patron's obsession. The task of acquisition had not yet acquired its aura.

Other American writers concentrated less on the ineffectual or frustrated aestheticism of the collector, and more on the ignorant vulgarity of self-made businessmen, using art to shore up shaky reputations. They had great fun. Finley Peter Dunne's Mr. Dooley found the new rich announcing their virtue by buying art. Until the top blew off the stock market the American millionaire had "bought his art out iv th' front window iv a news an' station-ry shop or had it put in be th' paperhanger." But having made their money here, the rich turned abroad to spend it. "Ye don't catch Higbie changin' iv anhy iv his dividends on domestic finished art. He jumps on a boat an' goes sthraight acrost to th' central depo." That depot was, of course, a Europe filled with clever dealers and enterprising fakers lying in wait for ambitious Americans. But the final victim was the community. The rich man might fill his home with the spoils of his travels, but when he died "he laves his pitchers to some definceless art museum." [13]

Another Chicago writer, Henry B. Fuller, also accepted as given the vulgarity of American collectors, but he added to his portrait the suggestion of civic duty that James had raised. In one Chicago collector's home room after room was "heaped up with the pillage of a sacked and ravaged globe," but its owner continued to study and learn. "I want to keep right up with the times and the people," Susan Bates told a young visitor. "We haven't got any Millet yet, but that morning thing over there is a Corot . . . people of our position would naturally be expected to have a Corot." [14]

The journalist and story writer Richard Harding Davis, writing in the early 1890s, also had sport with New Yorkers who "buy all those nasty French pictures because they're expensive and showy." [15] But he acknowledged the presence of another type, the sentimental art patron, taking more pleasure in nostalgic landscapes by a native painter than in the expensive pictures already imported from Europe. American landscapes could still evoke youth and innocence. But the European art brought higher prices.

Pompous, self-righteous, ignorant, and overbearing collectors made easy targets. The changes that could be rung on this theme were obvious by the 1890s, and were quickly joined to attacks on commercialism, materialism, and personal egotism. Americans abroad searched for canvases like carpeting. "Monet is making a great stir now," declared a visiting Chicagoan in Robert Herrick's *Gospel of Freedom*. "Mrs. Stevans has three of his. We must have at least one, and some Pizarros, and a lovely red Regnoir. [16] Yet pretension, greed, social climbing, and the shopping habit did not sum collectors up, particularly by the early twentieth century. The passions raised were too powerful, the human-object relationships too complex to be limited to lampoons and broad caricatures. Collecting represented dreams and fantasies of deep meaning, and suggested sensitivities and yearnings barely hinted at in conventional analysis.

Theodore Dreiser's epic portrait of Frank Cowperwood attempted one glimpse into the collector's passion. Cowperwood, modeled on the international traction tycoon Charles W. Yerkes, remains one of the compelling figures of the period's fiction. Dreiser developed his character within three different novels, published during the course of more than thirty years. But the first two portions of the *Trilogy of Desire* appeared during the Morgan era, and close upon Yerkes's death.

As Dreiser presented it, Cowperwood's early delight in pictures mingled powerful, undefined, semiconscious desires with a very self-conscious assault on respectability. Art could help the young Philadelphia businessman just getting established. But art also "fascinated him." Admiring nature "without knowing why, he fancied one must see it best through some personality or interpreter." [17] Cowperwood's passion for pictures grew; he paid more and more for them. And he developed a taste for fine furniture, for tapestries, porcelains, and oriental art as well.

The pull to art seemed primal. But intelligent planning and social goals also entered his calculations. "What could be greater, more distinguished than to make a splendid authentic collection of something?" Cowperwood wondered as he thought of representing the evolution of art within his own collection, on a scale possible only in great museums. This ambition came twenty years earlier to Cowperwood than to other collectors; Dreiser gave him special prescience. The logic seemed unassailable. Judgment and discrimination must "result in value as well as distinction? What was a rich man without a great distinction of presence and artistic background? The really great men had it." [18] So Cowperwood's passion could contain both a traditional quest for recognition and a compulsive urge for beauty, accompanied, to be sure, by a stunted if not primitive sense of moral issues.

The forced dispersion of his art at a public auction symbolized Cowperwood's Philadelphia downfall as poignantly as it revealed his superior judgment. The low prices suggested a taste that ran ahead of its time. In art as in business, Cowperwood possessed genius. A move to Chicago, the site of *The Titan*, the second volume, brought a resurgence of his collecting interests. Again he used art to push the road ahead, but his objects formed a courting arena as well as an outlet for personal sensuality. Cowperwood's sexual appetite was stimulated by women who appreciated his taste, who could discuss his art with him. His search for monumentality soon expressed itself by slavish devotion to the assembled objects. Cowperwood saw himself wandering in rapt communion with his pictures, his missals, his jade, and his sculpture. "The beauty of these strange things, the patient laborings of inspired souls of various times and places, moved him, on occasion, to a gentle awe." Wearied after strenuous days battling in the marketplace, he entered his gallery at night. Turning on the lights, he seated himself before "some treasure, reflecting on the nature, the mood, the time, and the man that had produced it," meanwhile exclaiming "A Marvel! A Marvel!" The businessman as artist, a theme midwestern novelists were exploring at just this time, was perhaps more easily expressed in the collecting than in the creating mode.[19] The patient and loving assembly of objects could draw on the imaginative urges and aesthetic leanings that also fed the artist's dream.

The relationships linking commercial sagacity, personal passion, cultivated taste, and high ambition were even more thoroughly explored in the fiction of Henry James. James designed a gallery of collecting types to populate the novels and short stories he wrote during a thirty-five-year period.[20] They assumed distinct shapes. There was the pilgrim abroad, Christopher Newman, who twenty minutes after buying the first picture of his life became conscious of "the germ of the mania of the 'collector,'" and began to think art patronage "a fascinating pursuit."[21] There were the Europeans themselves, penniless patricians like Valentine de Bellgarde, insatiable accumulators whose "walls were covered with rusty arms and ancient panels."[22] There were revolutionaries like Hyacinth Robinson, too poor to collect themselves but converted to the cause of civilization by "the splendid accumulations of the happier few," the "monuments and treasures of art," in which Europe so abounded.[23] There were the elect like Mrs. Gereth for whom "things" were the sum of existence. "She could at a stretch imagine people's not having, but she couldn't imagine their not wanting and not missing."[24] There were finely honed American tycoons like Adam Verver, engaged in a pursuit for perfection which applied "the same measure of value to such different pieces of property as old Persian carpets, say, and new human acquisitions." Here, at bottom, was the aesthetic principle "planted where it could burn with a cold, still flame; where it fed almost wholly on the . . . idea (followed by appropriation) of plastic beauty."[25] And there was, even more typically, the Yankee millionaire of *The Outcry*, Breckinridge Bender, in pursuit less of beauty than of some "*ideally* expensive thing," member of a conquering horde armed "with huge cheque-books instead of with spears and battle-axes."[26]

This spectrum of gifted, haunted, obsessive, and reckless types raised endless questions about the ties between taste and moral values, questions which later generations of critics are still trying to answer. Given James's knowledge of the Anglo-American scene it was possible that some impressions of Morgan may have entered several of his characters, notably the aspiring spirits of Adam Verver and Breckinridge Bender. James's subtle inquisition into the new connections between people and things, his portrayal of a world so encouraging to acquisition and cataloguing, probably did not penetrate the consciousness of most Americans. But the real counterparts to his fictional creations did march through magazine and newspaper pages, dazzling readers by their wealth and their grasp.

Among those so accessible in the first decade of the twentieth century was Mrs. Isabella Stewart Gardner in Boston, importing carefully chosen masterpieces while quarreling incessantly with the customs service and occasionally resorting to elaborate smuggling methods, which also made good newspaper copy.[27] By marriage and descent Mrs. Gardner was a millionaire. Benjamin Altman of department store fame collected on his own money, as did the Pittsburgh industrialist now resident in New York, Henry Clay Frick. The Philadelphia contingent included a Morgan associate, Edward T. Stotesbury, P. A. B. Widener, butcher, traction magnate, and corporate investor; and the eminent lawyer John G. Johnson, whose painting collection was larger, more distinguished, and less expensive than that of most of his fellow collectors. Charles L. Hutchinson and Martin Ryerson in Chicago, George Eastman in Rochester, Charles L. Freer in Detroit, Mrs. Collis Huntington in California, Charles Taft in Cincinnati, Otto Kahn, Jules Bache, Charles Yerkes, Clarence Mackay, and Mrs. Louisine Havemeyer, all enjoyed considerable public attention by reason of their avid pursuit of great art at large prices.[28] Without delving as deeply as did the novelists into psychological motives, newsmen were attracted by the new sport. The fortunes available outdistanced the combined national art budgets of several nation-states, and of depressed European curators entrusted with the growth of their collections.

Some comparisons make understandable the outrage and adulation greeting the new money. Before 1910 no picture had ever sold in America for more than $65,000, and this price was reached only occasionally. True, a Meissonier reached $66,000 at the A. T. Stewart sale of 1888, but it was accompanied by a self-portrait. Another nineteenth-century French painting, this time by Troyon, brought $65,000 at the Henry auction in the spring of 1907. But when Charles Yerkes's art collection was auctioned off in the spring of 1910, a spate of new records were set. A Corot brought $80,000, Turner's *Rockets and Blue Lights* managed $120,000, and a Frans Hals staggered the crowd at $137,000. All in all the Yerkes treasures garnered more than $2,000,000, some three-quarters coming from the painting sale, and $350,000 from rugs and tapestries. Headlines trumpeted the astonishing prices art could command.

But these figures paled alongside the sums Americans paid in Europe, not only for paintings but for decorative objects and groups of antiquities. In 1911 Henry Clay Frick parted with more than $1,000,000 in exchange for just three pictures, including a $500,000 Gainsborough. Otto Kahn purchased a Frans Hals family group for something more than $400,000, and Mrs. Huntington paid, that same year, about as much for a single Velasquez. A stunned *New York Times* observed that twenty years earlier $25,000 had been a handsome tribute for a single art work.[29]

Morgan helped set the new levels. To keep the Garland collection of oriental ceramics at the Metropolitan, he paid $1,000,000. In 1902 he spent $500,000 on a set of fifteenth-century tapestries once belonging to Cardinal Mazarin, having already purchased some Gobelins for more than $300,000. The Hoentschel collection of decorative art which he gave to the Metropolitan and various pieces from the Rodolphe Kahn collection in Paris commanded similarly staggering sums. This great price inflation occurred in a relatively short period, between the turn of the century and 1912 or so. Along with awe for the magnitude of the rise were questions about its meaning.[30]

The *New York Times* stood among the questioners. Even in 1904 it was wondering why the picture of a cow could fetch so much more cash than the cow herself, to say nothing of the pasture she grazed in. The price for such a canvas may well have constituted a simple tribute to technical skill, like the sums paid by spectators to see a man "keep ten brass balls in the air at once."[31] But the pricing logic reflected other things also. "Unique and nearly unique works of art which are desired by many tend to rise in value proportionately with the great modern fortunes," the *Times* observed. "The buyer foresees . . . that great fortunes can be made hereafter," but the finest works of art can be "bought at all, only now and then. It is the law of supply and demand in a highly accentuated form."[32] Any businessman could understand this formula; it made the swollen prices less surprising. The rich, the *Times* would argue several years later, could afford to ignore previous price levels, because art values were practically incomputable. The price for Rembrandt's *Night Watch* could one day surpass Holland's national debt.[33]

It was more than economic analogy that encouraged a tolerant view of collecting extravagance. Civic aims allowed it. At an earlier moment of national life these expenditures might well have generated greater hostility. And some reformers continued to criticize the huge prices, juxtaposing them with mass poverty. "Shall Fortunes Be Limited by Law?" remained a debate subject.[34]

Art, however, seemed a relatively wholesome outlet for the wealthy, one of the approved vents for great fortunes. As Morgan assumed the presidency of the Metropolitan Museum, the *New York Times* predicted that when the world had forgotten "the master mind which has directed the great railway combinations," it would still cherish his memory as an art collector. Art was the "monument which will carry his name 'down the corridors of time.'"[35] It was good to see rich men spending their money on "objects other than" yachts and automobiles, the *Times* observed several years later.[36]

Invested with public significance by the national press, American collections appealed as a civilizing force, an instrument for local pride, and a permanent tourist attraction. The Metropolitan's Hudson-Fulton Loan Exhibition of 1909, arranged in connection with a New York City pageant, revealed impressive American holdings of Dutch art. Visiting Germans were astonished by the Rembrandts, Vermeers, and Hobbemas they encountered. Max Friedlander of the Prussian Royal Art Museums plaintively noted that America had outstripped Germany in the number of Frans Hals canvases, and already contained seventy of the world's 650 known Rembrandts.[37] "We are gradually reaching the condition where New York is a true market for art," rejoiced the *Nation*, where the well-to-do fearlessly bought "objects of almost any description."[38] Privately owned art revealed national supremacy as clearly as steel production and coal tonnage did. And with almost the same ease of quantification.

International competition provided a justification for collecting energy beyond recreation for the rich or investment opportunity. The masterpieces purchased by millionaires were being taken away from France, Germany, Italy, and Britain. As European art lovers wrote angry letters to their newspapers, as legislatures debated (and occasionally passed) prohibitions against the export of art treasures, American readers devoured stories of humiliation and envy. "Fear for Europe Art Gems," ran one story in the *Times*. Morgan's election to the Metropolitan presidency induced alarm waves all over Europe. Georges Cain, director of the Musée Carnevalet in Paris, Adolpho Venturi of Rome's National Gallery, Siegfried Lillienthal, Berlin art critic, along with professors, journalists, and gallery keepers, pressed for action.[39] "American collectors are the terror of foreign curators," the *Times* reported happily.[40] "How We Strip Europe of Her Treasures of Art," became a popular theme for weekend writers.[41]

Occasionally Europeans rallied to their art. In Britain public subscriptions saved a few treasures. The Duke of Norfolk's Holbein, offered for sale in 1909, seemed safe only when a volunteer came up with £40,000 at the last moment.[42] British peers posed particularly mercenary demands that the nation ransom their great possessions from American millionaires. By 1911 the English were discussing imposition of an export tax on old masters. If (as was argued) as much as $10,000,000 worth of art left the country annually, a 10 percent duty might raise the funds for protection.[43] Even Wilhelm von Bode of Berlin, a museum director who with the kaiser's help had bought heavily in France, Italy, and England, complained about American raids. However, he observed reassuringly, Americans bought paintings with a yardstick. In selecting only those making for a big show, they left behind more elegant if unpretentious pieces for discriminating European buyers.[44]

Others, like Lord Clanricard, an Irish landlord, charged Americans with gullibility as well as vulgarity. Two-thirds of the old masters imported here were fakes, he insisted.[45] Not all Americans lacked judgment, however. When Morgan acquired the Amherst Caxtons for his library, and a gorgeous catalogue of

THE FLIGHT OF THE OLD MASTERS.

"The Flight of the Old Masters," by Hy Mayer, 1910

his holdings appeared, British connoisseurs bewailed the exhaustion of their "bibliographic and artistic treasures for the benefit of America," and hinted about "joint action of patriotic amateurs."[46]

The hundreds of stories like these brought immense satisfaction to American nationalists who reminded Europeans that their own art represented centuries of financial domination and military looting. "We ourselves largely took it away from somewhere, didn't we?" asked an English lady in a James novel. "We didn't *grow* it all."[47] American collectors were merely returning the favor. Movement was actually good for much of the art, boasted the *New York Times*. "The plaintive wail of the British writer on art, the arrogant ignorance of the German Kunstkritiker, and the groans of the French expert" filled the air of Europe, suggesting that the "objects thus changing hands were lost to the world." In fact they often stepped from dark, inaccessible nooks into commodious galleries generously organized for "the many. Sooner or later they reach the art museums of this big bustling country, where they are more needed than in Europe."[48] The American art collector, harmless, even benevolent, had been transformed into a "bogyman" by the Berlin art establishment, rattling bones to chill the blood of connoisseurs. The terrible picture emerged of Europe's treasures "taking ship for Yankeeland, never to return!"[49] In fact Europe's museums were already so crammed their art could barely be seen. Instead of complaints, American collectors deserved congratulations.

By purchasing undervalued schools and carrying off architectural fragments, the *Times* insisted, Americans increased European appreciation for their own art. When Burgos citizens rose angrily to protest removal of a staircase from the Casa de Miranda, the *Times* advised them to be grateful to Americans who had so stirred their pride and prodded them into protecting their heritage.[50] Swipes at Yankee meatpackers and grocers only encouraged American journalists the more to flail away at the snobbism of European connoisseurs, unwilling to spend the money to protect their treasures in an open market and unable to acknowledge that they were being bested by intelligent and discriminating (as well as wealthy) art buyers.[51]

To be sure, the millionaires were now laying siege to highlights of some celebrated collections. Americans, declared Jacques Seligmann, one of Morgan's favorite dealers, cared for "great age, for historical associations, for acquisitions that command the admiration and respect of museum experts, above all for pieces that reveal their beauty and character increasingly with disinterested familiarity."[52] This flattery may have been calculated, but a more neutral observer, recently appointed director of the Berlin National Gallery, denied that selling Americans art was like casting "pearls before swine. I make bold to say," he announced in 1911, "that the present-day artistic taste of Americans . . . will rank in all respects with European communities."[53] The recent concentration upon pedigreed masterpieces was one piece of evidence. Another was the prices. Some enthusiasts suggested that museums add purchase prices to the labels. This sight would reinforce "the value of the lesson taught."[54] Even the director of the Metropolitan, Sir Caspar Purdon Clarke, liked the idea, arguing that it would aid curatorial reputations.[55]

Fraud, of course, continued on its way. In Paris *La Patrie* reported (in 1910) that more than 15,000 fake old masters had been shipped to America during the previous twelve months. These included, it added slyly, 2,849 Corots, 1,812 Rembrandts, and 6,204 Teniers, along with hundreds of harpsichords once belonging to Marie Antoinette.[56] Reputable dealers denied that anything so horrendous could take place, but there were some extraordinary episodes. Spurious noblemen arrived in American cities with equally spurious pictures they presented to gullible buyers.[57] Mrs. Charles Hamilton Paine, the widow of a Boston broker and a resident of Paris, spent hundreds of thousands of dollars on sham art objects manufactured by a doubtful Comte d'Aulby. The English-born comte printed for Mrs. Paine a handsome catalogue in English and French, listing the royal provenance of the pictures he had sold her, adding after each, "Now belonging to the illustrious amateur of art, Mrs. Charles Hamilton Paine."[58] With his self-designed uniforms and his own order of nobility, the comte was a figure of notoriety in Paris, but this did not impair his ability to dominate Mrs. Paine. Eventually he was arrested for fraud. He had many colleagues.

American canvases were also subject to dispute. The most notorious incident provoked the trial of a New York art dealer, William Clausen, accused by a local collector of having manufactured a series of paintings by Homer Martin, an American landscapist. The lengthy and complex trial featured contradictory testimony from artists, critics, and connoisseurs. "Is there no quarter from which an authoritative announcement may come," plaintively asked the *New York Times*, "or must every man make up his mind for himself?" [59]

The sensational charges and countercharges, the revelations of dishonest dealers and active forgers, and the searching out of international networks did more than provide easy newspaper copy and still more publicity for the collecting passion. They also encouraged popular discussions which continue today. What was a real masterpiece? In 1910 the modern science of attribution was barely a few decades old. Giovanni Morelli's reexamination of Italian artworks in German galleries helped revolutionize connoisseurship, but it was published as late as 1880. Disciples like Gustave Frizzoni, Jean Paul Richter, and Bernard Berenson were soon establishing the principles and techniques for more careful judgments about authorship.[60] Scientific tests appeared to validate the age and origin of some decorative art objects. The expert, self-important and self-confident, was making novel claims. Scholarship, research, and systematic analysis replaced exquisite and undefinable sensations as the basis for conclusions. Of course scientific connoisseurs did make mistakes. They revised their opinions. And some dealers and collectors continued to insist that taste offered a better guide than extended scholarship. Nonetheless, by the early twentieth century artworks had to earn their labels, and this added to both the risks and the excitement of collecting.

The highly publicized changes of attribution, however, posed problems. Why should the simple change of an artist's name so affect the value and importance of a work? While its appearance remained the same, drastic consequences flowed from a single judgment. There was too much reverence for names, the *Times* argued. A picture or statue sold as the handiwork of a famous artist fetched a big price, and fought its way to a prominent museum. "Suddenly somebody comes along and denies . . . its 'authenticity.' At once, from being an object of worship by the elect and respect from common folk, it loses all value and is hastily removed to a cellar." Yet whatever beauty the object possessed before the discovery, it retained afterward. This "great mystery" contrasted with literature. Books, suggested the *Times*, "stand on their own merits. They are not liked the better because written by a noted author, or the worse because anonymous." [61]

What was the meaning of genuine? Research revealed that many famous artworks emerged from workshops rather than the master's hand. Renaissance geniuses not only copied one another's art, they employed assistants to actually paint, carve, and gild. Was it the age of the copy that made it important? Its quality? The copy's owner? Was the work of art simply a commodity whose cash value (and popularity) varied according to a supply and demand cycle? Reviewing the issues, the *New York Times* decided that the nouveaux riches who simply bought what they liked were on safer ground than more ambitious collectors determined to make important purchases. The vulgar might collect bad art but at least they were not victimized. The ambitious collector required expert advice "if not a guardian." The only infallible way to obtain art was to buy directly from its maker.[62] This meant visiting studios and patronizing the living. The alternative was to establish committees of experts who would then pass rulings (by majority vote) on art authenticity.

The discussion was, at a minimum, amusing. "The man in the street," wrote the *Times*, "to whom a picture is good if it appeals to his taste and bad if he does not like it," takes "a deal of enjoyment" in the disputes, particularly when they elevated to sudden glory a picture that had been hanging in relative obscurity for centuries. Paradoxically, its new prominence, by increasing its value, rendered it less accessible to the viewing public.[63]

Two other developments of the day further increased public interest in the cultural significance of art objects. While they testified to a new, more intense consciousness of their social meaning, they were disturbing and threatening to art lovers. The first involved the increased daring of art thievery. This was no new problem. The British crown jewels had been subject to ambitious conspiracies for many years; the nineteenth century had its own startling thefts (including a spectacular seizure of Gainsborough's *Duchess of Devonshire*, purchased by Junius Spencer Morgan and eventually housed in son Pierpont's own collection).

But during the first decade of the twentieth century the number and magnitude of thefts advanced. In France some thieves specialized in church treasures, hauling away reliquaries, monstrances, windows, manuscripts, carvings, statuary, and paintings. Headquartered in Clermont-Ferrand, one gang's technique was to persuade priests that the anticlerical government was about to sell their art. It offered to remove it for "safekeeping."[64] Rumors suggested the loot was then transferred to London before finding its way to American millionaires. The mysterious "anonymous millionaire" was invoked by Europeans on many occasions to explain why famous works of art, apparently unsalable on the open market, were taken. As Americans explained the growth of forgery and fraud, so they were pushed forward as the cause for expanded criminality.

No such exotic reasons were necessary. Much of the art crime was home grown and home inspired. This was never more true than in the single greatest outrage of the early century, one of the most brazen feats of knavery in the history of thievery. This was the August 1911 theft of the *Mona Lisa*, taken by an Italian carpenter in broad daylight right under the noses of Louvre guards, and kept hidden in Paris for more than two years until it was returned to the Louvre (via Florence) in early 1914.[65] No incident dramatized more clearly the ritual significance and singular status accorded to masterpieces in the Western world. "It is shocking to think that a thief could remove a fairly priceless painting from a famous gallery in the heart of a busy city," the *New York Times* editorialized.[66] French papers were less restrained. Noting the scandalous safety conditions of the Louvre, the inattention of the guards, the eating, cooking, and pipe-smoking that took place in the galleries, a writer in the *Revue bleu* charged that the museum had earned the world's contempt. "France is responsible in the eyes of every person of culture for this irreparable loss," he cried, and "the soul of the universe mourns and will mourn evermore." The theft had become the "crime of 21st August."[67]

Inevitably enough, stories appeared that Morgan had been offered the painting (which he angrily denied). According to the American press, the thief alleged he had tried to sell the painting to one of Morgan's representatives, as well as to dealers in several European cities.[68] Another rumor suggested that the theft merely disguised a transfer; the real *Mona Lisa* had already been sold to some American millionaire for a fabulous sum, and a reproduction had been hung in its place.

The fame of this painting, the length of time it was gone, and the size and reputation of the Louvre, all focused attention on the larger phenomenon of art thefts. A vague sense of danger and intrigue now hung over the collecting drama. Like his colleague the second-story man, then getting attention from elegant detective writers, the art thief became something of a romantic figure, stealing only from the rich (or the well-stocked) before facing his special problems of divestiture.[69] And accompanying his adventures ran the complexities of improved forgery and reproduction techniques, granting the successful collector a special note of triumph as he threaded his way amid criminals and impostors.

A second threat to the masterpiece also focused attention on its role as cultural icon. And this was the relatively recent device of attacking an artwork to express some personal or social grievance. In the summer of 1907 a young man with a knife slashed a Poussin canvas hanging in the Louvre. He explained afterwards that he did it to shame his parents, prosperous farmers refusing him financial aid.[70] Two months later an Ingres portrait was cut by a girl with a scissors. Inspired by the earlier slashing, she turned herself in to bring attention to the fact that so much money was "invested in dead things like those at the Louvre collections when so many poor devils like myself starve because they cannot find work."[71] In 1911 Rembrandt's *Night Watch* was badly damaged by a discharged naval cook, angry at the state because he had been dismissed by the Dutch navy.[72]

Such attacks provoked a series of responses. Some museums, like the Louvre, began to place valuable paintings under glass. This produced new complaints. Sticks and umbrellas (still carried into galleries) could break the glass, critics argued, and the reflecting surfaces now deprived students of effective study. Some suggested that admission to public collections be more carefully controlled, by instituting charges in previously free museums or by creating special galleries (of inexpensive objects) for more casual and potentially dangerous visitors.[73] Guard forces were enlarged, and greater vigilance preached. But there were no absolutely foolproof methods of protection, only a series of interim measures. For artworks, so prized a badge of culture, had also assumed other metaphorical burdens. They symbolized the margin, the surplus of wealth modern industrialization had achieved, now being applied to the purchase, display, and cataloguing of history's treasures. Alienation, quite properly, addressed these icons. Where else could civilization be wounded more cruelly? The attacks added to the glamour and notoriety the art enjoyed.

Through this extensive set of transactions, amid the fraud, the thefts, the great auctions, the happy meetings of impoverished Europeans and wealthy Americans, spreading rumors, making deals, granting interviews, wandered the dealers. This was, if not their greatest age, perhaps their most creative one. Wealthy English, German, and French collectors, assembling objects with feverish intensity, also needed dealers. But they were rarely as dependent on them as were the Americans. Linguistically, intellectually, even socially, American buyers relied on the dealers: to introduce them to artists, collectors, museums, and curators; to refine (or simply to change) their tastes; to stimulate their personal competition; to broaden their areas of interest and knowledgeability; even to correct their appearance and table manners. By the early twentieth century, the traveling agents of European houses had invaded eastern (and occasionally midwestern) cities, impressing the public with their cosmopolitanism, their aesthetic judgment, their claims to infallibility. They whetted appetites, nurtured egos, soothed hurt feelings, and established the rules of the hunt. Through dealers Americans discovered they could own masterpieces thought a few years earlier to be forever out of reach. Through dealers they were led backward in time from their own nineteenth-century favorites, and to regions of the world far beyond Western Europe. Both the older American firms and the Europeans—Scott & Fowles, Knoedler, Duveen Brothers, Durand-Ruel, Seligmann, Berolzheimer, Agnew—provided guidance, encouragement, and merchandise.[74]

Although dealers attracted less attention than did their clients or their art, they helped represent official opinion. At a time when museums had small staffs, when university-trained specialists were rare, when curators were just learning how to manage, dealers had the urbanity, articulateness, experience, and self-confidence to permit generalization about the art market. Museum directors like Wilhelm von Bode, his envy and outrage notwithstanding, paid them their due. Dealers, he admitted, had become "bearers of culture." "They are to thank that the American collectors seek only the best; that their sense of quality has developed in a measure quite unknown with us." As "pathfinders" dealers ensured that collecting implied the same high standards from coast to coast.[75] They were agents of high European culture, recreating its world. Museums were still too poor to constitute their principal customers. If art was bought at all, it was bought by individuals. And here the affectations and performance techniques, the flattery, promises, threats, and melodrama that some dealers employed, served as instruments in a good cause. To a large extent they were as much tastemakers as their clients.

The dealers had much more than the egos of their customers working for them. In early twentieth-century America they could exploit a powerful and competitive struggle for cultural dignity raging among the country's large cities.[76] The millionaires spoke not simply for themselves nor even for their personal reputations. All assumed they would be handing on their collections to public institutions. The private act of purchase was thus invested with public significance. The collectors had become spokesmen for their communities, already at work planning the civic monuments to announce their arrival on the world scene. Opera houses, orchestra halls, theaters, plazas, boulevards, statuary squares, universities, zoos, park systems, fairs, all testified to municipal grandeur. But the art museum was certainly a principal source of local pride. Ordering a great building and filling it with beautiful objects became a civic obligation. In Chicago, Boston, Philadelphia, and Cincinnati, in St. Louis, Pittsburgh, Baltimore, and Cleveland the collecting passion attracted popular support.

But while there was competition there was also dominance. Grand collecting coincided with the powerful claims of New York City, not simply to American metropolitan sovereignty but to rivalry with London, Paris, and Berlin as a center of learning and culture. Greater New York was created in 1898. During the next fifteen years the city's architecture, institutional growth, and financial power reflected a special surge of confidence and imperial desire. Millionaires flocked there from the countryside and from rival cities. On the boards of institutions like the Metropolitan, the New York Public Library, and the American Museum of Natural History, they protected the city's honor in the quest for treasure.[77]

Local pride and civic patriotism, at least on the part of the rich, seemed relatively new to New York. The *Times* observed in 1902 that it was traditional to think of this city as simply a camp to make money. Things, however, had changed. Once a desirable possession came on the market, some "public-spirited citizen" managed to secure it. "It was only the other day that Mr. Pierpont Morgan came forward to secure for the Metropolitan Museum the Garland collection, which it seemed in danger of losing. And now Mr. James Henry Smith comes forward to save for the city the famous Rubens which we were in danger of losing to Chicago."[78]

Vigilance was necessary, even for New York's magnificent future. The following month the *Times* struck a different, more petulant tone when it learned that Henry Walters of Baltimore was about to buy the Masaranti collection in Rome. "New York has lost the chance of a generation and at one blow Baltimore has raised herself far above all other American cities," mourned the *Times*. No New Yorker had bothered to go to Rome and buy these canvases and antiquities "like a sensible businessman." It was too bad, the *Times* concluded, that so little public spirit existed in the city. It made the Metropolitan "look silly" and placed the Walters Museum "on a level with the great public museums of London, Paris, and Berlin."[79] Sparring with other newspapers who warned about the collection's authenticity, harangued by readers who thought New York deserved a change of diet and a greater emphasis on modern art, the *Times* grieved to the last for the collection's loss, one which modern appraisers have found to be a mixed blessing for Baltimore.[80]

New York, however, was not to suffer many such losses. The wealth of Metropolitan trustees, the city's energy, its growth and development made it the drainage point for the siphon diverting so much European art. Stuffed with objects, by 1914 museums like the Metropolitan were being criticized as mausoleums, magnificent monuments crammed with a mass of objects, too many of them mediocre. The chief task of museums like the Met, warned Wilhelm von Bode in 1912, was the disposition of superfluous possessions.[81] Describing the "Land of Sunday Afternoon" in 1914, designer Lee Simonson condemned the "unending accumulation" making museums into caves in which "successive Niebelungen hoards recovered from a disintegrating past are accumulated in exactly the piles in which they were originally heaped."[82] The "aesthetic furniture of a plutocracy," Simonson wrote elsewhere, was poor building material for a civic institution.[83] The business of a museum was "not to store the past but to restore it, to restore to the scattered fragments of a dismembered age their meaning."[84]

Within a generation American collectors and the museums they stocked had grown from the weak and dependent children of European parents to so concentrated a level of wealth that plenitude was itself a problem. It had taken only twenty-five years (and several times that many millions of dollars) for the transformation. The celebration of collectors, the transformation of art objects into social talismans, and the consecration of museums as hallowed receptacles had aided the process. In the 1920s the art flow would expand and prices rise still further, but the pattern was now set.

And the pattern maker, the figure bringing together the trends and the paradoxes, the *beau idéal* of the private collector was Pierpont Morgan himself. As trustee and then president of the Metropolitan, as a benefactor of dealers and a patron of cataloguers, a focus for expert consultants, a bidder of huge sums at private sales and public auctions, as the recipient and then the restorer of stolen objects, as donor and preserver as well as pirate raider, Morgan the collector stayed continually in the public eye. When he outbid emperors other Americans rejoiced; when he entertained kings, queens, sultans, and pashas, the American press exulted. His lengthy campaigns against the art tariff—revised in 1909 and basically abandoned some years later—brought enthusiastic appreciation. His name figured in almost every major art rumor of the day and his travel plans received the attention today accorded only rock stars and royalty.[85]

Enhancing Morgan's capacity for fascination was, of course, his own personal collection, a fabulous assemblage of objects on display at the South Kensington Museum and his English houses. Its fate would become an international question, involving governmental figures as well as connoisseurs. It had been an obvious weapon in his war against the art tariff, but more than that it symbolized, to many of his countrymen, the larger transfer of treasure. When, in 1912, he announced he would transport his collection back to New York (some suggested to avoid the English death duties), it was front page news. This "amazing collector," gushed the *New York Times,* who "picks the fruit of European art from its parent tree with the zest and ease of a boy in an apple orchard," had shown the world what can be achieved by "the union of a genius for business with a taste for art."[86] When David Lloyd-George assured Morgan that his art would not be taxed if it remained (unsold) in England, alarmed Americans cried foul. "London museums have been enriched long enough," warned the *Times,* jealous for New York's reputation. And the inheritance tax was not the reason for Morgan's decision, it continued. He had always intended to bring the objects to America. New York was their destined home and "no promises to withhold taxation will serve to keep them on the other side of the Atlantic."[87]

Fears of the Exchequer's designs on his estate may have been a factor, but the *Times* had a point. Morgan's philanthropic career suggested an abiding

"Homeless," by
C. R. Macauley,
1912

intention to place his art objects in his native country, although for some time it was not clear just where they would go. But despite the spasmodic flamboyance of his many purchasing gestures, Morgan's civic interests were carefully thought out and directed toward national objectives. As with many other millionaires his passion for ownership was fed partly by the sheer pleasure of obtaining what was difficult to obtain. If the objects were rare or unique, if they were beautiful, and if they were important representatives of a style, a skill, or a civilization, Morgan could become aroused. He admired workmanship, valued associations, enjoyed precious materials, and had his particular aesthetic preferences.

But Morgan's buying transcended issues of taste or personal favor to assume, at moments, something of a military campaign. It was his single-minded pursuit of the priceless, his constancy in the hunt, and his willingness to commit fabulous sums which brought him contemporary fame. But it is the deeper ambitions and the institutional impact which deserve renewed attention today.

The adjectives "collected" and "possessed" conjure up contrasting sets of meanings. To be collected implies a state of calmness, composure, tranquillity, and placidity. Being possessed, on the other hand, insinuates a form of seizure, derangement, sorcery, or maniacal infatuation. Yet in the art world the two words frequently intertwine. Morgan's energy, his zeal, his compulsive fascination with objects suggest a degree of possession. His youthful fascination with bits of stained glass, a boyish obsession which eventually found expression in the windows of his library, was one small indication. His compulsive, lifelong pursuit of individual objects was another. But his philanthropic activities, his support of scholarship and cultural organizations, his larger collecting ambitions argue for something else. In those activities falling beyond either art or business, Morgan united elements of sentimentality, nostalgia, and personal conservatism. He was a devoted clubman, a breeder of dogs and cattle, a yachtsman, and something of a country gentleman. He delighted in his English stays and the great houses he visited might well have inspired some of his own collecting goals. His travels beyond England did not, as with so many Americans, emphasize France and Germany, sophisticated, modern, up-to-date, but Rome and Egypt. He hired scholars to produce careful and lavishly printed catalogues, which he distributed among research libraries. He was a generous contributor to the American Academy in Rome, a patron of neoclassical architecture, an active subscriber to many cultural associations. Finally, he was the most prominent lay member of the Episcopal Church of America, an enthusiastic participant at triennial conventions, the friend and host of prominent bishops, the warden of his own church vestry. Some of these activities reflected Morgan's own sense of self and position. His wealth and pride demanded that he contribute appropriately to various causes, that he be represented, handsomely, in the lists of purchasers and donors. His own taste for good things— to eat, to drink, to sail on—was fed by a lifetime of organized self-indulgence.

But beyond this Morgan pursued a larger task, one well adapted to his conservative values. By his purchases, his patronage, and his various gifts he was, in effect, preparing an historical record, shaping a research industry and stocking the cultural institutions that would dominate high scholarship and many forms of intellectual discourse for the rest of the century. At a time when many of these institutions were still plastic, Morgan's involvement stamped their future course of development.

This aspect of his influence received some comment. As he moved to the conclusion of his father-in-law's biography (despite its obvious bias, the best source for Morgan's life), Herbert L. Satterlee portrayed his subject at ease within the West Room of his famous library, surrounded by its Memlings, its Italian furniture, its Etruscan and Roman antiquities, its priceless books and manuscripts. "As Mr. Morgan sat among these ageless examples of the culture of past centuries," Satterlee wrote reverently, "he must have thought, not of the years of work and the money that he had put into them, but of the artists, authors, and students of future years who would be helped by them to create cultural standards that would give America a place of honor in the world of art and letters."[88] Such sentiments, fitting easily within a book of piety, can be dismissed as banal rather than revelatory.

But Satterlee had a point. Morgan's quest ensured impressive continuity between the connoisseurship and antiquarian traditions of Europe and the growing world of art history and scholarship in America. Noting the clamor for legislative protection against art exports in 1912, the London *Daily News* acknowledged the logic of the danger while it voiced its anxiety. "The American springs from the old civilization as truly as the European," it explained, "and can claim as authoritative [a] right as the European to share in its glories."[89] But it was really Morgan, with a few others, who made the connection so irresistible. The Anglo-American establishment, then forming and shaping the art museums and academies, saw the Morgan touch as ultimately reassuring.

Reassuring, because during the later years of Morgan's life two challenges to extant high culture were arousing some alarm. One was the enormous influx of tens of millions of European immigrants, workers and peasants for the most part, bearing popular tastes, social ideas, and folk memories that diverged from the gentilities that Morgan's class accepted as their standards. Fear of immigrants took many forms and had many sources. There is little evidence that Morgan absorbed any hysteria, though he undoubtedly held the prevailing bigotries of his friends.

But the task of educating, assimilating, and adapting immigrants to specific values, and transmitting to them certain aesthetic ideals, commanded considerable attention. For several generations the public schools, the newspapers, the stage, the saloon, the library, and more recently vaudeville and movies had been scrutinized as arenas of vice or theaters of virtue. Behind debates about school curricula and Sunday closings, comic supplements and newspaper sensationalism, spectator sports and pernicious advertising lay the sense that a war was raging for the hearts and minds of the new Americans.[90] This was often expressed in terms of shared behavioral norms, standards of political expectation, and adherence to economic values fundamental to a democratic and capitalist society. But there were issues of high culture at stake as well. Would this influx accept or reject the inheritance so cherished by the intellectual elites of

Anglo-America? Would traditional taste as well as traditional learning find an acquiescent audience? What would be the venerated texts and valued icons of the next generations? It was not altogether clear in 1912.

A second threat was quite different and more muted. Within Europe itself the forces of modernism had been mounting their own assault on tradition, challenging the criteria used to champion works of art, literature, and architecture, redefining the nature of narration, representation, and dramatic expression. The artistic version of this revolt may well have reached America later than its literary expression, but it did arrive. Several months after Morgan's death in the spring of 1913, and some months before his great loan exhibition went on display at the Metropolitan in February, 1914, the Society of Independent Artists launched its memorable Armory Show, introducing many Americans to post-Impressionism. The art establishment reacted with hostility; the popular press provided extensive coverage and a certain level of derision.[91]

Morgan showed little interest in contemporary art, to judge from his buying habits. But his collecting and administrative instincts helped set the Metropolitan (and other great museums) on a course which would distance them from the protean character of twentieth-century arts for some time to come. Morgan allied himself with the most valued art traditions of the past. He deliberately undertook to represent them to best advantage. Thus his strong personal response to individual artworks lay hidden within his larger collections.

Reviewing the Morgan Loan Exhibition in 1914, Frank Jewett Mather, Jr., described its effect as "wholly impersonal," lacking either adventurousness or individualism. Admitting the high quality everywhere, Mather argued in the *Nation* that the objects suggested "a standardization alien to the finest processes of artistic appreciation." The Morgan materials consisted of objects "which, by common consent of international dealers and their clients, are brevetted as of highest rarity." They formed an assemblage, not a true collection, dominated by pieces of curiosity rather than art.[92]

Such reactions helped establish a Morgan who seemed colder, more clinical, less involved in his treasures than he actually was. But the impersonality can be explained by the errand Morgan had undertaken. He was offering his countrymen an armory of standards, a series of sources, a group of canons to keep critics, connoisseurs, and museum visitors busy for generations.

Such didacticism enjoyed occasional notice. In an obituary editorial, the *Nation* described Morgan's distance from contemporary art, but in terms more positive than Mather's critical review suggested. Modern art—and here the *Nation* included both Impressionism and the Barbizon school—seemed too specialized, esoteric, and above all private to appeal to "so potent, public, and essentially simple a character as was Mr. Morgan's." A few critics attacked the

Medici mantle cast over Morgan's shoulders by admiring friends, pointing out that the Medici patronized the living. But, said the *Nation*, transported to the twentieth century, Medici patrons would have liked contemporary art no better than Morgan did. "It is the defect of our art . . . that its appeal to those who robustly do the world's work is so small."[93] Blame the artist, not the collector, for the failure.

The Morgan objects, then, projected a sense of obligation, appearing in the service of principles rather than in the grip of grand passions. Obituary editorials stressed again and again the benefits to a larger public which far outweighed any loss of visible personality. In art as in commerce, the similes in favor were military and imperial. Morgan was likened to Napoleon, to Caesar, to Bismarck, to Renaissance princes. His love of art came accompanied by strategic brilliance. "Mr. Morgan was no selfish collector of art merely for the gratification of his sense of that power which unlimited wealth supplies," wrote the *Philadelphia Evening Telegraph*. He had "a much broader and more un-selfish object in view," to bring Americans the greatest, most comprehensive set of art objects so that her aesthetic and educational ideals "might be built upon the true and lasting foundations of absolute finality."[94] There has been "no greater or more valuable achievement for the benefit of this nation in modern times," wrote the *New York American* in 1913 about the assembling of the Morgan collection.[95] And the *New York Mail*, while warning that transferring the entire collection to the Metropolitan might endanger the "just proportion" between past and present its exhibits represented, nonetheless admired it. Possession of the Morgan treasures "will do more to put the old world and the new upon an equality than all the trade balances that ever were written or even can be written."[96]

Morgan's death and the subsequent distribution of his art thus climaxed public approval of the collecting passion. The glamorous booty gained acceptance as an appropriate tribute to American economic growth. Art objects and the buildings enclosing them became the shrines for a secular religion that identified itself with the very pith of civilization. This was true in both Europe and America. Englishmen, Frenchmen, Germans, and Spaniards began to speak of what was "due to the nation" in possessing their art. Who is England "unless *I* am?" a bewildered Lord Theign asked those who insisted, in James's *Outcry*, that he keep his painting—done by an Italian several centuries earlier—for England rather than sell it to a Yankee. It had become a "national treasure" whose departure could be "dangerous to the . . . common weal."[97]

The union of high culture with nationalist ideals was clearly flourishing. Aided in the nineteenth century by bourgeois collectors and ruling houses, it was furthered in the twentieth by business corporations and public authorities.

"The French and the American Napoleons of Art," by J. Schuerle

Possession of art became a national touchstone in a world where tourism had begun to measure many of the qualities of civilization. As the United States acquired the institutional expressions of older societies, so also the physical evidences of continuity became increasingly valued. In supporting this transit of art objects Morgan and his fellow collectors, acting from many motives and many needs, served as popularizers as well as underwriters. Even the flamboyance, the dramatic exaggeration, the bidding wars, and the dealer manipulations thus acquired some use, heroicizing the art conquests of the day. As feeders and shapers of this high culture, the tycoons had an influence that went almost as far as the effects of their financial transactions. If it has not purchased them a serene immortality, at least to generations trained to scrutinize the meanings of personal display, it has added to their mystery. And this, the millionaires, Morgan particularly, would certainly have enjoyed.

● ● ●

THREE

The Changing Landscape

Spaced Out at
the Shopping Center

The year 1976 is an anniversary for all kinds of things besides American independence. It marks, for example, the twentieth anniversary of the South-dale Shopping Center near Minneapolis, the work of Victor Gruen & Associates. Southdale has a special place in the history of the American shopping center; it marked the debut of the large enclosed mall and set a pattern that has been extensively imitated and adapted in the last two decades. The regional shopping center is now so ubiquitous, that it is surprising how short a history it actually possesses. All the more reason then, to survey its varieties and social implications, as they become more apparent.

Early shopping centers, like so many modern innovations, developed in California during the 1920s and 1930s. Living in the first set of urban communities built entirely around the automobile, Californians quickly discovered the advantages of placing groups of stores around or within parking areas. Similar arrangements soon appeared in other part of the country. Richard Neutra designed a small shopping center for Lexington, Kentucky; New Jersey had the Big Bear Shopping Centers, built around giant groceries, with parking space for up to a thousand cars.

From *The New Republic*, 13 December 1975, pp. 23–26. Reprinted with permission of the publisher.

In the thirties also, chain and department stores, both vital to the future centers, began to adapt their businesses to the increasingly affluent suburbs and the ever mobile automobile. Until then, retail location in large American cities had been generally a function of existing transportation lines. But as automobile use spread, downtown location became more problematic. "The automobile emancipated the consumer but not the merchant," the *Architectural Forum* noted in 1949, and well before then firms like Macy's and Sears Roebuck had begun building in the suburbs or on the peripheries of metropolitan centers.

It was the union of department stores with the older ideal of grouping easily accessible smaller stores that produced the first regional centers. This was supplemented, of course, by the explosion of highway construction during the Eisenhower era. The period from the early fifties to the late sixties was the golden era of shopping center construction. By the end of the sixties more than 10,000 shopping centers of every size and shape had been built. The huge shift of wealth and population to the suburbs guaranteed their profits. Large department stores—like Hudson's in Detroit and Dayton's in Minneapolis—were eager to get a piece of this action. Instead of simply opening up more branches, department stores began to organize their own centers, hire architects and developers, and get mortgages from life insurance companies, whose huge supply of capital enabled them to influence the suburban landscape as powerfully as their huge downtown skyscrapers shaped the center cities.

By the middle fifties also, developers began to realize the crucial role of design planning. The department stores were the magnets, their drawing power and placement making or breaking the profits of their smaller neighbors. The straight lines of the early malls, like John Graham's Northgate in Seattle, began to yield to more informal treatments. In Chicago, whose suburbs offer a veritable encyclopedia of shopping center forms, Old Orchard in Skokie, and later Oakbrook, opened in 1962, contained several department stores and carefully landscaped courtyards, with flower beds, streams, ponds, bridges, fountains and seating areas. The rambling, informal lines of these centers, and the series of different sized quadrangles, produced a villagelike atmosphere, the large size (sometimes more than one million square feet) deliberately underplayed. At Mondawmin Shopping Center, in Baltimore, developer James Rouse used two levels to produce what contemporary critics found to be an intimate, casual setting, something like "a charming market town." By the late fifties two-level centers were increasingly popular; they cut down on the forbiddingly long walks between stores, a feature of older malls.

If the rambling, gardenlike centers of the late fifties and early sixties were profitable and inviting to shoppers, the Southdale model was the wave of the future. Gruen concentrated his buildings in a two-level mall, and in his en-

Southdale
shopping mall,
near Minneapolis

closed, air-conditioned structure he placed sculpture, trees, benches, so arranging the various spaces to give the impression of downtown bustle. Serenity
and village charm were not Southdale's goals; instead, it sought a replication of
downtown energy, exploiting the concentration that two enclosed levels, each
open to the sight of the other, permitted.

   Precedents existed. Glass-covered arcades like Milan's Galleria and London's Burlington Arcade were familiar to European-born designers like Gruen.

A few American cities—Cleveland and Providence among them—also possessed important arcades. But even more exemplary were the courtyards and light wells of American commercial buildings constructed at the turn of the century. Department stores, for example, had courts that were cathedral-like in their boast of space, sometimes topped by stained glass domes. Aware of being surrounded by hundreds of other shoppers, customers made their way in an atmosphere of bustle and activity.

The Cleveland Arcade (1890)

This kind of collective drama was what Southdale and many of its successors sought. Shopping centers, Gruen wrote in 1960, "can provide the need, place and opportunity for participation in modern community life that the ancient Greek Agora, the Medieval Market Place and our own Town Squares provided in the past." The new open spaces, he continued, "must represent an essentially urban environment, be busy and colorful, exciting and stimulating, full of variety and interest."

Thus two levels quickly became standard for most centers along with ramps, escalators, broad staircases and two-level parking lots. Ramps were particularly useful for women shoppers (the vast majority of customers), who could move strollers and high-heeled shoes easily up and down the undulating inclines, and catch a maximum view of other shoppers and store fronts. Even

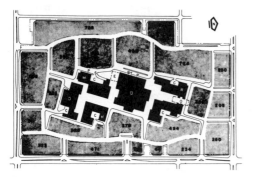
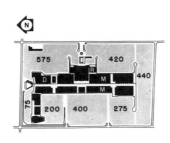
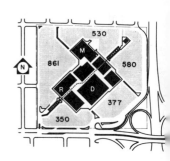

more than the verticality, it was the enclosed character of the new malls that delighted their users. Southdale was covered because of cold winters and hot summers, but areas with mild climates also sought temperature control. Marvin Richman, of Chicago's Urban Investment and Development Company, points out that the continued profitability of open centers like Oakbrook does not diminish the zeal of tenants to move into covered centers. "It is unlikely we will see any more of the large open centers constructed," he concludes.

If that is what customers want, that is what they will get. Little at the shopping centers is left to chance. Along with Disneyland they were early experimenters in the separation of pedestrian and vehicular movement, and the isolation of service activities from customers. Ingenious devices handled crowded parking lots, security problems, and the normal difficulties of congestion. Logos were adopted and incorporated into shopping bags, maps, and guard uniforms. Graphics and lighting experts facilitated shopping convenience. But nothing was given away, and efforts made only where they could show. Seen from the outside, from its vast acreage of parking lots, the typical shopping center looks like a pile of blocks. The elemental shapes of the center don't blend into the landscape—for there is no landscape to blend into—but they are not easily separable from it either. The streets are inside, so there is little reason to control facades which abut highways and parked cars.

But if clarity and concern are absent from the outside, the manipulation and self-consciousness become clear once the complex has been entered. Piped-in music, pavements designed to cushion noise, forced ventilation, controlled lighting, all screen the customer from distraction and aid his sense of location. The malls and arcades that lead to the main courts, writes an analyst and designer of shopping centers, Louis Redstone, "should strive for an intimate character and subdued atmosphere. The purpose is to have the shopper's eye attracted to the store displays." To encourage "shopping interest," when upper galleries are separated by large spaces, connecting bridges should promise con-

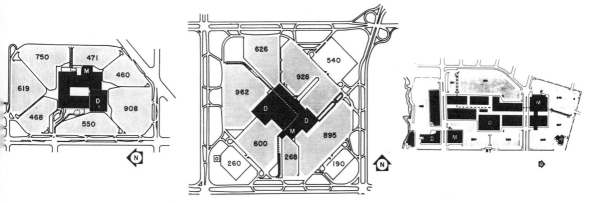

venient access and "give tempting views of the lower floor." Everything that goes into the center is organized to enhance the shopping act. "The typical shopper," according to one designer, "makes no thoughtful judgments concerning good or bad graphics, architecture or space design. He feels good or uncomfortable concerning buying or not buying, staying or leaving." Thus most shopping centers don't aim for good design as such; they seek an environment that will pull people in, keep them there, and encourage them to return.

Shopping mall plans

If the end is unambiguous, the setting is not. The desire for variety coexists with an insistence on order; the marvel of discipline and control yields impulse buying; the natural environment is destroyed in order to produce a replanted landscape; indoors and outdoors are blurred through climate control and the conceit of street lamps, trees, and occasionally aviaries and zoos.

There are legal as well as environmental ambivalences. In the past 15 years shopping center owners have had to fight a series of challenges that focus specifically on the public/private, or inside/outside character of their properties. The rights of freedom of speech and assembly, of picketing and distributing pamphlets, are not totally clear. The latest Supreme Court decision split 5–4 in determining that, in fact, shopping centers were not public thoroughfares but could limit activities normally permitted in public spaces. But it is probably not the last word.

The shopping center itself exemplifies how strongly boundary problems influence contemporary design and social life. One thrust of modern technology has been to permit and even to encourage acts which were once public and collective to be broken down into more private compartments. The automobile, which took the traveler out of a shared setting and allowed him to move either by himself or with selected companions, has spearheaded these changes, aided by the telephone, radio, and television. The potential for social violence, the threat of crime, and the nature of racial tensions have also served to limit the number of public occasions for casual mingling.

Compartmentalization, however, has inevitably produced reactions. The hunger for great, enclosed spaces that can provide dramatic settings for collective acts can be detected in the many new sports arenas, the Portman hotel interiors, the atriums and courtyards of a number of recent city skyscrapers. Substituted for streets, which are now so pervasively associated with danger and dirt, nodes of concentration in a sprawl that does not quite satisfy the urban memories of the displaced, the shopping centers permit suburbanites to shop, eat, attend films, exhibitions, lectures, even orchestra concerts and plays.

The designers offer several options. If some suburbanites seek to recall urban glitter and excitement, planners can oblige. Real limitations exist, of course. While all cities are attempts to control chaos, their control is frequently disguised because of the lengthy period of imposition. In the shopping center, artificiality is more obvious because nothing is any older than anything else. There is nothing worn, nothing used; even the flower beds stay fresh. But when the developer aims unambiguously at an urban mood—as in Woodfield Mall, near Chicago, or Eastridge, in San Jose—he produces, with hard materials and bright colors, exciting, dynamic interplays of light, texture, and movement: great hanging mobiles, huge open plazas, balconies, ramps, and stairways cutting with sharp angles across the empty spaces. From dozens of vantage points the shopper can gaze across what seem to be limitless vistas, depressing when they are empty, but exhilarating when they are filled with active people, a landscape in perpetual movement, assertive and ever changing.

Even cities need to recall what they once were, or are still trying to become. Many have built their own shopping centers, in an effort to retrieve the downtown. Chicago's Water Tower Place has carried the vertical possibilities of center design to new extremes. The shopping center, which supports a 22-story hotel and 40 floors of expensive condominiums, has seven levels. Seen from the outside its marble, windowless walls (which conceal the service corridors) could be housing a warehouse or convention hall. The street is as irrelevant to it as the suburban parking lots are to their centers. Inside, however, after customers arrive by escalators at the mezzanine, they encounter a seven-story atrium, bulging at the middle floors, crossed by three glass-enclosed elevators. Powerful lights pick out the prismatic colors of the glass, increasing the sense of movement within the center; five other small two- and three-story courts are scattered through the rest of this quintessentially urban setting.

The glitter and extravagance of Water Tower Place's atrium recall another period of Chicago design, the era of John Root and his partner, Daniel Burnham. Root provided, in the Rookery, the Masonic Temple, the Mills Building in San Francisco, Kansas City's Board of Trade, and the Society for Savings in

Woodfield Mall,
Schaumberg

Cleveland, a series of unforgettable light courts in glass and iron, surrounding delicately banistered staircases and filigreed elevator wells. Passage upward in those elevators, unlike the closed cabs of today, was an exhilarating adventure, playing lights and shadows against one another. "Through the constant interplay of dualities," writes Donald Hoffmann, Root's biographer, "of solid and void, structure and space, stasis and kinesis, opacity and transparency, darkness and light," the architect achieved a vital resolution. With its totally artificial lighting and very different materials it is not yet clear that Water Tower Place can approach the achievement of nineteenth-century masters like Root.

Water Tower But the effort to recapture the lost glories of courtyard, stairway, and elevator is
Place, Chicago a welcome one.

Water Tower Place and Woodfield, centers that are urban in spirit or place, form only one among many varieties. The developers of Water Tower Place have just opened another shopping center, this one in Aurora, Illinois. It maintains the conventions of size and enclosure, its retail space projected at well over one million square feet; but its very different approach to large space gives it another kind of personality. The Fox Valley Center is almost as large as Woodfield but much less urban in feeling: its use of wood and tile—in flooring, fixtures, railings, and columns—the subdued earth colors, the controlled scale of its courts and its lighting system, prevent this center from unleashing a sense of overpowering size or energy. The vast distances are disguised, and the center courts divided into two unequal parts, each a studied contrast to the other. Each department store has its own plaza, but they are or appear to be more intimate

than their cubic footage suggests. The shopper can still detect the several levels and come upon large, dramatic openings, but the wood and the foliage screen and break up the stark vistas, faintly echoing the villagelike qualities of the older, open centers like Oakbrook.

Ellicott Square Building, Buffalo (1892)

Not that the "rural" centers are any "softer," to apply Robert Sommer's term, any more flexible or responsive to individual needs. These are, on the whole, hard environments, their seating and traffic patterns clearly established and permanently fixed. The shopping itself can be disappointing. Because small, individually owned businesses do not generally have the capital to relocate here, chain stores and franchises dominate. One shopping center repeats the outlets found in another. The music, the fixtures, the forced air can all be dreadful. At certain times of day there is an inertness, a deadness about the centers which no city space ever quite descends to. They are dominated by homogeneous groups—housewives, older people, or teenagers—and thus lack the human variety of the street scene. And finally there is that single-minded devotion to the profit motive, the supervisory spirit which has outraged those critics who prefer to associate architectural innovation with more disinterested planning, and who find closed interiors to be oppressive.

But there is little evidence that many customers object to the total definition of the shopping center. There may indeed be relief at the lack of ambiguity, the limits on choice which the environment poses. All the attractions are controlled. One walks from the car to the center, and then tours the shops. Everyone seems there for a reason. Social transactions are simplified and dignified by the spatial drama of the great courts. Aware of the amphibious quality of contemporary American life, the merging of one function or activity into another, the studied informality to so many personal interchanges, developers have created integrated spaces with multiple uses that can handle anything from the most trivial errand to an evening on the town.

It is their capacity for visual surprise and contrast, and their impressive displays of technical virtuosity, that make the shopping centers stand out. The last architectural form that served American dreams so effectively was the movie palace of the interwar years, and it relied on decorative detail and costly materials. Architectural fantasy today employs space and lighting rather than eclectic stylistic quotation. Engineering technologies permit the shopping center to expand the achievement of their true ancestors, the great railroad stations: span a void in metal and glass, and use the proportions to honor the activity within. Space and light have always been luxurious, and few have exploited them as cleverly as the center designers. Conspicuous spatial consumption brings monumental status. In joining modern pleasure in large, unadorned surfaces to an older, baroque theatricality, the best of these buying machines remind us, once again, that the commercial spirit has nurtured much of our most interesting American design.

The Changing Landscape Living with Lobbies

I n an era of political corruption and influence-peddling, the word lobby, as noun or verb, usually refers to those representatives of special interests who attempt to win the blessings of legislators. Dictionaries, however, particularly those with historical interests, spend much more space on the word's architectural status; originally a covered walk in a monastery, or a passage which could be used as an anteroom, the lobby has also denoted, at various times, apartments under a ship's quarterdeck, a small enclosure for cattle,

From *The New Republic*, 8 May 1976, pp. 19–22. Reprinted with permission of the publisher.

INTERIOR PEOPLES GAS
BUILDING, CHICAGO

and an entrance hall in which members of Parliament met constituents, a usage *People's Gas*
which led to its modern political meaning. *Building, Chicago*

As an architectural setting, however, the lobby was relatively unimportant
until the nineteenth century and the growth of modern hotels, office buildings,
theaters, and apartment houses. As urban centers developed special institutions for amusement, lodging, and work, a new need appeared: to shelter
briefly, for purposes of convenience, movement, or communication, promiscuous assemblages of people.

Physical demands were supplemented, in the United States, by ideological constraints. Taught to suspect great demonstrations of private wealth,
Americans found a convenient site for collective fantasies in the public rooms
of commercial establishments like hotels. Forbidden palaces and castles, republican Americans enjoyed the opulence of fancy carpets, crystal chandeliers,
and elaborate furniture through the kindness of their local publicans, whose
huge establishments astonished foreign visitors and gladdened the heart of
every loyal patriot.

Moreover, because most American towns and cities neglected to provide
easily accessible and well-maintained sanitary facilities, lobbies (along with
restaurants and department stores) became havens for the frantic and the foot-
sore, their toilets and washrooms providing oases of comfort. Lobbies, of
course, served many other functions as well: they were centers for display,

arenas for assignation, spots to gain information and directions, and small shopping centers convenient for the purchase of cigars, toiletries, and postcards.

Hotel lobbies were particularly rich in their capacity to sustain social encounters. Filmmakers and novelists gloried in their profusion of furniture, foliage, and hidden corners, from which the house detective, the jilted lover, or a hated business rival might emerge at any moment. In the dozens of chairs which usually lined any well-appointed lobby sat the loungers, including pickpockets, the unemployed, and those simply waiting to meet friends or business acquaintances. The moral tone of the lobby was tolerant enough although, as Sam Spade told his friend Luke in *The Maltese Falcon,* cheap gunmen with suspicious bulges in their jackets didn't help much. With few settings that encouraged sauntering or quiet contemplation, Americans welcomed lobbies. The obvious services they performed disguised one of their true functions: a place one could go to rest and pretend to be waiting for something to begin, rather than, as so often happened, waiting for something to end.

The role of the lobby as refuge was explored by many novelists, among them by Theodore Dreiser in *Sister Carrie*. Dreiser used the lobby to signal Hurstwood's decline. The former restaurateur "knew hotels well enough to know that any decent-looking individual was welcome to a chair in the lobby." But taking that chair was a "painful thing to him. To think he should come to this! He had heard loungers about hotels called chair-warmers. He had called them that himself in his day. But here he was, despite the possibility of meeting someone who knew him, shielding himself from cold and the weariness of the streets in a hotel lobby."

Lobbies also supported more hopeful social encounters. Dreiser, again, this time in *An American Tragedy*, employed the Green-Davidson Hotel to initiate Clyde Griffiths into a taste for worldly luxury. The lobby was "more arresting, quite, than anything he had seen before. It was all so lavish. Under his feet was a checkered black-and-white marble floor. Above him a coppered and stained and gilded ceiling. And supporting this, a veritable forest of black marble columns," which surrounded "lamps, statuary, rugs, palms, chairs, divans, têtes-à-têtes—a prodigal display."

Lobbies, in effect, became stage sets, permitting a theatricality of manner that would have been out of place anywhere else. Making a return visit to the United States, Henry James caught the appeal of the "hotel spirit" to the display-conscious social climbers who moved through the public rooms of the old Waldorf-Astoria in a golden haze of clatter and publicity. It was the concentration, the accumulation, the intensity of the hotel world that absorbed James, its capacity to include almost everyone and to break down every barrier but two: the appearance of respectability and the filled wallet. "Protected at those two points the promiscuity carries, through the rest of the range, everything before it," parading "through halls and saloons in which art and history, in masquerading dress, muffled almost to suffocation as in the gold brocade of their pretended majesties and their conciliatory graces, stood smirking on its passage with the last cynicism of hypocrisy."

Such stage sets were naturally placed in the hands of free-spending decorators. The expense of the rugs, the antiquity of lamps and tables, the ornateness of grills and cuspidors, all formed part of every hotel or apartment house's pride. The Book Cadillac Hotel in Detroit, opened in 1924, chose a Venetian motif for its main lobby; lavish promotional literature described its walls "of beautiful colored Brèche Violette marble trimmed with white Alabama," while the bronze railings rested on black walnut beams which protected balcony promenaders. A ceiling of intricately designed gold leaf panels, emblazoned with the arms of Cadillac, the founder of Detroit, oversaw a selection of furniture which included several pieces "taken from Sarah Bernhardt's drawing room," as well as imported old Sèvres vases. Even the telephone booths and candy cases were made of walnut with marble bases, to carry out the motif chosen by the hotel's proud management. The Los Angeles Biltmore selected Spanish Renaissance for its theme: beamed ceilings, murals and painted panels, heroic antique lanterns, a giant Long Gallery, and a magnificent staircase adorned its public areas. The Book Cadillac and the Biltmore were matched in their splendors by hundreds of other hotels in every American city, fighting for patronage, as the Albert Pick Company put it in 1928, "through appeals to love of luxury and beauty." George B. Post & Sons, designers of the Statler hotels in Boston and Buffalo, New York's Hotel Roosevelt, and Seattle's Hotel Olympic; Schulze and Weaver, who planned the Los Angeles and Miami Biltmores, the Roney Plaza in Miami Beach, the hotels Pierre, Lexington, and Waldorf-Astoria; Weeks and Day, architects of San Francisco's Mark Hopkins and Sir Francis Drake, were among the major contributors to this outpouring of ostentation. And to this must be added, of course, the work of cinema designers like Rapp & Rapp, John Eberson, Thomas Lamb, and Walter Ahlschlager, whose lobbies made the gaudiest hotel interiors seem reticent by comparison.

Because the lobby established the personality of the building it introduced, managers did not begrudge its expense. And they understood the apparent deceits. In the case of theaters, it was legitimate, wrote Harold Rambusch in 1930, for the showman to hold sway at the entrance as well as the stage. "Even a very elaborate entrance and foyer has a certain effect after the excitement of the street. Lobbies may well be full of gold, mirrors and posters." The office building lobby, argued a designer of the 1920s, was meant to suggest

Peabody Hotel,
Memphis

"the prosperous conditions of the various business concerns housed in the building." And for apartment house dwellers, according to Lois Wagner in 1956, the elaborate lobby acted "to confirm the good fortune of the tenants who have secured leases to what may be an overpriced warren, and to create, by association, an aura of prosperity to dazzle their guests."

In the late twenties and early thirties many lobbies were created in a somewhat more restrained opulence than their predecessors. The greater austerity of art moderne relied on rich materials rather than a profusion of objects. Sleeker (and easier to keep clean), these lobbies used lighting more effectively to create the prosperous hush appropriate to expensive structures. But the crisis of the Depression and the pressures of postwar rebuilding interrupted this tradition of lobby luxury. Builders exploited the new savings possible by making lobbies simpler, smaller, and more utilitarian. Glass walls summoned the outdoors to the aid of illusion, blurred the boundaries between building interiors and exteriors and so achieved a spaciousness possible, at one time, only in large rooms with high ceilings. The furniture diminished in elaborateness, and gradually also the lobby's borderline role began to grow vaguely disturbing.

The trend appeared first in apartment houses and theaters, for new hotel construction did not really get under way until the 1950s. Apartment house owners grew concerned about security. With labor costs rising it was difficult to maintain the previously ubiquitous liveried doormen. Buzzers and room telephones began to take their place, but they were stationed in anterooms, cut off from the lobby itself. Why spend money on furnishings that thieves could rip off with effortless ease? Those locked in the building could gaze out at potentially threatening passersby or, better yet, stay safely in their own apartments. Lobbies grew smaller and in some instances practically disappeared. Movie theaters, particularly those featuring the new European art films, tended to be simpler and to treat the large decorated spaces of the older palaces as embarrassments. And motels, which mushroomed in the 1950s and for a time threatened to end all hotel construction, went even further. Where possible, the swimming pool, open only to registered guests, substituted entirely for the lobby's recreational pleasures. The chief exceptions here were the lavish resort hotels being constructed in places like Las Vegas and Miami Beach. In these gilded El Dorados, restraint was a cardinal sin.

Although some critics argued, in the 1950s, that the anonymity of modern buildings dressed in their glass and metal façades might lead to lobby extravagance as part of the search for personality, this did not happen. Instead, as security became a greater problem, the lobby's spatial shrinkage was accompanied by the disappearance of its social functions. A necessary pass-through, the lobby could be dominated by some large artwork (metal sculpture, hard to damage or to move, became increasingly popular) or by plantings. The foliage softens the hard-edged look of marble and metal and can be maintained on contract.

Thus in Chicago, a stroll through newer office buildings like the Standard Oil and Sears towers reveals clinically clean and smooth lobbies, with little to distract business people from making their appointed rounds. Simple fixtures and Alexander Calder's *Universe* dominate Sears's understated entrance. The shopping arcade is on a lower floor. Closed-circuit television cameras, aids to security guards, complete the sense of wandering through alien territory. Television cameras are also a feature of many apartment house lobbies. Where doormen can still be maintained, apartment houses attempt a show of elegance, but increasingly these lobbies are bare, quiet, and vacant.

The only lobbies that retain some of their older features and have not been converted totally into danger zones are hotel lobbies. But here, sad damage has been done. In the large urban hotels of the 1920s, while much of the ground and lobby floors was devoted to stores, the great central spaces were planned for the convenience of guests and visitors. Milwaukee's Hotel Schroeder (by Holabird & Roche), had a lobby of 53 by 86 feet, with practically all of the furniture "placed between the four large columns in the center of the room, leaving a passage around the columns to be used as a circulation space, insuring comfort and ease where people are sitting." Three steps away was a lounge, almost as large, with tables, lamps, couches, and other accessories.

Would that hotels continue to be so solicitous! In the 1950s and 1960s the lounges practically disappeared, and the lobbies were defaced by concessions and partitions. Although impressive spaces remain in some older urban and resort hotels—Chicago's Palmer House retains its grand stairway and 138-foot lobby—many hotels carved bars and cocktail lounges out of public areas, and new hotels, unhampered by legacies of generosity, could be still more efficient in their planning.

Within the last ten years, however, a burst of hotel planning has attempted to recapture, and even expand upon, these lost glories. Two diverging paths have been chosen. One is exemplified by Chicago's Ritz Carlton. The Ritz, seeking to inherit the *grande luxe* tradition, has spent a fortune to reinstate the lobby floor and make it a center for promenading, eating, and drinking. Once again the materials are rich and costly and the long promenade is impressive; moreover, the views, from its twelfth-floor location, are dramatic and enticing. Just as its advertisements try to evoke memories of Cesar Ritz and Escoffier, the hotel identifies itself with the era of palm courts, crystal chandeliers, and chamber groups playing for well-dressed diners and drinkers.

But the Ritz lobby is not completely satisfying, partly because the secure eclectic vision of the older hotels has been so weakened. It believes in luxury, but without stylistic conviction. The marble and the carpets don't really suit the furniture; in the main lobby, as opposed to the promenade, seating is inconspicuously placed in side sections rather than amply and invitingly in the center. Bars and restaurants, as well as the large central fountains and plantings, organize a traffic flow which is effectively shielded from wandering pedestrians by an elevator trip. The stage-set quality that absorbed Henry James is quickly apparent, but the Marshall Field showcases, which are scattered about every few feet, remind guests of the commercial urgency of the enterprise.

But if retailing intrudes, the Ritz lobby is rich, capacious, and even occasionally reassuring in its old-fashioned opulence. A very different model, in the lobby revival, has been developed by John Portman and applied in Chi-

Atlanta Hyatt

cago, San Francisco, Knoxville, and several other cities. And it has just been elaborated in its first home, Atlanta, by three huge new hotels which have either opened or are about to open. The Portman lobbies, and those which embody their principles, are special kinds of places. Enormous, dwarfing spaces, large enough to contain (as in Atlanta's Peachtree Plaza) an artificial lake and extensive plantings, they dazzle visitors, but they no longer function quite as lobbies once did. The layered tiers of floors, the activity and the multiple views are exciting but often dizzying; few nooks and corners permit quiet conversation or restful observation except, of course, for the bars and restaurants which exact a price for the privilege.

These new lobbies are not ceremonial stage sets or retreats for the tired and the expectant. They are closer to movie screens, illusionistic amusement parks whose glitter encourages activity, not repose, and speed in place of stateliness. No longer anterooms or border areas, these lobbies are the climaxes, the sum totals, the holy of holies of their respective buildings. They may soon need lobbies of their own. Miniature cities, with extensive shopping areas, avenues, and occasionally even re-created historic sites, they exemplify the closed landscapes that are increasingly being substituted for the wide open visions that used to form the American dream of space. Once American towns and cities differentiated themselves from Europe by their limitless, ungirdled vistas, the absence of defining walls, moats, and battlements; their attenuated streets stretched out to the infinite. "Instead of looking inward to a hermit realm of refuge," Fred Somkin argued in *Unquiet Eagle*, our antebellum towns "scanned the horizon with an exaggerated ambition bordering on the fantastic."

Now, befitting an older civilization, the lobby's function has become illusionistic: to reassure the anxious that it does, in fact, contain limits—doors, walls, roof—and yet can include every variety of nature, only more intensely than the outdoors itself. The glass elevators and revolving rooftop restaurants, both of which fit the conventions of distant spectatorship, allow these limits to be explored and experienced; once visitors have discovered them, they can revel in tours through the park and jungle of the lobby floor, punctuated by glances up at the enclosed heaven.

The success of these new interiors is partly a function of changing travel experiences. Railroads mixed ceremony in their stations with endless horizons on their tracks. But airlines join informality and rapid movement, at the airport, with enclosed transcendence of earth-bound limits, in their flights. The combination of enclosure and transcendence differentiates the new lobbies from the old. Border spaces once bridged public and private functions, their fulsome decoration serving as tributes to hidden resources of wealth and generosity. Their extravagance was a form of public flattery that humored masses of people into appropriate public behavior. The newer spaces disperse rather than concentrate social encounters, filtering not spotlighting meetings. No longer objectifying the social setting, the lobby overruns it, surmounts the environment by its own enclosure. Thus, like so many contemporary arrangements, the new lobby preserves the illusion of individualism by relying on secure controls. Vulgar and pompous the old lobbies were, but their elaborate decoration spoke more obviously of manipulation. Less has indeed become more.

Parking the Garage

All things come to those that wait. Opera houses, international trains, embassy ballrooms, and great country houses are natural favorites for lovers of intrigue and high drama. But modern life has dispersed the opportunities for mystery, giving generous doses of romance to the most mundane structures. Consider, for example, the parking garage, particularly its larger varieties. These concrete and steel structures now dot our cities or sprawl beneath our parks and squares, attracting little attention or interest. Humdrum, perhaps. But the seat of adventure as well. The great conspiracy of our era was, after all, cracked by clandestine meetings held with Deep Throat in garages. The hundreds of empty automobiles guarded against sudden intrusion: this was no site for the casual passerby. The purposefulness and intense efficiency of the garage give it, perhaps, some of its unique character. There are symbolic as well as practical aspects to the connection with bureaucratic insurgency that Deep Throat represented. The coming of the public garage is actually tied to central features of modern living, and is an artifact of our day without earlier analogues.

In pre-twentieth-century cities few could own their own horses and carriages. Those who did had stabling and coachmen who supervised the vehicles until the day's business, shopping, or visiting was completed. Hired cabs and horse-drawn public transit required barns or stables only at the finish of a working day. Scattered around the city were some private stables and coachhouses. In suburbs or in country towns more people owned animals or drove their carts and wagons themselves, but space was plentiful and livery stables could handle the overflow.

The appearance of the automobile and its penetration of built-up areas presented new problems. With horse-drawn vehicles, the major urban difficulty was congestion; with automobiles it was parking, and by World War I communities were discovering unhappily that their curbsides could offer only a limited amount of space. Commuters and shoppers, now using their own cars, began to complain, and merchants applied pressure on local governments to develop some solutions. Many ideas surfaced, including rooftop parking and banning the automobile from the city centers, but among other suggestions were proposals for large municipal garages, suggestions which multiplied in the 1920s. Dr. Carol Aronovici, city planning consultant for Berkeley, California, was one such

From *The New Republic*, 19 February 1977, pp. 21–24. Reprinted with permission of the publisher.

enthusiast, proposing to construct one garage of 10 stories that would cover two acres and accommodate 4000 cars. He pointed out that this was the equivalent of five miles of curbside.

Nothing so large as Aronovici's scheme was built, but just about all the basic elements of the modern garage appeared before 1930. According to a recent study by Hackman and Martin, at least 50 pubic garages had been built by 1929, most of them with ramps, elevators and staggered floors, this last idea developed by Fernand D'Humy shortly after World War I. Other variants also appeared, among them, push-button units, ferris wheels, and self-parking systems, as well as the underground garage, the first one built in Washington to accommodate the needs of United States senators.

While the Great Depression cut down on the availability of capital for investment in the large garages, parking congestion was eased considerably by the invention of the parking meter. First introduced in the summer of 1935, in Oklahoma City, within a year the meter idea had spread to many cities, promising not only greater control but welcome revenues. The *New Republic* excitedly hailed it as "the next great American gadget," admiring its ability to lighten traffic, make stores more accessible to potential customers, and lessen dependence on taxation. Apparently few motorists complained.

Although meters encouraged briefer parking and increased turnover, they could not create more curb space, and automobile possession was one of the few growth industries of the 1930s. By the end of the decade mammoth garages were being planned and built, not only in this country but in Europe as well. London's Cumberland Garage and Car Park, with five parking floors, contained most of the feature that contemporary motorists expect—staggered floors, passenger elevators, carefully graded ramps, color-keyed ticket stubs and floors, angled parking—and some features that would not become standard: areas for servicing and repairs, chauffeurs' rest room, a lounge and dressing rooms. There were other false starts. In the late 1920s one designer suggested that a billiard room would be appropriate for the garage while in a Baltimore building one parking level was set aside entirely for women drivers. And in the 1940s most large garages still relied heavily on parking attendants, advertising the speed with which cars could be retrieved: continuous elevators and fireman poles aided the nimble attendants as they ran and slid from floor to floor on their appointed rounds.

Although the war inhibited construction, it was in the summer of 1942 that the first great municipal garage opened, literally breaking new ground: San Francisco's Union Square Garage, for a time the largest structure of its kind. Its three million square feet could contain 1700 cars. Placed under the square, its construction had necessitated the removal of the park and the Dewey Monument, both of which were carefully put back. Newspapers and magazines spun out the details of this strange new structure whose heavy reinforced concrete roof made it an excellent air-raid shelter. Indeed, army experts helped to work out some of the air-raid features and designed the garage as a possible hospital, in the event of Japanese attack.

After the war's end, Detroit, Chicago, Los Angeles, Kansas City, Boston, and other cities began to plan their own underground garages. As might be expected, Chicago's effort was the largest. The Grant Park site was possible only after the city agreed to comply with court rulings barring any visible structure; the two-floor garage, which would hold almost 2500 cars, would have to be completely buried. Costing more than eight million dollars, the Grant Park facility developed elaborate ticketing systems, coupled with automatic issuing machines, to discourage chiseling. Boston's underground garage was buried under Beacon Hill, after decades of resistance by Brahmins, who declared it a desecration, and scandalous involvement by political figures like James Michael Curley and Bernard Goldfine.

To reassure their new publics, the underground garages boasted of the capacity of their ventilating fans, designed to change the air completely every few minutes, and of the presence of alarm systems which reported, electronically, changes in the carbon monoxide level. The central control stations resembled science fiction movie sets, their giant panels equipped with hundreds of lights and switches to report on air, traffic, and temperature conditions. Signs were created to permit parkers to select among various levels and sections, warning them when areas were full and placing curb barriers down to reroute traffic.

By the 1940s and 1950s, with several decades of experience, parking experts were debating the relative advantages of different ramp grades, surfacing materials, parking angles, centralized exit and entrance controls, accommodations for pedestrian traffic, and parking bay widths. As labor costs rose and urban congestion increased, plans became more ambitious. In 1953 William Zeckendorf unveiled plans for a 20-story, 5400-car mechanical garage, in which an operator simply pressed a button to take care of the parking. The ramp system, said Zeckendorf, "is old-fashioned and illogical; the Pharaohs used it to build the pyramids." If the center city were to survive, he continued, it needed mechanized, vertical solutions to parking and would have either to ban cars entirely or redesign the streets to cope with the increased traffic that would pour in and out of the great garages.

One new aid for the garages lay in flexible elevators which would move horizontally as well as vertically, and place cars precisely in prearranged spaces. A number of garages using the Bowser system were constructed in the midwest and southwest, employing a combination elevator and bridge crane. Running as high as 13 floors, and containing up to four of these elevators, they were built inexpensively. But, of course, they required attendants.

Today, the typical user of garages parks his own car; the great parking decks of airports and shopping centers, the underground garages of city centers, and the towering spirals of hotels, apartment houses, office buildings and hospitals have become intimate parts of the driving experience. As such, garages have been carefully designed to accommodate rapid movement, for profitability depends more on turnover than on the number of spaces. If a garage can use the same space four or five times each day, instead of twice, its economic returns increase. Planners thus sacrifice spaces to make for wider aisles and bays, and angle the car so that ordinary drivers can park and leave quickly.

Getting in and out rapidly has become, indeed, one of the crucial tests of the expert parker. For garages, like highways, have become tests of skill and competence, three-dimensional questionnaires whose rewards go to the swift and the sure. As the ordinary complexities of computers and transistors have sped beyond our capacities, as bodies age and the competition of the stadium becomes a memory of youth, there are few public arenas in which to demonstrate the sense of timing, the spirit of daring and superior experience that marks a champion. It is here that the giant parking garage acquires its certifying functions. Planners boast of how quickly garages can fill or empty, but initiates arriving at or leaving from ball games, concerts and jobs, or trying to catch a plane, or make an appointment, know how vulnerable these promises are. Much depends on split-second decisions, judgments about which aisle may hold a friendly space, and on patience in following a straggling pedestrian who may be about to find his car and release a berth. The electronic signals and the friendly attendants rarely help in crises. And so the driver is thrown back on his or her own resources, and the struggle for space becomes another episode of self-definition.

Identity is also at stake in these moments of panic when the parked car cannot be found. Somewhere in those thousands of automobiles is a familiar vehicle, but not every motorist heeds the advice of the signs and notes his aisle or quadrant. The color-coded tickets, the many efforts to force some kind of recollection (in Kansas City's Crown Center hearts, spades, diamonds and clubs are used for the different floors) sometimes go for naught. The interior of a garage then takes on the character of a de Chirico landscape, pitiless in its exposure of a faulty memory or bad planning. The endlessly repeating modules offer little chance of identification as the driver is reduced to the familiar experience of being one among many others, who has to obey the rules to fight his way out.

ZCMI garage, Salt Lake City

Garages, however, also produce their moments of satisfaction and even exhilaration. The great serpentine ramps, which demand nerves of steel and immunity to vertigo, can, in quiet moments, act as the poor man's racing track, their concrete walls threatening fenders and bumpers but offering a challenge that is hard to resist. The well-planned garage can also supply occasions for driver courtesy to surface, so long as the feeder lanes are clearly marked. In Chicago's Grant Park Garage, the post-symphony ritual has two lines of cars edging their ways to the exit, drivers from each lane alternating easily and precisely so that no one lane gains an advantage. The protocol is exquisitely fixed, and provides one of the rare moments when drivers exercise more restraint inside than outside their vehicles.

The external architecture, as opposed to the internal planning, has been late to develop. Many architects have felt ambivalent about building structures to house this intrusion into the landscape. The *Architectural Record* headed one story on an office complex in Portland, Oregon, "To Suppress the Visual Impact of the Automobile," and gauged the project's success by its ability to hide the presence of the car. Parking garages, concluded the *Architectural Forum*, are "an ever-present affront to the human consciousness; temples of Detroit where once men built cathedrals to the spirit."

A few architects, however, have responded to the challenge. Paul Rudolph, who designed New Haven's Temple Street Garage in the early 1960s, sought to make his garage "look like it belonged to the automobile and its movement"; Rudolph wanted to avoid "just another office building with glass." His garage became, for a time at least, the symbol of a commercial rejuvenation, a magnet rather than a background discreetly serving the needs of its connecting department stores. The long, modular building with its striated concrete finish stretches more than 700 feet and spans two city blocks. The handsome concrete lampposts and handrails, the giant curved forms seemed to answer the *Architectural Record*'s question, "Should a parking garage be an architectural tour de force, or should it be buried underground wherever possible?" New Haven has continued this architectural innovation by hosting, just a few blocks away, a Coliseum and Convention Center where Kevin Roche and John Dinkeloo have suspended a 2400-car garage over this auditorium and sports arena. The unusual placement has a practical as well as dramatic impact. And other architects have brought imagination and originality to the mundane task of housing the automobile.

But for the most part, parking garages have had as little to do with architecture as possible; their grill-like or glass-enclosed boxes and their underground cells have become as common as street signs and trash boxes. What makes them so representative of contemporary landscape development is their combination of great size and anonymity. Just as service functions now dwarf producers in our economy, so the peripheral, support structures of our culture dominate the nodes they are meant to serve. Much of this imbalance is caused by the automobile, which exhausts space even more enthusiastically than it consumes energy, but its effects are seconded by the airplane, the computer, and the record-keeping and monitoring systems that supervise and coordinate our political and ecological conduct. The formal rigidities and planning continuities of garages, some now basically unchanged for 50 years, indicate how utilitarian structures can protect design traditions. The machine's demands, once made, are less protean than the ever changing fashions of our artistic and cultural institutions. Compare the static quality of garages with the transformation of libraries, museums, and university campuses in the last 25 years. But its permanence in our topography has given the garage little grace or distinction; it remains a servitor, whose singleminded apprenticeship to the needs of movement and individual insulation project the tensions of the rush-hour, the income tax form, and the other penalites of living beneath the reign of numbers.

14

Iconography and

Intellectual History:

The Halftone Effect

The relationship between iconography and American intellectual history has been cold and distant. Intellectual historians have used words rather than images to define their subjects and provide their evidence. This has by no means confined the discipline to the history of ideas as a disengaged subject; institutionalists, psychohistorians, and social historians have examined the history of consciousness and provided other historians with models, issues, and arguments. But the energy concentrated upon written texts as points of departure has accompanied an indifference toward those shifts of style and form that belong to physical objects. The history of stylistic change has been left in the care of art historians.

As the study of pictorial description, iconography has involved, for the most part, the examination of stylistic transformations. Its students, evaluating changing inclusions and exclusions, placements, techniques, and visual formulations, have therefore treated iconographic identity as a stylistic problem. The ability to detect changes in the manipulation of images quite obviously

From John Higham and Paul Conkin, eds., *New Directions in American Intellectual History* (Baltimore: Johns Hopkins University Press, 1979), 196–211. Reprinted with permission of the publisher.

rests on familiarity with established conventions. The requisite discriminations belong to those who are habituated to the analysis of pictures and objects. The training of intellectual historians makes them unlikely candidates for substantial contributions, if iconography retains its current definition.

It would be possible, if time-consuming, to explore the historiography systematically and demonstrate how isolated the history of American art, architecture, and artifacts has been from the history of American thought. One could turn to classic texts and argue from omission or supply samplings from major journals and discuss trends. The *Journal of the History of Ideas*, for example, reveals fewer than a dozen articles in more than twenty years that confront changes in physical style, and these are almost entirely concerned with non-American subjects. The end results of such a survey would be to point with alarm and make promises for the future. But the reasons for failure are, as I suggest, obvious, and not easily surmounted.

Although traditional iconographic analysis rests upon a level of training achievable only by substantial reorganization of our various disciplines, there still remain unexploited possibilities, changes in image-making so gross and dramatic that they do not require the peculiar competence of art historians for study. They can and should be confronted by historians of mind and consciousness. For American historians, who operate within a more compressed time frame than most colleagues, this means, practically, considering changes in image-making produced by technological innovation or adaption. This task is not necessarily easier than the analysis of more traditional objects or works of art. In some cases it is far more complex. It requires sensitivities that span several areas of interest and a good deal of aggressive juxtaposition. But the integrative commitments of many intellectual historians, their concern for contextualizing, and their experience in establishing correspondences between mental processes and the possibilities or restrictions of social settings suggest their suitability for the task.

To indicate one such possibility I should like to examine an accomplishment that possesses great significance to the student of American thought and behavior during the late nineteenth and early twentieth centuries. So far as I know it has received little attention from anyone but historians of printing and photography. It is the coming of the halftone engraving process to American magazines, books, and newspapers. First appearing in the 1880s and early nineties, by 1900 it was firmly established as a major reproductive method for publishers of mass illustrated materials.

The halftone was developed to solve a problem that had bedeviled printers for a long time: securing a photomechanical method of reproducing images and doing this by using a printing block that was applicable to the same paper that accepted type. Decades of experimentation preceded Stephen Horgan's production, in 1880, for the New York *Graphic*, of a halftone reproduction of "A Scene in Shanty Town." In the newspaper's words, "There has been no redrawing of the picture. The transfer print has been obtained direct from the original negative." Horgan, according to Robert Taft, interposed "a screen of fine parallel rulings between the negative . . . made in the camera and the sensitive surface of bichromated gelatin. . . . The screen was made by photographing a mechanically ruled surface on the film of a wet collodion plate. . . . The film, after exposure and development, was stripped from the glass plate and became the half-tone screen."[1]

There were many improvements and refinements necessary before the invention could be put to daily use; Frederic Ives and Louis and Max Levy were among the Americans who helped perfect the screen. There were also many other experiments in photomechanical reproductions, in steady development since the middle of the nineteenth century. These included the collotype, photogravure, the Woodburytype, process line engraving, to name some of the major examples. But by the 1890s the power of the halftone to reproduce illustrations with shadows and tones, most of all its ability to reproduce photographs, was beginning to sweep all before it.

Until then photographs had been difficult to reproduce effectively in type-compatible printing. Some publishers, wishing to use photographs in books, had to slip in positive prints along with the pages of type. Newspapers and magazines employed engravers to reproduce photographs and paintings. There were, of course, many methods. Wood engraving, stipple and line engraving from metal plates, chromolithography, all obtained brilliant levels of technical excellence. And, for various purposes, these methods have been used in books and periodicals right through the present time.

But then came the screen halftone. This process, as several printing historians have pointed out, was more than simply a technological innovation; it was an iconographical revolution as well. Because what the halftone did was translate—or code—the original picture in a new way. It not only increased, geometrically, the mass of pictorial matter presented to the public, it also changed the quality of its appearance. It required adjustments and new expectations about appropriateness. And it stimulated extended commentary. According to one historian of the process, Estelle Jussim, the heart of the iconographical shift was the disappearance of the "sign function" of the reproduction; it became "an optical illusion with surrogate power."[2] Previously, Jussim argues, readers encountering illustrations were made aware of the subjective, contrived character of the pictures; these were obviously the product of an artist's mind and tools. And they still were, when the halftone reproduced a

painting or print. But with the halftone photograph, a photomechanical reproduction of a photochemical image, the illusion of seeing an actual scene, or
receiving an objective record of such a scene, was immeasurably enhanced.

To develop her point further, Jussim argues that in the 1880s, when the
screen halftone first appeared, magazines and books existed in a state of reproductive limbo, containing true multimedia experiences: wood engravings, full-
process halftones, white-line tonal wood engravings, line engravings, and combinations of all these type-compatible pictures were, in fact, mingled together.
But inexorably, the processed halftones, appealing to some deeper level of psychological satisfaction, began to drive out the wood engravings and pen drawings; phototechnology defeated the artist-mediated form of reproduction. In a
fascinating chapter that focuses on the picture books of world's fairs, Jussim
presents the scope of this change in the literature concerning Chicago's Columbian Exposition of 1893. Only 25 percent of the books published about the
Exposition, she points out, contained any process other than process halftone
and process line engraving.[3] The popularity of these books today owes a good
deal to this fact; with them, and with the periodicals that employed their systems of reproduction to publicize the fairs, we have entered the modern world
of visual reproduction. The contrast with the visual reproductions of just a
decade before is startling. Except for the addition of color, which would be
developed by improved processes in the twentieth century, the illustrations
match for persuasive power and technical impressiveness many of the photographic illustrations that appear in contemporary publications.

The Jussim argument may be a bit exaggerated. It fails to acknowledge
an extremely important aspect of visual reproduction: the permanent continuity
of nonphotographic reproductions as appropriate and popular illustrative and
informative devices, in newspapers and magazines particularly. One of the most
interesting results of this revolution, in fact, is the creation of categories of
appropriateness, in which certain kinds of visual reproduction—photographic,
drawn, painted—seem more valid in certain situations than others. I will return
to this later. But despite this caveat, what Jussim and other historians of printing reproduction point out is indisputable: in a period of ten or fifteen years the
whole system of packaging visual information was transformed, made more appealing and persuadable, and assumed a form and adopted conventions that
have persisted right through the present.

This, then, is an iconographical revolution of the first order, and should
be treated with careful attention. The single generation of Americans living
between 1885 and 1910 went through an experience of visual reorientation that
had few earlier precedents, although it would be matched by some twentieth-
century experiences. The one earlier parallel that seemed to possess even

greater scope and capacity for influence took place almost four centuries before, with the introduction of printing as a new code for transmitting verbal information. The Gutenberg Revolution has been the focus of sustained, elaborate, and controversial commentary, involving scholars from various disciplines. Some of its effects have been trumpeted too loudly, and more careful differentiations, distinctions, and tests have been introduced in the last few years to refine and qualify the glamorous generalizations that some associate with the name of McLuhan. And intellectual historians have played a major role in assessing the character of the printing revolution.

But American intellectual historians have done little with the history of our visual processing, although its impact, purely as a stylistic matter, was obviously great. The reasons for this failure are several, and their listing suggests, I think, some of the problems of subject definition that have restricted the appeal of intellectual history. First of all, the coming of pictures, either as replacements for written words or enticing and subversive supplements to them, has seemed to many thoughtful people of the late nineteenth century, and today, artistically and intellectually suspect. As students of the word, with a large investment in careful verbal analysis, intellectual historians, like colleagues in other fields, have tended to deprecate surrogates thrown up by the Industrial Revolution, surrogates that threatened the primacy of printed communication and menaced the very concept of authenticity itself. The mass of inexpensive, sometimes sensational illustrations that took up increasing space in periodicals represented degeneration. Once the phenomenon had been noted, and deplored, it seemed unworthy of serious study. Art historians, with no necessary bias against graphic communication, did not pay much attention to the halftone revolution, for one reason, because newspaper and magazine illustration in the prephotographic era was a minor art in itself, and for another, because photography, for a long time, seemed a mechanical device that did not require aesthetic analysis. So attention was given to other matters.

Second, the new reproductive methods were tied closely to commercialization, through both the forums that included them and the products associated with the pictures. The taint of money-making and profitable exploitation attached itself to this iconographic revolution; in general intellectual historians have given little effort to studying the history of American business and commerce. One evidence of that is the small number of serious studies of American advertising. European historians have, it must be admitted, been more assiduous in examining popularization processes and marketing, partly because their literary links have been better established and partly because the longer period of time that has separated the manufacture of evidence from its study has more easily legitimized the subject.

A third reason for the failure to take greater note of this change lies in the character of the innovations themselves. They were technologically complex and confusing in detail.[4] Assessment of their significance requires some absorption, not in the grand tradition of scientific theorizing, which historians of science do so well, but in minor, mundane, mechanical tinkering, bitterly disputed and often not explained with any degree of thoroughness. Since the history of technology in general has not formed a part of the usual training of American intellectual historians but has remained in limbo as a semi-independent field of specialization, the vocabulary and interests necessary to integrate this praxis with the history of thought are not widely available. Joining iconography and intellectual history, for recent American history, requires a sensitivity to changing modes of visual transmission. Not only type-compatible reproduction, but color photography, motion pictures, and television demand some immersion in operational details.

Fourth and finally, this kind of subject matter, once ignored, becomes provincial; its relationship to established issues within the field of intellectual history seems tenuous. What use is the demonstration of changes in visual coding unless some larger implications can be developed? This is, at the same time, the most important reason for the failure to develop historiographical ventures into new areas, and the most difficult to correct. It cannot be solved until the historiography itself develops.

Artistically suspect, commercially tainted, technically cumbersome, and intellectually isolated, the development of modern visual reproduction methods has failed to engage general historical interest. And until these problems are met, I believe that iconographical analysis will continue to suffer the isolation described at the beginning of the paper. The problem remains, however, of assessing the significance of the halftone process itself. And here one can turn to the considerable debate that took place, in the late nineteenth century, about changes in media form.

The literature of controversy is abundant, but its uses have been somewhat narrow. Because of present interests in the development of photography and its elevation to an important art form, claiming equal dignity (and prices) with painting, the late nineteenth-century discussion has been analyzed as combat about the aesthetic status of photography. It is this, to be sure, but it is also a dialogue about the nature of communication, and more particularly an early set of responses to the thrust of what would later be termed mass culture.

Starting from the early experiments of Daguerre, of course, painters and illustrators were concerned about the threat to their livelihood that photographers presented, particularly the portraitists.[5] If the creation of a memory piece was the principal motive powering a portrait commission, nonmediated, or apparently nonmediated, images processed an objectivity that seemed more satisfying to many customers. Landscapes could be and were idealized by the painter; so were history, allegory, and scripture, generally unavailable to the photographer in any case. But the human face and figure, off which so many artists lived, could be idealized only in a more limited way. It was a natural subject for literalism. The idealizing was generally done by friends and relatives, who would endow the physical lineaments of the subject with the memories and associations that belonged to it. Moreover, the subject of a commission demanded self-recognition, and could not be transformed into total sublimity without some questions being asked. The solution of painters, in some instances, had been to keep the essential features, warts and all, but select a setting and costume that dignified, beautified, or exalted the sitter, or in the case of some of our early nineteenth-century artists, proudly proclaimed doughty republican virtues and the advantages of a self-made background. Details of occupation and background added to conviction.

Daguerreotypists and photographic portraitists, however, could make the best of both worlds. While claiming objectivity for their cameras, they could establish studios that offered flattering trappings—exotic backdrops, lush foliage, interesting costumes, and accessories. They did not have to abandon entirely those conventions of portraiture which added allurement, and yet they could protect themselves from the customer's angry protests about what had been done to his face.

Impressed by the threat, painters, illustrators, and critics joined a vigorous and often angry discussion about the capacity and status of the camera and its products, and this was extended, of course, to include photographic illustrations. Few defended the values of literalism and objectivity as such, save for "subordinate" uses such as scientific research, documentation, or medical diagnosis. Since art as a category enjoyed such high repute in Victorian America, it was crucial to determine whether or not the photograph could compete with the painting or drawing as an object. So defenders of photography insisted that the photographer, like the artist, had available a wide range of choices. The selection of lenses, apertures, lighting, and distance made personal decision-making and judgment as vital to his work as it was for the painter. This was the position of Charles H. Caffin, an art critic with broad tolerances who published *Photography as a Fine Art* at the turn of the century.[6]

But culturally conservative journals, like the *Nation*, disagreed. The photographer's landscapes, "however modified in effect, must be always topographical, his figures must be strictly naturalistic in form." Photography "is not a fine art because it can invent nothing. It can give us a true record or a muddled and falsified one," and that was the only choice available.[7] What worried many critics of photography was a loss of mastery over events and occasions, a diminution of the artist's ability to create a comprehensive and self-sufficient achievement. The photographer, in their eyes, seemed too passive, a responder rather than a shaper, accurate or inaccurate, but never inspired or original. The coming dominance of photography, like that of so many other areas of modern life, seemed to spell a shrinkage of human effectiveness, even while it opened up vast new areas for amusement and recreation.

The nature of this bias was revealed in a semihumorous comment made by the same journal, the *Nation*, entitled "The Perils of Photography."[8] Here it acknowledged the manly, even heroic status of news photographers, who courted danger to record war, violence, and disaster. If the photograph was passive, the photographers surely were not. Nonetheless, events perversely refused to "adapt themselves to the photographer's eye." The moment when he chose to make the picture might not be the optimal moment to record the event; and sudden accidents could destroy the value of the image. More traditional artists, however, faced no such problems. The history painter was more in command. "His barons never get in the way of a clear view of King John at Runnymede; nor has he to erase any of the Roman populace with gray pigment," to reveal what "Mark Antony is offering to Caesar."[9] What had been gained in personal status by the photographic journalists was lost by the contingent character of their craft. Will Irwin's piece, "The Swashbucklers of the Camera," for *Collier's*, made a similar kind of point, at least by implication. The news photographer had to be patient, thick skinned, indifferent to danger, and "retain enough self-poise after long runs, frantic climbing of fences, struggles with policemen, persuasion of reluctant victims." But he needed these heroic virtues "to ply with certainty one of the most delicate and complicated trades known to modern life."[10] He bore, in short, the same relationship to art that the journalist bore to literature and, to conservatives at least, symbolized the way in which events were controlling man. All of this activity existed simply to record what was happening, simultaneously, to someone else.

The debate about loss of control, touched off by the reproductive improvements, was only one aspect of the cultural modernization that threatened to overwhelm older values. Distortion was another. The ease of reproducing images, drawn images as well as photographic images, excited attacks from those who felt that literary standards were being relaxed, perhaps fatally, by journals that would never have permitted these weaknesses to appear in their fiction or documentary reporting. Images were not only failing, in many instances, to complement the text, they were actually contradicting it. Tudor Jenks argued in the *Independent* that illustrators of fiction were exaggerating the purely pictorial aspects of stories and failing to supplement the plots. Modern illustrators, he insisted, were able to produce academically correct drawings, but they were a far cry from the greatness of John Leech, Felix Darley, and Doré; their work often bore little reference to the texts.[11] The *Atlantic Monthly* also argued that illustrators distorted fiction by raising passing details to unjustified importance and selecting the commonplace, instead of the unusual, as subject matter.[12] And one letter writer to the *Dial* protested against the deceptive and misleading illustrations to nonfiction. "Has not the time come," asked C. F. Tucker Brooke, "to demand that the pictures introduced into works on social and cultural conditions be subjected to the same investigation which is given to other testimony?" While Sidney Lanier was describing Tudor innyards, his illustrators presented eighteenth-century coaching inns; at other times hypothetical illustrations were passed off as an actual record. As "the rage for illustration" had now passed from magazines to serious textbooks, Brooke continued, it must be realized that "pictures irresponsibly selected, and inserted without adequate investigation, can easily lead to more serious misapprehension than would result from glaring error in the letter-press."[13] The picture's greater persuasive power made mistakes more dangerous.

Vulgarization and error, loss of control, these were complemented by another feature of mass culture: standardization. The increased number of images being produced by illustrators was an apparent response to categorical imperatives rather than to the needs of individual articles and pieces. Some conservative critics saw the origins of this in the sensational political cartoons, which, in the hands of men like Nast, Opper, Wales, and others, represented a pernicious influence. After words had lost their significance, the *Nation* argued, "pictures had to come sooner or later. The childish view of the world is, so to speak, 'on top.'" Soon the illustrated cuts, in their turn, would pall "and have to be supplemented by something more infantile still. The reader will demand and have to get a rattle, or a colored India-rubber balloon, or a bright ball of worsted, or a jack-in-the-box, with each year's subscription."[14] The *Atlantic*, proclaiming its horror of "the discolored supplement," and cartoons that defied "every maxim of morals and aesthetics," felt that the "tendency to mere symbolism" in newspaper pictures had become characteristic and deadly. "Buster Brown's costume is as fixed as the green tunic of St. Peter . . . Father Knickerbocker in buckled shoes, stockings, breeches, long waistcoat, flaring frock . . . Pitt in something like court costume; the late William Penn looking like an eighteenth-century publican . . . these are examples of symbolic figures which are probably destined to rival Uncle Sam and John Bull in permanence." Other cities besides Philadelphia, New York, and Pittsburgh would soon be developing their own emblems. This tendency to fixed symbolic forms was apparently a feature of "the decaying periods of all artistic nations," and resulted from the recurrent discovery "that imitation and fixed formulas were easier and more remunerative" than originality and initiative. Art, in short, had become a consumer product, reduced to immediate titillation by reliance upon formulas. "Emblematism" was a trifling artistic motive, raised to sudden importance by the mass audience.[15] The *Bookman,* surveying a recent rash of illustrations for romantic fiction, hinted darkly at a "Heroine Trust," grafting its uniform versions of feminine beauty on a range of unsuspecting readers.[16]

The case against the new iconography was summed up in a 1911 editorial in *Harper's Weekly,* entitled, significantly, "Over-Illustration." "We can scarce get the sense of what we read for the pictures," complained *Harper's.* "We can't see the ideas for the illustrations. Our world is simply flooded with them. They lurk in almost every form of printed matter." There were ancient origins, of course. "The knight of old, the castle, city, province," each had its own pictorial device, but these were minor forerunners to what had become literally an avalanche. Subordinated, illustrations aided thought, but improperly used, they became "a mental drug." "And it would be safe to say that a young mind, overfed pictorially, will scarcely be likely to do any original thinking." Because so many illustrations failed to illuminate their subjects, they precluded thought and actually prevented visualization. Thinking was a living process, "the athletics of the mind," and standardized images were crutches that discouraged active exercise.[17]

Had there been a pronounced decline in the quality of American illustration in the previous years, *Harper's* position may have seemed more understandable. However, its assault shared another quality with some of the diatribes against mass culture that our own century has witnessed—misplacedness. For *Harper's* was reacting to an iconographical shift rather than to decay and degeneration. The previous twenty years or so are now seen as one of the great periods of American illustration. Among the artists working for periodicals like *Collier's Scribner's, Century, Judge, St. Nicholas,* and for the publishing houses, were Blashfield, Bradley, Beard, Abbey, Christy, Frost, Castaigne, Davies, Fisher, Flagg, Parrish, Glackens, Luks, Sloan, Yohn, Denslow—some of the greatest names in the history of American graphic design.[18] *Harper's* itself had begun to use the halftone for illustration by the late 1880s, and steady improvements meant the easier reproduction of oil paintings and wash drawings, to say nothing of the photographs. The new iconography, then, was capable of provoking outbursts on the general thrust of modernity and stimulating its discontents.

But the halftone process did more than provoke comments on its belletristic aspects. It helped revolutionize the process of reporting news, and by the turn of the century the star photographer assumed a stance beside the crack journalist in purveying novelty to the mass audience. Now the unwanted snapshot took its place beside the aggressive interview as one of the hazards of

American journalism. The connections between photography and illustration, on the one hand, and the new craze for publicity, on the other, were multiple and momentous.

One such relationship between the packaging of information and larger social values involved the growing debate over privacy. Several historians, Alan Westin and David Flaherty among them, have argued for the antiquity of the notion of privacy. Western civilization, writes Flaherty, "has . . . always incorporated personal privacy into its system of values. . . . Privacy can surely be identified in a general sense as one of the cultural goals of sixteenth- and seventeenth-century English society." Colonial Americans carried on this older concern, and there was "no particular moment of decision in the country's history when the populace suddenly declared *de novo* that privacy was a good thing."[19]

Nonetheless, even if one allows this sometimes vulnerable argument validity, there was a moment when debates about personal privacy took on a special intensity. This moment began in the 1890s and continued through the period before World War I. The camera, and the ability to display and distribute accurate photographs, were vital elements in the new consciousness of the dangers—and benefits—of modern publicity.

The benefits had already been estimated by a number of social reformers. Jacob Riis, heavily involved in journalistic exposés, came in contact with flash photography in 1887. In the first published account describing the new technique, an article in the *New York Sun* of 12 February 1888, Riis explained that his object was to collect "a series of views for magic lantern slides, showing, as no mere description could, the misery and vice that he [Riis] had noticed in his ten years of experience." Aside from its strong human interest, he thought that this treatment of the topic would call attention to the needs of the situation, and suggest the direction in which much good might be done.[20] The *Sun* was still unable to reproduce the photographs by the halftone process, and ran instead twelve line drawings that copied the photographs; *Scribner's* published "How the Other Half Lives" in December 1889, illustrating nineteen of Riis's photographs, again through line drawings rather than halftones. His book, however, did not use only drawings; according to Alexander Alland it was the first American book to use a large number of halftones, seventeen of them, in addition to eighteen line drawings.[21] This was in 1890, only a year or two after the first extensive use of the still expensive practice had developed in magazines. Starting in the 1890s more books were published with halftones, and Robert Taft has chosen 1897 as "the advent of half-tone illustration as a regular feature of American newspaper journalism," with the *New York Tribune* and *Chicago Tribune* pioneering in their use.[22] Once Riis had set the pattern, others followed, especially Lewis W. Hine, whose photographs were published in

Charities and the Commons and *Boyhood and Lawlessness*. Hine's work was soon being commissioned by *Everybody's*, *McClure's*, and the *Outlook*, and helped contribute to the general progressive sense that dramatic publicity was the way to ensure public action and solve problems like child labor, slum housing, and industrial safety. The spirit of liberal reform was exemplified by muckraking efforts to make public the private business practices of American bankers and manufacturers, to force them to reveal the nature of interlocking and conflicting interests. It was difficult to argue with the dramatic results achieved by publication of revelations, accompanied, where possible, as in the *Pittsburgh Survey*, with photographs. Public astonishment fed upon this nurture, and along with it demands for legal and social changes grew.

But the same spokesmen for the public's right to greater knowledge were often anxious about how far the limits of this interest extended. The irony of Louis Brandeis's authorship of the first major discussion of the legal right to privacy just a few years before his published revelations of American finance released a firestorm of controversy was only the most theatrical of these paradoxes. The line had become blurred, warned the *Century* in 1913, between "the publicity which is for the good of the people, for the terror of offenders, and the publicity which is only gossip and scandal printed for no other purpose than to sell the papers and make money." Without proposing any remedy, the *Century* went on to argue that honest rights to privacy had been imperiled. "If Lady Godiva were to ride through the streets of Coventry to-day, there would be Peeping Toms in groups at every window with cameras and machines for making motion pictures." [23] The growth of gossip columns and the assault on the private lives of businessmen, socialites, athletes, actors, and actresses accompanied the camera's march and that of the illustrated supplement. John Gilmore Speed angrily protested these tendencies in an 1896 article for the *North American Review*. Disagreeing with court decisions that removed the right of privacy from public figures, he insisted that "the habit indulged in by so many actors of thrusting their portraits before the public, and filling the columns of daily newspapers with the most intimate as well as most trivial of their private affairs, does not take away from any member of the profession the right to be let alone." What drew his ire most severely was the new illustrated journalism, built upon surreptitiously taken photographs. "Indeed, it is a well-known fact that at least one of the newspapers of New York keeps a photographer busy in the streets of the metropolis taking 'snap shots' at every person who appears to be of consequence. These are used at once, or filed away." [24] The snapshot was still being taken "at" rather than "of" a subject.

But protests about intrusion came from both the innocent and the guilty. A developing press agentry and advertising managers sensed the rewards planted news and rehearsed photographs could bring. And they worked for politicians on the highest level. Both Theodore Roosevelt and Woodrow Wilson proved skillful at meeting the challenges of the new mass journalism and turning the public attention brought by photography to their own account. This meant inviting cameras in to record normal days at the White House and details of family living. As early as 1903 the *Century* noted the new willingness of government, at home and abroad, to encourage the publication of intimate glimpses of official life. Even the pope had permitted a photographer to enter his private chambers for a magazine article, and had subsequently allowed cinematographers and gramophone records to create publicity. The *Century* foresaw only good effects from this kind of self-advertisement, for mystery and dread were bound to recede under the new enlightenment. "When the mind is no longer awed and clouded by the dim and the unknown the appeal to reason must be reinforced. So far as publicity has to do with authority, secular or sacred, we believe the change effected is very great and likely to increase; and we believe that this change is, on the whole, better for humanity."[25]

Once again, it was easy to mistake the direction of change. Executive authority was not necessarily diluted by greater publicity; the cultivation of a more personalized relationship with the mass public was capable, if anything, of augmenting authoritarian power. But the expectation that a technological innovation would enhance the power of democratic, rational thought reappeared in commentaries on later inventions. Radio, for example, seemed to hold out the same promise. Isolated listeners, protected from the excesses of crowd psychology that were inevitably induced by mass meetings and political rallies, would listen dispassionately to the statements of elected leaders and candidates for office. No longer permitted the rhetorical bombast and exaggeration that the crowd loved, politicians would be forced to eschew demagoguery and offer clearheaded and restrained statements to their listening audiences.[26] By the mid 1930s the fallacy had been completely exploded by political demagogues who found they could exploit the radio waves as easily as predecessors had manipulated the laws of collective imitation. The passion for deliverance by machine dies hard.

Thus the debate about mass culture and a series of strategies toward it were furthered by the halftone revolution and the spread of pictorial journalism. The private lives of the great filled the new Sunday supplements and popular monthlies, orchestrated by their public relations experts and press managers. But issues of social reform, personal privacy, and political authority do not exhaust the effect of the outburst of pictorialism. Commodity advertising, school textbooks, pornography, and architectural and interior design were also affected. Not always evenly, of course. But few studies have attempted to chart the differing rates by which fields of thought and action were penetrated by the new coding system and the changing pace of specialized communication.

Some experiments were not successful. The illustrated novel, for example, a major source of illustrated commission during the nineteenth century, attempted to adjust by substituting photographs, often of staged versions; but this ploy was doomed by the effective competition of the photoplay. Photographed fiction could not match the silver screen, although in Europe the photographed serial seemed to do much better. And in magazines and newspapers, the photograph did not carry all before it; halftone reproduction of artists' drawings continued to be popular, as the twentieth-century success of illustrators like Leyendecker, Parrish, Rockwell, Flagg, Pitz, Artzybasheff, and the work commissioned by *Fortune*, the *New Yorker, Collier's*, and the *Saturday Evening Post* demonstrate.[27] But halftone photography was necessary accompaniment to certain kinds of stories—news, documentary, and travel, in particular.

All this, of course, requires much more research if the arguments are to be given appropriate conviction and precision. The question, I suppose, is who shall carry on the research, and how it shall be organized. Until now, historians of journalism and of art, along with the social scientist analysts of mass and popular culture, have not shown great interest in the history of nonmediated reproductive techniques and their intellectual and social impact. The literature of commentary upon the threats and promises of mass culture is now extensive and well established, its roots and conventions going back one hundred years or more. This in itself seems to me an important problem for intellectual historians to consider, but when it is combined with the specific stylistic changes in illustrated communication developed by technical innovators, it offers an opportunity to integrate aspects of commercial, industrial, technological, and administrative history with the history of taste, opinion, and artistic style. The study of these changes, treated narrowly, can result in a new antiquarianism, as recondite and self-limiting as the most abstruse problems of medieval, Byzantine, or Hellenistic reconstructions. Some recent work in the study of popular culture suggests this possibility. But viewed analytically by intellectual historians who are committed to explaining not only the origins of stylistic transformation but also their relationship to contemporary thought and opinion, they offer a way of incorporating iconography with classic subjects within the discipline. Models of analysis exist in dizzying number, provided, in general, by the anthropological and literary wings of the semiological schools. A great deal of highly personalized or overdetermined commentary has already appeared. Much of it needs correction and specification, in the same way that the McLuhanesque interpretation of the Gutenberg Revolution required evaluation and restriction. All this would, I fear, require another paper. It seems best, then, to stop with the proposal now. Arguments from abundance have a way of becoming their own worst enemies.

15

Color and Media: Some Comparisons and Speculations

T he literature on color and color theory is of huge extent and variety. Major contributors include Newton, Boyle, Descartes, Voltaire, Goethe, Gladstone, Havelock Ellis, Karl Groos, Schopenhauer, and Wilhelm Ostwald, to name just a few giants. For centuries color symbolism and color choices have fascinated philosophers, scientists, mystics, and artists. And fifty or a hundred years ago colors not only enjoyed therapeutic, religious, and cultural significance, but formed a popular subject for journalistic discussion.[1]

Despite all this attention, however, the relationship between color and the modern media has been only fitfully explored. We do know much about the progress of invention in process work and color photography. Impressive narratives treat the history of color printing in England and America; there are catalogues, exhibition lists, bibliographies.[2] But little attempt has been made to tie the quest for color reproduction to larger issues. What I wish to do here is to speculate about connections and comparisons not firmly established, and to propose some preliminary observations.

There are many directions in which one might pursue the study of color

From *Prospects* 11:7–28. Copyright © 1987, Cambridge University Press. Reprinted with permission of the publisher.

in a social context. The growing capacity to produce color has affected a range of expressions—in fashion, education, advertising, and mass production. These I will not describe. What interests me rather are contemporary reactions to the new advances in reproduction. Was color expected to change the transmitting media or the receiving audiences? What links the new technical skills with assumptions about media form? How did promoters and critics view the innovations? The vast expansion of pictorial representation has challenged traditional verbal description as an instrument of communication, as well as methods of critical evaluation. At stake in these debates is the definition of popular culture. The arguments, therefore, must hold meanings for us.

In some senses color can be termed the *most* pictorial of all the pictorial media's characteristics. In an economical, mass-produced, and accurate mode color has generally been difficult to reproduce, arriving after most other technical problems had been solved in black and white. But the coming of color was not purely a triumph. It could also be received as a threatening novelty by those who found safety in words or in older forms of visual representation. And its arrival could be seized as a moment for taking stock of the social impact of broad media novelties. Responses to color say something about the reception of illustrated experiences as a whole, and their assessment as either diminutions or enhancements of existing culture.

My procedure will be simple. First, as background, I will comment upon the lengthiest, best documented, and most complex example of popular color transmission: prints, and the illustration of books and magazines. I will turn next to the arrival of color in motion pictures and suggest the nature of expectations and responses here as well. Finally, I will treat the coming of color television. As we move from medium to medium we will see a growing coalescence of critical and commercial issues. This corresponds to changes in communications more generally and suggests a few reflections I will offer at the end. Because the stories are not easily available, I will need to supply occasional narrations. They are necessarily sketchy.

The development of printed illustration forms, of course, a major historical subject on its own. The search for inexpensive, aesthetically pleasing, and objectively faithful methods for reproducing color on paper dominated commercial printing in the nineteenth century. Processes and materials like ink and paper were continually modified from the middle of the last century onward. Any mere summary of the changes that took place from the invention of chromolithography to the development of three- and four-color methods fifty years later would be impossibly lengthy for our purposes. But although the individual steps were numerous and idiosyncratic, by the late nineteenth century color printing had become a force all its own, its terms entering the language to evoke institutions and periods: yellow journalism, color supplement, chromo-civilization. Inventors, critics, and publishers displayed self-consciousness about the impact of the new processes, particularly chromolithography. Histories of color printing appeared in number by 1910, like those by Martin Hardie, R. M. Burch, Courtney Lewis, and H. M. Cundall.[3] They moved back in time to fifteenth-century woodblocks; reviewed innovations by J. B. Jackson, William Savage, Jacques Le Blon, and George Baxter; and described experiments with colored mezzotints and stipple engraving before covering more recent innovators. All made but rarely examined the observation that the larger public sought color, of almost any kind. Or, as the famous American lithographer Louis Prang put it, "Color in a picture is always more satisfactory than the lack of it."[4]

But this sentiment concealed a problem. For while hand-colored aquatints and fine chromolithography possess delicacy, appeal, and vibrancy even today, the search for cheap color printing inevitably produced much that was clumsy and garish. Poor color quality stood out by contrast with the skillful subtlety of illustrations rendered more simply in black and white. Why then did color appeal so intensely? First of all it was an add-on, testifying to the greater wealth, ambition, or taste of its subject or purchasers. In prints, color was displayable. It was also attention-getting. In the form of posters it could be seen at great distances, and achieve a quicker impact than a black and white picture. Crudity did not seem to matter here; indeed it sometimes even helped get the message across. Some critics of color processes, therefore, seized upon them as symbols of the new pressures on art and taste coming from a democratizing age. Color seemed pretentious, aggressive, and an inadequate surrogate for something else. They were concerned not only about the specific problem of diluting art traditions, but by the larger issue of giving the public what it wanted instead of what was good for it. Insisting that the "touch of the master's hand on the canvas can never be reproduced by the press," the *Nation* advised chromolithographers to stay away from reproducing masterpieces. Imitating the effect of any original was bound to fail, as it was inherently vulgar. Framing a chromolithograph like a painting "would be an act of absurdity and as clownish as absurd."[5] Russell Sturgis complained that color printing had developed into a "pseudo-fine art," copies pretending "themselves, to be pictures, are in every print-shop and bookstore window." "That which makes an oil painting or a water-color drawing delicate or forcible, truthful or noble," these chromos had not, but all that "which makes human art poor beside nature, they have." It was fine for title pages on sheet music, but bad for great art. "Good color, that is, delicately gradated color, is not to be produced by the printing-press."[6]

Louis Prang wrote in to protest that "the business of this age is to make the products of civilization cheap," thus giving to all a share in the blessings of civilization; "what the people want and admire," he argued, "are not the dry bones or the syntax of art, but life pictures, full of the bloom and brilliancy of nature, to brighten their homes and make their own existence more pleasant."[7] But the *Nation* countered that chromos would do harm by accustoming people to ignoble and unhealthy forms of art. "The confusion of ideas which assumes that 'what the people want and admire' is the same thing as 'what the people need and ought to admire' is strange to see," wrote E. L. Godkin, who used chromolithographs to emblemize his dislike for all that seemed meretricious in modern civilization.[8] The debate about chromolithography, which Peter Marzio explores in *The Democratic Art*, was a confrontation with the apparently debasing forms of mass culture. In the early twentieth century, cheered by the return to favor of the artist lithograph—a medium graced by the work of men like Joseph Pennell, Frank Brangwyn, Whistler, Fantin-Latour, and the Senefelder Club in London—critics looked back in trembling at how narrowly the lithographic medium had escaped total vulgarization. The "very name of lithography passed into reproach," one recalled, "its commercial degradation" discouraging people from purchasing artists' work.[9] American customs officials once refused to deliver some artists' lithographs to an American gallery because the prints were described as lithographs, and the customs officials insisted they were not, their idea, one critic wrote, "being no doubt the flaming circus poster and the canned-goods label."[10] Lithography, wrote the *International Printer* in 1904, was a fine art, although at an earlier date, when Americans "aspired to the chromo in a garish scale of colors," and lithographers produced "monstrosities" in response to public taste, it would have been difficult to find its defenders.[11]

The coming of color, in short, was greeted by careful, self-conscious, critical appraisal, with much pondering of its impact upon established iconographic traditions. There appeared to be something worth defending in the history of the print, and of illustration, techniques of delicacy, standards of reception, which made color welcome only when it respected certain rules and did not vulgarize public taste.

Second, color illustration did not become, nor did anyone anticipate that it would develop into, a monopolistic form of expression. It was expected to coexist, into an indefinite future, with traditional, and even nontraditional, black and white techniques. Even when they are extensively illustrated, starting in the 1890s, books and magazines do not require color to sell, and even when they already include, at this date, some form of process color printing, they do not rely upon it exclusively. We are so used to this it scarcely attracts notice, but it is nonetheless significant. In printed reproduction color remains one of many modes. Illustrated books, then and now, contain a colored frontispiece and nothing more. Colors are icing on the cake. Most readers recognize them as such. Centuries of etching, engraving, woodblock, and other graphic techniques provided their own justification. Illustration and graphic art were well established long before mass-produced color had become a commercial possibility. In the case of modern magazines color appears, in impressive quantity or quality, principally through the advertising pages. Printers, artists, readers, and patrons were all aware that colored inserts were more expensive than black and white, and the special assessment would have to be borne by the principal beneficiary. While some periodicals used color to encourage sales or subscriptions—on the comic pages, for example, or the occasional reproduction of artists' work—only advertisers could afford elaborate color spreads on a regular basis. Indeed up through the recent past many popular journals have used far more color in their advertising sections than anywhere else. In the twenties and thirties, when artists' illustrations were more a staple of magazines than today, this was even more pronounced. Turning over the pages of the *Saturday Evening Post*, the *Ladies' Home Journal*, *Cosmopolitan*, the *Century*, and *Lippincott's*, one is struck by the uneven penetration of the commercial sector. Much was invested so that artists like the Leyendeckers, Parrish, Cleland, Phillips, Underwood, and Bird could sell cars, cereals, canned foods, beer, perfumes, tobacco, and clothing within the magazines, as well as design the beautiful covers that glowed on newsstands. There is no evidence of reader discontent, angrily denouncing the application of this expense and artistic energy to the selling of goods, or demanding that these organs of art, literature, and journalism spend more money developing color for their noncommercial sections. The color advertisements formed part of the magazines' appeal. Some of the most sophisticated journals of the century, like *Vogue* or the *New Yorker*, were content for their illustrations and cartoons to remain black and white, by contrast to the lavish use of color on their covers and advertising pages. Color was recognized as an ornamental instrument with mercenary capacities, of incidental appeal to the aesthetic and informational tastes served by noncolored print and illustration. Even while decrying public taste for garish color or comics, critics allowed color in commercial illustration to pass unscathed; reader discrimination in permitting spatial hierarchies of color and noncolor was demonstrable.

A third large feature of color reproduction in books, brochures, and journals, aside from its reception by an informed critical opinion and its station within an elaborate hierarchy of noncolor forms, was its slow, self-conscious, and still incomplete progress toward greater effectiveness and fidelity. Color printing never attains final perfection nor does it claim to. Glancing at even the most impressive and expensive forms of color reproduction during the past two or three decades, in magazines, newspapers, art books, or photographic texts, a reader is bound to be struck by the changes, long after color printing had become an accepted convention and its photomechanical capacities an object of admiration. Colors which seemed startlingly bold or lifelike in news photos or as art reproductions just fifteen or twenty years ago now appear faded, contrived, or distorting to contemporary vision, showing nothing more than the gap between our appetite for color and the technology or budget to support it. Expansion in contemporary color photography and our habituation to color on the film or television screen have raised or at least changed our standards. But the fact is that color reproduction methods are dynamic, and occasionally even volatile areas of research and experimentation. For seventy-five years printers' journals like *Penrose's* or the *Inland Printer,* or, more recently, *Print* and *Graphis,* have proudly featured innovations in paper, ink, and method, innovations which permit more subtle renditions of tone and hue. Enormous variations continue to be tolerated, for cheap color books maintain a market. But color quality remains a variable for reviews of book and magazine illustration to comment upon. With the longest history of color reproduction, the printing art maintains the liveliest debates about quality. Critics continue to debate the need or utility of color reproduction, and the relationship between reproduction and original values. Finality of technique is rarely, if ever, assumed.

Fourth, and finally, printed color is presumed to vary with cost, audience, and purpose of publication. Just as reader etiquette permitted color in advertising sections and black and white in textual illustration, so the audience for books and journals accepted formats which featured dramatically different color treatments. The concept of publishing a book in various editions, some limited in number and made more expensive by the presence of special paper, signatures, and original art inserts, was well established before the twentieth century, but it was then, particularly in France, that the craze for producing five or more renderings of the same text and pictures achieved new heights. In this country, with George Macy's Limited Editions Club and the growing perfection of offset printing, the practice became broadly dispersed. Limited Editions would publish its classic, signed by illustrator or author, using silk-screen, lino-cut, or hand-colored pictures, in numbered copies, while Heritage Books would print the same text and pictures in offset, on different paper, unnumbered. Printed color did not require total standardization. Different color effects could coexist within mass publishing. Even magazines could be produced in limited, numbered editions. Customizing remained possible.

The reception of color within printing media, then, reflected a culture with established iconographic traditions which accepted a variety of rendering techniques; was prepared to accept slow, indefinite progress as a condition; and demanded neither uniformity of technical quality nor pervasiveness of penetration. Colorists, indeed, were urged to develop their own conventions. Where color was condemned it was frequently because of unhappy imitation. But as original documents color prints could be admired in themselves.

When we turn to color and motion pictures, we find somewhat but not totally different circumstances. The commercial stakes are more defined (and much larger), the aesthetic standards more youthful, and the final product more standardized. But nonetheless there remains in evidence some resistance, some discrimination, and a framework of critical evaluation prepared to accept polychromatic and monochromatic diversity. In the end, however, total commitment to color emerges, along with an assumption of final perfection, in contrast to the print experience.

One tends to think that color entered motion pictures in a single convulsive movement, like sound. But its history is long and tortuous, almost as old as motion pictures themselves. The desire to marry color to movement was apparently visceral and immediate. In his exhaustive if technical examination of color and movies, James Limbacher reports that by 1894 Robert Paul was color-printing his one-reelers, and Georges Méliès was hand-tinting *A Trip to the Moon* and *An Astronomer's Dream*.[12] In the early twentieth century other filmmakers used pretinted film, giving one color at a time, for short sequences and sometimes for the whole work. David Griffith used tinted sequences for *Broken Blossoms; Intolerance; Down East;* and *The Birth of a Nation;* von Stroheim employed yellow for scenes in *Greed;* and Eisenstein tinted particular objects in some of his work, like the flying of the red flag in *Potemkin*. According to Limbacher's estimate, by 1920, 80 percent of Hollywood's features were being tinted in some way, partly by hand, the rest by tinted stock, in all the colors of the rainbow.

Meanwhile, color processes also developed, aiming to present everything in natural colors. A long line of inventors and processes appeared: Frederick Marshall Lee, Raymond Turner, Charles Urban, F. H. Ives, William Friese-Greene, Pathecolor, Gaumont Color, Biocolor, Cinechrone, Cinecolorgraph, Lippmann, Sanger-Sheperd, Kromoscope—some of them subtractive, some additive, most now forgotten. A few achieved momentary successes. Charles Urban created a huge impact with his 1908 London showing of the Durbar in Delhi, and somewhat later with a color film of George V's coronation.

But despite the many attempts, effective natural color was still a long way off prior to World War I. It would come only after lengthy and expensive experiments begun by two MIT graduates, Herbert T. Kalmus and Daniel Comstock, who incorporated in 1915 as Technicolor, Inc. The first Technicolor feature was made as early as 1921 in a two-color process, *The Toll of the Sea*. Despite its crudeness it grossed more than $250,000. Investment interest grew, for the

financial prize bid fair to be enormous. In 1926 another major production revealed some of the early concerns about movie color. This was Douglas Fairbanks's *The Black Pirate*. The decision to film in Technicolor indicated the fears
and hopes associated with color. Fairbanks himself believed that no one had
better captured pirate themes than the American illustrator Howard Pyle,
whose studio in the Brandywine Valley was a nursery for many American artists.
"Personally," Fairbanks wrote, "I could not imagine piracy without color." But
he admitted that cinematic tradition argued differently. Film color was still
imperfect and undermined "the simplicity and directness which motion pictures derived from the unobtrusive black and white."[13] By the mid-twenties,
with several decades of film art behind them, some purists still insisted that a
new variable like color violated the medium's iconographic character. Although
this position was less aggressive than hostility to sound as an irreparable cinematic danger, it did represent a segment of critical opinion. Not so vigorous an
anticolor lobby as the opponents of chromolithography, these voices deserve
further study before we can be confident about their number or influence. Fairbanks himself tied their arguments to older standards. Similar objections had
been made to scenery when it was first installed on the English stage, he wrote.
The Black Pirate was no masterpiece; color, presumably, could not damage it.
One critic found it just another typical Hollywood melodrama, adolescent in its
values, but he was impressed by the delicate shades. The public had become
"used to the queer colorless world of the movies," Charles Taylor wrote, so *The
Black Pirate* had performed a service in bringing natural color to the screen.[14]

Thus one argument was carried on between those believing that film possessed natural black and white properties and those who did not. But the larger
issue concerned the technical accuracy of the color process and its potential
for distracting attention away from the story line and characterization. Most
critics admitted that color was bound to come. They differed on how to handle
it. Two-color Technicolor had many problems: its palette was reduced and distorting; it was expensive. Nonetheless, during the late twenties the Technicolor
Company enlarged its facilities for film development, refined its cameras,
sharpened its cost control, and produced a series of twelve two-reelers on a
variety of subjects, ranging from Betsy Ross and the creation of the American
flag to the divorce of Napoleon and Josephine. The climax to silent Technicolor
came in 1929 with a Metro-Goldwyn-Mayer production, Irving Thalberg's *The
Viking*. Expensive and elaborate, it failed, according to Herbert Kalmus, because of too many whiskers; movie audiences of the twenties, he wrote later,
liked their lovers smooth-shaven.[15]

What really changed things was the sound revolution. It caused problems
for older color films, which could not be used because they blocked the light

signals transmitting sound. But Kalmus believed its impact was favorable. Sound required so many radical production changes that it became easier for studio executives soon thereafter to contemplate the need for the different lighting conditions, set and costume design, and overall coordination that color filming required. With so much else turned upside down, promoters of Technicolor could argue that only slightly more effort would adjust studio practices.

The very scope and suddenness of the talking revolution suggested, moreover, an analogy with color, indicating that movies could become something different than they had been. Sound divided film history into two separate parts; silent production quickly ended. Advocates of color could argue that their innovation would bring the same kinds of basic changes to the screen. Studios grew interested in the Technicolor experiments, Warner Brothers signing on for more than twenty features. One of them, *On with the Show*, became the first all-talking, all-Technicolor feature, still in two-color. Because so many studios placed orders with Technicolor for film and processing, too many were made. The larger project got a bad reputation, which again is reminiscent of the impact of chromolithography in cheap editions a century earlier. Color was seen as the last refuge of an incompetent picture, resorted to only after poor story, score, acting, or direction had conspired to doom the result. The flight to color was presented as further evidence of Hollywood's effort to turn brass into gold.

But the issue was complex. One reviewer in 1930 condemned *The Song of the West* as an insipid operetta, uncompensated for by its color. But he found color redeemed, on the other hand, in a version of Villon's *Vagabond King*. "The naive enthusiasts who have been denouncing color in favor of black and white as the only 'art' form of the movies must be either color-blind or simply ignorant of the art quality. . . . color is one of the most important means of cinematic expression." [16] The irony, he pointed out, is that while color was derided by those professing to be concerned with cinema art, it was being developed by those to whom art was only a tribute vice paid to virtue. As in printing, film color was held suspect by traditionalists, who resented it as an intrusion.

Technicolor benefited by new attention. Between 1929 and 1930 it appropriated three million dollars for new equipment and further research. But the Depression hurt. The extra cost and critical abuse cut into orders. Solutions came from three areas. One was Walt Disney, who after trying Technicolor for a 1932 *Silly Symphony*, used it in 1933 for the animated equivalent of the FDR inaugural, *The Three Little Pigs*. A second source lay in corporate investors like John Hay Whitney and Cornelius Vanderbilt. With a former head of RKO they organized Pioneer Pictures to produce feature-length Technicolor films. The third source was technological, a three-color Technicolor which vastly improved reproductive quality. After more than thirty years of experimentation, movie color was finally about to blossom. To help coordinate the new art, Pioneer Pictures brought in Robert Edmund Jones, a student of Max Reinhardt and a stage designer for both the Provincetown Theater and the New York Theater Guild. First Jones helped produce an experimental short, released in mid 1934, *La Cucaracha,* the climax to fifteen years of Technicolor research and an investment of more than $6 million. In two reels and twenty minutes this obscure musical film convinced watchers in the Waldorf Astoria's Sert Room that color had come to stay. The following year came the first three-color Technicolor feature, which premiered at Radio City's Music Hall. This was *Becky Sharp,* based on a turn-of-the-century Langdon Mitchell play itself built, of course, on Thackeray's *Vanity Fair.* The film starred Miriam Hopkins, and was directed by Reuben Mamoulian, with Jones again serving as the color designer. Here was the first major moment for critics and observers to evaluate the color revolution, and the future direction of film. Interestingly enough, comments were mixed. This was not an unambiguous revolution. Technicolor stock did rise twenty-five points, and *Newsweek* devoted its cover and a feature story to *Becky Sharp* and its breakthrough.[17] But the *Catholic World* labeled the picture a flop, Otis Ferguson called it stagy and sentimental, and Grenville Vernon concluded that it was still too early to conclude "whether this new process is going to oust the present method of screen projection."[18] Many reviewers enthused about some of the color effects, however. William Troy in the *Nation* marked *Becky Sharp* as a new stage in cinema history, for it supplied "one more of the qualities which still separate" motion pictures "from life." The problem, he argued, was that color was "too plainly being exploited for its own sake" and not sufficiently fused with the plot line. On the limited surface of a screen set within a darkened theater, colors were dangerously close to taking over everything. The contrast-montage employed so successfully by Russian directors would be far more difficult in color.[19] Directorial skills were suddenly overtaxed. The very preoccupation with color problems, some critics felt, was diverting directors from their actual task, although what was now labelled the "monotony of black and white" had finally been challenged for costume dramas. As Otis Ferguson argued in a review entitled "New Wine and Old Bottles," the problem was that color made the producer "a kid in candy land," and his product was "as pleasing to the eye as a fresh-fruit sundae, but not much more." Be patient, Ferguson advised readers; it would take time. Only when color was transcended as an issue would the question of color film be settled.[20]

Without admiring all of Hollywood's products or displaying absolute confidence in the power of color as a dramatic instrument, most film critics expressed hope about its future and respect for the medium's integrity. Movie color will come into its own, *Time* magazine argued, when "producers can forget about it."[21] While this suggested a different world from that of printing (where color continued to arouse debate long after its acceptance as an instrument of illustration had ceased to be questioned), it showed a concern for restraint, for subordination of color to higher values, which at least indicated that film itself was capable of operating within an understandable canon of theatrical accomplishment.

During the next three or four years a series of Technicolor features appeared, including *Dancing Pirate* set in old Spanish California; *A Star Is Born; The Garden of Allah; Nothing Sacred; The Adventures of Robin Hood;* and *The Trail of the Lonesome Pine*, a cinematic version of John Fox's gripping West Virginia novel, starring Henry Fonda, Sylvia Sidney, Fred MacMurray, and Spanky McFarland. This was the first Technicolor film shot out of doors, and to some came "pretty close to long-sought perfection," its natural color adding to rather than distracting from its dramatic impact.[22] On seeing it one columnist insisted "Within three years there can't be a movie made in black and white."[23] While others were more restrained, pictures like this convinced them that a color education program of vast importance was about to be unleashed. "Color atrocities will be relegated to the depths of oblivion," one enthusiast wrote in a printing journal, after talking with Henry Hathaway, director of *The Trail of the Lonesome Pine*. Manufacturers of furniture, rugs, and clothing would gradually abolish their gaudy, tasteless, highly ornamental items as color pictures led to a new conception of restrained harmony.[24] Like color printing a century before, it was still possible to think of the change in traditional terms, as part of a program of public refinement, enlightening and inspirational as well as entertaining.

In these first few years, reviewers evaluated the use of the new Technicolor medium specifically according to how color direction and camera work aided the larger intentions of the films.[25] But within three or four years of the first three-color production, the issue had been settled. By 1939 or 1940 some reviewers in newspapers and magazines were no longer bothering to mention that films they were considering had been shot in color, even though, prior to World War II, color productions still included only a small minority of all of Hollywood's features. Unlike sound, the problems color posed could not be instantly solved, nor was its logic so inescapable as to make black and white films obsolete.

But by the early forties the discussion had largely ended. Occasionally in later years a newly released film made special use of color and this would arouse comment. But these were rarities. Apart from technical journals color in films disappears as an aesthetic issue.

In fact it was not until the age of television began in the 1950s that color became standard. Seeking more obvious contrasts between movie-going and home television, film producers turned increasingly to spectacular techniques like the wide screen, three-dimensionality, and color. Increasingly black and white became a special effect, used only when budgetary limits demanded it, or when the director wished to make a statement through the self-imposed limitation of the black and white tradition. What black and white did for most viewers by the sixties, however, was to project a sense of time, giving the talking film an historic past. If the coming of color to periodicals had encouraged a sense of spatial hierarchy, compartmentalizing the illustrated function within different categories, the rise of Technicolor encouraged temporal distinctions, endowing the medium with a clearly defined tradition. But few noticed this. For while the Technicolor novelty had stimulated extraordinary excitement, this lasted only about four or five years, to be followed by critical indifference. Largely a self-conscious commercial strategy by monopolists who exacted royalties from all filmmakers, it had both a clear beginning and, apparently, an end. Most assumed color would be as pervasive as it was inevitable, although there were some lingering regrets about the loss of older conventions. Under some circumstances "Technicolor," as an adjective, would bear a faintly pejorative tone, but one much milder than "chromo-civilization." Unlike books or journals, films could not be customized. Once an improvement appeared it was difficult to avoid universal application. It was true that for a decade or two people viewed the screen in both color and black and white. Newsreels, serials, and half a double feature would frequently be without color. But these were by-stations on the road to a world that would soon be entirely in color.

If Technicolor modified many of the experiences and values associated with color printing, television exaggerated the contrasts still further. Its adoption of color revealed a world with fundamentally different standards, built around the presence of what many critics found to be a disappointing but dangerous medium. The search for technical perfection in television color proved more controversial than the slow achievement of Technicolor. It is a fascinating story of scientific intrigue, economic delay, and political postponement, climaxed by a sudden, overwhelming, and even unexpected victory for one of the competitors. If the achievement took longer than many at first expected, its diffusion was ultimately more impressive.

As a national system television was almost ready for deployment by the late 1930s, but the coming of the war put it into a holding pattern.[26] By the time of full demobilization in the late 1940s, television sets had begun to sell and stations to multiply. In the first days of this take-off many programmers and manufacturers believed color was imminent and expected it to have a stronger impact on television than on the motion picture. The screen was so much smaller that color would be able to provide a lot more information; it could even give the illusion of depth. It would make baseball and basketball easier to follow, and, above all, add attractiveness to the food, furnishings, and automobiles that advertisers wanted to sell. The stakes were high. Every commentator tried to estimate just how high they were.

Maneuverings began as early as 1946 when CBS tried to get an experimental system approved by the FCC; lagging technically, NBC forced a three-year postponement. But by 1949 the FCC, after assembling more than 11,000 pages of testimony, in some forty volumes, reported that only one color system seemed ready for American use, and that was a field sequential system developed in the laboratories of the Columbia Broadcasting System. Most who saw the CBS color admired it. The system employed a rotating color filter placed in front of the television camera, and required a color disc or wheel attached to the television set. Color seemed on the way.

In fact it would take another fifteen years for anything significant to happen. One reason was commercial rivalry. In printing, many individual inventors and entrepreneurs had promoted different kinds of improvement. In film, there was only the one major sustained effort involving Technicolor, and everything waited upon its perfection. But television had two major claimants. One was CBS. The other was RCA, the parent of the largest and most successful television network in the world. It was RCA which had forced a postponement in 1946 and which proposed to the FCC its own system. However, according to most observers, in 1949 that system was far from adequate. Describing it, *Variety* ran a headline entitled "RCA Lays an Off-Color Egg."[27] Neither the color fidelity nor the texture was acceptable; critics labelled it too soft and easily contaminated.

Racing for time, trying to improve their systems, RCA and NBC sought further postponements. They had one thing going for them. The CBS system not only required a mechanical color wheel, limiting the size of the screen; it meant that color broadcasting could not be received by existing black and white sets in any form, that is, not without buying and attaching a converter costing at least thirty or forty dollars. It was, in short, a noncompatible system. Sarnoff and RCA went on the offensive, attacking the CBS picture as a tin lizzie, a reversion to a mechanical scanning system, and the FCC as a dictatorship. Television manufacturers like Admiral, Emerson, Hallicrafters, and others, declared the FCC decision a threat to the American Way of Life, taking out full-page advertisements in major newspapers to develop their case further. Allen Dumont appeared on his own network ridiculing the CBS system as a Model-T picture, showing the huge wheel necessary for a thirty-inch screen. Some critics suggested that the reason manufacturers were anxious was that the black and white market had not yet been saturated, and a new color system raised the threat of uncertainty. In 1949 and 1950 there were millions of black and white sets still to be sold.[28] But how could manufacturers and retailers sell them when an entirely new color system lay on the horizon?

RCA and the appliance industry did more than simply protest. They took the FCC to court, and obtained an injunction in Chicago from three federal judges, suspending the FCC decision. CBS, meanwhile, was forced to delay its plans to broadcast in color. Finally, the FCC's argument won the day. The injunction was overturned, the color war was over, and on June 25, 1951, the first commercially sponsored color television program was broadcast by CBS over a five-city cable hookup.[29] Some sixteen sponsors lined up to present Arthur Godfrey, Gary Moore, Faye Emerson, and Ed Sullivan. There were in existence only thirty or so television sets able to receive this show, but CBS scattered them over the five cities, and began to anticipate the $150 million in royalties that it expected its system to provide. Again color television seemed to have arrived.

But had it? The critics were not certain what it all meant. The vigorous and bitter rivalry between the two networks had helped to emphasize, once more, the blatantly commercial objectives which had taken over programming. Those who were already suspicious of the cultural impact of television had their worst fears justified. Color is coming to television, Goodman Ace wrote in 1950. What will they think of next, he asked. And answered, "Good shows, may we hope?" Even with delicate colorings, he argued, the bad shows on television would remain lousy. The principal effect of color would be on commercials. "It is a little bleak looking at the new refrigerator stacked with all those heads of green lettuce, oblongs of yellow butter, bunches of red radishes," without the enhancement of color. "If you happen to be a refrigerator," Ace concluded, good for you, but at the moment television's problems of providing good entertainment were so basic that it seemed foolhardy to try to tackle the color question.[30] In another essay, written six months later, Ace extended his view that color was a transfusion television found necessary to arouse it from "its coma of monotony." Color was as old as Nature. And now, Ace concluded "that the gentlemen of television have borrowed color from Creation is it asking too much to hope for a little creation to go along with that color?"[31]

These opinions were seconded by Robert Lewis Shayon in his review of the first CBS colorcast. It was an heroic moment, said Shayon, a landmark in the history of invention. "The thrill of discovery is over—landfall. . . . Surely this is something for man to shout to the stars. . . . The lonely inspirations . . . the slow accumulation of operational knowledge in many lands . . . the brotherhood of science, the crescendo of invention, experiment, abstraction, finance, and mass production" had thundered to a climax. And yet, Shayon mused, there must be something more to the accomplishment than Ed Sullivan and Faye Emerson. "It cannot be that for this alone the scientific wizards of western civilization have prophesied and labored."[32] So suspiciously was television viewed by many critics then, that color sets, the most complex consumer commodity that had ever been mass produced (some producers argued proudly) seemed like a wooden victory, a source of shame, a measuring stick to berate all involved with the industry. Promise, wonder, and respect, associated with color innovations in previous media, were replaced by irony and a concentration on the financial and purely commercial aspects of the innovation.[33]

In any event, the 1951 promise of color television came to very little. As American involvement in Korea grew, so did military production; Charles E. Wilson, seeking to concentrate the limited number of electronic engineers on defense matters, asked CBS to postpone production of color television. CBS agreed immediately. In fact, *Time* suggested that Frank Stanton, plagued by rising costs and continuing technical problems, was probably relieved.[34] And the CBS effort totally and inexplicably stopped. It was replaced by an enormously expensive but sustained effort by NBC which saw its opportunity and took it, under Sarnoff's prodding. The 1950s were years of red ink, for Sarnoff plunked down some $130 million for development of cameras, picture tubes, and a system of producing effective color television sets. He got FCC approval in the early 1950s and spent the rest of the decade making slow but perceptible improvements. Ten years after the first CBS broadcast, on February 17, 1961, NBC ran what it called Color Day, programming all its shows that day in color. Patience was required to tune the sets in properly, and although critics commented on the "faintly unrealistic air" of color, they admitted that it enlivened daytime soap opera and variety shows.[35]

But as of this date fewer than 1 percent of American homes had color television sets; just 147,000 sets were sold that year, out of a total of six million television sets sold nationally, a pitiful 2.5 percent, and this after ten years and a huge dollar investment. But in 1961 the end of the beginning was in sight; other manufacturers besides RCA now began to interest themselves in the color field—Zenith, General Electric, Philco, Sylvania. While CBS had just about stopped its color broadcasting, and ABC did very little, NBC planned to offer more than 1600 hours of color in 1962. By 1963, sixty million black and white sets were operating in America, and 1.2 million in color, a small percentage, but the color sets were starting to take off. The signs of a massive shift had begun. Walt Disney left his black and white show on ABC to come to NBC and color. Eastman Kodak dropped the Ed Sullivan show on CBS to cosponsor the new Disney productions, while automobile manufacturers like Chrysler and food processors like Kraft were displaying new interest. By 1965 a boom was underway; 1.5 million color sets were sold, the price of the least expensive models came down to below $400, and NBC planned to broadcast 96 percent of its prime-time shows in color. Between 1963 and 1969 color went from having an outlet in 3 percent of America's TV households to 33 percent.[36] After all the premature expectations, manufacturers now found they had underestimated demand, and waiting lists developed. By the early seventies, eight years after the boom began, color dominated all network broadcasting.

It was particularly impressive, as Goodman Ace suggested, for commercials. Prophecies paid less attention to color's impact on the medium as an aesthetic device than to its selling power. Changes in packaging were seen as one likely result. Sol Polk, a major Chicago appliance dealer, predicted happily that color would produce a new form of obsolescence. Not only advertisements but programs as well could feature the latest color schemes in clothing, furniture, and accessories, training viewers in differentiating the up-to-the-minute from the passé.[37] Programming itself received little mention. "The addition of color," Leo Bogart wrote in an early study of television, published in 1956, would do little to the medium except to give it a "more realistic and natural character" and heighten the possibility for artistry in dramatic shows. But Bogart went on to admit that color would permit television to compete more effectively with magazines, whose color supplements until then had been the most sensuous translation of product quality to the buying public.[38]

Because television was so new when color appeared, there was little in the way of any aesthetic tradition to defend. The movies, at least, had thirty years of black and white cinematography behind them, and a corps of master directors. But television's Golden Age was entirely a retrospective invention. The views of Goodman Ace and Robert Shayon were shared by others like Saul Carson, who condemned the absence of experimental deviation. Video was imitating "radio's general mediocrity," he insisted, recapitulating the "race between merchants and moral innocents." However limitless the possibilities of television for education and entertainment, "what interests our TV planners most is putting war paint on Milton Berle."[39]

Thus, color for critics in the sixties as in the fifties, was a purely technical addition. They narrated the technological and commercial warfare, evaluated the technical improvements, and treated the entire episode as primarily an engineering and marketing adventure. Conflict continued as the RCA system competed with French and German versions for domination of Europe, just as Zeniths and Motorolas would compete with Sonys and Hitachis. But this was comparison shopping on an economic and technical level, newsworthy mainly for consumer magazines or international correspondents. By the 1970s television color had become a self-conscious commercial strategy designed to sell receivers. It was unhampered by any resistance based on a defense of existing aesthetic standards; it was succeeded by no subsequent critical reconsideration or continuing qualitative discussion; and it became even more pervasive in its spread and coverage than in its ownership.

For unlike printing, and even motion pictures, once a significant portion of the market had been penetrated television went over to color quickly and universally, even in local and educational versions. Advertisers, at first reluctant to spend the extra money, and then willing to do it under certain occasions, decided that they could not have commercials in color while sponsoring a black and white production, or permit commercials to be in black and white while accompanying a color show. In the one case they looked flamboyant; in the other, cheap. Unlike the pages of a magazine, or even the experience of a theatre's newsreels or second feature, television proved to be an all-or-nothing medium. Black and white merely demonstrated that the material was dated, historical, important from a documentary or aesthetic standpoint, or had been filmed under exacting and special circumstances, abroad, or in combat. Old films, newsreels, photographs, even old television shows appeared on the screen, but they represented history. Television color influenced the movie studios simply as a threat. As early as 1950 news reports had studio executives "trembling at the thought of being caught with their vaults full of black and white film when color TV comes along to keep moviegoers at home."[40] In any event, from then on most of Hollywood's movies were shot in color; in time this extended to just about everything.

Color television is not literally omnipresent. There are households without color, just as there are households without television. But they are a minority. And we seem better able to enjoy black and white in media other than television. Photographs, old movies, news magazines of the 1930s and 1940s, and of course, etchings and engravings exert extraordinary aesthetic appeal today. Indeed, they have something of the attraction Italian pre-Raphaelitism did for Victorians fatigued by the luxuriance of contemporary painting. But black and white television has little appeal in itself. Once tasted, color television seems difficult to give up.

If less dispensable, it can be argued that the color addition is also less influential. Although previous eras could be labelled as Chromo-Civilizations or Technicolor Generations, this is hardly a "color television age." Color was more obvious, perhaps, in an older day when blue shirts were worn on black-and-white television to guarantee white brightness. Nonetheless, this is a time when the ability to reproduce color is taken for granted and when its use—in buildings, dress, furniture, utensils—has become less inhibited than ever. This may owe something perhaps to the power of eclecticism in every area of design, to new materials and methods, and to the presumed relationship between personal fulfillment and visual expression. But some, surely, comes from the colors added to personal vocabularies through the mediation of photography, motion pictures, and television.

It remains, then, to determine the meaning of this movement of color from one medium to another. I admit that the survey may possess more interest than the destination. But there perhaps is one larger point. Although we live in an age with greater variety of color than ever before, with packagers, designers, and manufacturers endlessly debating the names and combinations of color for use in products and advertising, awareness of color as an intellectual problem seems much diminished. One hundred years ago color preferences could stimulate questions about the fate of public taste or the philosophical meaning of reproduction as a substitute for encounters with original art. Fifty years ago, the rise of Technicolor still touched off arguments about the canons of realism and the level of public culture. But by the time of the television age, color had become primarily a matter for commercial and technical translation. Its impact was to be measured almost entirely in the hours of television watched, the number of receivers sold, and the intensity of impact possessed by commercials.

This diminution has been accompanied by what seems to me a lessening of public interest in color theory, color therapy, and color ideologies writ large. I except, of course, the scientific and artistic communities. The impoverishment of color discussion exemplifies the complex relationship between words and pictures in an age of mechanical reproduction. The very specificity of color, its status as the best-protected bastion against two-dimensional replication, has made it an object of longing for inventors and promoters. But the closer color brought each medium to greater visual fidelity, the more it closed off any fundamental debate, for the ultimate aim of the designers was to make color natural and nondistracting. In printing this meant transcending the glaring vulgarity of chromolithography. For film it involved planning sets and camera work so that brightly colored objects would not distract from characterization or the actual story line. And in television it meant evaluating the claims of rival systems to determine which offered the most faithful representation. The better the process, the greater the illusion of perfect reproduction. But this involved, in effect, deflecting discussions of color symbolism, color moods, and color therapies, because once natural colors had been achieved there seemed no point to further development. Easy evocation has thus eclipsed even the larger history of color as an intellectual problem, except among technicians bent on recovering the history of invention.

In the twenties and thirties, excited by colored magazine ads, Technicolor, plastics, and home photography, modern Americans awaited a new era of color salvation.[41] Color was installed in asylum rooms to speed recovery: red chambers for depressives, yellow for hysterical paralytics, blue for the violent.[42] Engineers placed colors on moving machine parts to diminish fatigue and improve industrial safety. School boards experimented with yellow chalk on green blackboards. Hospital clinics substituted bluish green for white surgical smocks and theater walls. Color engineers showed stores how to increase sales, and factories how to improve production.[43] In Chicago Amos Alonzo Stagg fitted out two dressing rooms for his 1928 football team: a blue one for rest, a red one for fight-talks. Howard Ketchum, Faber Birren, Matthew Luckiesh, and others published attacks on "mental color-blindness." "The shackles of so-called culture are dissolved by the declaration of independence," Luckiesh wrote in 1938 of new color influences.[44] All this had been made possible by a chromatic revolution.

Printing and photography seemed to support these broader views. The promise of color movies nourished them. And television helped make them irrelevant. For so long a preoccupation, stimulus, and spur to cosmic views, color has been lost in colors. The search for technical perfection and universal audiences has succeeded in covering its tracks. Walter Benjamin used the phrase "reception in a state of distraction" to characterize changes in apperception.[45] The history of critical responses to color reproduction may suggest one way of determining how this developed, and places some of the responsibility, at least, on the critics as well as the media.

16

Pictorial Perils:

The Rise of

American Illustration

T he approaching end of centuries tends to produce retrospection. It was to be expected, then, that during the 1890s many commentaries on the evolution of American art during its first hundred years appeared in print. Written mainly by critics and artists, several of these summaries concentrated on a relative newcomer exhibiting unusual vigor and promise. This newcomer, of course, was book and periodical illustration.

As they surveyed the distance that separated the crude wood engravings of antebellum years from the flourishing engraving industry of a later day, commentators waxed eloquent about the triumphs of national skill. A galaxy of great names had sprung up, most within the previous quarter century, many associated with specialized techniques and subjects. There were illustrators who concentrated on military camps or western scenes, or upon farm and rural settings; there were those known for their presentations of women, of blacks, or of landscapes; still others who featured eighteenth-century America, sixteenth-century England, nineteenth-century France, or the exotic Middle and Far

From Gerald W. R. Ward, *The American Illustrated Book in the Nineteenth Century* (Winterthur, Del.: Winterthur Museum, 1987), 3–19. Reprinted with permission of the publisher.

East. However laggard the efforts of our sculptors and painters, a cohort of celebrities dominated the more intimate and domestic art of illustration—Pyle, Abbey, Pennell, Remington, Gibson, Frost, Kemble, Christy, and Smedley among them. "If we would find where in the world of art the artist is most sure of winning and keeping the heart of the people," Philip Paulding wrote in *Munsey's*, "we must turn to illustration. . . . Here the very practicality which has retarded our appreciation of ideal art is a potent factor in our enjoyment of the artist's work. We care less, as a people, for the lofty canvasses of some modern Rafael, than for the more tangible and useful excellences of beautiful books and handsome periodicals." "Perhaps in no other direction has America progressed more rapidly than in the making of attractive, illustrated books," Arthur Hoeber argued in the *Bookman* in 1899. And the progress was recent. Harold Payne, examining periodicals and children's books of the early part of the century, found them of "the crudest character, primitive in coloring as well as in expression." Hoeber himself, browsing through the first issues of *Scribner's*, fresh from the press only thirty years before, was amazed that "such performances could have passed current," their figures "wretchedly proportioned, ridiculously out of drawing and false in all the relations." Composition was even worse; "criticism fails here," Hoeber concluded, drawing a discreet veil over the more vigorous condemnation he might have employed.[1]

The growth achieved was multiple. Some involved the evolution of technique, a mastery displayed by the younger illustrators, particularly in their capacity to adapt to new reproductive media like the halftone. Further evidence of advancement was expanded international reputation, particularly in Europe, acknowledgment by laymen and other artists that illustration deserved critical attention and respect. And finally there were the salaries, glamorous and impressive on their own, testament to the conviction of publishers and editors that pictures paid. Running through the commentaries was a sense of new status for the illustrator, as distinguished American painters began to accept illustrated commissions and an increasing number of illustrators began to produce their own written texts. As early as 1882, William A. Coffin devoted an entire paper to painter-illustrators like Robert Baum, J. W. Alexander, William Merritt Chase, and Edwin Blashfield. These commanding figures brought to the field of illustration their insistence on autonomy. And, even more important, they transmitted a special individuality. Illustration would no longer have to rely on standardized if arbitrary conventions. These artists took orders from no one and insisted upon establishing their own style of design. This was still novel in the eighties and nineties. George Wharton Edwards, in an 1897 article describing how books were illustrated, argued that it was not until the 1880s that artists could even choose their own subjects within the text. "If Sir Galahad in the lines of the manuscript grasped the heroine by the arm, then the artist must so show him in the picture." The artist "was not expected to exercise his own imagination; and so art was still in fetters."[2]

These new artist-specialists, each associated with a personal style and a category of subject material, might well have been making New York, in William Hobbs's phrase, "the world's Bohemia of illustration" and American illustrators the envy of their European counterparts.[3] Few denied the skill or originality with which so many of these artists' generation tackled its commissions. But the achievement of this golden age was not without certain costs. Some among the celebrants grew suspicious about this new national dependence on pictures, raising questions not about artistic talent but about cultural meaning. I hasten to add that dissenters were far from a majority. Most Americans simply enjoyed their illustrations, and the literature of description is overwhelmingly favorable. But the discontents, if sometimes covert and disguised and invariably outnumbered, nonetheless exposed fundamental anxieties. And they have been largely ignored.

What were the objections to increasing illustration? They can be subdivided. First came concerns about accuracy. In this era of vigorous publication, verbal truthfulness was abused by many books and periodicals. But it was possible to check these facts; conventions and sources were clearly established. Visual inaccuracy, however, was more difficult to spot, at least without special knowledge or advance warning. And it was, apparently, common.

The *Nation*, for example, a leading critic of the excesses of illustration, grew exercised about some pictures in the *Philadelphia Public Ledger*. When it featured a story on a new French man-of-war, a ferocious, mastless boat with two towers of circular galleries for rifles and Gatling guns, the *Ledger* presented a cut of a three-masted ship under full sail. The *Nation* was furious. Absolute accuracy, it admitted, lay beyond the reach of most human beings. But newspapers had an obligation to cling to truth. The effort to feature pictures as a means of enticing readership was wrongheaded. "The reform . . . most needed in journalism today," the *Nation* concluded, "is not fresh or better means, like cuts, of spreading abroad 'things that are not so,' but improved means of making what appears in the paper more credible."[4]

The turn to pictures in documentary reporting was one thing, but many of the most prominent illustrators were tied to fiction. Here the issue of accuracy grew more complex. A series of angry letters and editorials, in bookish journals of the nineties and later, focused on a second concern: the artist's poetic license, apparently wider than the universe created by the written text. "I know that artists are privileged beings," one Edwin Carlile Litsey wrote in a letter to the *Critic*, "that they are supposed to possess attributes which would

blast a common mortal. . . . And yet, beneath all their glamour and high migh-
tiness," he continued, they ate, slept, and got sick just like everyone else. Why
should they be "given the right of way above their fellow artisans who labor
with letters and words?" Authors who used words incorrectly, or changed the
color of a heroine's eyes, received a torrent of abuse. Artists got little, although
they were themselves frequently inconsistent. When authors described ladies
in straw hats, the artists dressed them in derbies; they showed the heroine in a
carriage rather than on horseback as the writer intended; a wrecked auto was
drawn as it bumped into a tree, not a wall. "The ineptitudes of so-called illustrations," a Dorothea Moore wrote from San Francisco, "have become so common that every one expects them."[5]

The *New York Times* Saturday Review of Books and Art was a favorite
arena for critics of artistic carelessness to have their say. "It is sometimes hard
to decide at the present day whether we are glad or sorry to hear that a favorite
volume is to appear in an illustrated edition," the *Times* admitted. Prepared by
the author's words with a vivid mental picture, the reader was surely shocked
"to turn a page only to be confronted by an utterly commonplace or meaningless
illustration." Agreeing with the newspaper, Bret Gyle wrote in to ask the purpose of book illustration. He was confused. Pictures, he felt, appealed mainly
to those unreachable by words, "unable to feel and appreciate the inward spirit
of the writer." It was useless "if not absurd," he continued, "to illustrate such
works as Dickens, when the author takes chapters to bring an image before us.
Should our ideals, formed under the guidance of a master hand, be crushed or
perverted by the conception of another?" he asked. "Surely not," was the
equally emphatic answer. The spread of illustration endangered individual
thought.[6]

Naturally enough, defenders insisted that illustration was a harmless
pleasure which enhanced the impact of a great novel, but protests continued.
Even great figures like Howard Pyle, Howard Chandler Christy, and Henry Hutt
("chalky nothings that are an insult to both intelligence and taste") were not
immune. Why do publishers insist on illustrating everything? one letter writer
asked the *Times*. "Are they trying to pauperize our imagination, or do they think
the public hasn't any?"[7]

Some serious critics steered a middle course. Hobbs, a defender of illustration, did single out some poorly illustrated volumes and condemned the care-
less pictures of best-sellers like F. Marion Crawford's *Katherine Lauderdale*
(1894) and Charles Major's *When Knighthood Was in Flower* (1898). But he
enthusiastically supported literary-artistic collaboration. Praising Edwin Austin
Abbey's work for *She Stoops to Conquer*, Arthur Burdett Frost's illustrations for

Uncle Remus, and the achievements of Pyle, Rufus Zogbaum, and Thure de Thulstrup, Hobbs posited the sympathy between "the man of letters and the man of art" as a great contribution of the age, so successful that illustrators occasionally inspired authors to reshape their characters. In Hobbs's view, illustration had moved from merely embellishing the text "to the dignity of a literary performance. It can no longer be regarded as a mere accessory to, but rather as a part of, the book itself."[8] Because the drift of bookmaking was toward unity of design, this meant a more creative role for the illustrator, and Hobbs was all for that. He simply opposed unconscious liberties taken with an author's conception. When harmony characterized the relationship, Hobbs saw no danger from the enhanced status of the illustrator. The pictures, in his view, were simply an element in the larger work.

But other critics became alarmed, not by the mere presence of inaccuracy, but at the challenge offered by the illustrator's imagination. The importance of the reading experience and the integrity of the author's vision were both threatened. A picture, the *Atlantic Monthly* observed, could actually hinder understanding, for "the modern illustrator frequently leaves his author behind, and tracks off into the human wilderness in independent quest." The *Atlantic Monthly* admitted the value of pictures for obscure things and unusual people; essays on Tibet or China, descriptions of the making of a compass— these were subjects demanding illustration. But novels of Indian life were perfectly comprehensible without illustrated commentary; their pictures simply added a burden to the reader's shoulders. Certain illustrations could reduce "a book or a magazine to a mere picture album."[9]

Particularly at Christmastime, the new brand of illustrated holiday books, a genre in which the text was just about the least important aspect of the book, showed how far prettiness might go. Elaborate bindings, dreamy halftones, and extensive decorations all counted for more than any words. The illustrator was charged with making the popular book into an artifact, a commodity whose primary purpose was less to transmit an author's intention than to adorn a library table or make a properly expensive present. And when the illustrator insisted on his own artistic dignity, when he followed his own vision, he posed a danger because of textual diversions or inaccuracies. Seriousness of intention, then, was no absolute protection.

Some sensed the profundity of this shift toward pictorialism. As a device to obtain public attention, the picture was unrivaled. Pictures, as the *New York Times* pointed out in 1901, had existed before written language; the illuminations and woodcuts of the first printed books were "made to appeal to a wider audience." Books adopted the same techniques as the moralities in the miracle plays; both sought objectivity, "the one by drawings, the other by action." It was no wonder then that the contemporary writer "owed a large debt to his illustrator." [10]

But providing a traditional pedigree hardly described the expanded treatment pictures now received. Among other places, they were invading the classroom. One educator, Estelle Hurll, found the speed of the change breathtaking but admirable. "The curriculum of study has been largely disciplinary in character, intended to train the memory and the reasoning powers," she argued, constructed to supply the mind with information. Such an approach ignored the imagination and the aesthetic sense. Only the study of pictures, she suggested, could restore this part of the human sensibility. Distinct from the earlier movement to train future artisans and designers through drawing classes, the new art education reflected a sense that pictures formed an increasing basis for judgment and ideation. They required incorporation into the program of study. Pictures had long been accepted as a fundamental part of children's literature, and they dominated textbooks for the very young. But now the picture itself was proposed as a subject for popular study. Pictorialism constituted so large a part of the adult encounter with literature and popular journalism that preparation for its appreciation seemed vital. Progressive educators were, at just this time, seeking ways to reduce the distance between the classroom and the world of daily work and leisure. Picture study formed one bridge. [11]

But the association of bright and simple illustrations with juvenile reading tastes may have helped to raise still another issue associated with the new pictorialism: its threat to cerebration, its apparent regression to a more primitive system of communication. References to stained glass and miracle plays as instruments of enlightenment did not help. Reacting to a proposal by French critic and historian John Grand-Carteret for a series of historical picture books, the *Nation* turned to this line of attack. Grand-Carteret apparently believed that those "who come to scoff at history in uninteresting type" might "remain to pray over history tricked out with all the charm of the illustrator's art." There was logic to the proposal, the *Nation* admitted, but hardly ground for satisfaction. The problem was this notion that "the growing aversion to reading, and the increasing fondness for labor-saving and the thought-saving graphic representation" signaled progress. The *Nation* saw in it only a "distinct reversion to barbarism," being nothing more or less than "a recurrence to the picture-writing and sign-language of savages." The lengthy step from using images for thought conveyance to the more complex (but more accurate) method of language was, sociologically speaking, an immense advance. "Modern man can get along with the old ways," the *Nation* admitted; they might not, by themselves, destroy civilization. But it was a "civilization under difficulties, not its supreme and happy development." [12]

Several years earlier, the *Nation* had argued that dependence on pictures for news was producing a childish view of the world. Complex diplomatic disputes had been reduced to portraits of the protagonists. Youthful readers wanting to know something about the disturbances in Brussels were "satisfied with a picture of the King's palace." In fact, pictures were not, and never could be, up to the task of complex explanation. Only extended narratives could provide such interpretation. The increasing pictorialism of journalism, designed to provide a come-on for those who did not much enjoy reading, was bound to produce continuing degeneracy in mental powers and taste. Pictures, wrote John Hopkins Denison, were fine for untrained minds and children, but with "an educated audience a well-turned description is more effective."[13]

If pictures were not capable of adequately transmitting the complexity demanded by modern life, this was the more troubling because the expansion of book and magazine illustration was accompanied, at century's end, by a series of other changes emphasizing the power of the new pictorialism. And some of these trends attracted far more vigorous, aggressive criticism than did the illustrators. One such development was the rise of photographic representation. Photographs, in magazines, books, and newspapers, formed part of the new illustration; their presence appeared to relieve illustrators from certain tasks. Moreover, the popularity of photographic illustration directly involved the technological capacities of the halftone process, becoming a dominant form by century's end. However, it is not this aspect of photography that I single out here but the spread of camera ownership and the growth of the snapshot. By the 1880s Americans and Europeans were growing accustomed to photographs as renditions of people and places, particularly when they were prominent or newsworthy. What was new was the ability of millions of people, with relatively little training or money, to create their own illustrated records, to prowl the countryside, to stalk famous personalities, to pose family members, to attend great events like inaugurals and expositions, all for the mere purpose of accumulating photographic facsimiles, which could then be displayed as evidence of artistic skill or personal daring to friends or interested amateurs. The success of George Eastman in marketing his Kodak meant that the habit of picture-taking was now becoming as widespread, perhaps more widespread, than the habit of picture-looking.[14]

Each person could now be his own artist. And it was not simply a printed text but the life that lay around him that he illustrated. Pictures were becoming personal documents, increasingly a substitute for words as instruments of expression. For although the camera fiend brought many annoyances, including invasion of privacy, destruction of rural peace and solitude, monomaniacal obsession with lenses and lighting and posing (at the risk of personal friendship and social tranquility), there were other, more profound problems associated with the democratization of picture-making. One was analogous to the dilemma of illustrated inaccuracy: the possibility of staging photographs to make them more flattering or artistic. Because (whatever theorists have to say) photographs were popularly supposed to bear a special relationship to objective truth. A photograph that lied or exaggerated was more dangerous than a painting or an etching that did so. It was more dangerous because it seemed more convincing. Photographs, moreover, could be—and were—retouched in the late nineteenth century, and this occasioned considerable debate in amateur circles. But most important, perhaps, photographs could substitute for verbal description, and increasing reliance on them could impoverish both the imagination and the vocabulary.

It was difficult to make this argument in dealing with something as simple and innocent as family albums and casual snapshots. But once the photograph had been mounted on a piece of cardboard and sent through the mail, an entirely different sensibility stood revealed, one that could be effectively attacked. The rise of the picture postcard during the 1890s spelled just such an instance of a vulgarizing pictorialism to its many critics. Picture postcards could be assaulted from different directions. Many, of course, were simply illustrations, comic or sentimental, and could be derided on the grounds of their crudity, their sentimentality, or their silliness. But the increasing use of cards with photographed landscapes and architectural views suggested, on the one hand, an atrophy of descriptive powers and, on the other, dependence on standardized conceptions of the physical world. At one time the travel letter was a lengthy and fascinating document, highly personalized, filled with social commentary and extensive descriptions. These observations formed the basis of many books. Although much of the language, particularly the description of views, was highly standardized, the act of writing such letters forced a degree of self-consciousness, an attention both to what was being observed and to the letter's recipient. Written description seemed to demand more extended and more concentrated observation than did the selection of a small card, on which just a few lines could be scribbled, the picture substituting for more individualized responses. The picture postcard and the snapshot were, from one point of view, somewhat different eruptions of pictorialism. The postcard was anathema because of its easy standardization of response, the casual, nonthinking, passive approach to correspondence and to confronting experience that it suggested.[15] The snapshot was more personal and aggressive, since it involved a set of decisions and framing acts. But what they shared was a reliance on an image to make a point that had previously been made by words. Both involved a challenge to traditional devices of transmitting attitude and information, substituting the authority of the commercial entrepreneur, the postcard shop, and the tourist industry on the one hand, and a subjective, sometimes aggressively eccentric view of people and objects on the other. Neither form of pictorialization was content to accept the older, verbal canons. They were challenges to the rules.

A second large area of challenge involved the increasing dependence on pictures to sell products and experiences, in the form of commercial advertisement in newspapers and magazines and, more distressing perhaps, in the development of the poster. With our new regard for art nouveau and for fin de siècle graphic design, we look back fondly on the great age of Chéret, Steinlen, Beardsley, Klinger, Klimt, Mucha, Moser, and their American counterparts. Certainly the reputations of Bradley, Penfield, Leyendecker, and Parrish have never stood higher. But in fact, there were those who found the lurid colors, the distorted drawing, the sometimes grotesque juxtapositions of the new poster art to be disorienting, dangerous, and disturbing. Admittedly European artists were more radically subjective than Americans, but the American posters could still challenge the cause of careful draftsmanship and artistic propriety. This, along with other forms of pictorial advertising, was mercenary art in the service of selling products.[16] At one time art had been suspect because of its eager service to the cause of church and state, a willing prop to tyranny and superstition. Now, the cause was commercial rather than political, but the prostituting role of pictures and of artists was unmistakable. Advertising design could be charged, then, not only with challenging the conventions of drawing, coloring, and composition and with demeaning public taste but also with selling its services to the highest bidder. In its appeals to irrationalism, fed by psychological analyses of human motivation which began to appear regularly shortly after the turn of the century, the new pictorialism spelled a regression and an abandonment of the protections that verbal expression had brought with it to a credulous humanity.

A second aspect of the growth of a debasing and demoralizing pictorial art lay in the response to comic strips which, in Sunday supplements to newspapers, were beginning to attract attention in the 1890s and were perceived as a national menace not too long thereafter. Critics of the comics, like Ralph Bergengren writing in 1906, declared them to be a mechanistic, market-oriented menace, with "a confusing medley of impossible countrymen, mules, goats, German-Americans and their irreverent progeny, specialized children with a genius for annoying their elders . . . policemen, Chinamen, Irishmen, negroes, . . . boy inventors," a cast of characters without "respect for property, respect for parents, for law, for decency, for truth, for beauty, for kindliness, for dignity, or for honor." They were violent, brutal, coarse, and vulgar. "Physical pain is the most glaringly omnipresent of these *motifs;* it is counted upon

invariably to amuse the average humanity of our so-called Christian civilization" with a "saturnalia of prearranged accidents." They were worse, in fact,
than another target of conservative assault, the dime novel. That at least
propped up certain ideals of bravery and chivalry. "The state of mind that ac-
cepts the humor of the comic weekly," Bergengren insisted, might well be the
same as that which shuddered at Ibsen, yet the immorality caused by the Sunday comics was, in fact, far greater. There were exceptions like Peter Newell or
the inventor of Little Nemo, artists of taste, genuine humor, and wit, but the
comics seemed, for the most part, an example of the bad driving the good out
of circulation, a reduction of the mass audience to its lowest common denomi-
nator.[17]

It was the pernicious influence of the comics on the manners and morals
of the young that seemed most bothersome, and this applied as well to the
illustration of children's books. Walter Taylor Field, crying "better give him no
pictures at all than wrong ones," condemned the example of the comic-strip
youth who "shampooed his sister's hair, and anointed the poodle, with a mixture
of ink, glue, and the family hair-tonic." This suggested an artist who had little
sympathy with children. What he meant, presumably, was an artist who had
little sympathy with parents. The "picture is as important as the printed page
in forming taste and influencing character," Field argued. The comics aided
what Annie Russell Marble, writing in the *Dial* in 1903, called the "reign of
the spectacular" in American art, a "craze for pictures and pageants apart from
their essential or even relative value." The commercial demand for illustration
spared no calling or sphere of activity, from the pulpit to the presidency. And
even great lecturers, she added, were startled by the question, Haven't you
some talks with lantern slides?[18]

Snapshots, postcards, illustrated periodical articles, comics—these were
joined, at century's end, by still another, even more powerful and potentially
debasing form of pictorialism, the rise of the motion picture. The nineties were,
of course, the formative decade for the early, primitive efforts of filmmakers,
but soon after the turn of the century, about 1905, their efforts began to bear
fruit with the rise of the storefront nickelodeon theaters and the rash of one-
reelers filled with action-oriented adventure stories and sentimental romances.
The cry of concern and anxiety coming from teachers, clergymen, public officials, social workers, law and order groups, and moralists in general about the
menace of the motion pictures has been documented by a generation of film
historians. Immediately studies were launched to demonstrate the pernicious
effect the films were having on youthful morals, the unhealthy impact of the
crowded, germ-infested, firetrap theaters which lured the young away from
more vigorous outdoor play or even from gainful employment. Surveys at-

tempted to establish that motion pictures gained a kind of hypnotic suggestive power over the minds and eyes of viewers, that things presented on the screen, even the commission of violent crimes, were imitated by those who had little conception of the magnitude of their actions. A variety of schemes was launched, the better to control this new and powerful force.[19] Suggestions included closing down the theaters, creating local boards of review and censorship, and obtaining the cooperation of filmmakers in the production of less subversive and more uplifting films. In certain places and at certain times, these interventions succeeded in reorganizing the flow of films to a mass audience, at least for a period of time. As the financial stakes of picture-making and distribution grew more massive, self-policing on the part of the industry became more effective. But the appeal of film was too fundamental, too elemental to resist. That they were silents only made their challenge to the word more emphatic. Despite the occasional titles, the films were dependent not on dialogue, or literary referencing, or verbal wit, but on pictorialism pure and simple, for narrative, continuity, and persuasiveness. Quotation, if there was any, would have to be visual. In the end this meant that many of the traditional aspects of the theater, and their heavy reliance on literary skills, both for playwrights and authors, could be abandoned.

It is, to be sure, a lengthy jump from the illustrations of Abbey, Pyle, Reinhart, and Gibson to the pictures of Griffith, Chaplin, and Fairbanks. It would be exaggerated in the extreme to say that many contemporaries saw the connections between an expanded pictorialism in mass culture and the power of illustrated literature basking in its golden age. Nonetheless, there are parallels and continuities in these apparently disconnected areas: the publishing of serious fiction, history, and biography, all in illustrated form, and the appearance and astonishing development of cartoons and caricatures, snapshots, postcards, comic strips, and motion pictures. What all of these forms of expression shared was a diversion of authority away from its orthodox sources and traditional methods, in favor of new and apparently untried techniques. Ingenious, aggressively original, or incompetent illustrators could challenge the authority of the storyteller, as letter writers pointed out; cartoonists could challenge the honesty, patriotism, and, even more seriously, the dignity of pillars of the establishment, and so undermine their authority as setters of standards; movies could challenge the very persuasiveness of the written text as their translations of classics, scripture, or even modern stories held mass audiences in a thralldom that was as novel as it was intense. The new pictorialism was powerful precisely because an expanding range of techniques and a growing market permitted a degree of individuation. It no longer needed stock cuts, so inexpensively inserted alongside a written test. Formulas, of course, would develop with a vengeance, in every area of this new culture, but the formulas were complex enough to include considerable variety and to disguise their structure beneath a mass of arresting details.

But pictures were subversive, most of all, because they presented a new and apparently uncontrollable set of sources to the larger public. Guardians of the world had developed over the previous centuries: lexicographers, grammarians, rhetoricians, orthographers, rulemakers, critics, codifiers. The spread of reading and writing was accomplished, to a large extent, with their guidance and leadership. The rise of literacy was accompanied, of course, by bitter debates about the appropriate national, linguistic, and aesthetic models. There were furious cries of vulgarization attending the increased circulation of cheap novels, daily newspapers, and sentimental magazines. But control of the word remained in the hands of writers, publishers, editors, and teachers who were remarkably effective in demarcating the boundaries separating the acceptable and the unacceptable. The pictorial revolution, however, was too sudden, too comprehensive, and too appealing to be handled within just a few decades. Painters, photographers, caricaturists, filmmakers, and commercial printers had agendas of their own and pursued dreams different from those of the traditional establishment. In stylistic terms alone, fin de siècle art raised various problems for conservatives, but when to these challenges was added the further issue of image distribution on a scale and with a variety never before attempted, the consequences seemed profound and disquieting. Many, if not most American illustrators of the last century did not mean to challenge cultural authority as such. Their values may well have been as traditional as those of most of the authors they illustrated, but they were part of a larger movement which assumed a direction they could not control, or always understand.

By challenging the relationship between form and content, the new pictorialism appeared to subvert the hard-won discipline of verbal mastery. In the nineteenth century, still a handmaiden, a helpmate to the arts and sciences, an instrument spreading the results of other investigations, pictorial illustration was now launched on a career of its own. As we calibrate its rise to influence, we must not ignore the pangs of uncertainty and pain that accompanied its growth.

17

Designs on Demand:

Art and the

Modern Corporation

T he search for an enlightened American art patronage is as old as the republic itself. Even while it
dismantled bastions of political privilege, the
American Revolution challenged traditions of cultural authority as well. As students of history, many
Americans argued that princes and prelates had too
long employed artists to bolster their tyrannies.
Artist-mercenaries were the rule rather than the ex-
ception. The first generation of republican patriots suspected the spiritual
claims made for the visual arts and worried about the great fortunes needed to
support fine painting, sculpture, and architecture.[1]

During the nineteenth century many influences, including growing wealth
and a surge of nationalism, encouraged artistic survival in a country where
neither church nor state provided real sustenance. Voluntary societies to commission and distribute artworks were founded, and artists were trained. Academies, art unions, historical and antiquarian societies, and monument associations all kept an interest in art alive, often under discouraging circumstances.
But the burden of giving American artists work and importing masterpieces

From *Art, Design, and the Modern Corporation* (Washington, D.C.: Smithsonian Institution Press, 1985), 8–30. Reprinted with permission of the National Museum of American Art, Smithsonian Institution, Washington, D.C.

produced abroad fell increasingly upon wealthy individuals.[2] Often self-educated as well as self-made, these merchants and manufacturers, particularly during the middle years of the century, combined personal pleasure with civic duty. Admirers likened their involvement to the patronage of the Medici; indeed, because self-aggrandizement was not their goal, the modern patrons could claim the greater honor. Artists yearned for an increase in the numbers of patrons. From time to time critics bemoaned the American absence of Periclean statesmen who accepted a public obligation to support the arts. Defective private taste, reckless spending on old art, and increasing affection for European culture invited angry ripostes from practicing artists. But a system of art support based on voluntary personal expenditures and individual collecting seemed in little jeopardy. By the start of this century, American millionaires had begun to fill the first generation of our art museums with masterpieces once believed to be beyond the price or possibility of purchase.

All this changed, however, when the country moved from dreams of permanent prosperity in one decade to fears of total collapse in the next. Despite an unprecedented level of art purchases in the years following World War I, traditions of art patronage came under increasing scrutiny and reevaluation. Responding to changes in aesthetic taste, political ideology, shifts of economic power, and novel marketing principles, new patterns of support developed. What was tentative in the 1920s, experimental in the 1930s, and unusual in the 1940s, would eventually develop into a new system that would commission, conserve, exhibit, and publicize works of art.

One major element in this transformation was government—the federal government starting in the 1930s, followed by state and local governments in the 1960s and 1970s. The other ingredient—as legislative lobbyist, donor, exhibition supporter, organizer, adviser, management guide, and shaper of aesthetic philosophy—was the business corporation. None epitomized more powerfully this set of corporate claims and ambitions than Container Corporation of America, responding to the urgings of its chief executive officer, Walter Paepcke.

At least three different reasons underlay the corporate interest in art: first, a self-conscious concern with developing art in the interests of selling, thereby exploiting the possibilities of commercial design; second, a sense that modernism, still new to Americans in the 1920s, formed a visual vocabulary offering special opportunities to the business corporation; and third, a belief that the corporation could become a major patron, stimulating creativity even while it used art to enhance salesmanship, public relations, and employee efficiency. A number of American businesses prevailed in one or two of these areas, but sustaining all three was rare. Container Corporation's design program was early, enlightened, and continuous; its success was unusual but not unique. Business ambitions in the arts, prevalent in the United States since the 1920s, had even earlier origins in the world transformed by industrialization. Only by reviewing efforts made in nineteenth- and early twentieth-century Europe can the corporate art campaigns of twentieth-century America be set in any kind of effective context.

Historians have recently discovered that a self-conscious commercial interest in design, along with extensive employment of major artists, was well developed in eighteenth-century England, the most mature industrial culture of its day.[3] Producers of silver, ceramics, jewelry, beer, and clothing, working in a newly competitive market filled with alert consumers, recognized the commercial value of sculptors, etchers, and painters. Product lines and advertising campaigns were enhanced by Josiah Wedgwood, a brilliant market innovator who used artists like John Flaxman, Joseph Wright of Derby, and William Hackwood to decorate and design his pottery. Wedgwood commissioned paintings by George Romney and George Stubbs to further promote trade. Architects and landscapists, including James Wyatt, the Adam brothers, and Capability Brown, were cultivated for advice and counsel. Illustrators, typographers, and printers all participated in the expansion of eighteenth-century advertising. Continental manufacturers of fine porcelains, wallpapers, carpets, and other luxury items had long recognized the commercial advantages of skilled artists, but their markets were smaller than the English sought and their advertising somewhat less significant.[4]

During the nineteenth century both rewards and penalties for commercial design practices increased dramatically. Europeans made extensive efforts to strengthen the links between art and industry. So far-reaching were these programs that their history constitutes, to some extent, a social history of design itself. Among the institutional activities connecting the artist with commerce and industry were international expositions and their influential competitions, art schools and special apprenticeship programs, compulsory drawing classes in the public schools, tariff reform campaigns and official subsidies, contests, arts and crafts societies, trade shows and artisan lecture series, museum foundings, and specialized journals.[5] Prophets arose to denounce some traditions of industrial design, condemn the growing separation of the fine and practical arts, and celebrate specific traditions. Conservatives and reformers, whose ranks embraced major leaders of nineteenth-century thought (William Morris, John Ruskin, and Leo Tolstoy, for example) and a broad range of artists and educators, clashed on the spiritual, economic, aesthetic, and technological significance of art. Printing, book illustration, textile design, carpet-making, domestic architecture, stained-glass and furniture production, and industrial design (machine tools and transport vehicles) touched off debates invoking fundamental social themes. Industrial art could be seen as an underlying symptom of modern decadence or an encouraging instrument of redemption. From Birmingham, Glasgow, Manchester, and London to Paris, Lyons, Darmstadt, and Helsinki, groups of artists, pedagogues, and philosophers preached new doctrines. In some cases they found sympathetic responses from businessmen and industrialists. New national schools and workshops testified to the mutual interactions between art and industry that had become a major cultural issue by the early twentieth century.[6]

This was in Europe. Neither the scale nor the intensity of this movement was matched in America, although there were important echoes and some strident debates. Changes in public school curricula; the creation of major museums with public education and industrial training as objectives; craft guilds, private printing clubs, design schools, and aggressive decorating firms; and a distinctive intellectual response from a group of men and women suspicious of the claims of modern life evidenced the presence of interest in a cooperation between art and industry. The influence of designers, ranging from Ralph Adams Cram and Will Bradley to Frank Lloyd Wright and Gustav Stickley, was not sufficient, however, to make the role of decorative or practical art into the burning question it had become in Europe.[7] There was no involvement of the national government nor creation of any large workshops to compete with centers in Paris, Vienna, or Berlin. Although few American business corporations of any size acknowledged a particular responsibility for the arts, there were exceptions.

One came in the field of printing and publishing. New, middle-class journals of enormous circulation, typified by the *Saturday Evening Post* and the *Ladies' Home Journal,* assumed the guidance of public taste as part of their responsibility. They ran articles about art in the home, the need to clean up city streets and protect scenic landmarks, and the role of fashion in clothing and architecture; they also featured the work of progressive architects.[8] Magazine publicity popularized prairie school homes and mission-style furniture. Together with more professionally oriented and elitist journals, these magazines demanded improvements in the art of design as a national goal and occasionally set an example themselves.

When Edward Bok developed plans for a new editorial and production building on Philadelphia's Independence Square, he persuaded publisher Cyrus Curtis to install "good" art.[9] Bok commissioned seventeen panels from the painter-illustrator Maxfield Parrish for the huge dining room and contacted major academic muralists, including Edwin Austin Abbey and Maurice Boutet de

Monvel, for work on the lobby. In the end he succeeded in hiring Louis Comfort Tiffany to create a giant Favrile glass mosaic, which was based on Parrish sketches illustrating a dream garden. The Curtis Publishing Company possessed one of the most handsomely adorned business houses of the day.

As heavy users of illustration, magazines (and several newspapers) were quick to spot the talents of American poster designers in the 1890s and became some of the artists' most eager clients. Edward Penfield, Will Bradley, Louis Rhead, Will Carqueville, J. J. Gould, Frank Hazenplug, and their colleagues worked for *Harper's, Century, Lippincott's, Scribner's* and little magazines like the *Lark* and *Chap-Book.*[10] They also worked for publishers, printers, ink manufacturers, and papermakers who used their art in advertisements, posters, and sample books. There was no question that printing and publishing leaders were quick to recognize the effectiveness of established artists as fine commercial spokesmen.

By the early twentieth century there had also been several famous, even notorious, episodes of European businesses turning to distinguished artists for advertising aid. The best-publicized incident was the controversial purchase of Sir John Everett Millais's *Bubbles* by Thomas J. Barratt, a partner in the Pears Soap Company.[11] The sentimental painting had already been purchased for reproduction purposes by the *Illustrated London News*, and Barratt spent several thousand pounds to obtain both the picture and Millais's permission to use it as an advertisement. Angry debate broke out over the issue of artistic debasement. It threatened Millais's own reputation and raised now-familiar questions about the tendency of advertising to dilute art that was better left to the gallery and museum. Pears Soap, nevertheless, went on to feature *Bubbles* in its publicity and produce lavishly illustrated annuals containing presentation works by other famous artists. Moreover, the company incorporated additional designs into handbills and souvenir items.

Millais and Pears Soap were not alone. Walter Crane, Maurice Greiffenhagen, and Aubrey Beardsley did posters; Septimus Scott, John Hassall, and William Powell Frith were pressed into commercial service; Sir Edward Poynter designed an advertisement for the Guardian Assurance Company; Sir Hubert von Herkomer, R. A., produced further advertising art; and Lord Leverhulme became an active patron of important artists working for his various soaps. Leverhulme's 1889 purchase of a Frith painting, *The New Frock*, stimulated another lively spate of disputes; Leverhulme changed the title to *So Clean* before incorporating it into his ads.[12]

Outside of printers and publishers, few American businessmen systematically exploited painters and designers in advertising. One of them, however, Gordon Selfridge, on leaving Marshall Field's in Chicago to create his own giant

*Bubbles by Sir
Everett Millais*

London department store, provoked a sensation by using the works of Edmund
J. Sullivan, Robert Anning Bell, Walter Crane, and other leading artists as full-
page ads in the London dailies. Selfridge shrewdly disappointed his British

competitors who had hoped that "screaming methods" and "cheap and nasty" advertising in the "American manner" would cost him the loyalties of British customers.[13] Another American merchant, John Wanamaker, distributed around his department stores paintings that he had purchased in Paris.[14] Other business executives turned to architects as agents for publicity—Frank Woolworth's choice of Cass Gilbert to design his lavish corporate headquarters in New York City proved to be one of the most astute of such decisions. Insurance companies traded on the height, expense, and magnificence of their buildings while other firms sought out artists to create trademarks and company symbols for stationery and billheads.[15]

Before World War I such activity was, first of all, unusual; second, only rarely involved major artists; and third, tended to invoke the most traditional illustrative appeals—anecdotal, sentimental, and narrative in character. Although commercial artists in America were most accomplished and found plenty of work to do, they enjoyed a distinctly lower status than sculptors and painters. Many used the work simply as a bridge to a higher standing.

A few industrialists had greater ambitions for the commercial arts. Speaking to a group of advertising specialists in 1898 one businessman urged them to struggle for the dignity of commercial design. "Do not allow yourself to be snubbed by the snobocracy of art," he pleaded. It was a heresy to believe that "true art has no relation to practical things, and that a pictorial story is beneath the dignity of the true artist." In fact, advertising's highest mission might well be to unite "in some degree the fine and useful arts."[16] Distinguished typographical work and innovative illustration had made their appearance in American house organs, brochures, posters, and magazine ads, but the efforts, on the whole, were more traditional and less effective than the commercial graphics techniques that were being developed and strengthened in Germany, Austria, and France. American social and institutional life contained many new departures, but few of them had yet challenged the traditional hierarchy of the visual arts.

It was during the 1920s, the decade when Walter Paepcke created Container Corporation of America, that relations between art and industry began to change in this country. There were many reasons. American merchants and manufacturers, benefiting from dramatically changed product appearances and seeking to improve advertising, packaging, and architectural and display techniques, now openly recognized the importance of commercial designers. By implication, this awareness meant acknowledging the powerful influence of avant-gardists in the fine arts. Modernism had become infectious. Designers began to make more extended claims as they organized professional associations and interest groups. The decade as a whole was full of surprises.

World War I had acted as a catalyst. To begin with, it interrupted trade in traditional European imports, particularly luxury goods and manufacturing designs. Richard F. Bach, curator of industrial art at the Metropolitan Museum of Art, told the 1918 conference of the American Federation of Arts that the war had given American designers a unique opportunity. "It will be an evil day for manufacturers and dealers after the war if American taste must again go to Europe for its industrial art products."[17]

The war was also significant because it forged an alliance between major artists and propaganda goals. Seized with patriotic fervor, celebrated American painters and illustrators designed posters and car cards supporting military conscription, food drives, liberty bonds, conservation, and a host of other war-related activities.[18] Their success was impressive. Businessmen, some of whom were deeply involved with wartime mobilization, could not help but notice the impact of clever design on public opinion. They stored the lesson away for future use.

World War I and the economic depression that followed in Europe helped attract European artists to America, often for lengthy stays. Architects Eliel Saarinen, Richard Neutra, and William Lescaze and designers Raymond Loewy, Kem Weber, Frederick Kiesler, and Pola Hoffmann were part of this exodus.[19] Although it was smaller and less influential than the intellectual hegira provoked by Nazism in the 1930s, it made a difference.

It was the war's impact on the American economy that brought about the most revolutionary changes in American commercial design. The shift in world economic power, the growth of productivity, and the expansion of American trade during the 1920s, together with more widespread travel and communication with Western Europe, produced a culture newly appreciative of changing publicity techniques and commercial displays.[20] American retailers, manufacturers, and publishers now exploited the talents of Europeans like Paul Poiret, Marie Laurencin, Pierre Brissaud, Georges Lepape, Lucian Bernhard, Jean Dupas, Julius Klinger, Edgar Brandt, and Walter von Nessen. Some would eventually settle here. Their clients included B. Altman and Saks Fifth Avenue in New York, Condé Nast Publications, Gorham, Cheney Brothers, Cadillac, and a series of luxury-item makers and sellers. The fabled Exposition des arts décoratifs in Paris in 1925 elicited extensive and aggressive department store promotions in ensuing years; trade publications and new craft organizations brought further publicity. All increased the contemporary awareness that sophisticated design sold products.

European influences were only part of the story. Artists born and trained in America also spread interest in design as an instrument for selling. In this, nothing was more significant than the new sense of spirit and organization among American advertising artists. The most impressive symbols were the series of annual advertising art exhibitions sponsored by New York's Art Directors Club, which was established in 1919. In 1921 the club organized the first advertising art exhibition, in which hundreds of pictures by veteran illustrators and newcomers alike were displayed.[21] Edward Penfield, J. C. Leyendecker, Jules Guérin, Edward A. Wilson, Neysa McMein, René Clarke, Earl Horter, Maxfield Parrish, and Norman Rockwell—some of them veterans of the older poster movement—competed for prizes and attention. Their clients included important and nationally known companies, such as Johns-Manville, Victor Records, Wesson Oil, Lincoln Continental, Steinway and Sons, Paramount Pictures, and Adler Brothers Clothing. Writing a foreword to the first *Annual of Advertising Art in the United States,* which reproduced the pictures on display, Egbert Jacobson of Chicago argued that just as commerce was commissioning the most brilliant architects to serve its needs, it had also begun to engage the best artists to create its advertising; thus, a "second great national art expression based on usefulness [was] developed."[22]

It certainly was not clear that the best artists in America were now doing advertising, but the 1921 exhibition was, nonetheless, a revelation of beauty and power. In 1925, Earnest Elmo Calkins, a leading advertising executive and philosopher of the new commercial art, recalled that while serving on the publication committee of the National Arts Club, he had proposed the first exhibition of advertising art, which was held in 1908.[23] But the pickings were slim, and the ensuing show had to rely on magazine covers to fill its walls. This would not be the case for long, however. By 1921 a group of artists had developed into publicists for American commerce and industry, either as employees of advertising agencies or as independents. The same year that saw the first Art Directors Show witnessed creation of the Guild of Free Lance Artists in New York, an organization of several hundred men and women who did book and magazine illustration as well as advertising art but valued direct contact with the advertisers.[24]

The agency art directors, sponsors of the show, were crucial to this expanded art form. Their ranks had begun to multiply in the early twentieth century, when both advertisers and advertising agents found it increasingly difficult to make decisions about design, layout, and illustration. Art directors filled this gap. Often artists themselves, they were knowledgeable about the field of illustration and able to mediate between client and designer. They had also begun to introduce businessmen to the possibilities offered by distinctive art in packaging as well as advertising. In addition, a handful of major corporations began hiring their own in-house specialists to coordinate advertising with product design.

It was during the 1920s as well that a corps of aggressive and ambitious young men—few women were yet prominent in the field—developed the packaging of consumer products into a specialty of its own. Born mainly during the 1880s and 1890s, some even later than that, they sensed the role design could play in mass production and adopted rhetoric that reflected a national confidence in technological progress and business efficiency.[25] The business community of America was not content simply to rest on expanded production and a redefinition of potential consumer markets. It elaborated a dream that material prosperity, engineered by profit-seeking corporate executives, could lay the basis for a permanently peaceful, harmonious, and prosperous society. Purchasing the services of public relations specialists to interpret their motives and achievements before the mass media, corporations staked large claims on their own social and cultural significance.[26] These publicists, using their sometimes clamorous bombast, attracted the scorn of contemporary critics like Sinclair Lewis and H. L. Mencken. Nonetheless, designers such as Lurelle Guild, Donald Deskey, Egmont Arens, Norman Bel Geddes, Harold Van Doren, Henry Dreyfuss, and many others with backgrounds in art, merchandising, stage design, and advertising aided business ambitions by creating the profession of industrial design. These adviser-consultants reshaped everything from toasters and refrigerators to locomotives and alarm clocks, calling attention to the fact that new designs could stimulate new profits.

In 1930, as the Depression deepened, Earnest Elmo Calkins published an essay summarizing the prospects. Entitled "The New Consumption Engineer and the Artist," it ordained that contemporary beauty must grow out of industrial civilization. With their bath towels, fountain pens, radios, and typewriters, Joseph Sinel, Jay Hambridge, Edward A. Wilson, and Walter Dorwin Teague were making goods more saleable and advertisements more appealing. "Business can be and may be as stimulating a patron of the arts as the cardinals, prelates and popes who represented the church in the fifteenth century," Calkins contended, mingling together, as so many would do, art as salesman and art as product. There was no practical difference between Pinturicchio's frescoed history of Pius II on the walls of a Siena church and Ezra Winter's mural on the age of sail, designed for the great hall of New York's Cunard Building. There was "certainly none between Perugino's frescoes in the Cambio at Perugia and the murals by Boardman Robinson in the Kaufmann department store at Pittsburgh, except the ability and attitude of the artists."[27] Apparently the old quest for a neutral art sponsor, free from the authoritarianism of church and state, had finally been realized. Product design, advertising art, and environmental enhancement could all be mutually supportive. The desperate search for consumers in the hungry thirties only increased business interest in designers, in anyone who could make the commodity, package, advertising campaign, store, or showroom more enticing, more alluring, more dramatically satisfying.

By the end of the 1920s many magazines, brochures, and direct-mail advertisements were placing increasing reliance on distinguished artists and adapting the work of contemporary modernists. This was no longer simply calendar art, quoting selectively from established masterpieces, but an active and sometimes subtle exploration of vital themes and motifs. Colgate, Pepperell, Palm Beach Clothes, and many others employed important German artists— Lucian Bernhard, Robert Leonard, Hans Schleger, Hans Flato—attracting the attention of interested critics. *Westvaco Inspirations for Printers*, a paper company's periodical that compiled important advertising work, often featured artists such as Gerda Wegener, Ludwig Hohlwein, F. H. Ehmcke, C. O. Czeschka, and Otto Schulpig. Popular magazines were filled with arresting ads displaying distorted or abstracted figures, contemporary type fonts, and expressionistic juxtapositions. *Inspirations* noted in 1929 that one conservative magazine favored modernistic copy, typography, or layout in almost 40 percent of its 266 ads; another, more daring and highbrow, achieved a percentage almost twice as high.[28] Modernistic appeals were "rampant in current advertising effort," helping to sell everything from hosiery and luggage to housewares and department stores.

Celebrated French artists—Erté, Guy Arnoux, Iribe, Bénédictus, Jean Dupas, Kees van Dongen, Marc Chagall—also worked for American firms in the 1920s, and American modernists like Rockwell Kent and Edward Buk Ulreich were also much in evidence. Particular advertising agencies, notably Calkins and Holden, J. Walter Thompson, Philadelphia-based N. W. Ayer, and Erwin, Wasey, energetically exploited the decorative possibilities of modernist art.[29] The Thompson agency, for example, handled work for Edward Steichen, E. G. Benito, and Walter Dorwin Teague. Calkins and Holden clients, who were apparently satisfied with the nontraditional work of the agency's art directors—Merritt Cutler, E. A. Georgi, Walter Geoghegan, and René Clarke—included Heinz Foods, Hartford Fire Insurance Company, and Wesson Oil. N. W. Ayer employed, among others, Kent, Ulreich, the photographer Anton Bruehl, and Hugh Ferriss. These agencies and a few others developed reputations for artistic originality and contemporaneity.

By the late 1920s some clients were willing to identify themselves with modernism. These included not only the producers of expensive luxury items such as perfumes, jewelry, fine textiles, and automobiles, but makers of industrial products like batteries, roller bearings, shock absorbers, and pistons. Alcoa, Eveready, Timken, and Delco relied on arresting compositions and flirtations with surrealism to make their merchandising more effective. Reporting on the Seventh Annual Art Directors Exhibition in New York, Herbert Kerkow told British readers in 1928 that "American advertising art has gone modernistic."[30] "To know anything about modern advertising art," Brenda Ueland told *Saturday Evening Post* readers in 1930, "you will have to know about Cézanne, Gauguin, and Matisse." "Buckeye art" was now out.[31]

The change in artistic style was not total, however. Even though many art directors lobbied effectively for contemporary art, air-brushed modernism was popular, and some European artists found American clients, not all boundaries were passed. Reviewing one Art Directors Show in the twenties, Lloyd Goodrich found too much dullness and solemnity and too little humor as well as too much compromise and tentativeness. Advertising art in America seemed "still in its infancy—an enormously overgrown infancy, the body far too big for the brain."[32] If industry, as Forbes Watson put it, was "making violent love to art," it was all too often unrequited.[33] Commercial promotion abroad had moved far beyond America's tentative experiments with artistic innovation. This is evident by reviewing contemporary foreign journals, such as *Gebrauchsgraphik, Commercial Art,* or *Arts et metiers graphiques,*[34] the histories of major European art institutions, and case studies of corporate patronage. Commissioned before 1912, the work of Peter Behrens for Germany's great electrical trust, AEG, perhaps best exemplifies the distance between the two approaches.[35] Although Britain's Design and Industries Association, formed in 1915, was a forceful advocate, specific businessmen and bureaucrats were even more important.

The career of American designer E. McKnight Kauffer reveals the growing British willingness to take chances on serious modern art and cubism when American advertisers were still gingerly testing the waters.[36] Montana-born and Indiana-reared, Kauffer saw the famous Armory Show at the Art Institute of Chicago in early 1913 before he left for almost two years of travel and study in Europe. Attracted by the works of Van Gogh, Matisse, and Derain and influenced by contemporary British vorticists, Kauffer painted still-lifes and landscapes, became friendly with artists like Paul Nash and critics like Roger Fry, and simultaneously found himself designing audacious posters for newspapers, department stores, and most significant of all, the London Transport. During the twenties Kauffer's London Underground posters brought him considerable notoriety, thanks to the support of one of the country's great patrons, Frank Pick, who eventually became the managing director and vice-chairman of the London Passenger Transport Board. Kauffer also created labels for a cotton goods exporter; designed boxes, letterheads, and labels for a silk firm; worked for Sir William Crawford's advertising agency; designed for Percy Lund, Humphries, the printer; and found further opportunities at Eno's Fruit Salts, the Empire Marketing Board, Shell-Mex petroleum, and other corporations. Not uncontroversial—the Duke of Westminster refused to allow one of Kauffer's inn signs to remain on his estates—Kauffer maintained his status in the noncommercial art world as well. An exhibition of his posters at Oxford marked the first time a poster show had been held there.[37]

Kauffer had numerous colleagues in England. Graham Sutherland, Paul Nash, Henry Moore, Sir Jacob Epstein, Barnet Freedman, Ben Nicholson, Naum Gabo, Vanessa Bell, Rex Whistler, Tom Purvis, Barbara Hepworth, László Moholy-Nagy, and Eric Fraser were among the distinguished artists, many of them young and unconventional, who found employment with Shell-Mex, London Transport, and advertising agencies, such as W. S. Crawford and Stuart's, that specialized in modern publicity.[38] Executives knowledgeable about and friendly to contemporary art—Marcus Brumwell of Stuart's, Jack Beddington of Shell-Mex, Sir Stephen Tallents of the Empire Marketing Board and later the General Post Office, C. F. Snowden Gamble of Imperial Airways, Colin Anderson of the Orient Line, Peter Gregory of Cresta Silks, A. O. Simon of Steinthal and Company, and Frank Pick—were responsible for a series of innovative advertisements, brochures, posters, menus, show cards, tour guides, and documentary films. Printing firms such as Curwen and Westminster also played their own important role in this process.

Of them all, Frank Pick stood out. Nikolaus Pevsner called him the greatest art patron England had produced in the twentieth century and "indeed the ideal patron of our age."[39] Pick concerned himself with the design of stations, bus shelters, rolling-stock, signal cabins, waiting rooms, garages, lighting standards, platform seats, cartography, and lettering—in short, every aspect of the system he supervised. Clarity, elegance, comfort, and contemporaneity, insofar as designs could achieve them, were pursued by the more enlightened managers of British business. They were far from a majority. A thirties survey investigating more than one hundred manufacturers yielded depressing conclusions.[40] There were general complaints about the bad taste and clumsiness of much of British product and advertising design. But art-conscious business leaders constituted a recognizable group.

Before the late thirties it was difficult to find counterparts to a Pick or a Beddington in America. Though some stores, museums, advertising agencies, and manufacturers had dabbled with major designers or hosted exhibitions of contemporary design, few major executives had created comprehensive policies that married serious contemporary art with product promotion. Dozens of publications, organizations, and exhibitions testified to an interest in design, particularly in printing, but the corporate community still clung to traditional instruments of expression. When departures occurred they were usually led by public relations officers like Edward Bernays, who worked with French-born

HAMPTON COURT

BY BUS 14·27ᴬ·73·150·152·201·214·216

BY UNDERGROUND
to Wimbledon thence trolleybus 604
or to Hammersmith thence trolleybus 667

Hampton Court,
by Oleg Zinger,
1937

Henry Creange to revive the fashion leadership of Cheney Brothers Silks.[41] In general, American businessmen had not yet perceived patronage possibilities or the commercial utility of distinguished, avant-garde artists. More research will undoubtedly uncover many exceptions, for this history is still to be written.

The most dramatic signs of change were architectural, not graphic. Architects, sculptors, painters, metalsmiths, and ceramists—such as Samuel Yel-

lin, John Storrs, René Chambellan, Lee Lawrie, Leo Friedlander, Gaston La-
chaise, Stuart Davis, Joan Miró, and Joseph Urban—worked on the massive
business skyscrapers of Jazz Age America, smart shops and restaurants, expositions like Chicago's Century of Progress and New York's World of Tomorrow,
and above all, the Rockefeller Center.[42] A few great corporations took seriously
the challenge of tying the arts to their commercial identities. Outside of architecture, however, these practices were most often connected to special events.
There were no easy models available for American business leaders to copy and
few visible, centralized bureaucracies like the government bureaus of Europe.
American businessmen were Lorenzos only in their leisure hours, but that
would soon change.

Thus, the program that Container Corporation adopted in the mid 1930s,
while not without intimations and analogues, represented something of a new
start. That Walter Paepcke and his company were located in Chicago has an
interesting logic to it, insofar as the relationship between art and industry was
concerned.

Although New York remained the center of the nation's cultural and intellectual life during this period, Chicago artists and businessmen experienced
their own organizing impulse. Chicago possessed an Art Directors Club for local
exhibitions, a Guild of Free Lance Artists, a resident corps of illustrators and
industrial designers, a Business Men's Art Club, and an impressive complement of advertising agencies, all of which testified to the city's interests.[43] More
than 20 percent of approximately six hundred general advertising agencies
listed in a national handbook were located in Chicago, either as independents
(the vast majority) or branches of larger firms.[44] In addition, a general index of
American advertising artists and illustrators, with five thousand separate entries, found 750 in Chicago, albeit far behind New York but three times the
number offered by the next city, Philadelphia.[45] Chicago was also home to numerous art schools and academies, several of which specialized in commercial
design. In fact, the School of the Art Institute of Chicago, which enrolled more
than forty-five hundred students annually in the late 1920s, was the largest
single art school in the United States. Many of the nation's best-known illustrators, painters, commercial designers, and art teachers passed through its doors
in the late nineteenth and early twentieth centuries.

The wave of concern about the future of American design that followed
World War I motivated Chicago businessmen to found the Chicago Association
of Arts and Industries in 1922. Its primary object was to create a school of
industrial design. Although the association did much to encourage the larger
cause, it took fifteen years and a mass exodus of artists from Nazi Germany to
realize its specific goal—the founding of the New Bauhaus in Chicago, which

was directed by László Moholy-Nagy with the active support of a group of businessmen led by Walter Paepcke.[46]

Many reasons existed for Chicago's special attraction to commercial design and its predisposition to accept modernism in the cause of marketing. By the 1920s Chicago was well established as a printing center, specifically job printing. Engravers and photo engravers, lithographers, typographers, printmakers, printers, and manufacturers of printing machinery—including the internationally famous R. R. Donnelley, Barnes-Crosby, Blomgren Brothers, Ludlow Typograph, Curt Teich, the Franklin Company, Miehle Printing Press, Magill-Weinsheimer, and Barnhart Brothers and Spindler—were all headquartered in the city. Some of the firms employed their own design specialists, several of whom, like William A. Kittredge of Donnelley, enjoyed considerable celebrity.

Chicago was a center for printing mail-order catalogues, popular magazines, trade association journals, postcards, railroad literature, telephone books, tickets, labels, brochures, pamphlets, and advertising novelties. Its corporations, which focused on electronics, meat-packing and food-processing, drugs and pharmaceuticals, clothing, furniture, transportation, and home appliances, specialized in heavy consumer advertising. The city's department stores enjoyed powerful regional influence and hired their own art specialists. Their catalogues, newspaper ads, and window displays occasionally invoked the modernist spirit and provided employment for some of the young graduates of the area's art schools. The great mail-order houses, like Sears, Roebuck and Company and Montgomery Ward, also had in-house advertising specialists.[47]

Serious interest in modern design rested in the Renaissance Society and the Arts Club, which were founded during or just before World War I, and in some downtown galleries. These organizations provided places for enthusiasts to plan shows, host celebrities, and attend lectures. The *Inland Printer*, the best-known American journal in the field, had been published in the city since the 1880s, and the *Printing Art Quarterly* (formerly *Printing Art*), another distinguished periodical, moved from Boston to Chicago in the 1930s for its last years of production. Besides the Art Directors Club, the Society of Typographic Arts, and the Chicago Guild of Free Lance Artists, the city hosted its own Society of Photographic Illustrators and Society of Color Research, all of which came together in 1939 to open Art Center–Chicago.[48] Innumerable craft societies, art leagues, guilds, and neighborhood clubs also flourished.

With its history of manufacturing, merchandising, and distribution, Chicago's interest in the commercial uses of art was natural. As a printing, advertising, and educational center, the city attracted artists and art directors who were open to new approaches. Even in the early twenties the region's electric

*The Dunes
Beaches, by Hazel
Brown Urgelles*

railways—the Chicago Elevated and the South Shore and North Shore lines—
had developed an arresting series of posters and advertising graphics, which
were designed by artists like Ervine Metzl and Oscar Rabe Hanson and used
local landmarks for graphic depictions. The colorful renditions of parks,

beaches, and major structures suggested the sophisticated railway campaigns advertising French château country, or London's Underground, and attracted national and international attention.[49]

The city's lengthy involvement with the wood, paper, metal, and cardboard industries made it a node for the enormously dynamic packaging trade of the interwar years. From the mid-nineteenth century on, a series of remarkable innovations transformed the manufacture of containers (boxes, bags, tubes bottles, cans, cartons, jars, caps, and corks) and made possible the international distribution of consumer goods that would otherwise have been too fragile, perishable, bulky, or awkward to ship. These innovations included not only the materials from which the packages were constructed, but the machinery that made the packaging, the packaging designs, and the processes of construction. In addition to the arrival of plastics, cellophane acetate transparent paper, and solid fiber and folding cartons, the packaging industry was also affected by the growth of self-service food stores and the explosion in frozen food sales, which emphasized the enormous advantages of effective labeling and wrapping.

American packaging had several giants by the 1930s, including the Robert Gair Company of Brooklyn, which employed nearly four thousand workers in plants across the country, the Inland Container Corporation of Indianapolis, American Can of New York, and the Hazel-Atlas Glass Company of Wheeling, West Virginia. Chicago had more than its share, however—the Phoenix Metal Cap Company, the United States Bottlers Machinery Company, and the Container Corporation of America, to name a few.[50] During the years between the wars, manufacturers of bottles, cans, and containers were very active. Trade associations were organized and reorganized; journals—such as *Packaging Parade*, first published in Chicago in 1938. *Packaging Review*, begun five years earlier on the Pacific Coast, and *Modern Packaging*, which appeared in the 1920s—were established. These magazines featured reviews of innovative commercial designs as well as news of the trade.

Concern for effective appearance and consumer appeal dominated the industry. The first Packaging Conference, Clinic and Exposition was held in New York in 1931.[51] Sponsored by the American Management Association, it featured lectures, seminars, and competitions and displayed an impressive variety of boxes, labels, containers, tubes, tapes, papers, and caps. The second conference, held in March 1932, was hosted by Chicago. Thereafter the two cities dominated the convention sites. Artists and art students, paper and ink makers, manufacturers of plastics and packaging machinery, iron and steel makers, all paid attention to these deliberations, which focused on ways to make packages more durable, attractive, and efficient. Beginning in 1932 packaging awards named for Irwin D. Wolf of Pittsburgh's Kaufmann's Department Store (whose owner was a great patron of modern architecture) became high points of the meetings. Merchants, manufacturers, and advertising agents served as judges; winners, whose clients covered the range of American industry, from drug and beer companies to manufacturers of paints, vacuum cleaners, and cosmetics, included Henry Dreyfuss, Egmont Arens, Raymond Loewy, and Gustav Jensen.

Several package makers had already developed special relations with artists. The house organ of the Phoenix Metal Cap Company of Chicago, the *Flame,* received national recognition for its design. Moreover, packaging became a whole culture during the twenties and thirties, carrying a tinge of heroic romance. Its achievements seemed central to the growth of modern industry. Introducing a biography of Robert Gair, the Scottish immigrant who revolutionized late nineteenth-century packaging, Lewis Mumford argued that the development of paper containers linked institutions "so apparently remote" as the advertising agency, chain store, and apartment house. A critic of urban crowding, Mumford noted that without the folding box New York's street congestion "would be almost twice as great." He added that while the appearance of packages sometimes outdid the quality of their contents, consumers could console themselves "with the thought that, in its most characteristic material and product, our metropolitan world maintains a standard of excellence." [52]

Industry leaders made broad claims. "Packages induced people to buy," argued Alvin E. Dodd, president of the American Management Association in the 1930s. Manufacturers realized that a " 'mighty little man' of glass, or wood, or paper, or metal was ready to become their most vigilant salesman. . . . He was the package—with a bolt of sales lightning in each hand, and with a general air of 'buy' emanating from him." [53] Self-service stores, contended H. D. Chickering, merchandising director for Du Pont, were battlegrounds where thousands of products fought for customer dollars; without clerks to extol the merits of a particular brand, packages had to stand for themselves. If consumers reigned in such a domain, then "assuredly the display is the thing to catch the buying conscience of the king." [54] Intelligent design was the key to efficient display; packagers just might be the kind of business people to preside over the marriage of artists and manufacturers—for so long a promised but unfulfilled goal.

When Chicagoan Walter Paepcke decided to create a new corporate style in 1935 for his young company, he was working at a time, in a city, and within an industry that had already taken the problems of mass design to heart and begun to apply the lessons of artistic modernism. Packaging was a juncture where artists, engineers, printers, industrial designers, merchants, manufacturers, and advertising agents met. Container Corporation, formed ten years earlier, had been relatively conservative as a patron of contemporary design. Its artists won no awards, its projects attracted little attention. Walter Paepcke's growing interest in cultural renewal, the influence of friends and family as well as Chicago's own milieu, and his experiences at trade shows and expositions where modern packaging designs showed great effectiveness were important elements leading the company's transformation. They have been described elsewhere, together with the detailed steps Paepcke took to integrate contemporary art with effective salesmanship.[55] Here, rather than through the commercial display of old masters or patriotic icons, lay the route to the industrial art patronage that has become so important an aspect of our own culture.

One early step was installing Egbert Jacobson as director of design. A former art director for N. W. Ayer and J. Walter Thompson, Jacobson was an active leader among art directors. Container Corporation redesigned everything from its logo to its delivery trucks. Architectural journals featured its sales offices and showrooms as models of modernism; its factory interiors were replanned, with special attention given to the use of color.[56] Container's annual report featured some of the first changes. The fiscal report for 1934 (dated March 1935) sported a new typography; the following year the addition of photographs attracted the attention of Kent Currie, a student of this rather specialized genre. Annual reports could be taken as clues to a corporation's health and taste, Currie argued. Once the "orphan children" of company publicity, with improved layouts, printing processes, and pictorial matter, annual reports could boost investor confidence as well as customer interest.[57] Over the next few years, Container Corporation's reports, which included graphics and photographs, described the way paperboard products were manufactured, featured its new exhibition rooms, and included color reproductions of its innovative advertisements and ledger sheets.

It was through these advertisements that Container most impressed itself on the larger public and forcefully entered a world in which art directors, graphic designers, and typographic specialists were shaping a new art form. Despite the innovative work commissioned by American advertisers during the twenties and early thirties, a gap divided the tastes of corporate clients and the more sophisticated examples of visual art. Even when they turned to well-known artists, American corporations, with a few exceptions, tended to favor realism or sentimentality, or at least to demand obvious symbolic tie-ins with their products. American illustration and window display could occasionally be witty, charming, even surrealistic, but the task of promoting the product in a way that was readily understandable remained central.

Container Corporation of America, however, was not advertising a product as much as a sensibility, seeking to establish the importance of its paperboard

packaging by association. Specific renderings were less useful than clever al-
lusion, occasional irony, problematic juxtapositions, and arresting deconstruc-
tion of familiar objects and processes. Container's advertising art was simultaneously more austere in its references to traditional national settings and
sentiments, and richer in interpretive possibilities. While cubism and photo-
montage techniques had achieved some circulation in European advertising,
these methods were used less frequently in American advertising, which favored an airbrushed, streamline modernism. Seeking something different to
identify with his new approach, Paepcke turned to a specific advertising agency
and a specific art director. Charles T. Coiner of N. W. Ayer and Son was one of
the key figures behind the new collaboration, a midwife to the birth of modern
industrial patronage.

N. W. Ayer was one of the oldest agencies in the country. It had employed
art directors since 1910 and for more than a decade had been enlisting artists
in a memorable campaign for Steinway pianos.[58] In one dramatic gesture, Steinway, under Ayer's urging, paid $25,000 for a portrait of Ignace Paderewski by
the Spanish artist Zuloaga—an act which, Charles Coiner recalled, brought
several times that amount of free publicity.[59] In its magazine advertisements
Steinway, a bit breathlessly at times, tied artworks by Serge Sudekeine, Emile
Fuchs, Rockwell Kent, Earl Horter, N. C. Wyeth, Harvey Dunn, Covarrubias,
and C. Peter Helck to its promises of musical immortality. There was considerable support and admiration for the undertaking. "Great paintings have the
most irresistible form of salesmanship that has ever been created," wrote one
advertising spokesman in the mid twenties. "To accept an advertising commission for a really good painter, and to buy the work of a famous painter is certainly the surest way to greater returns for the manufacturer."[60]

By 1936 Ayer was running announcements in *Fortune*, a newly established showcase for distinguished commercial layouts, with titles like "Who
Says Beauty Doesn't Pay?" Ayer clients, the notices pointed out, had accumulated forty-one awards during the first nineteen years of the Art Directors exhibitions, far exceeding the number of awards—indeed by three times—won
by the nearest competitors. "Some people profess to think that Beauty is a
'sissy' and impractical thing," Ayer continued, "unworthy of the attention of
serious businessmen."[61] To the contrary! Ayer pointed out that beauty had been
an active ally of Steinway, Cannon Mills, Caterpillar Tractor, and Climax Mo-
lybdenum—all of them Ayer clients, all of them running ads with ambitious
and sometimes striking pictorial features. Other Ayer clients such as the
French Line and Marcus Jewelers were fond of Rockwell Kent designs in their
ads; De Beers Diamonds and Capehart, a radio manufacturer, used reproductions of paintings for their magazine publicity.

Advertisement for Container Corporation of America, by Edward McKnight Kauffer

Charles Coiner, director of Ayer's art department when Paepcke contacted him, was a painter who had begun his advertising career in Chicago with the firm of Erwin, Wasey. By 1930 he was outlining his ideas in the pages of the most sophisticated journal of American commercial art, the *Advertising Arts* section of *Advertising and Selling*, which signaled the beginning of a new cosmopolitanism in American advertising art. For the next five years it featured the most arresting commercial design available in Europe and America. Readers could learn about Sascha Maurer, Alexey Brodovitch, McKnight Kauffer, Herbert Roese, Otto Kühler, Ludwig Kozma, A. M. Cassandre, Joseph Binder, Julius Klinger, Otis Shepard, and Frederick Kiesler and encounter demonstrations of the latest techniques in printing technology and merchandise engineering. Coiner wrote several brief commentaries for *Advertising Arts*. These essays often focused on his work—for example, the Clicquot Champagne labels, the successful design for the famous blue eagle displayed by the National Industrial Recovery Act, and his decision to commission paintings by contemporary artists like Pierre Roy and Marie Laurencin for French Line ads.[62] "It would seem rather a bold stroke" to employ such artists, Coiner argued; yet France was "the source of virtually all that is new and significant in art." Even though Picasso, Dufy, and Rouault had inspired rug designs, the Ballets Russes de Monte Carlo had used sets by Derain and Dufy, and furniture, wallpaper, and page layouts had been profoundly influenced by French modernists, advertisers were not "going directly to the sources" for their commercial art.[63]

Coiner did. He ran his ads in "class" publications that attracted an educated, well-to-do audience. Well-informed, civilized readers, if "they [were] not already familiar with the artist [suspected] they should be." There was much progress to applaud, and Coiner praised in particular the Art Directors shows for their increasing modernism, which he found typified by artists Lester Beall, John Averill, Lucile Corcos, and Leo Rackow. If the "art director had proposed such art work to his clients a year or two ago," Coiner wrote in 1934, "he would have done nothing but infuriate them."[64]

Allowing the advertising agent to go directly to the sources, to important European modernists, and letting the art stand for itself, unencumbered with product messages, constituted the cornerstone of Container Corporation's departure in advertisements. After meeting with Jacobson, discussing Container's need, and examining domestic possibilities, Coiner turned away from American artists in favor of the Europeans he so admired. A. M. Cassandre, the Russian-born poster artist who had been working in France during the twenties, designed the first series of ads;[65] apparently Walter Paepcke himself suggested the second artist, Toni Zepf. During the late 1930s the work of Europeans, many of them recent émigrés, dominated Container campaigns. These émigrés included such notables as Herbert Bayer—probably the most distinguished European advertising artist working for Dorland in Berlin during the twenties and thirties—Herbert Matter, Gyorgy Kepes, Fernand Léger, and Jean Carlu, to name a few.[66] The advertisements were quickly rewarded by journals and professional groups, introducing Container to the select group of companies distinguished by their graphic presentations. Container's first appearance in the pages of the *Annual of Advertising Art* came in the sixteenth volume, published in 1937, which featured an airbrushed picture of a large boat by Fred Chance; the *Westvaco Inspirations for Printers* for 1936–37 included both Chance and Cassandre.[67]

This publicity increased during the forties and fifties with the famous series of themes—United Nations, United States, and Great Ideas. Container's reputation grew; the company became known for its understated, copy-minimal advertisements, which featured distinctive contemporary art commissioned from innovative artists without constraint on technique or subject. A new kind of corporate art patron had emerged, and others were standing in the wings.

Coiner and other art directors now found willing clients for fine graphic artists. Besides developing the French Line series and launching the Container program, Coiner helped plan many others. He sent Georgia O'Keeffe, Isamu Noguchi, Pierre Roy, and several others to Hawaii to create scenes that linked romance and pineapple juice. De Beers Diamonds, mounting a rescue operation to recover diamonds from the degradation of "kredit" jewelers, took Coiner's advice to associate itself with important artists; this would make the jewels more impressive and distinctive. Picasso, Dufy, Covarrubias, Marie Laurencin, and Derain participated in the De Beers strategy, which produced an impressive increase in sales.[68] Decades after the idea had been floated, major corporations came to realize that reproducing important art—traditional or contemporary, newly commissioned or already extent, connected to or disconnected from corporate themes, attached to copy or alone—sold the product and bought good will. From there it was only a short step to buying art for purposes of display, and surrounding the corporation itself, not simply its publicity, with the benefits art brought. And that step was quickly taken.

The rapidity and comprehensiveness of the movement that joined art with advertising and then went on to systematic corporate patronage was breathtaking. Almost nonexistent in the mid 1930s, it was so well established by 1946 that it evoked a number of significant commentaries, including a seminal essay written by Walter Abell, a faculty member at Michigan State University. That Abell's paper came only eleven years after Container's entry into modernism and offered perceptive insights into some major issues raised by the new trend justifies giving it attention.

Published in *Magazine of Art* (March 1946), Abell's article[69] argued that industrial patrons had raised artists to new levels of "recognition and affluence," transformed house organs into art museums, and stimulated the circulation of ideas and experiences by means of special exhibitions and art books. (The magazine cover carried a Ben Shahn illustration that was used in a Container advertisement.) Abell reviewed the work of Coiner and some of his lieutenants at Ayer (Leon Karp, Paul Darrow, Walter Reinsel, Leo Lionni); examined IBM's efforts to create (beginning in 1937) a painting collection based on artists from the dozens of countries in which the company operated; and summarized the work of Abbott Laboratories in Chicago, which had commissioned half a dozen separate projects involving war medicine, reproducing the art in its house organ, *What's New?* and repackaging it into special exhibitions.

Many campaigns were launched in the mid forties.[70] *Encyclopedia Britannica* commissioned paintings by American artists that were reproduced in its publications and assembled more than one hundred of the works for a national, five-year tour of American museums. Pepsi-Cola sponsored several Portrait of America competitions, which involved thousands of artists;[71] winners received cash awards and their works were reproduced in Pepsi calendars. Selected by independent juries without restriction of subject matter, this art was protected from interference. The advertiser, in Abell's words, had become the "patron of noncommercial painting rather than the purchaser of commercial adaptations of painting." Like Container Corporation of America, Pepsi-Cola reproduced the work of more "advanced experimental painters," such as Stuart Davis and Max Weber. By contrast with Coca-Cola glamour girls, "Pepsi-Cola really scores a 'pause that refreshes.'"

Standard Oil of New Jersey established still another patronage pattern. With the cooperation of the Associated American Artists, founded in 1934 to distribute fine prints and soon thereafter serve as a consultant to industrial art customers, Standard Oil commissioned sixteen artists to illustrate the industry's role in World War II.[72] Many of their paintings were reproduced in the company's in-house publication, the *Lamp.* Like Standard Oil and Abbott Laboratories, the Upjohn Company of Michigan made extensive use of graphic art in its internal bulletin. *Scope,* adapting existing art for use in its advertisements and distributing reproductions (suitable for framing) to thousands of physicians who displayed them in waiting rooms. Many bizarre paintings resulted from the Upjohn program, but it brought income to living artists. Abell also noted the involvement of department stores; for example, Ohrbach's in New York commissioned a set of city scenes and reproduced them in newspaper advertisements. It was Container Corporation of America, however, that maintained the most "consistently high standards of design and presentation."

There were other advertising campaigns as well: *Life, Fortune,* RCA Victor, Shell Oil, Pan American Airlines, Magnovox, and American Tobacco.[73] "Business, in a way, is assuming the role of patron held by the Church and aristocracy in past ages," Frank Caspers wrote in *Art Digest* (May 1943).[74] Industry was replacing the "tax-bereaved wealthy collector," Peyton Boswell commented in the same journal. Within ten years from the date when the bonds between art and industry had been limited and tentative, American corporations, in Abell's words, were establishing themselves as the "largest single source of support for the contemporary American painter."[75] Advertising campaigns, traveling shows, competitions, and collection development were impressive achievements. The outcome of important court cases and tax rulings encouraged corporate philanthropy: sponsorship of museum exhibitions on various themes, gifts for institutional needs and capital fund drives, matching contributions for employee gifts, and widespread use of art in corporate settings were established features of corporate programs by the late fifties and sixties.[76]

But even in 1946 the corporate impact was noticeable. Magazines and calendars bearing the newly commissioned art were viewed by millions; shows of corporate art, like the ones Container sponsored, set attendance records. Underpaid, underappreciated painters (and a few sculptors) obtained audiences and royalties on an unprecedented scale, and legitimacy came to contemporary subjects, including scenes of industrial work.

Pointing out these varied advantages, Abell also examined certain problems. The lure of easy money might lead some artists to lower their aesthetic standards, he admitted, and a few advertising campaigns had proven embarrassing because of commercial intensity or unhappy juxtapositions. Nonetheless, it was not unreasonable to hope for greater artistic freedom in the years ahead. And perhaps it was instructive to note that artists had always made compromises with the wishes of their patrons. Reynolds and Gainsborough had to please *their* sitters. "In the end it is not likely that the major production of any artist will be lower than his genius permits or his creative drive impels."

But despite the documented record of progress and his conviction that artists should not allow themselves to be coaxed into doing things they didn't really want to do, Abell's conclusions about the new relationship were not optimistic. Industrial patronage, he argued, was not the best foundation for a "true culture of democracy." Corporate art support rested neither on disinterested ideals nor superior discernment. It was merely that the "current profit system gives it larger concentrations of wealth." Once, a "handful of millionaires" decided that America should import old masters; now, a "handful of corporation executives" chose to sponsor certain kinds of painting. Or, as Dorothy Grafly put it at about the same time, the patrons had changed but the motives had not.[77] Most Americans, in any case, had little to say about the choices. Detecting "acute cultural malnutrition" in many areas of national life, Abell's primary complaint indicted the same corporate wealth that supported art patronage for contributing to unhealthy working conditions, child labor, and unemployment. Industrial advertising had enormous influence, and there seemed no instrument whereby the "social will and the cultural impulse of the American people [could] freely formulate themselves, independent of all industrial bias." The "ultimate ideals of a democratic culture," Abell concluded, would have to be realized by "other means than through patronage provided by industry." Two years earlier, his position had been even more dire: "Should all the arts come under the financial control of industry, and should industry continue to prove itself more interested in profits than in humanity, free men and free ways of life would have an appalling battle on their hands for the future." [78]

Both before and after these articles were published, American artists, critics, and social spokesmen debated the role of commercial patronage. Although certain artists, such as Thomas Hart Benton and Dale Nichols, advocated restraints on business interference, they welcomed the new opportunities. It was foolish and snobbish for artists to believe that commercial exploitation of their work destroyed their ideals, Nichols declared in 1940. "There is no need of a good artist living in poverty in America today, even should he be a painter of unpopular subjects." [79] Claude Fayette Bragdon, architect and graphic artist, had argued as early as the 1920s that a great body of aesthetic talent would suffer no blight through business associations. While the "highest type of artist" should avoid serving industry's needs, the rest of them should simply avoid fetters and time clocks; give the artist "plenty of air," Bragdon admonished business executives. [80]

There were, of course, artists who squirmed when advertising specialists proudly reported how much product their art had moved. [81] There were critics who complained about the traditionalism and sentimentality that continued to shape corporate preferences. But the chance to do art freely, no matter who paid, and the opportunity to view masterpieces, no matter who collected them, were attractive enough to allay many anxieties.

Optimists had other examples to point to besides Container. In a series of uncanny parallels, a Connecticut manufacturer of industrial lighting equipment remade product, salesrooms, advertising, and promotional campaigns in the image of modern art, while the owner and his wife, Burton and Emily Tremaine, expanded their collection of abstract art. [82] This shift in the Miller Company of Meriden, Connecticut, occurred in the 1940s. Some of the interest behind Miller's collection may have been more self-consciously practical than Container's art promotion. The effort, however, to display works by Van Doesburg, Braque, Mondrian, Miró, Picasso, Klee, Gris, Bolotowsky, and other abstractionists in order to influence the ideas of company engineers, sales personnel, and advertisers and increase the distinctiveness of the company product, fit a popular mood.

At the same time, critics Russell Lynes and Aline Louchheim were urging corporate clients to be businesslike in making artistic decisions, to be unafraid of finding needs and uses for their art. Abstract art could serve a sponsor such as the Miller Company as "directly as the art of the Renaissance satisifed the desires of the merchant princes who were its purchasers," Louchheim wrote in 1947.[83] Industry would do better by artists "if it [would treat] them less like glamorous recording angels and more like the serious observers and craftsmen that the best of them are," Lynes suggested in an important essay for *Harper's*.[84] The aim of business should be less that of becoming an art patron and more that of developing into a good employer and a discriminating consumer. The art that was purchased would, in the end, have to stand on its own anyway.

The next fifteen or twenty years brought impressive expansion. Contemporary and American art became the special interest of patrons like the Chase Manhattan Bank of New York, S. C. Johnson of Racine, Wisconsin, the First National Bank of Chicago, Prudential Insurance, Inland Steel, Sears, Roebuck and Company, Burndy Corporation of Norwalk, IBM, Reynolds Metals, New York Life, Joseph Seagram, Hallmark, and dozens of other companies.[85] In 1952 the Dallas Museum of Fine Arts, spurred on by a local patron, Stanley Marcus, mounted an exhibition entitled The Pictures Businessmen Buy.[86] In the fifties individual corporations, including Meta-Mold Aluminum of Cedarburg, Wisconsin, the Miller Company, Abbott Laboratories, and Container, put their own collections on display.[87] In 1960 the Whitney Museum of American Art presented Business Buys American Art and received hundreds of replies to its questionnaire from companies directly interested in some form of art patronage. As budgets and curatorial expertise mounted—between 1968 and 1974 the First National Bank of Chicago purchased thousands of art objects—so did the ambitiousness of the programs.[88]

There were those who continued to worry about business taste. The Johnson Collection of Contemporary American Art, acquired for the wax company because of the interest of Herbert F. Johnson, elicited wide praise. Lloyd Goodrich called it an "extraordinary collection." But Thomas Hess judged its general effect to be one of "flatness, timidity and compromise." Searching for the tangibles of culture-business, he discovered only its "mirrored image—the Safe and Sane look—which is a quality that helps to manufacture things and sell them, and which is disastrous to art." Despite its disappointments and continued artistic contempt, however, "Big Business remain[ed] fascinated, like an elephant transfixed by mice."[89]

Betty Kaufman was another who was not impressed by corporate standards. Reviewing the 1960 Whitney show, she detected little of the "ardor, richness or variety that one associates with the term 'art patron.'"[90] Unlike the church of an earlier day, business seemed neither to inspire nor foster any particular kind of art. On some levels it may have been reassuring to learn that, like most private buyers, corporations played it safe and relied heavily on the advice of specialists. But it was also disillusioning. With all the resources at their disposal it seemed a confession of inadequacy for corporations to order their art the way some hobbyists painted pictures, matching colors with numbers to achieve a formula-ridden expression of taste rather than an idiosyncratic statement of personal judgment.

Of course, timidity and standardization could be found anywhere. Museums themselves would be charged with imitating one another's collecting patterns and preferring predictable choices to the adventure of taking risks. And there were many private collectors who leaned heavily on dealers' advice or followed market trends. Individual patrons enjoyed no absolute superiority to the corporation.

A more fundamental question, perhaps, involved the privilege and wealth that art purchasing symbolized and the influence it brought the owner. Abell had seized on the heart of this problem—the issue of reflected glory. The confusion of realms that seemed so desirable a goal when industrial and fine arts were arbitrarily wrenched apart in earlier centuries, now developed into a new source of anxiety. Corporate commissioning, exhibiting, purchasing, and advertising of art involved a series of mimicries. It was not uncommon for corporate offices and showrooms to assume the character of museums; corporations to claim the status of sensitive patrons; artists to don the role of publicists; and cultural institutions to take on the appearance of branch offices. Attitudes to corporate interest in art depended as much on attitudes to the corporations as they did on views of the arts.

To those who found the capitalist free-enterprise system distasteful, unreasonable, or debasing, business exploitation of art was vulgar or threatening. It could occasionally even seem tyrannical. Some denounced redesigned office schemes featuring art objects because they were part of an efficiency scheme that turned employees into standardized robots. Workers could no longer move their furniture around at will or display family pictures on their desks; this disturbed the decorative scheme. When a "work of art is made to fit into a total design it is alienated from its aesthetic personality."[91] Paintings and people could be reduced to the level of things, if art objects became instruments through which to assert total control.

"The artist," wrote Peter Clecak in 1967, "pays an exorbitant price for this seat at the business table." Accepting financial aid from a corporate sponsor and remaining silent about that patron's unsavory exploitation of cheap labor or immoral interventions into foreign policy, only undermined the artist's vision. If the artist is an "indispensable part of civilization's survival plan, [that same artist] must demonstrate that the American corporation is not."[92]

More recently, and more politely, other critics (and administrators) have worried that exhibition subsidies might place museums "on the slippery road to becoming public relations agents for the interests of big business and its ideological allies." The choices of works to place on exhibition and their very forms of presentation "create a climate that supports prevailing distributions of power and capital and persuades the populace that the status quo is the natural and best order of things."[93]

The cohabitation of art and industry presents its own dilemmas. Art has always been "contaminated" with commerce, even when museums struggled to resemble classical temples. But the fiction that art represented a transcendent realm where connoisseurs and devotees could escape the clarion calls of commerce served a need. It may well have deflected attention from economic injustice and political absurdity, as some charge, but it also shielded aesthetic authority from the ongoing competition for economic gain. The insulation of art from commerce and industry disguised many connections. It limited commercial vocabularies to phrases and images that stood apart from the legacy of the great art traditions, and suddenly this almost royal prestige was available to anyone with the price of a subsidy or the space for an exhibition. Individuals had sought this distinction for millennia, it is true, so had monarchies and religious establishments. But in the mid twentieth century, they seemed less dangerous than the corporate dynasties still actively selling their myriad wares. Was it unfair, even sinister, for great corporations to attach to themselves the eternal splendor of art? How would they exploit these associations? And under whose auspices should the public view those objects that constituted its common heritage?

These questions demand thoughtful answers. In the United States the solution to fear of domination has been to encourage competition. Governments, individuals, universities, industries, and foundations contend for respect and affection. What marks the occasion of this exhibition with special effect is its reassertion of older patterns within an apparently novel world. The art commissioned by a corporation to enhance its reputation (as well as to succor artists, send a message, and interest the public) is now collectively moved to a public setting, just as the collections of princes and archbishops so often found their way by purchase, conquest, or appropriation to institutions enjoying civic legitimacy. The directions of today's corporate patronage and the ultimate destination of its accumulated treasures are difficult to discern. Company collections and workplace art seem to have secure futures, but not necessarily eternal ones. Art and authority have always faced the prospect of strong tensions and will continue to make mutual demands of one another. What counts in the end is the authenticity of each sphere and their occasional renunciations. If the artists represented here renounced, even fleetingly some of their absolute independence to serve a corporate client, it is reassuring to see their art renounced to the care of a more accessible setting. A business collection, developed in the interest of advertising, now arrives at the Smithsonian, a public institution that itself is named for a private donor. This confusion of realms promises, at least, only satisfaction and fulfillment.

NOTES

1

Four Stages of Cultural Growth:
The American City

1. The most extended treatment of antiurban thought can be found in Morton and Lucia White, *The Intellectual Versus the City: From Thomas Jefferson to Frank Lloyd Wright* (New York: New American Library, 1964).

2. I refer, among other books, to Sam Bass Warner, Jr., *Streetcar Suburbs: The Process of Growth in Boston, 1870–1900* (Cambridge: Harvard University Press, 1962); Sam Bass Warner, Jr., *The Private City: Philadelphia in Three Periods of its Growth* (Philadelphia: University of Pennsylvania Press, 1968); Gilbert Osofsky, *Harlem: The Making of a Ghetto—Negro New York, 1890–1930* (New York: Harper & Row, 1966); Seymour J. Mandelbaum, *Boss Tweed's New York* (New York: J. Wiley, 1965); John W. Reps, *The Making of Urban America: A History of City Planning in the United States* (Princeton: Princeton University Press, 1965); E. Digby Baltzell, *Philadelphia Gentlemen: The Making of a National Upper Class* (Glencoe, Ill.: Free Press, 1958); Stephan Thernstrom, *Poverty and Progress: Social Mobility in a Nineteenth Century City* (Cambridge: Harvard University Press, 1964); Roger Lane, *Policing the City: Boston, 1822–1885* (Cambridge: Harvard University Press, 1967); and James F. Richardson, *The New York Police: Colonial Times to 1901* (New York: Oxford University Press, 1970).

3. Raymond Williams, *Culture and Society, 1780–1950* (London: Chatto & Windus, 1958), passim.

4. The best survey of colonial cultural institutions can be found in two classic books by Carl Bridenbaugh, *Cities in the Wilderness: The First Century of Urban Life in America, 1625–1742* (New York: Ronald Press, 1938) and *Cities in Revolt: Urban Life in America, 1743–1776* (New York: Knopf, 1955).

5. Some of the cultural implications of an articulate nationalism can be found in Benjamin T. Spencer, *The Quest for Nationality* (Syracuse: Syracuse University Press, 1957); Lewis P. Simpson (ed.), *The Federalist Literary Mind: Selections from the* Monthly Anthology *and* Boston Review, *1803–1811* (Baton Rouge: Louisiana State University Press, 1962); Van Wyck Brooks, *The World of Washington Irving* (New York: E. P. Dutton, 1944); Neil Harris, *The Artist in American Society: The Formative Years, 1790–1860* (New York: G. Braziller, 1966); Lillian B. Miller, *Patrons and Patriotism: The Encouragement of the Fine Arts in the United States, 1790–1860* (Chicago: University of Chicago Press, 1966); and James T. Callow, *Kindred Spirits: Knickerbocker Writers and American Artists, 1807–1855* (Chapel Hill: University of North Carolina Press, 1967).

6. Among works of interest for this institutionalization are Carl Bode, *The American Lyceum: Town Meeting of the Mind* (New York: Oxford University Press, 1956); Thomas S. Cummings, *Historic Annals of the National Academy of Design* (Philadelphia: G. W. Childs, 1865); Eliot Clark, *History of the National Academy of Design, 1825–1953* (New York: Columbia University Press, 1954); Helen W. Henderson, *The Pennsylvania Academy of the Fine Arts* (Boston: L. C. Page & Co., 1911); Mary Bartlett Cowdrey (ed.), *American Academy of Fine Arts and American Art-Union, 1816–1852* (2 vols., New York: New-York Historical Society, 1953).

7. For information about urban audiences see David Grimsted, *Melodrama Unveiled: American Theater and Culture, 1800–1850* (Chicago: University of Chicago Press, 1968), chap. 3, and Blanche Muldrow, "The American Theatre as Seen by British Travellers, 1770–1860" (Ph.D. diss., University of Wisconsin, 1953). Biographies of famous actors such as Edwin Forrest and William Charles Macready, are also important sources for audience descriptions.

8. Some of these tours are described in Milton Goldin, *The Music Merchants* (New York: Macmillan, 1969), and Henry Knepler, *The Gilded Stage: The Years of the Great International Actresses* (New York: W. Morrow, 1968). For the Jenny Lind tour particularly see Gladys Denny Shultz, *Jenny Lind: The Swedish Nightingale* (Philadelphia and New York: Lippincott, 1962).

9. For Moses Kimball's Boston Museum see Claire McGlinchee, *The First Decade of the Boston Museum* (Boston: B. Humphries, 1940). For Barnum's museum activities see any of the editions of his autobiography. For the Peale family see Charles Coleman Sellers, *The Artist of the Revolution: The Early Life of Charles Willson Peale* (Hebron, Conn.: Feather & Good, 1939) and *Later Life of Charles Willson Peale (1790–1827)* (Philadelphia: American Philosophical Society, 1947). For the Western Museum in Cincinnati see Richard C. Wade, *The Urban Frontier* (Cambridge: Harvard University Press, 1959), p. 261, and Henry D. Shapiro and Zane L. Miller (eds.), *Physician to the West: Selected Writings of Daniel Drake on Science and Society* (Lexington: University Press of Kentucky, 1970), pp. 131–50.

10. For information on the art unions see Harris, *The Artist in American Society,* passim, and Miller, *Patrons and Patriotism,* chap. 14. The most detailed study of the American Art-Union can be found in Charles E. Baker, "The American Art-Union," in Cowdrey (ed.), *American Academy of Fine Arts,* 1:95–240.

11. Michael Aaron Rockland (trans. and ed.), *Sarmiento's Travels in the United States in 1847* (Princeton: Princeton University Press, 1970), pp. 141–45. Daniel J. Boorstin, *The Americans: The National Experience* (New York: Random House,

1965), pp. 134–47, contains a provocative discussion of American hotels.

12. Rockland (trans. and ed.), *Sarmiento's Travels,* p. 151.

13. No one work covers the history of these institutions. However, important information and observations can be found in the following books: Lewis Mumford, *The Brown Decades: A Study of the Arts in America, 1865–1895* (New York: Harcourt, Brace & Co., 1931); Lewis Mumford, *The Culture of Cities* (New York: Harcourt, Brace & Co., 1938); Arthur M. Schlesinger, *The Rise of the City, 1878–1898* (New York: Macmillan Co., 1933); Dixon Wector, *The Saga of American Society: A Record of Social Aspiration, 1607–1937* (New York: C. Scribner's Sons, 1937); John H. Mueller, *The American Symphony Orchestra: A Social History of Musical Taste* (Bloomington: Indiana University Press, 1951); Laurence Vail Coleman, *The Museum in America* (3 vols.; Washington: American Association of Museums, 1939); Walter Pach, *The Art Museum in America* (New York: Pantheon, 1948); Aline B. Saarinen, *The Proud Possessors* (New York: Random House, 1958); Russell Lynes, *The Tastemakers* (New York: Harper, 1954); and Daniel M. Fox, *Engines of Culture: Philanthropy and Art Museums* (Madison: State Historical Society of Wisconsin for the Department of History, University of Wisconsin, 1963). Individual histories include Winifred E. Howe, *A History of the Metropolitan Museum of Art* (2 vols.; New York: Gilliss Press, 1913–46); Calvin Tomkins, *Merchants and Masterpieces: The Story of the Metropolitan Museum of Art* (New York: Dutton, 1970); Walter Muir Whitehill, *Museum of Fine Arts, Boston: A Centennial History* (2 vols.; Cambridge: Belknap Press, 1970); Carl Wittke, *The First Fifty Years: The Cleveland Museum of Art, 1916–1966* (Cleveland: John Huntingdon Art and Polytechnic Trust, Cleveland Museum of Art, 1966); Charles E. Russell, *The American Orchestra and Theodore Thomas* (Garden City, N.Y.: Doubleday, Page & Co., 1927); H. E. Krehbiel, *The Philharmonic Society of New York* (New York: Novello, Ewer & Co., 1892); Philo A. Otis, *The Chicago Symphony Orchestra* (Chicago: Clayton F. Summy Co., 1925); Frances A. Wister, *Twenty-Five Years of the Philadelphia Orchestra,*

1900–1925 (Philadelphia: Published under the auspices of the Women's committees for the Philadelphia Orchestra, 1925).

14. Mueller, *The American Symphony Orchestra*, pp. 37–51, describes this phase of the Philharmonic's history.

15. See M. A. De Wolfe Howe, *The Boston Symphony Orchestra, 1881–1931* (Boston and New York: Houghton Mifflin Co., 1931).

16. Ibid., p. 40.

17. Ibid., p. 75.

18. Neil Harris, "The Gilded Age Revisited: Boston and the Museum Movement," *American Quarterly* 14 (Winter, 1962): 545–66, analyzes the motives of founding trustees.

19. Fox, *Engines of Culture*, p. 12.

20. Ibid., p. 13.

21. For a discussion of the expressions of this cultural separatism see the introduction in Neil Harris (ed.), *The Land of Contrasts, 1880–1901* (New York: G. Braziller, 1970).

22. Albert F. McLean, Jr., *American Vaudeville as Ritual* (Lexington: University Press of Kentucky, 1965), p. 42.

23. For nineteenth-century expositions see Kenneth Luckhurst, *The Story of Exhibitions* (London: Studio Publications, 1951). Although the great American fairs are frequently commented upon by historians, there exist no truly informative secondary accounts.

24. Nicholas Vachel Lindsay, *The Art of the Moving Picture* (Being the 1922 revision of the book first issued in 1915; New York: Liveright, 1970), pp. 247–48. Lindsay notes (p. 219), "The big social fact about the moving picture is that it is scattered like the newspaper."

25. This anecdote is told by Grace Glueck, "Power and Esthetics: The Trustee," *Art in America* 69 (July–August, 1971): 78. This issue of the journal was devoted to articles on museum history and values.

(2)

All the World a Melting Pot? Japan at American Fairs, 1876–1904

1. Clay Lancaster, *The Japanese Influence in American Architecture* (New York: W. H. Rawls, 1963). The book contains the best account of Japanese participation at American fairs.

2. Scholarly literature on the fairs is sketchy. The best survey is Kenneth W. Luckhurst, *The Story of Exhibitions* (London and New York: Studio Publications, 1951). The Crystal Palace has received more attention than any subsequent exhibition, although every international fair published at least one authoritative (and usually multivolume) history. Merle Curti, "America at the World's Fairs, 1851–1893," *American Historical Review* 55 (June 1950): 833–56, is one of the few recent articles. For more bibliography and an essay on the bibliographical problems and opportunities for writing the history of fairs see Richard D. Mandell, *Paris 1900: The Great World's Fair* (Toronto: University of Toronto Press, 1967), pp. 122–39.

3. Luckhurst, *Story of Exhibitions*, pp. 220–21, presents a tabular survey of exhibition costs, attendance, and so forth.

4. For a concise history of the Centennial Exhibition see Edward C. Bruce, *The Century: Its Fruits and Its Festival* (Philadelphia, 1877). The multivolume *United States Centennial Commission: International Exhibition, 1876* (Washington, D.C., 1880) contains massive amounts of information. James D. McCabe, *The Illustrated History of the Centennial Exhibition* (Philadelphia, Chicago, St. Louis, 1876) is helpful. A bibliography of material on the centennial can be found in Julia Finette Davis, "International Expositions, 1851–1900," in William B. O'Neil, ed., *The American Association of Architectural Bibliographers, Papers* 4 (1967):47–130. The most recent study of the Centennial Exhibition is John Maass, *The Glorious Enterprise: The Centennial Exhibition of 1876 and H. J. Schwarzmann, Architect-in-Chief* (Watkins Glen, N.Y.: American Life Foundation, 1973). Finally, see the provocative

essay on three American exhibitions by John G. Cawelti, "America on Display: The World's Fairs of 1876, 1893, 1933," in Frederic Cople Jaher, ed., *The Age of Industrialism in America: Essays in Social Structure and Cultural Values* (New York: Free Press, 1968), pp. 317–63.

5. Bruce, *The Century*, p. 65.

6. This account is based on *International Exhibition, 1876: Official Catalogue of the Japanese Section* (Philadelphia, 1876).

7. *United States Centennial Commission: Report of the Director General* (Washington, D.C., 1880), I, 54.

8. Ibid., p. 369.

9. *New York Times*, February 4, 1876, p. 1. For similar reactions see Scrapbook of Centennial Clippings, Historical Society of Pennsylvania (hereafter cited as HSP Scrapbook), p. 24; and *Philadelphia Graphic*, February 3, 1876.

10. W. D. Howells, "A Sennight of the Centennial," *Atlantic Monthly* 38 (July 1876): 97.

11. "Characteristics of the International Fair," ibid., p. 91.

12. Ibid., p. 89.

13. J. S. Ingram, *The Centennial Exposition* (Philadelphia, 1876), pp. 559–60, gives a clear description of the Japanese arrangement in the main building.

14. McCabe, *The Centennial Exhibition*, p. 446.

15. "Characteristics of the International Fair," *Atlantic Monthly* 38 (July 1876): 90.

16. HSP Scrapbook, p. 58.

17. Bruce, *The Century*, p. 141.

18. HSP Scrapbook, p. 92.

19. *New York Times*, June 24, 1877, p. 6.

20. "The Japs' Handiwork," HSP Scrapbook.

21. Bruce, *The Century*, p. 80.

22. HSP Scrapbook, p. 58.

23. Bruce, *The Century*, p. 141.

24. Ingram, *The Centennial Exposition*, p. 560.

25. [Marietta Holley,] *Josiah Allen's Wife as a P. A. and P. I. Samantha at the Centennial* (Hartford, Conn., 1878), pp. 440–45.

26. Ibid., p. 444.

27. "Characteristics of the International Fair," *Atlantic Monthly* 38 (July 1876): 91.

28. "Characteristics of the International Fair,"

Atlantic Monthly 38 (December 1876): 733.

29. For a discussion of Japanese appeals to American eclecticism see Lancaster, *The Japanese Influence*, p. 62.

30. Charles Wyllys Elliott, "Pottery at the Centennial," *Atlantic Monthly* 38 (November 1876): 576.

31. "Japanese Art," *New York Times*, June 24, 1887, p. 6.

32. *Philadelphia Bulletin*, July 2, 1875.

33. Bruce, *The Century*, pp. 244–45.

34. *Samantha at the Centennial*, pp. 444–45.

35. Bruce, *The Century*, p. 244.

36. HSP Scrapbook, p. 92.

37. Carl T. Western, *Adventures of Reuben and Cynthy at the World's Fair, As Told by Themselves* (Chicago, 1893), p. 101.

38. HSP Scrapbook, p. 92.

39. See Lafcadio Hearn, *Occidental Gleanings: Sketches and Essays Now First Collected by Albert Mordell* (Freeport, N.Y.: Dodd, Mead & Co., 1967) 2:209–40. Half a dozen of Hearn's articles are reprinted in this collection.

40. Good accounts of the Columbian Exposition can be found in Hubert Howe Bancroft, *The Book of the Fair*, 2 vols. (Chicago, 1894); D. H. Burnham, *World's Columbian Exposition: The Book of the Builders* (Chicago, 1894); H. N. Higginbotham, *Report of the President* (Chicago, 1898); R. Johnson, ed., *History of the World's Columbian Exposition*, 4 vols. (New York, 1897).

41. Gōzō Tateno, "Foreign Nations at the World's Fair," *North American Review* 156 (January 1893): 33–43.

42. "Unpacking Art Exhibits," *Harper's Weekly* 37 (April 15, 1893): 355.

43. "The World's Japanese Exposition: The Japanese Village," *Harper's Weekly* 37 (March 18, 1893): 259.

44. Lancaster, *The Japanese Influence*, p. 83. Lancaster presents a detailed description of the Hōōden.

45. *The Official Directory of the World's Columbian Exposition* (Chicago, 1893).

46. H. D. Northrop, *The World's Fair as Seen in One Hundred Days* (Philadelphia, 1893), p. 508. See also Mrs. Mark Stevens, *Six Months at the*

World's Fair (Detroit, 1895), p. 54.

47. Northrop, *The World's Fair*, p. 582.

48. Ibid., p. 591.

49. *Harper's Weekly* 38 (October 28, 1893): 1023.

50. [Marietta Holley,] *Samantha at the World's Fair, by Josiah Allen's Wife* (New York, London, Toronto, 1893), p. 402.

51. Ibid., p. 405.

52. Ibid., pp. 594–95.

53. Denton J. Snider, *World's Fair Studies* (Chicago, 1895), p. 230. Snider was an American Hegelian; his book is one of the most interesting interpretations of the White City published at the time.

54. H. G. Cutler, *The World's Fair: Its Meaning and Scope* (Chicago 1892), p. 286. This book was published before the fair opened and was designed to publicize the forthcoming exhibition.

55. Mrs. D. C. Taylor, *Halcyon Days in the Dream City* (n.p., n.d.), pp. 35, 42.

56. Julian Hawthorne, *Humors of the Fair* (Chicago, n.d.), p. 93.

57. Cutler, *The World's Fair*, p. 281. This, of course, was an exaggeration.

58. The figures can be found in Higginbotham, *Report of the President*.

59. Tudor Jenks, *The Century World's Fair Book for Boys and Girls* (New York, 1893), p. 144.

60. Western, *Adventures of Reuben and Cynthy*, p. 100.

61. "Quondam," *The Adventures of Uncle Jeremiah and Family at the Great Fair* (Chicago, 1893), p. 100. Other writers used the metaphor of reversing the direction of missionaries from East to West. See *Samantha at the World's Fair*, p. 594.

62. Bancroft, *The Book of the Fair*, 1:222.

63. *Official Directory of the World's Columbian Exposition*, p. 133.

64. Joseph Kirkland and Caroline Kirkland, *The Story of Chicago* (Chicago, 1894) 2:135.

65. Snider, *World's Fair Studies*, pp. 229–30.

66. Ibid., p. 231.

67. William Elroy Curtis, *The Yankees of the East: Sketches of Modern Japan* (New York, 1896, 1906), p. 561.

68. A Herbage Edwards, *Kakemono Japanese Sketches* (Chicago: A. C. McClurg, 1906), p. 209.

69. Gōzō Tateno, "Foreign Nations at the World's Fair," p. 43.

70. See, for example, the editorial, "The Japanese Indemnity Fund," *Harper's Weekly* 20 (February 19, 1876): 143. The money was paid back in 1893.

71. The history of the Japanese effort is described in Hajime Hoshi, *Handbook of Japan and Japanese Exhibits at World's Fair* (St. Louis, 1904); and Isaac F. Marcosson, "Japan's Extraordinary Exhibit," *World's Work* 8 (August 1904: 5146–53. This entire issue of *World's Work* was devoted to the fair. See also *The Exhibition of the Empire of Japan: Official Catalogue* (St. Louis, 1904).

72. For the St. Louis fair see *The History of the Louisiana Purchase Exposition* (St. Louis, 1904), a profusely illustrated book; and David R. Francis, *The Universal Exposition of 1904*, 2 vols. (St. Louis, 1913). Francis was the president and leading spirit of the exposition.

73. Plans showing the comparative size of American expositions can be found in G. H. Edgell, *The American Architecture of To-day* (New York and London: Scribner's, 1928), p. 52.

74. Baron Hirata Tōsuke, minister of agriculture and commerce, was the president of the commission; Tejima Seiichi was commissioner general.

75. Lancaster, *The Japanese Influence*, pp. 155–56.

76. *World's Work* 8 (August 1904): 5061.

77. The figures are printed in Francis, *The Universal Exposition*, 1:580–89.

78. [Marietta Holley,] *Samantha at the St. Louis Exposition, by Josiah Allen's Wife* (New York: G. W. Dillingham, 1904), p. 239.

79. Ibid., pp. 91–92.

80. Ibid., p. 242. This was certainly Samantha's most enthusiastic reaction to any of the three exhibitions Marietta Holley published books about.

81. Marcosson, "Japan's Extraordinary Exhibit," p. 5153.

82. "Lights and Shadows at the St. Louis Exposition," *Nation* 79 (September 1, 1904): 175.

83. Mabel Loomis Todd, "The Louisiana Exposition," *Nation* 78 (June 30, 1904): 511.

84. Francis, *The Universal Exposition*, 1:359. There also appeared highly sophisticated discussions of Japanese art efforts, the product, in part, of

years of writing and lecturing by men such as Ernest Fenollosa. See, for example, Charles H. Caffin, "The Exhibit of Paintings and Sculptures," *World's Work* 8 (August 1904): 5179–84.

85. "Is Japanese Progress Changing Japanese Character?" *World's Work* 8 (May 1904): 4726–27.

86. "Japan and the Jingoes," *Nation* 79 (September 29, 1904): 254–55.

87. "Japan's Rising Influence Won by War," *World's Work* 8 (July 1904): 4948. See also the interesting comments in "The Spirit of New Japan," *Harper's Weekly* 58 (December 24, 1904): 1982, where the ironies of military success as a device to gain world attention are canvassed. "We may be certain that the surface hardness which the fierce contests of material life have imposed upon Japan are for a time only," *Harper's* concluded, "and that, once her national well-being is assured, the old beauty and idealism will once more shine through." In its own way, therefore, *Harper's* also was worried about the effects of modernization in changing the distinctive character of old Japan. See also "The Japanese Spirit," *World's Work* 7 (June 1904): 4837, in which the writer argues that the new spirit demonstrated by the Japanese will be present in whatever enterprises they undertake, even after the war is over. Many American journals, overwhelmingly sympathetic to the Japanese side, were at pains to counter the Yellow Peril argument that Russians and others were propagating.

88. "Japan: A Paradox in Education," *Nation* 78 (April 28, 1904): 327.

89. Quoted in Barbara Solomon, *Ancestors and Immigrants: A Changing New England Tradition* (Cambridge, Mass.: Harvard University Press, 1956), pp. 57–58.

90. These included William James, Emily Balch, Jane Addams, and Charles William Eliot. See ibid., chap. 9.

3

Museums, Merchandising, and Popular Taste: The Struggle for Influence

1. For more on the ideals of early museum founders, see Daniel M. Fox, *Engines of Culture: Philanthropy and Art Museums* (Madison: State Historical Society of Wisconsin for the Department of History, University of Wisconsin, 1963); Helen Lefkowitz Horowitz, *Culture and the City: Cultural Philanthropy from the 1880s to 1917* (Lexington: University Press of Kentucky, 1976). See also Neil Harris, "The Gilded Age Revisited: Boston and the Museum Movement," *American Quarterly* 14 (Winter, 1962): 545–66. Many museum histories also contain statements by founders. Among others, see Winifred E. Howe, *A History of the Metropolitan Museum of Art* (2 vols.; New York: Gillis Press, 1913–46), vol. 1; and Walter Muir Whitchill, *Museum of Fine Arts, Boston: A Centennial History* (2 vols.; Cambridge: Harvard University Press, Belknap Press, 1970).

2. A useful summary of World's Fair activities can be found in Kenneth Luckhurst, *The Story of Exhibitions* (London and New York: Studio Publications, 1951). For the influence of fairs on American architecture and city planning, see John W. Reps, *The Making of Urban America* (Princeton: Princeton University Press, 1965), chap. 18; William H. Jordy, *American Buildings and Their Architects* (4 vols.; Garden City, N.Y.: Doubleday 1972), vol. 3, chap. 6; and Thomas S. Hines, *Burnham of Chicago, Architect and Planner* (New York: Oxford University Press, 1974), chaps. 5–6. The best recent study of an American fair is John Maass, *The Glorious Enterprise: The Centennial Exhibition of 1876 and J. H. Schwartzmann, Architect-in-Chief* (Watkins Glen, N.Y.: American Life Foundation, Institute for the Study of Universal History through Arts and Artifacts, 1973). See also David F. Burg, *Chicago's White City of 1893* (Lexington: University Press of Kentucky, 1976). For the impact of foreign displays, see chap. 2.

3. Sophia A. Walker, "An Art Impression of the Exposition," *Independent* 53 (July 18, 1901): 1678.

4. Information on these fair officials has been gathered from fair histories and from various biographical encyclopedias.

5. *The Chicago Record's History of the World's Fair* (Chicago: Daily News Co., 1893), p. 89.

6. "The New Art of Lighting," *Literary Digest* 32 (April 7, 1906): 515.

7. *Chicago Record's History*, p. 98.

8. In 1893 the *Nation* ran a long series of articles summarizing the exposition, examining and evaluating the buildings and exhibits.

9. "The First Week of the Exhibition," *New York Tribune*, May 18, 1876, p. 4. This kind of observation could be multiplied a hundredfold in the magazines and newspapers of the day. For example, see Alice Freeman Palmer, "Some Lasting Results of the World's Fair," *Forum* 16 (Dec. 1893): 517–23; Mary Clemmer, "The Opening of the Centennial," *Independent* 28 (May 18, 1876): 1–2; John Brisben Walker, "A World's Fair," *Cosmopolitan* 15 (July, 1893): 518–19; E. L. Godkin, "Refuse," *Nation* 57 (Oct. 26, 1893): 302.

10. Paul Bourget, *Outre-Mer: Impressions of America* (New York: C. Scribner's Sons, 1895), p. 231.

11. "The Exposition as an Educational Force," *Scientific American* 91 (Aug. 6, 1904): 90.

12. For department-store history, see John William Ferry, *A History of the Department Store*, American Assembly series (New York: Prentice-Hall, 1960); Daniel J. Boorstin, *The Americans: The Democratic Experience* (New York: Random House, 1973), pp. 101–9, and bibliographical notes, pp. 629–30.

13. For the history of Marshall Field and Company, see Lloyd Wendt and Herman Kogan, *Give the Lady What She Wants!* (Chicago: Rand McNally & Co., 1952), passim.

14. Hugh Dalziel Duncan, *Culture and Democracy* (Totowa, N.J.: Bedminster Press, 1965), p. 24.

15. Ibid., p. 116.

16. Ralph M. Hower, *History of Macy's of New York, 1858–1909: Chapters in Evolution of the Department Store* (Cambridge: Harvard University Press, 1943), p. 284.

17. Herbert Gibbons, *John Wanamaker* (2 vols.;

New York and London: Harper & Bros., 1926), 2:81.

18. Wendt and Kogan, *Give the Lady What She Wants!*, pp. 218, 308. Field's display of art objects and furniture was so impressive that the Art Institute of Chicago bought several of the interiors.

19. Carlos E. Cummings, *East Is East and West Is West: Some Observations on the World's Fair of 1939 by One Whose Main Interest Is in Museums* (East Aurora, N.Y.: Printed by the Roycrofters, 1940).

20. Douglas Haskell, "To-Morrow and the World's Fair," *Architectural Record* 88 (Aug., 1940): 65–72. For some perceptive observations on the changing appearance of American fairs, see John G. Cawelti, "America on Display: The World's Fairs of 1876, 1893, 1933," in Frederic Cople Jaher (ed.), *The Age of Industrialism in America* (New York and London: Free Press, 1968), pp. 317–63. For more on the changing nature of design during the interwar period and for excellent visual materials, see Donald J. Bush, *The Streamlined Decade* (New York: George Braziller, 1975); and Martin Grief, *Depression Modern: The Thirties Style in America* (New York: Universe Books, 1975).

21. Cummings, *East Is East*, pp. 39–40.

22. Lee Simonson, "Redesigning Department Stores," *Architectural Forum* 58 (May, 1933): 374–78.

23. Architectural journals of the 1920s and 1930s are filled with articles about the value of redesigning store interiors and exteriors. Among many others, see Ely Jacques Kahn, "The Modern European Shop and Store," *Architectural Forum* 50 (June, 1929): 789–804; John Matthews Hatton, "The Architecture of Merchandising," *Architectural Forum* 54 (April, 1931): 443–46; the entire issue of *Architectural Forum* 40 (June, 1924); James B. Newman, "A Modern Store," *Architectural Forum* 53 (Nov., 1930): 572–78; and "Store Modernization Gets Big Play," *Business Week* 454 (May 14, 1938): 38–40.

24. The Sack store is described in *Architectural Forum* 45 (Aug., 1926), pls. 22–24; Whittall's is described in *Architectural Forum* 49 (July, 1928): 86–87.

25. For department stores and cultural activities,

see Edith M. Stern, "Buy-Paths to Learning," *Reader's Digest* 32 (May, 1938): 90–92.

26. Quoted in Zelda F. Popkin, "Art: Three Aisles Over," *Outlook and Independent* 156 (Nov. 26, 1930): 515

27. Doublas Rigby and Elizabeth Rigby, *Lock, Stock and Barrel: The Story of Collecting* (Philadelphia, New York, and London: J. B. Lippincott Co., 1944), p. 503; for a detailed description of the department-store art sales, see pp. 499–503.

28. Forest H. Cooke, "Culture and Fatigue," *Century Magazine* 3 (Jan., 1926): 295; see also *Atlantic Monthly* 144 (Dec., 1929): 770–72.

29. John Cotton Dana, "The Use of Museums," *Nation* 115 (Oct. 11, 1922): 375.

30. "Art Museums Humanized," *Saturday Evening Post* 200 (March 31, 1928): 26.

31. Frederic Thompson, "Beauty for the Masses," *Commonweal Magazine* 10 (May 8, 1929): 14–15.

32. Lee Simonson, "Skyscrapers for Art Museums," *American Mercury* 10 (Aug., 1927): 401.

33. Ibid., 403.

34. Ibid., 404.

35. Laurence Vail Coleman, *Museum Buildings* (Washington, D.C.: American Association of Museums, 1950), pp. 4–6. For useful information on the evolution of art-museum designs, see also Joshua C. Taylor, "The Art Museum in the United States," in Sherman E. Lee (ed.), *On Understanding Art Museums*, American Assembly series (Englewood Cliffs, N.J.: Prentice-Hall, 1975), pp. 34–67.

36. See the study of Dorner by Samuel Cauman, *The Living Museum: Experiences of an Art Historian and Museum Director, Alexander Dorner* (New York: New York University Press, 1958), passim.

37. For a survey of these exhibitions and some interesting comments on the relationships between museums and department stores, see Jay E. Cantor, "Art and Industry: Reflections on the Role of the American Museum in Encouraging Innovations," In Ian M. G. Quimby and Polly Anne Earl (eds.), *Technological Innovation and the Decorative Arts* (Charlottesville: University Press of Virginia, 1974), pp. 331–54.

38. Among recent articles on shopping-center design, see "Shopping Centers," *Architectural Record* 147 (March, 1970): 119–23; Martha Weinman Lear, "A Master Builder Sites a Shopping Mall," *New York Times Magazine* 122 (Aug. 12, 1973): 12–13, 77–84; Gurney Breckenfeld, "'Downtown' Has Fled to the Suburbs," *Fortune* 86 (Oct. 1972): 80–87, 156–62; and see also chap. 13.

39. Among many relevant comments on the new museums, see *Time* 102 (Oct. 29, 1973): 108; and Douglas Davis, "The Museum Explosion," *Newsweek* 8 (Sept. 17, 1973): 88–89.

40. Douglas Davis, "The Streamlined Show," *Newsweek* 76 (Nov. 9, 1970): 99, and Lawrence Alloway, "Art," *Nation* 213 (Aug. 16, 1971): 124–26.

41. For an attempt to explicate this mood, see Neil Harris, "We and Our Machines," *New Republic* 171 (Nov. 23, 1974): 24–33.

42. For a comment on beaux art revivalism, see Ada Louise Huxtable, "Beaux Arts—the Latest Avant-Garde," *New York Times Magazine* 125 (October 26, 1975): 76–77, 80, 82.

Cultural Institutions and American Modernization

1. There is a vast literature relating to modernization theory. For one example of its application to American history, and some references to this literature, see Richard D. Brown, *Modernization: The Transformation of American Life, 1600–1865* (New York: Hill & Wang, 1976).

2. See the reference to Beard in one of these institutional histories: Gwladys Spencer, *The Chicago Public Library: Origins and Background* (Chicago: University of Chicago Press, 1943), p. xiii.

3. Daniel H. Calhoun, *Professional Lives in America: Structure and Aspiration, 1750–1850* (Cambridge: Harvard University Press, 1965); Roger Lane, *Policing the City: Boston, 1822–1885* (Cambridge: Harvard University Press, 1967); Michael B. Katz, *The Irony of Early School Reform: Educational Innovation in Mid-Nineteenth Century Massachusetts* (Cambridge: Harvard University Press, 1968); David J. Rothman, *The Discovery of the Asylum: Social Order and Disorder in the New Republic* (Boston: Little,

Brown, 1971); Anthony M. Platt, *The Child Savers: The Invention of Delinquency* (Chicago: University of Chicago Press, 1969, 1977); David F. Noble, *America by Design: Science, Technology, and the Rise of Corporate Capitalism* (New York: Knopf, 1977); Marvin Lazerson, *Origins of the Urban School: Public Education in Massachusetts, 1870–1915* (Cambridge: Harvard University Press, 1971); Stanley K. Schultz, *The Culture Factory: Boston Public Schools, 1789–1860* (New York: Oxford University Press, 1973); Helen L. Horowitz, *Culture and the City: Cultural Philanthropy in Chicago from the 1880's to 1917* (Lexington: University Press of Kentucky, 1976); Jerold S. Auerbach, *Unequal Justice: Lawyers and Social Change in Modern America* (New York: Oxford University Press, 1976); Laurence R. Veysey, *The Emergence of the American University* (Chicago: University of Chicago Press, 1965). These books, of course, vary enormously in method and point of view, and to them must be added many other monographs, and a growing literature on the impact of nineteenth-century professionalism and the organizational needs of modern society. Many of these are conveniently referred to in the notes to chap. 1 of Dee Garrison, *Apostles of Culture: The Public Librarian and American Society, 1876–1920* (New York: Free Press, 1979), pp. 248–50.

4. Bernard Bailyn, *Education in the Forming of American Society: Needs and Opportunities for Study* (Chapel Hill: University of North Carolina Press, 1960; New York: Vintage Books, n.d.), p. 4.

5. Ibid., pp. 9–11.

6. These influences, and interdisciplinary sources, are fully discussed by James A. Henretta, "Social History as Lived and Written," *American Historical Review* 84 (December 1979): 1293–1322.

7. Some of the influential texts here are Richard Hofstadter, *The Age of Reform: From Bryan to F.D.R.* (New York: Knopf, 1955); Robert H. Wiebe, *The Search for Order, 1877–1920* (New York: Hill & Wang, 1967); George E. Mowry, *The California Progressives* (Berkeley: University of California Press, 1951); Henry F. May, *The End of American Innocence: A Study of the First Years of Our Own Time, 1912–1917* (New York: Knopf, 1959); Gabriel Kolko, *The Triumph of Conservatism: A Reinterpretation of American History, 1900–1916* (Chi-

cago: Quadrangle, 1967); and Samuel P. Hays, *The Response to Industrialism, 1885–1914* (Chicago: University of Chicago Press, 1967).

8. See, for example, various anthologies of essays containing examples of these attitudes: Barton J. Bernstein (ed.), *Towards a New Past: Dissenting Essays in American History* (New York: Pantheon, 1968); Alfred F. Young (ed.), *Dissent: Explorations in the History of American Radicalism* (DeKalb: Northern Illinois University Press, 1968); Alfred F. Young (ed.), *The American Revolution: Explorations in the History of American Radicalism* (DeKalb: Northern Illinois University Press, 1976); Irwin Unger (ed.), *Beyond Liberalism: The New Left Views American History* (Waltham, Mass.: Xerox College Pub., 1971). See also many of the articles published in *Radical History Review* (1975—) and *Marxist Perspectives* (1978—).

9. Among the many texts that have reexamined the shaping of American culture are Christopher Lasch, *The New Radicalism in America, 1889–1963: The Intellectual as a Social Type* (New York: Knopf, 1965); James Weinstein, *The Corporate Ideal in the Liberal State, 1900–1918* (Boston: Beacon, 1968); Samuel Haber, *Efficiency and Uplift: Scientific Management in the Progressive Era, 1890–1920* (Chicago: University of Chicago Press, 1964); Carol S. Gruber, *Mars and Minerva: World War I and the Uses of Higher Learning in America* (Baton Rouge: Louisiana State University Press, 1975); Ann Douglas, *The Feminization of American Culture* (New York: Knopf, 1977); Stuart Ewen, *Captains of Consciousness: Advertising and the Social Roots of the Consumer Culture* (New York: McGraw-Hill, 1976). See also recent work in the *Journal of Interdisciplinary History* (1970—), *Journal of Social History* (1967—), and *Past and Present* (1952—).

10. In addition to many of the works already cited, several essays during the past few years have concentrated on the conservative objectives of the new professionals and the new institutions; among others, see Paul Finkelman, "Class and Culture in Late Nineteenth-Century Chicago: The Founding of the Newberry Library," *American Studies* 16 (Spring 1975): 5–22; Marvin E. Gettlemen, "Philanthropy as Social Control in Late Nineteenth-Century America: Some Hypotheses and Data on the Rise of Social

Work," *Societas* 5, no. 1 (Winter 1975): 49–59; Robert W. Rydell, "The World's Columbian Exposition of 1893: Racist Underpinnings of a Utopian Artifact," *Journal of American Culture* 1 (Summer 1978): 253–75; also, Kenneth L. Kusmer, "The Social History of Cultural Institutions: The Upper-Class Connection," *Journal of Interdisciplinary History* 10, no. 1 (Summer 1979): 137–46.

11. For summaries of recent thinking and research and references to the literature on professionalization and institution-founding during this period, see the essays in Alexandra Oleson and John Voss (eds.), *The Organization of Knowledge in Modern America, 1860–1920* (Baltimore: Johns Hopkins University Press, 1979). There has also been important research on the development of cultural institutions in Victorian Britain. See particularly H. E. Meller, *Leisure and the Changing City, 1870–1914* (London and Boston: Routledge & Kegan Paul, 1976); Peter Bailey, *Leisure and Class in Victorian England: Rational Recreation and the Contest for Control, 1830–1885* (London: Routledge & Kegan Paul; Buffalo, N.Y.: University of Toronto Press, 1978); many of the essays in H. J. Dyos and Michael Wolf (eds.), *The Victorian City: Images and Realities* (London and Boston: Routledge & Kegan Paul, 1973); Robert W. Malcolmson, *Popular Recreations in English Society, 1700–1850* (Cambridge: Cambridge University Press, 1973).

12. Dee Garrison, "Rejoinder," *Journal of Library History* 10, no. 2 (April 1975): 112, 115–16. I do find, in Dee Garrison, *Apostles of Culture,* many indications of the complexity of analyzing cultural relationships. See particularly pages 60–63.

13. Anthony M. Platt, *The Child Savers* (2d ed.), pp. xii–xiv.

14. In the vast literature that deals with these figures and their broad influence, students of American culture should find the following books particularly helpful: Roger B. Stein, *John Ruskin and Aesthetic Thought in America, 1840–1900* (Cambridge: Harvard University Press, 1967); Kermit Vanderbilt, *Charles Eliot Norton: Apostle of Culture in a Democracy* (Cambridge: Belknap Press of Harvard University Press, 1959); Raymond Williams, *Culture and Society, 1780–1950* (London: Chatto & Windus, 1958); Philip Henderson, *William Morris, His Life,*

Work and Friends (London: Thames & Hudson, 1967); Lionel Trilling, *Matthew Arnold* (New York: Norton, 1939); John Tomsich, *A Genteel Endeavor: American Culture and Politics in the Gilded Age* (Stanford: Stanford University Press, 1971); E. P. Thompson, *William Morris: Romantic to Revolutionary* (London: Lawrence & Wishart, 1955).

15. For more on this movement, see Susan Otis Thompson, *American Book Design and William Morris* (New York and London: Bowker, 1977); Freeman Champney, *Art and Glory: The Story of Elbert Hubbard* (New York: Crown, 1968); John Crosby Freeman, *The Forgotten Rebel: Gustav Stickley and His Craftsman Mission Furniture* (Watkins Glen, N.Y.: Century House, 1966); Oscar Lovell Triggs, *Chapters in the History of the Arts and Crafts Movement* (Chicago: Bohemia Guild of the Industrial Art League, 1902); David H. Dickason, *The Daring Young Men: The Story of the American Pre-Raphaelites* (Bloomington: University of Indiana Press, 1953); Joy H. Colby, *Art and a City: A History of the Detroit Society of Arts and Crafts* (Detroit: Wayne State University Press, 1956); Anthea Callen, *Women Artists of the Arts and Crafts Movement, 1870–1914* (New York: Pantheon, 1979); Herbert Peck, *The Book of Rookwood Pottery* (New York: Crown, 1968); Diane Chalmers Johnson, *American Art Nouveau* (New York: Abrams, 1979); Paul Evans, *Art Pottery of the United States: An Encyclopedia of Producers and Their Marks* (New York: Scribner's, 1974).

16. This connection is discussed in Neil Harris, "The Gilded Age Revisited: Boston and the Museum Movement," *American Quarterly* 14, no. 4 (Winter 1962): 545–66.

17. R. Jackson Wilson, *In Quest of Community: Social Philosophy in the United States, 1860–1920* (London and New York: Oxford University Press, 1970), p. 165.

18. Daniel M. Fox, *Engines of Culture: Philanthropy and Art Museums* (Madison: State Historical Society of Wisconsin, 1963).

19. Henry James, *The American Scene* (Bloomington and London: Indiana University Press, 1968), pp. 249–52.

20. Jorge Luis Borges, "The Library of Babel," *Ficciones* (New York: Grove, 1962), pp. 80–81.

8

Utopian Fiction and Its Discontents

1. Information about Lloyd can be found in Allan Johnson and Dumas Malone, eds., *Dictionary of American Biography* (New York, 1928—), supplement, 2:389–90. Hereafter cited as *DAB*.

2. *Etidorhpa; or, The End of Earth, the Strange History of a Mysterious Being and the Account of a Remarkable Journey*, 6th ed. (Cincinnati, 1896), pp. 383–86. *Etidorhpa* is *Aphrodite* spelled backwards, but this fact does not help much in explicating the book's details.

3. Lloyd, *Etidorhpa*, p. 97. See also pp. 80–81.

4. Amos K. Fiske, *Beyond the Bourn: Reports of a Traveller Returned from "The Undiscovered Country"* (New York, 1891). A brief account of Fiske can be found in *DAB* 6:416–17.

5. Fiske, *Beyond the Bourn*, p. 169.

6. Cyrus Cole, *The Auroraphone: A Romance* (Boston, 1890).

7. Ibid., p. 133.

8. Claude R. Flory, *Economic Criticism in American Fiction, 1792–1900* (Philadelphia: University of Pennsylvania, 1936), pp. 242–43.

9. One such exception is Kenneth M. Roemer, *The Obsolete Necessity: America in Utopian Writings, 1888–1900* (Kent, Ohio: Kent State University Press, 1976). Roemer's book is the most comprehensive published survey of American utopian fiction and treats a broad range of social, intellectual, and economic issues. Unfortunately, it reached me just as I was finishing the final draft of this paper. It contains extensive bibliographies and plot summaries of the utopian novels. I was gratified to note Roemer's emphasis on the anxieties of the utopian novelists and his attempt to qualify older, optimistic summaries of the novels.

Among the earlier studies that I read are Alleyn B. Forbes, "The Literary Quest for Utopia, 1880–1900," *Social Forces* 6 (Dec. 1927): 179–89; Walter F. Taylor, *The Economic Novel in America* (Chapel Hill: University of North Carolina Press, 1942); and Vernon Louis Parrington, Jr., *American Dreams: A Study of American Utopias* (Providence: Brown University Press, 1947). A number of unpublished dissertations have aided my work immeasurably. They include Robert L. Shorter, "The Utopian Novel in America, 1865–1900" (Ph.D. diss., Western Reserve University, 1936); Margaret Wilson Thal-Larsen, "Political and Economic Ideas in American Utopian Fiction, 1868–1914" (Ph.D. diss., University of California at Berkeley, 1941); Ellene Ransom, "Utopus Discovers America, or Critical Realism in American Utopian Fiction, 1798–1900" (Ph.D. diss., Vanderbilt University, 1946); Charles J. Rooney, Jr., "Utopian Literature as a Reflection of Social Forces in America, 1865–1917" (Ph.D. diss., George Washington University, 1968); and Lisle A. Rose, "A Descriptive Catalogue of Economic and Politico-Economic Fiction in the United States, 1902–1909" (Ph.D. diss., University of Chicago, 1935).

Two works that do indeed talk about various psychological aspects of American utopian fiction are Frederic Cople Jaher, *Doubters and Dissenters: Cataclysmic Thought in America, 1885–1918* (New York: Free Press, 1964), and the introduction in John L. Thomas, ed., Edward Bellamy, *Looking Backward: 2000–1887* (Cambridge: Harvard University Press, 1967). See also the very interesting essay by Virgil L. Lokke, "The American Utopian Anti-Novel," in Ray B. Browne et al., eds., *Frontiers of American Culture* (Lafayette, Ind.: Purdue University Studies, 1968), pp. 123–53.

There is also, of course, a major literature of commentary and description on utopianism more generally, as well as studies of specific national utopian traditions. I have found particularly helpful W. H. G. Armytage, *Yesterday's Tomorrows: A Historical Survey of Future Societies* (Toronto: University of Toronto Press, 1968); J. O. B. Bailey, *Pilgrims through Space and Time: Trends and Patterns in Scientific and Utopian Fiction* (New York: Argus, 1947); I. F. Clarke, *The Tale of the Future* (London: Library Association, 1961); Robert C. Elliott, *The Shape of Utopia: Studies in a Literary Genre* (Chicago: University of Chicago Press, 1970); many of the essays in Frank E. Manuel, ed., *Utopias and Utopian Thought* (Boston: Houghton Mifflin, 1965); and the extracts in Glenn Negley and J. Max Patrick, eds., *The Quest for Utopia: An Anthology of Imagi-*

nary Societies (New York: Henry Schuman, 1952).

10. The single most valuable analysis of science fiction is Thomas Dean Clareson, "The Emergence of American Science Fiction: 1880–1915; A Study of the Impact of Science upon American Romanticism" (Ph.D. diss., University of Pennsylvania, 1956). Clareson has also worked with the journal *Extrapolations*, which has published in various issues checklists of American science fiction, and analyses of particular themes. A recent book, David Ketterer's *New Worlds for Old: The Apocalyptic Imagination, Science Fiction, and American Literature* (Garden City, N.Y.: Doubleday, 1974), offers a provocative definition of the genre. Other helpful books on science fiction include Kingsley Amis, *New Maps of Hell* (New York: Harcourt, Brace & World, 1960); Mark R. Hillegas, *The Future as Nightmare: H. G. Wells and the Anti-Utopians* (New York: Oxford University Press, 1967); Robert M. Philmus, *Into the Unknown: The Evolution of Science Fiction from Godwin to H. G. Wells* (Berkeley and Los Angeles: University of California Press, 1970); and H. Bruce Franklin, *Future Perfect: American Science Fiction of the Nineteenth Century* (New York: Oxford University Press, 1966). Many of these critics spend a good deal of time distinguishing among science fiction, science fantasy, utopian fiction, and other related categories. Because my interest, in this essay, lies in charting a range of concerns which afflicted late nineteenth-century Americans, I have not pursued the matter of definition. Indeed, I have deliberately included in the utopian category much of this larger body of fiction. Most American utopian fiction, however, did employ the device that Philmus presents as basic to science fantasy, that is, "the rhetorical strategy of employing a more or less scientific rationale to get the reader to suspend disbelief in a fantastic state of affairs." Philmus, *Into the Unknown*, p. vii.

11. The Bestor comment I refer to was expressed most succinctly in Arthur E. Bestor, Jr., "Patent-Office Models of the Good Society: Some Relationships between Social Reform and Westward Expansion," *American Historical Review* 58 (Apr. 1953): 505–26. For some interesting comments on the relationship between the utopian novel and American technology, see John F. Kasson, *Civilizing the Machine: Technology and Republican Values in America,*

1776–1900 (New York: Grossman, 1976), chap. 5.

12. Henry Olerich, *A Cityless and Countryless World: An Outline of Practical Cooperative Individualism* (Holstein, Iowa, 1893), pp. 8–9. See also Albert Merrill, *The Great Awakening: The Story of the Twenty-Second Century* (Boston, 1899), p. 168.

13. Charles J. Rooney, Jr., in "Utopian Literature as a Reflection of Social Forces in America," has presented the most careful statistical analysis of the utopian authors. Of the forty-one writers for whom Rooney could find biographical information, all were engaged in professional, business, or public careers; more than ten were in journalism, with the others in teaching, politics, business, medicine, and engineering. Most utopian novelists were middle class. See Rooney, "Utopian Literature," pp. 13–15.

14. Olerich, *Cityless and Countryless World*, pp. 20–21.

15. H. E. Swan, *It Might Be: A Story of the Future Progress of the Sciences, the Wonderful Advancement in the Methods of Government and the Happy State of the People* (Stafford, Kansas, 1896), p. 142. See also [M. Louise Moore,] *Al-Modad, or Life Scenes beyond the Polar Circumflex: A Religio-Scientific Solution of the Problems of Present and Future Life, By an Untrammeled Free-Thinker* (Cameron Parish, Louisiana, 1892), p. 79.

16. Olerich, *Cityless and Countryless World*, p. 3.

17. There is little that is very helpful on the social and intellectual effects of the spread of electrical usage, but among the informative books are Harold C. Passer, *The Electrical Manufacturers, 1875–1900* (Cambridge: Harvard University Press, 1953); William T. O'Dea, *A Social History of Lighting* (London: Routledge & Kegan Paul, 1958); Harold I. Sharlin, *Making of the Electrical Age: From the Telegraph to Automation* (New York: Abelard-Schuman, 1963); and three essays, Bern Dibner, "The Beginning of Electricity," and Harold I. Sharlin, "Applications of Electricity" and "Electrical Generation and Transmission," all in Melvin Kranzberg and Carroll W. Pursell, Jr., eds., *Technology in Western Civilization* (2 vols; New York: Oxford University Press, 1967), vol. I.

18. For more details on the development of Niagara see Edward Dean Adams, *Niagara Power: His-*

tory of the Niagara Falls Power Company, 1886–1918 (Niagara Falls, 1927), passim.

19. Joseph Kirkland and Caroline Kirkland, *The Story of Chicago* (Chicago, 1894), 2:115–16.

20. Josiah Allen's Wife [Marietta Holley], *Samantha at the World's Fair* (New York, London, Toronto, 1893), p. 558. The prophetic tone that electricity induced is revealed in other Holley comments made in the Electricity Building: "But who—who shall map out this vast realm that Benjamin F. discovered? We stand jest by the sea-shore. We have jest landed from our boats. The onbroken forest lays before us. . . . A few trees have been felled by Morse, Edison, Field and others, so that we can git glimpses into the forest depths, but not enough to give us a glimpse of the mountains or the seas. The realm as a whole is onexplored; nobody knows or can dream of the grandeur and glory that awaits the advance guard." See also ibid., pp. 545–65, 569; and Josiah Allen's Wife [Marietta Holley], *Samantha at the St. Louis Exposition* (New York, 1904), pp. 125–27. In St. Louis, Samantha connected electricity with the coming of divine visitors, which someday men might be able to see and understand. See Lafcadio Hearn, "The Government Exhibit at New Orleans," *Harper's Weekly* 29 (Apr. 11, 1885): 240.

21. *Philadelphia Inquirer*, Jan. 4, 1890, p. 4. The article was a comment on the burning of an Edison building in New York City.

22. *Boston Evening Transcript*, Jan. 4, 1888, p. 4.

23. *New York Tribune*, Jan. 8, 1882, p. 6: "As the uses of electricity multiply, it is only fair that the belief in its dangers should multiply also; but, unlike most popular beliefs, modern experience has brought us practical verification of electrical perils."

24. Dexter W. Fellows and Andrew A. Freeman, *This Way to the Big Show: The Life of Dexter Fellows* (New York: Viking Press, 1936), pp. 172–73.

25. For a sample of Edison's rhetoric see Thomas A. Edison, "The Dangers of Electric Lighting," *North American Review* 149 (Nov. 1889): 625–34. New York newspapers were filled with the controversy over the use of the first electric chair and the limitations to be placed upon press attendance at the execution. For sample editorials, see *New York Tribune*, Jan. 22, 1889, p. 4; Mar. 16, 1889, p. 6; and

June 20, 1889, p. 6. A novel has been written about the first execution by electric chair, which took place in 1890, in Auburn Prison, New York. See Christopher Davis, *A Peep into the Twentieth Century* (New York: Harper & Row, 1971). The mode of execution was embroiled in a controversy between Edison and his followers, who favored continuous (direct) current, and representatives of the Westinghouse alternating current.

26. Park Benjamin, "The Infliction of the Death Penalty," *Forum* 3 (July 1887): 512.

27. A former resident of "The Hub" [John Bachelder], *A.D. 2050: Electrical Development at Atlantis* (San Francisco, 1890), p. 24.

28. Jack London, "Goliah," *Revolution and Other Essays* (New York, 1912), pp. 71–116.

29. William Alexander Taylor, *Intermere* (Columbus, Ohio, 1901), p. 138.

30. M. Auburré Hovorrè [Albert W. Howard], *The Milltillionaire; or, Age of Bardization* (Boston, 1895), p. 17. In James Cowan, *Daybreak: A Romance of an Old World* (New York, 1896), it rained only at night, to increase the pleasures of the day. Many utopias provided air-cooled buildings, covered or underground passageways, and huge hotels, all giving needed protection from rain or heat, if they were not controlled.

31. [Bachelder,] *A.D. 2050*, p. 56. Rev. W. S. Harris, *Life in a Thousand Worlds* (Cleona, Pennsylvania, 1905), p. 234, describes life on Ploid, a world of highest invention, which has a telephone employing photographic wires: "Persons can be in bed at night, if they imagine they hear a robber in any room they can first turn on the photograph current and then the light flash. In this way one can look, without leaving his bed, into each room of the house." See also Swan, *It Might Be*, p. 55; and Gustavus W. Pope, *Journey to Mars, The Wonderful World: Its Beauty and Splendor; Its Mighty Races and Kingdoms; Its Final Doom* (New York, 1894), pp. 66–67.

32. Cosimo Noto, M.D., *The Ideal City* (New York, 1903), p. 79.

33. Chauncey Thomas, *The Crystal Button; or, The Adventures of Paul Prognosis in the Forty-ninth Century* (Boston and New York, 1891), pp. 100–101. In Merrill, *The Great Awakening*, the horse is

practically extinct and found only in zoos, and in Paul Devinne, *The Day of Prosperity: A Vision of the Century to Come* (New York, 1902), a utopian host explains that electricity has made the horse superfluous. Moreover, since "robbery and stealing have gone out of fashion, we do not require watchdogs, and to keep dogs as a pastime . . . we should consider absurd," pp. 76–77. In Pruning Knife [Henry Francis Allen], *A Strange Voyage: A Revision of the Key of Industrial Co-Operative Government; An Interesting and Instructive Description of Life on the Planet Venus* (St. Louis, 1891), animals are also barred, to permit clean, odorless cities, pp. 62, 153. *Al-Modad* outlaws horses, cows, hogs, dogs, and cats. There were a few small wild animals "but no offensive pests. Not a gnat, fly, ant nor anything in the slightest degree obnoxious," p. 96.

34. There is little in print that is either comprehensive or scholarly on the history of American dietary reform. Some information can be found in Janet Barkas, *The Vegetable Passion* (New York: Scribner's 1975); E. Douglas Branch, *The Sentimental Years, 1836–1860* (New York: Appleton-Century, 1934), chap. 9; and Gerald M. Carson, *Cornflake Crusade* (New York: Rinehart, 1957). Related material is well covered in James Harvey Young, *Toadstool Millionaires: Patent Medicines before Federal Regulation* (Princeton: Princeton University Press, 1961). But the best source on diet and social control is unpublished—Stephen W. Nissenbaum, "Careful Love: Sylvester Graham and the Emergence of Victorian Sexual Theory in America, 1830–1940" (Ph.D. diss., University of Wisconsin, 1969). William J. McCrath, *Dionysian Art and Populist Politics in Austria* (New Haven: Yale University Press, 1974), pp. 92–97, contains some interesting material on European vegetarianism.

35. Edward Bellamy, *Equality* (New York, 1897; reprinted, Upper Saddle River, N.J.: Gregg Press, 1968), p. 286.

36. James Cowan, *Daybreak: A Romance of an Old World* (New York, 1896), p. 320.

37. Pope, *Journey to Mars*, pp. 234–35; Herman Hine Brinsmade, *Utopia Achieved: A Novel of the Future* (New York, 1912), p. 59. See also [Howard], *The Milltillionaire*; [Mary E. Bradley Lane], *Mizora:*

A Prophecy; A Mss. Found among the Private Papers of the Princess Vera Zarovitch, Written by Herself (New York, 1889); The Lord Commissioner [John McCoy], *A Prophetic Romance, Mars to Earth* (Boston, 1896); Prof. W[illis] Mitchell, *The Inhabitants of Mars: Their Manners and Advancement in Civilization and Their Opinion of Us* (Malden, Mass., 1895); [Moore], *Al-Modad;* and Noto, *Ideal City,* are also among the novels in which a vegetable diet assumes great importance. Many of the other utopian novels mention, simply as a matter of course, the vegetarian diets of their residents. So common a convention did dietary fads become among utopians that in his antisocial, dystopian novel *The Scarlet Empire* (New York, [1906]) David M. Parry played with various reforms, including laws compelling equal use of the muscles on both sides of the mouth for chewing—a reflection of Fletcherism—as well as laws controlling the trimming of fingernails and regulating the length of a step.

38. For explorations of this theme, with differing emphases, see John Higham, "The Reorientation of American Culture in the 1890s," in John Weiss, ed., *The Origins of Modern Consciousness* (Detroit: Wayne State University Press, 1965), pp. 25–48; Roderick Nash, *Wilderness and the American Mind* (New Haven: Yale University Press, 1967); and Peter Schmitt, *Back to Nature: The Arcadian Myth in Urban America* (New York: Oxford University Press, 1969).

39. Capt. Nathan Davis, *Beulah; or, A Parable of Social Regeneration* (Kansas City, Mo., 1904), p. 209.

40. W. D. Howells, *Letters of an Altrurian Traveller,* in Clara and Rudolph Kirk, eds., *The Altrurian Romances* (Bloomington, Ind.: Indiana University Press, 1968), p. 253.

41. W. D. Howells, *Through the Eye of the Needle,* ibid., p. 281.

42. Ibid., p. 372.

43. Noto, *Ideal City,* p. 180.

44. Olerich, *Cityless and Countryless World,* p. 65.

45. Bradford Peck, *The World a Department Store: A Story of Life under a Cooperative System* (Lewiston, Me.; 1900), p. 78.

46. Stewart Edward White, *The Sign at Six* (Indianapolis, 1912), p. 27.

47. L. P. Gratacap, *The Certainty of a Future Life in Mars, Being the Posthumous Papers of Bradford Torrey Dodd* (New York, Paris, Chicago, Washington, 1903), pp. 203–4.

48. Albert Chavannes, *In Brighter Climes; or, Life in Socioland: A Realistic Novel* (Knoxville, Tenn., 1895), p. 44.

49. Bellamy, *Equality*, p. 255. "It is a curious paradox," stated Mr. Barton, a spokesman for Bellamy's utopia, "that while the telephone and electroscope, by abolishing distance as a hindrance to sight and hearing, have brought mankind into a closeness of sympathetic and intellectual rapport never before imagined, they have at the same time enabled individuals, although keeping in closest touch with everything going on in the world, to enjoy, if they choose, a physical privacy, such as one had to be a hermit to command in your day."

50. Pope, *Journey to Mars*, p. 193 and passim. Another ribbon scheme was provided by Edgar Chambless in *Roadtown* (New York, 1910), a plan "to lay the modern skyscraper on its side and run the elevators and the pipes and the wires horizontally instead of vertically," p. 19. Continuous lines of houses, containing transportation systems as well as utilities, would stretch through the countryside, with farms on either side. In describing his future cities, Chambless intoned a catalogue of the evils distressing utopian novelists. There will be, he promised, "no streets, no street cars and no 'subway air'; no kitchens, no coal bins, no back yards or back alleys full of crime and tin cans; no brooms, no feather dusters, no wash day; no clothes line, no beating the carpet or shaking the rug out the window . . . no dish washing, no cooks, no maids, no janitors . . . no dust, no noise . . . no moving vans, no coal wagons, no garbage carts . . . no horses except for pleasure drives . . . no fire engines, no cabs nor taxicabs, no mixing of pedestrians and vehicles . . . no grade crossings and no 'death avenue'; there will be no bargain rushes, no small shops, no middleman's profits, no bill boards . . . no waste of money for little bottles and cans and bags, no adulterated food . . . no snow to shovel . . . no street cleaners, no

water wagons, no swill-tubs, no rain barrels, no manure carts . . . no beds to make . . . no fire escapes, no waiting in rain or snow to catch a car . . . no news boys, no messenger boys, no mail carriers, no traffic policemen, no teamsters . . . no street car conductors, no expressmen, no delivery boys, no peddlers, no pushcart men, no waiters to tip, no insurance agents . . . ," pp. 165–68. The emphasis throughout was on tidiness, economy of motion, lack of irritation, convenience, safety, and an end to the many varieties of brokers and middlemen that had come between the consumer and the products he used.

51. Uniforms can be found in, among other novels, Richard Hatfield's *Geyserland: 9262 B.C.: Empiricism in Social Reform, Being Data and Observations Recorded by the Late Mark Stubble, M.D., Ph.D.* (Washington, 1908); [Howard], *The Milltillionaire*; Peck, *The World a Department Store*; and Bellamy, *Looking Backward*.

52. Numbered tatoos were employed in William Wonder [Thomas Kirwan], *Reciprocity (Social and Economic) in the Thirtieth Century: The Coming Co-Operative Age* (New York, 1909), pp. 145–46. In Devinne, *Day of Prosperity*, everyone carries a permanent passport, which records his travels, birthplace, parents' background, schooling, marriages, etc., accompanying "its possessor from the cradle to the grave," p. 138. For an excellent description of a utopian parade, see John Ira Brant, *The New Regime, A.D. 2202* (New York, London, 1909), p. 22.

53. Olerich, *Cityless and Countryless World*, pp. 351–52.

54. Thomas, *Crystal Button*, p. 85.

55. Frank Rosewater, *The Making of a Millennium: The Story of a Millennial Realm, and Its Law* (Chicago, 1908), p. 50.

56. See, for example, Peck, *The World a Department Store*, p. 61; Rosewater, *Making of a Millennium*, pp. 78–79; and Henry Wallace Dowding, *The Man from Mars; or, Service for Service's Sake* (New York, 1910), p. 173.

57. For background on American reception of germ theory see Phyllis Allen Richmond, "American Attitudes toward the Germ Theory of Disease (1860–1880)," *Journal of the History of Medicine and Allied Sciences* 9 (Oct. 1954): 428–54.

58. Frank B. Vrooman, "Public Health and National Defence," *Arena* 13 (Aug. 1895): 425.

59. Among other examples, the *Literary Digest* 11 (June 29, 1895): 258; *Literary Digest* 11 (Oct. 5, 1895): 674; *New York Times*, Feb. 4, 1904, p. 8; *Boston Evening Transcript*, Jan. 4, 1888, p. 6; *New York Tribune*, Dec. 11, 1881, p. 6; *Independent* 59 (Dec. 1, 1905): 1492; *New York Times*, Aug. 5, 1900, p. 6; *Chicago Record-Herald*, Feb. 22, 1904, p. 6; and *Chicago Record-Herald*, Apr. 11, 1904, p. 6.

60. "Microbes in Books," *New York Times*, Feb. 8, 1904, p. 8.

61. "On Kissing," *New York Times*, Nov. 9, 1902, p. 6.

62. See the various extracts and the introduction to section 11 in Ray Brosseau and Ralph K. Andrist, *Looking Forward: Life in the Twentieth Century as Predicted in the Pages of American Magazines from 1895 to 1905* (New York: American Heritage Press, 1970), particularly "The Danger of Door-knobs," and "The Home of the Microbes," both on p. 282.

63. "The Mercenary Microbe," *Harper's Weekly* 38 (Dec. 30, 1893): 1243.

64. Jack London, "The Human Drift," in *The Human Drift* (New York, 1917), p. 21. "The Human Drift" was originally published in 1911.

65. Jack London, *The Scarlet Plague* (New York, 1912). See also Jack London, *Short Stories* (1914; reprinted, New York: Hill & Wang, 1960).

66. Thomas, *Crystal Button*, pp. 229–30.

67. Noto, *Ideal City*, p. 196.

68. W. N. Harben, *The Land of the Changing Sun* (New York, 1894), p. 66. For more on eugenic reforms see Fayette Stratton Giles, *Shadows Before; or, A Century Onward* (New York, 1894), p. 206; H. George Schuette, *Athonia; or, The Original Four Hundred* (Manitowoc, Wis., 1910), pp. 184–85; and Dr. W. O. Henry, *Equitania; or, The Land of Equity* (Omaha, n.d.), passim.

69. John Jacob Astor, *A Journey in Other Worlds: A Romance of the Future* (New York, 1894), p. 438.

70. Donald Meyer, *The Positive Thinkers: A Study of the American Quest for Health, Wealth and Personal Power from Mary Baker Eddy to Norman Vincent Peale* (Garden City, N.Y.: Doubleday, 1965), p. 48.

71. Many of the utopian novels incorporated rules concerning cremation as a healthier way of disposing of the dead than traditional burial methods. See, for example, Olerich, *Cityless and Countryless World*; and [Bachelder], *A.D. 2050*, p. 30.

72. For literary involvement with spiritualism see Howard H. Kerr, *Mediums and Spirit-Rappers, and Roaring Radicals: Spiritualism in American Literature, 1850–1900* (Urbana: University of Illinois Press, 1972). For American spiritualism, and up-to-date bibliographic references, see R. Laurence Moore, "The Spiritualist Medium: A Study of Female Professionalism in Victorian America," *American Quarterly* 27 (May 1975): 220–21.

73. Cowan, *Daybreak*, p. 65.

74. Pope, *Journey to Mars*, pp. 312, 314. See also Taylor, *Intermere*, pp. 116–18; Cole, *The Auroraphone*, passim; Alfred Denton Cridge, *Utopia; or The History of an Extinct Planet* (Oakland, Calif., 1884), passim; Francis Worcester Doughty, *Mirrikh; or, A Woman from Mars: A Tale of Occult Adventure* (New York, 1892), passim; and Fiske, *Beyond the Bourn*, passim.

75. Gratacap, *Certainty of a Future Life in Mars*; D. Mortimore, M.D., *The Spirit of God as Fire; The Globe within the Sun Our Heaven* (New York, 1870); Arthur Willink, *The World of the Unseen: An Essay on the Relation of Higher Space to Things Eternal* (New York, London, 1893). There existed, in the late nineteenth century, a literature of heavenly description, both inside the utopian genre and outside it. It could be argued, of course, that detailed heavenly description forms a utopian literature by itself. One such work is Edward Stanton, *Dreams of the Dead* (Boston, 1892). For more on heavenly description see Elmer F. Suderman, "Elizabeth Stuart Phelps and the Gates Ajar Novels," *Journal of Popular Culture* 3 (Summer 1969): 91–100; and Ann Douglas, "Heaven Our Home: Consolation Literature in the Northern United States, 1830–1880," *American Quarterly* 26 (Dec. 1974): 496–515.

9

The Drama of Consumer Desire

Since this essay's completion in 1978, a number of books and essays have appeared which bear upon its subject. Although these works could not be incorporated into the text, readers might wish to note the following: Gunther Barth, *City People: The Rise of Modern City Culture in Nineteenth-Century America* (New York, 1980); William Leach, *True Love and Perfect Union: The Feminist Reform of Sex and Society* (New York, 1980); Leonard Marcus, *The American Store Window* (New York and London, 1978); Lary May, *Screening Out the Past: The Birth of Mass Culture and the Motion Picture Industry* (New York, 1980); Jeffrey L. Meikle, *Twentieth Century Limited: Industrial Design in America, 1925–1939* (Philadelphia, 1979); Michael B. Miller, *The Bon Marché: Bourgeois Culture and the Department Store* (Princeton, 1981); and Elizabeth Stillinger, *The Antiquers . . . Changing Taste in American Antiques, 1850–1930* (New York, 1980).

1. There is a large literature on this theme. Edmund S. Morgan, *The Puritan Dilemma: The Story of John Winthrop* (Boston, 1958), remains an excellent and concise statement. Richard L. Bushman, *From Puritan to Yankee* (Cambridge, Mass., 1967), traces the interaction between the changing socio-economic ethic and the Puritan character. Perry Miller, *The New England Mind, from Colony to Province* (Cambridge, Mass., 1939, 1954), is a classic statement. Bernard Bailyn, "The Apologia of Robert Keayne," *William and Mary Quarterly,* 3d ser. 7 (Oct. 1950): 568–87; and Bernard Bailyn, *The New England Merchants in the Seventeenth Century* (Cambridge, Mass., 1955), are important studies of more specific episodes in the conflict between economic ambition and religious vision. A more recent work, Stephen Foster, *Their Solitary Way: The Puritan Social Ethic in the First Century of Settlement in New England* (New Haven, Conn., 1971), has important material bearing on the issue.

2. Again there is a very large literature on this subject. The most sophisticated discussion can be found in Gordon S. Wood, *The Creation of the American Republic, 1776–1787* (Chapel Hill, N.C.,

1969), particularly chaps. 2, 3, 10, 15. See also Neil Harris, *The Artist in American Society: The Formative Years, 1790–1860* (New York, 1966), chap. 2.

3. Fred Somkin, *Unquiet Eagle: Memory and Desire in the Idea of American Freedom, 1815–1860* (Ithaca, N. Y., 1967). This phrase is the title of Somkin's opening chapter.

4. This relationship (and the power of public opinion) was explored by many foreign visitors during the Jacksonian period. References and summaries are provided in Jane Louise Mesick, *The English Traveller in America, 1785–1835* (New York, 1922); and Max Berger, *The British Traveller in America, 1836–1860* (New York, 1943). An anthology of appropriate materials is *America through British Eyes,* ed. Allan Nevins (New York, 1948); the second and third sections are most relevant here.

5. Alexis de Tocqueville, *Democracy in America,* ed. Phillips Bradley (New York, 1945), 2:132–33. See also pp. 128–30.

6. "The Influence of the Trading Spirit on the Social and Moral Life in America," *American Review: A Whig Journal of Politics, Literature, Art and Science* (1 Jan. 1845), reprinted in abridged form in *Ideology and Power in the Age of Jackson,* ed. Edwin C. Rozwenc (Garden City, N.Y., 1964), pp. 48–54.

7. Carl Bode, *The Anatomy of American Popular Culture, 1840–1860* (Berkeley and Los Angeles, 1960), chap. 9, surveys this literature.

8. Alfred P. Chandler, Jr., *The Visible Hand: The Managerial Revolution in American Business* (Cambridge, 1977), contains the most authoritative discussion of marketing changes. Frank Presbrey, *The History and Development of Advertising* (Garden City, N.Y., 1929), remains, after fifty years, a useful source of information for this period. See also James P. Wood, *The Story of Advertising* (New York, 1958). Ralph M. Hower, *History of Macy's of New York, 1858–1919* (Cambridge, Mass., 1943); Herbert Adams Gibbons, *John Wanamaker* (2 vols.; New York and London, 1926); Robert W. Twyman, *History of Marshall Field & Co., 1852–1906* (Philadelphia, 1954); and John William Ferry, *A History of the Department Store* (New York, 1960), are all helpful on this subject. Above all, there is Hugh Dalziel Duncan, *Culture and Democracy: The Struggle for*

Form in Society and Architecture in Chicago and the Middle West during the Life and Times of Louis H. Sullivan (Totowa, N.J., 1965). This is the only book which has treated shopping as a culture; it contains important and stimulating discussions of Chicago stores, consumers, merchandising methods, and artists, and has an especially valuable commentary on Dreiser. I have benefitted greatly from reading the book, which has influenced my own formulation. See particularly chaps. 11 and 12.

9. "My Afternoons among the Drug Goods," *Harper's Weekly* 1 (31 Oct. 1856): 689–90.

10. Lillie Hamilton French, "Shopping in New York," *The Century* 61 (Mar. 1901): 651.

11. William D. Howells, *A Woman's Reason* (Boston and New York, 1882), p. 185.

12. See W. D. Howells, *The Rise of Silas Lapham*, intro. by Walter J. Meserve (Bloomington and London, 1971), chaps. 1 and 3, for Lapham's business methods, and the initial interviews between him and his architect about the new house. The most quoted episode in the book is the tragicomic dinner party scene, chap. 14.

13. W. D. Howells, *A Hazard of New Fortunes*, intro. by Everett Carter (Bloomington and London, 1976), p. 49.

14. Theodore Dreiser, *Sister Carrie* (Cleveland and New York, 1900, 1946), pp. 24–25.

15. Ibid., p. 75. Actually, Carrie is shopping alone while in The Fair, but Drouet joins her shopping expedition in the other stores.

16. Ibid., pp. 391–92, 431, 442.

17. Ibid., p. 556.

18. Theodore Dreiser, *The Titan* (New York, 1914, 1925), pp. 31–38, 56–61, 66–73, for Cowperwood's manipulation of the social scene, his use of possessions, and his passion for art. Consciousness of consumption and expenditure powerfully enters Dreiser's 1925 novel, *An American Tragedy*. For an interesting comment upon this subject see Michael Spindler, "Youth, Class and Consumerism in Dreiser's *An American Tragedy*," *Journal of American Studies* 12 (Apr. 1978): 63–80.

19. R. W. Sexton, *American Commercial Buildings of To-Day* (New York, 1928), pp. 153–44. For a discussion of the changing physical character of stores in the 1920s and a more general view of commercial influences on taste, see chap. 3.

20. John Taylor Boyd, Jr., "The Art of Commercial Display," *Architectural Record* 63 (Jan. 1928): 59.

21. Frederick J. Kiesler, *Contemporary Art Applied to the Store and Its Display* (New York, 1930), p. 79. See also Joseph Mayer, *The Revolution in Merchandise* (New York, 1939); A. T. Fisher, *Window and Store Display: A Handbook for Advertisers* (Garden City, N.Y., 1922); Ely Jacques Kahn, "Designing the Bonwit Teller Store," *Architectural Forum* 53 (Nov. 1930): 571; and Shepard Vogelsang, "Architecture and Trade Marks," *Architectural Forum* 50 (June 1929): 897–900.

22. For advertising techniques in the 1920s see Otis Pease, *The Responsibilities of American Advertising* (New Haven, Conn., 1958); Stuart Ewen, *Captains of Consciousness* (New York, 1976); Ruth Schwartz Cowan, "The 'Industrial Revolution' in the Home: Household Technology and Social Change in the Twentieth Century," *Technology and Culture* 17 (Jan. 1976): 1–23; and an excellent graduate seminar paper, Stephen Freedman, "Corporate Reach and the Family: The Social Context of Food Advertising in National Magazines, 1919–1929" (Chicago, 1978).

23. Floyd W. Parsons, "The New Day in Salesmanship," *Saturday Evening Post* 192 (4 June 1921): 28. Ewen, *Captains of Consciousness*, describes some of the manipulative strategies. Walter Dill Scott, *Psychology of Advertising* (Boston, 1921) was an influential text for students of the new methods.

24. Although this subject is not effectively brought together anywhere, there are suggestive hints in Margaret Farrand Thorp, *America at the Movies* (New Haven, Conn., 1939), chaps. 3 and 4; Leo C. Rosten, *Hollywood: The Movie Colony, the Movie Makers* (New York, 1941), chaps. 3 and 9; Hortense Powdermaker, *Hollywood, the Dream Factory: An Anthropologist Looks at the Movie-Makers* (Boston, 1950); the introduction and several of the articles anthologized in *Culture and Commitment, 1929–1945*, ed. Warren Susman (New York, 1972); Robert Sklar, *Movie-Made America: A Social History of American Movies* (New York, 1975), chaps, 8, 13,

14; and Garth Jowett, *Film: The Democratic Art* (Boston, Toronto, 1976), chap. 11.

25. See the homes documented in Arthur Knight and Eliot Elisofson, *The Hollywood Style* (New York, London, 1969), a cultural artifact of its own.

26. Dreyfuss, Bel Geddes, Loewy, and Teague are among the designers who published books on their own. The most useful recent survey on the movement is Donald J. Bush, *The Streamlined Decade* (New York, 1975), concentrating on the 1930s, when the most important work was accomplished. There were, however, some earlier intimations, in architecture and the decorative arts. See also Sheldon Cheney and Martha Cheney, *Art and the Machine* (New York, 1936), and Martin Greif, *Depression Modern: The Thirties Style in America* (New York, 1975).

27. Bush, *Streamlined Decade*, and Greif, *Depression Modern*, contain material on the fairs. See also chap. 3.

28. Alfred P. Sloan, Jr., *My Years with General Motors* (Garden City, N.Y., 1963), chap. 9, describes the introduction of the annual model change. Alfred D. Chandler, Jr., *Strategy and Structure: Chapters in the History of the Industrial Enterprise* (Cambridge, Mass., 1962). See also Daniel J. Boorstin, *The Americans: The Democratic Experience* (New York, 1973), pp. 546–55. This volume also has discussions of the department store (pp. 101–9) and many references to packaging, advertising, and merchandising in the twentieth century.

29. Mary E. Hoffman, *The Buying Habits of Small-Town Women* (Kansas City, Chicago, Rock Island, Atlanta, New York, 1926). The author was director of research for the Ferry-Yanley Advertising Company.

30. George Jean Nathan and H. L. Mencken, *The American Credo: A contribution toward the Interpretation of the National Mind* (New York, 1921), pp. 25, 28.

31. Lewis Mumford, "The City," in *Civilization in the United States: An Inquiry by Thirty Americans*, ed. Harold E. Stearns (New York, 1922), p. 9.

32. *The Portable F. Scott Fitzgerald*, intro. by John O'Hara (New York, 1945), from the unpaginated introduction.

33. John O'Hara, *Appointment in Samarra* (New York, 1934, 1946), passim.

34. F. Scott Fitzgerald, *The Great Gatsby* (New York, 1925, 1953), pp. 93–94.

35. F. Scott Fitzgerald, "May Day," *Babylon Revisited and Other Stories* (New York, 1960), p. 27.

36. Ibid., p. 32.

37. F. Scott Fitzgerald, *Tender Is the Night* (New York, 1933, 1963), p. 55. See also p. 97.

38. Sinclair Lewis, *Main Street* (New York, 1920, 1948), preface.

39. Ibid., p. 37. The tour is described pp. 33–38. See also chaps. 5 and 17, although consumer concerns touch practically every part of the book.

40. Sinclair Lewis, *Babbitt* (New York, 1922, 1961), pp. 320–21. Schorer wrote the afterword for this Signet edition.

41. Sinclair Lewis, *Babbitt* (New York, 1922, 1950), p. 75.

42. Ibid., p. 95.

43. Ibid., pp. 100–101.

44. Sinclair Lewis, *Dodsworth* (New York, 1929), p. 12.

45. Ibid., p. 58.

46. Ibid., p. 334. For contrast, see the description of Fran, p. 224. For more on buying and specifications of consumer goods, see pp. 183, 187–88, 371, 373.

47. Ibid., pp. 194–95. See also p. 363.

John Philip Sousa and the Culture of Reassurance

1. Comparisons between Sousa and Strauss have been numerous, both in the nineteenth and the twentieth centuries. See Wilfrid Mellers, *Music in a New Found Land* (London, 1964), p. 257; Paul E. Bierley, *John Philip Sousa: American Phenomenon* (New York. 1973), p. 5. Bierley's book is the most detailed study of Sousa's career. Sousa received the title of "March King" because a British author argued that if Johann Strauss, Jr., could be called the "Waltz King," Sousa deserved this new title (Bierley, *American Phenomenon.* p. 50).

2. As the notes will make clear, most of the citations for this essay are based on the Sousa Band press books, more than eighty volumes of clippings covering the Sousa Band between 1892 and 1931. The volumes are on deposit in the U.S. Marine Corps Museum in Washington, where I inspected them. Microfiche copies have been made, however, and I worked from these. I determined, therefore, to cite the sources according to the microfiche cards. These are numbered. The first number represents the series, usually coinciding with a date or season, and moving in roughly chronological order; the second number corresponds to the card number within the series. Each microfiche card is so identified. Although many of the clippings are identified, so far as date and newspaper are concerned, others are not. I will cite the newspaper and date when available, along with the fiche card; when I have not been able to identify the newspaper or date, I will merely cite the card, although the date (and often the place of publication) can usually be approximated. The citation for the scrapbook collection will be JPS.

3. For background on the nineteenth-century American band I have relied upon Jon Newsom, "The American Brass Band Movement," *Quarterly Journal of the Library of Congress* 36 (Spring, 1979): 114–39; Richard Franko Goldman, "Band Music in America," Paul Henry Lang, ed., *One Hundred Years of Music in America* (New York, 1961), pp. 128–39; Alberta Powell Graham, *Great Bands of America* (Toronto, New York, Edinburgh, n.d.); and a series of articles in the *Journal of Band Research*. For interesting comparative material see E. D. Mackerness, *A Social History of English Music* (London, Toronto, 1964), chaps. iv–v; and Ronald Pearsall, *Edwardian Popular Music* (Rutherford, N.J., 1975), chap. 8. Kenneth Young, *Music's Great Days in the Spas and Watering-Places* (London, 1968), contains fascinating material on another aspect of popular musical performance, again for Great Britain.

4. Matwood Darlington, *Irish Orpheus: The Life of Patrick S. Gilmore, Bandmaster Extraordinary* (Philadelphia, 1950) covers Gilmore's impressive career.

5. The early pages of John H. Mueller, *The American Symphony Orchestra: A Social History of Musi-*cal Taste (Bloomington, Ind., 1951), and Philip Hart, *Orpheus in the New World* (New York, 1973), contain some background on American symphonies. John Erskine, *The Philharmonic Symphony Society of New York, First Hundred Years* (New York, 1943); Edward Henry Krehbiel, *Philharmonic Society of New York* (New York, 1892); Max Maratzek, *Revelations of an Opera Manager in Nineteenth Century America* (New York, 1968) also contain relevant information. For comparison see William Weber, *Music and the Middle Class: The Social Structure of Concert Life in London, Paris and Vienna* (New York, 1975).

6. There is an enormous literature on many of these celebrities, the Jenny Lind bibliography alone being quite extensive. Milton Goldin, *The Music Merchants* (New York, 1969) contains sketches of some of the famous touring artists. Ivor Guest, *Fanny Elssler* (Middletown, Conn., 1970): Gladys Denny Shultz, *Jenny Lind: The Swedish Nightingale* (Philadelphia and New York, 1962); Adam Carse, *The Life of Jullien: Adventurer, Showman-Conductor . . .* (Cambridge, 1951), are among other useful texts here.

7. The immense German contribution to American musical life is recorded in a series of local studies like Bayrd Still, *Milwaukee: The History of a City* (Madison, 1948); F. Karl Grossman, *A History of Music in Cleveland* (Cleveland, 1972), among many others. Louis Moreau Gottschalk, *Notes of a Pianist* (Philadelphia, 1881), remarked in 1863 that a volunteer military band was assembled in Williamsport, Pennsylvania, on the major square. Is "it necessary for me to say that it is composed of Germans (all the musicians in the United States are Germans)?" p. 202.

8. Gottschalk was one of those offering severe comments about American audience taste. See Gottschalk, *Notes of a Pianist*, p. 17.

9. Carse, *Life of Jullien*, p. 11.

10. See Jack Felts, "Some Aspects of the Rise and Development of the Wind Band during the Civil War," *Journal of Band Research* 3 (Spring, 1967): 29–33; William Carter White, *A History of Military Music in America* (New York, 1944; Westport, Conn., 1975). Another important study, published after this essay was written, is Kenneth E. Olson,

Music and Musket: Bands and Bandsmen of the American Civil War (Westport, Conn., 1981).

11. Gilmore did attempt to persuade Congress to adopt his new national anthem, "Columbia," which he first presented Christmas Day, 1879, and whose words, he claimed, were dictated by an angel. However, it was his performing, rather than his composing or philosophizing, that earned him his popularity. See Darlington, *Irish Orpheus*, passim.

12. Thomas's career is examined in Ronald L. Davis, *A History of Music and American Life*, vol. 2, *The Gilded Years, 1865–1920* (Huntington, New York, 1980), chap. 1; and Rose Fay Thomas, *Memoirs of Theodore Thomas* (New York, 1911). Theodore Thomas, *A Musical Autobiography* (2 vols.; Chicago, 1905), George P. Upton, ed., remains a major source, and so does Charles Edward Russell, *The American Orchestra and Theodore Thomas* (Garden City, 1927).

13. J. Hecker to David Blakely, Elgin, September 16, 1891, Blakely Papers (hereafter BP), Band Correspondence, New York Public Library.

14. Jules Levy to Blakely, New York, May 8, 1891; Jules Levy to Blakely, Weehauken Heights, N.J., August 13, 1891; and Jules Levy to Blakely, Weehauken Heights, August 26, 1891, BP, Band Correspondence.

15. This subject is treated extensively in Martin J. Newhouse, "Artists, Artisans, or Workers? Orchestral Musicians in the German Empire" (Ph.D. diss., Columbia University, 1979); and Abram Loft, "Musicians' Guild and Union: A Consideration of the Evolution of Protective Organizations among Musicians" (Ph. D. diss., Columbia University, 1950), chap. 5.

16. Loft, "Musicians' Guild and Union," pp. 314–15.

17. New York *Evening Journal*, June 11, 1892, JPS 938-6.

18. John Philip Sousa, *Marching Along* (Boston, 1928), pp. 274–75.

19. J. H. Laine to Blakely, Indianapolis, April 13, 1891, BP, Band Correspondence.

20. Blakely to Hobart Weed, New York, June 23, 1892, BP, Band Correspondence.

21. J. H. Johnston to Blakely, Pittsburgh, January 5, 1893, BP, Band Correspondence.

22. *Musical Courier*, July 27, 1892, p. 13. By October 8, p. 15, the *Courier* was congratulating Sousa and looked ahead to a bright future. By February 1893 (Gilmore and Cappa were now dead), the *Courier* was calling him the most conspicuous figure in the band world. *Musical Courier*, February 2, 1893, p. 23.

23. Cappa had begun a series of Saturday and Sunday concerts in Central Park Mall, performing Mendelssohn, Beethoven, Wagner, Schubert, Bizet, Verdi, Gounod, etc. Born in Sardinia, Cappa enlisted in the U.S. Navy in the 1850s; went with Grafulla, another famous conductor, to the 7th Regiment Band when Grafulla became its leader, and conducted the 7th Regiment Band himself for twelve years.

24. Blakely to Elias Lyman, New York, June 18, 1892, BP, Band Correspondence. In the letter Blakely reviewed the profits he had made from the tours of the Gilmore Band, the Strauss Orchestra, two small tours by Theodore Thomas, and two tours by the U.S. Marine Band, led by Sousa. Between 1886 and 1892, Blakely told Lyman, he had made some $234,228 in profits.

25. Emily Howard to Blakely, St. Louis, October 1, 1893, BP, Band Correspondence.

26. Hartford *Times*, JPS 937-2.

27. Lowell *Journal*, JPS 937-2.

28. New York *World*, July 9, 1892, JPS 938-4. The *World* called Sousa's personality "intelligent and agreeable but severe and scholarly." However, it admitted there was great promise. The Wilkes-Barre *Record* was another newspaper arguing that "Sousa is not as magnetic as Gilmore," although it too appreciated his skillful training of the ensemble. JPS 937-3.

29. Both the Chicago *Inter-Ocean* and the Chicago *Times* were among those suggesting a name change. The Chicago *Times*, in a generally favorable review, wrote "The Marine Band of Washington has been so long famous that it would have been in better taste to have chosen an original name for the new organization. The encores were altogether too numerous and made the performance tiresome toward the end." JPS 937-2.

30. Chicago *Record*, JPS 937-2.

31. Hartford *Times*, JPS 937-2. The newspaper's

comment here came in the context of describing the backing of "Chicago capital and all that money could do."

32. Philadelphia *Times*, JPS 937-2. The newspaper was commenting on an 1892 concert in Philadelphia's Academy of Music.

33. Philadelphia *Enquirer*, JPS 937-2. This newspaper, among many others, was still referring, in 1892 and 1893, to the inadequate salaries the government paid its musical artists.

34. Kansas City *Star*, May 15, 1893, JPS 938-3. The Kansas City *Times*, May 15, 1893, JPS 938-3, complained about the small crowds coming to hear the Sousa Band on a Sunday, and also complimented Sousa for leading "the greatest military band in the country."

35. Boston *Herald*, JPS 937-2. "It will no longer be necessary to hold up the playing of the famous Garde Republicaine band of Paris as a standard of excellence."

36. Wilkes-Barre *Truth*, JPS 937-3.

37. "Coney Island," New York *Times*, July 18, 1880, p. 6. For some reason, during the summer of 1880, the *Times* was engaged in a campaign against brass bands, whose popularity it blamed on the Civil War's demoralization, long years of depression and poverty which had led many to "drown their miseries in brass" and the pernicious influence of bandmasters like Jules Levy. See "The Brass Instrument Habit," New York *Times*, July 28, 1880, p. 4; and "The American Brass Band," New York *Times*, August 25, 1880, p. 4.

38. Worcester *Telegram*, JPS 937-3.

39. This was a newspaper in Rockford, Illinois. JPS 937-2. The comment was made in 1892, while Sousa was making his first tour and expected to settle in Chicago.

40. Williamsport *News*, JPS 937-1.

41. Corning *Morning-Democrat*, JPS 937-1. In a similar genre, the Altoona *Tribune* observed of the Sousa Marine Band, "Its superior has never been heard in Altoona," JPS 937-2.

42. One fascinating commentary on this was William F. Apthorp, "Orchestral Conducting and Conductors," *Scribner's Magazine* 17 (March 1895): 384–92. The orchestra "has been converted into a

great, composite musical instrument on which the conductor actually *plays*," and a generation of conducting virtuosi have sprung up, "exercising the same fascination over the great crowd of music-lovers that other virtuosi have, time out of mind," p. 387.

43. Saginaw *Globe*, JPS 937-1.

44. Brooklyn *Daily Eagle*, July 13, 1893, JPS 938-4.

45. Ibid., JPS 938-4.

46. Duluth *Herald*, May 20, 1893, JPS 938-3.

47. Syracuse *Standard*, May 9, 1893, JPS 938-2; Lewiston *Journal*, JPS 937-3; Duluth *Herald*, May 20, 1893, JPS 938-3.

48. Syracuse *Standard*. JPS 937-3. The *Standard* believed that Sousa was at heart "a leader of strings and his ideal in brass band music is not blare and a great volume of sound but true harmony. He is the Theodore Thomas of band leaders." This was said during the first tour of the independent band, 1892-93.

49. Buffalo *Enquirer*, May 10, 1893, JPS 938-2.

50. Syracuse *Standard*, May 9, 1893, JPS 938-2; a Rockford newspaper in 1892, JPS 937-2. Countless reviewers likened Sousa to a general, emphasizing his qualities of leadership. "To be able to command men is a gift possessed by comparatively few, and the great general is no more difficult to discover then the great conductor. . . . Not the least enjoyable thing about a Sousa band concert is the masterly control of the leader over the human instrumentality before him." Detroit *Tribune*, April 6, 1899, JPS 944-23.

51. For more on this subject see "Music and Manliness," *The Nation* 75 (July 24, 1902): 66, which refers mainly to the English situation; and Edith Brower, "Is the Musical Idea Masculine?" *Atlantic Monthly* 73 (March, 1894): 332–39. "In the practical business world generally music has not been reckoned one of the manly arts," Edith Brower wrote, p. 333, but at the same time the vast majority of composers had been men.

52. An unidentified Buffalo newspaper in the summer of 1893, commenting on a Sousa concert at the Buffalo Music Hall, JPS 938-5.

53. A considerable literature has been devoted to

this theme. See, among others, Robert H. Wiebe, *The Search for Order, 1877–1920* (New York, 1976); Samuel Haber, *Efficiency and Uplift: Scientific Management in the Progressive Era, 1890–1920* (Chicago and London, 1964); Jerry Israel, ed., *Building the Organizational Society* (New York, 1972).

54. *Musical Courier,* February 8, 1905, p. 23. This was a reprint of an interview Sousa gave to the London *Daily Express.* In it, Sousa went on, "I know precisely what every one of my musicians is doing every second or fraction of a second that I am conducting. I know this because every single member of my band is doing exactly what I make him do."

55. Sousa, *Marching Along,* p. 153. There were limits, of course, to Sousa's showmanship. For a contemporary bandmaster, John S. Duss, who built his career primarily on showmanship and the work of a clever publicity agent, R. E. Johnston, see Richard D. Wetzel, *Frontier Musicians on the Connoquenessing, Wabash, and Ohio: A History of the Music and Musicians of George Rapp's Harmony Society (1805–1906)* (Athens, Ohio, 1976), chap. 6.

56. Unidentified New Britain newspapers, 1892, JPS 937-3.

57. Middlesex *Times,* 1892, JPS 937-2.

58. For an extended discussion of these issues see Joseph A. Mussulman, *Music in the Cultured Generation: A Social History of Music in America, 1870–1900* (Evanston, Ill., 1971). See also Arnold T. Schwab, *James Gibbons Huneker: Critic of the Seven Arts* (Stanford, 1963), for the development of a new kind of musical criticism and musical philosophy in America.

59. Gilmore to Blakely, St. Louis, October 18, 1891, BP, Band Correspondence.

60. New York *World,* July 9, 1893, JPS 938-4.

61. Kansas City *Journal,* May 15, 1893, JPS 938-3.

62. Elmira *Star,* undated, but during the first touring season, JPS 937-1.

63. Kansas City *Journal,* May 15, 1893, JPS 938-3.

64. Unidentified New York newspaper, July, 1893, JPS 938-5. Sousa was playing at the time at the Manhattan Beach Hotel, which was not, this newspaper continued, "a conservatory of music where taste is to be cultivated and people to be educated, but a pleasure resort where they come to be entertained."

65. Chicago *Herald,* June 28, 1893, JPS 938-4.

66. Duluth *Daily Commonwealth,* May 20, 1893, JPS 938-3. The St. Paul *Pioneer Press,* May 21, also found the program weak in places, arguing that Sousa's Salute of the Nations to the Columbian Exposition "is of the claptrap variety, and did not succeed in evoking much enthusiasm." JPS 938-3.

67. Springfield *Republican,* undated, but during the first touring season, JPS 937-3.

68. *Evening Wisconsin,* May 22, 1893, JPS 938-4.

69. Syracuse *Standard,* May 9, 1893, JPS 938-2. The brass band's function, the newspaper concluded, "is to play what Gilmore always called 'masculine music.'" And the Buffalo *Enquirer,* May 10, 1893, agreed that the band should play more military numbers and not try to imitate orchestral sounds. JPS 938-2.

70. Sousa interview in New York *World,* August 6, 1893, JPS 938-6. In this interview Sousa used medical analogies, arguing that the result is "being reached by homeopathic doses, so to speak; the allopathic treatment would not do at all in this case."

71. Sousa in Chicago *Herald,* June 27, 1893, JPS 938-4.

72. Chicago *Herald,* undated, during the first touring season, JPS 937-2. The *Herald* hoped that Sousa would bear in mind "that upon him, in a measure, devolves the responsibility of educating the taste of the people so that they may eventually learn to appreciate the higher forms of orchestral music. For band music always appeals to the masses and can thus be made a stepping stone to something higher."

73. Sousa in New York *Advertiser,* August 27, 1893, JPS 938-6. Here again, Sousa used the analogy of a skilled physician, saying he covered his pills with sugar.

74. Sousa, *Marching Along,* p. 275.

75. Ibid., p. 133.

76. Sousa in New York *Advertiser,* August 17, 1893, JPS 938-6. "The people who frequent my concerts are the strong and healthy," Sousa told an in-

terviewer. "I mean the healthy both of mind and body. These people like virile music. Longhaired men and shorthaired women you never see in my audience. And I don't want them." Houston *Post,* May 17, 1903, JPS 951-11. This interview was given in Paris.

77. For more on Sousa's rivals in the late nineteenth century see H. W. Schwartz, *Bands of America* (Garden City, 1957). Schwartz treats Gilmore extensively and devotes space to Liberati, Innes, Brooke, Creatore, Conway, Pryor, and Kryl.

78. *Musical Courier,* May 20, 1896, p. 23. In reprinting an article by W. S. B. Matthews, two years earlier, the *Courier* wrote, "The Sousa Band stands alone. It is at the head as much as the Boston Orchestra under Gericke was alone, or the Chicago Exposition Orchestra under Thomas was alone. Nothing has been heard better. . . . That is the beauty of Sousa. You can take culture from him without fatigue," *Musical Courier,* February 28, 1894, p. 21. And the same journal noted, in 1897, "Probably were men empowered and determined to plan an individual to fill the present position of John Philip Sousa invention would fall short in the detail of equipment which the brilliant leader so lavishly enjoys," *Musical Courier,* April 21, 1897, p. 26.

79. H. M. Bosworth, "Musical Comment," San Francisco *Examiner,* March 12, 1899, JPS 945-8.

80. Wilkes-Barre *Daily News,* April 19, 1899, JPS 944-18. "Gilmore's, Victor Herbert's," they are either past or "they never get close enough to the American people to make a comparison direct enough, generally speaking."

81. Dayton *News,* September 29, 1899, JPS 945-7.

82. New York *World,* August 18, 1899, JPS 945-3.

83. Wilkes-Barre *Sunday News,* no date indicated but probably April 1901, JPS 948-10. The article was an attack on critics who were hard on Sousa.

84. See, for example, the story in an 1898 New York newspaper about a local Richmond Hill lawyer, Darmstadt, who blackened his wife Martha's eye because she continually whistled the "Liberty Bell" march. He hit her and made slighting remarks about

Sousa. Their case went to court. JPS 942-19. The Rochester *Democrat Chronicle,* November 17, 1897, reported that a Mr. Godfrey Warburton of Tenafly, New Jersey, smote his wife in the eye because she kept whistling Sousa's "Liberty Bell." Curiously, Mmes. Darmstadt and Warburton whistled the march continuously for the same period of time, four days and four nights. The Sousa press agents had a stock of phrases, anecdotes, and observations, which they presented to the local press.

85. Sousa, *Marching Along,* pp. 187–88.

86. Ibid., p. 196.

87. Buffalo *News,* September 17, 1905, JPS 1018-2.

88. New York *Evening Sun,* September 2, 1905; and Denver *Republican,* September 11, 1905, JPS 1018-2. The Cleveland *Plain Dealer* noted, "One would as soon expect a Sunday school library story from D'Annunzio or a ragtime from Puccini as a novel by Sousa," objecting that the story was too ordinary. September 14, 1905, JPS 1018-2. Another Sousa novel, *The Fifth String,* received somewhat better reviews, but got its share of spoofs.

89. John Philip Sousa, *Pipetown Sandy* (Indianapolis, 1905), p. 253.

90. Oakland *Enquirer,* March 18, 1899, JPS 944-14. And newspapers echoed this thought. Sousa "has none of the musical crankiness, none of the intolerance and rabid jealousy that are quite too familiar," a Wilkes-Barre newspaper wrote in 1905. "He does not affect 'airs' or wear his hair in such a shape as to decorate his coat collar. He is a manly, healthful, wholesome American, loaded with genius. . . . Work is his delight." JPS 942-1.

91. Wilkes-Barre *Evening Leader,* April 9, 1897, JPS 942-1.

92. John Philip Sousa, "The Business of the Bandmaster," *Criterion,* August, 1905, JPS 946-6. In the article Sousa insisted: "After twenty years of organization and hard training, entailing the personal examination of more than fifty thousand musicians and the training of perhaps five thousand of them, I have no hesitation in affirming that I have approached the ideal standard."

93. Sousa, *Marching Along,* p. 266.

94. Ibid., pp. 131–32.

95. Fannie Edgar Thomas, "John Philip Sousa in Paris," *Musical Courier*, June 13, 1900, p. 16.

96. Ibid., p. 17. The European triumphs added immeasurably to Sousa's reputation. In December 1901, after Sousa had been decorated by King Edward, the Brooklyn *Eagle* wrote, "The fact that Sousa and his band played for the birthday celebration of Queen Alexandra . . . will give to his concerns an enhanced value in the eyes of the multitude when he comes back to Manhattan Beach." JPS 948-40. Or the Hutchinson *Daily News*, November 17, 1904, "Sousa and his band have come and gone and the only American bandsman who has been able to make kings and queens tremble at will has made Hutchinson another visit." JPS 951-31.

97. Unidentified Duluth newspaper, 1897, JPS 942-2.

98. Kansas City newspaper in 1897, commenting on a concert at the auditorium, JPS 942-3.

99. Lubov Keefer, *Baltimore's Music: The Haven of the American Composer* (Baltimore, 1962), p. 272. Note the Atlanta *Journal*, April 7, 1899, quoting one local figure that Atlanta must have band music in her parks. "Band music refines the people, it charms them . . . it whiles away the dull hours. It keeps people out of idleness." JPS 944-14. For more on music in the parks see Galen Cranz, *The Politics of Park Design: A History of Urban Parks in America* (Cambridge, Mass., 1982), pp. 10, 13, 258.

100. Everett Reynolds died in December 1905, and obituaries can be found in JPS 953-7. Reynolds's brother, Melville C. Reynolds, was business manager for the actress Helen Modjeska. And see the obituary for David Blakely, *Inland Printer* 18 (December, 1896), p. 321.

101. For more on the poster movement two contemporary works, Charles K. Bolton, *The Reign of the Poster* (Boston, 1895), and Charles Matlack Price, *Posters: A Critical Study of the Development of Poster Design in Continental Europe, England and America* (New York, 1913), are helpful, as are two later books, Victor Margolin, *American Poster Renaissance: The Great Age of Poster Design, 1890–1900* (New York, 1975); and Patricia Hills, *Turn-of-the-Century America* (New York, 1977). See also *Broadway Quarterly*, May 1901, JPS 948-7, for an interesting juxtaposition of Sousa's band and the magazine revolution.

102. JPS 953-11 contains many details on Sousa's statements. For a brief discussion of his attitudes see James R. Smart, *The Sousa Band: A Discography* (Washington, 1970), pp. 2–5. Sousa's hostility was extensive. He suggested that sales of musical instruments would lessen and that the vocal chords might become useless. "Wherever there is a phonograph the musical instrument is displaced. The time is coming when no one will be ready to submit himself to the ennobling discipline of learning music, whether instrumental or vocal. Everyone will have their ready made or ready pirated music in their cupboards." Sousa in New York *Morning Telegraph*, June 12, 1906, JPS 953-11. This was a period when canning was becoming an effective (and negative) metaphor. In 1906 "The Can Age" ran as an editorial in a New York periodical, treating illustrated books, slot machines, motion pictures, and simplified spelling. "If we can just crowd everything we want into a can and walk away with the original package, we are perfectly happy." JPS 153-14. And see "Canned Speeches," *Nation* 86 (January 16, 1908): 53–54, an editorial commenting on a new book *Ready-Made Speeches*. Sousa's most complete statement on the subject was "The Menace of Mechanical Music," *Appleton's Magazine* 8 (September, 1906): 278–84. There were strong replies to this in *Appleton's* 8 (November 1906): 638–40. For Sousa's extensive written work see Paul E. Bierley, *John Philip Sousa: A Descriptive Catalogue of His Works* (Urbana, Chicago, London, 1973), pp. 150–69. In his articles Sousa wrote on everything from baseball and horses to trap shooting, patriotism and, of course, music.

103. Unidentified Philadelphia newspaper, in early 1899, JPS 944-3. The Philadelphia *Inquirer*, January 15, 1899, conducted an imaginary dialogue between Sousa's body and the band, JPS 944-3.

104. New Haven *Leader*, May 8, 1899, JPS 944-20. "The conviction always presents itself afresh that if he laid down that stick the music would stop. Either he illustrates the music, or the music illustrates Sousa, one hardly knows which. When this original conductor turns his head on one side and gently trills the air with the left hand it really seems

as though the sound was made by the motion."

105. H. M. Bosworth, "Musical Comment," San Francisco *Examiner*, March 12, 1899, JPS 945-8. "Call this del Sarte or what you will, I call it genius. . . . Whatever he 'conducts' his gestures convey to the audience the proper acceptance of the musical intention."

106. Chicago *Tribune*, September 19, 1903. JPS 951-20. See also Portland (Me.) *Advertiser*, April, 1904, "Sousa's band couldn't be what it is without Mr. Sousa's curving figure, the graceful swing of his arms, his delightful nonchalance." JPS 951-27. There are hundreds of comments, scattered through the reviews, on Sousa's postures, gestures, mannerisms; vaudeville artists made their living imitating Sousa, notably Walter Jones. The Burlington *Hawk-eye*, February 15, 1898, wrote "Half the expressiveness of the Italian tongue, if one may venture an Irish bull, is in the gesticulation of the hands, and Sousa employs his after a very fascinating fashion." JPS 942-5.

107. Both quotations from unidentified newspapers, JPS 953-13. The Joplin *Globe*, September 18, 1906, insisted that mechanical music was "merely the instrument of awakening—just as great musicians have in childhood been roused to an ecstasy of delight and aspiration by the music of a humble street band." JPS 953-13.

108. Topeka *Daily Capital*, November 8, 1902, JPS 951-5. Some of the language employed by newspapers objecting to foreign bandsmen was nasty. A Newton, Kansas, newspaper wrote, November 17, 1904, that Sousa's Band contained only a "small number of foreigners of swarthy countenance, as was the case with Banda Rossa . . . most of them smoked cigars and not the nasty little cigarettes the foreign bandsmen seem to take to." JPS 951-31. The Bloomington *Pantagraph*, August 4, 1906, warned that the importation of Italian musicians threatened the existence of local musical organizations, and quoted a bandsman who prophesied that the local band would soon be a "crew of dark-skinned men from the country made famous as the home of Rome." JPS 953-13.

109. Springfield (Ohio) *Republican*, January 29, 1897, JPS 942-2.

110. Rev. M. F. Johnson, "Spiritual Suggestions from Sousa," A Sermon Preached in the Central Bap-

tist Church, May 16, 1898, JPS 942-11. For an example of the Sousa-inspired poetry see "How John Philip Sousa Impressed the Gallery," originally in the Detroit *Journal*, reprinted by the Toledo *Blade*, July 16, 1899, JPS 944-23; and "Uncle Silas Hears Sousa's Band Play," Kalamazoo *Morning Gazette-News*, March 23, 1901, JPS 948-8. An example of the latter:

So I went down to the opery house an' got a fust class seat—
There wuz music in the atmosphere an' music in my feet,
An' when the band come on the stage an' Sousy, too, no doubt,
I jined the folks around me an' jest stamped for all git out.

I had that happy feeling' that I feel onct long ago,
Being' when I got religion over at East Alamo,
When Elder Higgins come to me an' prayed, he did, that night,
An' we kneeled around the altar an' I saw I "saw the light."

111. Unidentified newspaper, JPS 942-26.

112. Unidentified newspaper, JPS 942-26. There was considerable surprise expressed by journalists at the enthusiasm of audiences at these concerts. The "conservative people of Pittsfield involuntarily rose to their feet and waved hats and handkerchiefs in a perfect furore of patriotic enthusiasm," while the band performed the "Star-Spangled Banner." The same thing happened at New Haven in the spring of 1898. In late March, 5,000 at the Metropolitan Opera House rose to their feet during the "Star-Spangled Banner." "It was as if a current of electricity had passed from stage through stalls, boxes and galleries to the very roof of the auditorium. Everyone jumped to his feet. Hats were waved and handkerchiefs fluttered." JPS 942-26.

113. Chicago *Times-Herald*, April 20, 1898, JPS 942-28.

114. New York *Mirror*, September 15, 1898, JPS 943-2.

115. Chicago *Times-Herald*, May 1, 1898, JPS 942-28. "Slam-bang eccentricities in band play may tickle for a time, but one cannot live perpetually on red pepper and musical fireworks."

116. The Syracuse *Standard*, August 18, 1899, in an editorial, "Brass Bands and King Sousa," quoted the Washington *Post* and added its own comments. JPS 945-5.

117. Chicago *Post*, March 16, 1901, JPS 948-10. "Anything so trivial as a Sousa concert ought not to be considered seriously," the newspaper began, acknowledging, however, that Sousa took himself so seriously that he forced some kind of rigorous response. See also Frederick Stevenson of the Los Angeles *Examiner*, October 26, 1907, who called Sousa the "Harriman of the Music World," one who knew advertising better than music. His band was fine, but played too much trash, Stevenson argued. JPS 953-21.

118. The Sousa interview which incorporated this remark was made in September 1903. It attracted widespread comment. See JPS 951-23. For more on the complex relationships among Sousa, ragtime, and jazz, see Edward A. Berlin. *Ragtime: A Musical and Cultural History* (Berkeley, Los Angeles, London, 1980), and William J. Schafer, *Brass Bands and New Orleans Jazz* (Baton Rouge and London, 1977).

119. St. Paul *Globe*, September 1903, JPS 951-23.

120. Rochester *Post-Express*, April 3, 1906, JPS 956-1. The following day the Geneva *Times*, April 4, 1906, condemned Sousa for playing common music like "Everybody Works but Father." It "seemed a prostitution and profanation of the art of music. This abominable song is such in itself. . . . But still greater was the disgrace that the people actually liked it." JPS 956-1.

121. "For Sousa has lost his gestures, his poses, his delsarte. No longer in great circles does his baton scrape the proscenium arch. The baseball swat and the ping pong volley are things of Sousa's past." San Francisco *Examiner*, October 17, 1904, JPS 951-30. "He is a subdued Sousa compared to what he used to be. Not that he was ever a contortionist. . . . He does not hump; he undulates." Irish *Independent*, February 16, 1911, JPS 966-5. "Perhaps the Sousa nonchalance is a bit accentuated; certain it is that he presents a more passive figure before his instrumental cohorts than of yore." Riverside *Press*, November 1, 1904, JPS 951-30.

122. "A band that has won such laurels in every great city of the world, and among foreigners jealous of and prejudiced against everything American, is something that does not come to Bakersfield every year." Bakersfield *Californian*, November 3, 1904, JPS 951-30.

123. "The Washington Post," New York *Times*, November 2, 1907, p. 8. The visitor was Arthur Walkeley, a drama critic for the London *Times*.

124. See New York *Herald*, June 29, 1918, JPS 979-2.

125. Oklahoma City *Oklahoman*, June 29, 1918, JPS 979-5.

126. Sousa indulged in attacks on various aspects of German culture during the war. At Willow Grove he announced, in the summer of 1918, "The greatest ambition of my life is to lead my band down the Wilhelmstrasse in Berlin playing 'The Star-Spangled Banner' for the delectation of the Hohenzollerns—or what is left of them." Philadelphia *Record*, August 19, 1918, JPS 979-5. On another occasion he declared, "The pro-German in America is the lowest, most sneaking, most cowardly thing on earth—he is even worse than a German in the German army, and that's about the limit of condemnation." Baltimore *News*, October 2, 1918, JPS 979-9. It should be pointed out that these remarks were not much different from many uttered by American cultural leaders at the same time; Sousa, once more, was quite representative.

127. *Musical Courier*, August 19, 1915, p. 22. Sousa was speaking to a reporter on the Spokane *Chronicle*.

128. And honest tunes provided another margin of safety in the postwar world. "If every Bolshevik were made to attend a week's course of concerts played by this famous band, the chances are that at the end of the week he would have caught the contagion and become a loyal citizen of these United States. You cannot think mean thoughts when you hear good music, and you cannot see Red Russia when you hear the 'Stars and Stripes Forever' or 'Who's Who in Navy Blue.'" Portsmouth (NH) *Times*, August 13, 1920, JPS 983-1.

129. D. C. Parker, "Sousa, Philosopher," *Musical Courier*, August 16, 1917, p. 32.

130. Sousa's interview with the Adelaide *Adver-*

tiser was reprinted in the *Musical Courier*, September 9, 1911, p. 31.

131. For more on high school music programs, see Edward Bailey Birge, *History of Public School Music in the United States*, new ed. (Philadelphia, 1928, 1937).

Who Owns Our Myths? Heroism and Copyright in an Age of Mass Culture

1. There are many accounts of the creation and development of "Superman." I have relied on, among others, E. Nelson Bridwell, *Superman: From the Thirties to the Eighties* (New York: Crown, 1983); and Gary H. Grossman, *Superman: Serial to Cereal* (New York: Popular Library, 1976).

2. For details on the early growth of the comic, see John Kobler, "Up, Up and Awa-a-y! The Rise of Superman, Inc.," *Saturday Evening Post* 213 (June 21, 1941): 14–15, 70+. For more on background, and for movie serials, see Jim Harmon and Donald F. Glut, *The Great Movie Serials: Their Sound and Fury* (Garden City: Doubleday, 1972).

3. Kobler, "Up, Up and Awa-a-y!" p. 70.

4. Slater Brown, "The Coming of Superman," *New Republic* 103 (Sep. 2, 1940): 301.

5. Heinz Politzer, "From Little Nemo to Li'l Abner: Comic Strips as Present-Day American Folklore," *Commentary* 8 (October 1949): 352. The essay is reprinted in David Manning White and Robert H. Abel, eds., *The Funnies: An American Idiom* (New York: Free Press, 1963), pp. 39–54. Along with other useful commentaries, the anthology contains a bibliography, pp. 293–304.

6. Kenneth Cavander, "Hercules Lives!" *Horizon* 17 (Summer 1975): 58–61.

7. These are the words of Jenette Kahn, president and publisher of DC Comics, as printed in Bridwell, *Superman*, pp. 7–8.

8. Pierre Couperie, Maurice C. Horn, et al., *A History of the Comic Strip* (New York: Crown, 1967), passim and p. 177. The principal example in this particular analysis is Flash Gordon.

9. Walter Ong, "The Comics and the Super State: Glimpses Down the Back Alleys of the Mind," *Arizona Quarterly* 1 (Autumn 1945): 34–48. Geoffrey Wagner, *Parade of Pleasure: A Study of Popular Iconography in the USA* (London: Verschoyle, 1954), pp. 71–112, launches a vitriolic attack on comics entitled "Comics: The Curse of the Kids," in which he cites McLuhan and Ong, among other critics. For more on the hostility to comic books generated by critics, see John E. Twomey, "The Anti-Comic Book Crusade," unpublished M.A. thesis, University of Chicago, 1955. By the mid 1950s, stimulated by figures like Dr. Frederic Wertham, senior psychologist for the New York City Department of Hospitals, there had been several legislative investigations, on both federal and state levels, of the impact of comic books. There were requests for bans on them and suggestions for various kinds of controls.

10. Gershon Legman, *Love and Death: A Study in Censorship* (New York: Breaking Point, 1949), p. 39.

11. This was a quotation from Sterling North, a leading early critic of comics, *Chicago Daily News*, May 8, 1940, cited in Legman, *Love and Death*, p. 40.

12. Arthur Asa Berger, *The Comic-Stripped American* (New York: Walker, 1973), p. 157.

13. See the conclusions in Morrie S. Helitzer, "A Political Analysis of Comic Strips, 1928–1947," unpublished M.A. thesis, University of Chicago, 1948. The strips, Helitzer concluded, reinforce "traditional beliefs and values in our society. The absence of competing ideologies, the repetition of familiar ideas, and the use of stereotypes, in effect, confirm and strengthen the reader's attitude toward his society" (p. 95).

14. Legman, *Love and Death*, pp. 39–40, provides a list of the superheroes.

15. For the history of copyright and for discussion of copyright cases, I have relied heavily on Benjamin Kaplan and Ralph S. Brown, Jr., *Cases on Copyright, Unfair Competition, and Other Topics Bearing on the Protection of Literary, Musical, and Artistic Works*, 2d ed. (Mineola, N.Y.: Foundation Press, 1974); and Melville B. Nimmer, *Nimmer on Copyright: A Treatise on the Law of Literary, Musical*

and *Artistic Property, and the Protection of Ideas,* vol. 1 (New York: Bender, 1983).

16. For early twentieth-century comments on the history of trademarks and the growth of litigation and charges of unfair competition, see Edward S. Rogers, *Good Will, Trade-Marks and Unfair Trading* (Chicago: Shaw, 1914); and Harry D. Nims, *The Law of Unfair Competition and Trade-Marks,* 2d ed. (New York: Baker, Voorhis, 1917).

17. *Empire City Amusement Co. v. Wilton,* 134 F. 132 (C.C.D. Mass. 1903).

18 *Hill v. Whalen & Martell Inc.,* 220 F. 359 (S.D.N.Y. 1914).

19. *Courier Lithographing Co. v. Donaldson Lithographing Co.,* 44 C.C.A. 296.

20. *Bleistein v. Donaldson Lithographing Co.,* 188 U.S. 239 (1902).

21. *Warner Bros. Pictures, Incorporated, v. Columbia Broadcasting System, Inc.,* 216 F. 2d 945 (1954).

22. *King Features Syndicate v. Fleischer,* 299 F. 533 (1924).

23. *Fleischer Studios, Incorporated, v. Ralph A. Freundlich, Inc.,* 73 F. 2d 276 (1934).

24. For some contemporary comments on this marketing, see "Ape-Man Business," *Fortune* 17 (March 1938): 18; "The Silly Symphony," *Fortune* 10 (November 1934): 88–95; and slightly later, "The Mighty Mouse," *Time* 52 (Oct. 25, 1948): 96, 98.

25. *Sheldon v. Metro-Goldwyn Pictures Corporation,* 81 F. 2d 49 (1932). Summaries of this case and many other appropriate cases, abridgements of the judgments, discussion of the issues raised, and references to many other cases are conveniently organized in Kaplan and Brown, *Cases on Copyright,* pp. 276–312.

26. *Detective Comics, Incorporated, v. Bruns Publications, Inc.,* 111 F. 2d 432 (1940).

27. This issue is discussed in various places, including Kenneth B. Umbreit, "A Consideration of Copyright," *University of Pennsylvania Law Review* 87 (1939): 932; and "Note: The Protection Afforded Literary and Cartoon Characters through Trademark, Unfair Competition, and Copyright," *Harvard Law Review* 68 (1954): 349.

28. For coverage of some of the suits, see *News-*

week 29 (Apr. 14, 1947): 65–66; and *Newsweek* 32 (July 19, 1948): 51–52.

29. "Marketing the Man of Steel," *MacLean's* 91 (Dec. 11, 1978): 46–50, contains some information on the relationship between Schuster and Siegel, on the one hand, and Warner Communications, on the other, in later years.

30. *Newsweek* 22 (July 12, 1943): 70.

31. *National Comics Publications, Incorporated v. Fawcett Publishers, Inc.,* 93 F. Supp. 349 (1950); and *National Comics Publications, Incorporated vs. Fawcett Publications, Inc.,* 191 F. 2d 594 (1951), the one a district court decision, the other, the decision on appeal, are the two cases of interest here; both are excerpted in Kaplan and Brown, *Cases on Copyright,* pp. 127–44.

32. *National Comics Publications, Incorporated v. Fawcett Publications, Inc.,* 191 F. 2d 603. Hand's decision actually reversed the district judge's ruling. For comments on comics at this time, taking them more seriously, see Leslie A. Fiedler, "Both Ends against the Middle," *Encounter* 5 (August 1955): 16–23.

33. Roderick Nordell, "Superman Revisited," *Atlantic* 217 (January 1966): 104–5. For more comments on the increasing interest in Superman and the aging of the hero, see the *New Yorker* 41 (Aug. 21, 1965): 23–24; *Newsweek* 65 (Feb. 15, 1965): 89–90; and Betty Rollin, "The Return of the (Whoosh! There Goes One!) Super-Hero," *Look* 30 (Mar. 22, 1966): 113–14.

34. "Marketing the Man of Steel," *MacLean's* 91 (Dec. 11, 1978): 46–50. See also *Newsweek* 112 (Oct. 9, 1978): 91.

35. Richard Manning, "Metropolis: Supertown," *Atlantic* 243 (May 1979): 16–21.

36. *Warner Brothers, Incorporated, Film Export A. G., and D C Comics, Inc. v. American Broadcasting Companies, Inc.,* 523 F. Supp. 615–16 (1981).

37. 523 F. Supp. 614.

38. *Berlin v. E. C. Publications, Incorporated,* 329 F. 543 (1964). This is actually Judge Kaufman's paraphrase of what the plaintiffs will not believe. By implication, given his conclusion, it is his own belief. In this decision Judge Kaufman cites a number of recently written law review comments involving

parody, burlesque, fair use, and copyright, among them "Comment: Parody and the Law of Copyright," *Fordham Law Review* 29 (1961): 570; and "Note: Parody and Burlesque—Fair Use or Copyright Infringement?" *Vanderbilt Law Review* 12 (1959): 459.

39. *Elsmere Music, Incorporated v. National Broadcasting Company*, 623 F. 2d 253 (1980). This was a decision confirming Judge Goettel, who had heard the case two years earlier, *Elsmere Music, Incorporated v. National Broadcasting Company, Inc.*, 482 F. Supp. 741 (1978). Judge Goettel obviously had a good time writing his decision, as he reviewed the lengthy efforts of New York to make war on its unsavory reputation, the development of the song "I Love New York" through an advertising agency, and the relationships linking the state, the city, and the lyrics.

40. *Loew's Incorporated v. Columbia Broadcasting System, Inc.*, 131 F. Supp. 165 (1955). Judge James M. Carter's decision was appealed, unsuccessfully, in *Jack Benny v. Loew's Incorporated*, 239 F. 2d 532 (1956). In the appeal decision, the court argued that up until then "no federal court, in any adjudication, has supposed that there was a doctrine of fair use applicable to copying the substance of a dramatic work, and presenting it, with few variations, as a burlesque" (239 F. 2d 536). On the following page the court went on to insist that whether the audience was tense with emotion or laughing "doesn't absolve the copier." Otherwise anyone could appropriate "in its entity, a serious and famous dramatic work protected by copyright merely by introducing" clownish garb, movement or facial distortion and "presenting it as burlesque." This, of course, was precisely what would happen in later years. The view that burlesque was essentially dramatic criticism, and thus not subject to action for copyright infringement, the court saw as "a parody upon the meaning of criticism."

41. *Columbia Pictures Corporation v. National Broadcasting Co.*, 137 F. Supp. 348 (1955).

42. *Berlin v. E. C. Publications, Incorporated*, 329 F. 545 (1964).

43. John T. Galloway, *The Gospel According to Superman* (Philadelphia: Holman, 1973).

44. Robert Warshow, "The Gangster as Tragic Hero," in *The Immediate Experience: Movies, Com-*

ics, Theatre, and Other Aspects of Popular Culture (Garden City: Doubleday: 1964), p. 85. This collection of essays also contains a piece by Warshow on comic books and the Wertham investigation.

Collective Possession: J. Pierpont Morgan and the American Imagination

1. There are a number of biographies of Morgan, dozens of essays and articles, and an enormous literature of observation and retrospection. No convincing, comprehensive, modern biography exists. Several of the books tend to repeat one another's anecdotes, albeit in some repackaged form. The first biography, Carl Hovey, *The Life Story of F. Pierpont Morgan: A Biography* (New York, 1912), takes a middle ground between adulation and condemnation and traces Morgan's love for art and collecting to his father. John K. Winkler, *Morgan The Magnificent: The Life of J. Pierpont Morgan* (New York, 1930), relies heavily on Hovey, is melodramatic, overwritten, and worshipful, although occasionally critical, presenting Morgan as a colossal adventurer, a genius, gifted with "incredible audacity, sublime self-confidence, unqualified courage." Lewis Corey, *The House of Morgan* (New York, 1930), and Frederick Lewis Allen, *The Great Pierpont Morgan* (New York, 1949), are the favored texts, better documented, although I have found them less helpful than the detailed study by Morgan's son-in-law, Herbert L. Satterlee, *J. Pierpont Morgan: An Intimate Portrait* (New York, 1939). Francis Taylor, *Pierpont Morgan as Collector and Patron, 1837–1913* (New York, 1970), is probably the most convincing picture of the man as a collector. Contemporary articles, cartoons, a still unpublished recollection by Bishop Lawrence of Massachusetts (much cited by Taylor), are available at the archives of the Morgan Library in New York. I am grateful to archivist David Wright for making scrapbooks and other materials available to me, and for many helpful suggestions.

2. For a summary of such generalizations see Neil Harris, "The Gilded Age Reconsidered Once Again," *Archives of American Art Journal* 23, no. 4

(1983): 9–18. Sigmund Diamond, *The Reputation of the American Businessman* (Cambridge, Mass., 1955), devotes a chapter to Morgan's obituary notices, but concentrates on things other than his art collecting.

3. Taylor, *Pierpont Morgan as Collector*, p. 39. Edward P. Mitchell, *Memoirs of an Editor: Fifty Years of American Journalism* (New York and London, 1924), contains an interesting interpretation of Morgan as collector, pp. 366–68, while also describing William Mackay Laffan, a journalist and specialist on oriental ceramics who often advised Morgan. The chapter on Morgan in Aline B. Saarinen, *The Proud Possessors: The Lives, Times and Tastes of Some Adventurous American Art Collectors* (New York, 1958), is also very useful.

4. The collecting patterns of this period, as they interact with patronage, are best summarized in Lillian B. Miller, *Patrons and Patriotism: The Encouragement of the Fine Arts in the United States, 1790–1860* (Chicago, 1966). The social setting for the art communities is examined in Neil Harris, *The Artist in American Society: The Formative Years, 1790–1860* (New York, 1966).

5. Francis Steegmuller, *The Two Lives of James Jackson Jarves* (New Haven, 1951), offers the fullest picture of Jarves's life. Saarinen, *Proud Possessors*, and W. G. Constable, *Art Collecting in the United States of America: An Outline of a History* (Toronto and New York, 1964), describe Bryan's attempts to create a comprehensive gallery.

6. For this later era see René Brimo, *L'Évolution du goût aux États-Unis* (Paris, 1938); and Wesley Towner, *The Elegant Auctioneers* (New York, 1970), alas entirely unannotated. For collecting and the art market on a worldwide basis see the volumes by Gerald Reitlinger, *The Rise and Fall of Picture Prices, 1760–1960* (London, 1961), and *The Rise and Fall of Objets d'Art Prices Since 1750* (London, 1963), vols 1 and 2 of *The Economics of Taste*.

7. For Avery and the development of American dealers see the introduction to *The Diaries 1871–1882 of Samuel P. Avery, Art Dealer*, ed. Madeleine Fidell Beaufort, Herbert L. Kleinfield, and Jeanne K. Welcher (New York, 1979), pp. vii–lxvii.

8. Towner, *The Elegant Auctioneers*, passim, describes these sales.

9. Several of these museums have their own historical monographs. For general overviews see Nathaniel Burt, *Palaces for the People: A Social History of the American Art Museum* (Boston and Toronto, 1977); Daniel M. Fox, *Engines of Culture: Philanthropy and Art Museums* (Madison, Wis., 1963); and Karl E. Meyer, *The Art Museum: Power, Money, Ethics* (New York, 1979), chap. 1. See also Walter M. Whitehill, *Museum of Fine Arts, Boston* (Cambridge, Mass., 1970), 2 vols; and Calvin Tomkins, *Merchants and Masterpieces* (New York, 1970), the last of which contains a good deal of material on Morgan's role in creating the Metropolitan.

10. Collecting as a literary theme has recently been examined in Rémy G. Saisselin, *The Bourgeois and the Bibelot* (New Brunswick, N.J., 1984), passim, but particularly chaps. 4–6.

11. Henry James, *Roderick Hudson* (London, 1879; Harmondsworth, 1969), p. 26.

12. Ibid., pp. 32–33.

13. [Finley Peter Dunne] "Art Patronage," *Observations by Mr. Dooley* (New York, 1902), pp. 42–43, 45.

14. Henry B. Fuller, *With the Procession* (New York, 1895; Chicago, 1965), p. 57.

15. Richard Harding Davis, "A Patron of Art," *Van Bibber and Others* (New York and London, 1892), p. 151.

16. Robert Herrick, *The Gospel of Freedom* (New York, 1898), p. 221. Interesting themes raised by collecting are featured in the group of short stories by the art critic Frank Jewett Mather, Jr., *The Collectors: Being Cases Mostly under the Ninth and Tenth Commandments* (New York, 1912).

17. Theodore Dreiser, *The Financier* (New York and London, 1912), pp. 115, 120. See also p. 187.

18. Ibid., p. 287.

19. Theodore Dreiser, *The Titan* (New York and London, 1914; New York, 1959), p. 378. This theme is addressed in Carl Smith, *Chicago and the American Literary Imagination, 1880–1920* (Chicago, 1984), chaps. 2–4.

20. There is an enormous literature of commentary on James's views of art, artists, and collectors. I have found Viola Hopkins Winner, *Henry James and the Visual Arts* (Charlottesville, Va., 1970), particularly chap. 8, especially helpful.

21. Henry James, *The American* (Boston, 1877; New York, 1963), p. 15.

22. Ibid., p. 91.

23. Henry James, *The Princess Casamassima* (London and New York, 1886; Harmondsworth, 1977), p. 352. These words are taken from the letter Hyacinth Robinson writes the Princess from Venice, revealing his weakened attachment to the revolutionary cause.

24. Henry James, *The Spoils of Poynton* (London, 1897; Harmondsworth, 1983), p. 20. This novella itself contains a spectrum of collectors, ranging from Mrs. Gereth to Mona Vetch's father, an accumulator whose "old brandy-flasks and match boxes, old calendars and hand-books . . . pen-wipers and ashtrays," foreshadow the "collectible" crazes of the mid-twentieth century.

25. Henry James, *The Golden Bowl* (New York, 1904; Harmondsworth, 1966), p. 160.

26. Henry James, *The Outcry* (New York, 1911), pp. 78, 131.

27. Mrs. Gardner's story is told in Morris Carter, *Isabella Stewart Gardner and Fenway Court* (Boston and New York, 1925); and Louise Hall Tharp, *Mrs. Jack: A Biography of Isabella Stewart Gardner* (Boston, 1965). For Mrs. Gardner's involvement with smuggling see *New York Times*, 20 August 1908, p. 9; and an editorial in the same newspaper, "Art and the Customs," 21 August, 1908, p. 6.

28. Several of these collectors are described in Saarinen, *The Proud Possessors*, and in separate biographies as well as in institutional histories. David Alan Brown, *Raphael and America* (Washington, D.C., 1983), contains an excellent discussion of the rise of this generation of old master collectors in America. Gerald Reitlinger, *The Economics of Taste*, vols. 1 and 2, is also invaluable on collecting tastes. For English collectors see the fascinating anthology compiled by Frank Herrmann, *The English as Collectors: A Documentary Chrestomathy* (New York, 1972). For the French see Albert Boime, "Entrepreneurial Patronage in Nineteenth Century France," in *Enterprise and Entrepreneurs in Nineteenth- and Twentieth-Century France*, ed. Edward C. Carter II, Robert Forster, and Joseph N. L. Moody (Baltimore and London, 1976), pp. 137–207, which is both thorough and suggestive.

29. See for example, "How We Strip Europe of Her Treasures of Art," *New York Times*, 19 February 1911, part V, p. 9. The *Times* had long been vigorously campaigning against the art tariff. It argued that the liberalization of the tariff schedules accomplished in 1909 would enormously increase art imports. See also "$50,000,000 Worth of Art Treasures for America in a Year," *New York Times*, 23 January 1910, part V, p. 2. I have drawn extensively on the *Times* to represent journalistic reaction during this period in large part because its subject index permits effective access to its coverage.

30. Comments on the huge inflation of this period, as well as the anticipations evidenced during the 1880s when the Rothschilds bought so lavishly at the Blenheim sales of the Marlboroughs, can be found in Gerald Reitlinger, *The Economics of Taste*, vol. 1, chap. 7: "The Treasures Depart"; and vol. 2, chap. 8: "The Apogee and Decline of Ritzy Taste." The *New York Times* not only covered great American purchases but did stories on major foreign sales of the day like the Doucet sale in Paris and the Weber sale in Hamburg. For typical comments on the price inflation see "Paintings Bought for a Song, Sold for Fortunes," *New York Times*, 18 June 1911, part V, p. 1.

31. "Topics of the Times," *New York Times*, 14 March 1904, p. 8.

32. "The Half-Million Tapestry," *New York Times*, 27 July 1902, part II, p. 6. This editorial was occasioned by the Morgan purchase.

33. "The Price of Pictures," *New York Times*, 20 March 1910, p. 10. See also "Comparative Values in Art," 9 April 1910, p. 10.

34. This topic was debated in *Century* 35 (April, 1888): 963–64. See also E. L. Godkin, "The Expenditure of Rich Men," *Scribner's* 20 (October, 1896): 495–501; "The Point of View," *Scribner's* 47 (April, 1910): 379–80; and Edward Chase Kirkland, *Dream and Thought in the Business Community, 1860–1900* (Ithaca, 1956), chap. 2.

35. "The Museum's New President," *New York Times*, 24 November 1904, p. 8.

36. "New York the Art Market," *New York Times*, 21 October 1906, p. 8.

37. *New York Times*, 16 January 1910, part III, p. 3.

38. "The Discovery of Artistic America," *Nation* 90 (27 January 1910), p. 96.

39. *New York Times*, 13 November 1904, p. 5.

40. "New York the Art Market," *New York Times*, 21 October 1906, p. 8.

41. *New York Times*, 19 February 1911, part V, p. 9.

42. The *New York Times* followed closely the campaign to save the Duke of Norfolk's Holbein in May and June of 1909. See 3 May 1909, p. I; "Holbein's Christina," 5 May 1909, p. 10; 30 May 1909, part III, p. 3; 31 May 1909, p. 4; "That Arundel Holbein," 1 June 1909, p. 8; "The Fate of That Holbein," 5 June 1909, p. 8.

43. *New York Times*, 11 May 1911, p. 1. By 1912 the Earl of Carlisle, Lord Ashburton, Lord Ilchester, Lord Warwick, the Marquis of Lansdowne, the Duke of Rutland, and the Duke of Sutherland had all sold art to Americans.

44. *New York Times*, 20 February 1911, part III, p. 2. Later that year Bode, making one of his American visits, paid tribute to American collectors. "I saw quite enough this time to explode the myth cherished so commonly in Europe that Americans are actuated by sheer snobbery in seeking to possess themselves of old masters." *New York Times*, 10 December 1911, part V, p. 2. For more on Bode, an extremely influential figure in the European museum world, see Edward P. Alexander, *Museum Masters: Their Museums and Their Influence* (Nashville, 1983), chap. 8.

45. *New York Times*, 27 February 1910, part III, p. 1.

46. *New York Times*, 13 December 1908, part IV, p. 2.

47. Henry James, *The Outcry*, p. 45.

48. "Planting Art Museums," *New York Times*, 6 July 1902, p. 6.

49. "The Bogy Man in Art," *New York Times*, 23 December 1906, part II, p. 6.

50. "The Pride of Burgos," *New York Times*, 3 November 1910, p. 8.

51. See the editorial attacking the socialist leader in Belgium's Chamber of Deputies who was concerned that King Leopold's pictures might end up in America, "Meat Packers and Art," *New York Times*, 29 May 1909, p. 8.

52. *New York Times*, 14 November 1909, part V, p. 7.

53. *New York Times*, 23 January 1910, part V, p. 2. Professor Justi, the giver of the interview, declared, "I shall long treasure in my memory the picture of Mr. Pierpont Morgan—whom Europe is fond of depicting as a self-centred and dollar-obsessed plutocrat—adjourning each morning to his magnificent library gallery, there to receive his visitors and to commune with art. . . . No mere materialist could ever assemble the collection over which Mr. Morgan rules in New York."

54. This suggestion was made by a New Yorker in a letter to the *New York Times*, 9 June 1908, p. 6, who pointed out that the South Kensington Museum put purchase prices on its labels.

55. Clarke's letter agreeing with the suggestion was published in the *Times* 10 June 1908, p. 6. But Clarke indicated that the South Kensington Museum was gradually abandoning the practice, because of dealer and collector pressure.

56. *New York Times*, 28 March 1910, p. 4.

57. *New York Times*, 3 April 1909, p. 1. This lengthy story was titled "Hotel Gotham Ousts a Picture Salesman." During the first decade of the century dozens of newspaper stories on frauds and art impostures appeared. For example see *New York Times*, 16 May 1909, part III, p. 2; "When Art Is Real and When It Masquerades," *New York Times*, 24 May 1908, part V, p. 3; *Chicago Tribune*, 10 October 1912, p. 1; *Chicago Tribune*, 13 October 1912, p. 1; *New York Times*, 5 January 1908, part III, p. 1; *New York Times*, 3 June 1907, p. 3; "Velasquez or Copy?" *New York Times*, 29 January 1905, p. 6; *New York Times*, 29 March 1910, p. 8.

58. The Paine case was front page news in the spring of 1910. See the stories, *New York Times*, 17–19 April 1910, p. 1.

59. The Clausen case was another sensation; it stimulated countersuits as well. The *New York Times* asked its question in an editorial, "The Clausen Case," 31 March 1910, p. 10, referring as well to the angry disagreement over Bode's purchase of a supposed Da Vinci bust in England, a debate that involved the Kaiser. Clausen, a picture dealer, was first arrested in the spring of 1908. See *New York Times* 15, 17 May 1908, p. 1. In another editorial

the *Times* remarked, "The man in the street, to whom a picture is good if it appeals to his taste and bad if he does not like it, must be pardoned for thinking that the pictures of Inness, Wyant, and Martin were as good pictures when they were painted as they are now." "The Bogus Pictures," *New York Times*, 17 May 1908, part II, p. 8.

60. David Alan Brown, *Berenson and the Connoisseurship of Italian Painting: A Handbook to the Exhibition* (Washington, D.C. 1979), provides an excellent introduction to the subject; so does Ernest Samuels, *Bernard Berenson: The Making of a Connoisseur* (Cambridge, Mass., 1977). By this time the expert art adviser had already worked his way into fiction. Robert Herrick put a venomous portrait of Berenson, in the form of a character named Simeon Erard, into *The Gospel of Freedom*. In James's *The Outcry* the crisis of the novel is precipitated by a reattribution put forward by Hugh Crimble, who was working at "the wonderful modern science of Connoisseurship—which is upsetting . . . all the old-fashioned canons of art-criticism, everything we've stupidly thought right and held dear," p. 34. Several of the short stories in Frank Jewett Mather's *The Collectors* revolve around scientific experts and their judgments. And see Simeon Strunsky, "The Complete Collector—II," *The Patient Observer and His Friends* (New York, 1911), pp. 189–99, for his sketch of a collector of frauds, who insists that gathering a genuine collection has become impossible. In *Post-Impressions: An Irresponsible Chronicle* (New York, 1914), pp. 53–62, Strunsky reprinted his fascinating essay, "Morgan."

61. "Topics of the Times," *New York Times*, 21 March 1910, p. 8.

62. "Bogus Art and Good Taste," *New York Times*, 24 May 1908, part II, p. 8.

63. *New York Times*, "The Bogus Pictures," 17 May 1908, part II, p. 8. See also Charles De Kay, "Ethics of the Pictorial Mart," *New York Times*, 4 March 1906, part IV, p. 8.

64. This ring was described in the *New York Times*, 13 October 1907, part III, p. 1. See also "A Long Way Round," *New York Times*, 10 October 1907, p. 8; and *New York Times*, 17 October 1907, p. 5. More on French art thievery can be found in the *New York Times*, 15 December 1905, p. 2.

65. The *Mona Lisa* theft is recounted in Seymour V. Reit, *The Day They Stole the Mona Lisa* (New York, 1981).

66. *New York Times*, 23 August 1911, p. 6. The theft stimulated a series of stories on other recent art thefts. See *New York Times*, "Famous Works of Art That Have Been Stolen," 27 August 1911, part V, pp. 1, 14.

67. Quoted in *New York Times*, 28 January 1912, part V, p. 11.

68. *New York Times*, 13 April 1912, quoted in Reit, *The Day They Stole the Mona Lisa*, p. 115.

69. Note the editorial, "The Gentleman Burglar Myth," *New York Times*, 18 September 1912, p. 10, attacking the idea that fictional thieves like Raffles or Arsène Lupin had many real counterparts.

70. *New York Times*, 8 July 1907, p. 1. See also *New York Times*, 28 July 1907, part III, p. 4.

71. *New York Times*, 4 September 1907, p. 3.

72. *New York Times*, 14 January 1911, p. 4. For other acts of vandalism see *New York Times*, 10 October 1909, p. 12; *New York Times*, 10 May 1911, p. I; and *New York Times*, 23 June 1912. This last involved the ink-splashing of a Boucher portrait. The accused declared she was out of work and maddened by the smiling figure of the picture dressed in "luxurious clothes." "I decided to mutilate her hateful face in the hope that perhaps . . . people would notice me and save me from starving."

73. *New York Times*, 10 October 1909, p. 12; and 24 October 1909, part III, p. 4.

74. For dealers in addition to the redoubtable S. N. Behrman, *Duveen* (New York, 1952), I have relied on Martin Birnbaum, *The Last Romantic: The Story of More Than a Half-Century in the World of Art* (New York, 1960); James Henry Duveen, *The Rise of the House of Duveen* (New York, 1957); Edward Fowles; *Memories of Duveen Brothers* (London, 1976); René Gimpel, *Diary of an Art Dealer* (New York, 1966); and Germain Seligman, *Merchants of Art, 1880–1960: Eighty Years of Professional Collecting* (New York, 1961). Of these the Seligman volume is most informative about Morgan. *Letters of Roger Fry*, ed. Denys Sutton (London, 1972), vol. 1, also contains many references to dealers, as well as a hostile portrait of Morgan. For Morgan's relations with dealers in Italy see Salvatore Cortesi, *My Thirty*

Years of Friendships (New York and London, 1927), chap. 6. For some rather amusing comments on dealers, American millionaires, and Morgan, see *How I Discovered America: Confessions of the Marquis Boni de Castellane* (New York, 1924), passim, but particularly pp. 34, 139–40, 170, 249. Ernest Samuels, *Bernard Berenson*, also contains a good deal of information about contemporary dealers.

75. *New York Times*, 28 January 1912, part V, p. 12. This was translated from an article in *Die Woche*.

76. For more on this large subject see, among others, Thomas Bender, "The Cultures of Intellectual Life: The City and the Professions," in *New Directions in American Intellectual History*, ed. John Higham and Paul Conkin (Baltimore, 1979), pp. 181–95; Paul Boyer, *Urban Masses and Moral Order in America, 1820–1920* (Cambridge, Mass., and London, 1978), chaps. 16–18; Peter B. Hales, *Silver Cities: The Photography of American Urbanization, 1839–1915* (Philadelphia, 1984), chaps. 2–3; Neil Harris, "Four Stages of Cultural Growth: The American City," chap. 1 in this volume; Helen Lefkowitz Horowitz, *Culture and the City: Cultural Philanthropy in Chicago from the 1880s to 1917* (Lexington, Ky., 1977); and Robert W. Rydell, *All the World's a Fair: Visions of Empire at American International Expositions, 1876–1916* (Chicago and London, 1985).

77. For the architectural expression of this surge to civic primacy see Robert A. M. Stern, Gregory Gilmartin, and John Massengale, *New York 1900: Metropolitan Architecture and Urbanism, 1890–1915* (New York, 1983).

78. "Civic Patriotism," *New York Times*, 20 April 1902, p. 6.

79. "The Masaranti Collection," *New York Times*, 11 May 1902, p. 8.

80. See "A Chance for New York," *New York Times*, 18 May 1902, p. 8; "Letter from an Art Lover," *New York Times*, 20 May 1902, p. 6; "Sober Second Information," *New York Times*, 31 July 1902, p. 8; "The Last Word Not Said," *New York Times*, 3 August 1902, p. 6. Some dealers suspected the authenticity of much of the collection and refused to become involved with the sale.

81. *New York Times*, 28 January 1912, part V, p. 12. Bode also criticized the architectural planning of American art museums, which he termed "edifices of empty magnificence with uncomfortable large and high rooms."

82. L. S., "The Land of Sunday Afternoon," *New Republic* 1 (21 November 1914): 22–23. Simonson was directly critical of the Morgan Collection display: "I had become inevitably as listless as any shopper in a huge showroom where nothing is for sale."

83. Lee Simonson, "Refugees and Mausoleums," *New Republic* 1 (9 January 1915): 24. Simonson did admire the Altman Collection, and the George Gray Barnard museum of Gothic fragments, which would eventually become the basis for the Cloisters.

84. Simonson, "The Land of Sunday Afternoon," p. 23. For another controversial view of American museums see the letter by John Cotton Dana, director of the Newark Museum, "Art Museum Palaces," *New York Times*, 31 October 1912, p. 12, and angry responses in the same paper, 4 November 1910, p. 10, and 5 November 1912, p. 12. Dana argued that American museum buildings were too magnificent and intimidating, were located too far from city centers, and thus were poorly attended. For more on Dana see Edward P. Alexander, *Museum Masters*, chap. 13.

85. It is difficult to convey a sense of just how closely newspapers like the *New York Times* covered Morgan's movements. He may well have been the most carefully watched private citizen of his day. It was front page news when someone tried to forge his checks; see *New York Times*, 11, 12 February 1903, p. 1. It was also news when his baggage was taken off an ocean liner ahead of passengers; *New York Times* 27 July 1906, p. 2. When his niece, living in St. Louis, had an argument about luncheon guests, the *New York Times*, 19 May 1909, put it on p. 1. But most of all his art buying, rumors of his art buying, his return of famous objects like the Ascoli Cope, his foreign honors, his gifts to American museums, his entertainments for (and by) monarchs and potentates, and his travels, really caught journalistic attention.

86. "An International Benefit," *New York Times*, 11 February 1912, part V, p. 12. See also the cartoon showing a British guard at the South Kensington Museum, pointing out to visitors the empty spaces

where Morgan's tapestries had hung, *New York Times*, 4 February 1912, part V, p. 16.

87. "Trying to Keep the Treasures," *New York Times*, 31 January 1912, p. 10. The Morgan collection never came as a whole to the Metropolitan for various reasons, including a delay by the New York City Council in appropriating money for a new wing. The *Times* worried that Hartford might take the whole collection, given Morgan's loyalty to his birthplace and his generosity in funding the memorial to his father. See "Morgan Art May Go to Hartford," 27 November 1912, p. 6.

88. Satterlee, *J. Pierpont Morgan*, p. 565. For Morgan's support of scholarly catalogues see George C. Williamson, *Behind My Library Door: Some Chapters on Authors, Books and Miniatures* (New York, 1921), pp. 101–16.

89. Quoted in *New York Times*, 7 May 1912, p. 3. The *Daily News* agreed with Prime Minister Asquith that immediate legislation requiring art owners to give the government an option on the purchase of valuable art was probably unnecessary, but it urged creation of a national art inventory and establishment of some priorities.

90. The literature on these subjects is vast. But some measure of the discussion can be gained from books like Gunther Barth, *City People: The Rise of Modern City Culture in Nineteenth-Century America* (New York, 1980); Frances G. Couvares, *The Remaking of Pittsburgh: Class and Culture in an Industrializing City, 1877–1919* (Albany, 1984); Lawrence A. Cremin, *American Education: The National Experience, 1783–1876* (New York, 1980); Lewis A. Erenberg, *Steppin' Out: New York Nightlife and the Transformation of American Culture, 1890–1930* (Westport, Conn., 1981); Dee Garrison, *Apostles of Culture: The Public Librarian and American Society, 1876–1920* (New York, 1979); Garth Jowett, *Film: The Democratic Art* (Boston and Toronto, 1976), chaps. 1–2; Stephen Hardy, *How Boston Played: Sport, Recreation, and Community, 1865–1915* (Boston, 1982); John F. Kasson, *Amusing the Million: Coney Island at the Turn of the Century* (New York, 1978); Arthur Mann, *The One and the Many: Reflections on the American Identity* (Chicago and London, 1979); Lary May, *Screening Out the Past: The Birth of Mass Culture and the Motion Picture*

Industry, 1896–1929 (New York, 1980); Michael Schudson, *Discovering the News: A Social History of American Newspapers* (New York, 1978); Alan Trachtenberg, *The Incorporation of America: Culture and Society in the Gilded Age* (New York, 1982); Kermit Vanderbilt, *Charles Eliot Norton: Apostle of Culture in a Democracy* (Cambridge, Mass., 1959); and Robert H. Wiebe, *The Search for Order* (New York, 1967).

91. For reactions to the Armory Show see Milton W. Brown, *The Story of the Armory Show* (Greenwich, Conn., 1963); and George H. Roeder, Jr., *Forum of Uncertainty: Confrontations with Modern Painting in Twentieth-Century American Thought* (Ann Arbor, 1980). For another view of the connection between the emergence of the avant-garde and old master taste see Brown, *Raphael and America*, p. 31.

92. F. J. M., Jr., "The Morgan Loan Exhibition," *Nation* 98 (26 February 1914): 220.

93. "Mr. Morgan as Art Patron," *Nation* 96 (3 April 1913): 234–35. The amateur, the editorial continued, must regard Morgan's artistic career "with something of awe and misgiving, not unmixed with pity, feeling the disproportion between his unwearied activities as a collector and the personal solace which he got from his royally abundant possessions." See also Gardner Teall, "An American Medici: J. Pierpont Morgan and His Various Collections," *Putnam's* 7 (November 1909): 131–43.

94. *Philadelphia Evening Telegraph*, 1 April 1913, Scrapbooks, Morgan Library, IV. My characterizations of the obituary editorials come from scanning the collection of Scrapbooks in the Morgan Library.

95. *New York American*, 21 April 1913, Scrapbooks, II.

96. *New York Mail*, 2 April 1913, Scrapbooks, IV. The *Evening Transcript* in Boston, 1 April 1913, wrote, "It is the manifest destiny of such art collections . . . to become eventually national or public possessions. . . . No critic would mistake the collection for that of a man who collects exclusively to gratify his own taste. . . . [W]hat would be a defect in a private collection . . . becomes, in the case of a great public collection, an advantage." Scrapbooks, III. Many editorials, written either on the oc-

casion of the transfer of some of the collection to the Metropolitan or on Morgan's death, stressed the immense national advantages which his privately gathered treasure obtained for the country as a whole.

97. James *The Outcry*, pp. 171, 20–21.

Iconography and Intellectual History: The Halftone Effect

1. Robert Taft, *Photography and the American Scene: A Social History, 1839–1889*, reprint ed. (1938; New York: Dover, 1964), pp. 437–38.

2. Estelle Jussim, *Visual Communication and the Graphic Arts: Photographic Technologies in the Nineteenth Century* (New York: Bowker, 1974), p. 288. This is the most complete modern analysis of the problem.

3. Ibid., chap. 9.

4. The varieties of photomechanical and other reproductive processes developed in the late nineteenth century are too complex to be adequately summarized in a few paragraphs. Dozens of newly patented methods appeared within a short time, promoted energetically by groups of supporters. Some of these varieties are detailed in the many periodicals and annuals devoted to printing and reproductive methods that appear about this time, among them the *Inland Printer*, which started publication in Chicago in 1883; *Printing Art*, published in Cambridge, Massachusetts, from 1903; and *The Graphic Arts and Crafts Year Book*, printed in Hamilton, Ohio, from 1907. Other serials of importance appeared in Britain and on the Continent. Extensive commentaries and bibliographies can be found in Harold Curwen (revised by Charles Mayo), *Processes of Graphic Reproduction in Printing* (London: Faber, 1967); Helmut Gernsheim and Alison Gernsheim, *The History of Photography, from the Earliest Use of the Camera Obscura in the Eleventh Century up to 1914* (London: Oxford University Press, 1955); Jussim, *Visual Communication and the Graphic Arts*, particularly pp. 45–76; and Geoffrey Wakeman, *Victorian Book Illustration: The Technical Revolution* (Newton Abbot: David & Charles, 1973).

5. Further discussion of this issue can be found in Gernsheim and Gernsheim, *The History of Photography*; E. H. Gombrich, *Art and Illusion: A Study of the Psychology of Pictorial Representation* (New York: Pantheon, 1960); Richard Rudisill, *Mirror Image: The Influence of the Daguerreotype on American Society* (Albuquerque: University of New Mexico Press, 1971); and Robert Taft, *Photography and the American Scene*.

6. Charles H. Caffin, *Photography as a Fine Art: The Achievements and Possibilities of Photographic Art in America* (New York: Doubleday, Page, 1901).

7. *Nation* 73 (19 December 1901): 475–76.

8. "The Perils of Photography," *Nation* 85 (11 July 1907): 28–29.

9. Ibid., p. 29.

10. Will Irwin, "The Swashbucklers of the Camera," *Collier's* 48 (3 February 1912): 11.

11. Tudor Jenks, "The Decadence of Illustration," *Independent* 51 (28 December 1899): 3487–89. For a more sympathetic view in the same journal, see Ella R. Boult, "The Illustration of Books by Artistic Photography," *Independent* 61 (13 December 1906): 1414–20.

12. "Handsomely Illustrated," *Atlantic Monthly* 93 (January 1904): 136–37.

13. *Dial* 51 (1 October 1911): 245–46. See also "The Illustrations That Do Not Illustrate," *Critic* 48 (June 1906): 498–99.

14. "Newspaper Pictures," *Nation* 56 (27 April 1893): 307.

15. "A Growl for the Unpicturesque," *Atlantic Monthly* 98 (July 1906): 141–42.

16. Laurence Burnham, "The Modern Heroine in Illustration," *Bookman* 25 (April 1907): 199.

17. "Over-Illustration," *Harper's Weekly* 55 (29 July 1911): 6. Articles about "overillustration" had been appearing since the 1880s.

18. Many of these illustrators are represented in the Delaware Art Museum catalogue, *The Golden Age of American Illustration, 1880–1914* (Wilmington: Wilmington Society of the Fine Arts, 1972). For more on American illustration see Walt Reed, ed., *The Illustrator in America, 1900–1960's* (New York: Reinhold, 1966); and *A Century of American Illustration*, a catalogue of an exhibition at the Brooklyn Museum in 1972.

19. David H. Flaherty, *Privacy in Colonial New England* (Charlottesville: University of Virginia Press, 1972), pp. 6–7. See also Alan F. Westin, *Privacy and Freedom* (New York: Atheneum, 1967), chap. 2.

20. Alexander Alland, Sr., *Jacob A. Riis: Photographer and Citizen* (New York: Aperture, 1974), pp. 26–27.

21. Ibid., p. 29. For a listing of books illustrated with photographs in the second half of the nineteenth century see Julia Van Haaften, "'Original Sun Pictures': A Check List of the New York Public Library's Holdings of Early Works Illustrated with Photographs, 1844–1900," *Bulletin of the New York Public Library* 80 (Spring 1977): 355–415. Before the late 1880s these books have mounted plates bound into them, and tend to be in limited and expensive editions.

22. Robert Taft, *Photography and the American Scene*, p. 446.

23. "Newspaper Invasion of Privacy," *Century* 86 (June 1913): 310–11.

24. John Gilmor Speed, "The Right of Privacy," *North American Review* 163 (July 1896): 64–74. See also George D. Richards, "Pictorial Journalism," *World To-Day* 9 (August 1905): 845–52.

25. "Some Effects of Modern Publicity," *Century* 67 (November 1903): 156.

26. See, for example, E. F. Barnard, "Radio Politics," *New Republic* 38 (19 March 1924): 91–93.

27. For a survey of later illustrators and their autobiographical experiences, see Ernest W. Watson, *Forty Illustrators and How They Work* (New York: Watson-Guptill, 1946). See also Susan E. Meyer, *America's Great Illustrators* (New York: Abrams, 1978).

Color and Media: Some Comparisons and Speculations

1. Two splendid bibliographies, both extensively annotated, provide an excellent introduction to various issues raised by color theory. Sigmund Skard, "The Use of Color in Literature," *Proceedings of the American Philosophical Society* 90, no. 3 (July, 1946): 163–249; and Robert L. Herbert, "A Color Bibliography," *Yale University Library Gazette* 49, no. 1 (July 1974): 3–52. Herbert built his bibliography around the presentation of the Faber Birren Collection of books on color to the Yale Library.

2. Major modern texts include R. V. Tooley, *English Books with Colored Plates, 1790–1860*, 2d ed. (London, 1954); Michael Twyman, *Printing, 1770–1970: An Illustrated History of Its Development and Uses in England* (London, 1970); Ruari McLean, *Victorian Book Design and Colour Printing*, 2d ed. (Berkeley and Los Angeles, 1972); Percy Muir, *Victorian Illustrated Books* (New York, 1971); Geoffrey Wakeman and Gavin D. R. Bridson, *A Guide to Nineteenth Century Color Printers* (Loughborough, 1975); Gordon N. Ray, *The Illustrator and the Book in England from 1790–1914* (New York, 1976); Joan M. Friedman, *Color Printing in England, 1486–1870* (New Haven, 1978); and Peter Marzio, *The Democratic Art: Chromolithography, 1840–1900—Pictures for a Nineteenth Century America* (Boston, 1979).

3. H. M. Cundall, *Birket Foster, R.W.S.* (London, 1906); Martin Hardie, *English Coloured Books* (London, 1906); R. M. Burch, *Colour Printing and Colour Printers* (London, 1910); C. T. C. Lewis, *The Story of Picture Printing in England during the Nineteenth Century* (London, n.d.).

4. Letter of Louis Prang dated November 6, 1867, *Nation* 5 (November 28, 1867): 438.

5. *Nation* 5 (October 31, 1867): 359.

6. (Russell Sturgis) "Color Printing from Wood and from Stone," *Nation* 4 (January 18, 1867): 36–37. Marzio, *The Democratic Art*, p. 120, cites the essay as being by E. L. Godkin, editor of the *Nation*, although it is unsigned. I prefer the ascription suggested by *Poole's Index to Periodical Literature*, rev. ed. (Boston, 1882, 1891), 1:246.

7. Louis Prang, *Nation* 5 (November 28, 1867): 438.

8. Ibid., p. 439.

9. (Elizabeth R. Pennell) "The Coming of Lithography," *Nation* 95 (December 5, 1912): 547.

10. (Elizabeth R. Pennell) "A Note on Lithography," *Nation* 97 (November 20, 1913): 492.

11. As quoted in "Lithography and the Fine

Arts," *Current Literature* 36 (January, 1904): 76. See also Ernest Knaufft, "Picture Books in Color," *American Review of Reviews* 46 (December, 1912): 759–65; and James B. Carrington, "Colored Pictures in American Periodicals," *Critic* 37 (September, 1900): 222–23.

12. James L. Limbacher, *Four Aspects of the Film* (New York, 1969, 1978), passim. This is the most extended discussion of film color I have found. Suggestive comments on the aesthetic implications of color are made by Stanley Cavell, *The World Viewed: Reflections on the Ontology of Film* (New York, 1971), chap. 13, "The World as a Whole: Color."

13. As quoted in H. T. Kalmus, "Technicolor Adventures in Cinemaland," *Journal of the Society of Motion Picture Engineers* 31 (December, 1938): 570.

14. Charles K. Taylor, "Doug Gets Away with It," *Outlook* 142 (April 14, 1916): 561.

15. Kalmus, "Technicolor Adventures in Cinemaland."

16. Alexander Bakshy, "Films," *Nation* 130 (March 19, 1930): 337.

17. *Newsweek* 4 (July 21, 1934): 16–17, covered the premiere of *La Cucaracha*, and reviewed the history of color in film. "Technicolor May Revolutionize the Screen," *Literary Digest* 119 (June 8, 1935): 24–25, gives an even fuller history of Technicolor. The *Newsweek* cover story ran in 5 (June 22, 1935): 22–23, and included further details on the history of Technicolor.

18. *Catholic World* 141 (September, 1935): 727–28; Otis Ferguson, "New Wine and Old Bottles," *New Republic* 83 (June 26, 1935): 194–95; Grenville Vernon, "The Play and Screen," *Commonweal* 22 (June 28, 1935): 243. A more admiring account is presented by Noel Carroll, "Becky Sharp Takes Over," in Michael Klein and Gillian Parker, eds., *The English Novel and the Movies* (New York, 1981), pp. 108–20.

19. William Troy, "A Penny-colored World," *Nation* 141 (July 3, 1935): 141.

20. Ferguson, "New Wine and Old Bottles."

21. *Time* 28 (November 30, 1936): 40. This was part of a cover story on *The Garden of Allah*, which starred Marlene Dietrich. "Unhurried by such outside spurs as the change in theatre equipment that transformed sound overnight from a pipe dream to a

necessity, other producers are still wary of color as an expensive and perhaps unhealthy precedent," *Time* went on, p. 40. For more on this film see *Newsweek* 8 (November 21, 1936): 20–22. No longer "was color crowded on the film with the naive prodigality of a butcher's calendar," *Newsweek* observed. And see *Literary Digest* 21 (November 14, 1936): 21.

22. *Commonweal* 23 (March 6, 1936): 524.

23. Quoted in *Literary Digest* 121 (February 29, 1936): 20. The critic was H. I. Phillips of the *New York Sun*. For less kind comments on the film see *Newsweek* 7 (February 29, 1936): 32–33. If "Nature wanted to sue for misrepresentation, she'd have good grounds," *Newsweek* observed, complaining that "Technicolor has dolled her up like a cocotte."

24. Joseph C. Gries, "Pictures and Color Printing," *Printing Art Quarterly* (1st Quarter, 1936), p. 69.

25. For examples of this see reviews of *A Star Is Born, The Thief of Bagdad,* and *Gone With the Wind.*

26. There is no single study that examines the coming of color to television. Innumerable articles consider the economic and legal aspects of the issue and give statistics on the extent and timing of the change. For information along the way see the cover story "At the End of the Rainbow," *Time* 56 (December 4, 1950): 52–58; Leonard Engel, "Should You Buy Color Television?" *Nation* 171 (November 11, 1950): 430–31; Charles Kirshner, "The Color Television Controversy," *University of Pittsburgh Law Review* 13 (Fall, 1951): 65–84; Walter Guzzardi, Jr., "R.C.A.: The General Never Got Butterflies," *Fortune* 66 (October, 1962): 102–7, 136–43; Sanford Brown, "Color Catches Fire," *Saturday Evening Post* 236 (August 17, 1963): 74–75; "Color TV's Astonishing Boom," *Newsweek* 65 (March 29, 1965): 70–72; and Martin Koffel, *The Impact of Color Television in Australia* (Melbourne, 1969), which includes a good deal of statistical information about the spread of color viewing in the United States. For several of these references I am indebted to Professor James L. Baughman.

27. Quoted in Engel, "Should You Buy Color Television?" p. 430.

28. This point was made, among other places, in *Time* 53 (June 13, 1949): 53.

29. For contemporary descriptions of all this see

"Color Climax," *Time* 56 (October 23, 1950): 66–68; "The Color War," *Time* 56 (October 30, 1950): 77; "Color Enigmas," *Time* 56 (September 11, 1950): 73; and "At Long Last, Color," *Newsweek* 38 (July 9, 1951): 57.

30. Goodman Ace, "La TV en Rose," *Saturday Review of Literature* 33 (November 25, 1950): 34.

31. Goodman Ace, "The Hue and the Cry," *Saturday Review of Literature* 34 (June 30, 1951): 24.

32. Robert Lewis Shayon, "2,591 Years of 'Progress': Thales, Paley & Sarnoff," *Saturday Review of Literature* 34 (July 28, 1951): 26.

33. See, for example, the same kind of comments made ten years later by Jack Gould, "The Hidden Costs of Color," *New York Times*, May 1, 1966, II, p. 15. Commenting on the added expense that color would bring to television production, he wrote that "For the dissenting viewer who complains that the networks have left him abandoned in a cultural barrel, the chains may have devised a novel type of response: Paint the barrel."

34. *Time* 58 (October 29, 1951): 48.

35. *Time* 77 (February 17, 1961): 67.

36. For data on television ownership see *National Survey of Television Sets in United States Households* (New York, 1969), a survey undertaken periodically by the Advertising Research Foundation, Inc., of New York.

37. Quoted in Sanford Brown, "Color Catches Fire," *Saturday Evening Post* 236 (August 17, 1963): 75.

38. Leo Bogart, *The Age of Television: A Study of Viewing Habits and the Impact of Television on American Life* (New York, 1956), p. 276.

39. Saul Carson, "On the Air: Color for What?" *New Republic* 121 (October 31, 1949): 20–21. Also see another column by Robert Lewis Shayon, "Black & White or In the Red All Over," *Saturday Review of Literature* 33 (December 1, 1950): 52–53. Color, Shayon concluded, "can never substitute for wit, imagination, and adult, creative programming. That is a gift horse of another color, and it is still galloping somewhere over the rainbow, untamed by either RCA or CBS." Fifteen years later Shayon was unchanged. Reviewing, in some statistical detail the growth of color and the international struggle for adoption among various systems, he concluded,

"There is vague talk of color enriching the esthetic consciousness of the nation, affecting our decor and design, but similar things were said when black-and-white television first made its bow. A look at the substance of next season's schedules offers no glint of any non-technological breakthrough. The world may look pleasanter on color television, but from all indications it will hardly be more significant." "Some Black Thoughts about Color TV," *Saturday Review of Literature* 48 (April 10, 1965): 83.

40. *Time* 53 (December 4, 1950): 58–58.

41. See Jeffrey L. Meikle, *Twentieth Century Limited: Industrial Design in America, 1925–1939* (Philadelphia, 1979), pp. 12–13; "The New Age of Color," *Saturday Evening Post* 200 (January 21, 1928): 22; "The Magic Wand of Color," *Reader's Digest* 35 (August, 1939): 112.

42. "The Color Cure," *Literary Digest* 91 (December 18, 1926): 21–22.

43. "Meet the Color Engineer," *Reader's Digest* 38 (June, 1941): 134–35. This excerpt from *Future*, May, 1941, described the work of Faber Birren, a New York color engineer, as well as innovations in color management taking place in the factory, the restaurant, the hospital, and the schoolroom. For an earlier version of this interest, not all of it serious, see "Making People Do Things by Wall Colors," *Everybody's* 34 (March, 1916): 398–99. See also "Emotions Due to Colors," *Literary Digest* 85 (April 25, 1925): 25, for a discussion by Matthew Luckiesh, then director of the Lighting Research Laboratory of General Electric. Luckiesh published a book, *Light and Color in Advertising and Merchandising* (New York, 1923), describing the benefits that an increased sensitivity to lighting and color might yield. All sorts of amusing figures and episodes appeared as part of this new color consciousness in the interwar years. For one of them, Raymond G. Twyeffort, a custom tailor, see the profile by Richard O. Boyer, "Color Nut," which appeared originally in the *New Yorker* 15 (September 23, 1939): 22–27 and was condensed in *Reader's Digest* 36 (January, 1940): 102–5.

44. Matthew Luckiesh, *Color and Colors* (New York, 1938), p. 5. The phrase "mental color-blindness" was by Luckiesh, but for other appeals for better color understanding see Howard Ketcham,

"Color Schemers," *Reader's Digest* 30 (March, 1937): 47–50, originally in *Harper's Bazaar,* and the writings of Faber Birren, in particular his ambitious survey, *The Story of Color: From Ancient Mysticism to Modern Science* (Westport, 1941).

45. Walter Benjamin, "The Work of Art in the Age of Mechanical Reproduction," in Hannah Arendt, ed., *Illuminations* (New York, 1968), p. 242.

Pictorial Perils: The Rise of American Illustration

1. Philip Rodney Paulding, "Illustrators and Illustrating," *Munsey's* 13, no. 2 (May 1895): 152; Arthur Hoeber, "A Century of American Illustration," *Bookman* 8, no. 5 (January 1899): 429 (this was stated in the seventh part of an eight-part article); Harold Payne, "American Women Illustrators," *Munsey's* 11, no. 1 (April 1894): 47; Arthur Hoeber, "A Century of American Illustration," *Bookman* 8, no. 4 (December 1898): 317.

2. William A. Coffin, "American Illustration of To-Day," *Scribner's Magazine* 11, no. 1 (January 1882): 106–17. Coffin would have agreed with Payne and Hoeber: "While it may be true that a good deal of the current illustration is inferior, it serves a useful purpose in the propagation of a love of art" (Coffin, "American Illustration," p. 108). George Wharton Edwards, "The Illustration of Books," *Outlook* 57, no. 14 (December 4, 1897): 817, 820.

3. William Herbert Hobbs, "Art as the Handmaid of Literature," *Forum* 31, no. 3 (May 1901): 371.

4. E. L. Godkin, "'Cuts' and Truth," *Nation* 56, no. 1453 (May 4, 1893): 326.

5. *Critic* 48, no. 6 (June 1906): 498, 499. "The Lounger," a regular feature of the *Critic,* featured three letters on illustration in this issue.

6. "Meaningless Illustrations," *New York Times* (April 7, 1900), Saturday Review of Books and Art, p. 232. For similar sentiments, see "Illustrations That Illustrate," *New York Times* (December 2, 1899), p. 816; *New York Times* (April 21, 1900), p. 493.

7. Katherine Gordon Hyle to the Editor, *New York Times,* November 5, 1904. An earlier letter from John K. Hoyt had criticized Pyle, M.P., *New York Times,* November 26, 1904, p. 812.

8. Hobbs, "Art as Handmaid," p. 380.

9. "The Contributors' Club," *Atlantic Monthly* 93, no. 555 (January 1904: 136–37.

10. "Author and Illustrator," *New York Times,* January 26, 1901, p. 56.

11. Estelle M. Hurll, "Picture Study in Education," *Outlook* 61, no. 3 (January 21, 1899): 174–76. For examples, see Elizabeth McCracken, "Pictures for the Tenements," *Atlantic* 98, no. 4 (October 1906): 519–28; and Caroline A. Leech, "The Gospel of Pictures," *Chautauquan* 37, no. 5 (August 1903): 484–86.

12. [Rollo Ogden,] "Knowledge on Sight," *Nation* 57, no. 1464 (July 20, 1893): 41–42. For an interesting earlier parallel, which unites this suspicion of picture-making to a Protestant hostility to pictorial propaganda, see Julia Ward Howe, *From the Oak to the Olive: A Plain Record of a Pleasant Journey* (Boston: Lee & Shepard, 1868), pp. 76–77.

13. [E. L. Godkin,] "Newspaper Pictures," *Nation* 56, no. 1452 (April 27, 1893): 306–7; John Hopkins Denison, "How to Use Objects as Illustrations," *Chautauquan* 27, no. 1 (April 1898): 34.

14. For more on the new pictorialism, see chap. 14. For more on Eastman, Kodak, and the marketing revolution involved in the spread of the camera, see Reese V. Jenkins, *Images and Enterprise: Technology and the American Photographic Industry, 1839–1925* (Baltimore and London: Johns Hopkins University Press, 1975).

15. A convenient summary of attitudes to picture postcards, as well as bibliographic references, can be found in George Miller and Dorothy Miller, *Picture Postcards in the United States, 1893–1918* (New York: Clarkson N. Potter, 1976). For one complaint about the growth of snapshots and postcards, and the contrast with earlier methods of recording one's travels, see [W. A. Bradley,] "The Lost Art of Sketching," *Nation* 90, no. 2343 (May 26, 1910): 530–31.

16. The poster literature is vast. One recent article that refers to hostile comments about poster art is Michael Patrick Hearn, "An American Illustrator and His Posters, Part One," *American Book Collector*

3, no. 3 (May–June 1982): 11–18. A useful summary and bibliography is in Victor Margolin, *American Poster Renaissance: The Great Age of Poster Design, 1890–1900* (New York: Watson-Guptill Publications, 1975). For a typical series of attacks on posters and billboards, see *Chautauquan* 51, no. 1 (June 1908): 18–81, featuring photographs of the offensive advertisements as well as speeches and manifestos. The assault on billboard art blended in with other areas of municipal and environmental reform which attracted progressive activists.

17. Ralph Bergengren, "The Humor of the Colored Supplement," *Atlantic Monthly* 98, no. 586 (August 1906): 270–73.

18. Walter Taylor Field, "The Illustrating of Children's Books," *Dial* 35, no. 420 (December 16, 1903): 460; Annie Russell Marble, "The Reign of the Spectacular," *Dial* 35, no. 417 (November 1, 1903): 297.

19. Convenient summaries of these responses can be found in Garth Jowett, *Film: The Democratic Art* (Boston and Toronto: Little, Brown, 1976), chaps. 4–5; and Robert Sklar, *Movie-Made America: How the Movies Changed American Life* (New York: Oxford University Press, 1975), pp. 30–32.

Designs on Demand: Art and the Modern Corporation

1. For more of this theme, see Wendell D. Garrett, "John Adams and the Limited Role of the Fine Arts," *Winterthur Portfolio* 1 (1964): 243–55; Neil Harris, *The Artist in American Society: The Formative Years, 1790–1860* (New York, 1966), chaps. 1, 2; and Gordon S. Wood, ed., *The Rising Glory of America, 1760–1820* (New York, 1971), introduction.

2. Lillian B. Miller, *Patrons and Patriotism: The Encouragement of the Fine Arts in the United States, 1790–1860* (Chicago, 1966).

3. See Neil McKendrick, John Brewer, and H. J. Plumb, *The Birth of a Consumer Society: The Commercialization of Eighteenth-Century England* (Bloomington, Ind., 1982), particularly the introduction, and the essay by Neil McKendrick, "Com-

mercialization and the Economy," which outlines Josiah Wedgwood's brilliant promotional campaigns.

4. A large literature treats the history of this luxury production. For a recent discussion of the cultural and economic role of innovative capital goods and the relationships between Continental and British products, particularly British cotton goods, see Chandra Mukerji, *From Graven Images: Patterns of Modern Materialism* (New York, 1983).

5. An abundance of monographs, synthetic narratives, biographies, and anthologies tackle this subject. For further reading and references, see Isabelle Anscombe and Charlotte Gere, *Arts and Crafts in Britain and America* (London, 1978); Elizabeth Aslin, *The Aesthetic Movement: Prelude to Art Nouveau* (New York, Washington, 1969); Reyner Banham, *Theory and Design in the First Machine Age* (London, 1960); Quentin Bell, *The Schools of Design* (London, 1963); Alf Boe, *From Gothic Revival to Functional Form* (Oslo, 1957); Ann Ferebee, *A History of Design from the Victorian Era to the Present* (New York, 1970); Fiona McCarthy, *All Things Bright and Beautiful: Design in Britain, 1830 to Today* (Toronto, 1972), chaps. 1, 2; Stuart Macdonald, *The History and Philosophy of Art Education* (London, 1970); Nikolaus Pevsner, *Studies in Art, Architecture and Design*, vol. 2 (London, 1968); and Tobin Andrews Sparling, *The Great Exhibition: A Question of Taste* (New Haven, 1982).

6. The work of C. R. Ashbee, Walter Crane, Lewis F. Day, Christopher Dresser, Charles Eastlake, William Morris, Hermann Muthesius, Gottfried Semper, Henry van de Velde, and other leading figures is available in modern editions. For commentary, narrative, and further references, see Yvonne Brunhammer et al., *Art Nouveau: Belgium–France* (Houston, 1976); Joan Campbell, *The German Werkbund: The Politics of Reform in the Applied Arts* (Princeton, N.J., 1978); Donald Drew Egbert, *Social Radicalism and the Arts: Western Europe* (New York, 1970); Thomas Howarth, *Charles Rennie Mackintosh and the Modern Movement* (London, 1952); Gillian Naylor, *The Arts and Crafts Movement: A Study of Its Sources, Ideals and Influence on Design Theory* (Cambridge, Mass., 1971); Nikolaus Pevsner, *Pioneers of the Modern Movement from William Morris to Walter Gropius* (London, 1936) and *Academies of Art,*

Past and Present (Cambridge, 1940); Maurice Rheims, *The Flowering of Art Nouveau* (New York, 1965); Robert Schmutzler, *Art Nouveau* (New York, 1962); Carl E. Schorske, *Fin de Siècle Vienna: Politics and Culture* (New York, 1980); and Robert Waissenberger, ed., *Vienna: 1890–1920* (New York, 1984).

7. For the situation in the United States, see *The American Renaissance, 1876–1917* (New York, 1979); *Arts and Crafts in Detroit, 1906–1976: The Movement, the Society, the School* (Detroit, 1976); H. Allen Brooks, *The Prairie School: Frank Lloyd Wright and His Midwest Contemporaries* (Toronto, 1972); *California Design 1910* (Pasadena, 1974); Freeman Champney, *Art and Glory: The Story of Elbert Hubbard* (New York, 1968); Kenneth Cardwell, *Bernard Maybeck: Artisan, Architect, Artist* (Santa Barbara, 1977); Robert Judson Clark, ed., *The Arts and Crafts Movement in America* (Princeton, N.J., 1972); Sharon S. Darling, *Chicago Ceramics and Glass* (Chicago, 1979), and *The Domestic Scene (1897–1927): George M. Niedecken, Interior Architect* (Milwaukee, 1981); John Crosby Freeman, *The Forgotten Rebel: Gustav Stickley and His Craftsman Mission Furniture* (Watkins Glen, N.Y., 1966); David A. Hanks, *The Decorative Designs of Frank Lloyd Wright* (New York, 1979); Diane Chalmers Johnson, *American Art Nouveau* (New York, 1979); Harvey L. Jones, *Mathews: Masterpieces of the California Decorative Style* (Oakland, 1972); William H. Jordy, *American Buildings and Their Architects: Progressive and Academic Ideals at the Turn of the Twentieth Century* (New York, 1972); Lionel Lambourne, *Utopian Craftsmen: The Arts and Crafts Movement from the Cotswolds to Chicago* (Salt Lake City, 1980); T. J. Jackson Lears, *No Place of Grace: Antimodernism and the Transformation of American Culture, 1880–1920* (New York, 1981); Randall L. Makinson, *Greene and Greene: Architecture as Fine Art* (Santa Barbara, 1977); Grant C. Manson, *Frank Lloyd Wright to 1910: The First Golden Age* (New York, 1958); Frederick C. Moffatt, *Arthur Wesley Dow, 1857–1922* (Washington, D.C., 1977); Robert Muccigrosso, *American Gothic: The Mind and Art of Ralph Adams Cram* (Washington, D.C., 1979); Richard Oliver, *Bertram Grosvenor Goodhue* (Cambridge, Mass., and London, 1983); Suzanne Ormond

and Mary E. Irvine, *Louisiana's Art Nouveau: The Crafts of the Newcomb Style* (Gretna, La., 1976); *A Rediscovery: Harvey Ellis—Artist, Architect* (Rochester, 1973); David E. Shi, *The Simple Life: Plain Living and High Thinking in American Culture* (New York, 1985), chap. 8; Susan Otis Thompson, *American Book Design and William Morris* (New York, 1977); Oscar Lovell Triggs, *Chapters in the History of the Arts and Crafts Movement* (Chicago, 1902); Douglass Shand Tucci, *Ralph Adams Cram: American Medievalist* (Boston, 1975); Kermit Vanderbilt, *Charles Eliot Norton: Apostle of Culture in a Democracy* (Cambridge, Mass., 1959); and Gwendolyn Wright, *Moralism and the Model Home: Domestic Architecture and Cultural Conflict in Chicago, 1873–1913* (Chicago, 1980).

8. For the role of these magazines, see Herbert E. Fleming, *Magazines of a Market-Metropolis* (Chicago, 1906); Frank Luther Mott, *A History of American Magazines* (Cambridge, Mass., 1957, 1968), vol. 4, 1885–1905, and vol. 5, 1905–30; and Selma Harju Steinberg, *Reformer in the Marketplace: Edward E. Bok and the Ladies' Home Journal* (Baton Rouge and London, 1979). Leonard K. Eaton, *Two Chicago Architects and Their Clients: Frank Lloyd Wright and Howard Van Doren Shaw* (Cambridge, Mass., and London, 1969), 229–31, discusses the influence of journals like *House Beautiful* and *House and Garden*.

9. Edward Bok, *The Americanization of Edward Bok* (New York, 1920), chap. 22, describes his efforts to decorate the building. "No other scheme of mural decoration was ever planned on so large a scale for a commercial building, or so successfully carried out." Bok reported proudly of the dining room murals.

10. For more on the American poster designers, see Victor Margolin, *The Golden Age of the American Poster* (New York, 1976).

11. This episode has been described in many places. For one summary, and for examples of Pears's advertising, see Mike Dempsey, ed., *Bubbles: Early Advertising Art from A. & E. Pears Ltd.* (Glasgow, 1978). The introduction, describing the painting's purchase, is by Tim Shackleton.

12. For further information on these trends, see Diana Hindley and Geoffrey Hindley, *Advertising in*

Victorian England, 1837–1901 (London, 1972), but particularly chap. 6; and Trevor Russell-Cobb, *Paying the Piper: The Theory and Practice of Industrial Patronage* (London, 1968), chap. 4. For Leverhulme's activities, see the interview with Viscount Leverhulme in "The Power of Art in Commercial Advertisement," *Commercial Art* 1 (August 1926): 103–6. Two surveys, especially valuable for the 1920s but useful for the earlier period as well, both profusely illustrated, are Percy V. Bradshaw, *Art in Advertising: A Study of British and American Pictorial Publicity* (London, n.d.); and W. Shaw Sparrow, *Advertising and British Art: An Introduction to a Vast Subject* (London, 1924).

13. Will B. Wilder, "'Art' and Advertising," *Fame* 18 (October 1909): 217–18.

14. The extensive Wanamaker art efforts are described in *Golden Book of the Wanamaker Stores: Jubilee Year, 1861–1911* (n.p., 1911), 245–56. For a broader, slightly later view of department store involvement with the arts that picks up the modernist interests of the 1920s, see Zelda Popkin, "Art: Three Aisles Over," *Outlook* 156 (November 26, 1930: 502–3, 515–16.

15. Commercial sensitivity to the functions of commercial architecture and to graphic arts pressed into the service of promotion can be seen by browsing advertising journals such as *Fame* and *Profitable Advertising;* architectural journals, *Architectural Record* and *American Architect;* and printing journals, *Graphic Arts, Inland Printer,* and *Printing Art.* I am speaking here of the pre–World War I era. Printers featured columns analyzing what they considered to be successful and unsuccessful designs. Some recent biographies of American illustrator-advertisers of the period are also helpful. See, for example, Coy Ludwig, *Maxfield Parrish* (New York, 1973); and Michael Schau, *"All-American Girl": The Art of Coles Phillips* (New York, 1975) and *J. C. Leyendecker* (New York, 1974). Surveys of American advertising art include Clarence P. Hornung and Fridolf Johnson, *Two Hundred Years of American Graphic Art* (New York, 1976); and Victor Margolin, Ira Brichta, and Vivian Brichta, *The Promise and the Product: Two Hundred Years of American Advertising Posters* (New York and London, 1979).

16. *Fame* 7 (May 1898): 180. The speaker was R. C. Ogden, a Wanamaker partner.

17. Richard F. Bach, as quoted in the *New York Times,* June 2, 1918, sec. 7, 15, quoted in Arthur J. Pulos, *American Design Ethic: A History of Industrial Design to 1940* (Cambridge, Mass., and London, 1983), 265. Pulos, pages 261–67 and 270–333, discusses increasing American interest in decorative and industrial design and its relationship to the war and European experiences in the 1920s.

18. For art and American propaganda, see George Creel, *How We Advertised America* (New York, 1920); Fairfax Downey, *Portrait of an Era as Drawn by C. D. Gibson* (New York and London, 1936), chap. 18; George Theofiles, *American Posters of World War I* (New York, 1973); Labert St. Clair, *The Story of the Liberty Loans* (Washington, D.C., 1919); and Stephen Vaughn, *Holding Fast the Inner Lines: Democracy, Nationalism and the Committee on Public Information* (Chapel Hill, N.C., 1980), chap. 8.

19. See Pulos, *American Design Ethic,* 274–76, for a discussion of some of these moves to the United States.

20. For more on American commercial, decorative, and advertising art in the 1920s, see Martin Battersby, *The Decorative Twenties* (New York, 1969); Karen Davies, *At Home in Manhattan: Modern Decorative Arts, 1925 to the Depression* (New Haven, 1983); Paul T. Frankl, *New Dimensions: The Decorative Arts of Today in Words and Pictures* (New York, 1928); Frederick Kiesler, *Contemporary Art Applied to the Store and Its Display* (New York, 1930); *The Other Twenties: Themes in Art and Advertising, 1920–1930* (Cambridge, Mass., 1975), a Carpenter Center exhibition by Stanislaus von Moos; Arthur J. Pulos, "William Lescaze and the Machine Age," Syracuse University Library Associates, *Courier* 19 (Spring 1984): 9–14 (this entire issue was devoted to Lescaze); Rudolph Rosenthal and Helena L. Ratzka, *The Story of Modern Applied Art* (New York, 1948); and Dorothy Todd and Raymond Mortimer, *The New Interior Decoration* (New York, 1929). An excellent contemporary account of modern European decorative art and architecture, describing its penetration of America, can be found in

a multipart article by C. Adolph Glassgold, "The Modern Note in Decorative Arts," which appeared in *Arts* 13 (March–May 1928). Jane S. Smith, *Elsie de Wolfe: A Life in the High Style* (New York, 1982), treats a prominent decorator and publicist, active before and after the 1920s.

21. The *Twentieth Annual of Advertising Art* (1941), 9–15, contains an essay by Nathaniel Pousette-Dart, "The Evolution of American Advertising Art," which reviews trends of the previous twenty years that could be found in the exhibition, assesses dominant influences, and singles out medal winners and important artists, agents, and clients.

22. *Annual of Advertising Art in the United States* (1921), ix. The jury of awards included artists and educators Edwin H. Blashfield, Arthur W. Dow, Charles Dana Gibson, Robert Henri, and Joseph Pennell. The show was reviewed in various places; see, for example, "A Declaration of Art in Advertising," *Arts and Decoration* 14 (April 1921): 464–65, 498.

23. *Fourth Annual of Advertising Art* (1925), introduction by Earnest Elmo Calkins. The earlier series, which Calkins helped begin, ran for several years before it stopped.

24. For the guild, see *Arts and Decoration* 19 (March 1921): 263–363, 406.

25. Jeffrey L. Meikle, *Twentieth Century Limited: Industrial Design in America, 1925–1939* (Philadelphia, 1979), is the best account. See also Donald J. Bush, *The Streamlined Decade* (New York, 1975); and Martin Greif, *Depression Modern: The Thirties Style in America* (New York, 1975). The bulk of the achievement and fame came during the 1930s, not the 1920s, but many of the designers were already at work by 1929.

26. For more on this subject, see Morrell Heald, *The Social Responsibilities of Business: Company and Community, 1900–1960* (Cleveland and London, 1970); Alan Raucher, *Public Relations and Business, 1900–1929* (Baltimore, 1968); and Richard S. Tedlow, *Keeping the Corporate Image: Public Relations and Business, 1900–1950* (Greenwich, Conn., 1979).

27. Earnest Elmo Calkins, "The New Consumption Engineer and the Artist," *A Philosophy of Pro-*

duction: The Business Bourse, ed. J. George Frederick (New York, 1927), 126–28. Several years earlier Winter had been likened to Pinturicchio and Raphael. Royal Cortissoz, "The Cunard Building: A Great Achievement in New York by Benjamin Wistar Morris," *Architectural Forum* 35 (July 1921): 1–8.

28. *Westvaco Inspirations for Printers*, no. 44 (1929). This issue was entitled "The Rising Tide of Modernism in America." Among others, no. 15 (1926) concentrated on German graphic artists; no. 33 (1928) used the title "Modernism as an Inspiration for Printers"; and no. 53 (1930) was "This Dynamic Spirit Which We Call Modern."

29. My comments are based on browsing through *Westvaco Inspirations*, various volumes of the *Annual of Advertising Art*, *Printers' Ink Monthly*, texts of the time like Frank H. Young, *Modern Advertising Art* (New York, 1930), popular magazines like the *Saturday Evening Post*, and anthologies like Robert Hunt, ed., *The Advertising Parade: An Anthology of Good Advertisements Published in 1928* (New York and London, 1930). Individual American firms had achieved international reputations—see the comments on Calkins and Holden in J. M. Bowles, "The Posters of Adolph Treidler," *Commercial Art* 3 (October 1927): 171–74. For comments and further references to modernism in advertising, see George H. Roeder, Jr., *Forum of Uncertainty: Confrontations with Modern Painting in Twentieth-Century American Thought* (Ann Arbor, Mich., 1980), 22–23, 154.

30. Herbert Kerkow, "The Seventh Annual Exhibition of Advertising Art," *Commercial Art* 5 (August 1928): 44. Kerkow singled out for attention Will Hollingsworth's Du Pont ads, Louis Fancher's work for Cunard, MacGregor Ormiston for Van Raalte Hosiery, Leo Rackow for Macy's, Helen Dryden for Stehli Silks, Willard F. Elms for the Chicago & North Shore Railroad, Rockwell Kent for A. G. Spalding, and Georgi for Heinz. During the 1920s and early 1930s, Kerkow reported sympathetically on American advertising. See his "Hupmobile Advertising," *Commercial Art* 8 (January 1930): 35–37; and E. T. Stiger, "American Commercial Art as It Is," *Commercial Art* 8 (January 1930): 68–73. Kerkow also focused on individual American artists including J. C. Leyendecker, Robert Foster, Edward

A. Wilson, and the German émigré, Robert L. Leonard. For the relationship between modernist ads and industrial advertising, see *Harvard Advertising Awards, 1930* (New York and London, 1931), with its concentration on modernist ads for Alcoa, Bakelite, and Northern States Power. The Harvard Advertising Awards were established in 1924.

31. Brenda Ueland, "Art, or You Don't Know What You Like," *Saturday Evening Post* 202 (May 24, 1930): 50, 52.

32. Lloyd Goodrich, "A Note on Advertising Art," *Arts* 9 (June 1926): 338–41. Another, more realistic note was struck by Alvin F. Harlow, "The Career of an Artist," *American Mercury* 4 (March 1925): 305–13.

33. Forbes Watson, "Hiring Taste," *Arts* 16 (October 1929): 71. This was an editorial. C. Adolph Glassgold regularly reviewed designers' publicity, architecture, and commercial interiors (Frederick Kiesler, Gilbert Rohde, Pola Hoffmann, Joseph Urban, Lucian Bernhard, Eugene Schoen, and Winold Reiss) or described store window displays (Franklin Simon, Lord & Taylor, and Arnold Constable) for *Arts*.

34. During the 1920s a rich set of European serials was devoted to contemporary advertising art and commercial design. *Gebrauchsgraphik* began in 1925 in Berlin; *Arts et metiers graphiques* was started two years later; *Commercial Art* was one of a series of journals on commercial art published by The Studio in England. For this group, see *The Studio—A Bibliography: The First Fifty Years, 1893–1943* (London, 1978). For serials on printing, advertising, and design, see Carolyn F. Ulrich and Karl Kup, *Books and Printing: A Selected List of Periodicals, 1800–1942* (New York, 1943), particularly 129–35. Of special interest is the *Annuario della Pubblicità Italiana* (1929–1931); *Archiv für Buchgewerbe und Gebrauchsgraphik* (which began in the 1860s but was particularly influential in the 1920s); *Graphicus*, published in Turin starting in 1911; *Reclame* (1922–27), a Dutch journal; and *Penrose Annual*, a review of British printing that had begun in the 1890s. In the 1920s the closest American equivalents were the *Modern Poster Annual*, which began in 1923; *Direct Advertising*, which started in 1912 as a sample book

of various American paper manufacturers; the *Printers' Ink Monthly;* and the *Printing Art.* In Germany in the 1920s the influence of the Bauhaus was radiating into many areas of commercial and decorative art as well as painting, sculpture, and architecture; the German graphic tradition had been innovative in commercial areas since the late nineteenth century, partly because of the technical skills of German printers. Walter F. Schubert, *Die deutsche werbe Graphik* (Berlin, 1927), contains a stunning collection of contemporary German graphic designs; there are numerous texts and catalogues on German poster art. For Britain, besides Percy Bradshaw, *Art in Advertising*, and W. Shaw Sparrow, *Advertising and British Art*, see R. P. Gossop, *Advertisement Design* (New York, 1927); and W. G. Raffe, *Poster Design* (London, 1929). For Austria, and the work of Klinger, Cosl-Frey, and Willrab, see *Poster Art in Vienna* (Chicago, 1923). The verve of contemporary French commercial and printing design is captured in A. Tolmer, *The Mise en Page: The Theory and Practice of Lay-Out* (London: The Studio, 1931). An excellent survey of European developments, particularly the graphic and typographic contributions of Bauhaus faculty and students, which would play an important role in Container Corporation advertising campaigns, can be found in Philip B. Meggs, *A History of Graphic Design* (New York, 1983), chaps. 15–18. Chapter 19 describes American developments, including Walter Paepcke's and Container's.

35. For more on this important episode, see Tilmann Buddensieg *Industriekultur: Peter Behrens and the AEG, 1907–1914* (Cambridge and London, 1984), a translation of a work originally published in 1979. Behrens's patrons at AEG were thought to have been Emil and Walther Rathenau, but Joan Campbell (*The German Werkbund*, 28), argues that it was Paul Jordan, managing director, who was most responsible for using Behrens so creatively.

36. Kauffer's career has been most recently and most extensively examined in Mark Haworth-Booth, *E. McKnight Kauffer: A Designer and His Public* (London, 1979). *Penrose's, Modern Publicity,* and *Commercial Art* spent a good deal of space illustrating Kauffer's work; the Museum of Modern Art held a Kauffer poster show in the 1930s. T. S. Eliot was

an outspoken admirer of his art. Kauffer returned to the United States for his last few years and did one of the Great Ideas of Western Man ads for Container, illustrating a passage by Dostoevsky. See John Massey, ed., *Great Ideas: Container Corporation of America*, no. 42 (Chicago, 1976). For more on Kauffer's milieu see Judith Collins, *The Omega Workshops* (Chicago and London, 1984).

37. Amos Stote, "McKnight Kauffer," *Advertising Arts* (April 2, 1930): 57–62. This was the second issue of this journal, which did not receive a separate volume number since it was printed as a section of *Advertising and Selling*.

38. For further discussion, and many more examples, see J. R. M. Brumwell, "Modern Art in Advertising," *Penrose Annual* 41 (1939): 17–21; Pat Gilmour, *Artists at Curwen* (London, 1977); Ashley Havinden, *Advertising and the Artist* (London, 1956); James Moran, ed., *Printing in the Twentieth Century: A Penrose Anthology* (Bradford and London, 1975); Nikolaus Pevsner, "Patient Progress Three: The DIA," *Studies in Art, Architecture, and Design*, vol. 2 (New York, 1968), 226–41; Herbert Simon, *Song and Words: A History of the Curwen Press* (Boston, 1973); Joseph Thorp, ed., *Design in Modern Printing: The Year Book of the Design and Industries Association, 1927–28* (London, 1928). Kauffer discussed the relationships between art and advertising in *The Art of the Poster, Its Origin, Evolution, and Purpose* (London, 1924). Although I have been concentrating on English commercial patronage during this period, even stronger comments could be offered for several other European countries. Wine and spirits makers, such as France's Nicholas and Dubonnet, seem to have been particularly innovative exploiters of graphic artists; for a discussion of the publicity techniques used by Italy's Campari Company, see Mario Ferrigni, *La Pubblicità di una Grande Casa Italiana* (Milan, 1937).

39. Nikolaus Pevsner, "Patient Progress One: Frank Pick," *Studies in Art, Architecture, and Design*, vol. 2, 309. This essay was originally published in 1942 in *Architectural Review*. Several collections of London Transport posters have been published; see, for example, *Art for All: The Story of London Transport Posters* (London, 1949).

40. The survey was in Nikolaus Pevsner, *An Enquiry into Industrial Design in England* (Cambridge, 1937). For a discussion of the book and the British lack of sympathy with the Bauhaus movement, see Fiona McCarthy, *All Things Bright and Beautiful*, 109–12. She points out that Breuer, Moholy-Nagy, Mendelsohn, Serge Chermayeff, and Walter Gropius all worked in England before leaving for America and better opportunities. This was in the mid or late 1930s, after American design and attitudes toward American design had undergone important changes. These included, as will soon be shown, several important new periodicals, the founding of the Museum of Modern Art and its vigorous crusade for design modernism in all the arts, and growing business interest as a function of the Depression. Indeed, a number of British advertising specialists found American commercial art, particularly newspaper and magazine layouts, to be more effective than their own. Some went even further. See Sir Charles Higham, "British and American Pictorial Advertising," *Commercial Art* 2 (March 1927): 89. For a contrast between traditions of press design and posters in Europe and America, see the review by Clayton Whitehill of a London Underground show at Philadelphia's Franklin Institute in *PM* 6 (April–May 1940): n.p. Actually, although the cover reads *PM*, its name had already changed to *A-D*. Begun in 1934, *PM* was an influential and sometimes avant-garde journal for advertisers, artists, and art directors. It ran only another two years after its name had changed, but during the 1930s it printed work by Bayer, Binders, Maurer, Rand, and Bernhard, examined innovations in packaging, and reproduced the work of contemporary painters.

41. Edward L. Bernays, *Biography of an Idea: Memoirs of Public Relations Counsel* (New York, 1965), 299–312. Creange was appointed by President Hoover to the official American delegation visiting the Paris Fair of 1925. Bernays also advised Cartier, Shelton Looms, Hart Schaffner & Marx, and other firms seeking fashion leadership. For a discussion of Bernays and a corrective to his claims of influence, see Richard S. Tedlow, *Keeping the Corporate Image*, 44–45, 55. Sidney Blumenthal of Shelton Mills, James McIntosh, vice-president of

Ovington Brothers, Joseph D. Little of the Gorham Company, Col. Michael Friedsam of B. Altman and Co., Frank R. Holmes of Lenox China, Inc., and furniture manufacturers John P. Adams and Ralph C. Erskine were among the American business leaders of the day who were concerned about industrial and commercial art. In the 1920s, at least, the group was less impressive and influential than its counterparts overseas.

42. See Walter Raymond Agard. *The New Architectural Sculpture* (New York, 1935); Alan Balfour, *Rockefeller Center: Architecture as Theater* (New York, 1978), pt. 4; Eleanor Bittermann, *Art in Modern Architecture* (New York, 1952); Rosemarie H. Bletter and Cervin Robinson, *Skyscraper Style: Art Deco, New York* (New York, 1975); Carol Hershelle Krinsky, *Rockefeller Center* (Oxford, London, and New York, 1978); and Francis V. O'Connor, "The Usable Future: The Role of Fantasy in the Promotion of a Consumer Society for Art," *Dawn of a New Day: The New York World's Fair, 1939/40*, ed. Helen A. Harrison (New York and London, 1980), 57–71.

43. Chicago's art institutions can be traced in the pages of the *American Art Annual*, which during most years of publication listed art institutions by community. For a brief history of the Chicago Guild of Free Lance Artists, see Chicago Guild of Free Lance Artists, Inc., *Presentation* (Chicago, 1942), with a foreword by William A. Kittredge and a statement of purpose and historical narrative by Norman Hall. The guild's publications included several annuals (beginning in 1927), bulletins (since 1934), and at least one exhibition catalogue for advertising artists. Major Chicago advertising artists of the day included the typography firm of Bertsch and Cooper, M. Vaughn Millbourn, Weimer Pursell, who worked for Abbott Laboratories, packaging consultants Paul Ressinger and Ernst A. Spuehler, John Averill, Andrew Loomis, Haddon Sundbloom, Joseph Chenoweth, William Welsh, Stanley Ekman, Elmer Jacobs, and Dale Nichols. In 1936 a group of commercial artists and typography specialists working in Chicago began to publish an annual, *Twenty-seven Chicago Designers*, containing examples of their work. The first volume noted, "In earlier days the Church, the kings and emperors were the patrons of artists and designers. Today, business has this privilege."

Sometime later a group of Chicago advertising artists began to issue a series of portfolios entitled *Nine Illustrators*, which came out irregularly for several years. Another Chicago figure, Frank H. Young, a student of the Art Institute of Chicago and for a time a Calkins & Holden art director, wrote several contemporary texts on the subject; one of them, *Modern Advertising Art* (New York, 1930), had a foreword by Earnest Elmo Calkins.

44. "Chicago Section," *National Edition of Advertising Arts and Crafts*, vol. 2 (Long Island City, 1926). These handbooks began to appear around 1924; the titles and nomenclature are confusing because several volumes were produced each year, for eastern, western, and national listings, and then were combined and recombined for the following year or two. The volumes were issued for only a few years.

45. This is from a "Complete General Index of American Artists and Illustrators," *National Edition* (1925), 129–84. Philadelphia had approximately 275 entries; Boston, 145; Los Angeles, 115; San Francisco, 72; and Detroit, 70.

46. For earlier background on Chicago interest in the arts, see Helen Lefkowitz Horowitz, *Culture and the City: Cultural Philanthropy in Chicago from the 1880s to 1917* (Lexington, Ky., 1976); and Ralph Fletcher Seymour, *Some Went This Way: A Forty-Year Pilgrimage among Artists, Bookmen, and Printers* (Chicago, 1945). Lloyd C. Englebrecht, "The Association of Arts and Industries: Background and Origins of the Bauhaus Movement in Chicago" (Ph.D. diss., University of Chicago, 1973), is indispensable for this subject. For general information on Chicago's background and Walter Paepcke's career and background, see James Sloan Allen, *The Romance of Commerce and Culture: Capitalism, Modernism, and the Chicago-Aspen Crusade for Cultural Reform* (Chicago, 1983), chaps. 1, 2.

47. By the 1920s the Chicago printing industry had more than fifteen hundred plants, employed more than thirty thousand wage earners, and valued its product at more than three hundred million dollars annually. See Emily Clark Brown, *Book and Job Printing in Chicago* (Chicago, 1931), 1. This is primarily a study in labor relations, however. A sense of the vigor of Chicago commercial printing can be

gleaned from trade journals like *Inland Printer. Chicago History* 13 (Spring 1984) is devoted to Chicago's role in cartography, with significant attention given to Rand McNally and Alfred Theodore Andreas, a leader in subscription publishing. George W. Engelhardt, *Chicago: The Book of Its Board of Trade and Other Public Bodies* (Chicago, 1900), 248–63, examines the city's printing, packaging, and labeling companies. Further evidence of Chicago's importance in commercial printing during the 1920s can be found in the sumptuous volume edited by Louis Flader, *Achievement in Photo-Engraving and Letter-Press Printing, 1927*, published in Chicago that year by the American Photo-Engravers Association. For more on related industrial capacities, see J. Seymour Currey, *Manufacturing and Wholesale Industries of Chicago*, 3 vols. (Chicago, 1918); Sharon Darling, *Chicago Furniture: Art, Craft, and Industry, 1833–1983* (New York and London, 1983); and Perry R. Duis, *Chicago: Creating New Traditions* (Chicago, 1976). There are a number of individual company histories for Chicago department stores, printers and publishers, and mail-order houses.

48. This is described by Norman Hall in Chicago Guild of Free Lance Artists, Inc., *Presentation* (Chicago, 1942). For an informal background on Chicago's art community in the late nineteenth and early twentieth centuries see Perry R. Duis, "'Where Is Athens Now?' The Fine Arts Building, 1898–1918," *Chicago History* 6 (Summer 1977): 66–78; for some modernist art interests, see Lynne Warren, *Alternative Spaces: A History in Chicago* (Chicago, 1984), 6–10.

49. Dana M. Hubbard, "How Chicago Elevated Is Advertising Chicago to Chicagoans," *Printers' Ink Monthly* 5 (November 1922): 53. Reproductions of these posters were printed in British journals, including *Posters and Publicity* (1924), 95; *Posters and Publicity* (1926), 19, 27. In 1927, Oscar Rabe Hanson won, posthumously, the Medal and Barron Collier Prize from the Art Directors Club. See *Sixth Annual of Advertising Art* (New York, 1927), 17, 77; and *Fourth Annual of Advertising Art* (New York, 1925), 11, 19, 36, 38, 41. Research is in progress on this campaign.

50. A Chicagoan supposedly received the first patent on making a paper box. Other companies included the Chicago Label & Box Company, which specialized in pill and powder boxes and druggists' labels; Baker-Vawter, developer of the loose-leaf ledger and a series of other office supplies; J. W. Sefton (eventually absorbed by the Container Corporation), maker of oyster pails, wooden butter dishes, and bottle-packing materials. Daniel J. Boorstin, *The Americans: The Democratic Experience* (New York, 1973), treats the fundamental role of packaging in modern life, 434–47. For further information see Harry J. Bettendorf, *Paperboard and Paperboard Containers: A History* (Chicago, 1946); Alec Davis, *Package and Print: The Development of Container and Label Design* (London, 1967); and Wilbur F. Howell, *A History of the Corrugated Shipping Container Industry in the United States* (Camden, N.J., 1940). During the 1920s and 1930s a series of books analyzed the important role of packaging, among them D. E. A. Charlton, *The Art of Packaging* (New York, 1938); Richard B. Frank and Carroll B. Larrabee, *Packages That Sell* (New York and London, 1928); and M. Luckiesh, *Light and Color in Advertising and Merchandising* (New York, 1923).

51. The first Packaging Conference is described in *Modern Packaging* 4 (June 1931): 33–34, 40. James O. Rice, ed., *Packaging, Packing, and Shipping: A Record of the Subjects as Developed through the American Management Association* (New York, 1936) contains a series of essays on related subjects and reviews participants and winners. The book itself was designed by a winner of the Irwin D. Wolf Trophy. Jurors included Richard F. Bach of the Metropolitan Museum of Art; Charles R. Stevens, specialist on American industrial design and vice-president of the Museum of Science and Industry in New York; Jack Straus of Macy's; as well as educators, publishers, writers, and art specialists.

52. These remarks can be found in Mumford's introduction to H. Allen Smith, *Robert Gair: A Study* (New York, 1939), vi.

53. Rice, *Packaging, Packing, and Shipping*, xv.

54. *Packaging Parade* 1 (May 1938): 12, 24.

55. This is done in James Sloan Allen, *The Romance of Commerce and Culture*, chap. 1.

56. *Container Corporation of America: The First Fifty Years, 1926–1976* (Chicago, 1976) reviews

many of these innovations. Container clients included Coca-Cola, Pepsi-Cola, Kleenex, Campbell Soup Company, Oscar Mayer, Swift, Armour, Salada Tea, Seagram's, Domino Sugar, Sunoco, Rheingold, Camel, Old Gold, Delco, and Havoline Oil. This represents an impressive and varied listing of some of the largest producers of consumer goods in the U.S.

57. Kent D. Currie, "Improving the Annual Report," *Direct Advertising* 22 (Winter 1936): 4–10. Lockwood Barr, "Annual Reports," *Advertising Arts* (September 1934): 21–22, had treated the subject two years earlier. The phrase "orphan children" is taken from the Lockwood Barr essay. The Container *Reports* were printed by Donnelley in Chicago; according to Currie, William A. Kittredge of Donnelley created a whole series of fine annual reports.

58. The Ayer story is told in one of the pioneering studies of American advertising history, Ralph M. Hower, *The History of an Advertising Agency: N. W. Ayer & Son at Work, 1869–1949* (Cambridge, Mass., 1949). Table 9, 326–27, lists the awards won by Ayer from 1921 to 1948 given by the Art Directors Club. Relatively slow to get many of the awards in the early 1920s, Ayer took off later in the decade. J. Walter Thompson took second place in this competition, followed by Young and Rubicam. Calkins and Holden, which had won most of its awards before 1931, placed fifth. However, pages 313 through 321 discuss the rise of art in advertising between 1920 and 1939. Several recent books illuminate the history of American advertising, among them Stephen Fox, *The Mirror Makers: A History of American Advertising and Its Creators* (New York, 1984); Daniel Pope, *The Making of Modern Advertising* (New York, 1983); and Michael Schudson, *Advertising: The Uneasy Persuasion* (New York, 1984).

59. Quoted in Walter Abell, "Industry and Painting," *Magazine of Art* 39 (March 1946): 83. See also Charles T. Coiner, "How Steinway Uses Modern Art," *Advertising Arts* (April 2, 1930): 17.

60. Raymond P. R. Neilson, "Advertising Paintings," *First National Edition of the Advertising Arts and Crafts*, vol. 1 (New York, 1924), 15. In the 1920s this argument was usually made in support of traditional art. See C. B. Larrabee, "When You Use a Famous Painting on Your Calendar," *Printers' Ink*

Monthly 6 (February 1923): 31–33, 82. Coiner's innovation, first developed through Steinway, was to rely heavily on contemporary artists and works that were contemporary in spirit.

61. This particular announcement ran in *Fortune* 13 (June 1936): 193.

62. The fullest profile of Coiner was presented by Alexey Brodovitch, "Charles Coiner Art Director," *Portfolio* 1 (Summer 1950): n.p. Brodovitch was, in the 1930s, an innovative art director of *Harper's Bazaar*, which featured adventurous fashion photography and was an important influence in the more cosmopolitan and sophisticated world of commercial design in 1930s America. Coiner wrote a good many short pieces in the 1930s, including his comments on Steinway in *Advertising Arts:* "Clicquot Redesigned," *Advertising Arts* (July 1934): 24–25; "Art for Government's Sake," *Advertising Arts* (September 1933): 23–24; and "Art with a Capital 'A'," *Nineteenth Annual of Advertising Art* (New York, 1940), 46–52. Coiner eventually illustrated a quotation by Marcus Manilius for the Great Ideas Series. He would go on to design civilian defense signs during World War II, see his paintings placed in major museums, receive the annual award of the National Society of Art Directors, and be elected to their Hall of Fame. By the time he encountered Walter Paepcke, he had been promoted to an Ayer vice-presidency. *Advertising Arts*, which printed so many of Coiner's pieces, had a total of thirty issues (January 1930–March 1935). It was created by Frederick C. Kendall, English-born publisher of *Advertising and Selling*, who was also editorial director for the *American Printer*. With its presentation of graphic designs, its coverage of foreign promotional methods and foreign designers, and its features on American packaging, industrial design, posters, photography, printing techniques, typography, and layout, *Advertising and Selling* must have seemed sensational in the early 1930s. Its publication helped disperse knowledge and influence taste among the most sophisticated designers in the United States.

63. Charles T. Coiner, "Atelier to Advertising," *Advertising Arts* (March 1934): 9–10.

64. Charles T. Coiner, "Exhibition," Advertising Arts (May 1934): 20. This was a review of the Art Directors Club show.

65. For Cassandre, see Robert K. Brown and Susan Reinhold, *The Poster Art of A. M. Cassandre* (New York, 1979). For Cassandre, Kauffer, and other interwar graphic designers, see Mildred Constantine and Alan M. Fern, *Word and Image: Posters from the Collection of the Museum of Modern Art* (New York, 1968), 55–62. Cassandre was the son of a French wine importer living in Russia. In 1936 the Museum of Modern Art held an exhibition of his posters. With Ayer's help he also worked for Ford, Dole, *Fortune* and *Harper's Bazaar.* His first Container ad appeared in *Fortune* during the spring of 1937. For further discussion of relationships linking modern art and modern poster art, see Dawn Ades, *Posters: The Twentieth-Century Poster, Design of the Avant-Garde* (New York, 1984).

66. Bayer's impressive record of commercial design is demonstrated in a Bauhaus Archiv catalogue, *Herbert Bayer: Das Kunstlerische Werk, 1918–1938* (Berlin, 1982). Arthur A. Cohen, *Herbert Bayer: The Complete Work* (Cambridge, Mass., and London, 1982), describes Bayer's work for Dorland. M. F. Agha, art director of *Vogue* and in time president of the Art Directors Club, hired Bayer to become art director for German *Vogue* after Bayer left the Bauhaus in 1928. Cohen argues in *The Complete Work* that Bayer's graphic design in America reflected the "undeniably cramping impact of the client and the client's advertising agency," insisting that even the best of Bayer's American work reflected the "presence in the United States of that overrated interpreter of public taste and corporate needs, the advertising expert." Bayer, however, went on to have a lengthy relationship with Container over the next several decades, serving as its design consultant and eventually chairman of its department of design, with special responsibilities for the advertising campaigns.

67. *Sixteenth Annual of Advertising Art* (New York, 1937), 77. The following year, Charles T. Coiner in "New Trends in Layout and Typography," *Seventeenth Annual of Advertising Art* (New York, 1938), 160–63, argued that Cassandre's high standards had "seriously hampered his acceptance in America." Cassandre's ads, both for Container and other American clients, are numerous in this volume of the annual. See Allen, *The Romance of Commerce*

and Culture, 29–31, for more on the early period of Container's advertising and Coiner.

68. These comments are taken from the Brodovitch essay on Coiner in *Portfolio.*

69. The quotations in the following paragraphs are taken from Walter Abell, "Industry and Painting," *Magazine of Art* 39 (March 1946): 82–93, 114–18.

70. By the late 1940s various magazines had begun to describe these campaigns. See, for example, "Art in Advertising," *Life* 18 (May 14, 1945); for Container Corporation, see Rosamund Frost, "This Business Ties Art into a Neat Package," *Art News* 44 (May 15–31, 1945); "Fine Art in Ads," *Business Week* (May 20, 1944): 76–80; for war reporting, see Rosamund Frost, "The Artist-Reporter: 1855–1945," *Art News* 41 (September 1945): 12–14; "For Prestige's Sake," *Business Week* (December 18, 1948): 38–46; and for Container Corporation, Maxwell House, U.S. Brewers, De Beers, and Abbott Laboratories, see Franklin Baker and Gladys Hinnus, "Does Fine Art Pay?" *Printers' Ink* 202 (January 2, 1948): 30–31. There is also a discussion of some of these campaigns and the growing role of corporate patronage in Virginia M. Mecklenburg, "Advancing American Art: A Controversy of Style," in Margaret Lynne Ausfield and Virginia M. Mecklenburg, *Advancing American Art: Politics and Aesthetics in the State Department Exhibition* (Montgomery, Ala., 1984), 35–64.

71. Described by Pepsi president Walter S. Mack, Jr., "Viewpoints: A New Step in Art Patronage," *Magazine of Art* 57 (October 1944): 228. Mack gave a general defense of industrial patronage. Industry "must take an active part in the community life of the country . . . helping to protect and develop this civilization under whose rules and laws it operates."

72. For more on Standard Oil's art involvement, see Gilbert Burck, "The Jersey Company," *Fortune* 44 (October 1951): 98–113, part of a longer, multipart article; and "Artists Recount the Story of Oil," *Art Digest* 20 (January 15, 1946): 5–7.

73. For more on several of these campaigns, in particular those of the American Tobacco Company and Hiram Walker, see Fairfax M. Cone, *With All Its Faults: A Candid Account of Forty Years in Advertis-*

ing (Boston and Toronto, 1969), 116, 156–59. An excellent bibliography covering these campaigns and corporate collecting is in Mitchell Douglas Kahan, *Art Inc.: American Paintings from Corporate Collections* (Montgomery, Ala., 1979).

74. Frank Caspers, "Patrons at a Profit—Business Discovers Art as a Selling Force," *Art Digest* 17 (May 1, 1943): 5. Caspers concentrated on the Capehart and De Beers series, but also mentioned Abbott Laboratories, *Life*, American Tobacco, Steinway, RCA Victor, and Pan Am.

75. Peyton Boswell, "Common Sense," *Art Digest* 20 (December 15, 1945): 3. Boswell noted a burgeoning controversy over sponsorship of New York Philharmonic broadcasts by the United States Rubber Co. Some found this demeaning to the orchestra; others welcomed it. The unprecedented tax structure of the New Deal, combined with heavy wartime expenditures, produced some doubt that wealthy individuals would be able to resume important patronage roles. This tax anxiety was somewhat exaggerated, given the recent history of collecting, museum founding, and institutional support, but it was an important point and produced some of the intensity behind the research for "new Medicis."

76. For more on corporate sponsorship, see "Businesslike and Beautiful," *Fortune* 49 (May 1954): 107–10; "Over the Water Cooler," *Newsweek* 45 (March 21, 1955): 71; "Wall Street Art Collection," *Look* 17 (November 3, 1953): 72–74; the entire issue of *Art in America* 44 (Spring 1956), which contains a series of articles devoted to art and industry; "Artists and Patrons," *Commonwealth* 64 (August 31, 1956): 529; Eloise Spaeth, "Art and Industry: Terence Cuneo's Paintings for International Nickel," *Art in America* 44 (Winter 1956/57): 48–51; Oscar Schisgal, "Our Newest Patron of the Arts," *Reader's Digest* 76 (May 1960): 192–98; "Art for Sales' Sake at Reynolds (A Portfolio)," *Fortune* 62 (November 1960): 158–61; and "Culture, Inc.," *Time* 83 (February 21, 1964): 85–86.

77. Dorothy Grafly, "The Weathervane: Industry—Art Angel," *American Artist* 11 (November 1947): 46–47.

78. Walter Abell, "Viewpoints: Can Industry Be Counted on as a Patron of the Arts?" *Magazine of Art* 37 (April 1944): 135. Abell had published an essay

discussing the future of art patronage one year earlier in this same magazine.

79. Quoted in *Art Digest* 14 (September 1, 1940): 22. See also Thomas Hart Benton, "Business and Art from the Artist's Angle," *Art Digest* 20 (January 15, 1946): 8, 31.

80. Claude Bragdon and Cleome Carroll, "Art and Industry," *Outlook* 158 (June 10, 1931): 178.

81. See the letter of Moholy-Nagy to his wife Sibyl, April 23, 1944, describing his (and Léger's) reaction to a polltaker reporting on how well modern artists scored against traditional commercial publicity. "We felt both ashamed in a strange sort of way that none of us had protested save under our breaths. I guess art directors buy artists to advertise advertising and to camouflage the mediocre quality of the anonymous designs. The provocative statement of modern art is constantly annulled by checkbook and cocktail party." Sibyl Moholy-Nagy, *Moholy-Nagy: Experiment in Totality* (New York, 1950), 215–16. On the other hand, some artists, sensitive to issues of corporate exploitation, found clients, including Container, unexpectedly sympathetic. See Selden Rodman, "Ben Shahn," *Portfolio, The Annual of the Graphic Arts* (1951): n.p.

82. Gregory Hedberg, *The Spirit of Modernism: The Tremaine Collection, Twentieth-Century Masters* (Hartford, Conn., 1984), 15–23, provides a history of the Tremaine Collection.

83. Aline B. Louchheim, "Abstraction on the Assembly Line," *Art News* 46 (December 1947): 53. Louchheim spent a good deal of time analyzing Mrs. Tremaine's background and her role as the company's art director.

84. Russell Lynes, "Suitable for Framing," *Harper's* 192 (February 1946): 168. This excellent essay, which treats the history of art in advertising going back to the early twentieth century and spends some time on Charles Coiner's various campaigns, was adapted for Lynes's influential book, *The Tastemakers* (New York, 1949), as chap. 16. "Taste—Tax Deductible." Significantly enough, Lynes entitled the third of the book's three large sections. "The Corporate Taste."

85. It is unnecessary to say much in detail about the history of corporate collecting in this period because of the comprehensive catalogue by Mitchell

Douglas Kahan, *Art Inc*. The introduction offers an indispensable overview to the subject.

86. "The Pictures Businessmen Buy," *Business Week* (May 3, 1952): 32–33, covered the Dallas exhibition.

87. For some of these shows and collections, see the citations in note 76 and "The Corporate Splurge in Abstract Art," *Fortune* 61 (April 1960): 138–47; "'ART: U.S.A. Now Thanks to a Wax Company," *Fortune* 66 (September 1962); Henry J. Seldis, "Business Buys Art," *Art in America* 52 (February 1964): 131–34; Charlotte Willard, "The Corporation as Art Collector," *Look* 29 (March 23, 1965): 67–72; *New Yorker* 91 (February 27, 1965): 23–24; "A Thing of Beauty Is a Profit Forever," *Newsweek* 69 (June 5, 1967): 76–78; "Art for the Corporation's Sake," *Business Week* (October 12, 1968): 82–84; for information on Container Corporation, see "Once They Were Ads, Now They Are Art," *Business Week* (August 19, 1961): 32–33; and "The Fine Arts for an Institutional Series," *American Artist* 30 (September 1966): 36–41, 66–67. Sam Hunter, *Art in Business: The Philip Morris Story* (New York, 1979), 132–39, analyzes one corporate story. This was sponsored by the Business Committee for the Arts, an organization set up in the late 1960s, in part from the urging of David Rockefeller, to encourage corporate support. Many of its reports and studies, conducted in the 1970s, were edited by Gideon Chagy.

88. The Whitney Museum show received wide coverage. For the First National Bank of Chicago, see *The Art Collection of the First National Bank of Chicago* (Chicago, 1974). Katharine Kuh was the art adviser. Even before this time, in the 1950s, for example, corporate headquarters began to receive more serious attention from architects, designers, and businessmen as statements of company personality and inviting places to work. The example provided by the Cummins Engine Company of Columbus, Indiana, is perhaps the most notable instance of contemporary architecture deployed as a corporate asset, in this case producing an outdoor museum of distinguished buildings, many of them concerned with municipal, religious and educational purposes, and business needs. Another important achievement was William Hewitt's campaign to get a nationally prominent architect for the John Deere administra-

tive center in Moline, Illinois; see Wayne G. Broehl, Jr., *John Deere's Company: A History of Deere and Company and Its Times* (New York, 1984): 636–41. For more recent interest in the subject, see Joseph Giovanni, "The Grand Reach of Corporate Architecture," *New York Times* (January 20, 1985), sec. 4, 1.

89. The Goodrich quote can be found in *Fortune* 66 (September 1962): 133. See Thomas B. Hess, "Big Business Taste: The Johnson Collection," *Art News* 61 (October 1962): 32–33, 55–56.

90. Betty Kaufman, "Who Buys American Art?" *Commonweal* 72 (May 20, 1960): 214.

91. Nicolas Calas, "ABC or LSD?" *Arts Magazine* 60 (September–October 1966): 15. See also the satirical essay by Frank Getlein, "Commerce and Culture: The Free Load," *New Republic* 145 (September 11, 1961): 22–23.

92. Peter Clecak, "The Aesthetics of Profit," *Nation* 205 (November 6, 1967): 469.

93. Hans Haacke, "Museums, Managers of Consciousness," *Art in America* 72 (February 1984): 15. This theme has been voiced again and again, often much less abrasively. See Lee Rosenbaum, "The Scramble for Museum Sponsors: Is Curatorial Independence for Sale?" *Art in America* 65 (January–February 1977): 10–14; and "Art's Growing Corporate Patronage," *New York Times* (February 5, 1985): 27.

ILLUSTRATION CREDITS

P. 33: Japanese builders at work, Philadelphia Centennial Exposition, 1876. From *Frank Leslie's Historical Register of the U.S. Centennial Exposition*, 1877.

P. 51: The Japanese Pavilion, St. Louis, Louisiana Purchase Exposition, 1904. From Stevens, *The Forest City*, 1904.

P. 60: Opening ceremonies at Memorial Hall, Philadelphia Centennial Exposition, 1876. Free Library of Philadelphia.

P. 62: Mines and Mining, Columbian Exposition, Chicago, 1893. From James W. Shepp and Daniel B. Shepp, *Shepp's World Fair Photographed*, 1893.

P. 66: *Left*, the Tiffany dome in Marshall Field & Co., Chicago. From Lloyd Wendt and Herman Kogan, *Give the Lady What She Wants!* (Chicago: Rand McNally, 1952). *Right*, entrance hall of the City Art Museum, St. Louis, Louisiana Purchase Exposition, 1904. From *Art in America* 59 (July–August 1971): 68.

P. 67: The Great Court in Wanamaker's, Philadelphia. Postcard, private collection.

P. 71: The Helicline, New York World's Fair, 1939. Photo by Alex Siodmak. From Helen A. Harrison, *Dawn of a New Day: The New York World's Fair, 1939/40* (New York and London: Queen's Museum and New York University Press, 1980).

P. 72: The hat department, Meier & Frank Store, Portland, Oregon, before 1933. From *Architectural Forum* 58 (May 1933): 366.

P. 73: The hat department, Meier & Frank Store, Portland, Oregon, after 1933. From *Architectural Forum*, 58 (May 1933): 366.

P. 74: Window display by Arthur V. Fraser, Marshall Field & Co., Chicago, 1925. From Leonard S.

Marcus, *The American Store Window* (New York: Whitney Library of Design, 1978).

P. 79: A Rembrandt on display at Parke-Bernet Galleries. From *The Museum World*, Arts Yearbook 9 (New York: Art Digest, 1967).

PP. 112–13: Palace of Education and East Cascade from Art Hill, Louisiana Purchase Exposition, St. Louis, 1904. From David R. Francis, *The Universal Exposition of 1904* (St. Louis, 1913).

P. 116: Chicago Day at the Columbian Exposition, 1893. Courtesy of the Chicago Historical Society (ICHi 02200).

P. 117: Early twentieth-century traffic congestion at Dearborn and Randolph, Chicago. Postcard, private collection.

P. 121: Machinery Hall, Columbian Exposition, Chicago, 1893. Photo by B. W. Kilburn. Courtesy of the Chicago Historical Society (ICHi 13673).

P. 122: Manufactures Palace and the Ho-o-den, Columbia Exposition, Chicago, 1893. Courtesy of the Avery Architectural Library, Columbia University.

P. 125: French Colonies, Columbian Exposition, Chicago, 1893. Courtesy of the Chicago Historical Society (ICHi 13661).

P. 130: The New York World's Fair, 1939. Library of Congress.

P. 153: "Confronted by a singular looking being," by J. Augustus Knapp. From John Uri Lloyd, *Etidorhpa*, 1895.

P. 162: Rubber suits for protection against electrocution. From *Judge* 1889.

P. 167: Utopian supply store, by Harry C. Wilkinson. From Bradford Peck, *The World a Department Store*, 1900.

P. 179: "The Dry-Goods Epidemic," 1857. From

Harper's Weekly, 31 October 1857; Smithsonian Institution neg. no. 81-508.

P. 188: Raymond Loewy's Evolution Chart of the Automobile. From Otto Mayr and Robert C. Post, eds., *Yankee Enterprise* (Washington, D.C.: Smithsonian Institution Press, 1981).

P. 261: "The Flight of the Old Masters," by Hy Mayer, 1910. From *The New York Times*, 27 February 1912. Copyright © 1910 by The New York Times Company. Reprinted by permission.

P. 270: "Homeless," by C. R. Macauley, 1912. From *World* 26 (November 1912). Courtesy of the Pierpont Morgan Library, New York.

P. 275: "The French and the American Napoleons of Art," by J. Schuerle. Source unknown. Courtesy of the Pierpont Morgan Library.

P. 280: Southdale shopping mall, near Minneapolis. From *Architectural Forum* 105 (December 1956): 118.

P. 281: The Cleveland Arcade (1890). Postcard, private collection.

PP. 282–83: Shopping mall plans. From Victor Gruen and Larry Smith, *Shopping Towns, USA: The Planning of Shopping Centers* (New York: Reinhold Publishing, 1960).

P. 285: Woodfield Mall, Schaumberg. Photo by author.

P. 286: Water Tower Place, Chicago. Photos by author.

P. 287: Ellicott Square Building, Buffalo. Photo by author.

P. 289: People's Gas Building, Chicago. Postcard, private collection.

P. 292: Peabody Hotel, Memphis. From *Architectural Forum* 54 (September 1929): 617.

P. 295: Atlanta Hyatt. Photo by author.

P. 301: ZCMI garage, Salt Lake City, designed by L. G. Farrant. From Geoffrey Baker and Bruno Funaro, *Parking* (New York: Reinhold Publishing, 1958).

P. 354: *Bubbles*, by Sir Everett Millais. From Mike Dempsey, ed., *Early Advertising Art from A. & F. Pears* (London: William Collins Sons, 1978).

P. 362: Hampton Court, by Oleg Zinger, 1937. From Michael F. Levey, ed., *London Transport Posters* (Oxford: Phaidon, 1976). Courtesy of the London Transport Museum.

P. 365: The Dunes Beaches, by Hazel Brown Urgelles. Courtesy of the Chicago Historical Society.

P. 370: Advertisement for Container Corporation of America, by Edward McKnight Kaufer. From *Art, Design, and the Modern Corporation* (Washington, D.C.: Smithsonian Institution Press, 1985).

INDEX

N